The Romanian Economy. A Century of Transformation (1918-2018)

Luminita Chivu / Valeriu Ioan-Franc /
George Georgescu / Jean-Vasile Andrei (eds.)

The Romanian Economy. A Century of Transformation (1918-2018)

Proceedings of ESPERA 2018

Volume 2

PETER LANG

Bibliographic Information published by the Deutsche Nationalbibliothek
The Deutsche Nationalbibliothek lists this publication in the Deutsche Nationalbibliografie; detailed bibliographic data is available online at http://dnb.d-nb.de.

Library of Congress Cataloging-in-Publication Data
A CIP catalog record for this book has been applied for at the Library of Congress.

ISBN 978-3-631-79204-9 (Print)
E-ISBN 978-3-653-06573-2 (E-PDF)
E-ISBN 978-3-631-70799-9 (EPUB)
E-ISBN 978-3-631-70800-2 (MOBI)
DOI 10.3726/978-3-653-06573-2

Peter Lang – Berlin · Bern · Bruxelles · New York · Oxford · Warszawa · Wien

This publication has been peer reviewed.

www.peterlang.com

Contents

Lucian LUCA
Two Decades of Functioning of the Agricultural Land Market in Romania 607

Carmen Beatrice PĂUNA, Tiberiu DIACONESCU, Raluca IORGULESCU, Gheorghe VOICU, Aurica SOARE
The Implementation of Advanced Technologies in Sustainable Agriculture: Best Practices in Romania 617

Elisabeta ROŞU
The Sustainable Rural Development Potential: Case Study 629

Romulus GRUIA, Radu REY, Liviu GACEU
Study on Animal Protein in Mountain Zoo-Products, a Reference for New Trends in Animal Husbandry in High Areas, as Adaptation to Climate Change 639

Daniela ANTONESCU
Sustainability and Mountains Biodiversity: A Survey and Perspective 653

Radu REY
Specific Elements for Organizing the Capitalization of "Mountain Products" on the Basis of Added Value, in the Associative-Cooperative System, in Favor of the Small and Medium-Sized Farmers. A Scenario for Organizing a "Pilot" Micro-Region in the Romanian Carpathians 671

Romulus GRUIA, Alexandru T. BOGDAN, George Florea TOBĂ, Marcel Th. PARASCHIVESCU, George-Leonard TOBĂ
Biodiversity and Evolution of Animal Genetic Resources in the Consolidation of the Romanian Natural and Food Patrimony 685

Marcel Th. PARASCHIVESCU, George Florea TOBĂ, Alexandru T. BOGDAN, Leonard George TOBĂ
Bioeconomic Significances of the Management and Marketing of the Conservation and Development Biodiversity of the National Herritage of Local Animal Genetic Resources Studied Intelligent and Eco-Innovating 701

Amalia-Gianina STRĂTEANU, Alexandru T. BOGDAN, Simona Nicoleta STAN, Lavinia UDREA
New Biotechnique Arguments, Based on Indicators of Meat Production in the European Union Countries, for the Zootechnization of Romanian Agricultural Production 711

Alexander S. CHERVINSKY
Methodological Problems of the Ecological and Economic Determination of the Natural Habitat Quality 725

Mariana GRODEA
Sheep and Goat Farming Sector in Romania – Development Opportunities and Perspectives on the Long Term 735

Alexandru ISAIC-MANIU, Stelian STANCU, Constanţa Nicoleta BODEA, Mihai Sabin MUSCALU
Structural Changes of Services Rendered to Enterprises, in Romania, during 2008–2016 745

Alina Georgeta AILINCĂ, Cătălin DRĂGOI
Correlations between Credit Default Swaps and Macroeconomic Developments in Romania 757

Elena Otilia MANTA
Challenges and Changes in the Microfinancing Policy in Romania 769

Irina A. CHERVINSKAYA
Theory and Practice of Antidumping Regulation as an Object of Economic Research 791

Anastasia VASILYEVA, Natalya BALYNSKAYA, Natalia IVANOVA, Inna KOBELEVA, Nina KUZNETSOVA
Study of Russian Commercial Banks' Lending Activities Management Efficiency: Comprehensive Approach 799

Emilian M. DOBRESCU, Edith Mihaela DOBRESCU
New Perspectives Regarding Rural Mountain Tourism in Spain and Romania – Comparative Study 811

Manuela Sofia STĂNCULESCU, Monica MARIN, Georgiana BLAJ
Social Services for the Elderly in Romania 821

Ioan I. GÂF-DEAC, Otilia Teodora RACHIERU
The Infrastructure of Mountain Areas in Romania, a Determinant Factor for Economic Diversification and Social Development 833

Elena BĂNICĂ, Valentina VASILE
External Trade and Employment in Foreign Capital Companies in Romania. Historical Approach 843

Gheorghe ZAMAN, Iulia Monica OEHLER-ŞINCAI
Romanian Trade Performance after 2001 as Compared to Poland in Terms of Neighbourhood Export Competitiveness 871

Mirela-Adriana RUSALI
Evaluations of Growth in the Foreign Trade with Food Products and Post-Accession Comparisons 881

Cristina BOBOC, Simona GHITA, Valentina VASILE
Characteristics of NEET'S in Romania 891

Ana-Maria CIUHU, Valentina VASILE, Nicoleta CARAGEA
The Unemployement in Romania – Evidences Based on the Philips Curve 903

Mimoza SERAFIMOVA
Entrepreneurship and Entrepreneurial Values: Evaluation of Macedonia 915

Cristina LINCARU, Speranța PÎRCIOG, Vasilica CIUCĂ, Gheorghe GHEORGHE
Tracking Human Capital thorugh Theory Based Evaluation in Mechatrec Sector 925

Irina BĂNCESCU
Analyzing Income Data Using Quantile Analogues of Gini Coefficients 939

Marioara IORDAN, Mihaela-Nona CHILIAN
Evolution of Economic Vulnerability of Households in Romania during the Pre-Accession and Post-Accession to the European UnionPeriods 949

Sorin AVRAM, Luminița CHIVU, Carmen Adriana GHEORGHE, Alexandru SIN
The Influence of Timisoara Urban Pole on Economic Growth and Socio-Demographic Dynamics 963

Florin-Marius PAVELESCU
Evolution of Gender Gap in Romanian Educational System during 1919–2017 Period 975

Bianca BULIGESCU
Atypical Employment for Young Graduates: Does it represent a Stepping Stone or a Trap? 987

Cătălin ZAMFIR, Virgil MUŞATESCU, Adina MIHĂILESCU
On the Residential Energy Consumers Vulnerability 1003

Vasile AVĂDĂNEI, Ioan SURDU, Iulia MEDVESCHI, Emanuela-Adina COCIŞ, Bogdan-Nicolae PĂCURAR, Alexandru-Sabin NICULA
Analysis of Discording Geodemographic Structures and Space Polarization in Regional Context Using GIS Technology Case Study: Apuseni Mountains Romania 1011

Mihnea PREOTESI
Precarious Employment-Poverty-In Work Poverty in Local Contexts of Social Underdevelopment 1023

Maria Livia ŞTEFĂNESCU, Stefan ŞTEFĂNESCU
Romania and Republic of Moldavia – Differences and Similarities between Some Socio-Human Values Accepted by their Respective Populations 1031

Gabriela-Mariana IONESCU
The Economic Polarization 1041

Cătălin BERESCU
Living Tomorrow. Housing in Romania in the Next 100 Years 1049

Cristina DEL-CASTILLO, Encarnación GONZÁLEZ-VÁZQUEZ, Jaime GIL-LAFUENTE, Alicia BLANCO-GONZÁLEZ
Spanish Universities' Reputation as a Determinant of the Country´s Competitiveness 1057

Marta-Christina SUCIU, Mina FANEA-IVANOVICI
The Role of Sponsorship, Patronage and Philanthropy for Supporting the Cultural & Creative Industries 1069

Ion STANCU, Georgeta- MĂDĂLINA MEGHIŞAN-TOMA
Sustainable Development Indicators for Education and Professional Training 1077

Cosmin ŞERBĂNESCU, Adrian VINTILESCU
Optimal Strategies for Organizing Public Internal Audit Departments 1085

Alexandru-Sabin NICULA, Iulia MEDVESCHI, Vasile AVĂDĂNEI, Ioan SURDU, Emanuela-Adina COCIŞ
Accessibility and Ecclesiastic Polarization of Monastic Settlements in the Romanian Carpathians. Case Study: Monastic Settlements on the Occidental Carpathians 1097

Paul MARINESCU, Sorin-George TOMA, Gheorghe-Florentin MIULESCU
Creativity and Innovation, Catalysts of Tomorrow's World 1109

Sorin-George TOMA, Paul MARINESCU, Andreea SĂSEANU
Smart Cities for Sustainable Development in the 21st Century 1121

Maria VIŞAN, Florin Gheorghe FILIP
Knowledge, Innovation and Heritage - Cross-Sectorial Support for Smart Development and Human Capital Transformation 1131

Zizi GOSCHIN, Elena DRUICĂ
A Composite Healthcare Index and its Relation with Romania's Regional Development 1141

Simona IVANA, Nicolae STARCIUC, Cristea COSTACHE, Delia COSTACHE
Innovations in Green Nanotechnology for a Circular Economy 1153

Diana Loreta PĂUN, Constantin Sorin PĂUN, Laurenţiu Alexandru CHIOTOROIU, Silvia CHIOTOROIU
Exogenous-Endogenous Associative Tensions in the Multitude of Threats to Human Health: Social and Economic Consequences 1167

Horia LĂZĂRESCU, Andrei KOZMA
Natural Halotherapeutic Resources – Cost-Benefits in the Context of Bio-Sanogenesis 1179

Adriana GRIGORESCU, Christopher DE FREITAS BRADLEY
Comparative Analysis of Health Care Systems in Romania and France 1189

Ilie Ionel CIUCLEA
Industrialization of Circular Economy in Romania 1201

Vlatko CINGOSKI, Biljana PETREVSKA
Preserving Environment by Clean Energy Public Transport: The Case of Skopje, Macedonia 1213

Ilie Ionel CIUCLEA
Life-Cycle Curve of Waste-Type Products 1223

Daniel CIUIU, Marina BĂDILEANU, Izabell Luminița GEORGESCU, Svetlana CIUMAC
Homogeneity Of The Granger Causality And Applications For Generated/Recycled Waste Dependence On Welfare 1231

Lucian LUCA[1]

[1] Institute of Agricultural Economics, Bucharest, Romania, email: luca@eadr.ro

Two Decades of Functioning of the Agricultural Land Market in Romania

Abstract *The Romanian land market evolution was the result of the gradual liberalization of the legislation on the legal circulation of agricultural land, starting with the very rigid provisions of Land Law 18/1991, relaxed through Law 54/1998 on the legal circulation of agricultural land and almost completely liberalized through the provisions of Title X of Law 247/2005 on the reform in the field of ownership and justice as well as some adjacent measures; upon the expiry of the transitional restrictions, Law 17/2014 on certain measures for regulating the sale-purchase of agricultural land outside the localities brought some corrections to the mechanism of farmland acquisition, without affecting the free operation of the land market.*

Keywords: *Land market, land prices, farmland acquisition, Romanian land legislation*

Introduction

Romania is in the situation of not being able to prove the different phenomena registered on the land market, as it does not have official data regarding the essential parameters of a functional land market. That is why we have decided to provide the best estimate of farmland prices at national and county level, on the basis of the individual data published by Ministry of Agriculture and Rural Development (MADR), and to continue the series referring to the volume of agricultural land transactions with land outside the built-up area of localities, based on the data supplied (on the demand of the Institute of Agricultural Economics) by the National Agency for Cadaster and Real Estate Advertising (ANCPI), which represents the best possible assessment of the Romanian land market, with data at county level.

The analysis of the situation in Romania can be organized into three distinct periods, namely 1996–2006 (before EU accession), 2007–2013 (the last years of the transitional restriction foreseen in the Treaty of Accession) and 2014–2017 (the period after restriction ending). The analysis of the land market in Romania is completed in the present paper by a comparison of the national and European legal provisions on the regulation of farmland sale-purchase.

1. Literature review

The efficient use of farmland from the economic point of view presupposes the existence of a functional land market. The efficiency of land markets is measured through their ability to transfer land from less productive to most productive users. The transactions costs, which complicate or hinder these transfers, lead to efficiency decrease. Several studies have shown that the agricultural markets from the countries that had already passed through the transitional period were characterized by the existence of significant transaction costs, which represented a constraint for the farms that intended to increase their size, also in the case of Romanian farms. These constraints came from the costs related to the asymmetric information, co-ownership of land (as result of the land restitution process), the precarious situation of the registration of properties, the high level of commissions and fees in connection to property transfers.

As EU membership implies the integration of all Member States into a single and free market (also as regards farmland), land transactions (land purchase by foreign people inclusively) contribute to productivity increase, improving the access to capital, knowledge and technologies, thus stimulating the economic development in the New Member States (Swinnen, Vranken, 2009).

The analysis of the European land market evolutions shows that there is a large variation in farmland prices and in the level of rent in the EU. Among the determinants of farmland value the following are worth mentioning: agricultural commodity prices, expansion of infrastructure, urban pressures, as well as land market regulation, period of leasing agreements, taxes on land into ownership and on land transactions and last but not least, CAP subsidies (Swinnen et al., 2013). As a trend, certain analysts consider that maintaining the present subsidizing system of agriculture in the EU has determined the significant increase of farmland prices, at least in the countries that joined the EU in 2004 and after. In this context, the role of the transitional restrictions these countries benefited from, usually for 7 years after the accession moment, was rather considered as non-determinative in the evolution of land price after the accession, more important being the specific land acquisition conditions by the local natural persons and legal entities (Swinnen and Vranken, 2010).

2. Land tenure and Romanian farm structure

Farmland leasing in was an important modality to establish large-sized farms in Romania. Land lease was regulated by Land Lease Law no. 16/1994, modified several times, and replaced since 2012 by the provisions of the New Civil Code (Particular rules for land lease).

The evolution of the leased areas from 2005 to 2016, by farm juridical status, shows the continuous process of farmland transfer from the individual households to those with legal status, through land leasing. Thus, the land areas into the

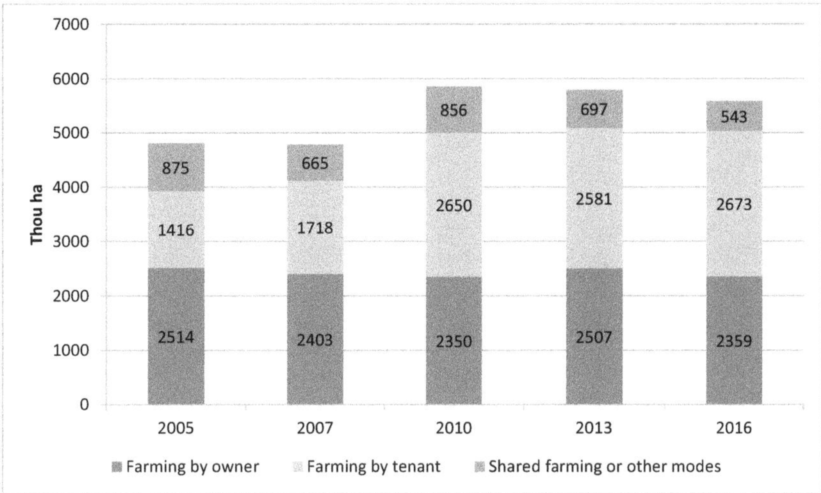

Figure 1: Land tenure by the Romanian legal entities farms
Source: authors' processing of Eurostat data

ownership of farms with legal status increased from 1.4 million ha in 2005 to around 2.7 million ha in 2016 (Figure 1). The most important change took place in the period 2007–2010.

3. Prices of farmland outside the localities

Prices of farmlands outside the localities (farmland with different utilizations – arable, pastures, hayfields, orchards, and vineyards) doubled on the average in the year 2005: from 247 euro/ha in 2004 to 884 euro/ha in 2005. This increase was probably due to the moment of accession coming closer (the negotiations had ended in December 2004) and to the expectations referring to an increase in prices in the post-accession period; yet this could also be the result of the change of legislation in the year 2005, in the sense of simplifying the procedure for changing the category of a plot of land outside the locality into land inside the locality (in this way it becomes buildable land, after the necessary authorizations are obtained).

After the spectacular arable land price increase in the year 2013, when the average arable land price was estimated at almost 3000 euro/ha in the counties with high agricultural potential, the increase continued year by year, so that in the year 2015 a detailed estimation (www.statista.com) showed that there were many situations when the farmland areas were sold at over 4000 euro/ha.

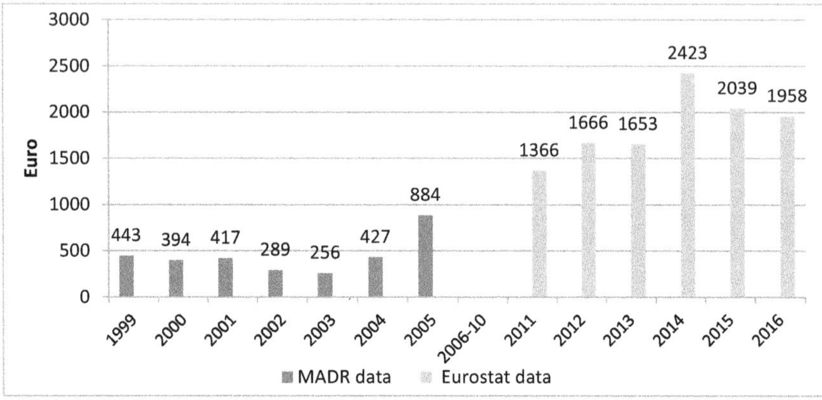

Figure 2: Annual average prices of farmland outside the localities in Romania
Source: authors' processing of MADR and Eurostat data.

In 2018 Eurostat published a new set of statistics on agricultural land prices, covering the period 2011–2016, completing the picture of land price evolution in Romania (Figure 2).

In the absence of official data on farmland prices (previously to 2018), their level was estimated starting from the public offers on the MADR website (for areas over 30 ha in the period June 2014 –September 2017) and on the websites of Agricultural Directorates in three counties (for areas under 30 ha): Bacău (for the period June –September 2017), Olt (for the period August –September 2017) and Mureş (for September 2017).

In the case of large areas, for which the offers must be published on the MADR site, the average price of the 264 sale offers after the coming into effect of Law 17/2014 was 3997 euro/ha (corresponding to an area of 12017 ha put for sale). Some offers with overly high prices, in the proximity of urban areas, were excluded in the data consistency checking stage. We can notice quite high differences between the farmland prices (mainly arable land) in the different counties from Romania: the highest prices are in Ialomiţa, Călăraşi and Timiş. In certain counties no large-sized transactions were registered in the last year (mainly the counties in the mountain and hilly areas).

By calendar years, the evolutions of areas and average prices reveal the transaction peak – as regards the transacted area – that was reached in 2015, under the background of the significant average price increase; after that price stagnation followed, with a diminution of areas put for sale in 2016 and 2017 (Table 1).

In the case of transactions with small-sized areas, the analysis of offers from the three selected counties (Bacău, Olt and Mureş) shows that most transactions involve areas under 1 ha. In the case of these offers, there are also great differences

Table 1: The national average prices of consolidated areas (offers over 30 ha)

Year	Number of offers	Cumulated area (ha)	Price (euro/ha)
National average 2014	51	2,227	3,771
National average 2015	90	4,242	4,073
National average 2016	67	2,856	4,052
National average 2017	56	2,686	4,005

Source: authors' estimations based on data from MADR website

Table 2: The agricultural lands prices (euro/ha) in selected counties (offers for land areas under 30 ha in the period July–September 2017)

	Bacău	Olt	Mureş
An average of all offers	5,559	2,097	3,561
Farmland in rural areas	2,362	2,098	1,843
Farmland in peri-urban areas	36,757	63,110	16,820

Source: authors' estimations based on data from Agricultural Directorates websites in Bacău, Olt and Mureş.

between the farmland in the proper rural area (used for agriculture) and those near the towns (rather destined to non-agricultural developments).

The average farmland prices for the three counties (Table 2) are calculated separately for the two zones. In the case of Bacău county, the 2362 euro/ha average results from 518 registrations with a total area of 267 ha; in the case of Olt county, the 2098 euro/ha average results from 734 registrations with a total area of 886 ha; in Mureş county, the 1843 euro/ha average results from 132 registrations with a total area of 73.7 ha.

4. Volume of transactions with farmland outside the localities

Farmland sale and purchase in Romania was possible after the adoption of Law 54/1998 on the legal circulation of land. The information referring to farmland transactions (areas and prices) centralized by the Ministry of Agriculture and Rural Development, on the basis of data from the period 1998–2005, represents the first official data on the land market in Romania. According to these data, throughout the period 1998–2005, 308 thousand of sale-purchase contracts of land outside the localities were registered. The total sold area was 513 thousand ha.

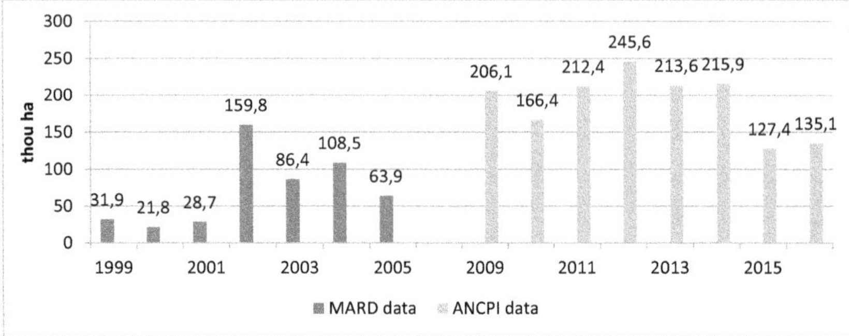

Figure 3: The volume of land transactions with farmland outside localities in Romania. Source: authors' processing of ANCPI data

In the year 2005, before Romania's accession to the EU, a few corrections were made to the agricultural ownership regime. Thus, by Law no. 247/2005 on the reform in the field of property and justice, as well as a few adjacent measures, new provisions were introduced with regard to the legal circulation of land (in the sense of land market liberalization). These provisions on the legal circulation of land simplified the legislation in this field.

After a period (2006–2008) when farmland transactions were not centralized any longer, starting with 2009 the information system of the National Agency for Cadaster and Real Estate Advertising (ANCPI) was gradually set into operation, county by county, which became fully operational in 2010. Comparing the ANCPI data after 2009 to those centralized by MARD until 2005, we can see that the land market has been much more active after the accession: while in the year 2005, the number of total (sale-purchase) transactions was around 33 thousand, with an area of around 64 thousand ha, in the year 2009 the number of transactions was about 118 thousand, with a total area of about 206 thousand ha. The total transacted farmland area exceeded 200 thousand ha in the period 2009–2013 (Figure 3).

To sum up, the evolution of land transactions after Romania's accession to the EU puts into evidence an intensification of farmland sale-purchase in the period 2011–2014, followed by a relative diminution in the years 2015–2016.

5. European and national debates on the land market

A debate on farmland utilization in the countries in the transitional period highlighted that the great differences between the values of farmland in the EU member states are due to agriculture restructuring in the last years, yet the problems noticed in the EU New Member States are mainly the result of differences in approaching the land reforms. (Swinnen, Van Herck and Vranken, 2013)

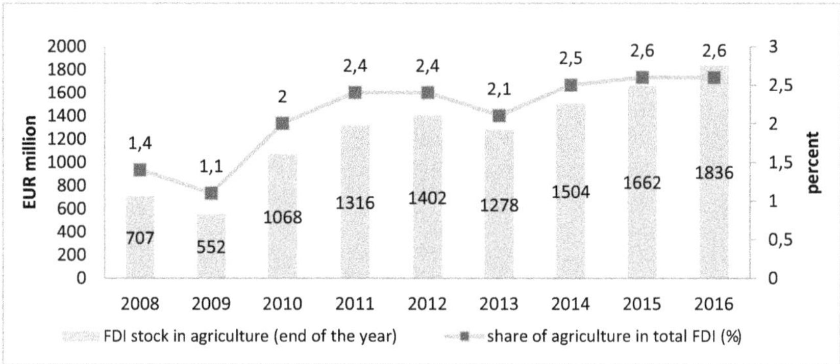

Figure 4: Foreign direct investments in Romania's agriculture
Source: authors' processing of NBR data

In many countries, land purchase by foreign investors was severely restricted through the transitional regulations that were enforced in the New Member States, as derogation from the EU legislation on the internal market. (Steriu and Otiman, 2013) Nevertheless, there were no restrictions on land use (through leasing) by the foreign investors. The percentage of leased land greatly varies and reflects the farm structures from the different countries (in Slovakia and the Czech Republic this represents more than 90 %, while in Poland about 30 %). The restrictions on farmland transactions have had a negative influence upon development, the laws on land ownership having an impact upon efficiency.

In reference to the direct foreign investments, it was considered (Swinnen, Van Herck and Vranken, 2013) that these would have mainly positive consequences for the countries receiving them, due to the capital flow and technology, and thus a complete liberalization of land markets in the EU New Member States was recommended.

The official research on Foreign Direct Investments (FDI), annually conducted by National Institute of Statistics in collaboration with by the National Bank of Romania (NBR), shows that the FDI balance in "agriculture, forestry and fisheries" on December 31, 2008 was 707 million euro, representing 1.4 % of total FDI in Romania's economy. By the year 2014, this balance already doubled (Figure 4), to reach 1836 million euro in late 2016, which represented 2.6 % of total FDI in Romania.

In Romania, one of the main concerns referring to the agricultural land market continues to be land purchase by foreigners (Ciutacu et al., 2017). Even Law 17/2014 was the result of a project initiated by MARD with the goal to limit the possibility of farmland purchase by foreigners. Although, in the end, a balanced Law was issued from the Parliament, the main novelty introduced by this, as suggested by certain studies (Luca, Cionga and Giurcă, 2012), i.e. the possibility for the Agency of State Domains (ADS) to use the pre-emption right to purchase land put for sale, was not implemented.

After more official debates at the level of the European Parliament, on the basis of some studies inclusively (Transnational Institute, 2015), the position of the European institutions in the matter of agricultural land was systemized in the Commission Interpretative Communication on the Acquisition of Farmland and European Union Law (European Commission, 2017). In this document, certain case law findings are described, that could provide member states guidance on the modalities to regulate the agricultural land markets, while complying with two essential principles, i.e. non-discrimination and proportionality. The 10 intervention elements analyzed are the following: a) Prior authorization, b) Pre-emption rights, c) Price control, d) Direct farming obligation, e) Vocational training in agriculture, f) Residence requirements, g) Interdiction to sell, h) Ceilings imposed in administrative terms, i) Privileges granted to local acquirers, j) Condition for reciprocity. From the perspective of this comprehensive document, in my view, the project of a new law debated in 2018 by Romanian Parliament is not acceptable.

However, there are certain improvements that can be made to the present law, and one of these is the application of the legal transfer procedure for all transactions (including the transfer of shares of firms owning land, and also in the case of forced execution of the debts for which farmland was pledged).

Conclusions

The land policy should be correlated with the policy orienting the farm structure. If the structure orientation policy has a goal established (for instance, ensuring the equilibrium between small and large-sized farms), the operationalization of a land settlement agency may prove useful, which should correct the effects of the simple operation of the land market.

For an efficient intervention on the land market, it is necessary that the land settlement agency is granted pre-emption right when buying farmland put for sale by its owners. By using the pre-emption right, the agency could contribute to farmers setting up or maintaining, to increase farm size, to keep a balance between different types of farms and to discourage land speculations.

The analysis of the legislation and of data collected from official sources and from special surveys and case studies reveals a better operation of the land market in the post-accession period, as against the pre-accession period; this is due to the continuous liberalization of the legislation on the legal circulation of land, and also to the strong economic growth context in the period 2004–2008, which also generated certain speculative actions. After the economic crisis and the emergence of the new legislation in 2014, the land market preserved its functional character.

By comparison with the effectively registered average prices until 2005 (that had reached about 900 euro/ha), after accession farmland prices have significantly increased, and in 2015 many large transactions (over 30 ha) were made at prices over 4000 euro/ha.

In the latest years, worries have existed in the Romanian society in relation to the land grabbing phenomenon, amplified by the mass media, as the prices of land transactions are much lower than the European prices, thus making the farmland very attractive for foreign capital.

A modality of rational management of the land market situation could be the ADS operationalization in the quality of intervention agency on the land market and strengthening its role in the implementation of a farm structure orientation policy.

References

Ciutacu, Constantin et al.: Land grabbing: A review of extent and possible consequences in Romania, in Land Use Policy 62 (2017) 143–150, 2017.

European Commission: Commission Interpretative Communication on the Acquisition of Farmland and European Union Law (2007/C350/05), in the Official Journal of the European Union of 18.10.2017, 2017.

Luca, Lucian: Piaţa terenurilor agricole din România după aderarea la Uniunea Europeană, in Otiman, P.I., Toderoiu, F., Sima, E. (editors), Cercetări de economie agrară şi dezvoltare rurală 1990–2010: realizări şi perspective, Editura Academiei Române, Bucureşti, 2011.

Luca, Lucian: Romanian Land Market Regulatory Framework: The Legislative Corrections in 2014, in Agricultural Economics and Rural Development Journal, Volume 11, Issue 2, pp.203–212, Bucureşti, 2014.

Luca, Lucian; Cionga, Cristina; Giurca, Daniela: Consolidarea exploataţiilor agricole, Editura Economică, Bucureşti, 2012.

Swinnen, Johan; Vranken, Liesbet: Land and EU Accession: Review of the transitional restrictions by new member states on the acquisition of agricultural real estate, report for the European Commission, CEPS, Brussels, 2009.

Swinnen, Johan; Vranken, Liesbet: Review of the transitional restrictions maintained by Bulgaria and Romania with regard to the acquisition of agricultural real estate, report for European Commission, CEPS, Brussels, 2010.

Swinnen, Johan; Van Herck, Kristine; Vranken, Liesbet: Land Market Regulations in the EU, in Swinnen, Johan; Knops, L. (editors), Land, Labour and Capital Markets in European Agriculture, CEPS, Brussels, 2013.

Swinnen, Johan et al.: Possible Effects on EU Land Markets of New CAP Direct Payments, study for the European Parliament, Brussels, 2013.

Steriu, Valeriu; Otiman, Păun Ion (editors): Cadrul naţional strategic pentru dezvoltarea durabilă a sectorului agroalimentar şi a spaţiului rural în perioada 2014–2020–2030, Editura Academiei Române, Bucureşti, 2013.

Transnational Institute: Extent of Farmland Grabbing in the EU, study made for the European Parliament (Policy Department B: Structural and Cohesion Policies), 2015.

Carmen Beatrice PĂUNA[1], Tiberiu DIACONESCU[2], Raluca IORGULESCU[3], Gheorghe VOICU[4], Aurica SOARE[5]

[1, 2, 3] Institute for Economic Forecasting, Romanian Academy, Email: carmenbpauna@gmail.com

[4, 5] „Dunărea de Jos" University Galaţi (UGAL), Faculty of Engineering and Agronomy Brăila

The Implementation of Advanced Technologies in Sustainable Agriculture: Best Practices in Romania

Abstract *In time, sustainable agriculture has demonstrated that there is no universally applicable system for soil exploitation, because of local differences, especially those related to the type of climate and soil, but also to the level of technology used in agriculture. The results of research have demonstrated that unconventional methods, when applied, like the minimum tillage system, have a particularly good impact, technically, economically and financially. The minimum tillage system, taken over from the USA, has rapidly extended to other countries, especially to Western Europe, but also to Romania, in Great Braila Island, the biggest agricultural holding in Europe. In this area of our country, the special conditions, the increase in the multiannual temperature and the rainfall deficit in the past few years have led to the successful application of the advanced technologies and unconventional methods, like this system. To this effect, the good practices, presented in this paper, have shown their impact on the holdings which use this system, thus upholding the need for replicating the positive experiences in other similar areas, as well. The advanced technologies contribute to achieving a conservation and sustainable agriculture by: the enhancement and improvement of the soil fertility and productivity; the rational conservation and management of the soil water.*

Keywords: *sustainable agriculture, minimum tillage, soil conservation, yield, Great Braila Island*

Introduction

Modern research in the field of soil conservation was carried out at the middle of the twentieth century in USA, in Michigan, Ohio and New York, on maize crops, under the name of "minimum tillage system". This paper discusses the implementation of technologies for unconventional soil work systems, in this case, the minimum tillage system. Depending on pedoclimatic conditions, were developed a couple of variants of the minimum tillage system:

a) The direct sowing system uses specialized equipment for a minimum preparatory work of the soil and sowing in a single passing.
b) Seeding in two passings: the first passing provides a deep mobilization of the soil without swath return and fertilizer application; the second passing is done by attaching a cultivator or disc harrow followed by a seed drill and a device to apply herbicides.

The technical advantages are: (i) storing more water in the soil; (ii) soil settles to a lesser degree; (iii) avoiding destruction of soil structure and settling (sinking); (iv) increasing the amount of soil organic chemicals; (v) reducing erosion; (vi) reducing loss of water by evaporation.

The economic advantages are: (i) by eliminating plowing, disking and harrowing the cost price is lower; (ii) economizes especially on fuel and lubricants and allows less wear of tractors and agricultural machinery (fewer passes, fewer works etc.); (iii) increased work productivity.

The minimum tillage system extended rapidly to other countries, especially to those in Western Europe but also to Romania, in Great Braila Island, the largest agricultural holding in Europe (since 2012 this farm adopted the minimum tillage system). Lucian Buzdugan, the chairman of the board for AGRICOST SRL explains (Agroinfo, 2013):

> "Great Braila Island is situated in an area lacking rainfalls, which actually required the use of the minimum tillage system on the soil. That is why, we introduced the minimum tillage system with Horsch machinery. We carry out minimum tillage works with Tiger machinery without inversing the furrows, which aerates the soil. If the furrow is turned over, no proper mineralization of the soil is obtained and, hence, there should be an increase in the quantity of chemical fertilizers per soil unit. In addition to that, we also lose the water in the soil, whereas microorganisms no longer find a proper environment to grow."

This paper builds on the experience regarding the implementation of the minimum tillage system accumulated in Northern Baragan by well-known agricultural holdings, like SC AGRICOST IMB Braila SRL, an experience shared with Lunca Agriculture Research Center – an academic research unit of the Dunarea de Jos University of Galati, the Faculty of Engineering and Agronomy Braila, which is based in Great Braila Island.

The paper is organized as follows: Section 1 presents a brief literature review, Section 2 introduces the minimum tillage system, and Section 3 discusses the case of SC Agritur SRL Braila agricultural holding. The last section concludes.

1. Literature review

In time, the sustainable development of agriculture has shown that there is no universally applicable system for soil tillage, because of local differences, especially those related to the type of climate and soil, but also the technology used. In consideration of these aspects, but also following the results of research that has been carried out in various areas, it was found that the crop production in the crop rotation system is also the result of the influence of the system on soil properties, plant density and weeds in the crops. Minimum tillage is a type of conservation agriculture (Berger et al., 2010), a tool for soil and water conservation (Kassam et al., 2014) and for reducing carbon and nitrous-oxide emissions to the atmosphere from agriculture. (Busari et. al, 2015)

For Romania, Rusu et al. (2006, p.265) compare the physical and chemical properties of the traditional/classic soil tillage system and four minimum soil tillage systems in Cluj-Napoca. They conclude that "advantages of minimum soil tillage systems can be taken into account as improving methods in weak productive soils with reduced structure stability on slope fields and as measures of preserving the soils on the rest of the surfaces". For the same area (Cluj-Napoca), Rusu (2006) reports on the yield of maize, soya-bean and winter-wheat in a study conducted during 1999–2001 considering different soil tillage systems.

The results show that for maize, productions are lower in the minimum tillage system compared to the classic soil tillage system. The author emphasizes that "the efficiency of the alternative systems is ensured only in the case of a crop rotation, case in which cultures rotation alternates with the systems of tillage" (Rusu 2006, p. 288). Boja et al. (2008) add to the literature of the field the results of a study conducted between 2005 and 2008 in Iarac forestry nursery Arad. The paper compares the effect of the conventional tillage system with the alternative minimum tillage system on some physical soil properties.

2. The minimum tillage system–a future component of advanced agricultural technologies

Following the good results obtained by holdings after applying unconventional methods, like the minimum tillage system, this system has become ever more known.

The example chosen briefly presents the results obtained by a Romanian representative holding in an agricultural area with tradition in Romania: the minimum tillage system in the agricultural holding SC Agritur SRL Braila. When initiating the first crops, this holding has until recently applied the conventional tillage system which has produced some major disadvantages – taking into consideration the pedoclimatic conditions of Northern Baragan area, where the holding is located.

Thus, following the numerous works that have been applied until recently in the technology used by SC Agritur SRL, specialists have found that the soil is compacted and its structure is spoiled, the soil gets dusty and loses its fertility. To sum up, its physical, chemical and biological characteristics are impaired dramatically. This degradation is also influenced by the process of desertification of the Northern Baragan area due to the increase in the multiannual temperature and to scarce rainfalls in the past few years.

In order to diminish these effects and disadvantages in the agricultural activity of SC Agritur SRL Brăila, it was suggested that there should be a reduction to the minimum of the soil preparation and sowing works, by applying the conservation technology. More exactly, the minimum tillage system, a system that will substantially contribute, in the future as well, to the enhancement and improvement of the fertility and productivity of the soil, with direct consequences on the economic efficiency of the agricultural holding.

In the conservation technological system, in the complex processes of enhancement, restoration and conservation of soil fertility, the decisive role is played by the process of soil aeration and mobilization.

From a pedological point of view, soil tillage is the most important technological component, as a matter of fact being also the major criterion making a difference between conservation and conventional agriculture, the reason why the minimum tillage system – ploughing and sowing is proposed.

The ploughing-sowing system is characterized by the fact that the main technical works are executed with single machinery for preparing and sowing the soil, in a single operation. The machinery can also be fitted with a device for dispensing fertilizers, herbicides and soil compaction on the sowed furrows.

In the vegetation period, one or two crop management works are carried out, a good opportunity for the additional nitrogen fertilization to be done.

The minimum tillage system has a series of advantages, from the agro technical and economic points of view, namely:

- It stores and better uses the water in the soil.
- The soil is less compacted.
- The soil structure is protected.
- The humus is better preserved.
- By eliminating works like ploughing, harrowing with discs, harrowing, the cost price is lower, producing fuel savings, as well.

In Table 1 are reproduced some of the results obtained in the U.S. with respect to soil quality, following the use of the two types of technologies (traditional and conservation – no and minimum tillage).

Table 1: The content of organic matter in the soil, after 20 years of maize crops, when using two technologies (traditional and conservation – no and minimum tillage)

Nitrogen N (kg/ha)	**Content of organic matter (%)**	
	Minimum-tillage	**Plowing**
0	4.10	2.40
84	4.93	2.53
168	4.28	2.45
336	5.40	2.73

Source: Thomas J. (1990) in Dobre, Marian (2011, p. 352).

The implementation of this system depends on a series of factors:

- In the droughty areas, this system is applied on the soils with a deep and crumbly structure.
- It is suitable for the coarse and medium texture, aired and well drained soils, not being suitable for soils with fine texture and poor drainage, on the soils strongly degraded by erosion or compaction.
- It requires eliminating weeds by chemical weeding and by using preventive methods (crop rotation).

3. The minimum tillage system in the SC Agritur SRL Braila agricultural holding

SC Agritur SRL has met the necessary requirements, which confirms the timeliness of replacing conventional technology by the conservation technology, through the minimum tillage system, applicable on all types of soil, after any plants cultivated before.

The SC Agritur SRL Brăila agricultural holding is located in an area of agricultural land included in group 1 of fertility. The predominant types of soils are black-coloured and brownish chernozems.

The holding carries out its activities in two directions:

- Crops of maize, wheat, barley, rape, sunflower and areas with seed maize and sunflower, the most profitable being the areas with hybridization of maize, with significant results on production and profitability by using the applied technologies.
- The subsidized ecological agriculture is strength for profitability, on the market. Irrigation ensures high yields annually, even in the droughty years.

The conventional technological flow used by SC Agritur SRL (Fig. 1) includes:

- Primary tillage (or main tillage) of the soil, which is carried out annually through the energetic aeration of the soil by ploughing with full or partial inversion of the furrow.
- The secondary tillage of the soil, which is carried out after the ploughing – is actually an element of aggression on the soil since, in most of the cases, it is leading to increased vulnerability of the soil, to degradation, on a longer term.
- The other technological steps: (a) seeds and sowing and (b) maintenance works (fertilization, eliminating weeds, fighting pests, irrigation).

SC Agritur SRL is applying all the types of technological steps, to be found in the specialty literature under the name of conventional systems or traditional agricultural systems.

During the use of conventional technology by SC Agritur SRL, the specialists of this holding found that the physical, chemical and biological characteristics of

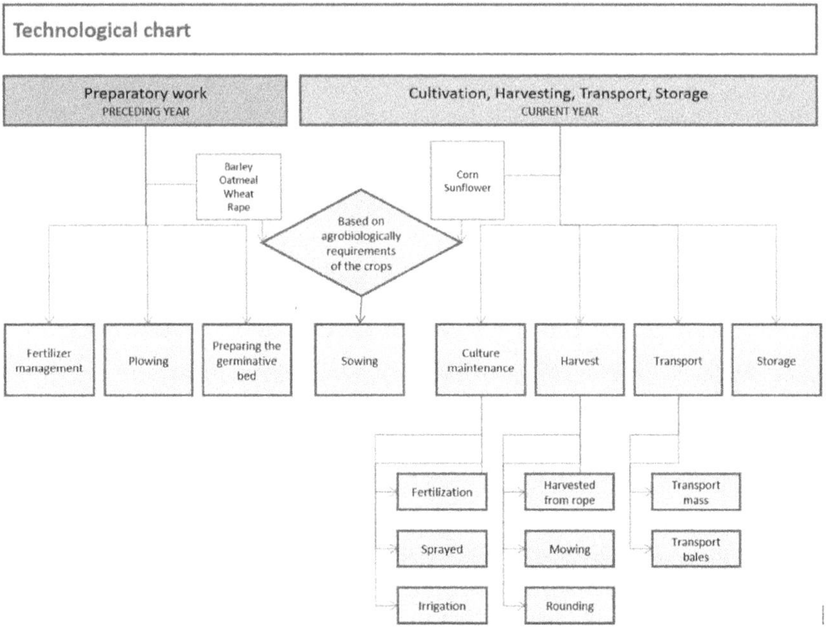

Figure 1: The conventional technological flow: The technological diagram SC Agritur SRL

Source: Agritur. Sistemele neconvenţionale de lucrare a solului, alternative agrotehnice şi economice pentru agricultura durabilă, Agricultura conservativa. Fişa informativa no. 5, May 2009

the soil got worse, due in particular to the process of soil desertification in the area of Northern Baragan (because of the increase in the multiannual temperature and poor rainfalls in the past few years).

With a view to minimizing the negative effects on the soil, and the disadvantages found in carrying out its agricultural activity, SC Agritur SRL decided to apply the conservation technology, the minimum tillage system, in order to reduce to the minimum the works for the preparation of the soil and for sowing. This system will contribute substantially to the enhancement and improvement of the fertility and productivity of the soil, with direct consequences on the economic efficiency of the agricultural holding.

The minimum tillage system has a series of agro technical and economic advantages: it stores and better uses the water in the soil; the soil is being less compacted; the soil structure is protected; the humus is better preserved; by eliminating the ploughing, harrowing with discs, the cost price is lower and fuel savings are made.

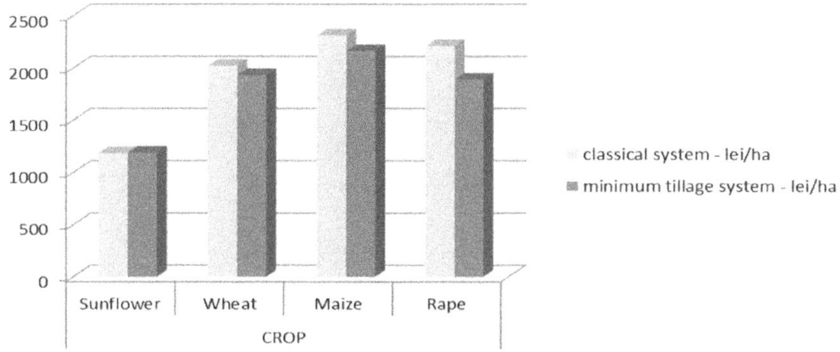

Figure 2: Comparative analysis of the cost of technology in the classical and minimum tillage systems

Source: Processing of the authors.

The technical-economic impact of applying the minimum tillage system refers to: a) savings of fuel and lubricants, and less wear and tear of tractors and farming equipment (less usage, fewer works etc.); growing labour productivity; c) minimizing erosion caused by water or wind; e) increased amount of organic matter in the soil; f) reducing the waste of water through evaporation, due to the partial modification of the soil etc.; (g) reduced production costs by hectare.

Estimation of the impact, technically and economically, of applying the minimum tillage technology, in the agricultural holding SC Agritur SRL, is based on the results of the technological charts drawn up for every type of crop (sunflower, wheat, maize and rape), and on the comparative analysis after using the two technologies, as shown in Figure 2.

As an example, Tables 2 and 3 offer a comparison between the detailed technological charts for the wheat crop, following the application of the two technologies, conventional and minimum tillage.

Conclusions

The minimum tillage of the soil presupposes giving up the basic soil tillage (ploughing) and carrying out works for soil preparation without turning over the furrow, totally or periodically, rationalization of the number of works, and preserving at the soil surface of at least 15–30 % of all the mulch, for the purpose of retaining the water in the soil, which is absolutely necessary for the process of seed germination. This system can be applied on all types of soils and after any plant cultivated before.

The success of this system depends on more aspects such as droughty areas (deep and crumbly soils), coarse and medium texture soils, aired and well drained,

Table 2: Technological chart – wheat crop – conventional technology

Work month	Work name	Diesel used		Costs of services provided by third parties			Expenditure on works executed on own account					Materials used				Total work (lei)
		Specific consumption (l/ha)	Amount (lei)	Area (ha)	Tariff (lei/ha)	Amount (lei)	Area (ha)	Amortization (lei/ha)	Costs of spare parts (lei/ha)	Remuneration (lei/ha)	Amount (lei)	Name	Necessary (U.M./ha)	Price (lei/U.M.)	Amount (lei)	
VIII	Ploughing	23.00	103.50				1.00	3.28	0.53	7.00	10.81			0.00	0.00	114.31
IX	Seeding bed preparation	8.00	36.00				1.00	3.28	0.53	7.00	10.81			0.00	0.00	46.81
IX	Fertilization with ammonium sulfate	1.70	7.65				1.00	0.15	0.02	5.00	5.17	Ammonium sulfate	250.00	1.10	275.00	287.82
X	Sowing	4.50	20.25				1.00	62.16	1.06	7.00	70.22	Seed	280.00	1.50	420.00	510.47
III	Fertilization with urea	1.70	7.65				1.00	0.15	0.02	5.00	5.17	Urea	200.00	2.00	400.00	412.82
IV	Weeding	2.00	9.00				1.00	1.71	0.27	3.00	4.98	Rival Superstar	20.00	3.00	60.00	73.98
IV	Treated with fungicide	2.00	9.00				1.00	1.71	0.27	3.00	4.98	Topsin	1.25	80.00	100.00	113.98
VI	Treated with insect-fungicide	2.00	9.00				1.00			3.00	3.00	Faster	0.15	120.00	18.00	30.00
												Bumper	0.80	150.00	120.00	120.00
VII	Harvesting			1.00	300.00	300.00										300.00
VII	Technological transport	2.00	9.00				1.00	0.10	0.01	3.00	3.11					12.11
	Total	**46.90**				**300.00**		**72.54**	**2.72**	**43.00**						**2022.31**

Source: Agritur. Fişe informative

Table 3: Technological chart – wheat crop –minimum tillage technology

Work month	Work name	Diesel used		Costs of services provided by third parties			Expenditure on works executed on own account				Materials used				Total work (lei)
		Specific consumption (l/ha)	Amount (lei)	Area (ha)	Tariff (lei/ha)	Amount (lei)	Amortization (lei/ha)	Costs of spare parts (lei/ha)	Remuneration (lei/ha)	Amount (lei)	Name	Necessary (U.M./ha)	Price (lei/U.M.)	Amount (lei)	
													0	0	
													0	0	
											Ammonium sulfate	250.00	1.10	275.00	
IX-X	Deep soil mobilization, basic fertilization and sowing in one pass.	18.00	81.00				45.60	20.20	28.00	93.80	Seed	280.00	1.50	420.00	869.80
III	Fertilization with urea	1.70	7.65				0.15	0.02	5.00	5.17	Urea	200.00	2.00	400.00	412.82
IV	Weeding	2.00	9.00				1.71	0.27	3.00	4.98	Rival Superstar	20.00	3.00	60.00	73.98
IV	Treated with fungicide	2.00	9.00				1.71	0.27	3.00	4.98	Topsin	1.25	80.00	100.00	113.98
VI	Treated with insect-fungicide	2.00	9.00						3.00	3.00	Faster	0.15	120.00	18.00	30.00
										0.00	Bumper	0.80	150.00	120.00	120.00
VII	Harvesting			1.00	300.00	300.00								0.00	300.00
VII	Technological transport	2.00	9.00				0.10	0.01	3.00	3.11				0.00	12.11
	Total	**27.70**	**124.65**			**300.00**	**49.27**	**20.77**	**45.00**	**115.04**				**1393.00**	**1932.69**

Source: Agritur. Fişe informative

and last but not least, weeds are eliminated by chemical weeding and by using preventive methods (crop rotation).

The firm discussed, SC Agritur SRL, has met all these requirements, which confirms that the proposal for the unconventional system implementation in this agricultural holding is a correct one, thus replacing the conventional technology with the conservation one. The major argument regarding the change of the system of soil tillage by using, as mandatory, the plough with moldboard (Boincean, 2011), is that with this system of soil tillage about 50–60 % of the amount of water from rainfalls during a year is lost by direct evaporation.

The data published by IPSO Agriculture indicate that the soil preparation by using the minimum tillage generates substantial fuel savings of up to 30 %, reduces the number of kilometers, and the time for preparing the seeding bed, because this technology uses machinery which is wider than the plough, for the same depth of tillage. In the conventional system, the estimated consumption is somewhat higher than in reality. In the ploughing technology, about 10–15 more liters of gas/ha are used as compared to the conservation technology.

References

Agroinfo. September 15, 2013. Available online at https://www.agroinfo.ro/vegetal/in-imb-s-a-renuntat-la-arat-lucrarea-de-baza-a-solului.

Berger, Amélie/Friedrich, Theodor/Kienzle, Josef: Conservation agriculture. In Soils, Plant Growth and Crop Production-Volume I, 2010, pp.79–105.

Boincean, Boris: Lucrarea solului - tendințe și perspective. In: Polemici academice 3(22), September 2011. Available online at www.akademos.asm.md/files/Lucrarea%20solului%20tendinte%20si%20perspective.pdf.

Boja, Nicu/Boja Florin/Cartis Mihaela: Influenta sistemului minim de lucrare asupra proprietăților fizice și a gradului de mărunțire a solului. In: STUDIA UNIVERSITATIS – Seria Ştiinţe Inginereşti şi Agro-Turism 3, 2008, pp. 79–88.

Busari, Mutiu Abolanle/Kukal, Surinder Singh/Kaur, Amanpreet/Bhatt, Rajan/Dulazi, Ashura Ally: Conservation tillage impacts on soil, crop and the environment. International Soil and Water Conservation Research 3, no. 2, 2015, pp. 119–129.

Dobre, Marian: Agricultura fără arătură (no till) – o opțiune revoluționară / Agriculture without plowing (no till) – a revolutionary option. In volume of Symposia 'Sisteme de lucrări minime ale solului', 2011, pp. 351–354. Available online at www.usamvcluj.ro/SMDT/Volum%20simpozion/34%20Dobre%20Marian.pdf.

Kassam, Amir/Rolf Derpsch/Theodor Friedrich: Global achievements in soil and water conservation: The case of Conservation Agriculture. International Soil and Water Conservation Research 2, no. 1, 2014, pp. 5–13.

Rusu, Teodor/Petru Guş/Bogdan, Ileana/Oroian, Ioan/Paulette, Laura: Influence of minimum tillage systems on physical and chemical properties of soil. Journal of Food, Agriculture &Environment, vol. 4 (3–4/2006), 2006, pp. 262–265.

Rusu, Teodor: The influence of minimum tillage systems upon the soil properties, yield and energy efficiency in some arable crops. Journal of Central European Agriculture, 6(3), 2006, pp. 287–294.

Agritur, Sistemele neconvenţionale de lucrare a solului, alternative agrotehnice şi economice pentru agricultura durabilă, Agricultura conservativa. Fişe informative 2009–2016.

IPSO Agriculture: http://www.ipso.ro/

Elisabeta ROŞU[1]

[1] Institute of Agricultural Economics, Romanian Academy,
Email: betty_rosu@yahoo.com

The Sustainable Rural Development Potential: Case Study

Abstract *The evaluating of the current state of development and the trends of evolution is important for the realistic design of the prospects of a sustainable development model in all its essential components: economic, social and environmental. The present study aims to elaboration and fundamentation a Sustainable Rural Development Index based on 5 criteria, with 18 indicators. The index has been applied at the level of six rural communities located in Braila County in order to determine the current state of affairs and also the tendencies of their sustainable rural development.*

Keywords: *current state of rural development, Sustainable Rural Development Index, typology*

Introduction

There are economic and social lacks of balance between the development levels of the country's regions, from one county to another, from one commune to another. It is necessary a realistic assessment of the rural space, starting from the available resources and ending with the favorizing and restrictive factors of the development. The main goal of the present study was the elaboration and fundamentation of the Sustainable Rural Development Index (SRDI) which was applied at the level of six rural communities (NUTS 5) situated in Braila County (NUTS 3).

The index included representative indicators for the economic sector, both agricultural and non-agricultural of the six rural communities, together with demographic, social, technical and environmental indicators. The SRDI values obtained by each commune have permitted, on the one hand the hierarchy and on the other hand the typology according to their level of development. The scope for which we tried to elaborate and fundament this index was to serve as support in the fundamentation of the strategic planning process of the present and future sustainable development of the six rural communities.

1. Literature review

In the last years there were issued some series of studies with major impact in the specialty literature in the socio-economic field. Starting from a multitude of aggregated indicators constructed on sets of variables defined at territorial level (country, region, locality) there were constructed indices measuring different development levels.

The Human Development Index (HDI) is an index used to compare the development level of a country, utilizing socio-economic indicators different from those utilizing its GDP per capita. In the year 2016 it was published the latest report (for 185 of the UN Member States). The index is measuring the life expectancy, the literacy degree, education, life standard, and life quality for all countries being a standard mean to measure the welfare. The index values are inscribing the countries into four human development categories: very high human development, high human development, medium human development, and reduced human development. Romania was inscribed in the category of the countries with a very high human development, place 50 (on the penultimate place of this category) (UNDP 2016, p.22).

In Romania, after1989 there were elaborated and fundamented some series of indices, of which:

- The Commune's Development Index (CDI), which was constructed on the concept of a measure of the community capital and which could be actualised with current data, different than those in the censuses. For the CDI construction it was realized "a grouping of 10 indicators in four groups, referring to particular aspects of the local development" (Dumitru Sandu 2009, p.2). According to CDI the communes in the area studied, were inscribed in two categories: very developed communes - Cazasu and Romanu and communes- medium developed: Siliştea, Vădeni, Traian and Tudor Vladimirescu.
- The Localities'Social Development Index (LSDI) was to be applied both for the communes and towns, within which there were utilized 7 indicators (Dumitru Sandu 2011, p.5). According to LSDI the six rural communities in the county Brăila were inscribed as: commune Cazasu – developed commune, the communes Siliştea, Traian and Vădeni –medium developed and the communes Romanu and Tudor Vladimirescu – poor developed. Both indicators, CDI and LSDI, were measuring the poverty degree of the communes in Romania, less the development potential of each.

2. Methodology

In the following passage we propose the fundamentation of a Sustainable Rural Development Index (SRDI) with which we could make a hierarchy and typology of the six rural communities in county Brăila, from the point of view of their development stage and potential.

For the elaboration of the theoretical analysis model of the present sustainable rural development of the six communities there were held in view 5 analysis criteria in which was operated a set of 18 indicators, the study year being 2015. Data were obtained from the official database of the National Statistics Institute, except those

Table 1: Sustainable Rural Development Index

SRDI
Criterion 1 – Human Resources
1. Number of inhabitants
2. Population density
3. Share of population with age between 0–14 in total population– young population
4. Share of population with age of 15–64 in total population– population of working age
Criterion 2 – Economy of agricultural sector
1. Agricultural area
2. Number of active enterprises in the agricultural sector / 1000 inhabitants
3. Number of salary workers in the active enterprises in the agricultural sector
4. Work efficiency in the agricultural sector
Criterion 3 – Economy of non-agricultural sector
1. Number of active enterprises in the non-agricultural sector /1000 inhabitants
2. Number of salary workers in the active enterprises in the non-agricultural sector
3. Work efficiency in the non-agricultural sector
Criterion 4 – Social and dwelling
1. Number of inhabitants /physician
2. Number of pupils/ teacher
3. Number of new dwellings built
4. Share of population connected at the network for edible water in total population
Criterion 5 – Environment
1. Share of areas with degraded and un-productive lands in total area of the commune
2. Share of forest area in total area of the commune
3. Area of sites of community importance at commune level

Source: own model to choose the criteria and component indicators.

referring to the area of community sites at the level of each commune, obtained from the official data of the Ministry of Agriculture and Rural Development.

Indicators were chosen in function of their relevance in describing the stage and present potential of sustainable rural development of the communes in the area studied, in function of their availability in the official statistical source, known being the fact that a series of indicators which would be more relevant for the analysis are not available at commune level and in function of their compatibility with other indicators, which are important for the describing of the level of sustainable rural development.

The first criterion of the analysis–human resource, the human potential, represents the most important resource of a rural community and is a factor with a maximum influence in the process of its economic development. Population is the one who produces, who consumes and who is benefiting from the socio-economic development of the territory in which it lives.

Number of inhabitants of the communes is important as it represents the human potential each commune has. The inhabitants of a rural have a double quality, they represent its labor force, an important production factor, but also are the consumers of the results of economic activities developed on that territory.

Population density represents the degree of a territory populating.

The share of population with age of 0–14 in total population of the commune represents the young population of the commune that who will enter on labor market in the near future and will actively contribute to the economic development.

The share of the population with age of 15–65 in total population of the commune represents the population of working age, the active population, who contributes in the analysis moment to the economic development.

For the analysis of the agricultural sector's economy there were chosen other indicators:

- Agricultural area - represents the area on which the economic activity is developed – agriculture, in a quantitative way this determines the specific of the rural community from point of view of economic activities.
- Number of the active enterprises in the agricultural sector /1000 inhabitants represents the density of economic agents which have as activity object - agriculture, hunting and annex activities at the level of the six administrative territorial units.
- Number of salary workers in the active enterprises in the agricultural sector is an indicator which shows how much of labor force exists in this sector.
- Labor productivity in the agricultural sector shows the degree of present human resource utilization degree.

For the analysis of the economy of non-agricultural sector, which comprised all the other economic activities developed at the level of the six rural communities, there were chosen the indicators:

- Number of active enterprises in the non-agricultural sector /1000 inhabitants represents the density of economic agents, having as object of activity- others than agriculture.
- Number of salary workers in the active enterprises in the non-agricultural sector represents the dimension of labor force in these sectors.
- Labor productivity in the non-agricultural sector, shows the utilization degree of the present human resource.

The social and dwelling aspect comprises indicators referring to the population's accessibility to health and education. The technical-dwelling equipment represents a basic element in ensuring the necessary conditions for a decent living, but also for the economic development of rural communities. Thus, the indicators comprised in this criterion are:

- Number of inhabitants/one physician represents accessibility of the population to qualified medical assistance and has connection with the general health state of population. As the healthier the population, as more apt to work the labor force is, contributing to the zone's development.
- Number of pupils/ teacher represents accessibility of rural population to instruction, education. The population with a precarious education is hardly integrated on the labor market while the population with a high instruction level contributes to the zone's development.
- Number of dwellings newly built is a modernity indicator, relevant for the living standard.
- The share of population connected to the network of edible water distribution in total population represents the access to water, an obligatory requirement for ensuring some minimum hygiene conditions which contribute also to the maintaining of the health condition in an adequate way, and also ensures the support for development of the different economic activities at the household's level.

In the context of the goal proposed – the environmental criterion comprises the available indicators and considered as most relevant for the six communes in the area studied.

- The share of areas with degraded and unproductive lands in total area of the commune shows the degree in which lands were affected by different degrading factors, be they natural, or resulted following the human activities.
- The share of forest area in total area of the commune is an indicator which in case of the six communes in the area studied has not an important contribution in the economy by exploiting the forest fund, but has an important role in the environmental protection by protecting against extreme weather phenomena (blizzards, strong winds, storms).
- The area of the natural areas in total area of the commune shows the concern of authorities for the environmental protection.

The indicators in the SRDI are indicators of maximum, except 3 of them, which are of minimum (number of inhabitants/one physician, number of pupils/teacher and respectively the share of area with degraded and un-productive lands in total area UAT). High values of them represent a low degree of accessibility to medical services, but also to the education ones, and on the other hand an expanded area of degraded and un-productive lands, represents a negative factor, both for a balanced development, and for the environment.

In order to avoid the possibility to obtain some negative values the indicators' normalization was realized by the formula: $v_1 = (v - vmin) / aa$, where: v_1 – represents the normalized value; v – represents the indicator's value; vmin – represents the minimum value registered by each indicator; aa – represents the absolute amplitude of each indicator.

It was obtained a value for each criterion for each commune, and by summing up all the values obtained for each criterion it was obtained a single value, that of the SRDI of each commune. On its basis, first it was made a hierarchy of the six communes, and secondly, a typology of them from the point of view of the stage and potential of rural development.

The data statistical processing was made with SPSS program being detached this way the causal determinative relationships, using factorial analysis (the method: Analyzing the Main Components).

3. Results and discussions

According to the methodology described previously, it was calculated a value for each criterion for each commune, and by the summing up of the obtained values at all five criteria, it was obtained a single SRDI value which permitted, afterwards, the hierarchy of the six communes.

The criterion: human resources positioned the commune Cazasu on the first place, on the last place being placed the commune Romanu. The commune: Cazasu has obtained the first place within the criterion of human resources, due to the high density of the inhabitants and the high share of the persons of working age.

The commune Traian was situated on the first place as regards the economy of agricultural sector supported being by the size of the agricultural area, by the big number of enterprises activating in this sector and by their big number of employees. Commune Cazasu situated on the last place, obtaining minimum points at three of four analyzed indicators. In conclusion, commune Traian has a strong agricultural sector, while the economy of Cazasu commune is not based on agriculture.

Table 2: Sustainable Rural Development Index (SRDI)

Commune	Human resources	Economy of agricultural sector	Economy of non-agricultural sector	Social and dwelling	Environment	SRDI	Hierarchy
Cazasu	2.65	0.93	2.54	3.19	0.68	9.99	II
Romanu	0.35	2.41	0.17	2.41	1.09	6.43	V
Siliştea	1.72	1.53	1.14	1.97	1.15	7.51	III
Traian	1.83	3.49	0.46	0.63	1.04	7.44	IV
Tudor Vladimirescu	0.50	1.17	0.00	0.87	1.04	3.58	VI
Vădeni	2.33	2.21	2.29	1.72	2.11	10.66	I

Source: own calculation

Whereas the economy of the non-agricultural sector positioned commune Cazasu on the first place, due to the big number of enterprises, activating in the non-agricultural sector and their big number of employees. The commune: Tudor Vladimirescu situated on the last place within this criterion, which means that its economy is not based on the non-agricultural sector.

The commune Cazasu situated on first place at the criterion: social and dwelling, supported being in this position, first by the dwelling indicators of the model (newly built dwellings in total dwellings and the share of population connected to the network of edible water distribution). The commune Traian situated on the last place at this criterion, due to the biggest number of inhabitants per one physician, but also to the lowest share of population connected to the network of edible water distribution. So, in the commune Cazasu the living standard is a high one, while in the commune Traian is the lowest within the area made of the six rural communities.

The commune: Vădeni situated on the first place at the criterion: environment, supported being on this position by the highest shares of foreast area in total area of the commune from the six communes of the studiead areal, but also by a significant area occupied by the sites of Natura 2000. On the last place within this criterion situated commune Cazasu, due to the fact that it has the smallest area with forest and forest vegetation and does not have on its territory community importance sites. To be remarked is the fact that although commune Tudor Vladimirescu has the biggest area with sites of Natura 2000 within the six communes in the studied area, it is the commune with the biggest percentage of degraded and un-productive lands.

Summing up the values resulted for each commune at each five criteria it was obtained a SRDI for each commune of the six of the studied area.

Thus, on the first place it was situated the commune Vădeni supported being by the human resources and by the economy of the two sectors, both non-agricultural and agricultural; on the second place it was situated the commune Cazasu due to the dwelling and social endowment, the human resources and the economy of the non-agricultural sector; on the third place was situated the commune Siliştea registering a rather balanced score within the component criteria; on the fourth place commune Traian was situated, supported mainly by the economy of the agricultural sector; on the fifth place was situated the commune Romanu supported also by the economy of the agricultural sector; on the last place it was situated the commune: Tudor Vladimirescu in which the non-agricultural sector is not present, only the economy of agricultural sector and the environment were the most important within the value registered by the index.

If we are to group the six communes by the score registered by the SRDI, into three categories, we can affirm that two communes situated in the first category: Vădeni and Cazasu, other three situated in the second category: Siliştea, Traian and Romanu and only one commune was situated in the third category: Tudor Vladimirescu. If, to each category was attributed a development level, then, the first category would be the one with a high potential of development, the second one with medium development potential, and the last one, with low development potential. According to the SRDI values obtained by each commune and the grouping of communes, the six communes in the studied area can be grouped as: communes with high development potential: Vădeni and Cazasu; communes with medium development potential: Siliştea, Traian and Romanu; communes with reduced development potential: Tudor Vladimirescu.

Processing of the data evidenced the fact that the accentuated development level of human resources and that of the agricultural sector determine the development level of the investigated rural zone. In this interactional mechanism, environment does not significantly influence upon the zone's development level.

The agricultural sector is characteristic for the studied zone, but the negative correlation with the non-agricultural sector means that the development of the agricultural sector is not made in the paradigm of modernization of the processing operations and implicitly of sustaining and increase of the non-agricultural sector development; the dependence between them is negative which shows an economic gap in the rural economy; the two types of economy are following their own development trajectories, do not potentiate each other and do not influence each other reciprocally, moreover in the conditions they are intersecting themselves this is made in their detriment (the correlation being negative).

The factorial analysis, through which the identification of factors was made, factors influencing the development level, clarified the following aspects: the variables chosen for the model of rural development are representative, between them existing significant statistic ratios. Communality is ensured because each of the variables chosen has a common variant with the variant of the other variables (human resources=0.94, non-agricultural sector=0.93, environmental=0.73). The values, very close, of all variables are suggesting the fact that they are well represented by the factorial model utilized. The variant explained by each factor is distributed as: human resources 47.3 %, agricultural sector 28.7 %, non-agricultural sector 11.9 %, social and dwelling 10.8 % and environment 1.3 %. The hierarchy of the determinative factors for the zone's development once made, the first two were evidenced: human resources (2.367) and agricultural sector (1.435). Using the Benzecri criterion (coverage criterion over 70 %) and the Keiser criterion (the criterion of the supra-unitary value) we extracted the factors that meet the two conditions: human resources and the agricultural economy. Thus, it can be said that the main factors influencing the development level are: human resources and agricultural economy.

Conclusions

The sustainable rural development index (SRDI) is useful for the establishing the present level of the sustainable rural development and for the identification of the potential for developing the studied area, being able to constitute an efficient modality of diagnosis and prognosis for the local authorities to establish the goals of local development, on long and medium term.

The indicators which have entered in the componence of the five SRDI criteria can be extracted anytime from the official statistical sources, being available on-line without depending on the statistical results obtained at great intervals of time (surveys, censuses).

Although the index was constructed only at the level of six rural communities, it can be adapted and utilized as model for all the communes in the county Brăila, it also can be utilized at regional or national level in order to assess the present stage and potential, but also the future development trends.

References

1. Dumitru, Sandu; Voineagu, V., Filoftia Panduru, (2009), Dezvoltarea comunelor din Romania, INS, SAS, http:\\dumitru.sandu.googlepages.com
2. Dumitru Sandu, (2011), Social Disparities in the Regional Development and Policies of Romania, în International Review of Social Research, volume 1, Issue 1, pag.1–30, https://www.researchgate.net/publication/276291942_Social_Disparities_in_the_Regional_Development_and_Policies_of_Romania
3. National Institute of Statistics (INS), database www.tempo-online, www.e-demos
4. MADR (2017), Lista ariilor naturale protejate Natura 2000, http://www.madr.ro/informari-dezvoltare-rurala/informari/actualitate-pndr-2014-2020/download/1994_9f17599376e2c9881422552a7af355e5.html
5. United Nations Development Programme (2016), Human Development Reports, www.undp.org

Romulus GRUIA[1], *Radu REY*[2], *Liviu GACEU*[1]

[1] Transilvania University of Brasov - Workstation Research and Study Centre for Agriculture and Forestry Biodiversity „Acad. David Davidescu"

and CE-MONT/INCE, Romanian Academy, Email: ecotec@unitbv.ro

[2] Center of Mountain Economy (CE-MONT), Romanian Academy; Email: cabinet_fmr@yahoo.com

Study on Animal Protein in Mountain Zoo-Products, a Reference for New Trends in Animal Husbandry in High Areas, as Adaptation to Climate Change

Abstract *Climate change is an obvious reality, it is the issue of adapting agro-zoo technical production to the new geo-climatic conditions. This review focuses on the mountain and piedmont area, where the zootechnics branch has all the chances to develop in the future and further, due to the climatic changes. The animals in the mountain area benefit from a high quality vegetation carpet, of great floral diversity, and will also produce zoo-products with special qualities. One of the traits studied is the amount and quality of protein in mountain products (meat, milk, eggs, and mountain fish) in relation to external factors (climatic, technological, managerial, ecological, etc.). The paper highlights the importance of the protein quality of zoo products, as well as the current situation of production, with the pluses and minuses registered in relation to the current market, with the health of consumers and the environment, on the principles of the bioeconomy, but also with the future requirements in a world in demographic, geo-political and climate change. In addition to this overall monitoring and diagnosis objective, the work is specifically aimed at identifying solutions in principle for future decades, conceptual and technological reorientation towards the mountain livestock economy.*

Keywords: *animals, bioeconomics, climate, montanology, protein*

Introduction

Climate changes emphasis is more and more evident. Effects are graver and graver, which results even when enumerating them: increase of annual average temperature; alternation between abnormally warm periods and abnormally cold ones; periods of time with precipitations much more over multiannual average in alternation with drought ones; the increase of summer day number and of tropical ones; decrease of winter day number; increase of the number of risk natural phenomena: tropical cyclones, hurricanes, tornados, hailstone rains, acid rains etc; decrease of the number of snowy days; increase of amplitude of extreme monthly and yearly temperatures; acceleration of iceberg melting rhythm with effects upon the growth of Planetary Ocean level. (Tomescu, 2013)

Consequences are frightening, as, for example, apparition of the hole in the ozone stratum in high latitude zone (in seems though that it has started to close), so important ozone stratum, that rises from almost 15 km high to approximately 40 km altitude and absorbs 97 %-99 % from high frequency ultraviolet radiations. (Bates et al., 2008)

It must be specified that in scientific world opinions concerning the real causes of climate changes are split. Most of researchers sustain the theory of planetary heating due to the negative action of the human factor and, especially, of the increase of the emissions of greenhouse effect gases, while a (smaller) part considers that we are in the period of an insufficient knowledge of the causes and consequences of this process. (Ardelean, Florinela, Colda Iolanda, Universitatea Tehnică de Construcții București) Beyond causes, the acute problem is represented by the ever more dramatic effects linked to climate changes, with unknown directions (there are theories indicating a climate cooling).

According to UNO's projects of the experts from the Intergovernmental Group regarding climate evolution (IPPC), until the year 2100, the increase of average temperature at globe surface will be between 1, 4 and 5, 7 Celsius grades, so that probably a 4^0 C change would have the same amplitude as the heating that put an end to the last ice age and that has radically modified the world's geographic-biologic map. Consequences will be dramatic, that may be also largely seen at present: catastrophic floods and prolonged droughts, season bouleversement, rapid passing from warm weather to cold one, from drought to rain abundance, traditional cultures affectation up to destruction. (Pachauri, Reisinger, 2008)

As for biodiversity, there is stipulated a real climate shock with temperature leaps that normally happen in thousands of years, allowing living creatures to adapt themselves at the environment, and that now happen in a century. Such a climate change may produce a biodiversity loss estimated to a third of all planet species up to the year 2050. There are scenarios that show that on long term (until 2100) it may be possible for the present life form to disappear and, probably, another new one may appear. The agricultural production will be compromise, looking for alternative solutions, especially linked to the lack of agricultural fertile land (as for example nodular agriculture in space and controlled environment). It is not excluded that mankind may become a "greenhouse species", continuing to survive only under artificially built conditions. The examples come especially from the highly affected areas, such as the Mediterranean ones, but where intense concerns and large countermeasures are found. (Olea, Sanmiguel-Aynz, 2006)

Practically, the northern zone of temperate climate strongly expands between the Tropic of Cancer, from approximately 23.5 grades northern latitude up to the Northern Polar Circle, at about 66.5 northern latitude. It is an area where Romania

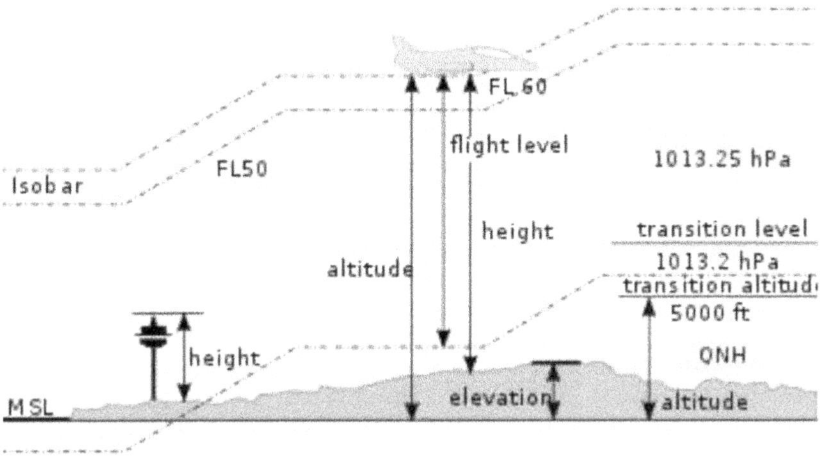

Figure 1: Classic model of exemplification of altitude and height difference

is in fact situated too and, of course, our country is not an exception from the climate change process. This process if an obvious reality and manifests itself, either concerning temperature (generally higher, with drought, especially in the south or south-east of Romania, and sometimes with cooling periods), or a reduced pluviometric regime, or concerning the alternation of meteorological indicators during extremely short periods (sometimes from one day to another). Therefore the question arises to adapt the agro-zoo technical production to the new geo-climate conditions. The average latitude imposes the climate realities all over Romania's territory, but a series of differences appear in relation to altitude, taking into consideration that there are important differences from sea level, up to over 2000 m altitudes. (Colda, Ardelean, 2004)

Analyzing especially altitude, we remind that the height of a point from the Earth surface in relation to a reference level, usually considered the still sea surface, called absolute altitude, or face to another reference point from the Earth surface, called relative altitude, as shown in figure 1 (Altitudinea).

In the paper we are approaching the territorial area of high altitude (mountain and submountain) where the animal breeding branch is well represented, but which has all chances to develop even more in the future, consequently to climate modifications. Global heating will make climate factors from plain and hill zones to be largely found in high altitude zones. In the future environment conditions animals bred in the mountain zone will benefit of a qualitative vegetable carpet, one of a high floral diversity, they will also achieve zoo-products with special qualities.

One of the pursued characteristics is protein quantity and quality from mountain animal products in relation to climate changes. In the paper, the made diagnosis underlines the importance of zoo-product protein quality, as well as the production present situation, with registered pluses and minuses. All these are analyzed in relation to present market, to consumers' and environment's health, to bio economy principles, but also to future demands in a world of demographic, geo-political and climate change at planetary level.

The hypothesis from which we start the analyses refers to climate changes (banded dynamics and intensity of climate factors, with ascendant trend of the average annual temperature) that impose animal breeding production adaptation on altitude gradients, because mountain and sub mountain zones will have other climate parameters (taking into consideration the global heating). Recent studies (Maruşca, 2012) show the impact of climate change on the agro-forest area is in some devastating areas so that gradually, high zones will offer more and more appropriate conditions for a diversified vegetable carpet with plants coming from other altitude zones, i.e. a fodder structure that will allow to maximize animal breeding activities. Average and high altitude zones may practically become the reservoir of animal protein, respectively of profound and efficient specialization of animal breeding in function of gradient of altitude.

In this context, the paper's general objective is to emphasize the importance of animal breeding and zoo-product quality in the mountain zone, in the idea to adapt activity at stipulated climate changes for the decades to come. An adjacent objective is to pursue protein quality from mountain products (meat, milk, eggs, mountain fish), in relation to external factors (climate, technical and ecological ones). The paper emphasizes the importance of zoo-product protein quality as well as the production present situation, in relation to consumers' health and the environment, on bio economy principles, but also to future demands in a world in demographic and geo-political change, as well as, considering what it has already been specified, linked to climate modifications at planetary level.

1. Material and method

There are used a series of data from the theme fields (climatology, biology, animal breeding, alimentary chemistry) for analyses of exhaustive and multicriterial type. There are monitored a series of species and races of animals as analyses material of genetic resource biodiversity from the mountain zone. The data of various authors are processed by our own analysis, on the axis: climatology – genetic amelioration – zootechnical production in zones of high altitude – protein structure and zoo-production quality.

2. Results and discussions

2.1. Premises linked to climate specificity

It is known that climatology field uses statistic data as, for example, to explain climatic heating by increase of the content of carbon dioxide from the atmosphere as a result of volcanic activity or anthropic activities. The best available proofs suggest that in the last three million years (!) it has never been registered such a level (average daily level over the threshold of 400 parts per million) on Terra, which announces massive changes in climate and in the level of planetary ocean.

Starting from factors that influence climate, especially solar radiation and region position (geographic latitude, altitude, relation sea / earth, existence of marine currents, existence of air currents), we may classify climatic zones in order to emphasize the altitude importance in the "equation" of climatic changes, respectively of mountain zones (Table 1).

As a general observation, we consider as probable climate "translation" in relation to altitude, namely the more frequent estimation in zones with average and especially high altitude, to find a tempered-continental climate. In this direction, beyond latitudinal specificity, we enumerate a series of aspects that we already largely observe at present in zones with high altitudes, respectively, we enumerate the following characteristics (Colda, Ardelean, 2004; Green Report):

- Summers are hot (the average monthly temperature during summer being 20–30 ^{0}C).
- Winters are severe (the average monthly temperature during winter being between -10 and -40 ^{0}C).
- The highest annual thermal amplitudes (i.e., the difference between the highest and the lowest temperatures registered in a year).
- Annual precipitations are approximately 500–800 mm and fall especially in spring and summer.
- There especially blow western winds.
- It has 4 seasons (although spring and autumn begin to shorten) etc.

We mention that, traditionally, in the east of Europe, tempered-continental climate is excessive, i.e. winters are long and severe and summers are short and hot. But in the last decades summers have become much hotter and winters "tamed themselves" as for the temperature, except for the mountain zone and mountain depressions.

In the mountain zone over 1800 m one may meet a cold tempered climate that certain people call boreal cold climate. It is the coldest climate within tempered climate, the region is characterized by poor boreal vegetation, with long winters, usually with very cold temperatures and short summers, with cool and mild temperatures. Taking into consideration that the polar climate zone will drastically diminish at high altitudes of the mountains from northern latitude, tempered-continental and cold tempered climate extends, which constitutes premises for a more abundant vegetation, that may improve biodiversity in this area. Consequently, it may be estimated that there appear better food conditions for animals too at altitudes of over 800 m, which entitles us to take into consideration the idea that high zones may represent a good reserve for the development of animal breeding. The immediate condition is to concentrate the research efforts in genetic amelioration and obtain new sorts of plants and animal races adapted to

Table 1: Probable dynamics of climatic modifications

A. PRESENT SITUATION		
I. Hot zone	II. Temperate zone	III. Cold zone
1. Equatorial climate 2. Subequatorial climate 3. Dry-tropical climate(desert) 4. Wet-tropical climate	1. Subtropical climate (Mediterranean climate) 2. Tempered-maritime climate 3. Tempered-continental climate 4. Cold tempered climate	1. Subarctic climate (sub polar) 2. Polar climate

B. PROBABLE DYNAMICS OF CLIMATIC CHANGES			
Extension of hot zone	Modification of tempered zone		Reduction of cold zone
	Low altitude (plain)	Average altitude (hill zone)	High altitude (pre mountain and mountain)
- Dry-tropical climate (desert / lack of water) - Wet-tropical climate (buffer with Probability of reduction of extension towards tempered zone)		- Subtropical climate (Mediterranean climate) - Maritime-tempered climate - Tempered- Continental Climate	- Tempered – Continental Climate - Cold-tempered climate (over 1800 m)

the mountain zone, respectively to the new environment conditions resulting from climate changes.

2.2. Biological impact of climate changes

It is obvious that climate changes have an unsuspected biologic impact upon all living creatures, including upon the human species. More than that, the impact is also linked to altitude gradient, as it has already suggested, which means that there are real chances to even more develop the animal breeding activity in high zones and to obtain particularly qualitative aliments for man's food. From recent analyzes (Maruşca, T, 2017) it was found that every 100 m altitude the temperature drops by 0.5^{0}C and if the average temperature in the Carpathians increases by 3^{0} C until 2070, it is expected to increase the floors vegetation with 600 m, where the subalpine and alpine floor will disappear. Instead of replacing them with more friendly vegetation levels, they will increase livestock and the protein quality of zoo products at high altitudes (over 1000 m). Put it otherwise, the mountain may become a reservoir of animal protein.

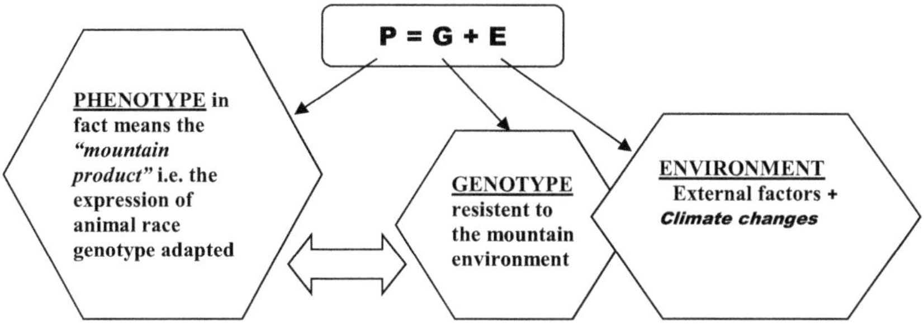

Figure 2: Explicative model of the conditions necessary to obtain qualitative mountain products

We analyze the problem having as basis the standard formula of genetic amelioration, in which the phenotype is the expression of genotype in relation to the "correction" of the environment factors: P = G + E (Figure 2).

"Mountain product" means animal (and resulting production) phenotype by expressing the animal race genotype and the vegetable fodder carpet, i.e. the sorts of plants adapted to the mountain zones, but also with the strong "correction" of the difficult mountain environment, sometimes hostile. At this rate, it becomes obligatory to improve animal races resistant at alternant dynamics of climate factors, i.e. to have a (genetically programmed) metabolism that stimulates a physical-chemical structure that will raise the quality level of the zoo-products obtained in these conditions.

2.3. Zoo-production quality in high altitude zones

In principle, the environment factors more "severe" in pre mountain and mountain zones (altitude levels as a rule over 800 m and, respectively, over 1000 m) have a beneficial impact upon the metabolism of vegetal and animal organism from this area, stimulating certain active biologic substances that considerably improve quality on the axis "fodder – animal organism – mountain product". What interests in this paper is to lay the basis of the manner how climate changes may influence this metabolic process of principle. It is thus opened a large field for future researches referring to energetic, metabolic, physic-chemical, sensorial etc. Biotransformation regarding animal products obtained in high altitude area.

A first idea would be the one referring to the reduction of certain parameters of zoo-product quality on terms of the growth of annual average temperature, taking as a reference, in order to exemplify, the probable protein degradation. It becomes opportune in this direction to remind some aspects concerning protein structure, namely that proteins are macromolecular organic substances formed out of simple or complex chains of amino acids and they are present in the cells of all living organisms in proportion of over 50 % from the dry weight. They are chemical compounds that mainly contain carbon, nitrogen, oxygen and hydrogen atoms. All proteins are amino acid polymers, in which their sequence is codified by a gene. Every protein has its unique sequence of amino acids, determined by the nucleolidic sequence of the gene. (Rey, R., 2013; Tamba-Berehoiu, R., 2015; Gruia, R., 2017; Calitatea proteinelor, 2016)

Offering an integrated perspective of proteins, both at cell but also at systemic level, this study suggests how biologic and climatic evolution determines proteins to adopt structures from the field, which combine themselves in order to get biologic results. The mechanism shows that protein association in dimmers (molecular machines and multi-enzymatic complexes) allows them to obtain a catalytic and functional efficiency of the manner in which proteins represent an up to date and authoritarian report of the protein function in the living systems. (Williamson, 2012)

As proteins are to be found in the majority of perishable food products, constituting basic sustenance in most of aliments of animal origin (meat, eggs, milk) and vegetable one (beans, peas, lentil, soya, etc.), they may be a reference element for modifications due to external factors (of environment or anthropical ones). Besides their energetic role, proteins especially have a plastic (formative) role, contributing to organism growth and destroyed tissue restoration by organism functioning and wearing out. They also enter in hormone, enzyme and antibody composition, with an important role in the organism metabolic functioning. (Damodaran, 1989; Choi, Park, 2002; Tamba-Berehoi, 2015; Proteina, considerente generale) Proteins of animal origin are easier assimilated in the organism than those of vegetable origin, which makes the mountain zone, favorite for animal breeding, be a "reservoir" of qualitative proteins.

If we analyze protein quality and the vulnerability of their degradation in conditions of high temperatures, either directly through processing, or indirectly through animal metabolism, we will take into consideration that muscular tissues, proteins, are to be found under the form of myofibril proteins, sacra-plasmatic proteins and proteins of the coupling tissues (collagen, elastin) (Banu,C. et al.,1997). Myofibril proteins are of interest, which determine the quality of muscle texture and the large capacity to couple water, reaching, for example, up to 75 % from the total of proteins from fish muscle and up to 50 % from the total of proteins at beef muscle. (Xiong, 1994; Iwata et al., 2000; Paschoalick, 2003)

Therefore, the creation of more favorable environment conditions at average and high altitudes by stipulated climate changes will allow the extension of the breeding of species that "donate" qualitative animal protein in premountain and mountain zones (mammals, fish, and birds). Unfortunately, it is not excluded that climate changes might be extremely destructive, through too large alternations of climate indicators, which will make life impossible in high altitude zones too.

2.4. Pragmatic elements of the capitalization of animal species adapted to the mountain zone in the conditions of stipulated climate modifications

Taking into account the scenario in which climate changes will allow animal production at high altitudes, we have in view the capitalization through valuable protein qualitative zoo-productions both of species from farms, and those coming from mountain fauna (from hunting and fishing). We are referring to obtain animal protein from species currently bred (poultry and pigs), as well as the one coming from the meat of species from mountain rivers and pisciculture (meat rich in amino acids, methionine and phenyl alanine). To be noticed is the fact that protein weight may diminish in favor of fats in function of stress factors (example high density in ponds). (Westphalen et al., 2005; Todoran, 2015)

The priority of exploiting animals in premountain and mountain zones is, of course, cow and sheep breeding and exploitation. Meat and milk quality is directly linked to the content in proteins, demarche sustained by specific technical and managerial elements. A series of practical aspects to be followed, at cow species, in order to successfully achieve animal protein obtaining in the high altitude area are presented in synthesis in table 2.

The meat cow may be an alternative for the mountain zone Romanian farmers, activity that may economically revive this area. Meat races are not very pretentious, they may resist to more difficult environment conditions, and the Carpathian Mountain climate is favorable for this, especially if we also take into consideration climate changes that have as an effect biodiversity extension towards higher and higher altitudes (very cold at present).

In that direction, there must be initiated programs to educate those who want to develop such an activity and be imagined programs to involve as many young people as possible from the mountain zone to develop farms (as for example those with 10–15 bovines for meat in conformity with the Bavarian or Alsacien model). We mean the Piemontese cow which is a meat race, but also with a good enough milk production (the conversion relation of food in meat is among the highest at this race, at which is also added a good sacrificing yield, of 66–68 %), comparatively to the Aberdeen Angus race, specialized only for meat production. In mountain zones, even at above 2.000 meters, during summer, cows are freely bred on high altitude lawns with advantageous results. (Dirzu, 2017; Grigoriev, 2017; Regulament de organizare ferma didactică agroturistică montană, 2007)

As is known, the quality of a protein source is measured by several parameters: the rate of protein efficiency, its biological value, degree of use or degree of digestibility, and so on. All of this indicates a future research direction to the issue of this review, which will continue the in-depth analysis of species and breeds with adaptability to the new climate conditions expected for the mountain area.

A considerable potential of animal protein from meat and milk from high altitude zones is represented by the sheep species. Sheep breeding, in the history of the Romanian people and of the Carpathian Mountains, not only accompanies the Romanian people history and the Carpathian Mountains, but, having well adapted races, the chance exists to ameliorate them in changeable climate conditions (the head with long muzzle is well adapted to the specificity of the vegetable carpet of high lawns). In addition, there also exists the great opportunity at European level, where sheep meat consumption in certain countries is completed, up to 50 %, from New Zeeland for example and not from European Unit countries (Consumul de carne de oaie, 2017). Besides, there are greater and greater demands from the

Table 2: Principles to obtain animal protein from beef meat and milk in the mountain area

Nr.	Specification	Animal Protein Cow Species	
		Meat	**Milk**
1	Importance as Mountain Zoo-Product ff High Proteic Quality	- Cow breeding is a traditional activity, especially of the population from pre mountain and mountain zones. The importance for the mountain zone also consists in potential diversity of the productions made by cow breeding, with more reduced consumption of energy and lawn flora texture and typology of high quality fodders. These are elements that confer cow breeding and exploitation, but also meat processing, the character of durable and of high perspective activity. Moreover, it assures labor force stability in mountain rural zone.	- Cow breeding for milk is a basic occupation in the mountain rural zone, achieving a strategic product with a particular protein impact upon children, aged persons, as well as upon those with different affections. - It assures superior capitalization of fodders got from surfaces of fodder basis in natural system (mountain lawns); but achieving an optimal animal load per surface unit in view of using the production potential of the mountain feeding basis. - Mountain milk and dairy products constitute the certain source for commercial exchanges with extra mountain zones.
2	Elements of Technical Program	- Stimulation of effective breeding in mountain zones that present opportunities in cow breeding as biodiversity with feeding potential extends in the area with higher and higher altitude, in function of climate warming measure. - Integration of the activity of cow effective amelioration at new environment conditions, but also in conformity with the EU norms and standards, as well as promotion of the activity of cow effective amelioration in direction of meat production increase and improvement. - Increase of matrix effective and birth rate in view of the increase of young cow effective meant to fattening and sacrificing at optimal weight.	- Sustaining the milk production sector, for its quantitative and qualitative increase, in view of alignment at European Commission standards - Processing and assuring population food security with milk and mountain dairy products of high protein quality. - Sustaining efficient capitalization of milk as raw material will allow achieving investments in activity changeover technic necessary to get controllable dairy products, with superior quality and deadline.

Table 2: Continued

Nr.	Specification	Animal Protein Cow Species	
		Meat	**Milk**
3	Management Principles	- Financial sustaining of exploitation organization in associations, in view of representing their interests in relation to input providers and beneficiaries of achieved products. - Assuring own incomes through the capitalization of the production as exportation merchandise. - Stimulation to organize exploitations in associations, in view of representing their interests in relation to inputs and finite product beneficiaries. - Stimulation to organize competitive and effective exploitations in rural and mountain zone, having as effect to increase own incomes and pass from self consumption to commercial production.	- Necessity of a financial support in order to balance the capitalization price at the inner producer with the one achieved in EU; without balanced adjustment of the price relation between the processing sector and production, it appears the risk to diminish animal effectives. - Stimulation to organize effective and competitive exploitations concerning the transition from the production dedicated to self consumption to commercial production and organizes farmers in associations in view of representing their interests in their relations with milk processors.

Arabian world, where temperature growth becomes more and more pregnant a limitative factor for animal breeding.

For Romania, protein from sheep meat may be a great chance in the decades to come, with the condition of intelligent policy and strategy. We mean a financing system for specialized races, either the meat ones or the milk ones, in order to be competitive on the unique European market. We mention here that competition is harsh enough (for example, in order to successfully enter in this market, it is obligatory to have the animal carcass at European standards, in case of meat races, with a good relation between proteins and fats). Also, to revive the mountain zone, it becomes obligatory NOT to export living animals, but processed animal products, i.e. aliments rich in protein, under the "mountain product" trade.

Conclusions

In the situation in which climate changes will not irrecoverably destroy favorable environment and biodiversity from the mountain zone, there is the probability that global warming moves to higher altitudes acceptable living conditions for living organisms, because they grow the vegetation floors by 600 meters starting with lower zones (plain and hill, with more and more desert surfaces), so that there may appear better conditions of food for animals at altitudes over 800–1000 m too.

The mountain, with its zones of average and high altitude, may practically become „the reservoir of animal protein" for future decades, respectively of well adapted specialization in function of altitude gradient, with animal species genetically ameliorated and animal breeding effectiveness, i.e. to have a metabolism (genetically programmed) that stimulates a physic-chemical structure that will raise quality level of the zoo-products got under hostile conditions.

"Mountain product" practically means animal phenotype and zoo-production achievement, through the expression of animal race genotype and plant sorts from the feeding carpet, but also with the strong "correction" of the mountain environment with changed climate parameters, "harsher" environment factors from the pre mountain and mountain zone stimulating certain more active biologic substances, especially protein "constellation", that considerably raises animal product quality on the axes "feeding -animal organism -mountain product".

Proteins of animal origin are easier assimilated in the organism than those of vegetable origin, which makes the mountain zone appropriate for animal breeding, a hope to get proteins of good quality, with an important energetic and nourishing role, with structures that belong to hormone, enzyme and antibody composition, all of these decisively contributing to organism growth, to destroyed tissue recovery and to harmonious metabolic functioning, so that the extension of the breeding of species „donors" of animal protein in pre mountain and mountain zones (mammals, fish, poultry, bees, from farms or hunting) may become of great interest in conditions of demographic and climate changes.

References

Ardelean, Florinela şi Colda, Iolanda, 2015: Cauzele schimbărilor climatice - un subiect controversat, comunicare Universitatea Tehnică de Construcţii Bucureşti, ardelean@333.org.

Banu, C., Alexe, P., Vizireanu, C.,1997: Procesarea industrială a cărnii, Editura Tehnică, Bucureşti, ISBN 973-31-2177-0, 643 pg.

Bates, B.C., Z.W. Kundzewicz, S. Wu and J.P. Palutikof, 2008: Climate Change and Water. Technical, Paper of the Intergovernmental Panel on Climate Change, IPCC Secretariat, Geneva, 210 pages, 2008, Intergovernmental Panel on Climate Change, ISBN: 978-92-9169-123-4 3.

Choi, Y.J., Park, J.W., 2002. Acid-Aided Protein Recovery from Enzyme-Rich Pacific Whiting. Journal of Food Science, 67, 2962–2967.

Colda, I, Ardelean, F., 2004: Meteorologie şi climatologie, Ed. Conspress, Bucureşti, 2004, 220 pag., ISBN: 973-7797-15-9.

Damodaran, S., 1989. Interrelationship of molecular and functional properties of food proteins. In: Kinsella JE, Soucie WG, editors. Food proteins. Champaign, Ill.: The American Oil Chemists' Society., 21–51.

Dirzu, I., 2017: Ferma de vaci de carne, o gura de oxigen pentru zona montană, Revista profilul agricol, 15.11.2017. 5–12.

Grigoriev, Al., 2017: Rase de taurine de munte, Revista Lumea Satului nr. 6, 16–31 martie, pag. 42.

Gruia, R., 2017: Resurse genetice în fermele agroturistice, Editura Clarion Braşov, 11–89.

Iwata, K., Ishizaki, S., Handa, A., & Tanaka, M., 2000: Preparation and characterization of edible films from fish-water soluble proteins. Fisheries Science, 66, 372–378.

Maruşca, T, 2017: Elemente de gradientică şi ecologie montană, ediţia a-II-a, Editura Universităţii Transilvania Braşov, 48–96.

Maruşca,T., 2012: Sistemul agrosilvopastoral durabil în contextul încălzirii globale a climei, Revista de silvicultură şi cinegetică, Braşov, anul XVI, 45–51.

Olea, L., Sanmiguel-Aynz, A., 2006: The Spanish dehsa. A traditional mediterranean silvopastoral system linkhing production and natural conservation, 21-th General Meeting of EGF, Badajos, Spain, 3–13.

Pachauri,R.K. et Reisinger, A.,2008: Bilan 2007 des changements climatiques: Rapport de synthès, Geneva, 103 pages, Groupe d'experts intergouvernemental sur l'évolution du climat, 2008, ISBN 92-9169-222-0 4.

Paschoalick, T. M., Garcia, F. T., Sobral, P. J. A. and Habitante, A. M. Q. B. 2003: Characterization of some functional properties of edible films based on muscle proteins of Nile tilapia. Food Hydrocolloids 17: 419–427.

Rey,R., 2013: Mountain product of high - biological quality. Meadows poliflora, organic fertilizer and sustainable mountain economy, ScienceDirect, Elsevier, Conf. ESPERA 2013. Procedia Economics and Finance, 8(2014), 622–631.

Tamba-Berehoiu, R., 2015: Chimia alimentului, vol.I, Ed, Stef Iaşi, 75–128.

Todoran, L., 2015: Cercetări privind aprecierea şi îmbunătăţirea indicilor de calitate într-o exploataţie salmonicolă, teză de doctorat, UASMV Cluj-Napoca, Facultatea de zootehnie şi biotehnologii, 225–244.

Tomescu,N., 2013: Încălzirea globală şi schimbările climatice, lucrare grad didactic I pe direcţie geografie - geologie, https://trovantisitafoni.wordpress.com/2.

Williamson, M., 2012: How proteins work, Garland Science, Taylor & Francis Group LLC, ISBN-13: 978-0815344469, ISBN-10: 0815344465.

Westphalen, A.D., Briggs, J.L., & Lonergan, S. M., 2005: Influence of pH on rheological properties of porcine myofibrillar protein during heat induced gelation. Meat Science, 70, 293–299.

Xiong, Y.L., 1994: Myofibrillar protein from different muscle fiber types: Implications of biochemical and functional properties in meat processing. Critical Reviews in Food Science and Nutrition, 34, 293–320.

Altitudinea - https://ro.wikipedia.org/

Green report, https://www.green-report.ro/

Proteina, considerente generale - https://ro.wikipedia.org/

2016: Calitatea proteinelor - https://www.dietaketogenica.ro/

2017: Consumul de carne de oaie - https://www1.agerpres.ro

2007: Regulament de organizare ferma didactică agroturistică montană, Monitorul Oficial al României, 26 iulie 2007.

Daniela ANTONESCU[1]

[1] Center of Mountain Economy CE-MONT and Institute of National Economy, Romanian Academy, Email: daniela.antonescu25@gmail.com

Sustainability and Mountains Biodiversity: A Survey and Perspective

Abstract *Relation between mountain regions and biodiversity is directly and inseparable because these areas represent, perhaps, the most important source of global and regional eco-systems, the core elements of the environmental and sustainable development policies. The mountains operate as true refuge for endemic species affected by uncontrolled human actions, while alpine meadows are exposed to losses of traditional pasture practices. Also, the mountains may be analysed also from the economic, social, cultural viewpoint, etc. as their multi-disciplinary nature is acknowledged both in the academic milieu but also by the decision factors involved in territorial development policy. The negative impact on the mountain area of economic activities is increasingly more visible both at high and low altitude and therefore it should lead to a sustainable approach regarding the state of the biodiversity for this area because affecting a habitat might attract also the destruction of the entire ecologic balance which is already very fragile nowadays. The present paper gives an overview of a relationship between the sustainability and the biodiversity of the mountain area and tray to identify the main implications of its impact upon economic and social development process. Also, by interpreting the finding of previous research and studies, the article presents the current knowledge of mountain biodiversity in Europe and Romania and its relation with sustainable development process.*

Keywords: *biodiversity, mountain region, sustainable development*

Introduction

The mountain areas cover about 22 % of the Earth's surface (32 million km2), sustain directly about 13 % of the world population (915 million inhabitants), 70 % of the rural population and provide approximate 60–80 % of the water resources of the earth. Due to the unique natural exquisiteness they host, most of mountain regions are declared "Protected Areas" and enjoy special attention. Thus, approximately 25 % from total land surfaces covered by mountains are framed within this category, as they represent the permanent dwelling of some rare species of fauna and flora, either relict or in peril (Blyth et al., 2002) or shaping unique habitats and ecologic shelter corridors for forest species, etc. (Körner & Ohsawa, 2005). The mountain regions hold 60 % from the biosphere's reserves and contribute by 15–20 % to tourism activities at global level and are covered in a share by 23 % with forests.

The mountains shape a living, captivating sometimes dangerous and relatively populated life-environment that is continuously and aggressively subjected to severe economic pressures (unemployment, migration, change of land use models, habitat fragmentations, deforestation, industrialisation, mining pressure, pollution and uncontrolled exploitation of natural resources, and environmental degradation, water deficit, etc.) all these contributing to decreasing their intrinsic value as natural owners of unique and non-replicable beauty. Mountain regions are found on all continents, at all latitudes and types of large ecosystems (from the arid desert and tropical rainforests to the polar zones) and they are in the permanent attention of all those who love or manage them.

From the relevance perspective, mountain regions play an important role in the economic, social, environmental development, and in culture and traditions etc., as they provide for essential eco-systemic goods and services. In dynamics, the mountain regions present a partial development even political and economic marginalisation and, in some cases, they are subjected to some territorial conflicts or reminiscences of the past. Mountain regions provide essential ecosystem services such as supplying and regulating water for communities in both mountain and lowlands areas. They also host a high diversity of habitats and species, many adapted to extreme climatic conditions. Mountain ecosystems are fragile and vulnerable, and are severely threatened by land abandonment or intensified agriculture, infrastructure development and rapid climate change.

From the perspective of sustainable management, the products and services provided by mountain ecosystems have vital importance for local communities as they are an important source of raw materials. The economic sectors specific to mountain areas, through the use of natural resources, affect biodiversity, sometimes causing inestimable damage, as follows:

- Impact of the agricultural sector on mountain biodiversity. There are mutual and complex interactions between agriculture and mountain biodiversity: agriculture needs biodiversity and it influences biodiversity. The mountain biodiversity is the one basis for agricultural production. On the one hand, it is the origin of all crops and domestic livestock and the variety within them. On the other hand, components of wild biodiversity in agricultural and associated landscapes provide and maintain ecosystem services that are essential to agricultural production. The heterogeneous mountain conditions contributed to the evolution of a significant variety of agricultural cultures adapted to the environmental conditions and human needs: many agricultural cultures (corn, potatoes, barley, sorghum, tomatoes, apples, etc.) and part of the domestic mammals (sheep, goats, etc.) originate from the mountainous region. Over time, the genetic diversity of the plants and animals from the mountain region knew an increase, being frequently associated with the cultural diversity and with the extreme variations of the environmental conditions. Currently, the mountainous biodiversity is threatened by the continuing modernisation processes of agricultural production, aspect that leads to the pauperisation of the ecosystem by using few sorts and lacking genetic variation[1]. The expansion of agricultural production on untilled land triggers the diminishment of habitats for some species and the deterioration of ecosystems, especially where the lands are not adequate to practicing agriculture. The mountainous agricultural ecosystems may bear invasions of some alien habitats, this aspect affecting local species and, implicitly, the local biodiversity as they are separated by valleys and mountain peaks.

- Impact of the forestry sector on mountain biodiversity. The vast majority of the mountainous area is made out of forestry ecosystems of low and medium altitude. Under certain conditions, the mountain forests provide basic produce and services to local communities. The forest ecosystems from the mountain areas are threatened by the expansion of agriculture and by the unsustainable methods of wood-cutting (uncontrolled, abusive wood-cutting, setting-up forest mono-cultures, etc.).
- Impact of the tourism sector on mountain biodiversity. During the last years, tourist activities in the mountain region had an important dynamic (winter sports, outdoor activities, etc.), fact which led to extending the tourist infrastructure and tourism services. This affected rapidly and in an uncontrollable manner the fragile ecosystems and the mountainous biodiversity. Just the same, the remodelling of mountain slopes for ski and other winter sports had a strong impact on the integrity of the mountain ecosystems (sometimes even their total deterioration), and the building of tourist infrastructures resulted in the urbanisation of some mountain areas and (total or partial) biodiversity loss.
- Impact of mining on mountain biodiversity. Ore, metal and other resources' exploitation has a negative impact on the habitats of mountain regions leading to severe water pollution and disturbs the downstream areas. Moreover, the elimination of trees, plants and soil in the areas where mining is practiced, or where opencast mining exist determined the destruction of landscapes, habitats, soil erosion and destruction of agricultural lands. At the same time, rains washed away the land of open strip mining and the removed sediments have polluted groundwater, poisoned fish and plants downstream, disfigured rivers and rivulets, generated flooding and landslides, etc. In this context, we refrain from mentioning the increased risk, as well, of chemical contamination of underground waters in case that the ores from sediments and rocks reach the mining sterile and infiltrate underground waters.
- Impact of the hydropower plants on mountain biodiversity. The mountains and mountain lakes are frequently used in building power plants for generating

1 According to a recent FAO estimate, 78 % of the world's mountain area is unsuitable or only marginally suitable for growing crops.

electricity. Even if they represent an important source of renewable (green) energy, their design has negative impact on rivers and ecosystems in the vicinity and, hence, they generate sometimes more wicked than good outcomes. The creation of artificial lakes and the alteration of water management determined also a negative change in the habitats, ecosystems and valleys in the immediate proximity.

Another process that has an important impact upon mountain biodiversity is climate changes. Mountain environments are very sensitive to climate change (Beniston, 2003, 2005). They appear among the most severely and rapidly impacted ecosystems, and can be affected by any change in temperature and precipitation patterns at all scales. (Zemp et al., 2009) Thus, the global warming affects negatively mountain ecosystems by the retraction and sometimes vanishing of some life forms from the alpine area. Endemic mountainous species pulled back at high elevations and some perished on the background of habitat loss. The changes in the precipitation periods and the increase in temperatures triggered the meltdown of glaciers and decline of snow covered mountain areas, thus reducing the capacity of preserving water. By a process of non-compliant water household management process for the mountain areas, both low altitude and vicinity areas were subjected to ecosystem changes.

Also, air pollution is a negative factor that influenced in negative sense the mountain biodiversity. In the mountain areas, the high rates of precipitations led to the depositing polluters' from the atmosphere in soils and/or their accumulation in the snow layers affecting on long-term ecosystems and vulnerable species. Acid rain triggered the destruction of trees while some negative effects are not visible yet (it involves intensive research and careful monitoring activities of polluters and main sources).

To combat the negative factors mentioned that have a direct or indirect influence on the biodiversity of mountain areas, a series of measures and actions are needed. Several important factors increase resilience to the major threats to mountain ecosystems. In addition to designating protected areas, measures to improve connectivity and ecosystem-based management are key for conserving mountain ecosystems, particularly helping adapt to climate change. Another action is needed to minimise the risk of local extinction of several species and to counteract the effects of habitat fragmentation and changes in land use. In the same time, national cooperation across European mountain regions can support improved integrated management practices.

1. Material and methodology

The article was conducted in European Union and Romania. The focus was given to biodiversity of the mountain areas. The information on characteristic of mountain biodiversity was collected on European Environment Agency site, which provides independent information on the mountain environment and on European

Environmental Information and Observation Network (Eionet). The specific information was collected from "Romanian National Plan for Territorial Arrangement" (PATN), Section III (Protected Areas), and also, from national and European Union legislation.

The main document reviewed for overall direction of the article is "Europe 2020 Strategy", Carpathian Convention, which has identified the main characteristics of the mountain biodiversity in the member state of EU. Similarly, documents produced at national level were studied; some major documents include different study reports of Food and Agriculture Organization of the United Nations (FAO), UNEP or Euro-Montana Forum.

2. Results

Irrespective of their localisation, the mountain chains are characterised by a relatively cold and harsh climate, high elevations, complex and varied topography (low slopes covered with forests and natural and semi-natural grasslands, high slopes without trees, alpine meadows, arid, wetland or shrubbery areas, etc.). To their vast majority, at different elevations, similar areas might be observed from the viewpoint of the vegetation covering them, while on steep slopes concentrated habitats can be seen which are differentiated by altitude.

2.1. Biodiversity of the Mountain European Area

In Europe, the mountain area covers 40 % from the total surface and hosts 20 % of the population[2]. On the continent, are found seven of the longest and highest mountain chains of the globs: the Alps (localized in the central area of Europe), the Apennines (Italy), the Pyrenees (at the border between Spain and France), the Scandinavian Mountains (in Sweden, Finland and Norway), the Carpathians (with the shape of an ark from Slovakia to Romania), the Balkan Mountains and the Rhodope Mountains (Bulgaria). The main mountain regions from Europe and its countries are presented in Table 1.

The extremely complex topography (south-oriented sheltered slopes, snow pockets, wind-blasted crags and rugged land covered by debris) explain the particularly rich biodiversity of the alpine areas (two-thirds of the plants are found in the mountain area) (Korner, 1985) (Table 2).

In the mountain areas of Europe, the extensive agricultural practices, the transhumance, forestry, etc. have contributed to creating an important diversity of landscapes and cultures (Huddlestone, 2003). Nowadays, this biodiversity is subjected to phenomena correlated directly to the activity of the local communities (and not only): abandoning the area, tourism and winter sports

2 http://www.turismulresponsabil.ro/wp-content/uploads/2017/01/2.-Danut-Ungureanu-Zona-montana.pdf

Table 1: Mountain areas and the countries involved

Countries involved	% of the EU territory	Regions
Belgium, Germany, Denmark, Spain, France, Ireland, Portugal, the Netherlands, the United Kingdom	18,4	Atlantic
Estonia, Finland, Latvia, Lithuania, Sweden	18,8	Boreal
Austria, Belgium, Bulgaria, Czech Republic, Germany, Denmark, France, Italy, Luxemburg, Poland, Romania, Sweden, Slovenia	29,3	Continental
Austria, Bulgaria, Germany, Spain, Finland, France, Italy, Poland, Romania, Sweden, Slovenia, Slovakia	8,6	Alpine
Czech Republic, Hungary, Romania, Slovakia	3,0	Pannonian
Romania	0,9	Steppic
Bulgaria, Romania	0,3	Black Sea
Cyprus, Spain, France, Greece, Italy, Malta, Portugal	20,6	Mediterranean
Spain, Portugal	0,2	Macaronesian

Sursa: http://ec.europa.eu/environment/nature/info/pubs/docs/biogeos/Steppic%20Region/KH7809607ROC_002.pdf

Table 2: Mountain chains in the alpine biogeographic region ofEurope

Mountains	Characteristics of the mountain biodiversity	Socio-economic characteristics
The Pyrenees (430 km.)	60 types of habitat are present (Habitat Directive). The mountains are characterised by numerous torrents, cascades and lakes and at elevations over 1000 m there are over 1500 lakes. The diversity of the flora is exceptionally high: 3000 species of plants, from among which at least 120 are endemic. The vast diversity of birds and animals (over 40 species of mammals, including rare endemic species). One of the extinct species is the Pyrenees Ibex[3].	The mountains are relatively low populated, the agricultural sector and sheep breeding being the main activities. In the past, the Pyrenees underwent an intensive deforestation process (and with visible traces mainly on the mountainsides). The beech was intensively used as firewood and in feeding the furnaces for ore extraction. Tourism is another economic activity of high intensity next to winter sports.

3 In January 2000, the Pyrenean Ibex was completely extinct. Nevertheless, scientists have attempted to clone this species by using DNA from one of the last females; such a clone died seven minutes after birth. Other sub-species survived: the Spanish

Table 2: Continued

Mountains	Characteristics of the mountain biodiversity	Socio-economic characteristics
The Alps (1200 km.)	The forests are in relatively natural state as at high elevations they are true refuge and ecological corridor for many large species (bears, birds of prey). The grasslands and alpine meadows make up 25 % of the mountain vegetation (the majority semi-natural, affected over time by moderate agricultural practices) and many of them are threatened by farmstead abandon. 84 types of habitat are listed, from among which 47 species of plants. The Alps have over 40 % of the European flora but also 200 species of birds (which lay their eggs here) and other 200 migrant birds. The Alps represent one of the most biodiversity richest mountain chains from European, but also one which is heavily exploited.	In the Alps live over 11 million inhabitants mainly in the urbanised valleys. To them are added 100 million tourists visiting the Alps with tourist or recreational purposes. These phenomena exert an important pressure on the mountainous environment which has a particular fragility.
The Apennines (1350 km)	. In the Apennines on the Italian side, during the last Ice Age the ice sheets advanced and after their meltdown the populations began their separate evolution. One of the species running the risk of extinction is the Abruzzo chamois (Rupicapra pyrenaica ornate) the reason being excessive hunting (450 individuals that are vulnerable to diseases and consanguinity).	The inhabitants are in small numbers and on a decreasing trend. Consequently, the traditional agricultural systems of cattle breeding are vanishing; however, efforts are made for repopulating the area due to the fact that these mountains are included in a network of interconnected national parks.
The Scandes (1400 km.)	The diversity of the species in the area of the Scandes is relatively low. Nevertheless, they represent an essential component of the European biodiversity due to their considerable size and the unaltered character. They are counted among the few locations in Europe where we might discover authentic wilderness. 44 types of habitat are represented, 29 species of plants and 18 species of animals (Habitats Directive).	The low presence of humans in the Scandes is not surprising. Some of the activities, such as river damming for generating hydroelectric power, reindeer herding, or the disappearance of summer grazing had negative impact at local level. However, the majority of the mountainous lands remain unperturbed by human presence, and therefore this remains one of the largest intact natural areas in Europe.

(*continued on next page*)

Table 2: Continued

Mountains	Characteristics of the mountain biodiversity	Socio-economic characteristics
The Carpathians (1450 km.)	The habitats have a long tradition regarding the exploitation of lands but also sheep and cattle breeding. The Carpathians host many species, with a high level of biodiversity: over 3500 species of plants from among which 481 endemic species. Here we find large carnivores, a varied selection of small mammals, many endemic species from among which the Tatra pine vole and the Carpathian marmot. Over 300 species of birds (the Ural owl, the white-backed woodpecker, the black stork, etc.).	In the Carpathians live about 18 million individuals, who are exerting pressure on maintaining and preserving the biodiversity
The Balkans[4] (550 km.)	These mountains display a typical alpine character and have a strong Mediterranean influence regarding the make-up of the species. Over 60 types of habitat (Habitats Directive) with a considerable forests' component, with many endemic species of trees (the Balkan pine, King Boris fir, and the black (Bosnian) pine. The area contains a huge variety of plant species and numerous large carnivore populations, and species of birds of prey (in Rhodope is found the largest agglomeration of day birds of prey from Europe).	The population density is extremely low. The mountains are in remote areas and still unexplored.

Source: processing after http://ec.europa.eu/environment/nature/info/pubs/docs/biogeos/Alpine/KH7809637ROC_002.pdf.

western Ibex, or the Ibex Gredos, and the Ibex from the south-eastern part of Spain, while the Portuguese Ibex is extinct. The last Ibex from the Pyrenees disappeared before scientists could analyse the species accordingly, the taxonomy of this sub-species being controversial.

4 They are constituted from three distinct mountain formations: the Rila Mountains, the Pirin Mountains and the Rhodope Mountains.

development, infrastructure development, urbanization, soil compaction, etc. The development of mountain tourism expanded practically over the entire continent, in parallel with the intensification of traffic and the building of the transport infrastructure (which turns into an important barrier for species migration[5]).

Damming the main rivers in the mountains for the electric power sectors or for agriculture has modified considerably the natural mountain environment. These activities influenced the biodiversity of the mountain areas, a fact mentioned in various reports and analyses at EU-level. As might be seen, most mountain areas from Europe are in an unfavourable preservation state (60.68 %) from among which 32.57 % are in a very bad situation, a fact which should impose the implementation of swift and drastic measures required for rebuilding the state of the affected habitats (Table 3).

The negative effects of climate changes led in time to promoting some actions that would counteract them and contribute to reinstating the natural balance. Some actions had as basis the specific legislation, promoted as of 1970 but also various cooperation agreements regarding the mountain regions from the Alps and Carpathians. Furthermore, as of 1975 the European Commission by the Directive on mountain and hill farming and farming in less-favoured areas no. 75/268[6], acknowledges the necessity of supporting agriculture from mountain areas. The European Union launches the first projects for sustaining Less Favoured Areas. Thus, in the mountain areas were determined areas with the statutes of less favoured area, as these cover about 69 % from the mountainous area. In the year 1978, at the Conference of the EU Council of Ministers responsible with regional planning (CEMAT) is launched the official paper "Pressures and regional planning problems in mountain regions"[7], which is the point of reference for all future development and regional planning strategies. After 2000, the mountain areas are an important component of the cohesion and regional development policy of the European Union being included in the thematic of the regions called 'permanent natural handicaps'.

From the biodiversity perspective, mountain regions are areas with high natural value requiring special attention. This attention consists in determining some areas where human actions of economic nature cannot take place and called Protected Areas. At EU-level, these protected areas represent up to 33 %[8]. Many of the mountain areas were declared as "Protected Areas" and they are the

---

5 Yearly, about 150 million individuals travel in the Alps, from among which 83 % travel on paved roads.

6 https://www.sciencedirect.com/science/article/pii/0264837786900621

7 http://www.bbsr.bund.de/BBSR/EN/Publications/IzR/2003/7DejeantPons.pdf?__blob=publicationFile&v=3

8 Only 5 % from the areas with high natural value are not included also in the category of less-favoured areas.

Table 3: Numbers of habitat types in each massif classified by conservation status (no.)

Massif	Favourable	Unfavourable (inadequate)	Unfavourable (bad)	Unknown	Total
Apennines	47	26	3	8	84
Balkans/South-east Europe	32	27	23	1	83
Atlantic islands	11	12	7	1	31
Nordic mountains	22	13	27	2	64
Central European middle mountains (Belgium and Germany)	16	18	12	2	48
Eastern Mediterranean islands	13	18	6	8	45
Carpathians	10	21	18	2	51
Alps	14	37	35	7	93
French/Swiss middle mountains	11	22	37	7	77
Western Mediterranean islands	7	17	14	15	53
Central European middle mountains (Czech Republic, Austria, Germany)	4	15	32		51
Pyrenees	3	19	30	36	88
British Isles	1	7	52	4	64
Iberian mountains		6	3	77	86
Total mountains (no.)	191	258	299	170	918
Total mountains (%)	20.81	28.10	32.57	18.52	100

Source: https://www.eea.europa.eu/publications/europes-ecological-backbone.

object of some Community or international programmes. For instance, "Natura 2000"[9] is the European network of natural protected areas comprising a representative sample of wild species and natural habitats of community interest. It was constituted not only with the purpose of protecting nature, but also for

9 Natura 2000, the widest world network of natural protected areas. In order to fight against the loss of natural areas, Europe drafted two important laws: the Directive Birds (1979) and Habitats (1992). These laws are the founding milestones for the

preserving these natural riches on long-term and for ensuring the resources required for the socio-economic development[10]. The reach degree of Protected Areas included in Natura 2000 differs from one country to another: Cyprus - 95 %, Slovenia - 83 %, Greece 82 %, Italy - 81 %, Slovakia - 79 %, Austria - 78 %, Spain - 73 %, Czech Republic 71 %, Romania – 65 %. In total, in the alpine region are 1.496 habitats of community importance (SCI) (Directive Habitats) and 365 areas of special protection (ASP) (Directive Birds)[11], as these areas with special protection statutes cover about 40 % from the total surface of the alpine region

Most of community importance (SCI) are found in the continental area (7475), followed by the Mediterranean (2928) and the Atlantic (2747) ones. Regarding the special protection areas (SPA) the most numerous are designated in the Continental region (1478) followed by the Boreal (1165). Nevertheless, the widest surfaces covered by habitats of community importance are found in the Black Sea region (71.8 %) and those of special protection in the Pannonian region (31.3 %)

2.2. Biodiversity of mountain areas in Romania

The statues of Protected Area presupposes a mix of actions regarding the strengthening of conservation, restoration and sustainable valorisation of biodiversity and landscape based on efficient management by harmonising the natural capital with its habitats and species, by preserving and promoting natural values.

The establishment by law of some protected natural areas was initiated with the purpose of obtaining a more efficient control over maintaining and protecting biodiversity (Popa, 2016). Thus, at the Earth Summit from 1992 (Rio de Janeiro) was adopted the Convention for Biologic Diversity. Romania ratifies the Convention in the year 1994, and the Government promulgates the Law 58/1994 regarding the biologic diversity by which the following major objectives were set: conservation of biologic diversity, sustainable use of biodiversity's resources and equitable distribution of benefits resulting from the use of genetic resources. In Romania, the main categories of Protected Areas are established by Law no. 5/2000 regarding the National Plan for Territorial Arrangement (PATN) in Section III (Protected Areas). In accordance with the law, Romania holds 845 protected areas classified in 5 out of the 6 IUCN categories (Table 4).

After Romania's accession to EU, the Emergency Ordinance no. 57 of June 20, 2007 is promulgated regarding the regime of protected natural areas,

environmental protection policy and led to setting up Natura 2000 the largest network of protected natural areas in the world covering - 1 million square kilometres of land, (over 18 % from the EU land surface) - 250.000 square kilometres of marine habitats (almost 4 % of the EU marine habitats), respectively 27.000 habitats and 1.000 species are under special protection.

10 https://natura2000.ro/ce-este-reteaua-natura-2000/

11 European Topic Centre for Biodiversity (European Environment Agency) http://biodiversity.eionet.europa.euOctober2008.

Table 4: Romania's Protected Area System

Type	Similar to IUCN Category/ International Designation	Number of Protected areas	Total area
Scientific Reserve		53	101,288 ha
National Park	II	11	300,819 ha
Natural Monument	III	231	2,177 ha
Natural Reserve	IV	542	117,265 ha
Natural Park	V	6	326,305 ha
Biosphere Reserve Danube Delta	Biosphere Reserve	Retezat (II) Rodnei (II)	576,216 ha. 38,138 ha 47,227 ha
Wetlands of International Importance	Ramsar Site	Danube Delta Small Island of Braila	576,216 ha 20,455 ha
Natural Sites for Universal Natural Heritage	Word Heritage Site	Danube Delta	
Special Areas for Conservation	SAC	None	
Areas for Special Protection of Bird	SPA	None	

Source: APPLETON M., 2012, Protected Area Management Planning, A Manual and Toolkit.

the conservation of natural habitats, of the wild flora and fauna (updated in 2016) by which are determined the areas considered of major public interest and which are included in the National Strategy for Sustainable Development Horizons 2013–2020–2030. In this Strategy is shown that Romania displays a relative variety and proportionality of landscapes, with unique characteristics in Europe and rare on the globe: 29.94 % mountain massifs (elevations over 1.000 meters), 42 % hills and plateaus (elevations between 300 and 1.000 meters) and 30 % flatlands/plains (elevation under 300 m) (Antonescu D., 2017). The total surface of the mountain area is of 71.381,48 square kilometres (29.94 % from total surface). The special biodiversity of the mountain area from Romania determined the inclusion of a share of 57 % from its surface in the ecologic network Natura 2000. In the mountain area are found 197 Natura 2000 sites (habitats), respectively 37 % from the number of national sites and 67 % from the protected area at national level. Romania holds also 54 % from the Carpathian Mountain Chain, mountains of mid-elevation (with an average of 1.136 metres) and only few peaks over 2.500 m.

In Romania the mountains represent the least anthropic changed part, with a low density of the inhabitant population and small localities which are almost depopulated as effect of internal and external migration because of the disappearance of some traditional practices (Avădanei V. et. al., 2016). This explains as well the location in the mountain region of 12 out of the 13 national parks and of 10 out of the 14 natural parks (NSSD)[12]: The forests from the mountain areas display increased biodiversity as here are found 150 types of forest ecosystems differentiated depending on the species or the group of dominant species of trees represented in the vegetal carpet, the type and quantity of humus in the soil, the water and ionic stress of the soil, etc., 227 types of forest which were classified into 42 types of vegetal layers and sub-shrubberies and 364 stations.

The forests shape one of the most important wood sources and other non-wood produce (berries, mushrooms, game, etc.). The surface covered by forests in the mountain area is of 4.4 million hectares, from which about 40 % are in private property, the rest being in public ownership of the state or of the territorial administrative units (the National Autonomous Administration of Forests, local councils, etc.). In view of protecting biodiversity of the mountain areas, Romania ratified the Framework Convention regarding the protection and sustainable development of the Carpathians (Law no.389/2006). The law stipulates that the Carpathian mountains represent a unique natural wealth of impressive beauty and ecological value, an important reservoir of biodiversity, the area from which main rivers flow, an essential habitat and refuge for numerous species endangered of plants and animals, and the widest area covered by virgin woods from Europe. (Rey R. et al, 2016) In the mountain area are 658 local administrative units (20 % from the country's surface, most of them in the counties Harghita (9.38 %), Hunedoara (6.92 %), Maramures (6.77 %), Alba (6.15 %), Suceava (5.85 %), Covasna (5.38 %), and Brasov (5.1 %). In the mountain area live about 3.354.041 inhabitants (24.92 % from total population) (Table 5).

---

12 a. 12 National Parks, four in the Oriental Carpathians (NP Rodnei Mountains, NP Călimani Mountains, NP in the Ceahlău Massif, NP Cheile Bicazului – Lacul Roşu (Red Lake) –Hăşmaş Mountains), six in the Mid-Carpathians (NP Piatra Craiului, NP in the Coziei Mountains, NP Buila – Vânturariţa, NP in the Jiului Gorge, NP Retezat, NP Domogled – Valea Cernei) and two in the Occidental Carpathians (NP Cheile Nerei – Beuşniţa, NP Semenic Mountains – Cheile Caraşului).
b. 10 Natural Parks, from which four in the Oriental Carpathians (NP Maramureşului Mountains, NP Mureşului Superior Gorge, NP Vânători Neamţ which breaks through also in the Neamtului Sub-Carpathians, NP Putna-Vrancea), four in the Mid-Carpathians (NP Bucegi, NP Grădiştea Muncelului-Cioclovina, Geoparcul Dinozaurilor (Dinosaurs' Geo-park) –Haţegului Country, Geo-park Mehedinţi Plateau which overlapps partially also with the areal of the Mehedinti Mountains) and two in the Occidental Carpathians (NP Apuseni Mountains, NP Cazanele Dunării-Porţile de Fier (Danube Cauldrons – Iron Gates). In the period 2007–2016 a series of changes were recorded regarding the surface of the protected mountain areas (increases or diminishments of the included surfaces).

Table 5: Mountain Local Units, distributed on counties (%)

	Territorial Administrative Units in the Mountain Area [13] (no.)	**GDP per capita (Euro/ capita) of the county**
Satu Mare	1	5944
Sălaj	2	6314
Timiş	3	10830
Arad	8	8268
Mehedinţi	11	4600
Gorj	12	7732
Dâmboviţa	13	5815
Cluj	14	11089
Bacău	16	5406
Bihor	19	6849
Mureş	20	6808
Vrancea	20	5181
Buzău	21	5344
Vâlcea	21	6110
Neamţ	23	4701
Argeş	24	7357
Sibiu	27	8849
Prahova	28	10717
Bistriţa Năsăud	33	6051
Braşov	33	10280
Covasna	35	5840
Caras Severin	38	6220
Suceava	38	4918
Alba	40	8411
Maramureş	44	6035
Hunedoara	45	6820
Harghita	61	5851

Source: http://www.gal-mt.ro/masuri/masura19.2/Anexa_12_Lista_localitati_din_Zona_Montana.pdf

13 LAU 2 – Communes, Municipalities and Cities

Conclusions

The importance of mountain areas is given jointly by the quantitative but especially by the qualitative size. Thus, the mountain areas cover important surfaces both at world level (22 %) and at national level (30 % of Romania's surface). In Romania, the mountain area is found in 27 out of the total 42 counties and the rural population of this area is represented by a share of 52.47 %, and is covered in a share of 59 % by forests. Next to the quantitative size presented above, the mountain area is characterised by high biodiversity this representing the qualitative side which requires increased attention and heightened interest for maintaining in good state the species of plants and animals, and all habitats which are in an easily to disturb balance.

The mountain areas characterised by high biodiversity are declared as Protected Areas and these are representing currently a surface of 25 % at world level, of 33 % within the European Union, and of 24 % in Romania. The particular biodiversity of the mountain area from Romania determined the attribution of a share of 57 % from its surface within the ecological network Natura 2000. In the mountain area are found 197 "Natura 2000 sites" (habitats), respectively 37 % from the number of national sites and 67 % from the protected surface at national level. The mountain areas are considered as important sources of biodiversity but, at the same time, they are faced with significant adjustment issues to new climate changes.

In Romania, the mountain areas should play a strategic role in the economic and social development constituting conducive environment, over time, for maintaining the continuity and durability of the Romanian people. It is imperative that the development vision in the field of Protected Areas –mountain areas pursues the protection, valorisation and recovery of the mountains' biodiversity, including eco-systemic services they provide (natural capital) by taking into account the intrinsic value that they display and their essential contribution to economic and social development. Because human activities (economic, social, cultural, etc.) cannot be omitted from this model, I consider that the basic principle of this evolution should be in a conservation framework for development, where the practices should aim both services of economic and social nature, and those of protecting ecosystems and biodiversity. Thus, development should meet the protection requirements of the mountain environment as in a contrary situation, biodiversity might undergo negative, sometimes irreversible changes caused by the loss of habitats, as result of converting agricultural lands to urban areas, by the emergence of some invasive alien species, and by the overexploitation of natural resources, etc. Overexploitation of services/products provided by biodiversity leads to influencing the natural balance with negative impact on human welfare and on the entire process of economic growth. These mountain areas with high biodiversity should benefit from specific, multidimensional policy that would take into account the principles of sustainable development and would contribute to diminishing ecologic and economic imbalances. The mountain policy might be considered as a true link that would ensure the good intercommunity and interregional cooperation, as well as partnerships at national and international level.

References

1. Antonescu D., (Co-author Chapter), Project No. 2 – Resursele naturale – rezerve strategice, ce folosim si ce lasam generatiilor viitoare, Strategia de dezvoltare a Romaniei in urmatorii 20 de ani – Sinteza, (Coordinator Acad., Bogdan C. Simionescu), Arii Protejate. http://www.academiaromana.ro/bdar/strategiaAR/doc14/Strategia-Sinteza.pdf, Publishing House Romanian Academy, ISBN 978-973-27-2756-0 pg.71–74; 2017.
2. Antonescu D., (Author Chapter), Strategic Resources of Romania. Dimensions of sustainable development, Coordinator: Acad. Bogdan C. Simionescu, Editors: Radu-Dan Rusu, Marcela Mihai, Publishing House StudIS, Iaşi, ISBN: 987-606-775-688-3, pag. 64–80; 2017
3. Beniston M. (ed.), Climatic Change. Implications for the Hydrological Cycle and for Water Management. Advances in Global Change Research, Kluwer Academic Publishers, Dordrecht and Boston, 503 pg.; 2002.
4. Blyth, R.E., Kaiser, M.J., Hart, P.J.B., Edwards-Jones, G. (2002) Conservation with voluntary management in an inshore fishery. Environmental Conservation 29: 493–508.
5. Avadanei V., Avadanei L., Mediocritas aurea – a possible and suitable solution for sustainable, smart and inclusive mountain development, Journal of Montanology vol. V, pg. 69, 2016
6. Huddlestone B., E. Ataman, L. Fed'OSTIANI, Towards a GIS-based analysis of mountain environments and populations Environment and Natural resources, Working Paper (Vol. 10). Food and Agriculture Organization of the U.N., Rome, 2003, http://www.fao.org/3/a-y4558e.pdf.
7. Korner C, Alpine plant diversity: a global survey and functional interpretations. In: Arctic and Alpine Biodiversity: Patterns, Causes and Ecosystem Consequences, F.S. Chapin III, and C. Korner (eds.), Ecological Studies 113, Springer, Berlin, 1985.
8. Radu Rey, R. Gruia, Responsible tourism in mountain area, an opportunity for local communities, Journal of Montanology vol. V, 2016.
9. I. Popa, Protected areas (forests) between strict protection and rural development engine, Journal of Montanology vol. V, 2016.
10. Ungureanu D., Dezvoltarea durabilă a zonei montane din România. Realități și perspective, 2017.
11. UNEP-WCMC, Mountains and Forests in Mountains. Cambridge, UK. Retrieved 27-03-2015, from http://www.unep-wcmc.org/resources-and-data/mountains-and-forests-in-mountains. U.S. Geological Survey, 1996. Global 30 Arc-Second Elevations (GTOPO30). In U.S. Geological Survey (Ed.), 2000
12. Zemp M, Hoelzle M., Haeberli W., Six decades of glacier mass-balance observations: a review of the worldwide monitoring network, Annals of Glaciology 50; 2009.

13. FAO (Food and Agriculture Organization of the United Nations), 2001. Global Forest Resources Assessment 2000, 512 pp. FAO, Rome.
14. Orientări Strategice Naţionale pentru Dezvoltarea Durabila a Carpaţilor – 2014–2020.
15. Munţii spre 2020 – Asociaţia Europeana pentru Cooperare si Dezvoltare a Zonelor Montane EUROMONTANA
16. Europe 2020 Strategy; Carpathian Convention.
17. Europe's ecological backbone: recognising the true value of our mountains, EEA Report No 6/2010. ISBN 978-92-9213-108-1 ISSN 1725–9177 DOI 10.2800/43450.
18. Legea nr. 5/2000 privind Planul de Amenajare a Teritoriului National (Zone protejate).
19. http://turism.gov.ro/wp-content/uploads/2016/02/Romania-tara-semnatara-a-Conventiei-Carpatice.pdf
20. http://www.greenpeace.org/romania/ro/campanii/rosiamontana/descriere/
21. http://www.turismulresponsabil.ro/wp-content/uploads/2017/01/2.-Danut-Ungureanu-Zona-montana.pdf.
22. Romania National Strategy for Sustainable Development 2013-2020-2030 (NSSD), http://www.un.org/esa/dsd/dsd_aofw_ni/ni_pdfs/NationalReports/romania/Romania.pdf
23. http://ec.europa.eu/environment/nature/info/pubs/docs/biogeos/Steppic%20 Region/KH7809607ROC_002.pdf
24. http://ec.europa.eu/environment/nature/info/pubs/docs/biogeos/Alpine/KH7809637ROC_002.pdf.

Radu REY[1]

[1] Senior Researcher, Center of Mountain Economy „CE-MONT", Romanian Academy,
Email: cabinet_fmr@yahoo.com

Specific Elements for Organizing the Capitalization of "Mountain Products" on the Basis of Added Value, in the Associative-Cooperative System, in Favor of the Small and Medium-Sized Farmers. A Scenario for Organizing a "Pilot" Micro-Region in the Romanian Carpathians

Abstract *The new visions that generated the EU/EC regulations on quality schemes and the idea of "mountain products" open a new perspective, safeguarding the agri-food economy, especially in emerging countries, with many economic and social benefits for small and medium-sized farmers and urban consumers. An essential "challenge" is how to organize the collection, transformation and marketing of guaranteed "mountain products", and the distinctive role of Grade I and II cooperatives in ensuring the directing of the benefits generated by the added value, with priority to farmers' families, increasing the profitability rate in the primary sector. To bring clarifications on some socio-economic aspects, various interests and predictable mentalities, it would be justified to create a "pilot" micro-region in the Romanian Carpathians, through which to select those components that have multiplicity value.*

Keywords: *"mountain product", cooperatives, added value, "pilot" micro-region, sustainability*

General considerations

The galloping demographic change to over 9 billion inhabitants of the planet at the 2050 horizon brings unprecedented attention to the provision of food resources, including mountain food producing areas, for both mountain and rural populations, as well as for a significant segment of urban consumers.

At the European level, within the EU and beyond, there are two great, partly different situations: on the one hand, mountain areas in developed countries - where cumulative investments over the last 50–60 years have been completed with a high level of equipping of the mountain territory with agricultural, forestry and tourism infrastructure, and investments in the fields of production, education and "mountain" lifestyle, as well as with many forms of stimulation and material support (roads, energy, water, productive animal breeds, hygienic and comfortable stables for both animals and humans, substantial financial compensation, development of mountain tourism and agritourism, attractive pension system, etc.); on the other hand, the emerging countries with mountains, newly admitted or with EU accession prospects are still at a yet insufficient level compared to their needs, not comparable to the Western European level.

In Romania, a country with a large mountain area, with inhabited mountains and multi-secular traditions in agro- zootechnology - the mountain remained non-collectivized, but the policy focused on the collectivist-statist system, until 1990, has profoundly marginalized the mountains, the mountain peasantry being left without "mountain type" professional schooling, agro-mountain scientific research being avoided, without specific agro - zootechnical modernization elements (small mechanization, hygiene in stables, etc.), mountain agro-tourism being unapproachable, etc. The Romanian mountain dealt with such a differentiated historical legacy until 1990.

After 1990, the agricultural policy in Romania, faced with major disruptions at APC (Agricultural Production Cooperative) and SAE (State Agricultural Enterprise) level, focused on large farms, including in agricultural education, with intense trends in land consolidation, the use of efficient mechanization, chemical fertilizers and pesticides, industrial animal husbandry forms, etc., based on the high fertility of the land in the plain and hilly areas.

Despite this, after 1990, a core of visionary specialists forced the creation of the first specialized institutions for the development of the mountain agro-zootechnical economy and rural area, under national "pioneering" conditions.

Some efforts have been initiated with the direct participation of the author as initiator and applicant at decision level, including the establishment of specialized institutions at the Ministry of Agriculture (Romanian Mountain Area Commission, 1990–1994; National Mountain Area Agency, 1994; Training and Innovation Centre for Development in the Carpathians – CEFIDEC; Montanology Institute and several agro–montanology faculties in Iasi, Cluj, Targoviste, Sibiu and Craiova; Centre for Mountain Economy CE-MONT / NIER – National Institute for Economic Research / Romanian Academy; the first Strategy for the sustainable development of the mountain area, 2004 and the first Mountain Law in Romania's history, 2004, revised and adapted in 2018).

Models of mountain households, small industries, etc., have been created with bilateral support from France, Germany, Switzerland, Austria, etc., and through projects with the World Bank, the European Commission, which allowed approaching certain agro-rural development models, especially evolutions in the development of certain scientific concepts - regarding the directions favourable to the development of the mountain agro-rural economy, with remarkable success in the field of tourism and mountain rural agro-tourism, where there are over 7,000 hostels in 2018, with beneficial economic and social effects.

An active role in these developments was played by the European association of mountain areas "Euromontana", within which evolved the new idea of the "mountain product"[1], made official in the EU by Regulations 1151/2012 and 665/2014 regarding quality schemes, and in Romania by the Government Decision no. 506/2016 and the Order of the Minister of Agriculture no. 52/2017 regarding the "mountain product".

It is important to note that, if for the developed mountain areas the valuable idea of the "mountain product" is a welcome addition, to the mountain farming of Romania and other emerging countries in Europe and elsewhere, it can represent a safeguarding chance, the key being preservation of the valuable diversity, of the mountain meadows' mix of flora - a phenomenon dependent, in a chain, of using all organic fertilizer resources (pasture, purine), an aspect directly dependent on the existence of ruminant animals (sheep, cattle, goats), all dependent on the existence of mountain farmers, with stable traditions and households in the mountain area. Hence the need and urgency for effective measures to encourage producers, especially young generations, with small and medium-sized households, with multiple functions connected to the environment and the cultural factor, hence the need for an educational system adapted to the mountain's specificity.

Mountain scientific research has an important mission to highlight micro-area differences and to design adapted methods of agro - zootechnic practice, solutions of small industrial activities, accessible according to the environmental specificity created by the environment, the good practices, the cultural traditions, the mentalities, discovering new reproducible resources, etc., to feed the decisional area with information and proposals for solutions tailored to the realities of the mountain, avoiding the creation of artificial conflicts between the "dominant large scale agriculture" and the "small mountain farming" always endangered by marginalization, which cannot compete with the agriculture in the low lands and hill areas based on high soil fertility, flat land, complete mechanization, high productivity in the vegetable and livestock sphere, aspects that are too little or incompatible with the specificities of the mountain areas (Rey, 2013).

The solution, almost unique, without also being exhaustive, is found in the superior quality of mountain food products, obtained mainly by animal husbandry, under conditions of feeding based on the natural mixed flora of mountain meadows, unpolluted waters and air, extensive breeding systems of ruminant

1 Radu Rey ("Euromontana" Vicepresident, 1994–2004): "Future in the Carpathians" (1979), Scrisul Românesc Press; "Mountain Civilization" (1985), Scientific and Encyclopaedic Press – Bucharest; "Mountains and the 21st century. Comparative study of European strategies for mountain areas, with particular reference to the Romanian Carpathians. M1-SEE Plan" (in Romanian and English), Terra Nostra Press, Iaşi – 2013.

animals, an aspect that includes sweating and elimination of toxins, and especially in the absence of chemical fertilizers and pesticides - an accumulation of conditions that generate both the superior (biological) quality of alimentary "mountain products" and the absence of chemical factors – generators of risks to the health of consumers.

Hence the appreciation of the fact that the guidelines of EU Regulation 1151/2012 and EC Regulation 665/2014 on quality schemes and the "mountain product" are beneficial to all mountain areas, but for emerging less developed countries they may be the primary solution to safeguard more and more precious "health carrying" but endangered agro-alimentary economy, both for the producers themselves and for a significant "niche" of urban consumers, which increases along with the demographic growth (over 3 million people in the Romanian Carpathians and surpluses for urban consumers outside the mountain area).

If the EU's large scale agriculture will remain the main source of food for an increasing population at global level, the food resources that the mountain territories can supply, which depend on the existence of mountain farmers, inevitably fall in the XXI'st century into a much higher cone of interest for a sustainable future (Rey, 2013).

Under the new CAP (Common Agricultural Policy) - post-2020, new, much-expanded provisions are needed to develop a distinct "mountain policy" at EU level, accompanied by "national mountain policies", given the significant differences between the mountain areas of developed countries and those from emerging countries. It is very relevant the European Parliament Resolution 2015/2279 – INI of 10 May 2016 addressed to the European Council and Commission regarding the cohesion policy in mountain regions.

The alarming emergency lies in the fact that smaller or medium sized mountain farms (large ones are not specific to mountain areas), once lost, can no longer be regenerated under the conditions of the 21st century, which is marked by new livelihood alternatives for the younger generation of mountain farmers (which did not exist in the 20th century) and which are the guarantee of continuity in the mountain agro-food economy, closely linked to the environmental protection factors and the cultural traditions.

Some elements specific to the mountain area

Natural factors

The fertile soil layer of mountain meadows is generally only approx. 10–25 cm, being particularly fragile, easily exhaustible by forcing plant productions (eg. with chemical fertilizers) with high acidity. A large period of time is needed for only one centimetre of fertile soil to form.

The input of organic fertilizers (manure, purine) supplied by ruminants (cows, sheep, goats), well-fermented, with alkaline reactions, is essential to create a natural flora with high-value as fodder, high economic value biodiversity, conditional on ensuring continuity for annual use. Scientific research and practical observations have shown that in the absence of organic fertilizers, valuable mountain flora degrades in 7–8 years through natural "return to wilderness" and are naturally replaced by plants of very low fodder or inedible value (e.g. Nardus, Spharagus). Restoration takes a long time and is costly, being dependent on the existence of livestock farmers and the correct annual use of all organic fertilizer resources (traditional good practices) (Rey, 2018).

Result: the urgency of interventions to limit the loss of small and medium-sized mountain farms through specific policies.

Social factors

An "inheritance" from the long period of "socialist agriculture" with effects in the non-collectivized mountain area of Romania was "the threat of collectivization", which terrified the mountain farmers and left deep traces that still exist in the collective mentality of elderly generations, who passed along their fears to the youth in their families. Surprisingly, the phenomenon remains in 2018, shaken but still anxiety inducing. Hence the need for the first action at the level of a mountain village to be devoted to a broad, convincing debate with farmers, to clarify that a mountain farming cooperative, in a European vision, does not affect private property (no "joining" land, no common stables, etc.).

The experience of the Mountain Area Agency/MARD – Ministry of Agriculture and Rural Development, the Romanian Mountain Forum and the Centre for Mountain Economy "CE-MONT"/NIER /Romanian Academy (2013–2018) in the mountain area has shown that this obstacle can be overcome, the first mountain agricultural cooperatives being created in the North, in the Bistriţa Năsăud and Suceava counties, with the idea of capitalizing on the "mountain products", on the raw materials, with prices higher than the current ones. But in the absence of "start-up aids" and an investment policy in operable transformation entities, the initial enthusiasm gets stuck quickly.

The unstimulating, even ridiculous prices (less than 0.20 euros / litter of milk, 1.2 euros / kg of living veal) practiced by new "industrialists" after 1990 for raw milk and meat and speculative actions of many "intermediaries" - have led to the discouragement of mountain agricultural youth, with the severe effect of agricultural abandonment and the search for better living solutions in cities and abroad. A newly emerging and disturbing phenomenon is found in the growth of disinterest for the development of own farms, managed by aging farmers.

In 2017, the Romanian Government, through the Ministry of Agriculture and Rural Development, began the first energetic measures explicitly aimed at the protection and development of the mountain agricultural and rural economy by including in the 2017–2020 governance program a distinct segment for the mountain area, followed by a new Mountain Law no. 197/20.07.2018 that provides one billion euros for a period of 10 years from the State budget. In this context, specialized institutions have been reactivated (National Mountain Area Agency, Training and Innovation

Centre for Development in the Carpathians) and a new "Mountain Law" has been elaborated, with complex provisions adapted to current and future needs. The Centre for Mountain Economy "CE-MONT" and the Romanian Mountain Forum have made a significant contribution to these advances in favour of Romania's mountain area.

Methodology

It was based on a vast experience of the author involved over 40 years as a practitioner and researcher in the Romanian mountain rural area and in 20 other countries with mountains from Europe as well as through the decision making functions of the institutions created for the mountain area, since 1990 (Secretary of State, General Director, Director - MARD; Vice-President of Euromontana and as 1st degree researcher) and direct contacts and information from mountain farmers and specialists.

Also, by participating in numerous events dedicated to mountain areas at national, European and world level - with own contributions (published papers) and the elaboration and implementation of agricultural and rural development projects, with national and external support (European Commission, World Bank, European Council, or bilaterally - from France, Germany, Switzerland, Austria), scientific analyzes, in different evolutionary stages, from economic, social and environmental point of view, in mountain areas. Direct participation in the creation of the first mountain agricultural cooperatives in the counties of Bistrita-Nasaud and Suceava.

Expected results

There is a need for a concept aimed at safeguarding and sustainable development of the mountain agro-food and eco-economy, aimed at transferring the surplus of high-quality agricultural food products left over from the consumption of mountain communities to national and foreign urban consumers. The concept involves changes and improvements firstly in the lifestyle of producers and consumers, simultaneously by organizing small and medium-sized mountain farms in cooperatives and through new technologies, maintaining traditional values and economic "good practices" in relation to the environment and culture; by raising awareness and increasing the demand from the "niche" of urban consumers interested in high-quality and health-guaranteed "mountain products" and willing to accept "a plus" of price for a quality that is achieved with greater efforts and costs; by orientating the valorization of "mountain products" for export with the best prices. A different evolutionary pace is foreseen between developed EU countries that have the experience of organic, traditional products with well-established brands, including quality schemes as PGI, PDO, TSG and a type of informed consumer and better financial means.

In this system, a "new financial source" can be created evolutionarily, one which contributes consistently to the sustainable maintenance and development of the production base, represented by the direct producers - mountain farmers, an aspect of special interest in Romania and similarly in other states in the South-East of Europe that have not yet found sufficiently efficient and dynamic solutions. A second "financial source" is the avoidance of spurious intermediaries, which constitute a dangerous "hurdle" for the present and future agricultural mountain economy. The third financial resource is found in the fact that in the cooperative system there are no patrons, the profit obtained from the valorization of "mountain products" returns to the cooperatives and, implicitly, also to the mountain farmers. Cumulatively, these financial sources will allow for higher prices for raw materials (milk, meat, etc.) and implicitly will increase the farmers' incomes, combat poverty and open up new perspectives and hopes for mountain agricultural youth, combined with other forms of support for agricultural producers and rural-mountain development.

The innovative character is found in two main aspects: the transition from the collectivist system of the production cooperatives practiced in Romania for about 30 years to the cooperatives for the valorization of "mountain products" (EU Regulation 1151/2012 on quality schemes and Regulation Delegate of the European Commission No. 665/2014) without interference in individual ownership, but without the existence of a historical precedent at European and world level, imparts an innovative character that entails a logical need for experimentation and modeling to avoid a chaotic evolution, lost time and money, with uncertain results.

The mission of the "associative cooperative mountain system", organized at the communal level and through strong enough inter-communal, inter-cooperative mountain associations, becomes to mitigate and stop the current decline, to restore the agricultural mountain economy, to revive the interest and hopes of the young generations of producers, to create production and capitalization entities for guaranteed "mountain products", to promote the modernization of traditional mountain farms to the limit allowed by the mountain environment, to halt mountain depopulation, to significantly improve the incomes of mountain farmers' families, to create new jobs and prospects for rural youth, combating poverty and agricultural abandonment.

The components of a "scenario" for the organization of a "pilot" mountain micro-area

The preparatory stage includes:

- The willingness to tackle a "pilot project" of sustainable mountain development at the central and local levels.
- The existence of a concept focused on knowledge and experience and the establishment of the main objectives.
- The financing of a complex study at the level of the mountain micro-region considered (Marketing study, impact study, technical and socio-economic study).

- The existence of support mechanisms at central, county and local level (Government / MADR, County and Local Administration).
- The existence of legislative support.
- Evaluating, through studies, the costs and material and human resources that can guarantee at least a moderate development without any substantial damage.
- In the project budget, it is necessary to provide for a "safety margin" of approx. 20 % - for unpredictable issues that will require corrective action along the way.
- Setting up a project management team - including the necessary experts by field.

The "pilot" project also includes the experimental research element that will highlight new issues that could not be foreseen in the design phase and require corrections to be made along the way without affecting the project basis. The results to be obtained will be multiplied in other similar mountain micro-regions, following the methodology used successfully in the experimental framework, avoiding the repetition of errors (horizon 2040).

The project management team will create contacts and experience exchanges with similar areas in advanced EU countries, with the "players" directly involved in the project.

The outcome of the marketing study will highlight the project's direction, regarding:

- The type of "mountain products" with real chances on the market (e.g. hard cheese, cold meats, vegetable products) on external and internal markets (different policies) and the best prices.
- The technical, reliable, assimilation-capable know-how elements.
- The specialization(s) with a sustainable perspective necessary for the mountain micro-region concerned (skilled labor training).
- The rational dimension of investments, correlated with local reproducible resources, related to the sustainable provision of ruminant feed and the limits of a sustainable development.

The preparatory phase includes the creation of agricultural cooperatives. Grade I cooperatives (a single cooperative / administrative unit), with an (early) profile of collection and capitalization of "mountain products" raw materials (with limited possibilities), whether through current industrial "transformers", with the possibility of negotiating better prices (e.g. for milk and live livestock) with larger quantities. Either by searching for and finding market niches with higher prices than those offered by industry, the trend remaining a shift to the Grade II cooperative, with own capacity to transform raw materials and value-added capitalization. And in this case, the key is to ensure a constant "market niche". More inspired is the solution of the organization, from the beginning, of a mountain farm cooperative focused on the valorization of the "mountain product", with its own raw materials transformation capacities (a single cooperative / administrative unit). And in this organizational formula it is essential to analyze, as a priority, market chances.

The general rules of a successful and sustainable concept with market success must be considered:

- Significant volume of goods (sufficiently interesting for the commercial system).
- Continuity throughout the year.
- The guaranteed quality wanted by consumers.
- Health guarantees.

Based on these considerations, it is necessary to get to the next step of associating the Grade II (or I) communal agricultural cooperatives at the mountain micro-region level (mountain basin, mountain valley) in an "Inter-cooperative Mountain Association", focused on the capitalization of "mountain products" under local brands, able to carve out a place for themselves on the foreign market and on the domestic market.

Only reaching this goal could be the complete solution for a sustainable mountain rural development that would meet the real needs of mountain farmers, small and medium-sized farmers by excellence, to increase family income based on renewable resources.

The necessary (hypothetical) investments:

- The first investment category: for Grade I or II agricultural mountain cooperatives - there is a need for a "start-up aid" (essential in the start-up phase to avoid a "block" of the initiative) with a "Task Notebook" that would establish the rational use of the funds. The amount of "aid" varies depending on the size of the cooperative.
- The second category of investments aims at organizing collection centers for raw materials (milk, fruit, and forest fruits) and small local bases for the collection of live animals - through the collection and acquisition system of the cooperative. For milk and fruit, there is a need for a central, refrigerated warehouse.

In the case of the development from the start of Grade II type cooperatives (single / administrative unit), the investments target the raw material collection centers, supplemented with a unit for their transformation in semi-fabricated or even finite, sellable "mountain products", depending on the provision by the agricultural communal cooperative of a constant "market niche", this objective being the most difficult to achieve and uncertain as longevity over time.

From the experience of recent years, it emerges that current solutions, through small cooperative associations in mountain villages have limited utility, cannot be sustainable on their own, being mostly unable to penetrate and resist on the markets that are able to provide a higher payment for a high quality commodity.

Investments (Category III)

It is the final solution for the organization of a mountain micro-region with similar geo-climatic features, traditions and commercial practices, which involves the association of agricultural cooperatives from geographically close administrative units (basins, valleys) in the form of "Inter-cooperative Mountain Associations", with approx. 4 investment objectives:

- Dairy factory (mainly focused on hard cheeses) with softening section.
- Slaughterhouse with meat processing unit and workshop for processing by-products.
- Vegetable mountain products factory.
- Central storage for "mountain products", with transport and maintenance services.

Within the Inter-cooperative Mountain Associations would activate the Commercial Service, which will ensure the prospecting of the foreign and domestic markets, the promotion of "mountain products" under their own brand, the signing of the contracts and the commercial organization, the Technical and Sustainable Development Service, the Supply and Maintenance Service and analysis laboratories.

For reasons of economic profitability, the four main objectives expected would be the equivalent of an "Eco-Food Mountain Park".

Financial resources

A detailed study is required. The financial sources for investments target EU funds and other resources, state contributions for less favored mountain areas, essentially non-reimbursable.

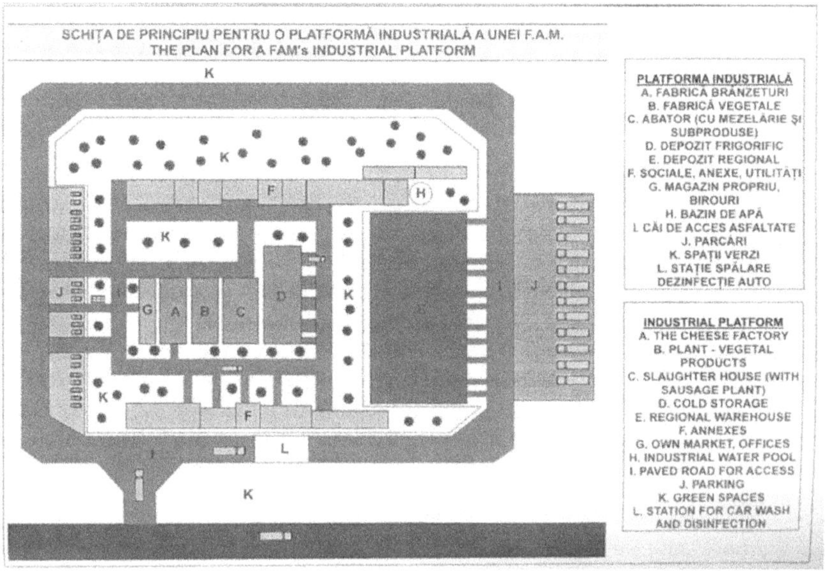

Figure 1: Draft scheme of an eco-food mountain platform

Figure 2: Private initiative from Dorna Basin, 2017 – small scale "emmentaler" cheese production unit – "mountain product" Discussions and debates

With researchers from Romania and abroad, with agricultural and forestry specialists, economists, mountain farmers and initiators of the first mountain agricultural cooperatives, administrative decision makers, top political and academic figures.

Comments and insights on various themes that are specific to the mountain areas, including the "mountain product" and the solution of mountain agricultural cooperatives, during twelve national and international scientific conferences organized by the Center for Mountain Economy "CE-MONT" Vatra Dornei (2015–2018) and within the "The CE-MONT Academic School of Mountainology" (papers published in the Journal of Mountainology - vol. I - VII).

Conclusions

The economic and social issues specific to mountain areas are complex, diverse and require appropriate, organizational and legislative approaches, based on mid-term and long-term studies. The orientation towards the high valorization of "mountain products" according to the EU and EC Regulations - on the "mountain product", is an inspiring direction for the safeguarding and sustainable development of the agro-food economy and the mountain society, taking into account the national and regional particularities and the approach in an integrated system, preceded by economic and social studies that provide an adequate scientific basis.

Limits of current research

They are found in the limited number of researches with sufficient accumulations for a holistic approach to mountain phenomenology and insufficient means for carrying out social economic research and studies useful especially in mountain areas of emerging EU countries and candidate countries - but also other mountain areas with food production possibilities.

Future research directions

Studying the renewable resources and the limits of the food productivity development of the territories with traditions, marketing studies aimed at the advantageous capitalization of "mountain products" for producers and studies on the selection of technologies appropriate to the mountainous peculiarities. Studying the needs of education and developing guidelines tailored to the mountain areas.

References

1. Agricultural- Co-operatives: Role in Food Security and Rural Development, Suleman Afam, (New York, 2009).
2. Bazin G., Les principaux resultats de l´evaluation de la politique agricole de la montagne en France, Commisariat general du Plan: La politique de la montagne, La documentation Française (Paris, 1999).
3. R.L. Brown – Plan B 3.0 – General mobilization to save civilization, Technical Press, Bucharest, 2008.
4. Caël Christian, Un plan de développement agricole durable pour la Montagne Nord (département des Vosges), Revue de géographie alpine, 1995.
5. Ebner, M. Raport provizoriu – cu privire la situaţia şi perspectivele agriculturii din zonele de munte şi deal, Parlamentul European – Comisia pentru Agricultură şi Dezvoltare Rurală – 2008/2066 – INI.
6. FAO. 2011, Global food losses and food waste: extent, causes and prevention, J. Gustavsson, C. Cederberg, U. Sonesson, R. van Otterdijk et A. Meybeck. Rome. www.fao.org.docrep/014/mb606e00.pdf.
7. Fiche d´information sur les coopératives et l´emploi rural (Genéve: 2007).
8. Fleury Philippe, Petit Sandrine, Dobremez Laurent, Implementing Sustainable Agriculture and Rural Development in the European Alps, Institut Supérieur d´Agriculture et d´agroalimentaire Rhône – Alpes (ISARA- Lyon), Institut National de la Recherche Agronomique (INRA), Cemagref – Institut de recherche pour l´inginérie de l´agriculture et de l´environnement, 2008.
9. Gerbaux Françoise, Les politique agricole et régionale européennes en faveur des zones défavorisées et de montagne, Revue de Géographie Alpine, 2004.

10. I.P. Otiman – Sustainable rural development in Romania, Romanian Academy Press, Bucharest, 2006.
11. Michel V., Hauwuy A., Chamba JF., Qualité des produis: practiques des producteurs et flore microbienne de laits, GIS Alpes du Nord, 2004.
12. Plăiaş, I. Agricultura montană – societate. Un necesar contract posibil. Munţii Apuseni, Edit. Libris, Cluj-Napoca, 1994.
13. Produits de montagne, Comment marier identité et qualité des élus de la montagne (ANEM), France, 2004.
14. Radu Rey – Factorii de zooigienă şi influienţa lor asupra sănătăţii şi producţiei bovinelor din gospodăriile populaţiei în zona montană Bazinul Dornelor. Economia agro-zootehnică montană încotro? Edit. Terra Nostra, Iaşi, 2018.
15. Radu Rey – Viitor in Carpati, 1979, Scrisul Românesc Press, Craiova, 1979.
16. Radu Rey – Mountain Civilization, Edit. Ştiinţifică Enciclopedică, Bucharest, 1986.
17. Radu Rey – Mountains and the 21st century. Comparative study of European strategies for mountain areas, with particular reference to the Romanian Carpathians. M1-SEE Plan. Terra Nostra Press, Iaşi, 2013.
18. Rey Radu – Multi-annual strategy for the Romanian Carpathians, Horizon 2040, Editura Terra Nostra, Iaşi, 2013.
19. Réponnes d´Euromontana á la consultation sur la politique de qualité des produits agricoles, Euromontana, 2008.
20. Ricard Daniel, Rieutort Laurent, Filiéres agro-alimentaires et moyennes montagnes françaises. Revue de géographie alpine, 2005.
21. Romanian Government Decision no. 506/2016.
22. Les Politiques Communautaires et la Montagne, Commision Européenne, 2003.
23. Minister Order (Ministru of Agriculture and Rural Development from Romania) no. 52/2017.
24. Report of the European Alpine Research Institute / ICALPE, European Parliament, July, 1998, Towards a European mountain policy.
25. Regulation 1151/2012 of the EU/EP regarding quality schemes.
26. Delegated Regulation 665/2014 of the European Commission regarding "mountain products".
27. Resolution of the European Parliament from 10 May 2016 regarding cohesion policy in mountain regions of the EU - 2015/2279 (INI).

Romulus GRUIA[1], Alexandru T. BOGDAN[2], George Florea TOBĂ[2]
Marcel Th. PARASCHIVESCU[2], George-Leonard TOBĂ[2]

[1] Transilvania University of Braşov, Research Centre EBIOTEFA & Brasov Workstation of Research and Study Centre for Agriculture and Forestry Biodiversity "Acad. David Davidescu", Romanian Academy, Email: ecotec@unitbv.ro

[2] Research and Study Centre for Agriculture and Forestry Biodiversity "Acad. David Davidescu", Romanian Academy

Biodiversity and Evolution of Animal Genetic Resources in the Consolidation of the Romanian Natural and Food Patrimony

Abstract *The paper proposes to analyze animal breeding and biodiversity to come in relation to the evolution or involution of animal genetic resources, as bases to find solutions to avoid imminent food crises, on the terms of the present demographic confusion and climate changes. There are made references at agri-ecosystems versus natural ecosystems, with the description of the reorientation frame of the agri-zootechnical production based on modular agriculture principles. Passing from general to particular, the paper makes an analyses and inventory of the zootechnical as an element of agricultural biodiversity and as a sub-set of general biodiversity. There is described genetic variability from natural patrimony, that includes all forms of life directly relevant to Romanian animal husbandry: plant varieties with feed potential and animal breeds (that is, in the generic direction of "farm biodiversity"), but also many other organisms such as soil fauna, predators, and all of the native animals ("wild biodiversity") existing on and having an economic potential for animal breeding farms. There is processed information in order to emphasise groups of genetic resources and, implicitly, of foods that by use of agricultural biodiversity, with focusing on those in tha Animalia regiment and afferent production methods, can contribute to food security and livelihood security.*

Keywords: *biodiversity, fauna, genetic resources, livestock, zoo-products*

Introduction

Biodiversity, in essence, represents life complex network that sustains us all and on which is based our whole food bank. Biodiversity protection doesn't mean only to save species and habitats, but also to assure in fact the access to food (and water) and, last but not least, to help ourselves in facing the most grave effects of climate changes. (Gustafson, 2005; Caroli, Pizzi, 2012; Bogdan et al. 2014; FAO, 2016)

The measures established by the World Convention upon Biologic Diversity to fight biologic erosion, show that every loss of a gene or species limits our future options. This situation not only menaces food security, but also creates difficulties in answering new provocations due to global heating. Biotechnology in general and especially the one linked to animal genetic resources, better lays stress on biodiversity economic and ecologic importance, offering new possibilities to transfer non transferable genes by sexual way. Every conserved gene, beyond its economic and scientific importance, means a careful and respectful attitude face to our fellow creatures and especially face to generations to come after us. That is why conserving and giving back animal species with economic potential become a priority for the present. (Gruia, 2017)

The animal biodiversity natural patrimony constitutes in fact the corner Stone of zoo- culture that feeds us all. It also provides clothing, medicines and other subsistence means for the major part of humanity. Social and economic importance being so big, we consider it opportune to analyze an extremely important component, namely the value of the biodiversity of animal genetic resources. Taking into consideration that many of these bio resources are to be found in zoo-productive ecosystems (Gruia, 1988) and, respectively, in the corresponding animal breeding farms, one may assuredly say that biodiversity is also essential in food security by the sub-set of animal origin food.

The food patrimony is thus enriched on the direction of nutrition quality and corresponding policies, especially because proteins of animal origin are absolutely essential in human body functioning, which shows the importance of animal diversified breeding. (Bogdan, Comsa, 2011; Hodges, 2012; Bennett, Jennings, 2013) As an argument for what has been mentioned, we remind that the main protein sources remain meat and fish, and, as quality, animal proteins are digested in a larger proportion, while the vegetal ones (having larger fiber content) have less digesting degree. Moreover, vegetal proteins are much poorer and do not contain at all certain essential amino acids, particularly important for the organism. Variants to replace animal protein frequently create important deficit of D, B12 vitamins, calcium, iron, iodine, zinc, whose repercussions are diminishing muscle mass, fatigue, muscular cramps, insomnias etc. That is why animal protein is of interest, for a diversified alimentation, within the general frame linked to health.

Animal protein diversity and health have as main relation the idea of metabolic equilibrium by food diversification and fructification to the full of the food patrimony and, implicitly, of biodiversity. (Rosegrant et al, 2013; Gruia, 2016; MADR, 2017) As for food patrimony, in the present paper animals are the main theme of the study of genetic resource from natural and artificial eco zones specific to animal breeding, that is, the species of economic interest for humans represented by the different types of fodder crops, part of the fauna and the farm animals. Proteins of animal origin or proteins with a high biologic value are generally to be found in products such as meat (of mammals, poultry, fish), eggs, milk and dairy products, that contain complete proteins (in the vegetal world soya is the only plant that contains complete proteins). Incomplete proteins do not assure an adequate contribution of aminoacids.

There must be mentioned that, out of the 20 known aminoacids, 8 are considered essential, as they may not be synthesized in the organism and have to be daily brought at the same time with food. (Sandu, 2014; Gruia, 2016) Consequently, food of animal origin becomes unreplaceable, which imposes animal genetic resources and, implicitly, animal breeding as a strategic branch of production and ever emphasized capitalization of the biodiversity of the Animalia world species.

All these things sustain the idea to develop investment policies in animal breeding and producing food industry (economy with high added value), which will be in connection with reasonable policies to diversify and genetically improve fodder cultures and races or lines of different animal species with potential of economic capitalization. (Steinfeld, 2006; Thornton, Herrero, 2009) In this context, natural and alimentary patrimony sustained by animal genetic resource biodiversity from the Romanian area becomes a real reserve both for Romania and for its contribution on internationally and especially European layout.

The paper general objective is linked to animal breeding evolution on direction of diversifying and valorizing the biodiversity of animal genetic resources, as a problem of large importance for Romania. The present demarche is also a warning concerning the weak interest and support for the growth of reproductive effectives and animal biodiversity conservation (such as conserving certain inland races). That is why the paper seeks for arguments for directions of action necessary to consolidate and adapt the existing natural patrimony in view of diversifying the present animal production. The present analyses may constitute a bases of biotechnical and bioeconomic start for Romania's "zootechnization", as a necessary component for food biodiversity and for adapting the feeding manner to unforeseeable conditions of demographic and climate evolution of decades to come.

The pursued specific objectives are to inventory and make a diagnosis of animal genetic resources with economic production potential existing over Romania's territory, then to develop an activity strategy based on a series of concepts (as for example: of modulization) with potential of adaptation and application to Romania's specific animal breeding situation. We are referring to the analyses of technical-biological and socio-economic benefits, which, by emphasizing the direct and integrative relation of biodiversity (natural patrimony) with worlds' food (alimentary patrimony), will have as a result the possibility to fix technical and managerial principles through which the Romanian phyto-zoo-food and natural area may be able to avoid potential alimentary crises, but also to become a real source of food export, especially at continental level. Another objective is to lay the conceptual bases in order to achieve the "Catalogue of animal biodiversity with zoo-technical and bioeconomic potential", as a working element in order to diversify the animal production.

Methodology

There are taken into consideration biologic-technical, managerial and statistic-economical analyses, that may estimate biodiversity and genetic resources from the ecosystems that are to be found in Romania's geographic space. Methodologically it is made a diagnosis, a data processing and a forecast, by the analyses centered on remediating the standard system of animal breeding production, in relation with animal biodiversity from Romania, necessary to apply methods based on bioeconomy principles to zootechnically capitalize animal bio resources. Methodologically, the analyses is made from general to particular: from Romania's flora and fauna biodiversity and biologic classifications, to enumerating terrestrial and aquatic animal genetic resources and their food sources represented by fodder plants and vegetables with fodder potential.

Results and discussions

After dates at our disposal (Gustafson, G., 2005; Steeg J. And others, 2009; FAO, 2016; MADR, 2017), there exist between 250,000 and 300,000 species around the world (including animals and plants), out of which only 150–200 are used in human alimentation (under 2 %). It results that a significant quantity of biodiversity is NOT capitalized. We practically refer to a real poverty of used genetic resources at present in agriculture, with repercussions upon food safety.

Starting from the hypothesis that Romania may keep and consolidate its animal biodiversity by intelligent policies, there may be foreseen the development of the natural and alimentary patrimony, based on the process of diversification and introduction of species with economic potential in the animal breeding circuit, necessary to equilibrate the requirement of animal protein in future decades and to avoid potential crises of alimentary nature. That is why it is of interest to identify potential animal categories from the zoological classification in order to understand the animal biodiversity structure. (Table 1)

Romania's geo climate diversity makes it possible to relate with the diversity of biologic classification in order to inventory in a synthesis the existing fauna, from which there may be selected species with economic potential and adapted at a diversified zootechnical production. Romania's fauna is one of the richest and varied in Europe, containing rare or even unique species on the continent. In Romania there live 732 species and subspecies of vertebrates and numerous (some thousands) species of no vertebrates. Among these ones, with potential in zoo-culture there are a series of vertebrates that are present in Romania's fauna: cyclostomes / aquatic vertebrates (4 species); fish (184 species and subspecies); amphibians (20 species and subspecies); reptiles (31 species and subspecies); birds (382 species and subspecies) and mammalians (110 species and subspecies).

On the other hand, on the line of natural patrimony of animal biodiversity, at world-wide level, there may be found a number of approximately 200 domestic species, starting with bovines and finishing with Drosophila and a series of

Table 1: Classification of animal biodiversity with economic potential

Biologic Group	Examples of biodiversity
Non Vertebrates (2 millions of species, as for ex.: jelly fish, starfish, octopus, fly or spider and others)	Mollusks – animals that have a soft segmented body rich in glands. The most important classes are: gastropods, lamellibranchiate and cephalopods. Arthropods – their feet are articulated, formed of 5–6 segments. Arthropods are divided in arachnids, crustaceans, myriapods and insects.
Vertebrates (fish, batrachians, reptiles)	Animals that have a vertebral column. They are divided in: Cyclostomes /Cartilaginous fish/Osseous fish. Amphibians – that live in aquatic and terrestrial environment, having pulmonary and cutaneous respiration (approx. 20 de species in Romania, ex.: frogs, salamanders and others) Reptiles – have scales; exclusively pulmonary respiration.
Birds	They present feathers, hull, pectoral muscles very well developed. Birds are Biped animals. The fish class is formed of acarenates and carenates. The Carenates are passeriformes, galiformes, ciconiformes, columbiformes, cuculiformes, pisciformes and anseriformes (Certain species are to be found in animal breeding).
Mammalians	They are animals that for the most part throw live young and feed them with milk from their mammals. They are divided in: - Monotremes – have a single orifice through which excrements, fecal matters and eggs are eliminated. - Marsupials – have a marsupial. - Placentals – are viviparous superior animals, with developed placenta = most of species from standard animal breeding.

microorganisms. To be noticed is the fact that in peri-urban and with industrial growth eco zones, the number of zootechnical species is much reduced (genetic poverty). In exchange, in mountain zones the species variety is a little bit higher, which imposes certain preoccupations to maintain genetic resources. The genetic reserve of the area of agri-zootechnical and agritouristic farms, presupposes a major preoccupation for future decades through special programs on bioeconomic animal breeding principles. (Gruia, R., 2016) But in general, out of all these animal species, only approximately 4 up to 20 are the object of exploitation for food, clothing and work production, inclusively in our country (Table 2).

Table 2: Genetic resources from Romania, with zoo-alimentary and clothing potential

Bioresource Group	Exemplification animal biodiversity
Genetic Resources of Farm Mammalians	Domestic pig (*Sus scrofa domesticus* or *Sus domesticus*)
	Cow of Ruminantia suborder (ruminants), Bovidae family
	Horse (*Equus caballus*)
	Domestic sheep (*Ovis aries*)
	Domestic goat (*Capra aegagrus hircus*)
Genetic Resources of Farm Birds	Hens (*Gallus gallus domesticus*)
	Turkey hens *(Meleagris gallopavo)*
	Domestic geese (*Anser cygnoides)*
	Domestic ducks *(Anatinae subfamily)*
	Quaits *(Coturnix coturnix)*
	Pigeons *(Columba livia)*
	Pheasants *(Phasianus colchicus)*
	Peacocks *(Pavo sp.)*
Genetic Resources of Small Farm Animals	Rabbits *(family Leporidae)*
	Chinchilla *(family Chinchillidae)*
	Coypu *(Myocastor coypus)*
	Muskrat *(Ondatra zibethicus)*
	Guinea pig *(subfamily Caviinae)*
	Polecat *(Mustela putorius)*
	Mink *(Mustela vison)*
	Polar fox *(Vulpes lagopus)*

From the perspective of today's reality, in the first decades of the 21st century (after the years 2009/2010, from governmental data), in Romania there were used 14 species, represented by 123 races and pure animal lines in animal breeding, that were found on the List of animal genetic resources either in critical estate (under 100 females), or in disappearance danger (between 101 and 1000 females), or in the attention zone of vulnerable ones (between 100 and 5000 females).

Besides the mentioned species, biodiversity also refers to species that belong to animal food, consequently to natural patrimony of fodder plants. As for the food of zoo-culture species, out of the several thousands of plants frequently met on the vegetable carpet, only 18 terrestrial species are to be generally found in fodder recipes and also other tens of aquatic plants (Table 3).

Table 3: Vegetable genetic resources with fodder potential met on the Romanian territory

Type of resource	Exemplification of biodiversity	Type of resources	Exemplification of biodiversity
Group of Fodder Plants	Winter fodder *(fodder peas + oat)* Potato *(Solanum tuberosum)* Hemp *(Cannabis sativa)* Beans *(Phaseolus vulgaris)* Orchard grass *(Dactylis glomerata)* Sudan grass *(Sorghum sudanense)* Flax *(Linum usitatissimum)*	Group of Aquatic Plants, with utilization potential in the food of Animalia world species They assure the life and food of aquatic species: - Aquatic plants from ponds, lakes, artesian fountains, aquariums etc., that assure water life; - Most of fish are omnivorous species, i.e. they eat small bodies that live in still and running waters (members of the zooplankton), warms, snails and larva of insects from mud, but, besides food of animal origin, and they also eat seeds, aquatic plant offspring, fruit, and dry parts of plants from mud that fall in water. - In artificial ponds there are used different types of cereals, agricultural auxiliary products, as supplementary fodder.	Reed Karka *(Phragmites karka Variegata)* Dwarf rush *(Typha minima)* "Calcea calului" *(Caltha palustris)* "Coada calului" *(Equisetum fluviatile or Equisetum scirpoides)* Calamus *(Acorus calamus variegatus)* "Planta Cameleon" *(Houttuynia cordata Chamaelon)* "Iarba Rosie de Balta" *(Imperata cylindrica Red Baron)*

(*continued on next page*)

Table 3: Continued

Type of resource	Exemplification of biodiversity	Type of resources	Exemplification of biodiversity
	Lucerne *(Medicago sativa)*		"Iris de Baltă" („Puddle iris") *(Iris ssp)*
	Fodder peas *(Pisum arvense)*		Water lily *(Nymphaea ssp.)*
	Barley *(Hordeum vulgare L.)*		"Rodul Pamantului" *(Arum italicum)*
	Two-row barley *(Hordeum distichon)*		Imperial Lilac *(Fritillaria michailovskii)*
	Perennial Raigras *(Lolium perene)*		"Rugina" *(Juncus ensifolius)*
	Sulla *(Onobrychis viciifolia)*		Lysichiton camtschatcensis *(Lysichiton camtschatcensis)*
			„Rachitan" *(Lythrum salicaria)*
			Miriophyllum aquaticum *(Miriophyllum aquaticum)*
			Reed *(Phragmites australis variegatus)*
			Water fern *(Thelypteris palustris)* *and other*

Note: the name in the quotation marks does not have an English correspondent.

It is to be noticed the fact that from biodiversity perspective, at international level, the attention is well directed and with justified hope towards aquatic species (Table 4), also taking into account the adaptation at different changing climate conditions (http://ec.europa.eu/fisheries/).

From the perspective of fish breeding biodiversity the Romanian natural patrimony benefits by a series of species that may more and more enrich the food patrimony (tab.5), at which there may also be added numerous species of sea fruit (but that are less present in Romanian alimentation and we do not mention them

Table 4: Elements of biotechnique and management from animal breeding branches of fish breeding and aquaculture, at European level

No.	Approached problems	Specification
1	Demands	At European level we need fish and sea fruits, but resources from nature are NOT sufficient to cover the existing demand, but complementarily, sustainable fishing goes together with fish breeding.
2	European fish breeding	There are bred very different species, among which there are shells, lobsters, tilapia, sturgeons and even some species that are very intensively fished in nature, such as turbot, codfish and sole. Lately, algae products has also developed.
3	Structure	Approximately 50 % from fish breeding farm production is represented by sea fruit, the most popular species being mussels and oysters. Sea fish such as salmon, sea bream and perch represent almost 27 % from the production, and sweet water fish, such as trout and carp, 23 %.
4	Consumption	The average of the last years shows that 68 % from the fish and sea fruit Europeans eat comes from extra continental import, and a large part is produced in fish breeding farms. Practically, only 10 % from the consumption comes from European fish breeding.
5	Perspectives - Species adapted at climate warming	Thermophilic species (bred in systems with warm water): • African salmon (*Clarias gariepinus*), • Species of tilapia (*Tilapia niloticus, T. mossambica, T. hornorum* or even their hybrids) • Baramundi (*Lates calcalifer*), • Eel (*Anguilla anguilla*). Species that are NOT thermophilic, but adapted at breeding in warm water systems: - European salmon (*Silurus glanis*), - Certain sturgeon species, zander (*Sander lucioperca*), - Perch (*Perca fluviatilis*), but also - Carp (*Cyprinus carpio*) especially varieties of ornamental carp (known under *Koi* name).

Table 5: Bioresources from animal and fish breeding in Romania

Typologic Group	Examples
Group of largely spread fish in Romania	Rapacious carp *(Aspius aspius)*
	Roach *(Rutilus Rutilus Carpathorossicus)*
	Beldita *(Alburnoides bipunctatus)*
	Perch *(Perca fluvialitis)*
	Sun Perch *(Lepomis gibbosus)*
	Crucian *(Carassius carassius)*
	Crucian carp *(Carassius gibelio)*
	Chub *(Leuciscus cephalus)*
	Carp *(Cyprinus Carpio Carpio)*
	Fusari *(Aspro streber)*
	Tench *(Tinca tinca)*
	Grayling *(Thymallus thymallus)*
	Eel-pout *(Lota lota)*
	Sucker *(Barbus barbus)*
	Ablet *(Alburnus alburnus)*
	Trout *(Salmo trutta fario)*
	Flounder *(Abramis brama)*
	Gudgeon *(Gobio gobio)*
	Rudd *(Scardinius erythrophthalmus)*
	Zander *(Sander lucioperca or Stiostedion lucioperca)*
	Broad snout *(Chondrostoma nasus)*
	Blue mackerel *(Scomber scombrus)*
	Waller *(Silurus glanis)*
	River pirate *(Esox lucius)*
	Loach *(Misgurnus fossilis)*
Group of fish acclimated in Romania	"Amurul alb" *(Ctenopharyngodon idella)*
	Batca *(Blicca bjorkna bjorkna)*
	Cteno *(Ctenopharyngodon idella)*
	Fitofagus *(Hypophthalamichtys molitrix)*
	"Sânger" *(Cornus sanguinea)*

here), but whose food potential is considerable and to be taken into consideration in the future.

The consolidation of natural patrimony of animal genetic resources has also in view other directions of biodiversity capitalization. Thus we mention a category, still little developed at present, but with great potential in the future, which is represented by insects. The group of food based on insects is considered to be the 21st century ecologic food (locusts, cricket, larva, enthomophagous bees etc.). To notice that we mean a category with numerous alimentary and non-alimentary qualities (Figure 1).

When speaking about modern farms, we refer to consecrated animal species and to those with economic potential at farm level, to zoo culture, i.e. the real „animal cultures" (ex. Poultry raising, sericiculture, apiculture, fish breeding etc.). Therefore, the farmer will more and more become an integrator of the zoo-alimentary act in specific modules, practically a specialist of phyto-zoo-alimentary culture systems.

In many farms only some species are bred, these ones replacing the numerous local species and lines from zoo culture, used before. After Kothari and Warner (1994), this situation is similar to a real "suicide", because it determines the loss of genetic diversity with grave consequences on productivity. Using the suicide phrase, wants to emphasize as striking as possible what the world's loss of genetic diversity for alimentary security means.

In this case it is observed that farmers and local peasants have a particular merit in achieving genetic diversity, but also in preserving this diversity, some of them still keeping today a series of local forms. But modern animal breeding creates new breeding systems (new modules), of high productivity, which, besides all demands they have, are solicited by breeders. In these conditions, farmers' demand for superior zoo-modules can't be stopped by invoking the necessity of biodiversity conservation. No matter how patriots farmers are, face to obvious economic and financial advantages, they will leave local species breeding in favor of new creations, which imposes to find solutions to preserve genetic resources.

The loss of genetic resources of animal lines bred in farms, but also of fodder cultures, constitutes a real threat all over the world where animal breeding rapidly evolves and where amelioration modern methods are applied. Although geneticists do not cease to express their worry face to the reduction of the genetic basis of most fodder cultures or animal species from farms, invoking immediate measures to save genetic diversity, fate irony makes that just the success of their work leads to this genetic narrowing. At that rate the idea to return to Nature model appeared, at the offer sustained by food biodiversity that may become a viable idea only if agri-zootechnical productivity growth may be assured and also a corresponding marketing, because mankind is confronted with strong urbanization and a particular population density.

The solution to solve the problem imposes a technologic rethinking. An example in this direction, besides others from literature, is a sub-set directed towards the idea of modular animal breeding (Gruia, R., 2010) where „modulization" refers

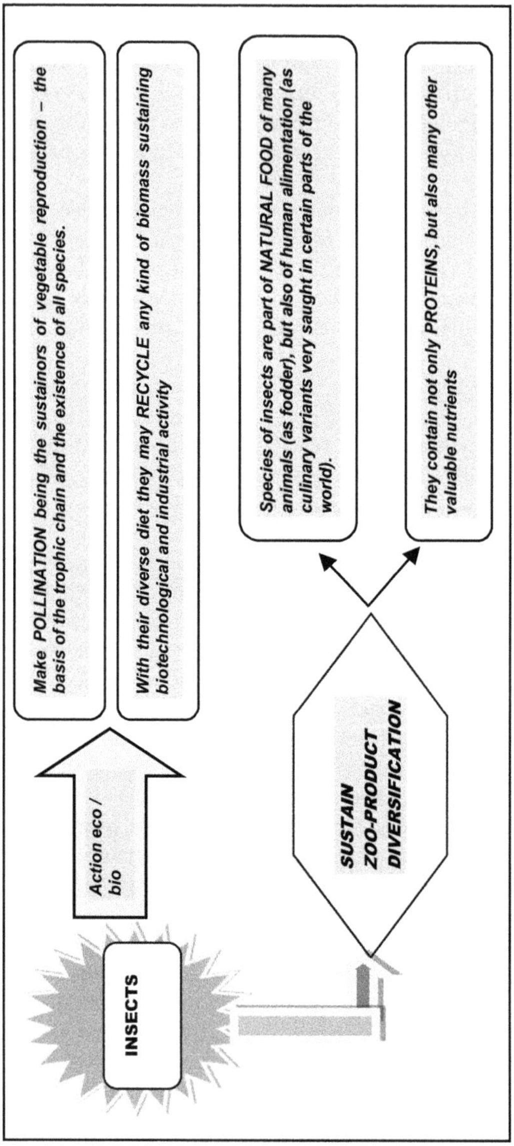

Figure 1: Insects – bio resources with huge potential in portfolio of zoo-products in biotechnological innovation

to approach to ecologic, bio economic and biotechnical principles in integronic dynamics, with operations and methods of breeding animals in complex systems. Within these ones, the flows will take into consideration trophic chains, to avoid pollution, eco-energetic interpretation (eMergetic) of module components, innovating technologies (biotechnologies, nanotechnologies, robotization, breeding in aquatic cages and others, and for fodder hydroponic, airponic techniques etc.). (Gruia, R., 2009)

In zoo-modules, activity goes on, from economic-social and managerial point of view, through emergently integrated elements in the logics of hyper complex systems of the type of zoo productive ecosystems, or of systems focused on special productions achieved by the controlled environment and space model (these ones being situated in the future in vertical farms in phyto-zoo-alimentary skyscrapers, farms built inside large cities, recovering thus the high deficiency of fertile land as a result of climate changes).

The basic idea in different types of zoo cultural modules is diversification, by capitalization of biodiversity and optimization of bio resource utilization, within the meaning of achieving an acceptable productivity and, respectively, of getting to such a threshold that the quantity of natural resources plainly consumed (i.e. the ones extracted for the first time from natural environment) not to put in danger their rhythm of natural remaking, in order to remain in sufficient quantities for future generations.

Conclusions

"Zootechnysation" in the future decades is based on change of paradigm by: retechnologization, application of bioeconomy principles and biodiversity capitalization, taking into account restructuration of animal breeding growth on direction of eco-traditional zoo-modules and of zootechnical bioindustry modules, either of ecosystem type, or of the type of the modules with controlled environment and space.

Animal breeding is sustainable bio industry within bio economy based on intelligent use of terrestrial and aquatic animal resources, by capitalization of Animalia world biodiversity (mammalians, birds, fish, vertebrate or no vertebrate different species), which may represent the mankind's reserve and salvation face to potential alimentary crises. Linked to this biodiversity, it is not modern practices that have been the main source of gene loss, but these ones have been lost before forming the present animal breeding bioindustry, that imposes to identify real factors that contribute to reduce biologic diversity.

In the future, Romanian animal breeding problem becomes productivity growth at the rate of optimizing bio resource use, within the meaning to get to such a threshold so that the quantity of consumed natural resources does not put in danger the rhythm of their natural remake, to remain in sufficient quantities for future generations.

Reconceptualization of animal breeding will emphasize the capitalization of animal genetic resources, from the perspective of species or population diversity and, respectively, of genetic amelioration, so that the analyses and stocktaking of bio resources become more than opportune in view of making the Catalogue of animal biodiversity with zootechnical and bioeconomic potential, as working element in the capitalization of food biodiversity of animal origin, so that zoo-products may become a pylon of national security and will be able to constitute a sub-set of Romania's country model for the 21st century, which, pragmatically speaking, will represent a food reserve of superior quality and an element of interest for the European Union.

References

Bennett,D. J. and Jennings, R. C. (eds.) (2013): Successful Agricultural Innovation in Emerging Economies, Cambridge University Press.

Bogdan, A. T., Comsa Dana (2011) - Eco-Bio-Economia o nouă paradigmă, în Solutii ecobioeconomice bazate pe biodiversitate agrosilvică pentru asigurarea independenţei şi suveranităţii agroali-mentare durabile a României europene şi euroatlantice, Ed. Libris Danubiu Bucuresti, p.34–38.

Bogdan, A. T., Gruia, R., Toba G. F., Pasalau Carmen (2014) - Scientific basis of a national, strategic and preference interest project, of agri-food bioeconomy, by innovative valorization of the Romanian territorial capital in the 21-st century, Journal of EcoAgriTourism, Publishing House Transilvania University of Brasov, Romania, ISSN 1844-8577, Vol.10, Nr.2, p. 9–10.

Caroli, A. M., Pizzi, F., (2012) - Livestock biodiversity: from genes to animal products through safeguard actions, Theor Biol Forum. 2012;105(2):71–82.

Gruia,R, (1988): Fiabilitatea ecosistemelor zooproductive, Zootehnie și Med. Veterinară,nr.10, 54–58.

Gruia, R., (2009) - Theory of Ecoemergent Integronics (General Theory of Ecological Emergence Integration), (wseas_brasov), The 2nd International Conference on Environmental and Geological Sciences and Engineering – WSEAS, Proceedings ISSN: 1790-2769, ISBN: 978-960-474-119-9, Transilvania University of Brasov, Romania, September 24–26, 168–172

Gruia, R., (2010) - Modular agriculture – paradigm of globalization dynamics within the context of climatic and scientific changes, Environmental Engineering and Management Journal, „Gheorghe Asachi" Technical University Iasi, ISSN 1582-9596, Vol.9, nr.12, 1601–1606.

Gruia, R., (2016) - Zootehnia bioeconomică, Editura Lux Libris Brașov, ISBN 978-973-131-357-3,36–58.

Gruia, R., (2017) - Res. genetice în fermele agrotur., Ed.Clarion Brașov, ISBN:978-606-94470-0, 29–241.

Gustafson, G., (2005) - Biodiversity as a tool in animal husbandry, Ekologiskt lantbruk, Utgivare SLU, Centrum för uthålligt lantbruk ISSN 1102-6758, ISRN SLU-EKBL-EL--29--SE, ISBN 91-576-6881-7, 45–69.

Hodges, M. (2012): The politics of emergence: Public-private partnerships and the conflictive timescapes of apomixis technology development, Biosocieties, 7: 23–49.

Kothari, S.P., Warner, J.,(1994) - Econometrics of event studies, Handbook of empirical corporate finance 1, 3–36.

Rosegrant, M.W., C. Ringler, T. Zhu, S. Tokgoz, and P. Bhandary, (2013): Water and food in the bioeconomy: Challenges and opportunities for development. Agricultural Economics, International Association of Agricultural Economists, vol. 44(s1), p. 139–150, November. doi:10.1111/a gec.12058.

Sandu, Mariana (2014) - Assessment of romanian livestock sector available from the perspective of animal food product, postdoctorat Institutul de Economie Mondială / Academia Română, 123–131.

Steeg J., Freeman H. A., Li X., Parthasarathy Rao P., (2009) - Drivers of change in crop– livestock systems and their impacts on agro-ecosystems services and human well-being to 2030. CGIAR Systemwide Livestock Programme. International Livestock Research Institute, Nairobi, Kenya. Google Scholar.

Steinfeld H., Gerber P., Wassenaar T., Castel V., Rosales M., de Haan C., (2006) - Livestock's long shadow: Environmental issues and options. FAO, Rome. Google Scholar

Thornton P. K., Herrero M., (2009) - The inter-linkages between rapid growth in livestock production, climate change, and the impacts on water resources, land use, and deforestation. World Bank Policy Research Working Paper, WPS 5178. World Bank, Washington, DC. Google Scholar.

FAO, (2016) - Sustainable agriculture for biodiversity / Biodiversity for sustainable agriculture I6602EN/1/12.16 www.fao.org, 47 p.

MADR - 2017: Raport de activitate, Agenția Națională pentru Zootehnie „Prof. Dr. Gh. K. Constantinescu", 822/25.01.17, 130 pag.

xxx - http://ec.europa.eu/fisheries/cfp/aquaculture/species/index_ro.htm.

Marcel Th. PARASCHIVESCU[1], *George Florea TOBĂ*[1], *Alexandru T. BOGDAN*[1], *Leonard George TOBĂ*[2]

[1] Research and Study Centre for Agriculture and Forestry Biodiversity, Romanian Academy, Email: cscsbas@yahoo.com;

[2] Cabinet attorneys, Bucharest Bar, Romania, Email: leonardtoba@yahoo.com

Bioeconomic Significances of the Management and Marketing of the Conservation and Development Biodiversity of the National Herritage of Local Animal Genetic Resources Studied Intelligent and Eco-Innovating

Abstract *Eco-innovation involves „improving or introducing a new product, service, process, organizational change or marketing strategy, which reduces resource consumption and reduces emissions of toxic substances throughout the life cycle." Management and marketing of natural resources of animal genetic biodiversity in animal husbandry is primarily a historical recognition and a certificate of existence in our country breed Grey Steppe, Pinzgauer, Bazna, Țigaie of Suseni etc. and preservation of the cultural traditions and the current bio-economic, animal enhancement rustic, resistant and adapted to the natural environment in which they were created and maintained. A reproductive biotechnology increases male fertility by artificial insemination (AI) or female embryo transfer (MOET). Moreover, current techniques of cryogenic preservation of gametes (eggs and semen) and embryo genetic banks, allows to keep „ex situ" for a very long time and unchanged genetic information of a population. Applying one or other reproductive biotechnologies is based on the risk status of the population. If the active population is applied biotechnologies producing genetic is progressing.*

Keywords: *management, marketing, eco-innovation, genetic resources, biotechnologies of reproductions*

Introduction

Bioeconomy research on the relationship between genetic resources and management of the organization and functioning of banks showed that bioinformatics is up to the national interest, for the reasons that follow (Tobă et al., 2014; Drucker, Gomez and Anderson, 2001):

- Bioeconomy activity is the enhancement of natural resources to meet the needs of existence of humans. (Georgescu-Roegen, 1996)

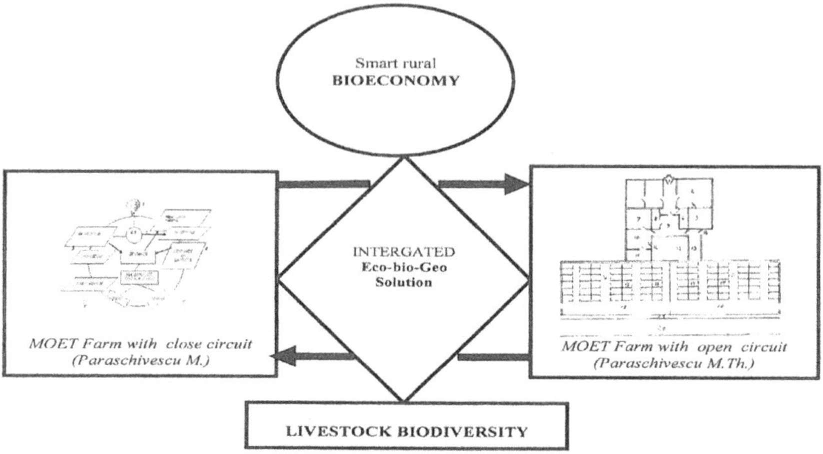

Figure 1: Approach eco- innovative smart rural bioeconomy in the context of livestock biodiversity

Source: Authors.

- People's main needs are food - agro necessary security and safety; protection from pests' biota components; energy - needed first two requirements. (Bogdan et al, 2009)

The management of animal genetic resources using bioinformatics banks should lead to: balance poly-gastric animals with forage resources in natural grasslands; balance livestock for humanity production requirements; improving the genetic potential of animals for production and raising the converting feed resources; using domestic livestock without harming the natural environment. (Sandu, Tobă, Paraschivescu, 2014)

Eco-innovation involves improving or introducing a new product, service, process, organizational change or marketing strategy, which reduces resource consumption and reduces emissions of toxic substances throughout the life cycle.

The marketing of animal genetic resources was done by using the following biotechnologies of reproductions: artificial insemination and embryo transfer. Thus Romania's first artificial insemination in cows was made in 1953, using fresh sperm.

Breeding use of biotechnology in the development and conservation of animal genetic equally ensure local access to the diversity of animal genetic resources at global and transferring them with zoo veterinary advantages, which diminishes the economic crisis and adapting to new environmental conditions.

In 1957, were set up 16 large centers of artificial insemination (C.I.A.) with 261 points insemination (P.I.A.V.), in 1959 there were 40 centers with 650 points, while in 1960–52 the centers with 1,500 points, which used diluted semen and stored at 0–4^0 C. This new organization of artificial insemination was extended gradually and used in parallel the Cattle Artificial Insemination network stations (S.I.A.V.) and for the sheep (S.I.A.O.). The number of cows inseminated in 1960 was 379 608 and 2,500,000 sheep, representing almost 28 % of the total number of sheep. Since 1961, it has extended its network of artificial insemination by setting up 115 sub-centers (S.I.A.) and gradually eliminating S.I.A.V. and S.I.A.O. from artificial insemination and the number increased from 1500 to 3663.

In 1961–1965, the number of artificial inseminations increased for a C.I.A. from 8978 to 18493 cows and breeding and selection Central Station (S.C.R.S.) performed artificial insemination to 71 906 cows and 55 600 sheep. In 1965 artificial insemination with diluted and preserved sperm was done across the country on 1.122.700 cows and heifers, and in some regions such as: Bucharest, 141.800 females; Ploieşti, 77.500 females; Galaţi 91.600 females; Banat, 77.500 females, etc. The number of used bulls as donors of semen in the same year was 1.155, out of which 1,098 bulls were classified as class and elite record.

In early 1997, 4.884 P.I.A.V were running nationally, wherein about 5.600 artificial inseminations operators were working.

Currently 2.627 P.I.A.V national sites are functional and 2.619 operators are working in the artificial insemination.

The first research on embryos transfer in our country was initiated by N. Lunca in 1955 and taken over by V.Oţel; the first works were carried out in 1964–1965 by V. Oţel and T. Feredean, who obtained the first pigs. (Tobă, 2014) The research was continued by V.Oţel et al. to the sheep in 1966–1967 when they obtained the first calves. The first center for embryo transfer was inaugurated in 1975 at SCPCB Tg.Mureş, and in 1977 it's been set up the second center to ICPCB Baloteşti.

In 1978, Silvaş E. et al., obtained the first calf in our country at SCPCB Tg.Mureş, using the surgical collection and embryos transfer, and in 1979 another 3 calves were obtained, by the same team, by mixed cropping non-surgical method and surgical transfer. In 1980, N. Ilinca and V. Negoiţă (from ICPCB Baloteşti) obtained the first calf through non-surgical collection and transfer method.

In June 1987 Silvaş E. et al., obtained the first bull received from a cryopreserved embryo at SCPCB Tg.Mureş, and in February 1988 a second calf was born from a frozen embryo for 42 days, by the non-chirurgical transfer method being performed.

In 1988 N.Ilinca et al. have frozen the first sheep embryos harvested by surgical technique to ICPCB Baloteşti. These were stored for 74 days in liquid nitrogen, than were thawed and surgically transferred to the receiver sheep from Palas Constanţa synchronized by Dr. Stela Zamfirescu, yielding two lambs in March 1989. In 1989 Vintilă et al., have obtained two pairs of twins, identically genetic, by cutting into two, two embryos.

In 1990 Vintilă et al. obtained the first monozygotic calves in our country, by cutting into two an embryo at the age of 7.5 days, at blastocyst stage. In the same year N. Ilinca et al. have succeeded severing a blastocyst and installation of two identical twins gestations on a receiver heifer which aborted after 6 months of gestation. In 1994 was founded the Romanian Association Embryo Transfer (ARET), which was shortly affiliated to AETE and it creates the statistics since 1995. In 1995 four regional centers E.T. (Wallachia, Moldavia, Transylvania and Banat) were established within the National Centre for Breeding with Selection.

Material and method

On signing the Convention in Rio de Janeiro the problem of vulnerable species and biological activity was formalized thus triggering the state of risk of biological species in nature acknowledgement in order to prevent their disappearance caused by the natural ecosystems' anthropization (United Nation Environment Programme, 2011) (Sandu, Tobă, Paraschivescu, 2014).

In nature the existence of biological species is sustained by the natural reproductive isolation mechanisms controlled by the genetic information whose support is.

Because of the wild animals' reproduction function isolation, there are biological populations in which the variability of genotypes is distributed according to the law of chance, Gregor Mendel's great discovery (see Mendel's Laws) (Paraschivescu et al, 2010).

The risk status of species extinction was downgraded to a simple criterion that on the number of species individuals (adults). So it's been decided, even if we repeat, that the biological species (populations) is safety which have a flock of more than 10,000 individuals, vulnerable populations with 1,000–10,000 individuals, populations in danger with 100–1,000 individuals and critically populations with less than 100 individuals. Status of population's extinction risk became one of the biological criteria for estimating the sustainable development of human economic systems, and is an indicator of degradation of the natural environment through human intervention. (Paraschivescu, 2013). Apparently simple, this criterion is perfectly valid as reproductive isolation mechanisms of natural cause's limited risk of species extinction for the inter-relationships and the effects of inbreeding.

The idea of risk status was extended to artificial biological populations created by culture. Initially, to assess the risk of extinction of biological culture populations (breed and animal varieties or cultivars to plant) to take up the same numerical above mentioned criteria as such, ignoring the fact that biological populations in culture have not genetic identity defense by natural mechanisms of reproductive isolation, being at the crossbreed risk.

Although the numeric criteria in question was formally accepted by FAO, the world organization that took over the management of risk status of natural and artificial biological populations, that reached after the proposal of several criteria for classifying artificial biological populations by the degree of extinction risk, one of the criteria that imposed the pace of population decline.

Following this idea and selecting the authors' proposals who got involved in the states risk classification criteria issue of populations extinction in culture, the following points of view have to be kept in mind:

- Engaging the populations in crop production supporting for the market, which is reflected in their inclusion in breeding programs in pure breed (directional selection = grading up).
- The decrease or increase trend of the livestock effective.
- Number of female puberty (livestock) population.
- The number of families where male breeders are grouped with sexual activity in the population or at least the number genitors males.
- Inbreeding coefficient or rhythm.

Results

By combining the above criteria, a more acceptable and adequate classification, generally speaking, would be:

- Working population with large effective livestock, reproductively isolated by "Herd Book" and reproducing after genetic improvement programs in progress.
- Safely populations that have economic utility, have a large number of livestock without lowering tendency are reproductively isolated and not by islanding territorial improvement programs.
- Vulnerable populations, with uncertain role for product market and slow decrease of livestock.
- Populations threatened with fast decreasing of the herd or livestock of 100–1000 animals and less than breeding 6 families' species, regardless the genetics.
- Population in critical condition with a livestock effective of up to 100 animals and less than 4 active breeders.
- Constitution or reconstitution of the population works either by creating lines or breeds by structuring the families, or by identifying new specimen's works and completion of the herd.

In comparison with the classification version of the animal populations by the state of risk launched by FAO, common for both wild species and domestic population, there are some major differences intended to approach the classification proposed by the own reproductive isolation particularities of the domestic animals, because without reproductive isolation there is no population. (Tobă et al, 2012)

Thus it was included among the assessing criteria of the risk status of populations in culture and the existence of operational improvement programs that exclude genes infusion from other population, in addition to the livestock population. Therefore the Pinzgau breed and the Indigenous Carpathian Buffalo from Romania fall in the safe condition population category after the herd size but not under active populations because they do not have breeding programs. Thus it results that they have some risk, because not being a subject to improvement will respond much less to the breeders' requirements and they might become vulnerable in the future.

A second difference is the fact that FAO does not mention that the vulnerable population on whose actual livestock drops sharply, although in artificial population this might be produced easily even though the livestock is initially very high, due to crossbreeding. This happened with flocks of Merinos produced in previous step of the raising sheep strategy in Romania when, before 1990 the target was the production of fine wool, and after 1990, when there was no longer any demand for the production of wool and they have become worthless. As happened with the horse species when the tractors where implemented in agriculture. Such a phenomenon was followed 50–60 years ago by the Grey Steppe that in the planned economy stage was replaced by west European mixed races of milk and meat and after the number of livestock is safely now, at least in intention, in the population category (re)establishment. We can mention the development programs management in collaboration with 25 associations of breeders that include biotechnology type MOET adapted to each species. (Paraschivescu, 2013) (Tobă et al.,2010)

In between 2006–2013, in Romania, the indigenous livestock biodiversity, in various states of risk, is shown in table 1, 2, 3 and continuously monitored by the Ministry of Agriculture and Rural Development (MAPDR) through the National Agency for Animal Sciences (NAAS.) in collaboration with associations of breeders and Research and Study Centre for Agroforestry Biodiversity (CSCBAS).

In this artificial population risk statement classification it might also be included some indication of the number of families in which the animals group by breeding males. This knowledge is absolutely necessary for endangered domestic animal

Table 1: Dynamics in conservation herds of cattle during 2006–2017

Year	Grey Steppe	Pinzgauer	Romanian Buffalo
2006	29	17782	118
2007	34	16122	119
2008	45	16491	221
2009	51	12940	228
2010	55	13662	433
2011	135	12996	1005
2012	218	10857	960
2013	67	11353	289
2014	59	-	94
2015	59	-	94
2016	37	-	93
2017	38	-	93

Source: Authors based on dates from National Agency for Animal Sciences 2017

Table 2: Dynamics of sheep in conservation during 2006–2017

Year	Tigaie v. Ruginie	Rațcă	Karakulul of Botoșani	Merinos of Palas	Merinos of Suseni	Merinos Transylvanian	Merinos of Cluj	Meat Breed Palas	Milk Breed Palas	Black Head Sheep Teleorman
2006	337	183	3,278	3,521	0	0	0	0	0	2,186
2007	462	1,727	3,391	4,395	624	0	0	0	0	3,121
2008	1,151	2,058	3,646	4,160	789	2,163	202	0	0	4,030
2009	1,271	2,371	3,669	4,415	978	2,396	202	0	0	4,030
2010	1,434	2,889	3,091	6,138	1,011	4,703	314	0	0	3,382
2011	3,603	3,447	4,537	7,074	1,011	4,567	314	0	0	3,833
2012	3,074	3,447	4,314	6,914	842	4,280	240	0	0	3,031
2013	1,120	3,680	2,342	4,364	300	268	203	635	224	3,438
2014	802	3,811	2,761	4,552	1,489	203	635	224	3382	2,014
2015	802	3,811	2,761	4,552	1,489	203	635	224	3382	2,015
2016	947	4,085	3,093	5,813	1,144	277	-	-	-	2,016
2017	1,045	4,600	3,476	4,124	1,470	97	-	-	-	2,017

Source: Authors based on dates from National Agency for Animal Sciences 2017

Table 3: Dynamics of swine in conservation during 2006–2017

Year	Bazna	Mangalița
2006	0	53
2007	11	66
2008	79	548
2009	79	548
2010	226	457
2011	226	317
2012	45	161
2013	22	55
2014	22	36
2015	22	36
2016	22	283
2017	38	453

Source: Authors based on dates from National Agency for Animal Sciences 2017

population in critically and (re)constitution state, to avoid genetic drift resulting from inbreeding. They are also needed to preserve the rare populations, native or exotic, the "ex situ" bank organized gene. The above differences regarding the criteria of the artificial populations risk statement, essentially changes the vulnerability of the animal farms population in a highly mobile market and their workforce biodiversity conservation.

To avoid the risk statement degradation for the upper classes up to vulnerable population class can be done by activating the animal farms population. This activation MOET (Paraschivescu, 2013) (Tobă et al, 2010) can contribute to obtain a larger number of offspring individuals with genotype appreciated phenotype, which has consequently the genetic accelerate progress in animal farms population in which is used. An important result of the use of MOET (Tobă et al, 2014) is a short time animal farm population transfer and replacing them with the missing population.

Regarding the population preserved in situ where the collective growth is economically unacceptable and the possibility of activation is not possible, MOET may interfere through the increase of the artificial fertility for some families to balance family size and increase the chance of maintaining variability in population. There is no doubt that the growth of fertility that can be obtained by MOET (Tobă et al, 2012) for some genotypes of interest can spur success in the formation works or population reconstitution.

Conclusions

1. Using biotechnology breeding equally ensure access to animal genetic resources diversity worldwide and their transfer, with advantages that deplete crisis bio and adapting to new environmental conditions.
2. For maintenance, preservation and development of indigenous genetic biodiversity of animal resources should be set up, authorize and operating laboratories A.I. and ET and branches in the territory.

References

1. Bogdan A. T., Dorina Bogdan, I. Groza, M. Paraschivescu, G. F. Tobă, S. Chelmu, D. L. Diaconescu, Amalia Străteanu, I. Surdu, M. Th. Paraschivescu: More animal production in Agrifood Green Power Development, a New Paradigm of Concept regarding Sustainable Rural Bioeconomics and Eco – Economics, Bulletin-Veterinary Medicine vol.66, 2009, pag.416–423, U.S.A.M.V.Cluj;
2. Drucker Adam G., Veronica Gomez and Simon Anderson: The economic valuation of farm animal genetic resources: a survey of available methods, Ecological Economics, 2001 pag. 1–18;
3. Georgescu-Roegen N. Legea entropiei şi procesul economic, Colecţia Bibliotecii Naţionale nr.13, 1996, Editura Expert;
4. Rege J. E. O. J.P. Gibson: Animal genetic resources and economic development: issues in relation to economic valuation, Ecological Economics Volume 45, Issue 3, 2003, pag. 319–330;
5. Paraschivescu M. Th., A. T. Bogdan, M. Paraschivescu, Iudith Ipate, G. F. Tobă: Degree extinction risk in farm animal production, Simpozionul Prospects for the 3rd milenium agriculture, Bulletin - Agriculture vol.67 (2), U.S.A.M.V.Cluj, 2010. pag.87–91;
6. Paraschivescu M. Th.: Virtuţi şi servituţi ale aplicarii MOET la animalele de fermă în relaţie cu biodiversitatea lor - Lucrare finală Scoala Şcoala Postdoctorală de Biodiversitate Zootehnică şi Biotehnologii Alimentare, 2013, Bucureşti;
7. Sandu Mariana, G. F. Tobă, M. Th. Paraschivescu: Bioeconomical research on biodiversity of animal food resources in Romania, Romanian Biological Letters ISSN 1224–5984, 2014;
8. Tobă G. F., A. T. Bogdan, M. Th. Paraschivescu, M. Cornilă, L. Ioniţă, L. G. Tobă, F. Bănăţeanu: Use MOET programme for development and conservation of some races of bovine in Romania, Simpozionul Contribution of the scientific research to veterinary medicine progress, Bucureşti, Scientific Works C series: Veterinary medicine, Volume LVIII (4), 2012, pag. 380–387

9. Tobă G. F., M. Th. Paraschivescu, A. Bogdan, Mariana Sandu: The bio-economic impact of the MOET program for development of vulnerable genetic resources trough eco-innovative reproduction biotechnologies, Procedia Economics and Finance 8 iii–vi, 2012, pag. 696–703;
10. Tobă G. F.: Biotehnologiile de reproducţie la taurine şi impactul lor bioeconomic, 2014, Editura Economică, ISBN 978-973-709-708-8, Bucureşti;
11. Tobă G. L., S. Chelmu, G. F. Tobă, A. T. Bogdan, Iudith Ipate, M. Th. Paraschivescu, Mariana Sofronie, Elena Ruginosu, Adriana Pop: Preservation of national genetic fond of Sura de Stepa race by frozen embryos and their storage in genetic banks, Lucrări Ştiinţifice Vol.21,ISSN 2067-8983, 2010, pg.13–23, Editura CERES Bucureşti;
12. *** United Nation Environment Programme: Keep Tracking of Our Changing Environment: From Rio to Rio+20(1992-2012), 2011, Nairobi.

Amalia-Gianina STRĂTEANU[1], *Alexandru T. BOGDAN*[1],
Simona Nicoleta STAN[2], *Lavinia UDREA*[3]

[1] Center for Study and Researches of AgroForestry Biodiversity "Acad. David Davidescu", Romanian Academy, Bucharest, Romania, Email: strateanuamalia@gmail.com

[2] Bioterra University, Bucharest, Romania,

[3] Valahia University of Târgoviște, Târgoviște

New Biotechnique Arguments, Based on Indicators of Meat Production in the European Union Countries, for the Zootechnization of Romanian Agricultural Production

Abstract *The authors present analytically and synoptically comparative data on the annual dynamics of meat production (bovine, swine, sheep and goats) performed in Romania for more than 25 years (1990–2016), as well as the annual dynamics of exports and imports of live animals and meat of Romania (1990–2017), related to the economic value of the crop production. It is considered that the biodiversity of farm animals is an eco-economic territorial capital necessary for the zootechnization of Romanian agriculture for the sustainable bioeconomic development of Romania as a green agrifood and industrial agar-green biopower, in the third millennium perspective, for a "healthy economy" in a global changing world. The paradigm of "healthy economies" is based on the integrating health of the ecological environment on the "soil-plant-animal-food-man" trophic chain, through strategic and performant management for food security and nutrition. It is specified that Romania in 2016 is ranked 12th in the world in maize and the world's 18th place in wheat, which materialized in an average production of 51 kg meat per capita; by doubling this meat production to 102 kg per capita, Romania can and must be in the top 15 producing countries in the world.*

Keywords: *zootehnization of the agriculture, zootechnical biodiversity, healthy economy*

Introduction

As is well known, the 2011–2020 period has been carried out and finalized United Nations Decade of Biodiversity, which has three main strategic objectives, namely the support framework for the implementation of the Strategic Biodiversity Plan 2011–2020 and the Aichi Biodiversity Objectives at national, regional and international level; guidance for regional and international organizations, as well as raising public awareness of biodiversity issues (http://biodiversitate.mmediu.ro/convention/). On this line, at ESPERA 2018, with the occasion of the symposium under the aegis of the Centenary of the Great Union, respectively 100 Romania, "The Romanian Economy. A Century of Transformation (1918–2018)", it was considered that an objective assessment of the potential for the growth of farm produce is necessary through the understanding, development and deepening of the inter-war European concept on the zootechnization of Romanian agriculture.

1. Literature review

Based on the Romanian and international bibliography in the field, the authors of this scientific article reasonably believe that the post-war periods (respectively after World War I and World War II) were undoubtedly dominated, in many scientific, technical, journalistic and social aspects by the fruitful prestigious activity of the Romanian scholar and patriot Gheorghe K. Constantinescu (Viaţa şi opera Prof. G. K. Constantinescu. 120 de ani de la naştere, 2008), founder of modern Romanian zootechny. After the removal of the Romanian monarchy on 30 December 1947 and the establishment of the Romanian People's Republic on January 1, 1948, our country moved to a centralized economy and the socialist transformation of agriculture, continued and generalized after 1965, when the Romanian Socialist Republic was proclaimed. All these social and economic aspects turned the concept of zootechnization of Romanian agriculture into a major national objective.

Thus, in the decade 1970–1980, an efficient "National Program for the Development of Zootechnics" was developed and applied in our country by a valuable team of prestigious specialists made up of university professors at the four Faculty of Zootechny (from Bucharest, Cluj-Napoca, Iaşi and Timişoara), by certified scientifical researchers from institutions and stations for research-development-innovation zootechnical and graduates of zootechnical and veterinary higher education, validated by performant results obtained in farms and zootechnical complexes belonging to the centralized economy of our country at the time, called State Agricultural Enterprises (IAS) and State Agricultural Cooperatives (CAP).

2. Material and method

The study material consists of the main species of farm mammals, meat producing, namely bovine, swine, sheep and goats. The financial evaluation of the zootechnization of the Romanian agriculture also took into account the economic value of the milk production obtained from bovine (which, in the official statistics, is the production of milk from cattle and bubaline) and, respectively, from sheep and goats in lactation (ie in the postpartum period and after the weaning of the millets and goatling). The official statistics of the United Nations Food and Agriculture Organization (UNO through FAOSTAT), the European Union (through EUROSTAT) and recognized international organizations such as the Organization for Economic Co-operation and Development (OECD) and United States Agency for International Development (USAID) have been used.

Statistical data from governmental, technical and scientific public institutions in Romania were used as well, from: National Institute of Stratistics (INS), Ministry of Agriculture and Rural Development, Romanian Academy, Academy of Agricultural and Forestry Sciences, National Sanitary Veterinary and Food Safety Authority (ANSVSA), National Agency for Amelioration and Reproduction in Animal Breeding (ANARZ) “Prof. Dr. G. K. Constantinescu”.

3. Results

3.1 Zootechnization of Romanian agriculture through the annual national dynamics of exports and imports of live animals and meat

The sources of statistical documentation presented under point 2 “Material and method” show that the dynamics of the animals in the mammalian class, in Romania, for one hundred thousand hectares of land, between 1990 and 2016, by the indicator of the animals in this particular area, for bovine went down from 38,000 in 1990 to 15,400 in 2016 (with a minimum of 14,600 heads in 2010); swine from 127,300 in 1990 to 53,700 in 2016 (with a minimum of 47,500 heads in 2001); sheep and goats over the same time range from 106,300 to 85,500 (with a minimum of 54,400 heads in 2001).

It is also noted that since December 1989, all meat-producing livestock categories (some of them also milk producers, being mixed breeds) with periods of distinct reproductive or productive activities, have determined that our country holds the largest number of households of peasants / farmers in all the rural area of the European Union. This digital aspect must also be considered in the light of the fact that each peasant/farmer in Romania receives in absolute value the lowest subsidy in euro per hectare or per household.

Because this scientific article was presented and discussed in the 2nd Workshop entitled “Natural resources patrimony – Costs and benefits of capitalization” of the International Symposium ESPERA 2018, in the conference room “Prof. Dr. G. K. Constantinescu” from the Center for Studies and Research for AgroForestry Biodiversity “Acad. David Davidescu”, it was considered necessary and useful to calculate and systematise the numerical values related to the export and import of live animals and meat of Romania between 1990 and 2017, in thousands of euros and thousands of tons.

It is obvious that in the dynamics of the 28 years studied, the highest economic values of livestock exports amounted to 421.551 million euros in 2017 (for the equivalent of 192.048 million heads) and the lowest values were recorded in 1990 of 12.934 mill. Euro (for the equivalent of 126.0 thousand heads).

The import analysis shows that the largest number of live animals heads was registered in 2014, namely 59.906 mill. with an equivalent of 187.162 mill. euros,

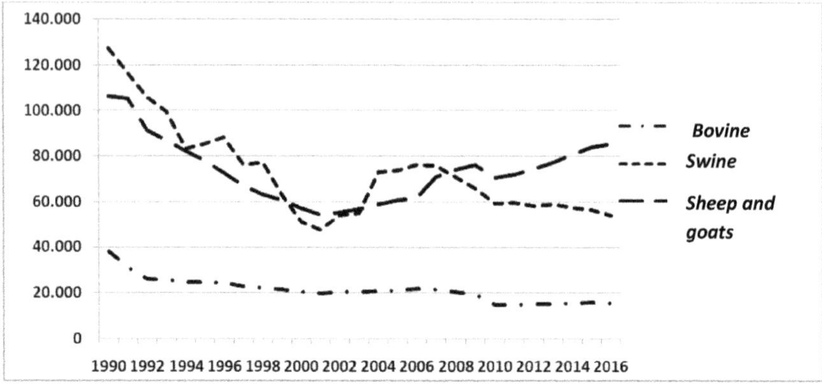

Figure 1: Biannual dynamics of livestock in the mammalian class (bovine, swine, sheep and goats), in Romania, at one hundred thousand hectares of land, between 1990 and 2016

Source: Biannual data taken from the Statistical Yearbook of Romania, published by the National Institute of Statistics in 2017 and processed by our team.

and the lowest number (except 1990, where the value published by NIS is 0.00), it was 979.0 thousand heads in 1997, with the equivalent of 2,840.3 thousand euro.

In explaining the numerical variations presented in Table 1 and Figure 2, in addition to the strategic management and performant marketing factors, there was also a lack of professional and decisional concerns related to the zootechnization of Romanian agriculture. This finding is also substantiated by the fact that the multiannual average for live animals is 23.750 mill. imported heads and 92.923 mill. exported heads, obviously inappropriate in terms of the zootechnization of Romanian agriculture.

Concerning the export and import of meat, in the dynamics of the 28 years studied, the highest economic values of meat exports were of 280,.694 mill. euros (in the year 2017, equivalent to 131.849 mill. tons), while the lower values were recorded in 1990 of 2,694 thousand euros (equivalent to 1,739 thousand tons).

The analysis of the imports shows that the largest quantity in thousands tons of meat was recorded in 2006, namely 469,593, with the equivalent of 519,530 thousand euros, and the smallest quantity was in 1991, representing 11,493 thousand tons, with an equivalent of 8,422 thousand euros. The multiannual average for meat is 232,682 thousand tons for import and 46,094 thousand tons for export, obviously inappropriate to the potential of domestic territorial capital.

Regarding the zoo-economic interpretation of the average values expressed in thousands euro for exports and imports of live animals and meat of Romania, in the cases presented in Table 1 and Figure 2 and discussed in the previous phrases,

Table 1: Annual dynamics of exports and imports of live animals and meat of Romania, in the period 1990–2017

Year	Exports				Imports			
	Live animals		Meat		Live animals		Meat	
	Mill. heads	Mill. euro	Mill. tons	Mill. euro	Mill. heads	Mill. euro	Mill. tons	Mill. euro
1990	0.126	12.934	1.739	2.694	...	44.287	183.328	157.833
1991	58.156	51.232	47.765	5.202	2.004	2.264,4	11.493	8.422,
1992	78.336	58.415	54.877	6.396	2.070	3.082	39.019	2.9197
1993	60.981	47.822	75.983	7.858	2.431	2.728	42.447	28.702
1994	83.465	72.832	97.185	97.649	1.208	2.337	54.965	48.790
1995	82.071	67.400	42.040	48.421	5.300	8.800	51.218	53.747
1996	73.325	58.469	40.308	47.777	2.125	6.587	14.159	12.012
1997	77.616	69.819	62.681	83.043	0.979	2.840	20.269	19.391
1998	43.398	47.945	10.175	15.419	2.059	7.225	97.160	103.832
1999	75.785	77.575	5.269	5.749	2.807	5.070	49.139	57.304
2000	91.763	106.721	1.637	3.442	19.966	23.622	66.273	83.090
2001	83.857	111.818	2.456	6.088	44.551	64.229	154.912	185.840
2002	81.491	114.466	3.126	7.517	29.692	43.714	223.689	200.665
2003	104.278	136.166	5.066	12.632	13.848	19.637	224.497	164.912
2004	105.452	141.235	6.763	17.964	12.579	23.596	301.749	276.391
2005	82.711	142.278	6.266	18.182,	12.015	35.467	443.068	503.086
2006	89.223	153.279	6.487	15.911	12.620	37.489	469.593	519.530
2007	104.593	181.210	13.427	27.039	19.258	47.389	387.643	553.429
2008	92.509	177.037	21.770	41.632	47.039	102.434	436.827	729.878
2009	83.820	173.347	41.742	74.411	45.893	116.888	432.312	642.047
2010	97.044	195.639	76.675	129.312	38.500	95.704	360.612	515.172
2011	102.582	234.153	99.454	221.171	38.285	106.832	295.084	456.909
2012	130.313	304.381	115.140	262.688	50.027	140.152	318.245	479.420
2013	134.530	314.495	101.565	225.977	52.827	163.657	297.746	487.173
2014	136.069	313.510	94.387	212.200	59.906	187.162	348.815	551.691
2015	154.426	319.466	110.279	247.646	53.620	160.175	381.096	571.891
2016	183.365	373.203	113.987	238.586	48.601	165.128	390.446	645.828

(*continued on next page*)

Table 1: Continued

Year	Exports				Imports			
	Live animals		Meat		Live animals		Meat	
	Mill. heads	Mill. euro	Mill. tons	Mill. euro	Mill. heads	Mill. euro	Mill. tons	Mill. euro
2017	192.048	421.551	131.849	280.694	44.806	178.399	419.302	762.439
Multiannual average	92.923	159.943	46.094	90.008	23.750	64.175	232.682	316.022

Source: The digital data is taken from the data provided by the National Institute of Statistics (NIS) (Export_Import_1989_2017_capitole_NC_01_02_03_04_05_10_Tone; Export_Import_1989_2017_capitole_NC_01_02_03_04_05_si_10_Mii Euro) at the request of the authors and processed by our team.

a very important role had it the government policies, noting that their quantitative and qualitative level was somewhat mediocre or even inappropriate, although the use of stimulus financial measures was attempted through various technical schemes of subsidies.

3.2 Zootechnization of the Romanian agriculture by evaluating of the crop and animal production for the year 2016

Table 2 shows the crop and animal agricultural branch production, calculated in hundreds of thousands of lei at current comparative prices in Romania and for each of the four macroregions of economic development.

An inedit aspect of our biotechnological arguments for the zootechnization of Romanian agriculture, which allowed the transition from the classical approach of zootechnization through biotechnological interpretations based on predominantly zootechnical arguments, to our new approach, because the authors of this scientific article have more scientific studies and researches related to complex bio-eco-geo-economic issues (Bogdan et al, 2010; Bogdan et al, 2015; Udrea, 2017; Udrea, 2018; Stan, 2017; Străteanu, Stan, 2018; Străteanu, Enache, 2018), represents it the zootechnization of the Romanian agriculture assessed in 2016 for each of the four macroregions of economic development and the whole country, as well as the eight regions of economic development, are presented in Tables 2 and 3.

From this table we can see that for the year 2016 the total production of agricultural branches in Romania was 693.486 mill lei at current prices, out of which the crop production of 451.551 a nd the animal production of 232.935 mill. lei at current prices; in relative terms the crop production was 65.11 % of the total value of the Romanian agricultural production, and the animal production was 33.58 %, namely almost half the value, although in the whole interwar period and respectively after the decades that followed World War II, all other countries, both in Central Eupora

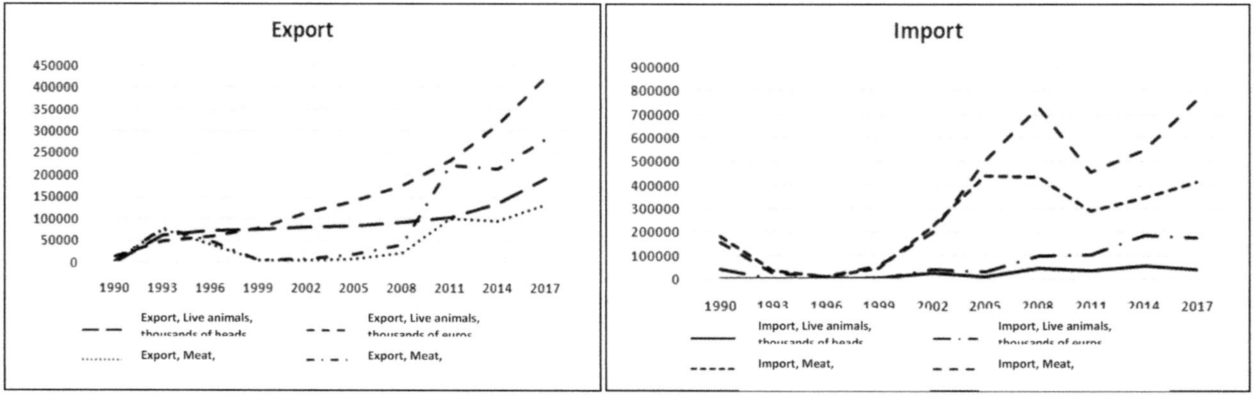

Figure 2: The triennial dynamics of exports and imports of live animals and meat of Romania, in the period 1990–2017

Source: National Institute of Statistics, imports and exports of Romania for live animals and meat, including offal, between 1990 and 2017; primary statistical situations provided by the INS at the request of the authors.

Table 2: Zootechnization of Romanian agriculture evaluated in 2016 for each of the four macroregions of economic development

Economic development macroregions of the Romania	**Production of agricultural branches (mill. lei at current prices)**					
	Total Romania	**Crop production (CP)**	**CP from total RO %**	**Animal production (AP)**	**AP from total RO %**	**AP from CP %**
1	2	3	4	5	6	7
Total Romania (RO)	693.486	451.551	65.11	232.935	33.58	51.58
Macroregion I	166.476	98.622	59.24	67.344	40.45	68.28
Macroregion II	231.610	150.070	64.79	78.228	33.77	52.12
Macroregion III	141.052	98.682	69.96	38.495	27.29	39.00
Macroregion IV	154.347	104.176	67.49	48.867	31.66	46.90

Source: The digital data are taken over and processed after the Romanian Statistical Yearbook, published by the National Institute of Statistics in 2017.

Table 3: Zootechnization of Romanian agriculture evaluated in 2016 for each of the eight regions of economic development

Economic development regions of the Romania	**Production of agricultural branches (mill. lei at current prices)**					
	Total Romania	**Crop production (CP)**	**CP from total RO %**	**Animal production (AP)**	**AP from total RO %**	**AP from CP %**
1	2	3	4	5	6	7
Total Romania (RO)	693.486	451.551	65.11	232.935	33.58	51.58
Nord - Vest	87.604	53.706	61.30	33.692	38.45	62.73
Centru	78.872	44.915	56.94	33.652	42.66	74.92
Nord - Est	111.365	65.109	58.46	45.601	40.94	70.03
Sud - Est	120.244	84.961	70.65	32.626	27.13	38.40
Sud - Muntenia	132.614	93.868	70.78	37.219	28.06	39.65
Bucureşti - Ilfov	8.437	4.814	57.05	1.276	15.12	26.51
Sud - Vest Oltenia	78.174	54.286	69.44	23.342	29.85	42.99
Vest	76.172	49.889	65.49	25.524	33.50	51.16

Source: The digital data are taken over and processed after the Statistical Yearbook of Romania, published by the National Institute of Statistics in 2017.

and especially in Western Europe, have definitely had different national strategies regarding the fundamental importance of agricultural zootechnization for each country. In contrast, although in the interwar period Prof. Dr. G.K. Constantinescu strongly advocated for the zootechnization of a performing Romanian agriculture, however, both the great landowners in our country and the governmental decision-makers of that period, promoted directly and indirectly agricultural policies based on excessive cerealism, with many unfavorable consequences on the Romanian rural economy and especially through a unperforming national zooeconomy.

It is understood that in each of the eight economic development regions of Romania there are actually statistically significant differences between the main indicators of economic activities, including agriculture, which have various explanations of economic historiography. It is worth mentioning that in this table 3 are also presented the statistical data for the economic development region called Bucharest-Ilfov, which we do not consider when discussing the minimum values because this region of economic development of Romania has an atypical character, because it includes only the capital of our country, and Ilfov County practically represents the majority of the metropolitan area of Bucharest.

Therefore, the results of our investigations presented in Table 3 (which we are not discussing comparatively Bucharest-Ilfov region for the reasons shown) show that these differences are sometimes from simple to double values in hundreds of thousands of lei at current prices. Thus, for example, the crop production for the Center Region is 44.915 mill. lei, and in the South-Muntenia Region of 93.868 mill. lei. The animal production ranges from 23.342 mill. lei in the South-West Oltenia Region to 45.601 mill. lei in the North-East Region.

3.3 Zootehnization of Romanian agriculture by Redesigning, Rethinking and Revival the National Program for Development of Zootechny

From the content of these points of view of our collective it is clear that only in the decade mentioned by the National Program for Development of Zootechny (PNDZ), respectively in the decade 1970–1980, Romania had a modern approach in the economic policies regarding the zootechnization of agriculture. Therefore, although it has been over eight decades since Professor G. K. Constantinescu (1931) has consistently and documented supported the need for our country to pass on the utilization of a part of the country's crop production by raising livestock and increasing its production, but the national and international statistical results show that Romanian livestock has fallen to absolute and relative values, that is unfortunately, at the lowest in all European Union countries, related to the country's surface and population. In this sense, our team considers there are priorities from the professional point of view Redesigning, Rethinking and Revival a New National Program for Development of Zootechny in Romania, with new biotechnological arguments and bio-eco-geo-economic solutions.

3.4 Zootechnization of Romanian agriculture by elaboration, development and implementation of patents for reproduction biotechnology

A new biotechnological argument brought by our team for the effective realization of the zootechnization of Romanian agriculture is inventiveness, by the elaboration, realization and implementation of patents of invention necessary in reproduction biotechnology. It is known that through complex, biochemical, biophysical and cryobiological scientific researches, have been developed and implemented in our country several patents granted by State Office for Inventions and Trademarks necessary for collection and dilution of semen from bulls (Bogdan et al, 71898, 1979), from boars (Bogdan et al, 71899, 1979) and from the ram (Bogdan et al, 71894, 1979)], as well as various instruments and devices for the biotechnical collecting of semen from stallions (Bogdan et al, 78812, 1981) and boars (Bogdan et al, 78813, 1981), including for harvesting and biotehnical identification of zygotes in zootechny (Bogdan et al, 78827, 1981) and (Bogdan et al, 79903, 1981). We underline that all these biotechnological breeding methods have obtained zooeconomic benefits through bioeconomic improvement of the eco-economic potential of feed, under the pedoeconomic constraints of the national land fund. In this way, the national genetic patrimony of Romanian zootechny has been and should be used at maximum yield with socio-economic advantages of food biosecurity.

Another interesting biotechnological argument in the favorable aspect of biological synergy is the existence of a distinct patent as a bio-scientific foundation, namely that which allows increasing the quantitative and qualitative of the production of seminal material from the reproduction males tested genetic improvers, by biostimulation with micromineral premix based on zinc, copper and manganese (Salanţiu et al, 1982) All these patents ensure increase the quantitative and qualitative of meat production through the superior bioconversion of feed in productions and produce of animal origin (Salanţiu, 1982).

Conclusions

By studying the exports and imports of live animals and meat during the period 1990–2017 in Romania, it is found that there is a real potential for quantitative and qualitative growth with the superior zooeconomic valorization of the domestic territorial capital. It has been confirmed that the highest value of exports in Romania in the period mentioned was in 2017 for 192.048 mill. heads and 421.551 mill. euro, while for the meat exports of 131.849 mill. tons and 280.694 mill. euro.

From the point of view of imports, the highest value was in 2014 for 59.906 mill. heads and 187.162 mill. euro, and for meat imports the highest value was in 2006 of 469.593 mill. tons, corresponding to 519.530 mill. euro, with the fact that the highest economic value of meat imports during the reference period was 762.439 mill. euro in 2017.

Using the zootechnical biosciences advances, finalized by patents, applied for zootechnization of Romanian agricultural production, allows direct participation in the prevention and combating of world food insecurity through the safety, security and food defense.

Thus, Romania already has an international recognition for the year 2016, which places it on the 12th place in the world for maize (INS, 2017, p. 757) and on the 18th place in the world for wheat (INS, 2017, p. 756), what materialized only in an average yield of 51 kg meat per capita (INS, 2017, p. 762). In this sense, it is considered that the doubling of this meat production, namely to 102 kg per capita, can lead us to the world's 18th place, and if we integrate the numerical increase of the livestock then definitely Romania can and should be in the top 15 great producing countries in the world, a real green agri-food power.

References

1. Asociaţia General a Medicilor Veterinari din România: Viaţa şi opera Prof. G. K. Constantinescu (120 de ani de la naştere). ISBN 978-973-87716-7-3, Editura AgroTehnica, 2008, pp. 5–134.

2. Bogdan A.T., Vioara Miresan, Al. Mironov, S. Chelmu,Viorica Boboc, I. Surdu, R. Burlacu, D. Diaconescu, Amalia Strateanu: Prospects of Agrifood Green Power in 2050 and Forecasting for 2100 with Sustenable Solutions Based on Ecobioeconomics new Paradigm, Bulletin UASVM Animal Science and Biotechnologies, 67(1–2)/2010, Print ISSN 1843-5262; Electronic ISSN 1843-536X, 2010, p. 1–18.
3. Bogdan A.T., A. Şonea, Dorina Bogdan, V. Miclea, G. F. Tobă, Amalia-Gianina Străteanu: Soluţii bioeconomice pentru criza zootehniei, prin asigurarea independenţei şi suveranităţii agroalimentare durabile a României euroatlantice (cu semnificaţii bioeconomice ale sănătăţii integrate a mediului şi protecţiei complexe a consumatorului) Ediţia a III-a revizuită şi completată, ISBN 978-973-27-2517-7. Editura Academiei Române, Bucureşti, 2015.
4. Constantinescu G.K.: Zootehnicizarea agriculturii. Ziarul "Cuvântul", 16.10.1931.
5. Udrea Lavinia: Directions of Growth, Improvement and Prospects for Efficiency of the Productivity of Sheep Breeds Tigaie in the Context of Zootechnical Bioeconomy. The Annals of "Valahia" University of Targoviste, Volume 11: Issue 2, 2017, p. 29–35.
6. Udrea Lavinia: New Approach for Bio-Economic Integrated Management in Sheep Growth. The Annals of "Valahia" University of Târgovişte, Volume 12: Issue 1, 2018, p. 1–6.
7. Salanţiu Dorina: Cercetări asupra suplimnetării unor microeelemente în furazarea taurilor şi efectul lor în procesul de dermatogene, Teză de doctorat, USAMV Cluj-Napoca, 1982.
8. Stan Simona Nicoleta: Impactul biotehnologiilor de reproducţie la taurine asupra trasabilităţii şi siguranţei agroalimentare în relaţie cu bioetica rurală şi legislaţia în domeniu a României europene, Ed. Moroşan, Bucureşti, 2017, ISBN 978-606-626-100-5, pp. 168.
9. Străteanu Amalia-Gianina, Mihai Liviu Enache: The influence of environmental and social factors on agricultural biodiversity and food security. The Annals of "Valahia" University of Targoviste, Volume 11: Issue 2, 2017, p. 46–49.
10. Străteanu Amalia-Gianina, Simona Nicoleta Stan: New Bio-Scientific Interpretations of the Eco-Economic Zootehnization of the Romanian Performing Agriculture. The Annals of "Valahia" University of Targoviste, Volume 12: Issue 1, 2018, p. 39–43.
11. Bogdan A.T. et al: Pahar izoterm pentru recoltarea şi diluarea materialului seminal. Certificat de inventator nr. 71894, OSIM, 1979.
12. Bogdan A.T. et al: Pahar izoterm pentru recoltarea şi diluare materialului seminal la tauri. Certificat de inventator nr. 71898, OSIM, 1979.
13. Bogdan A.T. et al: Pahar izoterm pentru recoltarea şi diluarea materialului seminal la vieri. Certificat de inventator nr. 71899, OSIM, 1979.

14. Bogdan A.T. et al: Vagin artificial pentru recoltarea biotehnică a materialului seminal de la armăsar. Certificat de inventator nr. 78812, OSIM, 1981.
15. Bogdan A.T. et al: Vagin artificial pentru recoltarea biotehnică a materialului seminal de la vier. Brevet de invenţie nr. 78813, OSIM, 1981.
16. Bogdan A.T. et al: Aparat pentru recoltarea biotehnică a zigoţilor în special la animale. Certificat de inventator nr. 78827, OSIM, 1981.
17. Bogdan A.T. et al: Recipient izoterm pentru identificarea zigoţilor. Certificat de inventator nr. 79303, OSIM, 1981.
18. Salanţiu Dorina (Popa) şi col Supliment de microminerale pentri tauri de reproducţie, Certificat de inventator nr. 80019, OSIM, 1982.
19. Institutul Naţional de Statistică: Anuarul statistic al Romaniei 2017.
20. Export_Import_1989_2017_capitole_NC_01_02_03_04_05_10_Tone.
21. Export_Import_1989_2017_capitole_NC_01_02_03_04_05_si_10_Mii Euro.
22. http://biodiversitate.mmediu.ro/convention/.

Alexander S. CHERVINSKY[1]

[1] Institute of Philosophy, National Academy of Sciences of Belarus, Minsk, Belarus;
Email: a.chervinski@gmail.com

Methodological Problems of the Ecological and Economic Determination of the Natural Habitat Quality

Abstract *Anthropogenic expansion into the system of ecological complexes poses to science questions of the dependence of the quality of the natural habitat on the conditions of nature consumption. Therefore, an urgent problem of normative definition of the quality of the natural habitat is the development of evaluation principles, the correlation of functional complex criteria, and the rationale for the hierarchical structure of environmental quality indicators.*

Keywords: *quality of the natural habitat, methodological principles of evaluation, criteria, payment for nature use, intangibles*

Introduction

When assessing the quality of the natural environment under different conditions, various evaluation criteria are traditionally used. In one case, quality indicators can include: the richness of species diversity, the diversity of forms and elements in trophic chains, the level of ecological plasticity of the species, etc.

To assess the quality of polar biocoenosis, the indicators of saving metabolism, the ability to deposit nutritional reserves in the body and provide the necessary level of autonomy from the fluctuations of external conditions.

Specific qualitative assessment of cultural ecosystems - agrocoenosis, which are limited in the manifestation of protective functions: nutrient cycling, population management, increase in species diversity, duplication of systemic links, etc.

Assessment of each of the marked natural complexes requires the use of specific techniques. Functional incompatibility of such evaluation methods is a serious obstacle in the development of social ecology as a scientific discipline.

A methodological analysis of the problem studied, based on the principle of the interdependence of natural and social factors, is described in the works of many researchers. (Elliot, Gare, Goodin, Warren, Attfield, 1993; Sagoff, 1996; Siebert, 1981)

A special role belongs to the works of Vernadsky V.I, who developed the biogeochemical concept of the biosphere. Biogeochemical approach, in which the object of study is not a separate organism but systemic integrity, allows a complex of organisms to be represented as carriers of their geochemical energy (Vernadsky, 1967, p. 218).

In Vernadsky's concept, the basis of the biosphere system is the organization of biogeocoenosis in the transformation of real-energy and information flows. This approach allows us to examine in qualitative and quantitative terms the complex relationships between organisms and their habitat. The peculiarity of these relations is that the quantitative invariance of the mass of living matter is combined with the qualitative changes in life forms, and is manifested in the rearrangement of chemical elements in the biosphere.

Vernadsky formulated the basic biogeochemical principles: biogenic migration of atoms of chemical elements in the biosphere tends to maximum manifestation; the evolution of species leading to the creation of sustainable forms of life, goes in the direction of increasing the biogenic migration of atoms in the biosphere.

The works of these researchers create a serious basis for solving the problem of environmental quality, and contribute to the development of criteria for the optimality of socio-natural relations.

At the same time, such questions as the justification of the environmental normative quality assessment have not yet been resolved; the hierarchy of normative criteria in the assessment of environmental quality is not defined; the methodological principles of integrated assessment have not been developed. The article is devoted to solving these problems.

It is necessary to investigate the quality of the natural environment as a normative characteristic of social and natural systems, which allows preserving the optimality between the processes of nature protection and the processes of industrial exploitation of natural resources.

1. Principles for the integrated assessment of environmental quality

Assessment of the quality of the environment requires the formation of appropriate criteria and principles, taking into account the level of anthropogenic determination of natural processes. It is possible to propose criteria that make it possible to identify the characteristic features of the dependence of natural processes on the social factor.

The main criterion for assessing the level of social determinism of natural processes is associated with the preservation of the traditional structural and functional certainty of ecological systems. In each individual case, this indicator will have a specific expression: the preservation of a specific biotope over a long period of time, the preservation of species diversity, the ability to perform functions in the biosphere system, the ability to maintain and maintain the existing dynamic equilibrium, ponents through the implementation of internal reserves, etc.

The next criterion is the importance of anthropogenic activity in maintaining the normal regime of the existence of ecological systems. Anthropogenic impact on natural systems can be ambivalent: either act as an external, alien factor or as a necessary condition. So, in relation to cultural ecosystems, human participation in the transformation of matter and energy is a necessary condition for the conservation of natural complexes.

From this circumstance logically follows one more evaluation criterion of division of a natural environment according to the degree of anthropogenic determination measure of human participation in the development of the ecosystem.

In accordance with this interpretation, a set of evaluation principles designed to ensure the effectiveness of the evaluation procedure in determining the level of optimality in social and natural interaction can be proposed.

The principle of qualitative-quantitative conjugation in social ecology is designed to perform a correlation of different, but interdependent quantities. In this sense, it can be manifested as a specific, regulated within the framework of the development of social and natural relations, the option of identifying cause-effect relationships in complex, multifunctional processes. Directional structural changes in the biocoenosis necessarily necessitate functional deformations in the system of socio-natural relations, leading in the final expression to the degradation of one of the aspects (usually biogeocoenological) of sustainable development. An analysis of the cause-effect relationship between structural and functional changes in the "human-nature" system constitutes an essential aspect of the evaluation procedure carried out in accordance with the social criteria of the quality of the environment.

The transformed environment, which has lost its traditional functional status, should be presented in a differentiated expression in the evaluation structure. Substantial changes should be interpreted as qualitative, expressing the peculiarities of the new factor in the systemic organization of the biocoenosis of the factor, and attributive, in turn, as derivatives that express the quantitative representativeness of the factor. Estimated conjugation of these two aspects of the factor (representation and significance) allows to achieve sufficiently adequate reflection of the existing ecological situation in the conceptual expression of sustainable development.

Interaction of environmental characteristics implies a certain mutual adaptation, with a change in the structural ordering of the interacting components:

- The quantitative interpretation stage involves abstracting from a qualitative expression, focusing on the relationship between comparable aspects of social and natural mutual adaptation.
- The qualitative expression is associated with changes in the functional characteristics of the object, therefore the evaluation process must have the same sequence, i.e. functional changes in the system of socio-natural relations should be evaluated as derivatives of structural transformations.

Structural changes in biocoenosis cause functional deformations in the system of social and natural relations. Deformations lead to the degradation of one of the aspects (usually biogeocoenological) of the quality of the natural environment.

Analysis of the causal relationship between structural and functional changes in the system “man - society – nature” is an important aspect of the evaluation procedure, which is carried out in accordance with the social criteria for assessing the quality of the natural environment. Artificially transformed natural environment loses its traditional functional status. In the evaluation framework, it should be presented in a differentiated expression. Substantial changes should be interpreted as qualitative, expressing the importance of a new factor in the systemic organization of the biocoenosis. Attributive changes should be treated as derivatives that express quantitative characteristics.

Estimated interaction of these aspects (presence factor and factor of significance) allows to adequately reflect the existing ecological situation in the conceptual expression of the quality of the environment.

Modern ecological systems on the planet (with the exception of individual, actually unique highland, polar, island, etc. sites) are not natural. Therefore, the functions of the anthropogenic factor in the structure of the biocoenosis, its role (both destructive and constructive) in ensuring and maintaining the structural and functional organization of the ecological complex should be taken into account when determining the level of socio-natural optimality.

The conditions for social and natural adaptation at the level of cultural ecosystems differ fundamentally from the conditions, interactions with natural and industrial complexes: a forest biotope, a river ecosystem, etc. Therefore, the specifics of the assessment of the quality of the environment, depending on the anthropogenic factor, should be reflected.

Correlation of two levels of assessment: social, which determines the qualitative level of the rehabilitative interaction of society and nature and biogeocoenological, based on ecological criteria, (the degree of species diversity, the balance of trophic connections, ecological plasticity of species, etc.).

The principle of the hierarchy of qualitative characteristics of the state of the natural environment is effective in studying the consequences of anthropogenic impact, differentially influencing the organization of the biosphere. Such an evaluation structure of the criteria may take the form of centralization, or decentralization.

The centralized form of the hierarchy reflects the quantitative characteristics of the “more-less” principle. This form of hierarchy is effective in determining the quantitative composition of a biocoenosis containing different elements of flora and fauna. For a comprehensive assessment, it is of fundamental importance to identify the conditions for preserving the biotope as a system.

The hierarchical rigidity of the criteria depends on the level of optimality or the extreme nature of the interpreted ecological situation. Estimation of ecologically extreme regions assumes a more rigid hierarchy, and ecological optimality assumes a decentralized hierarchy. Probably the decentralized hierarchy has more prospects in assessing socio-ecological structures.

The principle of pyramidality of the evaluation structure is derived from the principle of hierarchy, and is realized in the situation of ecological catastrophe.

Ecologically extreme environment is a combination of natural conditions, in which life is impossible. Staying in such conditions contains the danger of irreversible changes in the state of human health.

2 Ecological and economic aspect of integrated assessment

The assessment of the quality of the natural habitat on the basis of economic and environmental indicators is carried out by comparing the observable (ie, fundamentally measurable) states of biospheric components with environmental standards. In the case of significant mismatch of indicators, there is a need for a comprehensive correlation of the situation on the basis of environmental and economic indicators.

The situation of such a mismatch does not allow us to approach the evaluation with the same criteria. The object should be estimated by at least two parameters:

- Firstly, how much it is qualitatively socially, and here the main indicators are the productivity of the ecosystem, its aesthetics, industrial efficiency, etc.
- Second, how well it performs the functions of an element of the biosphere. In this case, the indicators will be: the stability of the biocoenosis, ecological plasticity, the richness of species diversity, etc. These indicators are not yet subject to economic evaluation. It is characteristic that the latter indicator (quantitative indicators of species diversity) is in direct contradiction with economic criteria, since species diversity does not agree with the productivity of cultural ecosystems in which monoculture dominates.

In the theory of social use of the natural environment, the possibility of an ecological assessment of natural complexes as a resource of industrial raw materials is of great interest. The functioning of modern industrial complexes in the system of socio-natural relations does not allow the use of mono aspect criteria. In such a situation, functional contradictions between various aspects of the quality of natural complexes are inevitable, therefore the problem of priority of the quality criteria will have an applied solution each time. However, an integrated approach is needed to adequately assess both negative and positive consequences of anthropogenic impact.

The approaches that are preserved in the modern economy are mainly represented by the development of mechanisms for assessing the materially significant characteristics of natural complexes. The natural environment surrounding a person, as a rule, is interpreted in strictly economic traditions of rent and mountain rent. Rent itself as the right of economic use of land is quite abstract, and the economic evaluation of the quality of the environment is realized as a quantitative assessment of the resource. As you know, rent in the economy is treated as "a given god", and in reality is a specific form of receiving material goods. It is connected with the realization of the right of ownership ofland.

The approaches that are preserved in the modern economy are mainly represented by the development of mechanisms for assessing the materially significant characteristics of natural complexes. The natural environment surrounding a person, as a rule, is interpreted in strictly economic traditions of rent and mountain rent. Rent itself as the right of economic use of land is quite abstract, and the economic evaluation of the quality of the environment is realized as a quantitative assessment of the resource. As you know, rent in the economy is treated as "a given god", and in reality is a specific form of receiving material goods. It is connected with the realization of the right of ownership ofland.

The appraisal approach from the point of view of revealing economic benefits is based on the identification of quantitative characteristics and is expressed in monetary estimates. Sometimes such an assessment of the natural environment is carried out in scores, but this does not lead the assessment situation beyond the utilitarian approach. The functional orientation of such an assessment is still based on the idea of the economic feasibility of a natural complex. This shows the limitations of the traditional economic approach.

The utilitarian orientation of the economic evaluation is related to the consideration of the natural environment surrounding a person as a condition for ensuring the material vital activity of a person. It does not take into account the value of the environment itself, regardless of man. This approach is limited, since the anthropocentrism present in it does not imply preservation of the natural environment as a system that preserves self-sufficiency and self-sufficiency. In this case, from the assessment, a significant part of the element of the natural habitat falls: the forest is undergoing changes; industrially not exploited, but representing the ecological value of the lake; bogs that do not have economic significance before they are drained, but at the same time perform the functions of air purification, carbon dioxide absorption, efficient oxygen production; providing the necessary atmospheric composition for life.

This approach does not allow us to consider the "weightless", economically insignificant values of the pristine nature and, moreover, to find in them a source of serious economic benefits. From the mono aspectual economic evaluation, value characteristics that improve the quality of human life fall out. Loss of economic benefit due to a single-factor, resource-raw material interpretation leads to the domination of the consumer approach to the benefits of the natural environment. For example, the forest ecosystem, while retaining its traditional ecological quality, does not represent economic benefits as a source of raw materials.

The indirect nature of relations in the system "man-nature" creates real preconditions for discrepancy, and mutual contradiction in the evaluation structures of the economy and ecology. This probability of mismatch manifests itself in a proportional dependence on the degree of mediation of social and natural connections. If in relation to cultural biocoenosis, the ecological quality of which is a direct condition of normal vital activity, it is possible to identify environmental and economic criteria, then in the case of natural ecological complexes such identification is methodologically difficult.

Estimated autonomy, however, does not mean conceptual independence from common grounds for the whole social ecology: the systemic nature of natural complexes of any level of organization; presence of subject-object relations in social-natural interaction, etc.

As an economic tool in ensuring the processes of social and environmental optimization can serve as payment for nature use. The introduction of payment for nature management is a means of economic regulation of economic use of nature. The highest efficiency is paid in the sphere of consumption of natural resources.

The development of market mechanisms in the regulation of sustainable development is largely based on the need to expand the approach to the problem of man-made pollution of the natural habitat. The allocation of quotas for pollution, as well as the trade in these quotas on the international market, is not directly related to the perception of the environment as a source of raw materials. It is based on the recognition of the uniqueness of biogeocoenological functions of natural biogeocoenosis.

If the land plot belongs to the property of the business entity, the results of the practical operation of this site should be evaluated. If a piece of land on which there are ecological systems that have not been subjected to anthropogenic transformation is assessed, then this site can not be considered as a source of raw materials. Since abstract land does not exist, on each scrap something grows and according to this, the complex can be evaluated either within natural conditions or artificial ones.

Without transforming such a plot of land, the material benefit can be obtained from the exploitation of its ecological significance. Value can be determined by unique species of valuable species of flora and fauna. In this case, a specific form of evaluation arises. It includes both economic and environmental indicators.

The most appropriate task to identify the stages, level and system characteristics of the phenomenon of the ecological and economic approach is the method of pair comparison, in which mutual comparative comparison of factors with the definition of transitivity is carried out.

As applied to the problematic, the transitivity can be presented in a simplified form: if the environmental factor A is given priority over the economic factor B, and the factor B, in turn, relative to the economic factor C, factor C can not be more important than the environmental factor A.

The transitivity of the assessment seems to be a fairly effective technique in determining the situation by the parameters of environmental and economic viability, since it involves an assessment of the most characteristic feature - the ability to influence the systemic organization of social and natural relations. The ability to reflect the factor of anthropogenic impact in the total expression makes it possible to quantify the situation, which makes it possible, on the one hand, to achieve a larger presentation, on the other hand, provides estimated representativeness.

This approach poses the task of conceptual integration of quantitative indicators from the position of environmental and economic assessment. Ecological and economic assessment of the biocoenosis of any degree of organization assumes the definition of its role both in the system of socio-natural relations and the identification of its functional status in the biosphere system.

The development of such a mechanism creates the prerequisites for an economic assessment for the provision of environmental services. If the state is the owner of the land, the withdrawal of income can be made in the form of an environmental tax for the use of intangible and non-physical expressions of the values of the ecological complex.

Rationalization of social nature management in accordance with such criteria can bring significant environmental dividends.

Conclusions

The methodological aspect of the problem under investigation is: in promoting the development of new methods and cognitive procedures at the time of the transition of scientific knowledge to a new level of analysis of sociocultural links; development of the conceptual apparatus in connection with the expansion of cognitive activity and the inclusion of research on qualitatively new aspects; justification of principles in the development of an overall strategy of environmental safety at the present stage of socio-natural interaction.

Important is also the question of the direction of the assessment process, aimed at finding the best options for interaction between man and nature and thus providing the necessary basis.

In the complex ecological and economic assessment of the quality of the natural habitat, it is necessary to take into account the multifunctionality of biosphere complexes in the following system of indicators: a generalized characteristic of the ecocomplex as a subject of protection and rational nature management; the economic significance of the complex, the degree and nature of social exploitation; functions of the complex in the biosphere system (water regulation, soil protection, climate, etc.); spontaneous processes and anthropogenic factors causing disturbances in biogeocoenosis (storms, droughts, artificial and natural salinization of reservoirs, changes in runoff regimes, etc.); a complex of measures for reclamation of complexes, renewal of functional characteristics and restoration of lost states.

The results of the methodological development of the problem can serve as a basis for the formation of a set of applied methods for assessing the quality of the natural environment, which will allow to form an integrated assessment of the quality of life of a person.

References

1. Butlin J.A., Mcade J.E., Heal G.M., Page T., Grout P.: Economics and resources policy. Longman. 2001, p. 206.
2. Vernadsky V.I.: Selected Works on Biogeochemistry. Thought: Moscow, 1967, p.376.

3. Campbell K.O.: The role of agricultural economists in the conservation of natural resources. Minerva: 1991, p. 632–639.
4. Carpenter R.A., Dixon J.A.: Ecology meets economics. Environment: Wash., 1985. p. 6–11.
5. Elliot R., Gare A., Goodin R., Warren M.A., Attfield R.: Environmental philosophy. Univ. of Queensland press: 1993, p. 303.
6. Sagoff M.: Process or product? Ethical priorities in environmental management. Athens, 1996. p. 121–138.
7. Siebert H.: Economics of the environment Lexington. Toronto, 1981, p.230.
8. Young O.R.: Natural resources and the state Berkeley. Univ. of California press, 1991, p.227.

Mariana GRODEA[1]

[1] Institute of Agricultural Economics, Romanian Academy, Bucharest,
Email: marianagrodea@yahoo.com

Sheep and Goat Farming Sector in Romania – Development Opportunities and Perspectives on the Long Term

Abstract *In the period 2003–2017, Romania became an import export source of live sheep and goats, both for the intra-Community trade and for third countries in particular. From food security perspective, for Romania, sheep and goat meat (accounting for 3.5 % of total meat consumption in the year 2016) has a particular importance both for dietary diversification and for the complex contribution to putting into value the country's agricultural resources, the sheep species having the exceptional capacity to valorize the land from the areas with natural handicaps (80 % of these areas are valorized by the ovine species). Although Romania ranks 6th in EU-28 in terms of total sheep and goat herds, it ranks 10th in terms of meat production (in carcass equivalent), yet on the rise compared to the pre-accession period. The paper intends to identify new opportunities for sector development on the long term, both for relaunching domestic production and consumption growth and for the creation of export availabilities. The growth of middle-income population from Asia, Latin America and Middle East and the increasing demand of ovine meat implicitly represent an export opportunity that Romania has to valorize, also having in view that Romania, as supplier of live animals, is also appreciated for raising animals under extensive grazing system.*

Keywords: *sheep and goat meat production, consumption, trade*

Introduction

The livestock sector in Romania has experienced a difficult period, due to landed property fragmentation, decreasing trend of livestock herds, insufficient national financial support, as well as to the fact that only a small number of livestock farmers are eligible for receiving coupled livestock support (additional payment from EU funds introduced in the year 2015).

In terms of food security, sheep and goat meat (accounting for 3.5 % in the structure of total meat consumption, in the year 2016) is quite important for Romanian consumers, both for dietary diversification and for its complex contribution to the valorization of the country's agricultural resources, the ovine species having an exceptional quality to put into value the land in the areas with natural handicaps (80 % of these areas are used by ovine species).

The growth of medium-income population from Asia, Latin America and Middle East, and implicitly the growing demand of sheep meat, represent an export opportunity that needs to be valorized, also taking into consideration that Romania, as a supplier of live animals, is also appreciated due to the livestock farming system based on extensive grazing.

From this point of view, the paper intends to identify new opportunities for the development of the sheep and goat farming sector, on the long term, both for the domestic production relaunching and consumption increase, and for the creation of export availabilities.

1. Literature review

The sheep and goat meat production increased by 4.3 % in the first half of the year 2017 (+19500 tons), as against the same period of the previous year, both in EU-15 and in EU-13 (European Commission, 2017). This increase fully results from sheep slaughter (+5 %), while goat slaughter decreased by almost 2 %. About 50 % of this increase can be attributed to the United Kingdom, while the difference to Ireland (14 %), Germany (9 %) and Romania (6 %).

It is estimated that the world total meat production (in carcass equivalent) will increase up to 357454 thousand tons by the year 2025. Sheep and goat meat production will also increase significantly, from 14137 thousand tons (2013–2015 average) to 17438 thousand tons in 2025, the developing countries contributing significantly to the increase of sheep meat production on the long run. It is estimated that the following countries will largely contribute to this increase: China by about 45 % and the Saharan Africa Sub-Region by about 27 % (FAO, 2016).

The EU exports, mainly the exports of live animals (about 8 % of its total production) mainly go to Middle East and North Africa, while meat and meat products have mainly the Far East as main destination. The EU imports, around 212 thousand tons in the year 2016, mainly came from New Zealand and Australia (94 %), accounting for about 23 % of the EU's consumption (European Commission, 2017).

Although the European Union improved its access to the Asian market, the competition from North America and South America will make it difficult to fully fructify the advantage of this opportunity. Australia and New Zealand will continue to be world leaders in the sheep meat market, meeting the medium-income population demand, on the rise, from China and Middle East (FAO, 2016).

The sheep and goat sector in EU-28 can be described as vulnerable, as this is facing significant challenges, i.e. low incomes at farm level, dependence on direct support, low productivity, and old-aged sheep farmers. However, there are certain positive opportunities for the sector, including its position as supplier of top quality products on an EU market with only 88 % self-sufficiency (2015).

One can add the positive role of sheep farming in improving the environment, managing natural resources and biodiversity, especially in areas with natural and other specific constraints, where other agricultural enterprises are not sustainable, as well as the socio-economic role in labour employment and economic activities in the rural areas (Carlier, Chotteau, 2017).

In this sense, the financial support provided to the sheep and goat sector, as well as the maintenance and consolidation of coupled support under the future reform of the Common Agricultural Policy (CAP) in order to reduce the abandonment of these productions in the European Union, as well as state aids and compensations of 100 % in case of attacks by wild animals, represent proposals that are in the attention of the European Parliament Committee on Agriculture and Rural Development (Sime, 2018).

Sheep meat consumption worldwide will reach 2.1 kg per capita by the year 2025 (FAO, 2016). In Australia and New Zealand, countries with high sheep meat consumption per capita, it is estimated that consumption will slightly decrease, due to competition from other cheaper meat types. Sheep meat consumption will increase instead in countries like China and in those with tradition in sheep meat consumption like Middle East, under the background of middle class enlargement and population growth.

In the last 15 years, in the European Union, the yearly average sheep meat consumption decreased by 40 %, from 3.8 kg/capita in 1999 to 2.1 kg/capita in 2015, this accounting for only 2.9 % of total meat consumption. As a result, at the European Commission level, a program promoting sheep meat was initiated, in order to reconnect consumers to sheep meat consumption in the European Union, highlighting the positive attributes of sheep meat (European Commission, 2017).

As regards the price of sheep meat in carcass equivalent (2015), we must mention that there is a significant gap between the EU price (5,097 euro/ton) and the world price (3,229 euro/ton) due to the protection of the European Union's borders. On the long term (2026), due to the steady increase of demand in Asia (in China in particular) and in the Middle East (mainly in Saudi Arabia), it is estimated that the EU sheep meat price will increase to 5,224 euro/ton (European Commission, 2017).

2. Methodology

The research work for the period 2007–2016 targeted a wide area of study. Data were collected, statistically processed and analyzed, concerning the evolution of sheep and goat herds, milk and meat productions, consumption and self-sufficiency, as well as the import – export balance of live sheep and goats, in Romania and in the European Union area, with 28 member states.

Self-sufficiency in sheep and goat meat in the investigated period was calculated using an analysis model (of food balance sheets) used by the National Institute of Statistics, in conformity with the FAO and EUROSTAT methodologies, the main indicator being the utilizable production, on the basis of which the supply availability is obtained (by adding imports and subtracting exports). The ratio of utilizable production to supply availability, in percentage terms, represents the self-supply level (indicator expressing the self-sufficiency rate for the respective product).

The documentation and synthesis of the main ideas necessary to conduct this study was based on the consultation of materials from the national and international literature on the sheep and goat market evolution at European and world level (reports, studies, forecasts, other EUROSTAT and FAOSTAT publications).

As information source, we mention the "Tempo-online database" – time series – National Institute of Statistics, ANSVSA data, "Food Balance Sheets" and "Population's Consumption Availabilities", as well as EUROSTAT and FAOSTAT data for the period 2007–2016.

3. Data and estimation results

3.1. Evolution and development of the sector after accession

Unlike other livestock farming sectors (cattle, pigs), the accession to the European Union in the year 2007 has contributed to the revival of the sheep and mainly goat farming sector in Romania, the goat herds steadily increasing, without being affected by the crisis. In the investigated period 2007–2016, the total goat herds increased by 71 %, while the sheep herds by 16 %.

The support to the sheep and goat sector by EU funds, as well as the Romanian consumers' demand for sheep and goat milk products represented motivational factors for farmers, materialized into a relatively constant milk production in the investigated period.

With a meat production (carcass weight) of 9.3 thousand tons in the year 2015, Romania ranks 10th among the 28 member states, although it ranked 4th as regards the total sheep and goat herds, after the United Kingdom, Spain and Greece.

Keeping in top four was due to programs aimed at stimulating the organization of farms or associations for young sheep raising and fattening to provide meat to the domestic and foreign markets, to increase farmers' incomes through the sale of marketable production and to modify the priority operating directions for meat – milk production.

At the same time, the sheep breeds for meat production have been improved by using artificial insemination and breeding rams for meat production, by size structure improvement of farms for young sheep fattening and introducing the carcass classification grid, according to EU standards.

Although the share of slaughter in specialized units increased from 3 % (1.8 thousand tons) in 2007 to 16 % (8.5 thousand tons) in 2016, it continues to remain low compared to other European states. In this context, we mention that sheep farmers signal out a stringent problem they are facing, namely the lack of animal slaughter centers. The operation of a larger number of such centers, with sanitary-veterinary accreditation, would make it possible for sheep farmers to sell better their meat production, and consumers would have the guarantee that the high food safety standards are respected.

As regards the average slaughter (carcass) weight in specialized units (slaughterhouses), Romania ranks among the countries with the lowest average weight (12.8 kg/head), as against Denmark (22.2 kg/head), Germany (20.5 kg/head) or the United Kingdom (20.4 kg/head).

3.2. Development opportunities for the sector

As it has been mentioned before, Romania has a numerous sheep population. However, the consumption of sheep meat is mainly occasional, with maximum values in the Easter period. The yearly average consumption (consumption availability) of sheep and goat meat reveals a slight decrease, in percentage terms, in the structure of total meat consumption per capita, from 5.6 % in 2000 to 3.5 % in 2015. The Romanian consumers' preferences for sheep meat differ across regions; higher consumptions are met in the regions Sud-Est, with Greek and Turkish influences, and Centru, with tradition in sheep grazing.

Compared to other countries from EU-28, consumption in Romania (3.3 kg/capita) is higher than that in Poland (0.05 kg/capita), Hungary (0.1 kg/capita), Germany (0.8 kg/capita), Italy (1.1 kg/capita), close to that of Spain (2.7 kg/capita) and France (3.3 kg/capita), yet lower than that of Greece (12.8 kg/capita) or Iceland (22 kg/capita).

In order to stimulate sheep meat consumption in Romania, and the consumption of Romanian products in general, in the year 2017, the Ministry of Agriculture and Rural Development initiated the program "Choose the Sheep" with two axes: program popularization throughout the country and developing the infrastructure, i.e. opening specialized stores to meet the consumer needs in sheep meat and products.

This program also aims at capitalizing on sheep meat production, increasing the export value through processed products, attracting labour force in the sheep meat processing sector, while preserving the sheep-based food traditions, mainly in the mountain areas.

The final objective of this campaign is to inform consumers on how to cook sheep meat and meat preparations, as well as to develop a culinary culture based on sheep meat consumption. At the same time, the program intends to provide support to sheep raisers and to establish a wholesale market that will represent an intermediary between the sheep farmers and the marketing channels (retail and proximity shops).

Another opportunity for sheep farmers in Romania is that there is a growing demand for wool for the textile industry and tourism industry on the world markets and for the domestic market. From this point of view, Government's Decision no. 500/2017 was adopted on the scheme "De minimis aid for the implementation of the program supporting sheep farmers for selling wool". In this direction, the measure for the identification of wool collection centers was implemented. Thus, at present, there are 20 centers that collect wool from sheep farmers, with a total capacity of about 30000 tons. These are located throughout the country, in

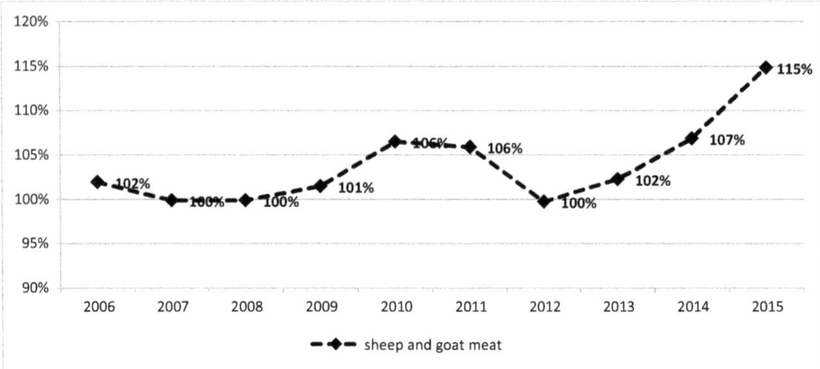

Figure 1: Evolution of self-sufficiency level in sheep and goat meat, 2006–2015 - %
Source: author's own calculations, Food Balance Sheets, National Institute of Statistics.

the counties: Bacău, Bistriţa Năsăud, Brăila, Constanţa, Galaţi, Maramureş, Sibiu, Suceava, Tulcea and Vaslui. The context of adopting this de minimis aid scheme to support sheep farmers is that from experts' estimates it resulted that about 70 % of the wool obtained was not valorized.

The value of financial support representing this de minimis aid is 1 RON/kg of wool. The financial resources necessary to implement this scheme total 36000 thousand RON and are paid from the state budget, within the limit of budgetary provisions approved for this destination by the Ministry of Agriculture and Rural Development in the year 2018.

The effects of the scheme also target the wool selling price: while before the scheme was initiated, the wool price was far from farmers' requirements, at present, on the basis of competition, a certain price began to be formed, depending on quality, which currently ranges from 2 to 4.5 RON/kg.

The justification of the low sheep meat consumption by the Romanian consumers is based on the consumption habits and the relatively high price, as compared to poultry or pig meat. Yet the sheep carcass weight (under 13 kg), priced 236.8 euro/100 kg, is one of the lowest in EU, compared to France (623.1 euro/100 kg) and to the EU-28 average (493.3 euro/100 kg).

In the year 2016, the Romanian farmers received 7.5–8 RON/kg live weight (1.7–1.8 euro/kg) at the export of live sheep, which is a low price if we take into consideration that on the Arab market the live weight price is 4.8–5.2 euro/kg. This is why the Romanian farmers are discontented, as they consider that for them 2.5–3 euro/kg live weight would be a satisfactory price to cover their costs and to obtain profit.

The analysis of self-supply level (indicator expressing the self-sufficiency rate) in the period 2006–2016 reveals 100 % and over self-sufficiency from domestic production (107 % in 2014, 115 % in 2015). The significant growth of imports starting with 2012 (2.3 times compared to previous year) and the exports that dropped more than half resulted in a higher self-sufficiency level in the year 2015 (Figure 1).

The trade balance in live sheep was positive in the period 2003–2016, due to permanent export growth. Since 2009, Romania has no longer imported sheep and goats from the extra-Community area. The imports from intra-Community countries have significantly increased instead, mainly after 2013, 72 % of imports originating from Spain and 19 % from Hungary, in the year 2016.

The sheep export almost fully depends on the export orders from North Africa and Middle East and has as main destinations the following extra-Community countries: Jordan (58 %) and Libya (26 %). In the year 2016, according to the data from the National Institute of Statistics, Jordan was the main export destination, with a value of 73.4 million euro, representing 58 % of the total value of extra-Community sheep export. In the intra-Community area, the export destinations include Greece, Italy and Bulgaria.

Conclusions

With a meat production of 9.3 thousand tons, Romania ranks 10th in EU-28; however, it ranks 4th in total sheep and goat herds, after the United Kingdom, Spain and Greece. Its position in top four was due to the programs that targeted the organization of farms or associations for young sheep raising and fattening in order to provide meat on the domestic and foreign markets.

The financial support to the sheep and goat sector from EU funds and the increased consumer demand for goat milk and dairy products represented motivational factors for farmers, materialized into a constant sheep and goat milk production in all the regions from Romania. In the period 2007–2016, farmers preferred to slaughter their animals in specialized units, and so the slaughter production increased from 3.7 thousand tons live weight in the year 2007 to 18.6 thousand tons in 2016.

Although the share of slaughter on specialized units increased from 3 % in 2007 to 19 % in 2015, it is still low compared to other EU member states; as regards the average slaughter weight, Romania is among the countries with the lowest average weight (12.8 kg/head).

The average farm size is low (29 heads/sheep farm and 11 heads/goat farm) and makes it difficult to adapt to the new performant technologies as a result of insufficient own financial means and reduced access to other funding sources.

Ovine meat consumption is mainly occasional, with maximum values in the Easter period, and Romanian consumers' preferences for sheep and goat meat varies across regions, high consumptions being found in the Sud-Est region, with Greek and Turkish influences and the region Centru, with sheep grazing tradition. Self-sufficiency was over 100 %, in the period 2000–2016.

Sheep export is almost fully dependent on the orders from North Africa and Middle East, Romania permanently ranking 1st in EU-28 in the export of live sheep.

The support to the sheep sector under the future Common Agricultural Policy is necessary as besides the food source there is also the secondary product – wool; at the same time, sheep and goats contribute to the cultural wealth of European landscape. The support to the sector contributes to maintaining an important number of jobs, in the great agricultural areas from the EU, vulnerable from this point of view. In the absence of support measures, many sheep farmers will have to abandon this activity, with serious consequences as regards jobs, social dynamics in the countryside, environment and cultural heritage.

Romania initiated and implemented two important schemes to support sheep farmers. These refer to "De minimis aid for the implementation of the program supporting sheep farmers for selling wool" and "Choose the sheep" – scheme for promoting sheep meat and meat preparations consumption. The effects of these schemes, both initiated in 2017, began to be seen in the first months of 2018, in the collection of important quantities of wool in the wool collection centers and the slight increase of meat consumption.

References

European Commission (2016): Short-term outlook for EU agricultural markets in 2017 and 2018, https://ec.europa.eu/agriculture/sites/agriculture/files/markets-and-prices/short-term-outlook/current_en.pdf.

Food and Agricultural Organization (2016): OECD-FAO Agricultural Outlook 2016–2025, ISBN 978-92-5-109296-5, http://dx.doi.org/10.1787/19991142; http://dx.doi.org/10.1787/agr_outlook-2016-10-en.

European Commission (2017): The Policy Roadmap for the EU Sheep Meat Sector Recommendations from the EU Sheep Meat Forum https://ec.europa.eu/agriculture/sites/agriculture/files/sheepgoats/forum/recommendations_en.pdf.

Marie Carlier & Philippe Chotteau, GEB – Institut de l'Élevage: The EU sheep sector. A global player?, 2017 https://ec.europa.eu/agriculture/sites/agriculture/files/sheep-goats/forum/workshop-1/presentation-1-eu-sheep-sector_en.pdf.

Liliana Sime: Noi ajutoare pentru crescătorii de ovine Agroinfo 2018, https://www.agroinfo.ro/cresterea-animalelor/exclusiv-ultima-ora-de-la-bruxelles-vesti-excelente-pentru-subventiile-acordate-crescatorilor-de-ovine?utm_source=agroinfo&utm_medium=email&utm_campaign=newsletter_1792

European Commission (2016): EU Agricultural Outlook for the Agricultural Markets and Income 2017-2030", https://ec.europa.eu/agriculture/sites/agriculture/files/markets-and-prices/medium-term-outlook/2017/2017-fullrep_en.pdf.

European Commission (2016): EU Agricultural Outlook for the Agricultural, Prospect for EU Agricultural Market and Income 2016-2026, https://ec.europa.eu/agriculture/sites/agriculture/files/markets-and-prices/medium-term-outlook/2016/2016-fullrep_en.pdf.

Ro.aliment, Revista specialiştilor din industria alimentară (2018), Programul Alege oaia, http://www.roaliment.ro/stiri-industria-alimentara/programul-alege-oaia-ridicat-consumul-de-carne-de-oaie-randul-romanilor-la-37-de-tone-lunar/.

Ştiri agricole (2018), O nouă oportunitate pentru crescătorii de ovine, https://www.stiriagricole.ro/o-noua-oportunitate-pentru-crescatorii-de-ovine-iata-in-ce-judete-se-vor-infiinta-centre-de-colectare-50276.html.

EUROSTAT: Meat production statistics, http://ec,europa,eu/eurostat/statistics-explained/index,php/Meat_production_statistics#Beef_and_veal_,28bovine_meat,29, 2015

OECD/FAO (2015), Agricultural Outlook 2015-2024, http://www.fao.org/3/a-i4738e.pdf

Tempo online, National Institute of Statistics.

Alexandru ISAIC-MANIU[1], *Stelian STANCU*[2], *Constanţa Nicoleta BODEA*[3], *Mihai Sabin MUSCALU*[4]

[1] Centre for Industrial and Services Economics, Romanian Academy, Email: alexandru.isaic@csie.ase.ro

[2] Informatics and Economic Cybernetics Department, Bucharest University of Economic Studies; Centre for Industrial and Services Economics, Romanian Academy, Email: stelian_stancu@yahoo.com

[3] Informatics and Economic Cybernetics Department, Bucharest University of Economic Studies; Centre for Industrial and Services Economics, Romanian Academy, Email: bodea@ase.ro

[4] Centre for Industrial and Services Economics, Romanian Academy, Email: msmuscalu@yahoo.com

Structural Changes of Services Rendered to Enterprises, in Romania, during 2008–2016

Abstract *By 1990, in Romania, the statistical evidence of services was made only for the services rendered to population. Two indicators were used in this regards: the number of service units and the activity value. Comparability with the developed countries was achieved only after the transition to the National Accounts System after 1990. Gradually, as the service activity expanded, the statistic was aligned, the last change being made after the accession of Romania to the EU and the use of the CAEN-Rev.2 classification system. In recent years, the general economic evolution has also been accompanied by a series of qualitative changes in national production, the most significant being the increase in the volume of services and major changes in their structure. The objective of the paper is to identify the main changes in the structure of the services rendered to enterprises. This topic is relatively rare from the analysts' concerns mainly due to the fact that the pursuit of this activity is relatively recent. After the selection and adaptation of the main methods of measuring the structure, the concentration / diversification of services, the dynamics of the structure of the services rendered to enterprises is characterized. The final paper objective was the formulation of some strategic directions of action, the acceleration of the process of convergence of the Romanian economy in the group of developed countries from the EU.*

Keywords: *structure of services, services rendered to enterprises, quantitative indicators, concentration*

Introduction

One of the features of modern economies is the high share of services in national production. In Romania, in the last decade of the communist period, the industry contribution at the Social Product (PS) was 63.0–66.9 %, the agriculture contributed with 13.0–11.3 %, the movement of goods with 4.5–3.5 %, the constructions with 9.8–8.9 %, the transport and telecommunications with 4.8–5.3 % (Statistical Yearbook of Romania 1990, CNS, pg 232, tab. 125). It is necessary to mention that, as a basis of the construction and functioning of the economic mechanism of the society, the Marxist ideology had distinguished between productive and non-productive labor.

The macroeconomic statistics carried out the calculations accordingly, based on the principles and methodology of the Material Production System (SPM) so that activities such as defense and public order, health, administration, education, culture, etc. were not considered creators of new value, therefore these activities were not included in the macroeconomic aggregates as: Social Product and National Income. After 1990, when the political system was changed, the concepts of calculating the macro aggregates were replaced, starting from the premise behind the calculations in the National Accounts System (the specific version recommended by the UN Statistical Commission).

After the collapse of the economy, in the early years of transition, gradually, with the economic recovery, both the volume and the diversity of services increased. Especially after the accession to the European Union, the volume of services has increased as a volume, but has also diversified, and their share in national production has increased. In 2016, the GDP growth was 104.7 % compared to the level registered in 2015, the value value reaching 759.23 billion lei (169.0 billion euros), the structure by sectors being: 23.1 %, agriculture 3.9 %, constructions 6.0 %, commerce 18.1 %, real estate transactions 8.2 %, public administration and defense 10.2 % and, as a new one, computer science and communications 5.6 %.

Remarkable is the growth of telecommunications and IT services, whose share in GDP almost equals the entire construction sector and significantly outpaces agriculture (this activity was included until 2010 in the same group with commerce, hotel activity - restaurants), generating in 2016 a value of 42 billion, up 14.2 % compared to 2015. The figure 1 illustrates the dynamic of the services rendered to enterprises, in total and the dynamic of one of its component, the information and communications services.

1. Literature Review

The review of the literature was carried out in two main directions: the first one aiming to reflect the scientific concerns related to the typology of services rendered to enterprises, and the second one focusing on the methodological approaches related to the analysis of the service structure. Referring to the theoretical bases of the services, Hill (1999) proposes their classification based on the

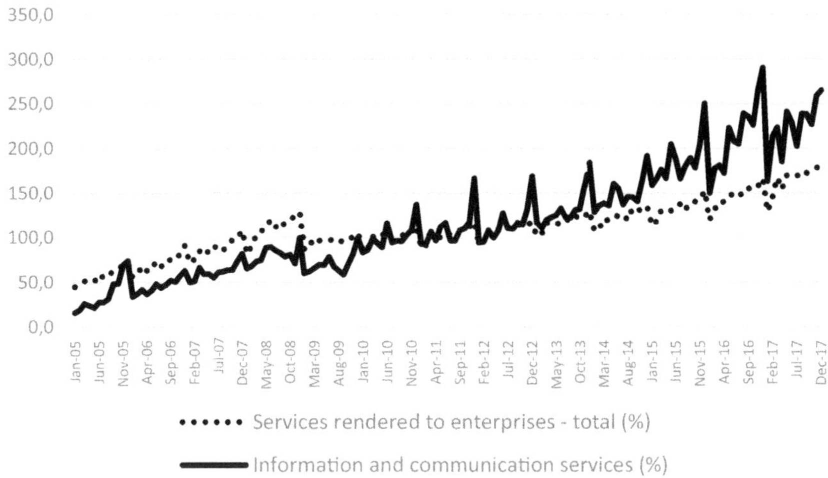

Figure 1: Turnover dynamics of the services rendered to enterprises (%) - base year 2010

Source: Institutul National de Statistica

distinction between products and services that has traditionally been interpreted by economists as being equivalent to the differentiation between raw materials and finished products, as tangible materials on the one hand and immaterial or intangible products on the other. An in-depth approach is made by Harte and Dale (1995) by separating and defining professional services as "intangible outputs rather qualitative than quantitative, the main criteria for customer being satisfaction and accessibility". Wemmerlov (1989) undertook a service structure analysis, by using a detailed service processes database. Several works of Silvestro, Fitzgerald and Johnston (1992) are also related to the classification of services and their differentiation from tangible goods.

Significant contribution to the theorization and systematization of service activity makes Bell (2008) taking the road from ideas, concepts, design to the IT management services. In an interesting scientific communication, Leung and Bockstedt (2008) highlight that over the past two decades, the quantitative analysis of enterprises has advanced significantly in line with advances in information technology using OLAP. An interesting conclusion of a dissertation thesis (Itkonen, 2015) aims to clarify the most appropriate definition for services. Jaakkola and Halinen (2006) highlight the specific organizational behavior of medical services. On the field of human resources services, Austin (2012) develops a real case study on the situation of social assistance organizations. A macroeconomic analysis of services in the US is conducted by Sanders (2013). Using a database of 168 service processes, Larson (2008) provides a methodological guide for those interested, but also develops the concepts of what tends to become "Service Science". Interesting is the Schmenner's (1986) argumentation in the field of strategic services management, for the establishment of service networks, as a way of increasing these performances, reducing the "mortality rates" of companies. Borangiu, Dragoicea and Nóvoa (2016) are the editors of a volume that brings together the scientific connotations of national and international experts in the field of service science.

The work of Tovissi, Scarlat, Tasnadi (1979) is remarkable in terms of the quantitative approach of services, as distinct activity in the national economy, offering the most extensive and rich monograph in Romanian of methods for characterizing the structure of economic systems. An area that has provided a whole set of methods applicable in the study of economic systems is the spatial statistics. The work of Stein and Allard (2015) brings together a rich collection of scientific materials. In the field of professional services and in the context of membership in the EU, the analysis of the competitive advantage of the national industry measured by the RCA (Revealed Comparative Advantage) performed by Russu (2011) shows that Romania has a real comparative advantages in the group of these countries.

Hackl and Westland (1991) bring together the contributions of several authors in the field of quantitative methods for the measurement of structural displacements. Popescu (2012) performs an analysis of structural disparities in the orientation of foreign investments in Romania. Dragan and Isaic-Maniu (2017) provide an alternative to the usual measures of structural displacement measurement. Li and Liu (2017) address the topic of the land usage and degradation by analyzing the changes in the land structure. Lesschen, Verburg and Staal (2005) present the results obtained from field studies, by using as data processing methods the spatial regression, cluster analysis and the Bayesian analysis. In the same field, Steininger et al. (2016) develops the analysis of climate scenarios and socio-economic implications of the land degradation. Aiginger (2002) analyzes structural differences between US and EU economies.

2. Data gathering

Due to the transition to the market economy and the implementation of CAEN Rev.1 another classification of services emerged. Compared to the communist period, this new classification extracted the services from the large group that included the internal trade, the supply of services to the population and the hotel tourism activity. The CANE Rev.2 interrupted the continuity of the data series on the activity of the services in 2008, the differences regarding the activity classification, the type of aggregation and the degree of detail, and since 2011, only the values on the total economy are registered, the private sector becoming the majority. Managing information on the collection, processing and dissemination of information is based on a series of official regulations in the field, harmonization with those of EUROSTAT.

According to CANE Rev.2, the market services provided mainly for enterprises include the following activities: transport and storage (divisions 49–52), post and courier (division 53), information and communications (divisions 58–63), real estate transactions (division 68), professional, scientific and technical activities (divisions 77, 78, 80–82), entertainment, cultural, recreational activities (divisions 90–93), other service activities (divisions 95–96). The data are collected by the National Institute of Statistics, mainly on the basis of two surveys: Structural Survey in Enterprises (AS'2016), and Industrial Short-Term Industry Indicators (IND TS). The selection of enterprises and their inclusion in the research sample is done from the REGIS survey, the random and optimal stratified surveys (Neyman variant), the selection variables being the size of the firm and the main activity object. Enterprises with more than 20 employees are fully researched, the values are recorded in current prices, and dynamics are calculated at prices comparable to the base year 2010, by Laspeyres indexes. About 5500 enterprises are regularly investigated.

3. Methodologies for determining structures and their modifications

3.1. Theil Index

Gini coefficient is considered as the starting point in the analysis of structural changes. Several quantitative methods were introduced for measuring the structural discrepancies, such as: Theil Index, Atkinson index or generalized entropy index (Novotný 2007; Parker 2015; Haughton and Khandker 2009; Greselin and Zitikis 2018). The Theil index was defined developed based on the entropy indicators, starting from the following hypotheses:

- The amount of information of an event with the probability of realization p_i is $\ln(1/p_i)$.
- For a certain event, with the probability of realization 1, the information is null.
- If the probability of occurrence of an event is low, then the information held by it is high. Entropy of a system consisting of k elements, determined in relation to the probability vector $\mathrm{p} = \left[p_{1,} p_{2,} \cdots p_k \right]$, with $p_i \geq 0$ and $\sum_{i=1}^{k} p_i = 1$, is calculated by:

$$H(p) = -\sum_{i=1}^{k} p_i \cdot \ln(p_i) \tag{1}$$

With values in the range of values $[0; \ln k]$. Entropy can be used to analyze the degree of concentration of service categories across the entire sector (Onicescu and Stefanescu, 1979).

Element p_i, as a measure of the degree of concentration in the Theil variant, is determined as the difference between the maximum value of the entropy of this event and its entropy:

$$T(p) = \ln k - H(p) \tag{2}$$

If the distribution is equiprobable, so with maximum diversification, the value is zero and in the case of maximum concentration the value is $T_{max}(p) = \ln k$.

3.2. The length of the structure vector

For calculating the length of the structural vector, the one-dimensional distribution series is considered $(x_i)_{i=\overline{1,n}}$, for which the values are summed directly. The length of a vector in the Euclidean space is defined as the distance between the origin and the point determined by the vector $\mathrm{x} = [x_1, x_2, \ldots x_n]$, (Tovissi et al, 1979; M.Bădiţă et al, 2004; Isaic-Maniu et al, 2004) being determined by:

$$\| x \|_n : x \to E,\ E \subset \mathbb{R}_+ \tag{3}$$

Concentration is maximal when all population units belong to a single group, in which case the distribution series is represented by $\mathrm{x} = [\sum x_i, 0, \ldots 0]$, and the upper limit becomes:

$$\| x \|_{max} = \sqrt{(\sum x_i)^2 + 0^2 + \ldots + 0^2} = \sum x_i \tag{4}$$

If the values are evenly distributed, so there is maximum diversification, the lower limit of the value range is:

$$\| x \|_{min} = \sqrt{\left(\frac{\sum x_i}{n}\right)^2 + \ldots + \left(\frac{\sum x_i}{n}\right)^2} = \frac{\sum x_i}{\sqrt{n}} \tag{5}$$

The following two observations are important:

i) The value of the indicator is influenced by the number of series classes and the magnitude of the values;
ii) The indicator is expressed in the characteristic measurement unit, so it cannot be used in the comparisons with different characteristics. This limitation can be overcome by the indicator normalization:

$$C \| x \| = \frac{\| x \|_n - \| x \|_n^{min}}{\| x \|_n^{max} - \| x \|_n^{min}} \in [0,1] \tag{6}$$

Where $C \| x \|$ is dimensionless, its size is directly proportional to the concentration level of the series.

3.3. The length of the weight vector

For x values which can be summed up directly, the characterization of the degree of concentration / diversification is made also by the length of the weight vector: $g^x = [g_1^x, \ldots, g_n^x]$, with $g_i^x = x_i / \sum_{i=1}^n x_i, i = \overline{1,n}$, respectively with the length:

$$\| g^x \|_n = \sqrt{\sum_{i=1}^n (g_i^x)^2} \tag{7}$$

The length is minimal if the values (or weights) are evenly distributed, so it is constant for any index, being the maximum if the values are placed in a single group, so $g_i^x = 1$, and $g_j^x = 0, (\forall) j \neq i$ with $j = \overline{1,n}$, the range of variation being:

$$\frac{1}{\sqrt{n}} \leq \| g^x \|_n \leq 1 \tag{8}$$

It is also useful the relationship: $\| x \|_n = \| g^x \|_n \cdot \sum_{i=1}^{n} x_i$ which highlights the dependency of $\| x \|$ to a quantitative and a qualitative factor. In comparisons over time, it is necessary to use comparable prices.

3.4. Transformed Gini index and measurement of the concentration

For a simple distribution series, represented by $(x_i)_{i=\overline{1,n}}$, in order to define a necessary indicator for the analysis of the concentration (Yitzhaki, 1982; Greselin and Zitikis, 2018; Iacob and Andrei, 2004), the series of pairs of values is formed $(x_i, x_j)_{i,j=\overline{1,n}}, i \neq j$ with $n(n-1)$ components, and Gini index is calculated from the average of the absolute differences of the differences x_i şi x_j, as a ratio between the average of the deviations and the arithmetic mean of the series terms:

$$G = \frac{\Delta}{\overline{x}} = \frac{1}{n(n-1)\overline{x}} \cdot \sum_{\substack{i,j=1 \\ i<j}}^{n} \left| x_i - x_j \right| \tag{9}$$

which can also be calculated according to the area of the concentration area: $G = 2S$.

The above-mentioned indicators have a major inconvenience in imposing the "system condition", which requires that all parts of the whole be known, so $\sum x_i$ or $\sum f_i = 1$. For such cases, Dragan and Isaic-Maniu (2017) proposed an alternative, using a uniparametric statistical distribution with subunit values, of density (Isaic-Maniu and Vodă, 1987):

$$x : f(x;\theta) = \frac{1}{2}\theta^3 x^{\theta-1} ln^2 x, x \in (0,1], \theta > 1 \tag{10}$$

Restriction $\theta > 1$ is required for that $\lim_{x \to 0^+} f(x,\theta) = 0$. The non-centered moment of order n is:

$$E(X^n) = \frac{1}{2}\theta^3 \int_0^1 x^{n+\theta-1} \cdot ln^2 x \, dx = \left(\frac{\theta}{\theta+n} \right)^3 \tag{11}$$

With media and dispersion given by:

$$E(X)=\left(\frac{\theta}{\theta+1}\right)^3,\text{ respectiv } Var(X)=\left(\frac{\theta}{\theta+2}\right)^3-\left(\frac{\theta}{\theta+1}\right)^6 \tag{12}$$

Estimation of the parameter θ can be done either by the Pearson method or by the maximum fidelity (Fisher). Let's consider $0 \le x_i \le 1$ a random sample of X. By making $\bar{x}=n^{-1}\sum x_i \le 1$ with *E(X)*, it is immediately obtained the θ estimation by the moments method: $\hat{\theta}_{MM}=\frac{(\bar{x})^{1/3}}{1-(\bar{x})^{1/3}}$ the condition $\hat{\theta}>1$ implying $\bar{x}>\frac{1}{8}=0.125$.

By using the maximum likelihood method (ML) it is obtained: $\widehat{\left(\frac{1}{\theta}\right)}_{ML}=\frac{1}{3n}\sum \ln\frac{1}{x_i}$.

The verification of a simple statistical hypothesis $H_1:\theta=\theta_1\left(\theta_0<\theta_1\right)$ has the significance of a hypothesis on the state of the system at one time, but also of the structure shift, the purpose in which we use the Wald test (SPRT - the sequential test of the verosimility report):

$$r_n(x)=\frac{\prod_1^n f(x_i;\theta_1)}{\prod_1^n f(x_i;\theta_0)}=\left(\frac{\theta_1}{\theta_0}\right)^{3n}\cdot\prod_{i=1}^n x_i^{\theta_1-\theta_0} \tag{13}$$

If α and β represent the risks associated with the two hypotheses, and A and B are the decision constants of the sequential test, $A\approx(1-\beta)/\alpha$ and $B\approx\beta/(1-\alpha)$, then the area delimited by the two limits indicates the absence of significant structural movements:

$$\left[\ln B-3n\ln(\theta_1/\theta_0)\right]/(\theta_1-\theta_0)<\sum_{i=1}^n \ln x_i<\left[\ln A-3n\ln(\theta_1/\theta_0)\right]/(\theta_1-\theta_0) \tag{14}$$

Conclusions

The main results are shown in Table 1.

The interpretation of data and results obtained based on authors' calculations can be synthesized as follows.

Apart from the amplification of the service activities, another significant process was the services outsourcing, which is hard to be quantified, from the general dynamics of services;

Major changes took place after 2008 as a result of NACE Rev. 2 classification of the activities, which make the comparisons over time very complicated;

There has been a strong increase in the volume of services rendered to enterprises, a process carried out in parallel with the increase of the economic

Table 1: Indicators of the structure of the services rendered to enterprises

Year	2008	2009	2010	2011	2012	2013	2014	2015	2016
Total xi (mil lei)	162,289.4	154,458.2	162,542.8	178,467.2	195,969.1	201,505.9	220,478.9	239,515.2	247,705.8
Vector |x|	46,104.4	43,592.5	45,627.8	50,543.6	55,607.5	58,843.8	64,762.1	70,650.9	73,460.5
Vector |p|	0.2841	0.2822	0.2807	0.2832	0.2838	0.2920	0.2937	0.2950	0.2966
Total p_i^2	0.0807	0.0797	0.0788	0.0802	0.0805	0.0853	0.0863	0.0870	0.0879
Dynamics compared to 2010	0.9984	0.9503	1.0000	1.0980	1.2056	1.2397	1.3564	1.4736	1.5239
$\|x\|/\|x_{2010}\|$	1.0104	0.9554	1.0000	1.1077	1.2187	1.2896	1.4194	1.5484	1.6100
$\|p\|/\|p_{2010}\|$	1.0139	1.0062	1.0000	1.0102	1.0125	1.0464	1.0534	1.0585	1.0651
$\|x\|/\|x_{2010}\|$ * $\|p\|/\|p_{2010}\|$	1.0244	0.9613	1.0000	1.1191	1.2339	1.3495	1.4952	1.6391	1.7147
$C_{\|p\|}$	0.2565	0.2546	0.2530	0.2556	0.2562	0.2647	0.2665	0.2678	0.2695
Dynamics $C_{\|p\|}$ (%)	101.4	100.6	100.0	101.0	101.3	104.6	105.3	105.8	106.5

Source: Authors calculations.

activity at national level. For example, in 2016, the national production increased by + 4.8 % and the services by +7.5 %, of which the IT services +20.1 %.

As compared to 2010, the dynamics of the services to the enterprises was 181.2 %, and the informatics services by 268.5 %;

The impact of the crisis in 2008–2010 on the volume of service activity during compared to the economy as a whole was less dramatic. Compared to 2008, in 2009 the GDP rate was -5.9 %, while services dropped only by -4.8 % and the informatics increased by +7.4 %; And the recovery after the crisis has been more vigorous in the sphere of services, proving that there were gaps in the dynamics between the economy, in general, and those of the services;

There were strongly differentiated evolutions of some categories of services, notably those of the IT area. For example, compared to 2010, in December 2017, the increase rate was + 168.5 %. For the same period, the rate for water transport was - 36.2 %;

The structure dynamics of the services sector is mostly influenced by the extensive rather than the intensive factors (1.61 compared to 1.065 for the year 2016, which denotes the existence of strong reserves for performance improvement);

In 2008, Gini coefficient was 0.081, and, in 2016, it was 0.088, indicating a relative concentration, the dynamics recorded being +4.5 %;

The structure of the values vector has evolved from 46.1 in 2008 to 73.5 in 2016, reflecting the relative concentration of activities on the 27 specific services;

The integration of the organizations providing services to enterprises into networks, consortia, alliances, associations could enhance the service activity because this integration can leads to synergy of efforts and, by consequence to performance increase and competitive position strengthening;

Other solutions for performance increase and competitive position strengthening are the collaborations with European companies by providing access to their infrastructure in exchange of advanced know-how and the enrollment in the benchmarking networks, in order to align the process of modernization and alignment with the field performers;

Also, the organizations providing services to enterprises could adapt and diversify the range of services they provide in order to fulfill increasingly sophisticated demands of the market;

And finally, diversifying and expanding government support for service companies, alongside the entry of outsourcing firms represents examples of public policies which could have a positive impact on the service sector dynamics

References

Aiginger, K.: Speed of Change, European Commission, DG Enterprise, Working Paper, Standford University, 2002.

Austin, D.: Human Services Management: Organizational Leadership in Social Work Practice, (Foundations of Social Work Knowledge Series), 2012, Kindle Edition, Columbia Univ.Press.

Bădiţă, M. et al: Specializarea in servicii - opţiune de dezvoltare economică a Romaniei - Metode şi modele, Economia. Ser. Man., 2004, Vol. VII, No. 2 - Special, pp.92–107

Bell, M.: Service-Oriented Modeling: Service Analysis, Design, and Architecture, 2008, J.Wiley, Hoboken, New Jersey.

Borangiu, Th. et al.: Exploring Services Science- 7th International Conf., IESS 2016, Springer.

Dragan, I. M., Isaic-Maniu, A.: An Alternative for Indicators that Characterize the Structure of Economic Systems, Entropy, 2017, 19(7), 346.

Hackl, P., Westland, A. (Eds.): Economic Structural Change-Analysis and Forecasting, 1991, Springer, Berlin.

Harte, G. H., Dale, G. B.: Improving quality in professional service organizations: A review of the key issues, Managing Service Quality, 1995, 5(3), pp. 34–44.

Haughton, J., Khandker, S.: Handbook on Poverty and Inequality, The International Bank for Reconstruction and Development, The World Bank, 2009.

Hill, P.: Tangibles, intangibles and services: A new taxonomy for the classification of output, Canadian Journal of Economics, 1999, 32(2), pp. 426–446.

Iacob, A. I., Andrei, T.: L'analyse de la concentration géographique du développement économique en Roumanie, XXXVI mes Journées de Statistique, 24–28 mai, 2004, Montpellier, France.

Isaic–Maniu, Al., Vodă, Gh.: A method for the analysis of subunitary values. An uniparametric distribution, Econ. Comp. Econ. Cyb. Stud. Res., 1987 vol. XXII, nr. 3, pp. 53–60.

Isaic-Maniu, Al. et al: Proiectarea modelelor de masurare a specializarii fortei de munca in profil teritorial, Economia. Seria Management, 2004, V.7, Nr.2, pp.216–235.

Itkonen, M.: Analyzing the Technical Structure of Service Product, Master's Thesis Industrial Engineering and Management Degree Programme in Process Engineering, January 2015.

Jaakkola, E., Halinen, A.: Problem solving within professional services: Evidence from the medical field, International Journal of Service Industry Management, 2006, 17(5), pp. 409–429.

Larson, C. R.: Service science: At the intersection of management, social, and engineering sciences, IBM Systems Journal, 2008, 47(1), pp. 41–51.

Lesschen, P.,J., Verburg, P., Staal, St.: Statistical Methods for Analysing the Spatial Dimension of Changes in Land Use And Farming Systems, LUCC Report Series No. 7, Edt. LUCC Focus 3 Office, 2005, Kenya, International Livestock Research Institute Wageningen Univ. Netherlands.

Leung, T. Y., Bockstedt, J.: Structural Analysis of a Business Enterprise, Service Science, 2009, 1(3), 169–188.

Li, Y., Liu, G.: Characterizing Spatiotemporal Pattern of Land Use Change and Its Driving Force Based on GIS and Landscape Analysis Techniques in Tianjin during 2000–2015, "Sustainability", 2017, 9, 894.

Maleyeff, J.: Analysis of Service Processes Characteristics across a Range of Enterprises, J. Serv. Sci. & Management, 2009, 2: 29–35.

Novotný, J.: On the measurement of regional inequality: does spatial dimension of income inequality matter?, The Ann. of Reg.l Science, Sept. 2007, Vol. 41, Issue 3, pp 563–580.

Onicescu, O., Ştefănescu, V.: Elemente de statistică informaţională şi aplicaţii, Editura Tehnică, Bucureşti, 1979.

Parker, L: Racial and Ethnic Segregation, "In the News and On PolicyMap", 2015.

Popescu, C.: Foreign Direct Investments and Regional Development in Romania, Rev. Roum. Géogr./Rom. Journ. Geogr., 2012, 56, (1), pp. 61–70, Bucureşti.

Russu, C.: Revealed Competitive Advantage of the European Union and Romanian Manufacturing Industries, Bulletin Vol. LXIII No. 3, 2011, Economic Sciences Series, Petroleum-Gas University of Ploiesti, pp. 50–58.

Sanders, G. et al: Structure and Dynamics of the U.S. Federal Services Industrial Base, 2000–2012, Center for Strategic an International Studies-CSIS, Rowman & Littlefield, 2013, N.York.

Schmenner, W. R.: How can service businesses survive and prosper?, Sloan Management Review, 1986, 27(3), pp. 21–32.

Silvestro, R. et al.: Towards a classification of service processes, International Journal of Service Industry Management, 1992, 3(3), pp. 62–75.

Stein, A., Allard, D., Ed.: Spatial Statistics 2015: emerging patterns, Procedia Environmental Sciences, 2015, vol. 26, Elsevier.

Steininger, W., K. et al.: Consistent economic cross-sectoral climate change impact scenario analysis: Method and application to Austria, Climate Services, 2016, Vol. 1, pp. 39–52.

Tovissi, L., Scarlat, E., Tasnadi, A.: Metode si modele ale analizei economice structurale, Editura Stiintifica si Enciclopedica, 1979, Bucuresti.

Wemmerlov, U.: A taxonomy for service processes and its implications for system design, International Journal of Service Industry Management, 1989, 1(3), pp. 20–40.

Yitzhaki, S., Stochastic dominance, mean variance, and Gini'mean difference, American Economic Review, vol. 72, no 1, 1982, 178–185.

(***) Acte normative: Regulamentul CE nr.1165 /1998, Regulamentul nr. CE 1158 /2005, Regulamentul CE nr. 1503 /2006, Regulamentul CE nr. 586 /2001, Regulamentul CE nr. 1893 /2006, Regulamentul CE nr. 656 /2007, Ordinul Presedintelui INS nr. 932 /2005, Ordinul Presedintelui INS nr. 808 /2011.

Alina Georgeta AILINCĂ[1], *Cătălin DRĂGOI*[2]

[1] Scientific researcher III, "Victor Slăvescu", Centre for Financial and Monetary Research, Romanian Academy, Email: alina.glod@gmail.com

[2 1] Scientific researcher, "Victor Slăvescu", Centre for Financial and Monetary Research, Romanian Academy, Email: hipercub@gmail.com

Correlations between Credit Default Swaps and Macroeconomic Developments in Romania

Abstract *Generally, the literature and the practice consider the credit default swap (CDS) as an efficient backup mechanism against the situations of non-payment by the creditors, being signals of the healthiness, therefore, stability of the financial market of a country, or even a region of the world. They have the power of influencing the evolution of the macroeconomic reality and to reveal, by their rates, possible positive or negative signs of the macroeconomic evolutions. Therefore, this paper aims to show the relation between CDS rates, the sovereign risk rates for Romania given by the main international rating agencies and the main macroeconomic indicators of Romania. Based on empirical analysis, we may say that the CDS are closely connected to the macroeconomic realities of Romania, being important signals of the financial market which, in turn, can contribute to maintaining the macroeconomic balance and the financial stability in Romania.*

Keywords: *credit default swap (CDS), Sovereign risk, GDP, Inflation, Exchange Rate*

Introduction

Introduced for the first time in 1994 by JP Morgan Chase, the credit default swap (CDS) represents a credit derivative contract concluded between two sides, being some king of insurance policy, by which the buyer (seller of the risk) makes periodical, quarterly or monthly, payments to the seller (buyer of the risk) in exchange for the right to cash a payment in the case of default (unfavourable or devastating event which prevents the fulfilment of the contractual obligations), or of another credit event regarding a third party, which is the entity of reference (generally insurance company, bank of hedging fund).

Most of the CDS provide protection against the unfulfillment of obligations, or cover the bankruptcy risk of a debtor regarding support assets such as sovereign debt, corporate debts and municipal bonds. They also protect against the credit risk of junk bonds, collateralized debt obligations and mortgage-backed securities.

According to Eurostat (2016), the CDS for the credit risk are a mechanism ensuring against events such or creditors failing to pay their debts, while the CDS for sovereign debts are usually regarded as extremely relevant signals and instruments of the financial market.

This article aims to identify the implications of the macroeconomic evolutions on the CDS and vice versa. Although the empirical evaluation is not the focus of the paper it will, nevertheless, use this type of methodology for the case of Romania, to show both the implications of the CDS for the economic environment and the implications of the economic environment evolutions on the CDS and on the sovereign risk rating. This paper is a partial result of the 2017 research project "Globalization and the country risk" coordinator Cătălin Dragoi, within the research program of the Centre for Financial and Monetary Research „Victor Slăvescu", of INCE and the Romanian Academy.

1. Literature review

According to Greenspan (2004), CDS are efficient vehicles for credit risk transfer. Nashikkar, Subrahmanyam and Mahanti (2011) consider that CDS trading affects market efficiency, liquidity and quality, while Massa and Zhang (2012), the use of CDS provides a plus of liquidity, quality and efficiency, because the hedging reduces the risk despite the possible degradation of the bonds. According to Ashcraft and Santos (2009), the CDS can have a positive impact on the financial market by an easier discernment of credit quality: the solvable creditors will have lower borrowing costs, while the companies with problems and higher risks, will be punished by higher borrowing costs. Ismailescu and Phillips (2011) prove empirically that the public bonds become more informationally efficient with the use of the CDS, while the spreads of the bonds decrease. On the other hand, the CDS were used in certain circumstances as vehicles for speculations against other investor or governmental assets, by boosting the unpayment of the support debt.

This aspect was noticed during the global economic and financial crisis, when the CDS, unregulated until 2009, contributed to the Lehman Brothers bankruptcy and had a negative contribution to the onset of the crisis by bursting the real estate bubble (Fostel and Geanakoplos 2015) and by blocking the capital markets and the banking credits (Stulz, 2010). At the same time, the deceptive feeling of security lead to the sovereign debt crisis of Greece, in 2012, which had, besides a high rate of the public debt in the GDP, a sizeable volume of investors in CDS, CDS which covered extremely little of the risks of an increasing debt.

The fact that the CDS are traded on the financial markets often makes their price fluctuate significantly depending on the circumstances of the international, regional or national context, and of the particular debtor. It is noteworthy that the buyer of CDS pays a price which entitles him, in case of bankruptcy of the issuer of the support assets, to receive an amount of money set through the contract, which can trigger speculations and even to "assisting" or "helping" companies, municipalities or even states, to enter a state of default, so that the holders of CDS or of other types of financial derivatives, can cash much more money than usually.

The hedging funds or the speculative funds are often accused of buying a default insurance, with no right of property on the support asset, actually covering the credit risk, not the creditors, thus altering the nature of the indebting instruments, which can cause distortions, difficult economic situations and bankruptcy both for the issuers of a private debt, and for the issuers of public debts. On the background of the sovereign debts crisis, the literature describes such dangers (Portes 2010, Subrahmanyam, Tang and Wang 2014 etc.); this caused a legal, temporary or even permanent, interdiction of CDS trading in the European Union (such as in December 2012, as mentioned by Augustin, Subrahmanyam, Tang and Wang 2016).

Regarding CDS determinants, according to Heinz and Sun (2014, p. 36) and the Global Financial Stability Report Old Risks, New Challenges (April 2013), the most important factors that determine the CDS spreads of Central and South Eastern European countries are their own economic fundamentals, global investor sentiment and CDS market liquidity conditions. Thus, the changes in market perception of macroeconomic fundamentals have been primarily associated CDS spreads, sovereign CDS spreads reflecting economic fundamentals such as growth prospects, forward looking fiscal indicators and current account forecasts.

2. Data sources and methodology

This paper studies preponderantly the impact of the macroeconomic indicators of Romania on the CDS, and vice versa, the implications of CDS evolution on the macroeconomic indicators. Thus, the adaptation of the CDS to the Romanian macroeconomic realities can be sustained, at least partially, by a rather simple economic analysis (e.g. correlation, regression). We used the least squares method and Excel Data Analysis to determine the parameters of the used regressions. For this paper we accessed national and international statistics databases, but we will mainly used Romanian National Bank data. For the econometric analysis we used 2013–2017 data, with monthly frequency. This frequency was required by the necessity of producing a relevant number of observations (60, in this case), and by the way of systematizing the surveyed indicators.

CDS is a very liquid instrument for the Romanian sovereign debt, thus we used CDS quotas on sovereign debt instruments issued by Romania. We used for rating classifications of international rating agencies (Moody's, S&P and Fitch) the state bonds for denominated contracts on long term, in foreign exchange. We computed monthly data as average daily values, and we took into consideration the 2013–2017 monthly data because we had limited access to the CDS spreads quotations before 2013. The Romanian sovereign CDS market is relatively small compared to other countries but it takes shape, being more or less compared to the government bond market. The article tries to reveal the importance assigned to the information delivered by CDS in assessing the country risk and its impact on the economy.

3. Results and comments

Many studies approached the influences sent and received from/by the CDS. Few, however, approached the situation of the CDS in Central and East European countries, and even fewer approached the connection between the sovereign debt CDS and the evolution of the main macroeconomic indicators in Romania. Thus, for Romania, if we look at the CDS in correlation with the main macroeconomic indicators for 2013–2017 (monthly series), we may notice (Table 1) a correlation matrix with somehow expected results.

We may, therefore, notice that the CDS display strong, positive correlations with the foreign direct investments, with the number of employees in the economy, with the long-term external debt, with the interest rates applied by the credit institutions for loans to the non-financial societies and to households for operations in lei (balance, % annual percentages) and, of course, with the ratings from the main international rating agencies, among which Moody's and S&P. Thus, to develop the regression equation for CDS determinants, we considered only the indicators with a rather strong correlation [0.75; 1]. The simplified regression equation is:

CDS = f (FDI, NE, LTED, IRACI, SR-Moody's, SR-S&P) (Table 2)

Analysing the value of the coefficient of determination (R2), used to measure the strength of the correlation between the endogenous variable and its determinants, one can notice that the value of 0.942 is very good. The adjusted R2 is 0.935 for the sample of 60 observations, which suggests a very strong correlation between the variables of the model. Table 2 shows that, although most coefficients are different from zero, their associated probability, the p-value, is much over 0.05; only NE and SR-S&P, have the p-value 0.004 and 0.000, respectively, which confirms that only they are significant within the total statistical population, and that only for these indicators, the null H0 hypothesis is rejected. Thus, for these indicators, the pattern has been correctly specified, identified and evaluated; therefore, we may consider that the influence on the dependent variable (CDS) comes only from these two factors.

At the same time, in order to analyse the relation between the macroeconomic variables and the CDS, we also used regression equations, keeping only the indicators with a rather strong correlation, within the [0.75; 1] interval. Thus, the regression below regards the level of determination of the long-term external debt by the CDS and by the number of employees in the economy. The simplified formula is: LTED = f (CDS, NE) (Table 3)

If we analyse the relation between the long-term external debt and the indicators mentioned above, one can see that for both indicators, the p-value is much below 0.05, which confirms that both indicators are significant within the total statistical population and that the null H0 hypothesis is rejected, the model being properly specified, identified and evaluated.

In order to capture the relation between the average interest rate used by the credit institutions for loans and the evolution of the CDS, of the number of

Table 1: Correlation matrix between the CDS, implicitly sovereign risk rates and the main macroeconomic indicators of Romania

	CDS	IP	CAB	FDI	NE	HICP	ER	LTED	LTFDS	BCGG	IRACI	SR-Moody's	RR-S&P	RR-Fitch
CDS	1													
IP	0.24	1												
CAB	0.54	-0.16	1											
FDI	0.75	0.22	0.70	1										
NE	-0.84	-0.06	-0.73	-0.70	1									
HICP	-0.06	0.33	-0.40	-0.10	0.14	1								
ER	-0.57	0.16	-0.74	-0.49	0.77	0.35	1							
LTED	0.88	0.25	0.56	0.67	-0.91	0.11	-0.63	1						
LTFDS	-0.01	-0.04	-0.30	-0.22	-0.10	-0.06	-0.09	-0.02	1					
BCGG	-0.17	-0.35	0.54	0.03	-0.06	-0.39	-0.35	-0.11	-0.34	1				
IRACI	0.95	0.25	0.55	0.73	-0.89	0.09	-0.65	0.94	-0.03	-0.14	1			
SR-Moody's	0.90	0.24	0.59	0.73	-0.92	0.04	-0.64	0.88	0.11	-0.05	0.92	1		
SR-S&P	0.92	0.34	0.38	0.76	-0.67	0.10	-0.43	0.77	-0.08	-0.29	0.89	0.81	1	
SR-Fitch	-0.60	0.19	-0.74	-0.52	0.83	0.47	0.70	-0.61	-0.10	-0.31	-0.60	-0.67	-0.37	1

Source: Authors' processing, NBR data, Financial Stability Reports and monthly bulletins No.1 for the period 2013–2017. For December 2017, data are from Asset Macro (https://www.assetmacro.com). Abbreviations: CDS – credit default swap; IP - industrial production (annual percentage change); CAB - current account balance (mil. EUR); FDI - foreign direct investment (mil. EUR); NE - number of employees in the economy (thousands people); HICP – IAPC (%); ER - Average exchange rate of the EUR / RON; LTED - Long-term external debt (mil. EUR); LTFDS - Long-term foreign debt service (mil.EUR); BCGG - Balance of the consolidated general government (mil RON), IRACI - Interest rate applied by credit institutions for loans, (percent per year); SR-Moody's - sovereign risk from Moody's for Romania; SR-S&P - sovereign risk from S&P for Romania; SR-Fitch - sovereign risk from SR-Fitch for Romania. Colour notations: white - correlations of and over 0.75, very light grey - correlations that can fall within the range [0.50–0.75), grey - correlations with values between [0.25.0.50), very dark grey - correlations below threshold 0.25.

Table 2: Result of the regression equation regarding the relation between the CDS and the foreign direct investment (mil. EUR), Number of employees in the economy (thousands people), Long-term external debt (mil. EUR), Interest rate applied by credit institutions for loans (%a.p.) and ratings from Moody's and S&P

Regression Statistics								
Multiple R	0.970							
R Square	0.942							
Adjusted R Square	0.935							
Standard Error	9.268							
Observations	60							
ANOVA								
	df	*SS*	*MS*	*F*	*Significance F*			
Regression	6	73704.089	12284	143.00831	6.434E-31			
Residual	53	4552.5519	85.8972					
Total	59	78256.641						
	Coefficients	*Standard Error*	*t Stat*	*P-value*	*Lower 95 %*	*Upper 95 %*	*Lower 95.0 %*	*Upper 95.0 %*
Intercept	-199.665	212.655	-0.939	0.352	-626.197	226.867	-626.197	226.867
FDI	-0.001	0.001	-0.743	0.461	-0.003	0.002	-0.003	0.002
NE	-0.075	0.025	-2.971	0.004	-0.125	-0.024	-0.125	-0.024
LTED	0.000	0.001	0.144	0.886	-0.002	0.002	-0.002	0.002
IRACI	2.257	3.449	0.654	0.516	-4.662	9.176	-4.662	9.176
SR-Moody's	-2.801	10.198	-0.275	0.785	-23.255	17.654	-23.255	17.654
SR-S&P	55.972	10.103	5.540	0.000	35.708	76.237	35.708	76.237

Source: authors processing based on NBR's dates and publications. The notations of Table 1 are maintained.

employees and of the long-term external debt, we use the following simplified equation: IRACI = f(CDS, NE,LTED) (Table 4). Analysing the value of the coefficient of determination and of the adjusted coefficient of determination, one can notice that the values of 0.950 and 0.948, respectively, are very good for the sample with 60 observations, which suggests a very strong correlation between the model variable.

Regarding the relation between the average interest rate used by the credit institutions and the CDS, the number of employees and the long-term external debt, one can see that only for the CDS and the long-term external debt, the p-value is much below 0.05, which confirms that these two indicators are significant for the

Table 3: Result of the regression equation regarding the relation between the long-term external debt (mil. EUR) and CDS and the number of employees in the economy (thousands people)

Regression Statistics								
Multiple R	0.930310637							
R Square	0.865477882							
Adjusted R Square	0.860757807							
Standard Error	1617.169597							
Observations	60							
ANOVA								
	df	*SS*	*MS*	*F*	*Significance F*			
Regression	2	959065498.6	479532749	183.36107	1.481E-25			
Residual	57	149068537.9	2615237.5					
Total	59	1108134036						
	Coefficients	*Standard Error*	*t Stat*	*P-value*	*Lower 95 %*	*Upper 95 %*	*Lower 95.0 %*	*Upper 95.0 %*
Intercept	130038.972	11186.136	11.625	0.000	107639.122	152438.822	107639.122	152438.822
CDS	46.637	10.783	4.325	0.000	25.045	68.230	25.045	68.230
NE	-13.735	2.163	-6.350	0.000	-18.066	-9.404	-18.066	-9.404

Source: authors processing based on NBR's data and publications. The notations of Table 1 are maintained.

Table 4: Result of the regression equation regarding the relation between the interest rate applied by credit institutions for loans (%a.p.) and CDS, the number of employees in the economy (thousands people) and the long-term external debt (mil. EUR)

Regression Statistics								
Multiple R	0.975							
R Square	0.950							
Adjusted R Square	0.948							
Standard Error	0.444							
Observations	60							
ANOVA								
	df	*SS*	*MS*	*F*	*Significance F*			
Regression	3	210.452	70.151	356.174	1.964E-36			
Residual	56	11.030	0.197					
Total	59	221.482						
	Coefficients	*Standard Error*	*t Stat*	*P-value*	*Lower 95 %*	*Upper 95 %*	*Lower 95.0 %*	*Upper 95.0 %*
Intercept	-9.423	5.636	-1.672	0.100	-20.714	1.868	-20.714	1.868
CDS	0.027	0.003	7.973	0.000	0.020	0.034	0.020	0.034
NE	0.000	0.001	-0.559	0.578	-0.002	0.001	-0.002	0.001
LTED	0.000	0.000	5.619	0.000	0.000	0.000	0.000	0.000

Source: authors processing based on NBR's data and publications. The notations of Table 1 are maintained.

total statistical population and that the null H0 hypothesis is rejected, the model being properly specified, identified and evaluated.

If we study the determination of the sovereign ratings in relation with the evolution of CDS ratings and with the main macroeconomic indicators, we can see that for a simplified equation, such as SR-Moody's= f (CDS, NE, LTED, IRACI), although the coefficient of determination is 0.906, while the adjusted coefficient of determination is 0.899, the p-value is much below 0.05 only for NE and IRACI, which confirms that these two indicators are significant within the total statistical population and that the null H0 hypothesis is rejected.

Using the correlation matrix to analyse the relation between the S&P ratings and several macroeconomic indicators, we employ the following simplified formula: SR-S&P= f (CDS, FDI, LTED, IRACI, SR -Moody's), shown in Table 5.

Table 5: Result of the regression equation regarding the relation between S&P rating and CDS, the foreign direct investment (mil. EUR), the long-term external debt (mil. EUR) and the interest rate applied by credit institutions for loans (%a.p.)

Regression Statistics	
Multiple R	0.946
R Square	0.895
Adjusted R Square	0.885
Standard Error	0.134
Observations	60

ANOVA

	df	*SS*	*MS*	*F*	*Significance F*
Regression	5	8.264	1.653	92.093	3.5592E-25
Residual	54	0.969	0.018		
Total	59	9.233			

	Coefficients	*Standard Error*	*t Stat*	*P-value*	*Lower 95 %*	*Upper 95 %*	*Lower 95.0 %*	*Upper 95.0 %*
Intercept	15.777	1.373	11.493	0.000	13.025	18.529	13.025	18.529
CDS	0.007	0.002	4.389	0.000	0.004	0.010	0.004	0.010
FDI	0.000	0.000	2.172	0.034	0.000	0.000	0.000	0.000
LTED	0.000	0.000	-3.787	0.000	0.000	0.000	0.000	0.000
IRACI	0.171	0.043	4.014	0.000	0.085	0.256	0.085	0.256
SR-Moody's	-0.194	0.118	-1.638	0.107	-0.431	0.043	-0.431	0.043

Source: authors processing based on NBR's data and publications. The notations of Table 1 are maintained.

The analysis shows that R2 and adjusted R2 are rather good for the sample with 60 observations, which suggests a strong correlation between the model variables; the p-values are below 0.05 for all selected indicators, except for Moody's rating, which confirms that these indicators are significant for the total statistical population and that the null H0 hypothesis is rejected, the model being properly specified, identified and evaluated.

Conclusions

The paper aims to show that the CDS, on the one hand, is a valuable instrument to evaluate the sovereign risk premium, affecting the financing costs of Romania, while on the other hand, it can send serious signals on the evolution of the main macroeconomic indicators. The econometric analyses using monthly data from the 2013–2017 for Romania, show clearly the informational power of the CDS for the evolution of the main macroeconomic indicators, confirming and supporting, at the same time, the hypothesis that the sovereign ratings are very strongly related to CDS evolution, and vice versa.

The provision of political and economic stability can bring direct and indirect benefits to the evolution of the main macroeconomic indicators, implicitly reflecting positively on the evolution of CDS rating for the sovereign debt instruments of Romania, implicitly on the country risk.

The financial stability can be affected on the background of a higher and faster volatility of the exchange rate and of the prices in the economy, which can bear adverse effects on the evolution of the sovereign debt market, affecting the country risk and CDS ratings. However, our analysis with the specified model show a rather weak relation between the CDS and the industrial production (annual percent modification), and even negative relation regarding the inflation. The paper, showing a case study on Romania, reveals that CDS ratings can corroborate the multitude of information flows of the main macroeconomic indicators and can also send then back, afterwards.

References

Ashcraft, A.B./Santos, J.A.: Has the CDS market lowered the cost of corporate debt?. J. Monet. Econ. 56:514–23, 2009.

Augustin, P./Subrahmanyam, M.G./Tang, D.Y./Wang, S.Q.: Credit Default Swaps: Past, Present, and Future, Annu. Rev. Financ. Econ. 2016. 8:10.1–10.22, The Annual Review of Financial Economics is online at financial.annualreviews.org, 2016.

Eurostat: Manual on Government Deficit and Debt. Implementation of ESA 2010, 2016 edition. Publications Office of the European Union, Luxembourg, 2016.

Fostel, A./Geanakoplos, J.: Financial innovation, collateral and investment Discuss. Pap. 1903R, Cowles Found. Res. Econ, Yale Univ, 2015.

Greenspan, A.: Economic flexibility. Remarks at Her Majesty's Treasury Enterprise Conference, Jan. 26, London, 2004.

Heinz, Frigyes Ferdinand/Sun, Yan: Sovereign CDS Spreads in Europe - The Role of Global Risk Aversion, Economic Fundamentals, Liquidity, and Spillovers. IMF Working Paper WP/14/17, European Department, January, 2014.

Ismailescu, Iuliana/Phillips, Blake: Saviour or Sinner? Credit Default Swaps and the Market for Sovereign Debt. This draft: August 4, 2011. Online at:http://www.uis.no/getfile.php/1346846/Konferanser/paper_IulianaIsmailescu.pdf.

Massa, M./Zhang, L.: CDS and liquidity provision in the bond market. Work. Pap., INSEAD, Paris. 2012.

Nashikkar, A./Subrahmanyam, MG./Mahanti, S.: Liquidity and arbitrage in the market for credit risk. J. Financ. Quant. Anal. 46:627–56, 2011.

Portes, R.: Ban naked CDS. Eurointelligence, March, 2010.

Stulz, RM.: Credit default swaps and the credit crisis. J. Econ. Perspect. 24:73–92, 2010.

Subrahmanyam M.G./Tang D.Y./Wang S.Q.: Does the tail wag the dog? The effect of credit default swaps on credit risk. Rev. Financ. Stud. 27:2927–60, 2014.

World Economic and Financial Surveys: Global Financial Stability Report Old Risks, New Challenges. International Monetary Fund, April, 2013.

*** Buletin lunare no.1, National Bank of Romania (BNR), 2013–2017, Rapoarte de stabilitate financiară, 2013–2017.

*** Riscul de ţară: aspecte teoretice şi abordări metodologice comparate, Editura Lucretius, 1998.

*** Moody's Sovereign Rating: A Ratings Guide, Moody's Investors Service, Global Credit Research, March 1999.

Elena Otilia MANTA[1]

[1] PhD, Centre for Financial and Monetary Research "Victor Slăvescu", Romanian Academy, Email: otilia.manta@icfm.ro

Challenges and Changes in the Microfinancing Policy in Romania

Abstract *Financial policy, including microfinance policy in the current context of each EU and world state, primarily targets national objectives in line with the community directives and international financial policy. Since each state is an integrated part of a family (as is Romania's EU), no country is isolated, but has more or less extensive economic relations with the rest of the world, which leads us to affirm that microfinance policy it needs to take global targets into account, being the biggest challenge in developing sustainable finance.This is also due to the fact that Romania benefited from EU funds received from the EU budget in the period 2007–2017, amounting to approximately 45.7 billion euros, representing an average of 2.8 % of GDP annually with a direct impact on the financing policy, including microfinance. Of this amount, € 37.1 billion were funds from the EU budget related to the 2007–2013 multiannual financial framework, the remaining € 8.6 billion being received under the current multiannual financial framework, i.e. 2014–2020. EU funding programs for microfinance represent the great challenge of the development of this sector, so vital to the sustainability of the rural environment. Microfinance is an instrument in the sustainable development of the rural environment.*

Keywords: *finance, microfinance, rural sustainable development*

Introduction

The approach of the research paper is based on personal professional experience in the economic financial field (we have experienced the phenomenon of microfinance with an effective and direct involvement in the process of financing the small rural entrepreneurs in Romania), but also based on extensive documentation from other microfinance models in UE and India.

At the scientific level, there was a wealth of theoretical and empirical literature that investigated the consequences of changes in access to the financial intermediation and loans to households and small businesses in rural areas, whose loans have seen many challenges throughout history in terms of structure and size, and with a direct impact. However, there is a growing recognition that access to credit can be possible without the negative impact of those in need of funding and without affecting households through general equilibrium effects, such as: changes in the "price" factor resulting from large-scale changes in access to credit. Over the course of history two important channels have arisen in connection with the reduction of the volume of credit markets and the negative results of the labor market:

- First of all, the investment and financing channel / financing network: firms in need of financing can reduce demand for labor in response to a negative impact of the credit offer policy, leading to a decrease in wages and employment workforce.
- Secondly, aggregate demand for credit: consumers can lower demand for goods and services when they face more difficult borrowing restrictions. The decline in aggregate demand may lead to a fall in demand for labor, exerting downward pressure on wages and employment, especially in the non-commercial sector.

Both channels seem to have worked the US financial crisis, was mentioned in the paper (Chodorow-Reich, 2014; Mian, Sufi, 2014). In this paper, we are trying to measure the impact of the balance between the volumes of microcredits in Romania based on the historical results corroborated with the current situation and to draw some conclusions on the current situation as well as proposals on microcrediting at national level. While global loans are usually very low (about $ 200 each at market exchange rates), the impact of micro-credit is a major one especially in social policy to create new jobs, micro-credit playing an important role in sustainability economic, social and environmental factors. On the one hand, microfinance serves as a means of financing investments in rural microenterprises and small entrepreneurs (Banerjee et al, 2018, 2017) and, on the other hand, allows households to accelerate consumption, especially the purchase of consumer goods (Devoto et al, 2012; Tarozzi et al, 2014; Ben-Yishay et al, 2017). Thus, both the investment-financing channel and the aggregate microfinance demand can in principle be an instrument of economic equilibrium.

The theoretical work examining the role of microcredit in developing countries has largely focused on the investment and financing channel (Banerjee, Newman 1993; Evans, Jovanovic 1989; Aghion, Bolton, 1997). Especially in connection with our approach is Buera et al (2017), which theoretically explores the overall balance of microfinance for labor through the investment-finance channel. Thus, the evaluation of the microfinance phenomenon was carried out by testing the impact on the creation, expansion, employment, profitability and survival of a micro-firm by accessing microcredit - in a partial balance - little evidence being found that the average microfinance leads to growth of transformation businesses.

Literature review and Methodology of scientific research

In order to underpin the research methodology, the classical observation and examination instruments, research methods based on the basic principles of scientific research, namely: "competence, objectivity, truth, methodical, demonstration, correlation, evaluation of results, utility and psychomoral" (Ristea, Franc, 2013). It will use procedures based on factual analysis, intensive documentation at the level of domestic and international literature, using the databases and the scientific material existing in the endowment of the libraries of specific institutes in Romania and internationally.

The methodology of the paper has as direct instruments the collection of data and information from the literature and from the existing practice in public and private institutions, but especially scientific articles published on specialized research networks (Research Gate, Academia.edu, etc.), articles published in different journals, relevant books in the field of reference, legislation, analyzes and studies, official documents of various tax bodies, tax documents and interactive database of the National Bank of Romania, other relevant sources identified at the libraries: CCFM, Romanian Academy, INCE, IEN, BNR, National Library, INS, etc. Moreover, we analyzed the documents using the comparative, analytical, descriptive method, the nonparticipative and participatory observation, the use of a set of information sources, the collection of financial data in the established databases. Also, the paper will be based on annual reports, publications, consolidated statistical data provided by the National Bank of Romania, the European Central Bank (ECB), the International Settlement Bank (BRI), the European Commission, OECD, published annually, data to be processed in order to be able to provide a general and analytical picture of the most important changes taking place in the European Union as a whole, but also globally - considered to be representative of the understanding of the phenomena studied, and especially in Romania.

The information support of the research was provided by the monographs, books, scientific papers, materials of the scientific conferences, the balance sheets of SMEs during 2008–2017, as well as other materials, which are presented in the scientific papers and publications on the official pages of national and international research institutes, international financial institutions (research centers), etc.

Documentation on the basis of the existing works in the study services of the National Bank of Romania in the period 1918–1962, works in the library of the Romanian Academy, my paper "Microfinance. Concepts and Application in Rural Environment", Harvard University Microfinance Studies, and last but not least, European Microfinance Network (Brussels). The preparation of the documentation framework starts from the successful model in India, being one of the reference books in the literature. On October 28, 2010, the Wall Street Journal held the title "Major India's crisis in micro-loan: Loans involving small amounts of money were a good idea, but the explosion of interests back." Several papers, such as Khwaja and Mian (2008), have shown that in various situations, the bank's negative liquidity shocks are often passed on to borrowers by reducing lending. See also Paravisini (2008), Khwaja and Mian (2008) and Schnabl (2012). Other related documents include Chodorow-Reich (2014), Jiménez et al. (2014) and Greenstone et al. (2014), Imbert and Papp (2015), Muralidharan et al. (2017), Jayachandran

(2006), Mobarak and Rosenzweig (2014), Akram et al. (2017). (SHG). On November 4, 2010, Harvard Business Review published an article entitled "The microfinance crisis in India is a battle to monopolize the poor."

Results and discussions

Despite the recognition that microfinance also allows households to reduce consumption over time, there has been little knowledge of how microfinance affects the real economy through the aggregate demand channel, in line with the model mentioned in this paper.

In the romanian rural area (but also in the rural environment at the global level) the model includes two sectors of the rural economy, namely the agricultural sector for marketing and non-agricultural non-agricultural sector, and direct action on the labor force, both highly qualified and low on the local labor market. Rural households also consume cash from non-tradable goods (earnings plus credit). It is important that the product market for non-tradable goods is limited to local demand.

In the simplest version of this framework, the households borrow only is to meet the current needs, respectively for the consumption of goods and services strictly necessary. A contraction in credit supply will reduce the cash available to households, thus lowering their total consumption demand. This triggers a decline in demand for non-tradable non-agricultural crops and a further fall in demand for labor in the non-commercial sector, which puts pressure on wages, or on their decline.

Because the aggregate demand channel is, by definition, a balancing phenomenon, the empirical approach to its importance is a first challenge. In order to balance the effects of microfinance on the labor markets, a shock is needed for access to microfinance, which is exogenous, large-scale, and which takes place at the level of the entire labor market.

In order to reflect the microfinance phenomenon at national level, we start from the following indicators:

1. Evolution of the Banking Income of Population in the Period 2007–2015

   Indicator: Population Income Banking Ratio (Rbv)
   The calculation formula is as follows:

$$Rbv = \frac{CRP + DEP}{VDB} \times 100$$

Where: CRP = Population Loans; DEP = Population Deposits; VDB = Gross disposable income of the population: the balance of the income account and measures the part of the created value of the population for final consumption and gross economy (from which the financial savings are made).

Determination of indicator for the analyzed period:

Table 1: Evolution of the banking income of the population in the period 2007–2015

	2007	2008	2009	2010	2011	2012	2013	2014	2015
CRPs mill.lei	80,460	113,589	116,452	120,195	121,578	122,628	122,130	120,513	107,953
DEPs mill.lei	64,990	80,518	94,930	105,388	113,068	123,595	132,287	139,559	146,780
CRP+DEP mill.lei	145,450	194,107	211,382	225,583	234,646	246,223	254,417	260,072	254,733
VDB mill.lei	411,816	543,839	539,190	562,635	604,013	638,427	665,880	663,392	659,595
Rbv %	35.3192	35.6920	39.2036	40.0940	38.8478	38.5671	38.2076	39.2034	38.6196

Source: author based on the National Bank of Romania's databases (from the National Financial Accounts 2007–2014 and the monthly bulletins from 2008 to 2015) and the National Institute of Statistics (Statistical Yearbook of Romania, editions 2011–2014, Monthly Statistical Bulletin December, 2010–2015, Financial State of Romania, CCFM - 2016 edition.

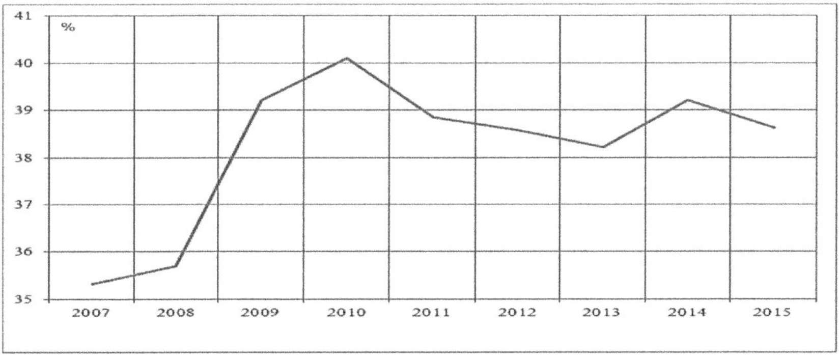

Figure 1: Evolution of the household income banking rate (%)

Source: author based on the National Bank of Romania databases (from the National Financial Accounts 2007–2014 and the monthly bulletins from 2008 to 2015) and the National Institute of Statistics (Statistical Yearbook of Romania, editions 2011–2014, Monthly Statistical Bulletin December, 2010–2014), Romania's Financial Condition, CCFM - 2016 edition

The evolution of this indicator, determined as a ratio of a stock variable to a flow, highlights the increase in the population's involvement in bank flows, banking of population incomes, reflecting the increase in the banking system's potential to influence the available income of the population.

The two components of bank flows to and from the population, loans and deposits increased in value during the period, while the increase in loans (by 34.17 % higher in 2015 compared to 2007) was lower than that of deposits 125.85 % higher in 2015 compared to 2007), so that if the loan / deposit ratio was 1.24 in

2007, it was 0.73 in 2014, which means that the population tends to or an absolute indebtedness to the banking system.

2. Economic and financial results in the real economy in rural areas

Using the economic, financial, informational and human potential has led to a series of economic and financial results, of which we have selected as significant: turnover, operating income, total income, operating profit / loss, total profit / loss, debts.

Indicator: Turnover (CA)

Most often, the size of total turnover is determined by summing the earnings from the core business (VB) with the income from other activities (VA):

The calculation formula is as follows:

$$CA = VB + VA$$

Where: VB-reflects the turnover of the enterprise's core business and refers to the sale of products resulting from the core business of the enterprise; VA - reflects industrial or non-industrial turnover.

Fiscal value - one of the most important results of business activity, which cannot be missing from economic analyzes, is turnover. In the period 2007–2015 in the real economy, there were significant increases in average unit turnover (an increase of 57.44 % as at 31 December 2015 as compared to 31 December 2007). Synthetically, on December 31, 2015, as well as between 2007 and 2015, real economy firms, divided by total economy and agriculture, recorded on average the average turnover according to the data in the following table.

In the branch "Agriculture, forestry and fishing", due to the size of the structure of the SMEs and micro-enterprises, respectively the total value of the economic potential, as well as the demand for the products of this branch, the average turnover per unit has the levels of the SMEs in 2015, about 262.79 times higher than

Table 2: Evolution of the level of turnover achieved by SMEs and micro-enterprises active in agriculture in 2007–2015 (%, 2007 = 100)

	Period							
	2008	**2009**	**2010**	**2011**	**2012**	**2013**	**2014**	**2015**
Total real economy	122.42	109.49	118.59	137.14	141.97	141.82	146.68	157.15
Total agriculture, forestry and fishing, of which:	133.13	134.57	149.83	206.17	226.87	222.21	243.90	238.14
-SMEs	133.23	126.93	147.09	196.69	220.49	232.07	235.38	262.79
-Microenterprises	114.33	132.83	160.72	218.89	239.04	242.04	269.55	278.09

Source: author based on data provided by the Ministry of Public Finance (annual financial statements of active companies in the real economy of Romania).

the value registered in 2007, and the micro enterprises registered an increase of approximately 278.09 % compared to the reporting year. It should also be noted that the turnover in primary branches such as agriculture is a very important cost element for firms in other branches and ultimately determines the performance of the entire real economy.

From a territorial point of view, there is an obvious asymmetry, the companies in the development region Bucharest - Ilfov have, on average, the highest turnover (more than 1.44 times the country average), while the region South-West development is the smallest (the ratio between these two regions was 2.50 times on December 31, 2015). The highest dynamics were registered in the North-East Development Region, where, between 2007 and 2015, the company increased its average turnover by 39.03 %.

Operating profit /loss

A significant indicator of the quality of utilization of the production potential is the profit / loss from exploitation. As profit-making and loss-making companies are analyzed at national level, the average profit, average loss, and algebraic sums can be used in the analysis. We preferred to reflect the evolutions of both the average profit on the trading company and the average loss on the trading company.

Indicator: Operating profit

The calculation formula is as follows: OP = SP – CP, where: OP – Operating Profit or Gain: If the selling price is more than the cost price, the difference between

Table 3: Evolution of turnover achieved by active SMEs of agriculture, grouped by development regions, between 2007 and 2015 (%, 2007 = 100)

	Period							
	2008	**2009**	**2010**	**2011**	**2012**	**2013**	**2014**	**2015**
Total SMEs in agriculture, forestry and fisheries, of which:	133.13	134.57	149.83	206.17	226.87	222.21	243.90	238.14
North – West	129.55	141.02	158.42	195.38	236.36	245.59	45.32	303.42
North – East	129.90	158.54	186.84	232.51	275.97	310.37	337.24	332.74
South – West	54.44	99.79	84.19	106.75	128.44	139.43	196.76	137.85
South – East	124.26	128.57	182.00	262.59	280.71	240.90	103.33	275.02
South	150.41	156.09	206.88	304.37	293.97	336.27	429.56	346.57
Centre	115.00	132.97	151.81	180.17	205.20	200.46	528.57	258.72
West	126.46	150.50	185.27	249.98	290.39	253.24	205.22	305.55
Bucharest – Ilfov	90.06	103.46	128.82	204.42	184.99	237.83	428.77	344.97

Source: author based on data provided by the Ministry of Public Finance (annual financial statements of active companies in the real economy of Romania)

them is the profit incurred; SP - Selling price: This is the price at which an article is sold; CP - Cost price: This is the price at which an article is purchased.

If the selling price is less than the cost price, the difference between them is the loss incurred.

Indicator: Operating Loss

The calculation formula is as follows: OL = CP – SP, where: OL – Operating Loss; Profit or Loss is always calculated on the cost price; CP - Cost price: This is the price at which an article is purchased; SP - Selling price: This is the price at which an article is sold.

Marked price: This is the price marked as the selling price on an article, also known as the listed price.

Discount or Rebate: This is the reduction in price offered on the marked or listed price.

Indicator: Gross Profit

The calculation formula is as follows: GP = NS – CGS, where: GP - Gross Profit; NS – Net Sales; CGS - Cost of Goods and Services

Net operating profit

Between 2007 and 2015, due to developments in average operating expenses and net operating income, significant changes in net operating profit were recorded in the agricultural sector (a decrease of 5.04 % in 2009, but also a an increase of 33.75 % in 2014 as compared to 31 December 2007). In 2015, firms recorded on average an operating net profit of 32.20 % higher than the 2007 level. Synthetically, on 31 December 2015, as well as in 2007–2015, the net profit on the company in agriculture, distributed to SMEs and microenterprises is presented in table.

Indicator: Net operating profit. The calculation formula is as follows:

NP = GP – (TOE + I + TX + A + D), were: NP - Net Profit/Net Income; GP - Gross Profit; TOE - Total Operating Expenses; I – Interest; T – Taxes; A – Amortization; D – Depreciation.

Table 4: Evolution of net profit achieved by SMEs and microenterprises active in agriculture between 2007 and 2015 (%, 2007 = 100)

	Period							
	2008	**2009**	**2010**	**2011**	**2012**	**2013**	**2014**	**2015**
Total real economy	93.80	101.79	109.13	83.56	96.13	107.53	117.75	134.92
Total agriculture, forestry and fishing, of which:	118.47	94.96	133.61	248.77	245.35	235.91	296.26	310.47
-SMEs	125.11	99.23	149.97	277.51	246.70	247.73	305.66	342.64
-Microenterprises	113.70	92.34	121.95	247.24	217.68	234.26	316.87	311.87

Source: author based on data provided by the Ministry of Public Finance (annual financial statements of active companies in the real economy of Romania)

From the territorial point of view, and in the case of the net operating profit there is an obvious asymmetry, the companies from the Southeast development region record the highest values of this indicator (over 393.59 %), while the companies from the development region Bucharest- Ilfov has the lowest values (the ratio between these two values was 1.66 times on December 31, 2015). The largest dynamics were recorded in the South Development Region, where, over the period 2007–2015, firms increased on average their operating profit by more than 3 times. It should be noted, however, that the companies in the Bucharest - Ilfov region registered the gains lower in this period, namely only 2.36 %. However, in 2015, on average, all firms in the development regions recorded a higher operating profit compared to 2007.

In view of the above mentioned results, we identify the causal impact of microfinance by using the variation in the balance sheet, each borrower's exposure to loans in the affected region, before the crisis, interacted with the pre-crisis variation in the geographical footprint of each external creditor. We use this differentiated analysis method on the microfinance market as a source of quasi-exogenous variation to study the effects of credit supply cuts in consumption, entrepreneurship, wages and our empirical strategy that only takes into account the regions have not been directly affected by the crisis and where people have not lost their obligation to pay the loans. This natural experiment is a unique opportunity to

Table 5: The evolution of the net profit level achieved by the active SMEs of agriculture, grouped by development regions, between 2007 and 2015 (%, 2007 = 100)

	Period							
	2008	**2009**	**2010**	**2011**	**2012**	**2013**	**2014**	**2015**
Total SMEs in agriculture, forestry and fisheries, of which:	118.47	94.96	133.61	248.77	245.35	235.91	296.26	310.47
North – West	93.87	93.93	93.62	166.98	204.65	158.06	0.41	291.87
North – East	93.14	99.35	118.19	192.22	197.87	212.83	231.48	249.51
South – West	104.56	95.20	183.01	257.96	299.74	273.18	388.89	369.88
South – East	145.61	101.00	134.73	323.44	235.16	304.56	111.66	393.59
South	136.81	92.27	157.87	368.91	254.39	271.77	472.80	350.17
Centre	70.78	86.47	90.67	141.48	114.14	153.50	512.75	256.62
West	81.40	89.37	101.66	213.35	238.41	218.00	147.40	260.79
Bucharest - Ilfov	149.85	71.70	74.13	159.58	158.84	198.50	448.75	236.88

Source: author based on data provided by the Ministry of Public Finance (annual financial statements of active companies in the real economy of Romania)

study large, exogenous, labor-market shocks to microfinance credit supply in a place where there were no shocks of competing demand.

The impact of this reduction in microcredits was large enough to affect the labor market.

The growth process of "lending to the real economy is an indispensable condition for relaunching the investment process and ensuring the Romanian economy re-enters a new growth cycle. Also, the need to boost lending is also based on the fact that one of the main difficulties for SMEs is difficult access to finance. Thus, in 2013, 91.52 % of SMEs were self-financing, 22.43 % obtained bank credits, and 2.36 % of enterprises leased out" (Nicolescu O, 2015) and the correlation of this with the increase in the number of jobs in each region.

The aforementioned data reflect the current situation of small enterprises in the Romanian rural area, but returning to the topic of our research, i.e. the link between the microcredit offer correlated with the salary incomes of the rural household, we make the following points: the decrease in the credit offer determines a decrease in salary incomes for the average rural household, moreover a possible financial exclusion. We also note that household experience has led to significant reductions in non-sustainable and sustainable consumption. Decreasing wages implies that implied non-borrowed workers can have wage and earning decreases when the local economy is affected by low credit access. While agricultural products are marketable and should not respond strongly to changes in local demand, non-agricultural enterprises are mainly involved in services, construction, or minor transactions, all of which are non-tradable and sensitive to changes in local demand.

Indeed, we find that wage response in agricultural sectors with high exposure is almost three times higher for non-farm wages than for agricultural wages, suggesting that aggregate demand for canals is an important part of the ramifications of the financial crisis in rural areas that still in certain regions both in the country and abroad exist.

We directly look at sectoral results for the tradable sector by studying the financial indicators of the agricultural sectors. On the one hand, businesses in the commercial sector that do not have a shock on credit demand will benefit from lower wage levels. But, on the other hand, some of these firms may be forced to drop salary again, as liquidity constraints are more closely linked to the crisis. Thus, the net impact on the production of the marketable agricultural sector is ambiguous. We find a precise "zero" effect for a yield index in the agricultural sectors with high values. This suggests that, as a whole, a balance and a correlation between any benefits and a reduction in wages are offset by a reduction in the size of production by constrained enterprises.

Then we take into account the implications of the credit transmission channels / microfinance network in contracting microcredit, aggregating them in the two sectors. In addition, we find that middle-income households, whose ability to accelerate consumption (or invest in a business) may be most dependent on microfinance, experience the largest drop in net sustainable consumption.

The fair effects of investment micro-credit on implicit effects on business profits, with implicit effects on business profits falling within the range of estimates in the literature. Moreover, we can say that the salary results are in line with our proposed microfinance model. A series of robustness tests to support our identification strategy, such as the Khwaja and Mian (2008) approach, to further support our assertion, the identification strategy captures a change in the microcredit supply and adapting it to needs, rather than demand. We also demonstrate that our results are robust for a number of alternative specifications.

The paper is directly related to an active debate on the role of microfinance as a tool for economic growth and poverty reduction. A recent wave of works uses specialized studies to measure the impact of the partial balance of microcredit spreads. Angelucci et al. (2015), Augsburg et al. (2015), Attanasio et al. (2015), Banerjee et al. (2015a), Crépon et al. (2015) and Tarozzi et al. (2015), all find similar results in a diverse set of countries and settings.

These papers present in the short and medium term a consistent picture of the most impactful microfinance models globally. It has generally been found that increased access to partial microfinance is linked to modest business creation and business expansion. Although there is evidence that borrowers buy more durable goods and business goods, there is almost no support for the major average impact on business profits or on non-sustainable consumption from one year to two years after the intervention. In a quasi-experimental study, Kaboski and Townsend (2012) find in response to short-term consumption the expansion of micro-credit from a village in Thailand, in line with many households using consumer loan income. Fink et al. (2017) shows that in Zambia, access to poor season credit is associated with rising consumption and wage levels in the village. In our case, we can say that this situation occurs in the interwar period, according to studies by Madgearu V. and Taşca Gh.

Our study differs from other specialized studies as the most important for microfinance is the magnitude and magnitude of shock in crisis / crisis. The financial crisis has made the credit in rural areas fall both in size and level per beneficiary. This paper is also based on the literature on macroeconomics and finance, the impact of credit supply shocks and the balance of firms in rural areas. Our work is also related to the recent work examining the overall balance, i.e. the effects of large-scale microfinance programs and the economic shocks in less developed countries where the microfinance phenomenon is present. Last but not least, we consider that the results of our research complement the specialized scientific literature, microfinance, although apparently in terms of financial flows seems to have modest effects, from a social point of view it has a major impact on the global level, being one of the most used financial instruments in the process of global social and financial inclusion (Manta O., 2017).

Framework of Microfinance Model

In this section we will present a simple and illustrative microfinance model structured on credit supply, aggregate demand and the labor market. First of all, we focus on the aggregate demand channel for several reasons. A first empirical evidence that microfinance has limited effects on business expansion for business. Another is to illustrate that the aggregate demand channel is capable of generating a number of testable predictions, for which we will find support in the data presented. Another aspect is given by the fact that some households have the opportunity to invest in a business, but the lack of assets / guarantees to do so, makes there another reason to borrow.

The model comprises two periods - today and the future - the desire to access microfinance combined with the prediction of revenue growth creates the appetite to bring consumption in a timely manner and therefore a demand for consumer credit. The economy comprises two sectors: tradable (mainly agricultural goods) and non-tradable (local goods and services).

Consumers and workers-households acquire utility from consumer goods from both sectors, tradable (T) and non-tradable (NT) through a Cobb-Douglas aggregator:

$$c_i = c_{T,i}^{a} \, c_{NT,i}^{1-a} \qquad (2.1.)$$

Consumers are risk neutral, but impatient, and discount period 2 consumption by *3* <1. Moreover, each household is endowed with deterministic non-labor income in each period, y_t. We assume this income is growing over time: y_2 > y\. This, along with ;*3* < 1, ensures a consumption smoothing motive for borrowing

All households are endowed with fixed amounts of two types of human capital: high- skilled (e.g., numeracy), and low-skilled (e.g., physical strength).[1] We assume for simplicity that households supply labor inelastically. The aggregate endowment of low-skilled human capital is N^e, and that of high-skilled human capital is N^h.

Micro-loans and the financial crisis

We model microfinance as a source of a fixed amount of credit. If the microfinance is available in a community, the non-bank financial undertaking will be willing to extend the repayment period of the B-loan to the R gross interest rate to all those who wish to borrow. Credits are paid during period 1 and reimbursed over the period[2]. Assuming that all micro loans have the same terms of payment fit to the fact that our non-banking financial institution standardizes their loan offer.

---

1 We refer to the two labor types as high- and low-skilled for simplicity, but the distinction could also capture horizontal differentiation, such as interpersonal skills vs. mechanical skills.

2 shows that increases in agricultural productivity in rural India increase the labor share of the non-agricultural sector.

We model the effects of the crisis, reducing the value of microcredit available in rural areas, so that households, which in the absence of the crisis could have borrowed more to bring consumption before, are now more constrained.

Firms and equilibrium is the following: in both the tradable and non-tradable labor markets, wage is set in each period by market clearing, so that labor supply equals labor demand for both high and low-skilled labor.

Labor markets are likely to be somewhat, but not completely, segmented (Emerick, 2017). Thus, we ally for imperfect segmentation across high- and low-skilled labor markets. We assume that the tradable (agricultural) sector employs only low-skilled labor, but the non-tradable (non-agricultural) sector employs both low- and high-skilled labor, which are combined through a constant elasticity of substitution aggregator. Production functions in each sector are:

$$y^{T} = A^{T} L^{T\,e} y \tag{2.2}$$

$$Y^{NT} = A^{NT} (L^{NT} y + d(L^{NTh})^{p\,p} \tag{2.3}$$

In equilibrium, the wage must be such that the non-tradable sector employs the full endowment of high-skilled labor, and the tradable and non-tradable sectors together employ the endowment of low-skilled labor. The tradable good price is normalized to 1 and the relative price of the non-tradable good is pinned down by supply and demand.

With partially segmented labor markets, it is not possible to obtain closed-form solutions for the high- and low-skilled wages.[3] The following result gives the signs and relative magnitudes of how high- and low-skilled period 1 wages respond to credit supply *B*.

Proposition: When high- and low-skilled labor are imperfect substitutes in the non-tradable sector, $df^{\sim B} h > dB^{jB} t > 0$.' dB w^{h} dB W

The proposal implies that the highly qualified balance of salary, wage 1 falls when B decreases due to the aggregate demand effect. Moreover, a reduction in aggregate demand also induces non-tradable firms to replace the now-cheaper, cheaper labor force, pushing lower wage levels with low skill levels in both sectors. There is a higher elasticity of highly qualified wages on loans than wages with low loan qualification. The proposal also implies that if the marginal product of the highly qualified workforce is higher than that of low-skilled workers, it will lead to a reduction in access to credit in rural areas and will also lead to lower wages of high qualification.

Empirical experiences

The Indian model taken as an example for the topic of our paper and can be compared to the Romanian microfinance model, provides some key predictions about

3 We consider the case of fully segmented labor markets, which has the advantage of producing closed form solutions.

the effects of exposure to the financial crisis. The model also foresees a decrease in total labor income for all households at t = 1. Consumption decreases, both in response to wage decline and in reducing credit consumption.

Investment channel. The above framework only allows microfinance to affect the balance by reducing consumption and, therefore, reducing aggregate demand during the crisis in the non-commercial sector. However, a wealth of theoretical literature analyzed the potential for credit towards poor households to count through the expansion and expansion channel (e.g. Banerjee and Newman 1993, Buera et al. 2017, Ahlin and Jiang (2008)). In practice, some businesses providing rural areas do not belong to urban shareholders, but to rural households that may face credit constraints.

Adding an investment channel within our framework would increase the magnitude of the predicted effects of low access to microfinance on marketable and non-commercial wages, earnings and consumption. If (some) enterprises are forced to fall back on employment or close their businesses because of the direct effects of the credit decline, this will cause labor demand to decline both in the tradable sectors and in the non-tradable, increasing the salary drop suddenly. Moreover, in an occupational scale model (Banerjee and Newman 1993), adding this channel suggests that the effects may be heterogeneous throughout the distribution of wealth. However, in order to be able to formulate some conclusions regarding microfinance in Romania, we present in some pictures the microfinance situation at European level according to the report "Microfinance in Europe: A Survey of EMN-MFC Members. 2014/2015 ".

Microloan providers use a variety of institutional models to operate in heterogeneous legal and regulatory frameworks: survey participants are primarily non-bank financial institutions (60 %) and NGOs (31 %) but also include other legal forms (i.e. commercial banks, cooperatives/credit unions, government body). The European microcredit sector, as depicted by the 149 surveyed MFIs, is diverse, relatively young and dynamic. The majority of respondents (77 %) initiated their micro lending activities after 1995. Approximately half of the sample started lending activities between 1995 and 2004 (EMN, 2017).

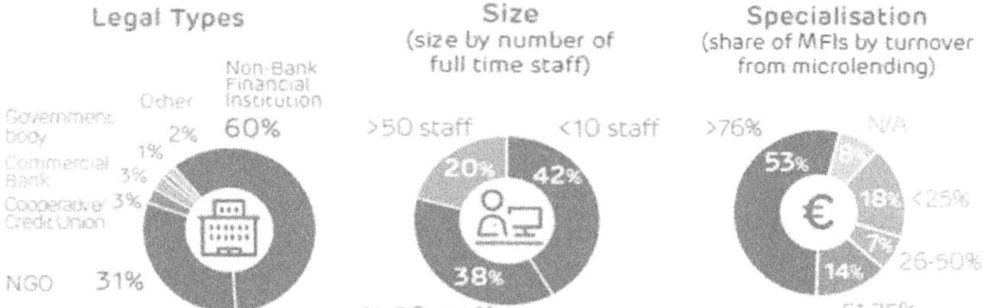

Figure 2: Institutional diversity

Source: author based on Microfinance in Europe: A Survey of EMN-MFC Members. 2014/2015.

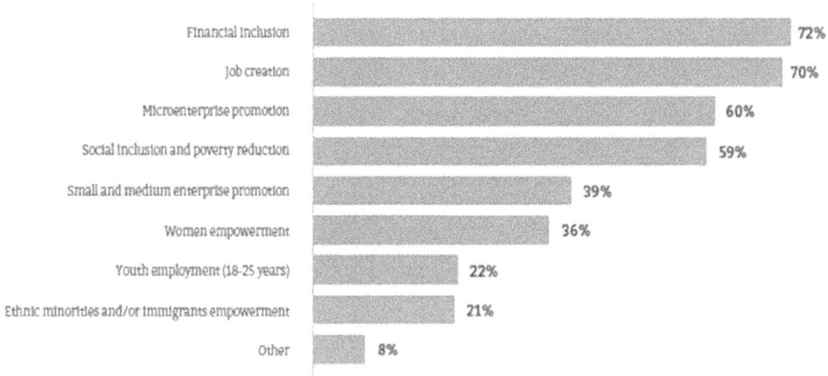

Figure 3: Mission of MFIs

Source: author based on Microfinance in Europe: A Survey of EMN-MFC Members. 2014/2015.

The vast majority of responding MFIs selected financial inclusion (72 %) and job creation (70 %) as their primary missions, followed by microenterprise promotion (60 %) and social inclusion and poverty reduction (59 %). A smaller share of respondents' mission statements (20 %) emphasize ethnic minorities and/or immigrant empowerment as well as youth employment (18–25 year) goals.

More than half of the surveyed MFIs are specialized in microlending activities, which contribute to more than 75 % of their overall turnover. The total number of paid staff reached 7,076 full-time equivalent employees in 2015, with a substantial share of women staff (56 %) and a significant presence of MFIs with less than 10 employees (42 %) (EMN, 2017).

In the period 2014–2015 both the total volume and the number of microloans disbursed showed a growing trend. In 2015, the MFIs surveyed disbursed a total of 552,834 loans (+12 % compared to 2014) with a total volume of almost EUR 1.6 billion (+16 %).

Overall in 2015, surveyed institutions served 747,265 active borrowers (+13 % compared to 2014), and the gross microloan portfolio outstanding reached EUR 2.5 billion (+15 %). The outstanding portfolio is predominantly allocated for business purposes (71 % of the total in 2015, 75 % in 2014). Nevertheless, the overall distribution is shifting towards personal loans (29 % of the total in 2015) due to the fastest grow of number and value of personal microloans disbursed compared to business microloans.

In 2015 the number of active borrowers supported by business microloans reached a total of 402,365. During the year the MFIs surveyed disbursed a total of 220,305 business microloans (+8 % compared to 2014) corresponding to a total lending volume of EUR 917 million (+6 %).

The survey shows also that a minimum of 207,983 enterprises were supported with business microloans in 2015 with informal businesses and self-employed

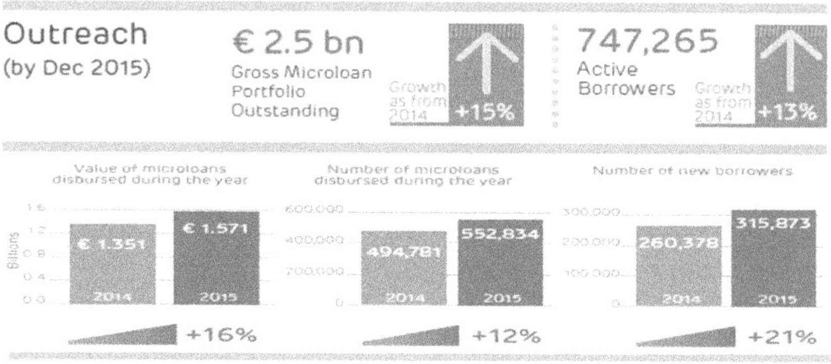

Figure 4: Recent trends in microlending activities
Source: author based on Microfinance in Europe: A Survey of EMN-MFC Members. 2014/2015.

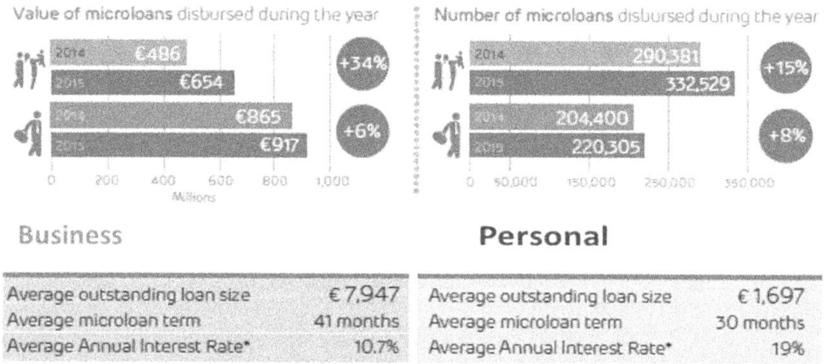

Figure 5: Recent trends in microlending activities: Business & Personal microloans
Source: author based on Microfinance in Europe: A Survey of EMN-MFC Members. 2014/2015

representing the main clients segment served. The reported number of enterprises supported by the MFI surveyed increased by 9 % from 2014 to 2015.

In terms of personal microloans, in 2015 MFIs surveyed disbursed a total of 332,529 microloans (+15 % compared to 2014) corresponding to a total volume of EUR 654 million (+34 %). During the same year, the number of active borrowers supported by personal microloans reached a total of 344,900 (EMN, 2017).

Business and personal loan products differ greatly with regards to their terms and conditions. In terms of average characteristics personal microloans are much smaller in size than business microloans (EUR 1,697 vs. EUR 7,947), are offered on shorter terms (30 months vs. 41 months) and are pricier (19 % interest rate vs. 10.7 %).

Overall, in terms of clients served with both business and personal microloans, surveyed MFIs show a partial commitment to the different target groups proposed in the Survey: rural or urban population, unemployed people or people on welfare, women, ethnic minorities and/or immigrants, youth aged 18–25 years old, disabled people, and financially excluded individuals. MFIs diversify their portfolio risk by serving multiple categories of disadvantaged borrowers (more than 4 on average), each of them representing a limited share of total active borrowers served (EMN, 2017).

Conclusion

The issue of micro-credit is more than ever on the agenda of any state, as a result of global financing policy and financial and social inclusion policy, micro-credit being an instrument. The same microfinance institution will need to finance tomorrow in the current context of regular daily wages, total labor supply of rural households, total labor income, involuntary unemployment and entrepreneurship. The outcome model described in this paper is consistent with the projected impact of a negative impact on labor demand through the business investment channel, which affects both tradable and non-tradable, combined with a reduction in aggregate demand, leading to a further drop in pressure on employment and wages in the non-commercial sector.

Asymmetric treatment of wage and employment effects suggests that a reduction in aggregate demand is important as a factor driving declines in labor demand and, therefore, wages. It also has an impact on agricultural production, given that at national level the number of semi-subsistence farms (rural households) is around 3.5 million, which leads us to affirm that micro-credit will have an equilibrium effect both financial, economic and social point of view. The fair effects of microcredits are related to wage policy, earnings and consumption. It shows that despite the small size of the loans, microfinance can have significant effects on rural economies.

Microfinance is especially, for rural areas, one of the research areas of great interest in the contemporary society in Romania and in the world, both. Based on the theoretical and methodological approaches in the field and the more or less sustainable realities of the microfinance process, our research provides a perspective picture of this field (Manta, 2017).

In the current complex and dynamic economic and social context, which decisively influences the good functioning of the companies, the research carried out brings to question one of their most pressing problems, namely the microfinance of their own businesses. Following the researches undertaken, the main conclusions and proposals are synthesized as follows:

- The stage of development and the complexity of the global financial structure have a decisive influence on the variables of financial management action, the terms of their specific problems, and the nature of the solutions offered, in particular;

- Each type of financial environment delimits the space targeted by the entrepreneur's financial management (SME, micro-enterprise and rural household), determining its objectives, issues and means of action;
- capital analysis in order to "direct" the microfinance policy towards optimal and cheaper capital sources, which contribute to maximizing the market value of the firm and to the best satisfaction of the interests of the parties involved in its activity or direct needs of beneficiaries;
- The financial structure of the household must be one of the areas of applicability of the optimization, because its components, being variable, can be combined so as to maximize the value of the company while maximizing the cost of capital (human, material and financial) procurement;
- The optimal structure of microfinance is based on: knowledge of the microfinance needs of SMEs or micro-enterprises, i.e. knowledge of the investment and financing channel; the sources of microfinance and their weight in meeting the microfinance needs of the household / firm in rural areas; the cost of microfinance sources; the financial environment at macroeconomic level and the financial policies promoted in a given period; the behavior of market actors and their position on risk and the psychological effects of indebtedness, as the financial structure of the small entrepreneur highlights the attitude of financial decision makers towards the risk of indebtedness;
- If, in theory, it is possible to achieve an optimal microfinance structure, in practice, this objective is difficult to meet because of the quantification of the various variables involved in the medium and long-term microfinance decision;
- There are no free financial resources anywhere, which is why a good knowledge of the cost of capital by financial managers is a necessity (even grants for micro-enterprises bear costs);
- In adopting microfinance decisions, firms must have rigorous criteria that allow them to choose and combine these resources, and the cost of microfinance is the main criterion in choosing funding resources; for Romanian companies, even in the economic crisis, exogenous microfinance through microcredit is the main solution to cover the microfinance needs of both current activity and its own development projects;
- In order to improve the microfinance activity of rural businesses through microcredit specific banking products we propose the following measures: eliminating the formal character of the preliminary discussions and advising support services for microfinance of the representatives of the companies related to the specificity of the micro-credit activity, and complete the documentation required to obtain the microcredit; by the most appropriate regulations to provide firms with the necessary conditions to effectively negotiate with banks the conditions for micro-credit (microcredit volume, lending period, interest rate, grace period, etc.); the reimbursement schedule is to be drawn up according to the cash flow made by the small entrepreneur and the specific nature of his activity (especially in the field of agriculture, the reimbursement is according to the harvesting campaign) and the monthly repayment term is not fixed date, but

a refund (for example between 25–30 of the month to avoid additional costs or penalties due to non-payment on that day); the size of micro-loans is determined by the activity carried out and by the nature of the microcredit (for example, in the case of investments in tangible assets, the guarantees may be established on the one hand by already existing assets in the firm and on the other purchased) and adjusting the magnitude and evolution of interest and commissions to the level and real market trend;
- The global and regional trends of micro-insurance in rural areas are favorable both at global and European level;
- As far as micro-guarantee is concerned, it has grown considerably, ranked second in the volume of guarantees for SMEs.

We appreciate that the analysis of the need for microfinance in the rural area, at the level of the companies according to the complexity of the activities carried out, must be achieved by an optimal combination of the presented microfinance sources. In this case, it is recommended to use short-term microcredit combined with micro-guarantee and micro-insurance, i.e. medium- and long-term micro-credit combined with other microfinance products such as microleasing.

Romania can have a valuable and varied potential for microfinance and support services to provide resources for new microfinance institutions and to provide the opportunity to develop this new sector of activity with significant benefits for the country's economy.

The Romanian rural environment has a specific specificity, both in terms of the organization of agricultural holdings (most of which are rural agricultural households that can be financially supported to become integrated family farms), as well as the current situation of SMEs, rural communities and micro-enterprises (Manta, 2017)

The economic activities generated by the new business models of microfinance services can have a multiple impact on the sustainable development of the Romanian village and the Romanian business environment.

References

Aghion, P., Bolton P. (1997): A theory of trickle-down growth and development, The Review of Economic Studies, 64, 151–172.

Angelucci, M.; Karlan, D.; Zinman, J. (2015): Microcredit Impacts: Evidence from a Randomized Microcredit Program Placement Experiment by Compartamos Banco, American Economic Journal: Applied Economics, 7, 151–82.

Attanasio, O.; Augsburg, B.; De Haas, R.; Fitzsimons, E.; Harmgart H. (2015): The Impacts of Microfinance: Evidence from Joint-Liability Lending in Mongolia, American Economic Journal: Applied Economics, 7, 90–122.

Augsburg, B.; De Haas, R.; Harmgart, H.; Meghir, C. (2015): The Impacts of Microcredit: Evidence from Bosnia and Herzegovina, American Economic Journal: Applied Economics, 7, 183–203.

Banerjee, A.; Breza, E.; Duflo, E.; Kinnan C. (2018): Do Credit Constraints Limit Entrepreneurship? Heterogeneity in the Returns to Microfinance, Working Paper.

Banerjee, A.; Duflo, E.; Glennerster, R.; Kinnan C. (2015a): The Miracle of Microfinance? Evidence from a Randomized Evaluation, American Economic Journal: Applied Economics, 7, 22–53.

Banerjee, A.; Duflo, E.; Hornbeck R. (2017): How Much do Existing Borrowers Value Microfinance? Evidence from an Experiment on Bundling Microcredit and Insurance.

Banerjee, A.; Karlan, D.; Zinman J. (2015b): Six Randomized Evaluations of Microcredit: Introduction and Further Steps, American Economic Journal: Applied Economics, 7, 1–21.

Banerjee, A. V.; Newman A. F. (1993): Occupational Choice and the Process of Development, Journal of Political Economy, 101, 274–298.

Ben-Yishay, A.; Fraker, A.; Guiteras, R.; Palloni, G.; Shah, N. B.; Buera, S. F. J.; Kaboski, J. P.; Shin Y. (2017): The macroeconomics of microfinance, Working Paper.

Burgess, R.; Pande R. (2005): Do Rural Banks Matter? Evidence from the Rn Social Banking Experiment, American Economic Review, 95, 780–795.

Chodorow-Reich, G. (2014): The employment effects of credit market disruptions: Firm-level evidence from the 2008–9 financial crisis, The Quarterly Journal of Economics, 129, 1–59.

Crépon, B.; Devoto, F.; Duflo, E.; Parienté W. (2015): Estimating the Impact of Microcredit on Those Who Take It Up: Evidence from a Randomized Experiment in Morocco, American Economic Journal: Applied Economics, 7, 123–50.

Devoto, F.; Duflo, E.; Dupas, P.; Parienté, W.; Pons, V. (2012): Happiness on tap: Piped water adoption in urban Morocco, American Economic Journal: Economic Policy, 4, 68–99.

Emerick, K. (2017): Agricultural productivity and the sectoral reallocation of labor in rural R.

Evans, D. S.; Jovanovic B. (1989): An Estimated Model of Entrepreneurial Choice under Liquidity Constraints, The Journal of Political Economy, 97, 808–827.

Botti, F.; Diego, L.; Dagradi, L.; Torre, M.; Benaglio N. (2017), Microfinance in Europe: A Survey of EMN-MFC Members. Report 2014/2015, Journal of Financial and Monetary Economics, 2017.

Field, E.; Pande, R.; Papp, J.; Rigol N. (2013): Does the classic microfinance model discourage entrepreneurship among the poor? Experimental evidence from R, The American Economic Review, 103, 2196–2226.

Greenstone, M.; Mas, A.p Nguyen H.-L. (2014): Do credit market shocks affect the real economy? Quasi-experimental evidence from the Great Recession and normal economic times, NBER Working Paper.

Imbert, C.; Papp J. (2015): Labor market effects of social programs: Evidence from R's employment guarantee, American Economic Journal: Applied Economics, 7, 233–263.

Jayachandran, S. (2006): Selling labor low: Wage responses to productivity shocks in developing countries, Journal of political Economy, 114, 538–575.

Jiménez, G.; Mian, A.; Peydró, J.-L.; Saurina J. (2014): The Real Effects of the Bank Lending Channel, Working Paper.

Kaur, S. (2015): Nominal wage rigidity in village labor markets, Tech. rep., NBER Working Paper No. 20770.

Khwaja, A. I.; Mian A. (2008): Tracing the impact of bank liquidity shocks: Evidence from an emerging market, The American Economic Review, 1413–1442.

Manta, O. (2017): New challenges in economic science, LAP LAMBERT Academic Publishing, Germany.

Manta, O. (2018): Microfinance. Concepts and application in rural environment, LAP LAMBERT Academic Publishing, Germany.

Meager, R. (2016): Understanding the Impact of Microcredit Expansions: A Bayesian Hierarchical Analysis of 7 Randomised Experiments, Working Paper.

Mian, A. R.; Sufi, A.; Verner E. (2017): How Do Credit Supply Shocks Affect the Real Economy? Evidence from the United States in the 1980s, Working Paper.

Mobarak, A. M.; Rosenzweig M. (2014): Risk, insurance and wages in general equilibrium, Tech. rep., National Bureau of Economic Research.

Morvant-Roux, S. (2011): Is microfinance the adequate tool to finance agriculture? in The Handbook of Microfinance, World Scientific, 421–436.

Muralidharan, K.; Niehaus, P.; Sukhtankar, S. (2017): General equilibrium effects of (improving) public employment programs: Experimental evidence from R, Tech. rep., NBER WP.

Paravisini, D. (2008): Local bank financial constraints and firm access to external finance, The Journal of Finance, 63, 2161–2193.

Schnabl, P. (2012): The international transmission of bank liquidity shocks: Evidence from an emerging market, The Journal of Finance, 67, 897–932.

Documentation sources from virtual space:

(2013): Social economy and social entrepreneurship, European Commission.

(2012): Microfinance as a support to senior entrepreneurship and to the transfer of competences, European Microfinance Network aisbl, Brussels.

(2012): EMN study for Youth entrepreneurship, European Microfinance Network aisbl, Brussels.

(2011): Microfinance and business. What can we learn from the outh? European Microfinance Network aisbl, Brussels.

(2010, 2011, 2012, 2013, 2014, 2015), National Bank of Romania, Report on Financial Stability.

Irina A. CHERVINSKAYA[1]

[1] Institute of Economics of the National Academy of Sciences of Belarus, Minsk, Belarus; Email: a.chervinski@gmail.com

Theory and Practice of Antidumping Regulation as an Object of Economic Research

Abstract *Methodological aspects of evaluation normativity justification in development of basic criteria for determination of the normal price of export goods are studied. The possibilities of optimization of analogue variant choice in the situation of anti-dumping claims against domestic exporters are analyzed.*

Keywords: *dumping, anti-dumping regulation, transitive economy, mechanism for determination of normal price*

Introduction

The theoretical aspects and the current practice of applying modern mechanisms, in the first place, anti-dumping measures, are investigated. The problem is relevant for countries with a transitional economy. It proposes to consider and determine the main directions for the formation of a mechanism for the application of special anti-dumping measures, taking into account the aggravation of competition for markets.

Theoretically, the relevance of the study is determined by the fact that the ongoing improvement of the system of state support for domestic producers allows us to trace the dynamics of the real process, identify the main trends and problems, and also to identify the possibilities for making changes in the chosen directions, forms and methods of adjusting the system of state anti-dumping policy. This will help the transition from a one-dimensional treatment of anti-dumping mechanisms to a comprehensive understanding of the policy of protecting the interests of commodity producers and, thereby, will contribute to a significant enrichment of the methodological potential of domestic scientific developments.

1. Literature review

Certain aspects of the problem were covered in the specialized literature on the analysis of the role of anti-dumping measures in international trade (Bruce A Blonigen, 2005). Significant developments in the methods of applying anti-dumping measures in connection with possible threats to the national security of participants in world trade were performed by Messerlin (2002), Gunnar (Gunnar, Kate, 2006), Bown (2007) and others.

Of great practical importance are studies aimed at analyzing the prospects for the development of the current anti-dumping situation, and in this regard particular mention should be made of theoretical works and applied developments realized by Messerlin (2002), Gunnar, Kate, (2006), Rutkowski (2007) etc.

These works create a theoretical basis for further research on the problem of anti-dumping regulation, contribute to the development of criteria for optimality in the system of international economic relations. But the questions of substantiating the basic criteria of the normal price of the goods, against which antidumping claims are presented, have not yet been properly resolved. The development of a general system for regulating the export of goods has also received insufficient attention.

2. The effect of dumping in a transitional economy

The development of export dynamics for countries in a transitional economy has its own specific features, the ignoring of which in practice can provoke the emergence of a complex of trade conflicts, the final solution of which is largely due to the manifestation of voluntarist tendencies on the part of economically developed countries, which are usually neither legal nor moral framework in the competitive struggle.

Therefore, in practice, countries with economies in transition have to overcome not only the conditions of an objectively developed situation, but also demonstrate readiness for compromise solutions to the situation, which involves not only acquaintance with the fundamental principles on which WTO activities are conceptually based, but also competent use of professional operating co- materials on the basis of which a normative study of the current situation of the conflict is carried out. This situation particularly actualizes the problem of determining the normal price for countries with non-market economies with the prospect of preparing a set of applied methodological recommendations for domestic exporting enterprises.

Quite often there are questions connected with the definition of the domestic price of the imported goods, originating from so-called countries with non-market economy "non-market economy country" or third countries.

Although the countries with economies in transition among the complaints about market access most often mention quantitative restrictions (including voluntarily accepted as a result of anti-dumping proceedings), the peculiarity of the anti-dumping procedures applied by the EU and the US with respect to these countries, and their impact on the export of countries with transition economies have not been systematically investigated.

In a market economy, the normal price is determined on the basis of the EXW producer's shipping prices for unrelated buyers in its domestic market, taking into account the cost of transportation, the physical characteristics of the goods, the terms of sale and insurance. This is done in order to make it comparable to the price of manufacturers of similar goods shipped for export. (Bloningen, 2005, p. 413).

In countries with economies in transition, prices for products calculated in local currency on the domestic market are not considered as a real basis for calculating a normal or "fair" price. This decision is based on the fact that in a centralized economy, non-convertible currencies and price control mechanisms are subject to political and administrative influence and do not reflect the normal "market" value of goods. The US Treasury Department developed a method by which a producer from a country with a non-market economy needs to document its actual costs: the costs of materials, labor, energy and capital (the method of the constructed price, the constructed cost). The normal cost is determined by evaluating these factors of production in another country, which is a market economy and is approximately at the same level of economic development, based on the GDP per capita. The difference is added to the price of the supplier from a country with a non-market economy. As a surrogate, countries that also produced this type of goods were to be selected.

Legislative, six criteria were set for classifying a country as a non-market economy: whether the country's currency is freely convertible; whether wages are established as a result of free trade between the employee and the employer; conditions for the operation of enterprises with foreign participation; the limits of the state's ownership of the means of production or control over them; limits of state control over the allocation of resources and prices, as well as decisions on the volume of production of enterprises.

Other factors that are considered relevant, in particular the existence of an institution of bankruptcy.

The decision as to whether the exporter is a representative of a market or non-market country is taken in each individual case, mainly on the basis of the allegations of the dissatisfied firm.

The normal value established by the method described above is compared with the export price (for both market and non-market economies). In the case where the export price is lower, a dumping margin is determined reflecting the difference expressed as a percentage of the export price. A dumping margin of less than 2 % is considered to be of minor significance and has no enforcement force. But in the case when the margin exceeds the limit of two percent, the conclusion should be made of the cause, or the threat of causing material damage.

It should be noted that the status of a country with a non-market economy and the use of different methods for determining normal value can have a significant impact on the probability of detecting a dumping event. Also, many of the problems that the country faces with both the market economy and the so-called "third countries" are associated with the lack of knowledge of anti-dumping legislation and procedures by foreign enterprises and with the requirements to respond immediately in English to detailed technical questionnaires on prices and costs on production. In the absence of accounting practices (including accounting) in a number of countries that meet international standards, this causes serious problems.

Definition of dumping is basically a judicial procedure, during which both companies claiming damage caused, and foreign exporters have the opportunity to provide evidence to substantiate their claims. In cases where respondents representing market or non-market countries are not in a position to provide detailed information on prices and costs in a certain format, decisions are made on "available facts". This often actually permits the use of those data and those methods of determining the presence of dumping that are deemed appropriate. In addition, exporters from the countries with transition economies have less experience in administrative support for foreign trade operations and, as a consequence, they are more difficult to cope with procedures accompanying anti-dumping investigations. As a result, anti-dumping measures may affect them more severely than on other exporters.

The provisions of the WTO GATT grant freedom to individual countries to develop their domestic legislation to determine the normal value in the context of anti-dumping legislation. However, in principle, there is no incompatibility between the procedures adopted by countries and WTO requirements, which are the primary source for the anti-dumping legislation of individual countries.

In trade with the EU, a country is classified as a country with a non-market economy by the decision of the EU Council on the basis of whether it can be considered that it has taken sufficient steps to follow the market principles of organizing trade and production. There are no opportunities for individual exceptions, nor for legal counterarguments. In other words, the partial recognition of a particular company as functioning in a market economy, provided that the whole country as a whole has the status of a country with a non-market economy is impossible. In general, in the European anti-dumping practice, countries with non-market economies face serious problems. This is not least due to the difficulties in preparing the documentation and completing the questionnaires, as well as with obvious procedural uncertainty in determining the normalprice.

Accession to the WTO also does not guarantee protection against the application of the analogue country methodology, if the country is not considered "market". The only reliable way to avoid the application of the price of a third country as normal is to obtain the status of a country with a market economy.

The use of third-country (analog) countries' prices to determine the dumping margin and has enormous difficulties faced by countries in transition due to poor familiarity with administrative procedures in the US and the EU, as well as with international accounting practices, which jeopardized the export of these countries. Moreover, this method of determining the normal cost undoubtedly increased the risks associated with exports, opening up the possibility for arbitrariness and bias on the part of European and American officials during the conduct of anti-dumping proceedings.

The very practice of determining the presence of dumping, domestic prices of a third country, chosen on the basis of preferences, rather than rigidly defined rules, may be sufficient to reduce exports. The fact that Poland has found it profitable to accept the status of a country with a non-market economy in determining the normal value of some of its products is the same evidence of the existing arbitrariness and lack of economic content in the procedures for determining the most normal value.

Legislative methods for determining the normal price for countries with non-market economies are tantamount to. In practice, under the conditions under which one of these methods is chosen on the basis of preferences, and not regulated rules, there is a danger that the preference will be given to the method in which the exporter would be immune to charges of dumping. A country with a non-market economy, faced with the method of an "analogous country" and a hidden threat of a possible choice of an unfavorable analogue country, may be vulnerable and, therefore, most likely agrees to an out-of-court settlement, i.e. assumes voluntary quantitative restrictions or raises the price. Consequently, thus potential constraints can be as effective as real limitations if the threat of their application is large enough.

Thus, for countries with non-market economies, anti-dumping measures are, in fact, a veiled form of ordinary protectionism, and not the protection of the domestic market from "dishonest" trade. Moreover, placing the blame for the problems of domestic firms on poorly performing foreign competition firms, this practice provides an extremely attractive opportunity for manufacturing firms to request, and the state to provide protection without formal violation of WTO principles on trade liberalization throughout the world.

3. The problem of normative falsification in the sphere of antidumping regulation

A good example of falsification of the procedure for determining the normal price for a product imported from a country with an unrecognized market economy may be manipulations with the procedure for calculating the dumping margin, carried out using the so-called "zeroing method".

Practical implementation of this method can be presented in a procedural way in such a sequence: the initial stage of the evaluation procedure can be limited to the definition of the normal price for the exported goods. Traditionally, such an assessment is usually carried out on the following grounds: on determining the price of the imported goods in the domestic market of the exporting country; on the identification of the price of sales of the same products in the markets of other countries that export in similar, or similar in terms of their economic and geopolitical parameters; on the determination of the cost of production of the exported goods in the country of the producer. Determination of the normal price of products for the reasons listed above completes the first stage of the evaluation procedure.

The next stage is connected with the operation of comparing the normal price of products with the price of its sale in the market of the country carrying out the import. At the implementation of the evaluation procedure at this stage, its thoroughness and operational consistency are fundamental. Comparison of the normal price of the product with its selling price in the importing country is made separately for each transaction made, the result is summarized, the arithmetic mean is determined and on its basis the dumping margin is calculated, which is the difference between the price of the detected normal price and the price in the country importer. In the event that the excess of the normal price is detected above its price in the country of sale, this excess is strictly fixed by the evaluating party, and in the future, as a rule, is reflected in the procedure for calculating the dumping margin.

But in a situation where the normal price is smaller than the price of selling the goods in the importing country, the normative rigor of the procedure is finally lost. Its final stage, objectively derived from all previous appraisal operations, is the implementation of the procedure for subtracting the resulting amount from the integrated value of the definitively determined dumping margin to the opposite in the valuation procedure. The results of a comprehensive assessment, contrary to the original goal, are ignored without sufficient justification, and the cost of a particular transaction is reset.

In some cases, the average weighted average price can be compared with the prices of individual export transactions if one finds a standard in determining export prices, which, as a rule, differ significantly among different buyers, regions and at different time periods.

Obviously, when detecting the existence of a dumping effect, calculation methods based on different time bases can be applied. If a semi-annual (six-month) period is taken for a temporary unit, the dumping margin will be equal to one indicator (possibly zero). But if the monthly (thirty-day) period is considered as a time interval, then it becomes possible to falsify the indicators.

In foreign economic activity, it is often the case that some members of the WTO, in order to prevent the zero value of a set of foreign trade transactions, deliberately deduce from the calculation of transactions that have a negative dumping. Most often this is done by an arbitrary, convenient for the interested party choice of the final settlement schedule, often with a decrease in the time interval. This method allows unfair competitors, members of the WTO to "zero" the indicators of negative dumping, and in essence ignore and out of the final calculation its results.

The peculiarity of using this method is that if at least one transaction is ignored and dropped from the final calculation, then if desired, dumping will inevitably be detected by unscrupulous competitors. As a result of this approach, actions that have signs of violation of the principles of functioning of the free market, declared in the WTO regulations, are implemented.

The practice of implementing such a method, which has been conventionally called the "zeroing method", leads to an unjustified, and in fact voluntaristic, increase in the dumping margin, which opens up wide possibilities for unjustified introduction of protective duties. Countries with a transitional economy are especially vulnerable to such voluntarism.

The application of this practice does not comply with the norms of the World Trade Organization, therefore it is necessary to abandon the vicious practice of "zeroing" in the implementation of various anti-dumping investigations (Rutkowski, 2007, p. 476).

Regulation of dumping has three main features: first, it is carried out by the executive authorities; Secondly, there are a number of basic conditions for determining dumping and dumping; thirdly, in order to introduce anti-dumping duties, it is necessary that damage is done or there is a threat of damage to industry.

Anti-dumping measures implemented by the state in order to protect national producers from the adverse effects of dumped imports. They are applied by introducing an anti-dumping duty, including a temporary anti-dumping duty, or by accepting price obligations by the exporter.

Foreign trade activity clearly demonstrates a certain tendency when exporters of transit countries with a high share of the raw material component in the export structure experience the main share of the action of anti-dumping measures, on the one hand, and, as a rule, insufficient experience of normative support of foreign trade dynamics processes, on the other hand.

Both of these circumstances make transitional economies particularly vulnerable to various kinds of falsification by WTO member countries with some experience of manipulating the methodology for determining the facts of dumping. One of the most specific and widespread methods of falsification is the so-called "zeroing method", the practice of which is based on the continuing conceptual incompleteness of the traditional normative criteria for calculating the dumping margin. A wide variety of available techniques creates the prerequisites for an artificial imitation of the dumping situation on the part of certain competing firms that are not burdened by the need to follow the traditions of a market economy.

The calculation of the "normal price" in real practice of international economic relations does not yet have strict criteria, which contributes to the development of voluntaristic tendencies, both in determining the very fact of dumping and in adopting anti-dumping measures.

Greater use should be made of the potential of the allies of the enterprises - the processing companies of the EU and various consumer associations interested in the supply of national products. Since the potential threat of anti-dumping hangs over many goods, preventive work with a view to preventing new anti-dumping sanctions is of particular importance for preserving and increasing the volume of exports. Due to the fact that the anti-dumping mechanism is included through the procedure for filing complaints from competing companies and their unions and associations, close contact should be established with them to eliminate possible conflict situations even at the stage of their origin. If the complaint has already been received by the EC, it is necessary to conduct prompt consultations with a view to withdrawing the complaint from the EC prior to the commencement of the official investigation procedure.

Conclusions

To reduce the risks of anti-dumping investigations, the following actions are necessary:

- Application of anti-dumping legislation as a response to investigations against national enterprises.
- The inclusion in the texts of contracts provisions providing for the reimbursement by buyers of costs for the services of law firms in the event of the initiation of anti-dumping procedures.
- Development of scientific forecasting of anti-dumping procedures, based on analysis of domestic production dynamics, demand, consumption and exports, in the context of development of the world, regional and sectoral economy.
- Coordination of volumes of deliveries to certain geographical sales markets by joint efforts of domestic manufacturers and traders.
- Participation in the WTO as a full member, so that questions about anti-dumping measures are regulated on a common for all international legal basis.

The problem of anti-dumping regulation marks the need to train qualified national personnel who possess modern knowledge on various aspects of foreign trade.

It seems advisable to supplement the curricula of higher educational institutions with special courses on such a problem as minimizing the likelihood of imposing anti-dumping sanctions against national producers.

References

1. Blonigen, Bruce A. The Effects of NAFTA on Antidumping and Countervailing Duty Activity. World Bank Economic Review: 2005, p. 407–424.
2. Bown, Chad China's WTO Entry: Antidumping, Safeguards, and Dispute Settlement. National Bureau of Economic Research Working: 2007, p. 345–378.
3. Gallaway, M.C, B.A. Blonigen, and J.E. Flynn: Welfare Costs of U.S. Antidumping and Countervailing Duty Laws. Journal of International Economics: 1999, p. 211–244.
4. Messerlin, Patrick: China in the World Trade Organization: Antidumping and Safeguards. The World Bank Economic Review, 2002, p. 105–130.
5. Niels, Gunnar and Adriaan ten Kate: Antidumping Policy in Developing Countries: Safety Valve or Obstacle to Free Trade. European Journal of Political Economy: 2006, p. 618–638.
6. Rutkowski, Aleksander: Withdrawals of Antidumping Complaints in the EU: A Sign of Collusion. The World Economy: 2007, p.470–503.

Anastasia VASILYEVA[1], *Natalya BALYNSKAYA*[1], *Natalia IVANOVA*[1], *Inna KOBELEVA*[1], *Nina KUZNETSOVA*[1]

[1] Magnitogorsk State Technical University n. a. G.I. Nosov, Magnitogorsk, Russia, Email: anastasiavava@rambler.ru

Study of Russian Commercial Banks' Lending Activities Management Efficiency: Comprehensive Approach

Abstract *The current macroeconomic situation propels research in the field of development and implementation of the commercial bank's lending policy contributing to understanding the nature of credit management as a continuous system of measures to prevent crises and minimize their negative consequences. In this regard, the problem of effective management of lending activities, contributing to the increase of public confidence in commercial banks, is now becoming particularly acute and deserves detailed and comprehensive study and discussion. The article reflects the results of the development of the comprehensive approach, which is relevant for the current conditions of commercial banks functioning and which determines lending activities management efficiency level. The expediency of practical application of the proposed approach to the commercial banks registered in the administrative borders of the Russian Federation, the loan portfolio leaders according to the national rating, was studied in the process of credit exposure management efficiency monitoring. The article contributes to the development of comprehensive assessment of the commercial banks' lending activities management efficiency in the national financial science and provides an opportunity to modernize existing approaches to diagnostics.*

Keywords: *commercial bank, comprehensive approach, lending activities, loan portfolio*

Introduction

Until recently, commercial banks have been seeking to rapidly expand their client base and territory and increase their share in the lending market. The desire to capture the full benefits whittled down the defences of commercial banks, which often provided loans to dubious borrowers. Therefore, at the moment of macroeconomic instability, characteristic for 2013 and the subsequent period, they faced huge volumes of defaults that have been causing financial losses up to the present day. Therefore, the problem of modernization of existing and development of new approaches aimed at assessing the efficiency of credit management became especially acute.

The purpose of this research is to improve existing methodological approaches to assessing the efficiency of lending management of the commercial banks registered and operating in the territory of the Russian Federation.

The designated purpose defined the research objectives:

- To systematize the basic criteria and financial indicators characterizing credit exposure based on the results of the comparative analysis of diverse approaches to assessing the efficiency of the commercial bank's loan portfolio management.
- To develop and theoretically substantiate comprehensive methodical approach to assessing the efficiency of managing the lending activities of commercial banks in the Russian Federation, to present its mathematical algorithm.
- To study the feasibility of the practical application of the proposed approach and the presented mathematical algorithm to assessing the efficiency of lending activities of commercial banks registered in the administrative borders of the Russian Federation, the loan portfolio leaders according to the national rating.

1. Literature review

The problem of assessing commercial banks' lending activities management efficiency is characterized by a variety of aspects. It is studied by many scientists and specialists: the fundamental theoretical concepts of the commercial bank's lending policy development and implementation are reflected in the works of Ageeva S. D., Mishura A. V. (Ageeva, Mishura, 2016), Balakina R. T., Galdetsky P. V. (Balakina, Galdetsky, 2014), Brodsky I. (Brodsky, 2007), Bass A. B. (Bass, 2016), Gorkina T. I. (Gorkina, 2015), Kuklin A. A., Schneider E. A. (Kuklin, Shneider, 2007), Nesvetaylova A. (Nesvetaylova, 2010), Solomin S. K. (Solomin, 2009), Tavasiev A. M., Murychev A. V. (Tavasiev, Murychev, 2012), Stanley T., Roger C. (Stanley, Roger, 1996) et al.; economic and mathematical methods and tools used to assess credit exposure was proposed by Ayvazyan S. A., Afanasyev M. Yu., Afanasyev A. M. (Ayvazyan, Afanasyev, Afanasyev, 2009), Borzykh O. A. (Borzykh, 2016), Chortareas G., Girardone C., Ventouri A. (Chortareas, Girardone, Ventouri, 2012), Dubova S. E. (Dubova, 2013), Egorova N. E., Smulov A. M. (Egorova, Smulov, 1998), Nivorozhkina L. I., Ovcharova L. N., Sinyavskaya T. G. (Nivorozhkina, Ovcharova, Sinyavskaya, 2013), Nishikawa T. (Nishikawa, 2002), Summer M. (Summer, 2003) et al.

In the course of the studied issue development degree analysis, it was revealed that the number of publications on the development of comprehensive approaches to assessing the commercial bank's lending activities management efficiency is very small. Most of the works are based on the analysis of certain criteria for credit exposure assessment and do not address the issues of taking consolidated assessments. These include the works of Becht M., Bolton P., Röell A. (Becht, Bolton, Röell, 2011), Ezrokh Y. S. (Ezrokh Y. S. 2014), Laeven L., Levine R. (Laeven, Levine, 2009), Stukalo N. V., Bilay O. S. (Stukalo, Bilay, 2012), Taylor J. (Taylor,

2002). Thus, evaluating the results obtained by the authors mentioned, we consider it necessary to note that there are still many aspects that require in-depth analysis, elaboration and revision.

2. Research methods

The comprehensive approach to assessing the efficiency of commercial banks' lending activities management proposed by the authors involves four stages.

First, the determination of commercial banks' lending activities efficiency criteria groups' weights management by classical formula (1):

$$P_i = \frac{\alpha_i}{\sum_{j=1}^{n} \alpha_j}, \qquad \alpha_i = \sum_{z=1}^{k} \beta_{iz} \tag{1}$$

Where:

P_i – weight value of ith group of lending activities management efficiency criterion;
α_i – overall rating for ith efficiency category.
β_{iz} – estimation of ith efficiency category by zth group of experts.
n – number of groups of criteria for the efficiency of lending management.
k – number of expert groups.

Second, the introduction of financial ratios matrices characterizing the efficiency of commercial banks' lending activities management which is carried out by dividing the entire set of ratios into two matrices: the first one includes the ratios that independently characterize a certain efficiency category (according to the results of the approach approbation, they are loan portfolio risk ratio, general loan portfolio efficiency and security ratio and credit turnover ratio); the second indicates the ratios that characterize a category in a certain aggregate with the other ratios (according to the results of the approach approbation, these are NPL ratio, loan loss coverage ratio, bank's lending activity level, loan policy "aggressiveness – caution" ratio, loan portfolio profitability ratio, bank margin ratio, lending efficiency ratio). In addition, if the values of the ratios called "The bank's lending activity level" and loan policy "aggressiveness – caution" ratio do not fall within the range of optimum values, the deviation from the recommended value is taken into account in the calculation process.

Third, the significance of individual financial ratios for the relevant category, indicating effective commercial bank's lending activities management, is defined by introducing the weight values matrix. In this case, the significance of individual financial ratios is reasonable to be calculated only if the efficiency category is represented by two or more ratios.

Schematically, the ratios weights matrix can be represented in the form of formula (2):

$$Q=\begin{pmatrix} q_{11}=\gamma_1/\sum_{j=1}^{2}\gamma_j;\, q_{12}=\gamma_1/\sum_{j=1}^{2}\gamma_j;\, q_{13}=0 \\ q_{21}=\gamma_3/\sum_{j=3}^{4}\gamma_j;\quad q_{22}=\gamma_4/\sum_{j=3}^{4}\gamma_j;\, q_{23}=0 \\ q_{31}=\gamma_5/\sum_{j=5}^{7}\gamma_j;\, q_{32}=\gamma_6/\sum_{j=5}^{7}\gamma_j;\, q_{33}=\gamma_7/\sum_{j=5}^{7}\gamma_j \end{pmatrix}, \quad (2)$$

Where γ_j – an overall estimate for jth financial ratio of the relevant lending activities management efficiency category.

Fourth, the calculation of the aggregated indicator characterizing commercial banks' lending activities management efficiency.

3. Results

The article attempts to analyze the expediency of practical application of the proposed comprehensive approach in the process of assessing the efficiency of management over the lending activities of the commercial banks registered in the administrative borders of the Russian Federation, the loan portfolio leaders according to the national rating. The key characteristics of commercial banks that form the research polygon are reflected in Table 1.

It should be noted that in the process of approbation of the approach developed by the authors, the opinions of experts – the staff and clients of the designated commercial banks (8 expert groups were formed for the research) – as well as the provisions of the main approaches to assessing lending activities management efficiency suggested by leading specialists in the field under study were taken into account.

The results of the first stage, which involves the identification and systematization of the most significant groups of efficiency criteria for the commercial bank's lending activities management and associated financial ratios, as well as determination of their weight values, are reflected in Table 2 and in Figure 1.

Solving the problem the experts often disagree when it comes to assessing the research objects, in the process of ranking the groups of criteria for the commercial bank's lending activities management efficiency it is necessary to take into account consensus degree, for example, using the concordance ratio proposed by Kendall, which can be calculated by formula (3) (Yakovenko, 2015):

$$W=\frac{12}{m^2(n^3-n)}\times S,$$
$$S=\sum_{j=1}^{n}\left(\sum_{i=1}^{m}R_{ij}-\frac{m(n+1)}{2}\right)^2, \quad (3)$$

Table 1: The key characteristics of commercial banks registered in the administrative borders of the Russian Federation, the loan portfolio leaders according to the national rating

Name of commercial bank	Date of registration by the Central Bank of the Russian Federation	Authorized capital, RUB, thousand.	Presence of the General License for Banking Activities	Volume of loans granted to legal entities, RUB, thousand.	Volume of loans granted to individuals, RUB, thousand.	Dynamics for the period from 1st January 2017 to 1st January 2018
PJSC "Sberbank"	06/20/1991	67,760,844	+	11,731,510,967	15,879,842,991	↓
PJSC "Bank VTB"	10/17/1990	651,033,883	+	5,643,244,963	5,574,379,181	↑
JSC "Bank of GPB»	01/23/1992	194,996,181	+	3,507,509,606	3,783,696,878	↑
JSC "Rosselkhozbank"	24/04/2000	384,848,000	+	1,578,348,107	1,892,395,027	↓
PJSC "Moscow Credit Bank"	05/08/1992	27,079,709	+	1,498,327,365	1,577,033,866	↑
JSC "Alfa – Bank"	01/03/1991	59,587,623	+	1,389,153,346	1,612,320,223	↓
PJSC "Otkritie Bank"	12/15/1992	138,000,000	+	750,545,880	791,577,084	↑
JSC "UniCredit Bank "	11/15/1991	40,438,324	+	571,314,587	697,478,821	↑
PJSC "Promsvyazbank"	05/12/1995	0.001	+	643,512,351	675,597,115	↓
JSC "AB "Rossia"	12/29/1991	547,311	+	401,467,903	385,742,085	↓

Source: authors' development.

Table 2: Set of criteria and financial ratios affecting the commercial bank's lending management efficiency to the maximum extent

Criteria for assessment	Indicator
Lending activities risk assessment	Loan portfolio risk ratio
Loan portfolio performance assessment	Loan performance ratio
	Loans losses coverage ratio
Lending security assessment	Total loan portfolio security ratio
Bank's lending activities assessment	Bank's lending activity level
	Lending policy "aggressiveness-caution" ratio
Lending turnover assessment	Lending turnover ratio
Bank's lending activities efficiency assessment	Loan portfolio yield ratio
	Bank margin ratio
	Lending efficiency ratio

Source: authors' development.

Where:

n – the number of objects analyzed.
m – number of expert groups.
R_{ij} – the rank of jth object, which is assigned to it by ith group of experts.

Usually, the specified value of the concordance ratio is 0.5, hence:

- for W> 0.5, the experts' conclusions are more consistent.
- for W <0.5, the estimates cannot be regarded as sufficiently consistent.

In the process of studying the feasibility of the practical application of the proposed comprehensive approach, the concordance ratio was calculated using the OpenOffice Calc and, ultimately, the ratio value amounted to 0.591 that indicates the consistency of the expert groups in ranking the significance of the efficiency criteria for the commercial bank's lending activities management.

To increase the reliability of the research results, it is also recommended to determine the weights of financial ratios within the groups of criteria for the commercial bank's lending activities management efficiency, which include more than one indicator. The results of ranking the significance and determining the weights of the financial ratios that form the criteria for the commercial banks' loan portfolio and lending activities and their efficiency assessment using a five-point scale are shown in Table 3.

The next stage of comprehensive commercial bank's lending activities management efficiency assessment suggests determining the direction of the impact of each financial ratio included in the aggregated indicator criteria, the results of

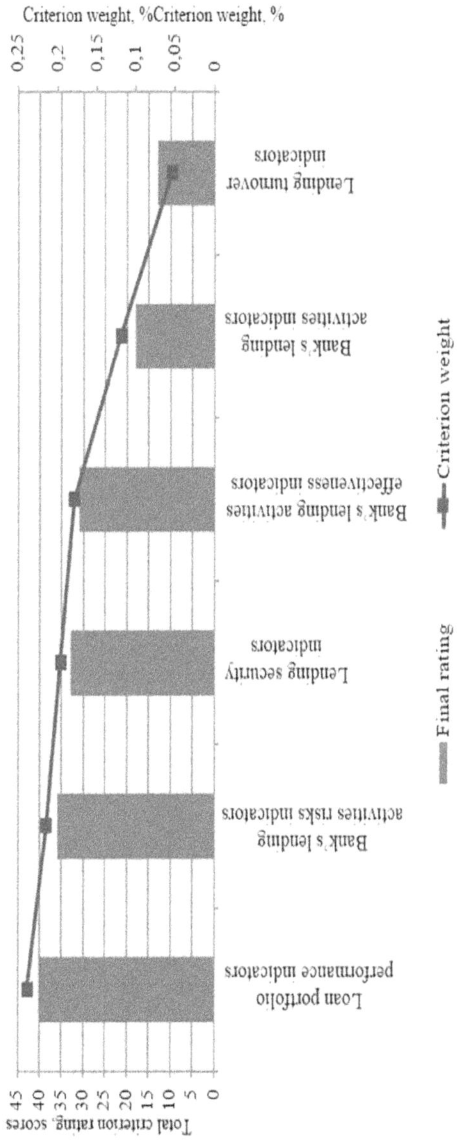

Figure 1: Ranking of the criteria importance for commercial bank's lending activities management efficiency

Source: authors' development

Table 3: Significance ranking and determination of the financial ratios weights that form the criteria for commercial banks' loan portfolio and lending activities performance and their efficiency assessment

Indicators	**Indicator weight**
Criterion – non-performing loans	
NPL ratio	0.75
Loans losses coverage ratio	0.25
Criterion – commercial bank's lending activities	
Bank's lending activity level	0.42
Bank's credit policy "aggressiveness-caution" ratio	0.58
Criterion –the commercial bank's lending activities efficiency	
Loan portfolio yield ratio	0.35
Bank margin ratio	0.40
Lending efficiency ratio	0.25

Source: authors' development

which are presented in Table 4. The results of the research indicate the opposite effect of financial ratios on the quality of loan investments that should be taken into account in the process of calculating the aggregate commercial bank's lending activities management efficiency indicator.

The use of the above importance weights for criteria and financial ratios, their impact directions, as well as a set of historical data characterizing commercial banks – leaders according to the national rating of the Russian Federation in terms of credit exposure – allows us to express the aggregate credit management efficiency index in the form of formulas (4.5):

$$K = \sum_{i=1}^{n} (P_i \times \sum_{j=1}^{K_j} Q_{ij} K_{ij}), \tag{4}$$

$$\begin{aligned} K = 0{,}214K_1 - 0{,}238 \times 0{,}75K_{10} + 0{,}238 \times 0{,}25K_2 + 0{,}196K_3 \pm 0{,}119 \times 0{,}425K_8 \pm \\ \pm 0{,}119 \times 0{,}575K_9 + 0{,}054K_4 + 0{,}179 \times 0{,}35K_5 + 0{,}179 \times 0{,}4K_6 + 0{,}179 \times 0{,}25K_7, \end{aligned} \tag{5}$$

Where:

P_i is the score weight for ith group of financial ratios, or the significance of a separate group of financial ratios in the general financial assessment.

Q_{ij} is the score weight for jth financial ratio in ith group, or the significance of an individual ratio in the corresponding group, $\sum |Q_{ij}| = 1$. In the event that the growth of jth financial ratio positively affects the loan portfolio quality, then $Q_{ij} > 0$; otherwise, and also if the calculated value of jth ratio does not fall within the range of optimal values, $Q_{ij} < 0$.

Table 4: Assessment of financial ratios impact on commercial bank's lending activities management efficiency

Indicator	Indicator designation
Indicators increasing the efficiency of lending activities	
Loan portfolio risk ratio	K_1
Loans losses coverage ratio	K_2
Total loan portfolio security ratio	To $_3$
Lending turnover ratio	K_4
Loan portfolio yield ratio	To $_5$
Bank margin ratio	K_6
Lending efficiency ratio	To $_7$
Indicators with intermediate value	
Bank's lending activity level	K_8
Bank's credit policy "aggressiveness-caution" ratio	To $_9$
Indicators reducing lending activities efficiency	
NPL ratio	To $_{10}$

Source: authors' development

K_{ij} is jth financial ratio included into ith group, or its deviation from the optimal value, if it does not fall within the range of optimal values.

–n is the number of indicators groups (in our case, n = 6).

–k_i is the number of financial ratios in ith group.

The results of the calculations presented in Figure 2 indicate that the vast majority of commercial banks under study began better addressing new challenges posed by the socioeconomic system in unfavorable external conditions.

4. Conclusions

Thus, the research resulted in:

- A comprehensive methodical approach to assessing the effectiveness of Russian commercial banks' lending activities management taking into account the impact directions and the significance level of the criteria characterizing credit exposure.
- It was stated that the proposed tool allows regular monitoring the achieved lending activities performance indicators, compare the efficiency of loan portfolio management in different periods and assessing the level of competitive banks' credit exposure, and also increasing the interest of commercial banks in

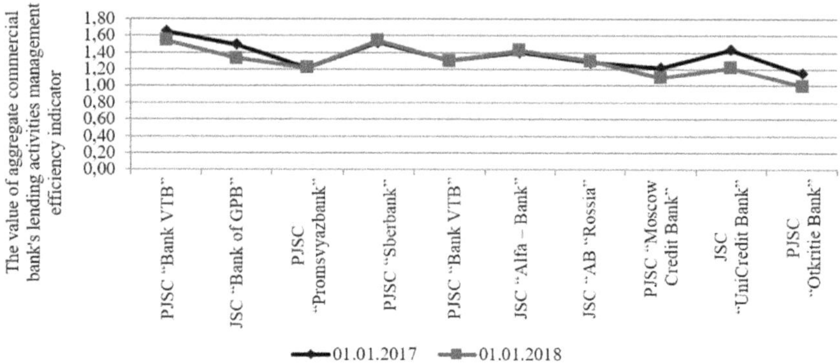

Figure 2: Dynamics of the aggregate Russian commercial banks', the leaders according to the national loan portfolio volume rating, lending activities management effectiveness indicator

Source: authors' development.

improving the system of protection from insufficiently qualitative structure of the loan proceeds allocated.

- Factors that adversely affect the Russian commercial banks, leaders according to the national rating by the volume of the loan portfolio, lending management effectiveness were identified – aggressive credit policy and the growing volume of non-performing liabilities.

References

Ageeva, S.D./Mishura, A.V.: Regional disparities in the development of banking institutions, Regional Research of Russia 4 (6), 2016, pp. 304–313.

Ayvazyan S. A./Afanasyev, M. Yu./Afanasyev, A. M.: Estimation of economic efficiency of the bank's activities on advertising of credit products, Applied Econometrics 4 (16), 2009, pp. 46–59.

Balakina, R. T./Galdetsky, P. V.: Theoretical aspects of managing the bank's loan portfolio, Bulletin of Omsk University. Series: Economics 1, 2014, pp. 198–206.

Bass, A. B.: Current problems in the quality of the loan portfolio, International Scientific Journal Innovative Science 4, 2016, pp. 42–46.

Becht, M./Bolton P./Röell A.: Why bank governance is different, Oxford Review of Economic Policy 3, 2011, pp. 437–463.

Borzykh O. A.: Anti-Effectiveness of Liquidity in the Russian Banking System, Economic Journal of the Higher School of Economics 3 (20), 2016, pp. 377–414.

Brodsky, I.: Investment Activities and Russian Banks, World Economy and International Relations 2, 2007, pp. 101–107.

Chortareas, G./Girardone, C./Ventouri, A.: Bank supervision, regulation and efficiency: Evidence from the European Union, Journal of Financial Stability 8, 2012, pp. 292–302.

Dubova, S. E.: Development of risk-oriented approaches in banking supervision and regulation: monograph. Moscow: Flinta 2013, 180 p.

Egorova, N. E./Smulov, A. M.: Mathematical methods for financial analysis of banking activities (the case of a large savings bank), Financial Analysis of Banks 2, 1998, pp. 75–146.

Ezrokh, Y.S.: Bank consumer lending in Russia from the point of view of foreign experience: competition and ways of development, Studies on Russian Economic Development 2 (25), 2014, pp. 184–193.

Gorkina, T.I.: Regional structure of the Russian banking system at the present stage, Regional Research of Russia 1 (5), 2015, pp. 23–30.

Kuklin, A. A./Schneider, E. A.: Some approaches to planning the commercial bank's interest policy for lending, Economics of the Region 2 2007, pp. 216–229.

Laeven, L./Levine, R.: Bank governance, regulation and risk taking, Journal of Financial Economics 93, 2009, pp. 259–275.

Nesvetaylova, A.: Enigmas of global credit breakdown, or illusion of liquidity, Economic issues 12, 2010 pp. 33–58.

Nishikawa, T.: Credit risk estimation for small businesses based on a statistical method, Asia-Pacific Financial Markets 2 (9), 2002, pp. 101.

Nivorozhkina, L. I./Ovcharova, L. N./Sinyavskaya, T. G.: Econometric modeling of consumer loans non-payment risk, Applied Econometrics 2 (30) 2013, pp. 65–76.

Solomin, S. K.: Bank credit: problems of theory and practice. Moscow: Justicinform, 2009.

Stanley, T./Roger, C.: The logic of strategic management of your loan portfolio, Bankers Magazine 1 (179), pp. 51–57.

Stukalo, N.V./Bilay, O.S.: Системний підхід до управління проблемни ми кредитами в банківській діяльності, Економічний часопис-XXI 6, 2012, 55–58.

Summer, M.: Banking Regulation and Systemic Risk, Open economies review 14, 2003. pp. 43–70.

Tavasiev, A. M./Murychev, A. V.: Banking: Credit Organization Management. Moscow: UNITY 2012, 668 p.

Taylor, J.: Stress testing a commercial loan portfolio, Commercial Lending Review 2 (17), 2002, p. 10.

Vasilieva, A.G./Zaitseva, E.M./Ivlev, A.V./Puzankova, E.A./Rakhimova, L.M.: Russian experience of practical application of banking supervision tools and techniques, Journal of Applied Economic Science 3 (49), 2017, pp. 709–718.

Yakovenko, S. N./Markelova, A. S.: The Commercial Bank's Loan Portfolio Quality Management and Assessment Optimization, Economics and Entrepreneurship 6–2 (59–2), 2015, pp. 596–601.

Emilian M. DOBRESCU[1], *Edith Mihaela DOBRESCU*[2]

[1] Senior Researcher, Institute for National Economy, Romanian Academy, Bucharest, Romania, Email: dobrescu@acad.ro

[2] Senior Researcher, Institute for World Economy, Romanian Academy, Bucharest, Romania, Email: edithdobrescu@gmail.com

New Perspectives Regarding Rural Mountain Tourism in Spain and Romania – Comparative Study

Abstract *Rural mountain tourism developed as active tourism, in the nature or agritourism, are increasingly used alternatives both in Romania and Spain - the first European tourist country by results and tourist infrastructure - for family vacations, friends groups as bonuses or facilities offered by management or employees, for business meetings and for relaxation. The number of hotel rooms for rural tourism has also increased due to the diversification of economic activities in rural areas and with the main aims of preventing the depopulation and the exodus of people to large urban agglomerations. In Spain, perhaps more than in any other part of Europe, as a result of the rich experience of promoting tourism very well, rural tourism activities have been subsidized through rural development programs. The Spanish society suffers today profound transformations at economic, social and spiritual level, found at high levels and in rural tourism.*

Keywords: *rural mountain tourism, Romania, Spain*

Introduction

The study shows the favorable issues of the mountain rural tourism from Spain and Romania as similarities and differences. At the same time are presented new perspectives of rural tourism in the two countries and the evolutionary paths.

The aim of this paper is to present the current state of rural tourism in regions with exceptional environmental and cultural values with the role in the development of rural tourism of the selected countries - Spain and Romania.

The contribution of the authors of this study consists in the comparative analysis of the main aspects of rural tourism in the most developed tourist country - Spain, and the development of tourism in Romania, where the authorities make substantial efforts for a favorable evolution in this important sector of the economy.

Research methodology

The main source of data for the present study was Eurostat Community Methodology on tourism statistics. In order to identify significant trends of ecotourism, agro-tourism and rural tourism in the European Union, focusing on the New Member States, given the available statistics.

Rural mountain tourism in Spain

Spain is the country whose knowledge needs to be deepened even through mountain rural tourism. In the mountainous areas of Spain, as in all rural areas of this country, there are networks of hotels, hostels and rural houses, all endowed with special services tailored to the needs of the most diverse categories of tourists. Spain is a major recipient basin for the demand for mountainous rural tourism. The “white villages” of Andalusia - in the south of the country, Flamenco music and dance, bullfighting, as well as the many traditional accommodation places are special attractions for visitors arriving in the Spanish mountainous countryside.

The rural Andalusian environment includes municipalities with agricultural activities, forestry, river fishing and livestock farming that are not found in the influential zones of coastal areas; rural Andalusia also contains municipalities with less then 20,000 inhabitant. (Blancas et al., 2011)

Accommodation in rural areas is provided through guesthouses, huts, equestrian farms, han farms, guest rooms grouped in rural tourism associations such as the Basque Agrotourism Associations and Balearic Agrotourism, historical buildings such as those belonging to the Paradors, established as early as Franco’s dictatorship, as a way to finance the reconstruction, but also to save historical buildings that have been renovated and turned into comfortable rural hotels.

Rural zones with more consolidated tourist activity are located in areas with enormous natural beauty, great ecological diversity and strongly protected natural areas. These protected areas include nature reserves that constitute their main tourist attraction. In addition, these destinations have an important cultural heritage. The character of these destinations promotes tourism activities aimed at getting “in touch” with nature, such as botanical activities (ie, collecting wild fruit), observational activities (ie, bird and mammal watching), hunting, sport fishing, aquatic activities and other outdoor activities (ie, mountain biking, horse riding, shooting, paragliding, canoeing and hiking cultural routes). (Blancas et al., 2011)

In a scientific articles (M.V. Sanagustín Fons et al., 2011) was shown that with regard to the average night-stay specifically in rural tourism houses, the leading province in Aragon is Teruel, with a yearto-year variation of 3.32 %, as against 0.76 % in Huesca and a fall of 5.13 % in Zaragoza. The average year-to-year variation in rural tourism accommodation by provinces shows that Teruel and Huesca have a better year-to-year variation than the rest of Spain, being Teruel a really notable case in the country as a whole, being placed behind such well-established tourist destinations as: Granada (14.84 %), Malaga (12.91 %), Seville (11.50 %), in the first, main block, and provinces such as Burgos (8.18 %), Lerida (7.15 %), Murcia (3.67 %) and Tarragona (3.77 %), in the second block. It is apparently the support given by all social agents in Teruel for Quality Rural Tourism has undoubtedly thrown very good results.(Eurostat 2011)

Spain was the third top tourist destination in the European Union, with almost 46 million arrivals in hotels and similar establishments in 2010. (Eurostat, 2011)

Between February and March 2013, an exchange of experience was carried out through which five groups of beneficiaries of the e-learning program "Entrepreneurs in tourism" - Pensions in Romania went to Spain to visit 24 successful tourism business.[1] and know how access to European best practices. Following the selection since July 2012, 100 beneficiaries of the e-learning program participated in the exchange of experience in 5 different periods in the mentioned months.

As in other parts of Europe and the world, including in Romania, individual owners make rural Spanish mountain tourism the main means of subsistence; In addition, in many cases, a contribution is made to preserving the natural environment through activities carried out in mountain rural areas. The more important objectives to reach for the tourist attracted by the Spanish mountainous environment blend harmoniously in each case with ethnographic, folklore and cultural traditions. We can talk about a specific mountain mountain tourism in the Balearic Islands or Tenerife, as well as a specific of this type of tourism existing in all mountain areas of the various continental Spanish provinces.

In Spain, there are several incentives for mountain rural tourism. In 2013 a study (Blasco D. et al., 2013) were identify four types of mountain tourism zones ranging from high to low tourism intensity. Some of the most tourism-intensive types were located in the central and peripheral coastal regions of the mountain range and have the highest international cross-border intensity.

Type I mountain tourism zone includes only one of the areas, Cerdanya–Andorra. This type of tourism area is characterized by being highly cross-border (with up to six borders, both international and regional), by having the highest number of accommodation units, a medium-sized population for a mountain area and the highest level of intensity, specificity and variety of attractions.

---

1 The 24 successful Spanish businesses visited by Romanian entrepreneurs were:1. Bodegas y Vinedos Laujar; 2. Casa Rural Domingo en el Valle; 3. Complejo Rural "La Marmita de Ahlam"; 4. Grupo Playas y Cortijos – Hotel Dona Paquita; 5. Ferma El Sotillo şi Hotelul El Palacil; 6. Casas Rurales Los Albardinales – Fabrica "Oro del Desierto"; 7. Camping de Sierra Maria; 8. Hotel Plaza Vieja; 9. Casas Rurales El Picachico; 10. Hotel Rural La Posada del Candil; 11. Hotel de Naturaleza Rodalquilar; 12. Hotel Venta El Museo; 13. Complejo Rural Sol de Taberno; 14. Cortijo Rural Loz Velez; 15. Hotel Cortijo El Paraiso; 16. Hotel Cala Grande; 17. Hotel Cortijo Los Malenos; 18. Beach Golf Resort Playa Macenas; 19. Cortijo Relente; 20. Villa Turistica de Laujar; 21. Hotel Almirez; 22. Cortijos Rurales Reúl Alto; 23. Hotel Rural Las Fuentes, şi 24. Hotel Catedral

Type II mountain tourism zone is composed of Oriental Pyrenees and Basque Pyrenees tourism zones. This type of tourism zone is the most populated with the highest variety of attractions and medium values of intensity and specificity of attractions, accommodation units and cross border intensity.

Type III mountain tourism zone includes the areas of Atlantic Pyrenees and Aragon Pyrenees. This type is characterized by medium levels of accommodation units, intensity and specificity of attractions and low levels of population, variety of attractions and cross-border intensity.

Type IV mountain tourism zone is composed of Navarra Pyrenees, Aran–Haute Pyrenees, Pallars–Ariege and Ariege–Aude, and is characterized by very low levels of all attributes.

The study also was reveal that in terms of international cross-border intensity, the central Cerdanya–Andorra tourism area is the most relevant, followed by Basque Pyrenees, Aran–Haute Pyrenees and Ariege–Aude. The rest of the zones only have one border, being international in the cases of Oriental Pyrenees and Pallars–Ariege and national in the other two cases

Regarding the state's financial support for the development of the citizens' accommodation activity in Spain consists in: a) Granting subsidies for the rehabilitation of the patrimony in the localities with less than 2,000 inhabitants, such as those in Catalonia or the Canary Islands (Tenerife); b) grant investment grants to Galicia and Asturias; c) lack of taxation for businesses developed by firms and associations operating in the field of rural tourism, including mountain tourism. For example, the Basc Agrotourism Association received subsidies from the European Union, amounting to up to 50 % of the total subsidy received from the entire province; through the tax regime adopted in the province, all associations with activity in the field of mountain rural tourism were not subject to taxation.

Rural tourism, active tourism, nature tourism or agritourism, all hosted in Spain's mountain areas, are increasingly used for family vacations, groups of friends as bonuses or facilities offered by management companies or employees, for business meetings and relaxation. The number of hotel rooms for rural tourism has also increased due to the diversification of economic activities in rural areas, to prevent depopulation and exodus to large urban agglomerations; In addition, mountain rural tourism activities are subsidized through rural development programs. Through successful business, especially in the years of deep economic crisis in Spain (2012–2013) and beyond, this country is also considered a European model for mountain rural tourism.

Mountain Rural Tourism in Romania

Rural tourism in Romania is has always practiced, spontaneously, sporadically, accidentally and especially unorganized.[2], its forms of materialization being

2 Puiu Nistoreanu, Romania, "Turismul rural european", coord. Emilian M. Dobrescu, Puiu Nistoreanu, Craiova, Editura Sitech, 2018.

represented by pilgrimages, visits to the mansion / cottage, spending some days in the hermitage or the monasteries, or from the 20s-30s of the twentieth century the accommodation of occasional visitors in to a house of rural settlement

Starting with July 16, 1973, according to the Order of the Ministry of Tourism number 744/1973, the following 14 rural settlements were declared experimental villages of tourist interest: Lereşti and Rucăr (Argeş), Poiana Sărată (Bacău) Fundata and Şirmea (Braşov), Bogdan Voda (Maramureş), Tismana (Gorj), Sibiel (Sibiu), Vatra Moldovitei (Suceava), Racos (Timiş), Sfântu Gheorghe, Murighiol and Crişan,Vaideeni (Vâlcea)[3]. The following year, Decree 225/1974 prohibits the accommodation of foreign tourists in private dwellings, the tourist villages becoming inoperable for international tourism. However, given that part of the mentioned tourist villages were included in the programs of cultural and folkloric character of the National Carpathian Tourism Office Bucharest and contracted on the foreign market, there is a break for the villages: Lereşti, Rucăr, Sibiel, Murighiol and Crişan.

The short period of "formalization" of rural tourism did not make it possible to organize the tourism activity or to properly arrange the tourist villages. In many localities, the households that met the accommodation conditions (Rucăr, Vatra Moldoviţei, Vaideeni) were not approved, while in others the accommodation of the Romanian tourists was done in an unorganized manner and without keeping a record (Crişan, Fundata, Rucăr), and some localities have not registered any tourist activity (Tismana, Bogdan Voda, Vaideeni). With only a few exceptions, this situation lasted until 1989. Since 1990, interest in mountain rural tourism has been rebounding.

The Association with the highest resonance in rural tourism activity in Romania - the National Association of Rural Ecological and Cultural Tourism (ANTREC), was founded in 1994. It brought together more than 2,000 members, organized in 15 branches at the end of 1995. The touristic activity took place in 1,240 equipment (farms, hostels or peasant farms), which attracted 18,500 tourists - of which 3,500 foreign tourists - with an average stay of 4 days / tourist. The next year (1996) saw an increase in size to 25 subsidiaries and the upgrading of the level of equipment, services and the whole activity. ANTREC was concerned with raising the level of professional training of rural tourism service providers by organizing: seminars, colloquia and tourism and tourism marketing courses, centralized or zonal in the regions with significant tourist traffic (Brasov, Maramures, Bucovina, etc.). Also in 1996 began the first Phare Program for rural tourism in our country.

In the third year of existence (1997) of ANTREC, the number of its members reached almost 3,000, and that of its subsidiaries at 28. The association managed to publish the first CD-rom, the first catalog of the hostels and tourist farms, participated in numerous promotional events (fairs and exhibitions, meetings and congresses) and was concerned with the realization of a decentralization climate

3 http://old.madr.ro/pages/dezvoltare_rurala/Raport_SEA_PNDR.pdf, p.45

for his actions. The sustained activity of the first millennium of the third millennium led ANTREC to a structure of 32 county branches, which employs more than 3,500 members - owners of tourist and agrotourist pensions from 800 localities[4].

Touristic (mountain) villages are those of rural (mountain) communities, which, through their particularity and particularity (settlement, natural resources, architectural or historical monuments, ethno-folklore tradition, etc.) can be a rural tourist product, while being prepared to satisfy a wide range of motivations of domestic and international tourism. Areas of rural tourism, including mountainous, are variously classified.

The Romanian village is a unique tourist product for both the national and the world market. Obviously by practicing tourism in the countryside, the Romanian village can contribute to discovering our country as a possible tourist destination, as a place that offers a wide range of experiences, quality holidays and even business opportunities. The statement is based on: the broad range of natural and cultural resources; various tourist facilities and experiences; the specificity and uniqueness of our country: people (different groups and religions), history (buildings, events, legends), culture (written, art, costumes, music, dance, theater, crafts, topography (Black Sea coastal beaches, wild animals in the Danube Delta, mountain areas, etc.), existing within the Romanian village, as part of our natural heritage (especially in affection and in the common one[5]).

At the same time, the Romanian village, including the mountain area, combines: a) important scenic scenic rivers; b) Invaluable religious and cultural heritage; mineral and thermal waters; c) novel flora and fauna; d) old traditions, appreciated and respected internationally: art and crafts (theater, music, poetry, dance, painting, sculpture); e) a varied range and good quality of attractions and facilities. The fitting, harmonization, concertation and assimilation of some of the perennial values of the village in some tourist arrangements leads to the production of Romanian rural tourism products of a certain value and of a unique unmistakable character.

New perspectives of rural tourism in the two countries are represented by the following evolutionary paths[6]:

- Attracting new investments, including foreign, by providing banking and financial facilities[7], of production and customs, by central and local authorities.

---

4 http://www.infotravelromania.ro/interviu100_antrec.html

5 C. C. Negri, "Bazele economiei mediului", Bucharest, Editura Didactică şi Pedagogică, 1996, p. 32

6 Ideas inspired by the rural realities of the analyzed countries, as well as the reading of the paper "Turism rural. Note de curs", de Cristian Tălângă, Editura Credis, Universitatea din Bucureşti, 2010, p. 11

7 For example, granting interest-bearing loans, preferential deposit bonuses slightly higher than in the rest of the country, creating a system of tax advantages including discounts for obtaining construction, operating licenses, etc.

- Better attraction of female labor, usually over, in activities specific to rural tourism.
- Creating new local economic units of production (for clothing, knitwear, local fabrics and toys) or restoring existing rural patrimony.
- Development of local services activity, especially those specific to rural tourism.
- The development of handicraft or folk art through private initiatives - individual or family by which the future generations can be preserved or handed over - customary traditions, unique artisanal crafts specific to certain ethnographic regions.
- The revaluation of old buildings, which can obtain tourist functions and where the interior decorations and decorations must respect ethnography and local traditions specific to certain historical periods.
- Implementing specific forms of marketing and promotion that make better use of local rural tourism products and attract as many customer segments as possible.
- The restoration and preservation with modern means of the rural and movable rural patrimony; a special place is occupied here by the architectural and historical monuments, which should enjoy greater concern from local rural authorities and constitute a defining element for local history and culture.
- Clear settlement and then observance of the specificity of the tourist village that the tourist tourist settlement concerned (tourist village: a) ethnographic-folkloric; b) artistic and craftsmanship; c) with climatic and landscape valences; d) hunting and fishing interest; e) of pastoral, fruit or vineyard interest; f) for practicing summer or winter sports.
- Support for pluriactivity, through which agricultural, craft, handicraft, reception, leisure and leisure activities can be developed through better use of off-farm times.
- Better use of household animals for rustic walks by carriage, harness, sleigh, etc. or for equitation.
- The use of degraded land with reduced agricultural return, ecological restoration or reforestation, which can be made available for rural tourism investments.
- Better use of rural agricultural products - so larger quantities of vegetable or animal products can be made available to rural tourists directly for local consumption or at home.

For the development of the above directions, it is necessary to resort to the services of tour operators, trained and specialized for the rural area, to the media services, to travel agencies, to the creation of own networks of promotion and information centers, fairs and exhibitions dedicated to rural tourism.

If the above directions are considered to have a positive impact and influence, there are also situations that are considered to have a negative effect, such as:

- Less beneficial attitudes towards local tourists.
- Increasing the level of pollution of the rural environment through unattended or harmful tourist activities at the respective places.
- The degradation of local tourist resources by important flows of tourists reaching the rural area.

There are also cases where the over-estimation of rural development (smaller demand at the expense of supply too high) in some areas in Spain and Romania has led to the stagnation and regression of the economic profitability of local tourist offerings and its authenticity. The response of the local tourist market to demand and supply is the barometer needed to increase or decrease the local rural tourism market. Among the dimensions and indicators of the success of local rural tourism are the following:

1. the level and profitability of investments in the rural area concerned;
2. professionalism in achieving local hospitality;
3. Integration into local and national marketing and promotion networks of the product;
4. the development of rural tourism activities in close connection with the evolution of the natural, economic, social and spiritual environment of the local communities concerned.

The past, present and future evolution of mountain rural tourism in the two countries must also take into account local dysfunctions, such as: a) overstating the qualities and effects of this form of tourism; b) considering mountain rural tourism as the only preferred form of development; c) failure to take into account the specific risks that occur permanently (climate and environment factors, pollution, the prevalence of secular behavioral characteristics of the local population, etc.).

Conclusions

The achievements obtained by the two countries surveyed in the field of rural tourism demonstrate that this is a factor and a means of multi-level development of the respective rural areas. Rural tourism in Spain and Romania contributes greatly to preserving the viability and stability of localities that promote this form of tourism, based on geographic, historical, environmental and climate realities, on local traditions, culture and spirituality.

In last decades, the development of local rural tourism is a variant, a possibility to help reduce the mobility of the local population, increase the quality of its life, while preserving and promoting local traditions. Some rural systems in the two countries surveyed - such as those specific to rural tourism in. Canary or Balearic Islands, from Maramures or the Danube Delta, etc. - have been built on true models praised by universal rural tourism.

Annex 1: Tourist objectives in the two countries entered in the UNESCO World Heritage

In Romania: The Danube Delta (1991); Horezu Monastery (1993); The painted churches in northern Moldavia (1993); Saxon settlements with fortified churches from Transylvania (1993); Dacian fortresses from the Orastie Mountains (1999);

Wooden Churches in Maramures (1999); The old historical center of Sighisoara (1999).

In Spain: Güell Park, Palau Güell and Casa Milà in Barcelona (1984); Monastery and Escorial, Madrid (1984); Burgos Cathedral (1984); Alhambra, Generalife and Albaicín, Granada (1984); Historic Center of Córdoba (1984); Monuments of Oviedo and the Kingdom of Asturias (1985); Caves in Altamira (1985); The old town of Segovia (1985); The old town of Santiago de Compostela (1985), The old town of Ávila and the extra-mural churches (1985); architecture of the Aragon muddies (1986, 2001); National Park Garajonay (1986); The historic old town of Cáceres (1986); The historic old town of Toledo (1986); Cathedral, Alcazar and Archivo de Indias of Seville (1987); The historic old town of Salamanca (1988); Poblet Monastery (1991); Archaeological Site of Mérida (1993); Royal Monastery of Santa María de Guadalupe (1993); The pilgrimage route to Santiago de Compostela (1993); Doñana National Park (1994); Fortified City of Cuenca (1996); La Lonja de la Seda, Valencia (1996); Palau de la Música Catalana and Hospital de Sant Pau, Barcelona (1997); Las Médulas (1997); Monasteries of San Millán de Yuso and Suso (1997); The bustling art of the Mediterranean Arc of the Iberian Peninsula (1998); University and the old historical center of Alcalá de Henares(1998); Isle of Ibiza, biodiversity and culture (1999); San Cristóbal de La Laguna (1999); Archaeological sites in Sierra de Atapuerca (2000); Elche palm grove (2000); Catalan Roman Catholic Churches in Vall de Boí (2000); The Roman fortifications of Lugo (2000); Archaeological Ensemble of Tarragona (2000); Cultural Landscape of Aranjuez (2001); Renaissance monumental ensembles in Úbeda and Baeza (2001); Vizcaya Bridge (Biscaya) (2006); Teide National Park on Tenerife Island (2007); Torre de Hércules (2009); Cultural Landscape of Serra de Tramuntana on Mallorca Island (2011); Almadén (historical site of mercury extraction) (2012).

References

Barbu, I., Approach to the Concept of Rural Tourism. Scientific Research. Agricultural Management, 2013, pp.125–28.

Bran, Florina et al., Turismul rural. Model european, Bucureşti, Editura Economică, 1997.

Blasco, Dani; Jaume Guia; Lluís Prats, Tourism Geographies, Tourism destination zoning in mountain regions: a consumer-based approach, An International Journal of Tourism Space, Place and Environment, 2013.

Darău, A.P.C.M.; Brad, M.L.; Avram, E., The Concept of Rural Tourism and Agritourism. Studia Universitatis "Vasile Goldiş" Arad, V (1), 2010, pp.39–42.

Dobrescu, Emilian M., Spania, in Turismul rural european, revised edition, coordinated by Emilian M. Dobrescu and Puiu Nistoreanu, Craiova, Editura Sitech, 2018.

Dupeyras, A.; MacCallum, N., Indicators for Measuring Competitiveness in Tourism: A Guidance Document. OECD Tourism Papers, February, 2013, pp.20–24.

F.J. Blancas; M. Lozano-Oyola; M. González; F.M. Guerrero; R. Caballero, How to use sustainability indicators for tourism planning: The case of rural tourism in Andalusia, Science of the Total Environment 412–413 (2011) 28–45.

M.V. Sanagustín Fons; José A. Moseñe Fierro; María Gómez y Patiño, Rural tourism: A sustainable alternative, Applied Energy 88 (2011) 551–557.

Negri, C. C., Bazele economiei mediului, Bucureşti, Editura Didactică şi Pedagogică, 1996, p. 32.

Stoian, Mihaela şi Voinea, Oana, Modele de dezvoltare a turismului rural în ţările iberice, Universitatea "Constantin Brâncuşi", Tg. Jiu, preluare de pe site-ul http://www.utgjiu.ro/revista/ec/pdf/2007-01/47, vizitat pe 4 iunie 2015, orele 8:10.

Tălângă, Cristian, Turism rural. Note de curs, Editura Credis, Universitatea din Bucureşti, 2010, p. 11

Turismul rural şi de pensiune. Studii de caz de succes în Spania, iunie 2011, pe site-ul www.interprinzatorturism.ro, cisited pe 4 iunie 2015, orele 8:00

Eurostat Comunity Methodology on Tourism statistics, on site http://ec.europa.eu/eurostat/documents/747990/6278123/Community-methodology-+tourism-EN-CA0196228ENC-002%5B1.pdf/47e09270-b7b6-436f-941a-79474f51ddf0?version=1.0.

Manuela Sofia STĂNCULESCU[1], *Monica MARIN*[2], *Georgiana BLAJ*[3]

[1] Senior Researcher, Research Institute for Quality of Life, Romanian Academy, Email: manuelasofia.stanculescu@gmail.com

[2] Senior Researcher, Research Institute for Quality of Life, Romanian Academy, Email: monicatoba@hotmail.com

[3] PhD student, Faculty of Sociology and Social Work, University of Bucharest, Email: blaj.geo@gmail.com

Social Services for the Elderly in Romania

Abstract *This article presents an analysis of social services for the elderly in Romania. The research findings presented are based on a census of the public and private suppliers of social services for the elderly, according to the official data available in April 2014. The results are grouped around the following key topics included in the questionnaire: (a) capacity of providing services, (b) accessibility of the services, (c) financing of the services, (d) human resources and (e) plans for the future.*

Keywords: *social services; elderly; Romania*

Introduction

The primary motivation behind this study was the lack of specific research on social services for the elderly[1] in Romania. The topic is increasingly important given the demographic pressures Romania has to face, similar to other European countries. The demographic prognosis developed by the National Institute of Statistics (INS) shows a constant increase of the share of people aged 65 and above, from over 19 % in 2020 to 26 % in 2060 (INS in CNPV 2014a, p.63). Aging of the population is significantly higher in small communes located far from the urban areas, in particular in small and isolated villages[2] (Teşliuc et al. 2015, p.373). Hence, this results in substantial consequences for the system of benefits and social services.

The paper analyses the current status of development of social services for the elderly in Romania, based on the data resulted from a survey of providers of services of care and assistance for the elderly. The questionnaire was sent by post mail and e-mail (where possible) and it was self-filled in. This survey was conducted by

1 The term "elderly" is defined by the Law 17/2000 as referring to all persons at or over the official Romanian age of retirement.

2 Based on Population Census Data.

the World Bank in June 2014, as part of the background studies for the National Strategy for Social Inclusion and Poverty Reduction 2015–2020.[3] All public and private providers from the list of social services as of April 2014, from the Ministry of Labour and Social Justice (MMJS),[4] were included in the survey. Out of a total number of 505 providers of care and assistance for the elderly at national level, the survey registered a total response rate of 54 % (271 providers answered the survey).

Providers from all counties answered, except for Giurgiu and Mehedinti. The rate of response varied, however, being above 70 % for the providers of day-care services, 58 % for the providers of residential services and 40 % for the providers of home-care services. The response rate was of just 42 % for the private providers of social services, compared to 69 % for the local level services (SPAS) and 91 % for the county level (County Directorates of Social Work and Child Protection-DGASPC/ County Council) providing services for the elderly. Consequently, the results of the analysis are affected by a somehow underrepresentation of the private providers, particularly among those providing home-care services.

1. Literature review

Most of the few published research studies on social services for the elderly in Romania focus on topics related to quality of life for the elderly (CNPV 2013; CNPV 2014d); social assistance for the elderly (CNPV 2014c; Roş 2012; Costachescu 2015), including a theoretical analysis of policies regarding social assistance and protection for older people in a comparative perspective between Romania and Switzerland (Vranceanu 2015); demographic projections, general gerontological research (CNPV 2014b; Bodogai 2013), specific types of social services (Mirişan 2017); attitudes towards the elderly in Romania (Rusu 2016), or descriptive analysis on available social services for the elderly at local level (Petrescu et al. 2011). There are also few data regarding the quality of services[5] offered as part of the social services in Romania. Among these, some of them report extreme cases of breaking human fundamental rights, particularly in residential centres for mental health (CRJ 2013).

Previous studies conducted by the National Council for the Elderly conclude there are several key problems in the development of social services for the elder people in Romania: (i) a poor development of social services for the elderly compared to other vulnerable groups (children, people with disabilities); (ii) a poor development of specific organizational structures at the level of local public authorities (for instance within the county councils); (iii) lack of specialized personnel (social workers, geriatric physicians, carers, occupational therapy and kinetic therapy specialists, etc.), (iv) lack of communication within the multidisciplinary team (at

---

3 Government Decisions no. 383/27 May 2015.
4 Previously named Ministry of Labour, Family and Social Protection.
5 Quality standards for the social services for the elderly have been approved by the Ministerial Order no.2126 from November 5, 2014.

the county level); (v) unbalanced distribution of service providers at national level; (vi) a too small capacity of residential services compared to the number of requests, as well as (vii) a hyper centralization of services in the public services (at county level – Directorates of Social Work and Child Protection) resulting in the development of much too large services which are difficult to be managed (CNPV 2014c, 2014d).

Similar or complementary problems related to the development of a network of specialized services have been reported in post-communist countries, in relation to: (i) differences in population size and structure between Estonian municipalities, which further results in a specific demand structure for social services (Reiljan et al. 2015); (ii) the situation of family carers/ informal care and its impact on the development of long-term care in Czech Republic (Wija 2015); (iii) the insufficiently transparent funding of the services and an artificially divided system of funding between ministries in the Slovak Republic (Hrozenská 2011)[6] and (iv) a substantial gap between the needs and the availabilities of long-term care arrangements in Slovenia (Kavšek and Bogataj 2017).

This article fills in this gap of knowledge on the specific structure of social services for the elderly in Romania, with national level data on both the number and type of services, as well as detailed information on their capacity, accessibility, financing, human resources and plans for the future.

2. Survey Findings

The national network for social services for the elderly developed substantially during 2014 and 2018 in Romania, for the whole range of services (particularly for the residential services), both in the public sector and in the private one.[7] At present time (January 2018) there are 740 social services for the elderly (in some cases with other vulnerable groups) holding a provisional operating licence and an operating licence awarded by the Ministry of Labour and Social Justice.[8] Hence, these social services fulfil the minimum quality standards, at least in a share of 75 %.[9]

There are significant discrepancies in the national distribution of these services by county. For instance, in the county of Botosani, there are only 2 centres for the elderly (one public and one private), 5 medical and social centres (all public) and a

6 A similar survey to the one presented in this article is presented for the case of the structure of services provided in selected social facilities in Slovakia in Ležovič, 2009.

7 Based on a comparison of official data from MMJS in 2014 and 2018. More than two thirds (65 %) of the total number of units suppling social services for the elderly people, authorised at January 8, 2018, come from the private sector.

8 In addition, there are also 469 social assistance public institutions for adults with disabilities, which are coordinated by the National Authority for People with Disabilities (ANPD), as of September 2017. Yet, there are no disaggregated data on provision of services for the elderly people by these institutions.

9 Art. 11, alin. 5, c, Law no. 197/2012.

public unit for home care services. In the counties of Alba, Cluj, Sibiu and Bihor, day care and home care services are much more numerous and are managed by private entities. In Alba county there are 15 centres for the elderly (out of which 11 are private), 8 protected dwellings (with 5 of them private), 4 day care, assistance and rehabilitation centres (1 private), 6 centres for socialization and spending spare time (2 private), 1 social and medical unit and 29 home care units (with 27 of them private). Hence, access of a beneficiary residing in Botosani County is much more limited and less diversified than of one from Alba County.

More than two thirds (65 %) of the total number of units suppling social services for the elderly, authorised at January 8, 2018, come from the private sector.[10] However, at the level of the residential services, the beneficiaries of services provided by private entities account for less than a third of the total number of beneficiaries. On the other hand, at the level of the day-care and home-care services, the beneficiaries of services provided by private entities (mainly NGOs, foundations, associations and religious organisations) predominate, accounting for about two thirds from the total number of beneficiaries. This highlights the trend of the public institutions to focus rather on the development of residential services, while the private organisations focus on the development of day-care and home-care services.

The survey from 2014 revealed that, actually, there are entities which supply a mix of services, which prevents their classification in one of the main three types of services. The analysis will therefore deal with these entities providing a mix of services (residential and/or day-care/ home-care), as a fourth, a distinct type of providers.

Residential services account for almost half of the sample (with the homes for old people accounting for most of the entities, while 7 % are medical social centres). About 20 % are day-care services, most of which are centres for socialization and spending the free time (club-type). A quarter of the sample services are home-care providers, while about 7 % are entities providing a mix of services.

Both at the level of the national network of social services for the elderly, and at the level of our sample, about 30 % of the providers are located in the rural areas, with a maximum of about half of the total number of providers, in the South and South-West regions.

The regional distribution of the providers of social services for the elderly was highly imbalanced in 2014 (both at the national level and for the sample). As mentioned, the situation remained unchanged until 2018. A very low number of services were and still are developed in Bucharest-Ilfov, South-West and South regions, while two regions, North-West and Centre, cover almost half of the existing number of providers.

The survey questionnaire included responses on the following topics: (a) capacity of providing services; (b) accessibility of the services; (c) financing of

10 Source: MMJS, 2018, www.mmuncii.ro.

the services; (d) human resources, and (e) plans for the future. These topics are presented below.

(A) Capacity of providing services

Among the providers of social services for the elderly in Romania there are entities with tradition, established as early as in the inter-bellum period, but the providers of services established between 1930 and 2001 account for just a quarter of the total number of providers. As of 2002, after the adoption of Law 17/2000 concerning the social assistance of the elderly, the development of such social services boomed.

Most providers supply a wide range of services and activities. As a general rule, the residential providers supply a higher number of services and activities for the beneficiaries than the day-care providers and the home-care providers (an average of 12–13 services/ interventions, compared to 8).

The residential services for the elderly vary considerably in terms of capacity, from a minimum of 6, to a maximum of 295 beneficiaries. The largest entities are the homes for the elderly and the medical and social residential centres, particularly those managed by a SPAS/local council (with an average number of 66 old people). In contrast, the centres for palliative care and the protected homes are the smallest (with an average number of beneficiaries >20).

The capacity of the residential services for the elderly was (in 2014, and remained so in 2018) insufficient related to the needs. Thus, most providers have waiting lists with a rather large number of people waiting for an opening. The highest average number of potential beneficiaries in the waiting list is registered for the entities providing a mix of services, including residential services, while the highest share of services with a waiting list is in the case of residential centres.

The dominant profile of the beneficiaries shows people aged 75 and more and/ or people completely dependent, which explains why about two thirds of the exits from these services are due to death. On average, a beneficiary spends about 4.5 years within a residential service, with a minimum of 3–4 months and a maximum of 20 years. The period spent in an institution ranges from 6.7 years in the centres providing a mix of services to 2.9 years in the centres for palliative care, with a minimum of 3–4 months in the centres for palliative care.[11]

The endowment of the residential services for the elderly improved/ was modernized a lot in time, including the period between 2014 and 2018. At the time of the survey (2014), for almost half of the providers of social care services, the rooms with 1–2 beds accounted for about 54 % of the total number of rooms, but just

11 Because most homes for the elder are managed by local councils (SPAS), the beneficiaries of services provided by SPAS/local councils entities tend to spend more years in the institutions compared to the period spent by the beneficiaries of the other services which are supplied by counties (DGASPC) or by private entities (about 6 years, on the average, compared to 3–4 years).

about a third of the sleeping rooms had their own bath. Furthermore, more than half of the centres had courtyard, library and multimedia room, or areas where the beneficiaries could spend actively the spare time.

Overall, even as early as in 2014, the providers of residential services for the elderly, with no significant difference depending on the type of service, or between the public/ private entities, were evaluating[12] the conditions provided to their beneficiaries as being: (i) "very good" regarding the conditions of preparing and serving the food, and regarding the possibilities of the beneficiaries to communicate with people outside the institution (mean score 4.5); (ii) "good" regarding the conditions of accommodation and spending the spare time indoor and outdoor (mean score around 4).

The capacity of the home-care services for the elderly was (in 2014 and remained so until 2018) insufficient compared to the requirements, just like in the case of the residential services. Unlike this, the day-care services seemed to have just a slightly undersized capacity compared to the demand. Accordingly, only in the case of the home-care services, most providers (57 %) stated that during the last year there were periods when the demand for services exceeded their capacity. This proportion decreased to 24 % in the case of the day-care services, while 33 % of the multifunctional centres reported such problems.

Anyhow, the demand for day-care services depends strongly on the attitude of the elderly towards the activities and services provided by such entities. Thus, along with the changes in the society, it is very likely that the demand for day-care services (particularly the demand for services of socialization and of spending spare time) will increase significantly among the elderly.

While the public institutions provide services for the elderly only in the county of residence, the private entities may expand their activity in several counties. Thus, about 15 % of the private providers supply services for the elderly in 2–6 counties. Furthermore, about half of the home-care providers for old people, operate in just one locality, while the other half operate in 2 to 107 localities. On the average, a provider covers 6–7 localities, with the observation that while local social assistance services/ local councils provide home-care services only in their locality of activity, the private entities cover about 9 localities (on average).

At the level of all the providers of services for the elderly, irrespective of their type, the providers declare[13] that the following factors affect negatively their capacity of supplying quality services to the beneficiaries: (i) "very little" or "at

---

12 On a scale from 1 to 5, where 1 means "very bad", and 5 means "excellent", how would you evaluate your institution in terms of the following aspects?: Accommodation, Possibilities of spending the spare time indoor, Possibilities of spending the spare time outdoor, Conditions of preparing and serving food, Possibilities for the beneficiaries to communicate with people outside the institution.

13 How much do each of the following factors affect your capacity of supplying quality services to your beneficiaries? Responses on a scale from 0 – "at all" to 4 – "to a great extent". Factors: 1. Lack of financial resources; 2. Lack of infrastructure / space / proper endowments; 3. Lack of trained staff; 4. Legal issues; 5. Lack of or difficult

all" – lack of, or difficult cooperation with the local authorities or with other organisations; (ii)"to some extent" – legal issues, lack of trained staff and lack of infrastructure / space / adequate endowments; (iii) "rather a lot" – lack of financial resources.[14]

(B) Accessibility of the services

The beneficiaries access the existing services in various ways: the beneficiaries (or the family members) identify and come alone at the particular provider; the beneficiaries are identified directly by outreaching activities conducted by the providers, or they are redirected there by the local authorities, by specialists, by hospitals, the church or by other beneficiaries. In this regard, only two types of services show a different pattern. In the medical-social centres people generally get there being sent by a third party, while regarding the home-care services, the bulk of beneficiaries are identified by outreach activities (specific to the private providers of social services, and very seldom used by local social work services). Regarding the other services, most of the beneficiaries get to be there by themselves (or with the assistance of their family).

Generally, the day-care services are accessed by the elderly living in their proximity. Living close to the provider of services is thus and important factor for the use of these services. This is just why most day-care services don't provide free transportation services, because their beneficiaries can access these services either by public transportation, or just walking.

In the opinion of the providers[15], the main factors which limit the access of the potential beneficiaries relate both to the demand (low level of demand because of the potential beneficiaries' mentality), and to the offer (which was rather limited, at least in 2014). However, for particular types of services there also are specific factors. For instance, the providers of services consider that the access to

---

cooperation with the local authorities; 6. Lack of or difficult cooperation with other organizations.

14 There are significant differences between the public and private providers. Thus, financing is a problem particularly for the private entities and for the SPAS/local councils, while the DGASPC/county councils are less affected by the lack of funds. The lack of trained staff is stated as a major adverse factor by the public providers and less by the private providers. The lack of cooperation with the authorities is an issue mentioned only by the private suppliers of social care services.

15 In your opinion, which are the main factors which limit the access of the potential beneficiaries to services such as those provided by your unit? Multiple answer. Factors: 1. The existing offer of services is quite limited; 2. The services are located mainly in towns and it is difficult for the rural people to access them; 3. The quality of the services is rather poor; 4. Too high costs for the potential beneficiaries to access/ use the services; 5. The potential beneficiaries don't trust the providers; 5. Mentality of the beneficiaries/their families; 6. Other.

multifunctional day-care centres is limited for the elderly living in rural areas because these centres are generally located in urban areas. Concerning the medical and social centres, the high costs incurred by the beneficiaries are an important obstacle for the use of these services. Other factors which limit the access to these services regard both the low (insufficient) number of seats within the existing services, and the lack of information and mistrust which characterize most of the potential beneficiaries, as well as their families.

(C) Financing of the services

As already mentioned, financing is a factor with an important impact on the capacity of the providers to supply quality services to their beneficiaries. The problem of financing the social services for all vulnerable groups, not just for the elderly, remained a problem that is yet to be solved even in 2018. The situation must be treated with priority and highly seriously, more so as even 73 % of the private providers (and all the public providers) rely on public funds.

(D) Human resources

The lack of, or insufficient human resources is "to some extent" a factor which affects adversely the capacity to provide quality services, as previously shown, particularly for the public providers.

Irrespective of the type of services, the main problems[16] concerning the human resources, mentioned by the providers of social services for the elderly, are as follows: (i) "to some extent" – it is hard to fill in the open positions because of the current regulations applying to the public institutions; the offer of trained people is very limited for particular qualifications, especially for the home-care services; (ii) "to a rather large extent" – difficult to employ additional staff because of the budget constraints; low wages compared to other sectors of activity (mentioned only by the public providers); working in this job is rather demanding (emotionally, physically, etc.), in the case of the staff from the medical-social centres.

16 To what extent your unit, as provider of services, is confronted with the following problems which affect its capacity of ensuring the staff required to supply services? Scale of response from 0 – "at all" to 4 – "to a great extent". Problems: 1.We cannot afford to hire additional staff because of the budget limitation; 2. Filling in the open positions is difficult because of the current regulations applying to the public institutions (we are not allowed to hire staff); 3. The low wages compared to similar positions in other sectors of activity; 4. Very limited offer of trained staff for particular qualifications that we need; 5. Working in this job is very demanding (emotionally, physically, etc.).

(E) Future plans regarding the services

The future plans of the providers of services, mentioned in 2014, were announcing the process of development which took place between 2014 and 2018, as has been previously mentioned. Most of the public and private providers stated in 2014 that they were planning to expand their capacity to provide services, so as to include as many elder beneficiaries as possible; they also aimed to diversify the range of services/activities supplied to their beneficiaries.

Therefore, the network of social services for the elderly experienced a sustained process of development over the recent years. However, it is yet to meet the increasing requirement for assistance and care for the aged people, more so as under the conditions of a massive immigration of the young people and changing of the dominant pattern of care within the family.

Conclusions

This article presents an analysis of social services for the elderly provided in Romania. The research findings presented are based on a census of the public and private suppliers of social services for the elderly, according to the official data, as of April 2014. The census registered a response rate of 54 %. The results are grouped around the following key topics included in the questionnaire: (a) capacity of providing services, (b) accessibility of the services, (c) financing of the services, (d) human resources and (e) plans for the future.

The residential services for the elderly vary considerably in terms of capacity, from a minimum of 6, to a maximum of 295 beneficiaries. The largest entities are the homes for the elderly and the medical and social residential centres. The dominant profile of the beneficiaries of residential services shows people aged 75 and more and/or people completely dependent, which explains why about two thirds of the exits from these services are due to death. The capacity of the home-care services for the elderly was (in 2014 and remained so until 2018) insufficient compared to the requirements, just like in the case of the residential services. Unlike this, the day-care services seemed to have just a slightly undersized capacity compared to the demand.

The main factors which limit the access of the potential beneficiaries relate both to the demand (low level of demand because of the potential beneficiaries' mentality), and to the offer (which was rather limited, at least in 2014), as well as to specific factors such as: most of the centres are located in urban areas, high costs of services provided in medical and social centres, or an insufficient number of seats within the existing services.

The study also draws attention to the problem of financing the social services for all vulnerable groups, not just for the elderly, an issue that is yet to be solved even in 2018. In addition, the lack of, or insufficient human resources is "to some extent" a factor which affects adversely the capacity to provide quality services, as previously shown, particularly for the public providers.

To sum up, the network of social services for the elderly significantly developed over the past years. Nevertheless, there still are serious challenges to be addressed, such as the increasing requirement for assistance and care for the aged people, more so as under the conditions of a massive immigration of the young people and changing family structure which affects provision of family/ informal care for the elderly.

References

Bodogai, Simona/Cutler, Stephen J.: Aging in Romania: Research and Public Policy. The Gerontologist 54(2), 2013, pp. 147–152.

CNPV - Consiliul Naţional al Persoanelor Vârstnice: Evoluţia condiţiilor de viaţă ale populaţiei vârstnice din România în perioada 2007–2012. 2013. Available at: www.cnpv.ro

CNPV - Consiliul Național pentru Persoane Vârstnice: Situația persoanelor vârstnice din România. 2014a. Available at: www.cnpv.ro.

CNPV - Consiliul Național pentru Persoane Vârstnice: Proiectarea populației vârstnice a României la orizontul anului 2060. 2014b. Available at: www.cnpv.ro.

CNPV - Consiliul Național pentru Persoane Vârstnice: Asistența socială a persoanelor vârstnice furnizată la nivelul comunităților locale. 2014c. Available at: www.cnpv.ro.

CNPV - Consiliul Național pentru Persoane Vârstnice: Calitatea vieții persoanelor vârstnice din România. 2014d. Available at: www.cnpv.ro.

CRJ – Centrul de Resurse Juridice: Raport vizită inopinată de monitorizare pentru observarea modului în care sunt respectate drepturile persoanelor cu dizabilităţi mintale din Cãminul de vârstnici şi adulţi cu dizabilităţi Aldeni, judeţul Buzău — centru privat de recuperare şi reintegrare socială a persoanelor cu dizabilităţi mintale. 2013. Available at: http://www.crj.ro/userfiles/editor/files/Raport%20CRJ%20_Caminul%20de%20batrani%20Aldeni.pdf

Costăchescu, Daniela: Romanian Social Protection System for Elderly People. Scientific Annals of the "Alexandru Ioan Cuza" University, Iaşi. New Series Sociology and Social Work Section 8(2), 2015, pp. 113–132.

Hrozenská, Martina: Long-Term Care for Older People in the Slovak Republic: Current Problem and Urgent Challenge. Revista de Asistență Socială X (2), 2011, pp. 89–100.

Kavšek, Marta/Bogataj, David: Towards new quality standards of long-term care in Slovenia. Journal of Universal Excellence 6(1), 2017, pp. 11–24.

Ležovič, Mário: Analysis of long-term care in the context of social and health services in social institutional facilities in Slovakia. Cent Eur J Public Health 17(3), 2009, pp.128–132.

Petrescu, Claudia/Toth, Alexandru/Bojinca, Marian/Kedves, Maria: Studiu privind situația existentă a serviciilor sociale în Municipiul Bucureşti. 2011 Fundația pentru Dezvoltarea Societății Civile. Available at: http://www.fdsc.ro/library/Studiu%20privind%20situatia%20existenta%20a%20serviciilor%20sociale%20in%20Bucuresti.pdf.

Reiljan, Janno/Ülper, Aivo/Puolokainen, Tarmo: The Impact of Demand Factors on the Supply of Local Public Services în Estonian Municipalities. Public Finance & Management 15(1), 2015, pp. 24–46.

Roş, Nicolae: Protecţia socială acordată persoanelor vârstnice în România. Fiat Iustitia 6(2), 2012, pp. 76–99.

Vrânceanu, Elena Simona: Migration and Social Protection Policies in Romania and Switzerland Promoting Active Aging in the Welfare State. Scientific Annals of the "Alexandru Ioan Cuza" University, Iaşi. New Series Sociology and Social Work Section 8(2), 2015, pp.83–100.

Rusu, Horaţiu: Solidarity with the Elderly in Romania. Revista de cercetare și intervenţie sociala 52, 2016, pp. 130–144.

Teşliuc, Emil/Grigoraş, Vlad/Stănculescu, Manuela Sofia (coord.): Background Study for the National Strategy on Social Inclusion and Poverty Reduction 2015–2020. 2015. Bucharest. World Bank Available at: https://openknowledge.worldbank.org/handle/10986/23830.

Wija, Petr: Formal and Informal Long-Term Care and the Role of Family Carers. European Journal of Mental Health 10, 2015, pp. 233–244.

Ioan I. GÂF-DEAC[1], *Otilia Teodora RACHIERU*[2]

[1] Senior Researcher, Center of Mountain Economy, Romanian Academy, Email: editurafmp@gmail.com

[2] PhD, RNP Romsilva, Bucharest, Romania, Email: otilia.ciutacu@yahoo.com

The Infrastructure of Mountain Areas in Romania, a Determinant Factor for Economic Diversification and Social Development

Abstract *The article examines the national capacity to assume the sequential, sub-structural development of the mountain areas in Romania that do not have enough amplitude of communication and connections in relation to the requirements and speed at which transformations take place, in the sense of economic and social development, in the mountains Europe. In Romania there are also disadvantaged mountain areas, which are categorized as special territories / areas, of national interest, due to the economic, social, cultural and environmental potential. The authors propose the establishment of Regional Agro-Technology Alliances for the Mountain Areas, in which regional generic contractors will work to promote the collaborative mountain economy. At the same time, it is proposed to rally to an important general trend of "collective-collectivization" in the new mountain economy. For Romania, it is appreciated that, in fact, the most important requirement in the retellistic context of the new mountain economy is to identify the ways of conceptualization / formalization of the network / networks. A network must be "a structural one." If an "anomaly" (such as a shortcoming, a failure, a dysfunction, etc.) of a member firm / member of the group occurs, the network is meant to "rectify the market" and "hierarchies" so that the whole of the association, (so for all components) to achieve an expected economic positivity.*

Keywords: *mountainous holistic development, collaborative mountain economy, networking mountain economy mountain development*

Introduction

The fundamental objective of Romania's development can be achieved by creating a functioning market economy, compatible with EU principles, norms, mechanisms, institutions and policies. The evaluation of the resources and possibilities, of the national development context also takes into account the mountain economy of Romania.

Until now (2018), an adequate, representative, quasi-complete, quantitative and qualitative picture of the structure, functionality and expected contribution of the mountain economy to the overall economy of Romania is not formalized. However, the participation of mountains and people, exploiting their natural resources, to the overall development of the country, is recognized statistically and pragmatically.

The mountain economy contributes to the orientation of the national development direction, opens / provides ways of social inclusion and cohesion in local communities. It is also part of a social economy, starting from the reality of the supremacy of participation and influences from social actors, people and social objectives on capital.

Economic development is closely linked to social-political development and human development. We appreciate that the mountainous social and economic development is a sum of micro and macroeconomic processes when economic growth is registered.

The linear transformation of the mountain society is today relatively inadequate, in the conditions of generalization of communication and movement without frontiers of people and goods, in accelerated, complex, nonlinear regime.

The central issue of mountain development is to identify solutions by which communities in these areas overtake their traditional work, living and well-being. The concrete mechanisms through which mountain development is actually achieved are the result of new knowledge in multidimensional society in which Romania objectively engages and immerses, according to the global unstoppable tendencies towards evolution towards a universal, universal well-being.

In the context, an explanatory model of the theory of the dependence of the mountain infrastructure of infrastruture is more present than necessity, more than ever, for Romania.

1. Literature review

Economic diversity and social development in mountain areas is a widely debated issue in world literature. In particular, vulnerabilities are identified and concerns are being sought to find solutions to difficult and specific mountain development issues.

For exemple, Jodha S. Narpat (2005), afirm that "In the context of socio-economic vulnerability, the mountain circumstances can be seen as the cause of risky and limited range of earning and sustenance options for mountain communities. Thus, due to fragility, some mountain areas cannot withstand the activities involving high resource use (which is often associated with increase in productivity) and creation of infrastructure (which could catalyze resource use intensification). Because of relative isolation, mountain communities are unable to fully harness <niche opportunities>, which could enhance the range of earning options. Inaccessibility and isolation restrict the access and hence, the reliance on external support and force the mountain communities to depend on the limited options and local resources."

Garcia-Ruiz J.M., et al., (1996), show that "Internal and external factors explain the great changes that have occurred in the mountains of developed countries, especially in Western Europe. (...) Rapid depopulation, due largely to changing social expectations rather than a decrease in crop production (...). This led to the break down of the traditional social system and to the progressive marginalization of agriculture. (...) The most significant changes in the land use have been: 1) the decline of sheep and the expansion of cattle farming; 2) the shrinkage of the cultivated area; 3) the decline in cereal production and increase in meadows; and 4) the reforestation of many abandoned hillslopes."

On the other hand, it is considered that the "Depopulation is responsible for a marked ageing of the population and a decrease in the number of members per family, which in turn caused the disappearance of transhumance and a crisis in sheep farming. In a parallel way tourism, forest policy and hydrological policy also contributed to the general spatial disorganization." (Garcia-Ruiz J.M. and Lasanta T., 1993)

In Overcoming Poverty Together, 2014–2019 Progress Report, (2018) it is shown that "Social development is about improving the well-being of every individual in society so they can reach their full potential. The success of society is linked to the well-being of each and every citizen.", and Petrescu Claudia, (2013), emphasizes that "Local development includes activities carried out both with the participation of community members and those carried out by public authorities in order to increase the quality of life of members of a community."

In essence, there is also a certain redundancy in discussing the topic among the specialists. Thus, Toderean Olivia, (2004), reports that "So much is discussed about underdevelopment, developed countries, developing countries, sustainable development, human development, political development, that the very ubiquity of the term raises signs of question on his clear, appropriate understanding."

2. Research Method. Data Collection and Preparation

Mountain development is essentially linked to the industrial transport sector. The Romanian carriers' area is participating in the country's development by 5–6 billion euros, equivalent to 5 % of Gross Domestic Product (GDP). (National Institute of Statistics, 2017)

The major obstacle to the development of the field and, in broad terms, to the national economy proves to be the infrastructure. It brings together only 800 km of the highway and 60 more kilometers planned to be operational in 2018. As a consequence, the mountain sub-zones do not have enough inter-unitary connections. (National Union of Road Transports in Romania, 2017)

According to WEF Global Competitiveness Index, Romania lost six positions in 2017 compared to 2016 in terms of infrastructure quality. (World Economic Forum, 2018)

In fact, infrastructure quality measures, - indicatively, the competitiveness of global economies. In this chapter, Romania has ranked 68th in 137 countries. (Euler Hermes Economic Research, 2018)

As such, the national capacity to assume the sequential, sub-structural development of mountain areas with insufficient amplitude of communication and connections in relation to the requirements and speed of the transformations, in the sense of economic- in the mountains of Europe.

Some estimates show the need to invest in Romania's transport infrastructure by almost 70 billion euros, of which positive affection for mountain areas has a reflection of approx. 9–11 billion euros. (ZF & Deloitte, 2018) Mountain areas require support for specific protection, development and management as they are environmentally vulnerable areas.

In Romania there are also disadvantaged mountain areas, which are categorized as special territories / areas of national interest, due to their economic, social, cultural and environmental potential. The ecological fragility of mountain areas in Romania is reflected in the consequences of excessive actions, activities and commitments to exploit specific resources, or in neglecting the modeling of specific local balances. Thus, the unreasonable exploitation of forest resources, the absence or intermittent use of organic fertilizers, cause the qualitative degradation of natural pastures and meadows.

Insufficient commitment to protect and exploit mountain resources in conditions of climate change and demographic evolution, lack of road infrastructure, access roads and subsistence transport, all articulate to the matrix of local defensive elements in mountain structures.

According to the Romanian Mountainous Sustainable Development Strategy (2009), and the National Strategic Guidelines for the Sustainable Development of the Less-favored Mountain Area (2014–2020), a disadvantaged mountainous area in Romania consists of ATUs designated according to the following criteria: 1) Administrative-territorial units located at average altitudes greater than or equal to 600 m, the limits of which are those of the physical blocks (identified in the Integrated Administration and Control System) belong to these ATUs; 2) UATs located at medium altitudes between 400–600 m and having an average slope equal to or more than 15 %, the limits of which are those of the physical blocks (identified in the Integrated Administration and Control System) belonging to these ATU's.

On the other hand, large distances and inadequate transport infrastructure, plus the lack of concentration of supply, cause mountain products not to be fully exploited. The number of accommodation units in the less-favored mountain area increased by 22 % in the last decade. The closure of some industrial units in mountain areas has led to labor migration, witnessing depopulation.

Exploitation of mountain natural resources is not yet sufficiently competitive, due to the lack of financial resources for technological upgrading. Lack of the road network leads to increased anthropogenic pressure on protected natural areas.

The Strategic Guidelines for Mountain Development are articulated with the provisions of the Europe 2020 Strategy document and aim at: 1) smart growth (developing the knowledge-based mountain economy); 2) Sustainable growth (promoting a competitive green economy, making better use of resources); 3) inclusive growth (promoting a high-employment economy generating social and territorial cohesion).

The principles for mountain development refer to: 1) sustainable / sustainable development, 2) precaution and prevention, 3) public-private partnership 4) programmatic approach 5) ecological balance, biodiversity and habitat conservation 6) adequate living standards for all residents.

According to a study by the European Commission, cited by Oprea Cornel, (2013), 19.7 % of the utilized agricultural area is found in the mountainous area in Romania, 18.5 % of the labor force directly involved in agriculture, 17.6 % of the total number of farms and 19.5 % of the number of animals. The average size of the farm is 3.9 ha (the third smallest of the mountain countries), the economic size of the farm per hectare is 253 Euros, and the annual unit of work is 1,631 euros (the smallest of mountain countries).

There are eight economic and social development regions in Romania, including mountain areas. These are conditions for the incipient preconditions of formalizing mountain agro-industrial clusters. The dynamic economic coverage of each region can be achieved by using alliance and cooperation formulas. For example, the Regional Agro-Technology Alliance for Mountain Areas may be set up to operate a regional generic contractor to promote a collaborative mountain economy.

Contextually, in the new mountain economy, in our appreciation, alliances must be formalized in the regime of competitive advantage (generators). That is why the upper stage in the evolution of the mountain economy of the future is fundamentally related to the emergence / establishment of innovative alliances, providing quasi-continuous, cumulative exponential competitive advantages.

Mountain companies in alliances will have a predisposition to strong interrelationships. Proximity or local support leads to wider information and immersion in the phenomenon of mountain industrial climate dominated by "collective advantage".

We propose to rally an important general trend of "collective – collectivization" in the new mountain economy.

Visibly, the contemporary economic world, including mountain areas, allies / accepts conventionally, without significant reservations, organizational and functional processes that relate to: 1) association; 2) accession; 3) communion; 4) access, 5) multiculturalism; 6) generalized information; 7) consensus; 8) generalized distribution and consumption; 9) unification; 10) foreign investments; 11) cross-border relocations; 12) cohesion, solidarity; 13) international affairs; 14) liberalization, redistribution; 15) harmonization; comparative advantages; 16) competitive advantages; concentration, 17) collective advantages; 18) alignment; increasing complexity; 19) convergence; 20) the acquis communautaire; clustering; 21) economics; internationalization; 22) regionalization; globalization; 23) integration; 24) globalization.

All the above system vectors contain intricately the property of gathering, gathering, summing, respectively cumulating, approaching, tangent of factors and conditions of mountain development - in other words, interrelation, articulation, osmosis, connection, multipotential and n-dimensional connection.

Essentially, a certain “collectivization” of the actions / activities, respectively, of the infrastructure and the life of human communities in the mountain areas is accepted and implemented.

The productive-economic strategic execution is the one that becomes the real factor of business orientation towards superior performance in mountain areas in Romania. In fact, the formalization of the mountainous strategic development network for diversified, social and economic development takes place.

In the new mountain economy there is always a knowledge management map, operational real-time. Achieving the competitive advantage in the new mountain economy is characterized by the actions of the companies, which have to face different managerial attempts at the individual level. Therefore, the whole of the new mountain economy is marked by a competitive advantage as new knowledge is formalized in slow processes, characterized by increased attention to the application of scientific / specialized data / information, codifying the abilities and tasks of human resources in an innovative, flexible environment and demand-oriented.

Low freight costs, increased dissemination of information (knowledge), liberalization of markets, disappearance / mitigation of restrictive boundaries between different market areas, expansion of marketable goods and services, facilitation of markets, extension of marketable goods and services, facilitation of delocalisation, to which new types of specific management are added in the productive / reproductive and distribution / consumption entities are formalizing prerequisites for the new economy in mountain areas in Romania.

For Romania, we consider that, in fact, the most important requirement in the retellistic context of the new mountain economy is to identify the ways of conceptualization / formalization of the network / networks.

A network must be “a structural one.” If there is an “anomaly” (such as a drawback, a failure, a dysfunction, etc.) of a group member / group member, the network is meant to “rectify the market” and “hierarchies” so that, on the whole associations (so for all components) to achieve an expected positiveness.

Therefore, the collective solution of the problems of the firms in the network of the new mountain economy refers not only to the aspects related to the interconnections in the markets and hierarchies, but to the correct applications from the transactional cost theory, by improving the functions of: 1) coordination, 2) information and 3) control through / using network structures.

Between the usual transaction costs and those related to the network that ensure the mountain development in Romania there are differences of favorability, the positive predominance being found, first of all, in the local network of proximity. (Figure 1).

It is appreciated that in the mountainous areas of Romania the competitive advantage has the more favorable chances of appearance and manifestation in the new economy, as the productive-economic re-utilization is achieved with a high degree of consolidation and functionality.

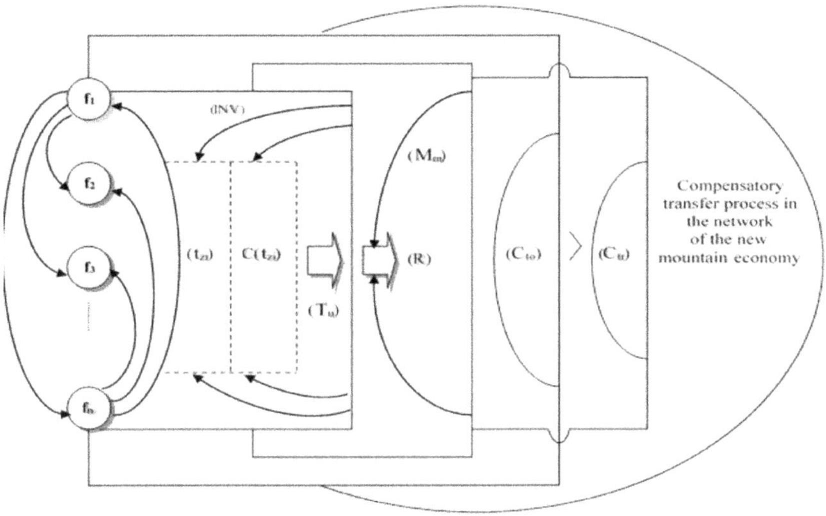

Figure 1: Manifestation of the favorable compensatory transfer process in the network of the new mountain economy

Source: Author, 2018.

Note: f1, f2, f3,...,fn= mountain businesses/ firms; (Mm)= mediation mechanism; (Ctr)= network transaction costs; (R)= network; C(tzi)= transaction costs; (Tu)=single transaction; (tzi)= transactions; (Cto)= common transaction costs; (INV)= invisibility of the initial transactions.

We note that the systemic vision of the "all-encompassing mountain economic complex" suggests the holistic development of the quasi-fully articulated, "architecturally" Romanian mountain ensemble, in which any inter-relationship and any multi-dimensional and multidimensional reporting between the constituent elements is possible.

Therefore, in order to formalize in real terms the perceptible new mountain economy proves useful the approach of reintegration, which ensures the diversification and the development of the multilateral socio-economic development.

For now, economic reintegration (the retailing economy) represents - in our opinion - the conceptual alternative of proximal applicability in the Romanian mountains.

Conclusions

The major obstacle to the development of the mountain range in Romania and, in a broad view, of the national economy proves to be the infrastructure.

Insufficient commitment to protect and exploit mountain resources in conditions of climate change and demographic evolution, lack of road infrastructure, access roads and subsistence transport, all articulate to the local disfavoring matrix, affecting the development of mountain structures.

The strategic guidelines for mountain development in Romania are articulated with the provisions of the Europe 2020 document and aim at: 1) smart growth, 2) sustainable growth, and 3) inclusive growth.

The dynamic economic coverage of each region can be achieved by using alliance and cooperation formulas. For example, the Regional Agro-Technology Alliance for the Mountain Areas in Romania can be set up, in which a regional generic contractor, to promote the collaborative mountain economy, will operate.

The ensemble of the new mountain economy is marked by a competitive advantage as new knowledge is formalized in slow processes characterized by increased attention to application of scientific / specialized data / information, codifying the skills and tasks of human resources in an innovative, flexible and oriented environment on request.

References

1. Garcia-Ruiz J.M., Lasanta T.- Land-use conflicts as a result of land-use changes in the Central Spanish Pyrenees. A review. Mountain Research and Development, 13(3): 213–223, 1993.
2. Garcia-Ruiz J.M., et al. - Land-use changes and sustainable development in mountain areas: a case study in the Spanish Pyrenees, Landscape Ecology, vol. 11, no. 5, pp. 267–277, SPB Academic Publishing bv, Amsterdam, 1996.
3. Jodha S. Narpat, - Adaptation strategies against growing environmental and social vulnerabilities in mountain areas, Himalayan Journal of Sciences, Vol. 3, Issue 5, Jan.-June 2005.
4. Oprea Cornel, - Agricultura in zonele montane va beneficia de o strategie dedicata de dezvoltare, groRomania.ro, July 2013.
5. Petrescu Claudia (coord.), - Economia socială în contextul dezvoltării locale, Ed.Polirom, Iaşi, 2013.
6. Toderean Olivia - Dezvoltare economică, dezvoltare social-politică sau dezvoltare umană? O retrospectivă asupra gândirii consacrate despre dezvoltare (development thinking), Revista Transilvană de Ştiinţe Administrative, 2(11), 2004, pp. 145–156.
7. Date statistice, Institutul Naţional de Statistică, 2017.
8. Date statistice, Uniunea Naţională a Transportatorilor Rutieri din România, 2017.
9. Global Competitiveness Index 2017–2018, World Economic Forum, 2018.
10. Major Companies in Romania 2018, Report by ZF&Deloitte, 2018.
11. Modalităţi de plată, Euler Hermes Economic Research, 2018.
12. Orientări strategice naţionale pentru dezvoltarea durabilă a zonei montane defavorizate (2014–2020), Anexă memorandum, www://madr.ro.

13. Overcoming Poverty Together, 2014–2019 Progress Report, The Economic and Social Inclusion Corporation, New Brunswickers, Smallacts.ca/resources, February, 2018.
14. Strategia dezvoltării durabile a zonei montane din România, www.enciclopedia-economica.ro, 2009.

Elena BĂNICĂ[1], *Valentina VASILE*[2]

[1] Romanian Academy and National Institute of Statistics, Bucharest, Romania, Email: elenabanica77@gmail.com

[2] Institute of National Economy, Romanian Academy, Bucharest, Romania, Email: valentinavasile2009@gmail.com

External Trade and Employment in Foreign Capital Companies in Romania. Historical Approach

Abstract *In the last century, foreign capital was present in Romania, contributing to economic development, diversification of economic activity, promotion of technological progress and employment. Involvement was unequal, as well as economic and social efficiency. This analysis illustrates, from a historical perspective, the main similarities and differences of the presence of foreign capital during the periods of market economy of Romania, respectively the interwar period (1918–1948) and after 1989, in terms of the importance of foreign capital in Romania, its productivity and commercial policies adopted at national level. It presents the overall evolution of the foreign trade activity from the point of view of the goods, which are subject to the international transactions, and the main partner countries of Romania. For the period after EU accession, it is presented the relationship between foreign capital, employment generated in the economy and foreign trade in goods activity. This relationship is based on the theory according to which the symbiosis between financial resources, human capital and advanced technology used in productive processes lead to market competitiveness, both on microeconomic and macroeconomic levels. The competitiveness of foreign trade companies is mainly defined by the technology used in production of goods destined for external markets. It is identified the specialization or diversification of the activity of the companies with foreign capital from the point of view of the economic sectors. The historical analysis revealed that the national production potential can be valued through foreign trade activity. The role of foreign-owned firms is very important for a developing economy but their contribution is limited to the comparative advantages they can obtain.*

Keywords: *export, foreign capital, employment, market economy, competitivity*

Introduction

The Great Union in 1918 led to the creation of the modern Romania and of an important industrial base. By joining the new Romanian territories to the Old

Kingdom, the economic potential increased by more than 2 times: the population by 2.2 times, the total area of Romania and the cultivated agricultural area by 2.1 times, the length of the railways network by 2.5 etc. (Manoilescu, 1921). The contribution of the regions was different from the perspective of the economic potential: Transylvania and Banat have increased the industrial character of Romania, while Bessarabia the agricultural one. (Arcadian, 1936).

The foreign capital strongly influenced the economic life of Romania, being important part of the business environment during the development period of the competitive economy, respectively during the interwar period (1918–1948) and the period of active participation in the process of globalization (1989–2017). The period from 1948 to 1989 was excluded from this study because it is characterized by a centralized economy where, through the nationalization of assets, foreign capital has considerably been reduced, having a limited role in influencing the business environment.

The two periods characterized by open economy and competitive business environment, despite the over 4 decades separating them, have important similarities. On the one hand, the peace treaties concluded by the end of the First World War led to the opening of new economic opportunities in the Romanian space for the national and foreign companies. The return to the market economy after 1989 had the same effect, followed by privatization and free access of foreign capital for economic modernization and diversification. On the other hand, the development of the FDI sector, with available financial resources and important market shares, has influenced the dynamics of the domestic business environment, including the local one (through economic integration on the value chain of some goods / services) and ensuring high level of employment and increased productivity. Similarly, in both periods of analysis, foreign capital has accessed strategic areas of the Romanian economy, such as the mining and petroleum industries, the processing industry, and has taken over an important part of banking services, commerce and transport infrastructure development.

There are also important differences between the two periods, which stem from the increasing process of globalization in which Romania has actively participated since 1990, as well as from the development of technology, of communications or working conditions. The market capitalisation of the current opportunities for relocating of economic activities through FDIs and foreign trade on new markets differs substantially in the period after 1989 from the interwar period. This process differently affects every industry; the competitiveness of the firm depends on the reaction on market opportunities. The very large amount of information available on the market - facilitated by ICT services - leads to the need to integrate the companies (including small and medium-sized) on the production chains of MNEs, already leaders of the product market.

The close relationship between foreign capital, employment and external trade in goods is a self-generating factor of economic development at the level of companies. The symbiosis between the availability of financial resources, adequate human capital and advanced technology in productive processes leads to market competitiveness, both at microeconomic and macroeconomic level, ensuring a better capitalization of resources and stimulating the development of domestic capital.

Foreign capital has accessed the Romanian market primarily through the technology with which it participates in the economic activity. The import of the next generation technology in various sectors leads to increased performance, regional and local development where the productive places of foreign investment is located. Benefits might be obtained from both specialization and diversification on productive branches; for Romania it is essential to negotiate its advantages obtained from the presence of the foreign capital and its economic activity in our country.

Romania's foreign trade was influenced by the main political, economic and social events of the last century: the First World War, the post-war reconstruction period and the development of the market economy, the imminence of the Second World War, the centralized economy (1947–1989), the period of return to the market economy in 1990, integration into European structures in 2007 and active participation in the globalization process (Figure 1).

Two aspects, with strong effects on the national industrial structure and activities, influenced Romania's industrial development, as a weaker developed country in Europe: a) the political conditions of development of the Romanian state and b) the interests of the capitalist economies influencing the national development through export markets and FDIs.

In both analysed periods, the start-up period was characterized by instability and economic and social disruption, affecting the external trade activity, generating trade balance imbalances (Figure 2):

a) During the period 1918–1947, Romania functioned for the first time as a unitary state, in a social and business environment integrated into the new national borders. Territorial expansion through the joining of Transylvania, Bucovina, Crişana, Maramureş, Banat and Bessarabia was accompanied by the increase of the labour force and the resources of the land and the subsoil with those of the former territories in possession of the Austro-Hungarian Empire and of Russia, respectively. (Vasile et al., 2018). In 1918, the economic activity, production and export, were subject to the protectionist laws, in force at the beginning of the 20th century, mainly represented by the Costinescu's customs tariff (1906) and the incentive laws in various industrial branches (textile industry, beer, alcohol, flour) (Scărlătescu, 1939).
b) After the events of December 1989, chaotic economic restructuring and privatization (with any price) were accompanied by a renunciation of the foreign trade markets; consumption austerity in the nineteenth decade of the 20th century led to increases in consumption of imported goods.

In both situations, due to the chronic shortage of economic resources for rehabilitation / reorganization, respectively development / diversification, foreign capital easily accessed the business environment, developing sectors and activities of

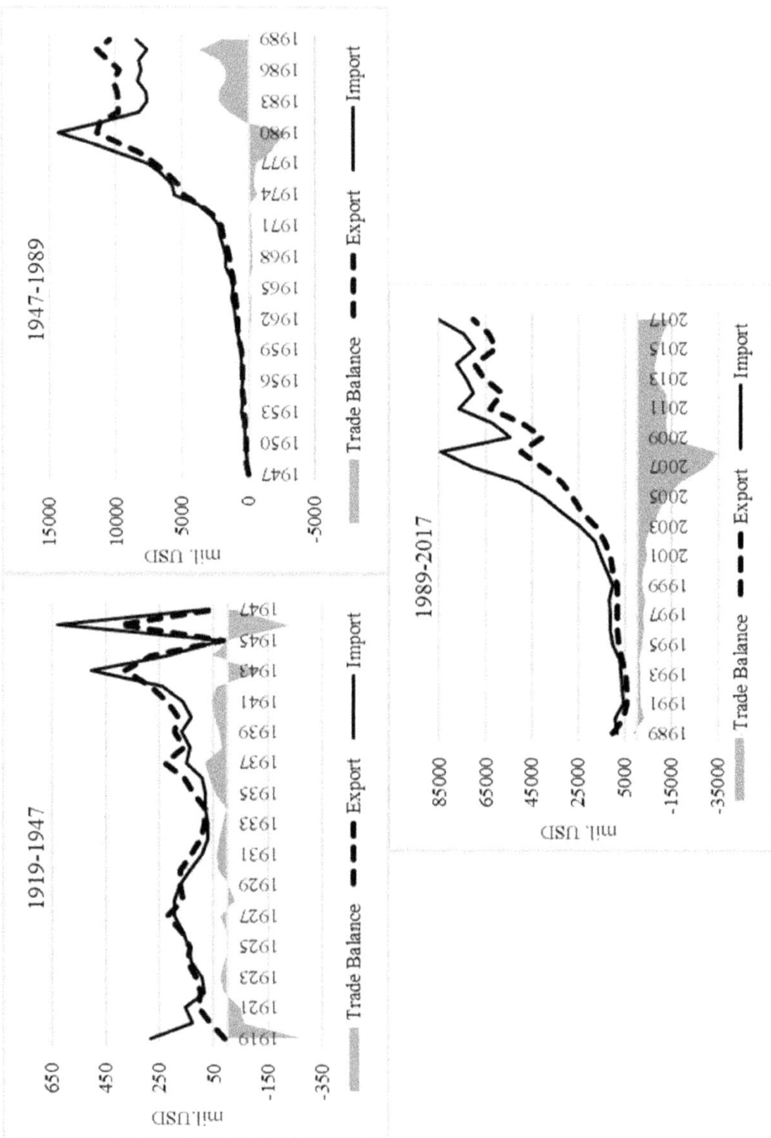

Figure 1: Romania's external trade, 1918–2017 (mil. USD, current prices)
Data sources: Romanian Statistical Yearbook, editions 1939, 1990, TEMPO Online databases (www.insse.ro)

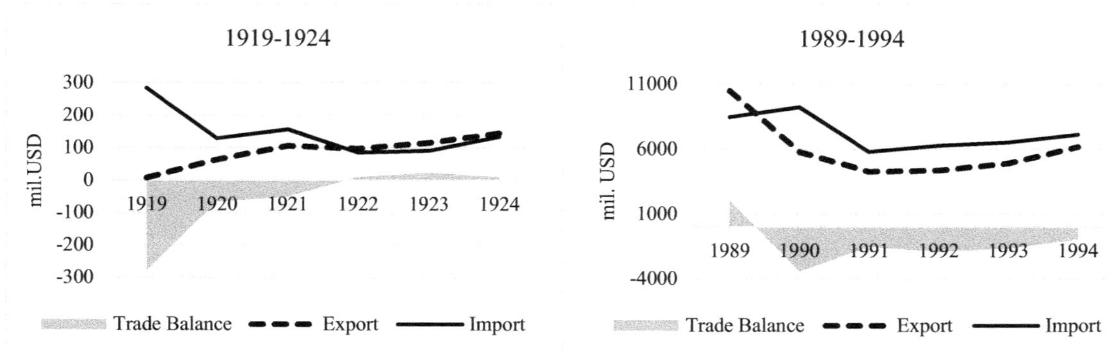

Figure 2: Romania's external trade during 1919–1924 and 1989–1994 (mil. USD)

Data sources: Romanian Statistical Yearbook, editions 1939, 1990, TEMPO Online databases (www.insse.ro)

interest - the banking system, industries with important local resources, activities that capitalised the strategic wealth in the domain of construction and transport.

The main stages of the economic cycle which Romania underwent in the periods with market economy (1918–1947 and 1990-present) can be subdivided, each substage presenting specific characteristics, some of them similar in both periods or, on the contrary, divergent. In all cases, we considered the overall effect of the foreign trade activity, namely the trade deficit or trade surplus.

Each stage presented in the above table has its own balancing mechanisms, but after 1990, the trade balance was exclusively negative. On the one hand foreign capital is oriented towards exports of goods on the own value chain, where export prices are reduced and, on the other hand, the domestic firms capitalizes the opportunities found on foreign markets, and the share of high tech.

1. Goods imported and exported by Romania

During 1918–1938, Romania exported mainly raw materials and agricultural products, wood and mineral oil. The share of vegetable products in the total export increased by 16 % in 1938 compared to 1919, while the share of fuels, ores and their derivatives decreased by over 22 %. After the Great Union, the import of vegetable textiles held the largest share in the national import (31.3 %), but in 1939 goods such as iron, goods of iron, machinery and appliances accounted for over 61 % of total imports. (Figure 3).

Prior to the crisis of 1929–1933, Romania's exports were mainly made up of immediately available products (cereals and their derivatives), but after 1934, mineral oil became the main exported product. The import was carried out to cover areas where the availability of goods on the Romanian market could not be assured (machinery, installations, industrial products and various raw materials).

After the period of centralized economy, the structural changes had strong impact on the supply of goods on foreign markets. The collapse of formerly state-owned industries, the privatization of large industrial companies and the reopening of the economy to foreign capital led to a reduction in the share of manufacturing goods in national exports and to the increase imports of machinery and equipment of next generations needed for re-launching of national industry (Annex 3).

After 1989, industrial products, which generated important exports during the centralized economy, experienced strong reductions as a share in national exports: petroleum products from 18 % in 1989 to 3 % in 2016, metallurgical products from 13 % to 5 %, chemical industry products from 10 % to 3 % over the same period. There were economic sectors that have registered significant growth, such as the road transport industry, which grew from 7 % to 21 % in 2016, due to FDIs.

Other industries have maintained their share in total exports, regardless of political or economic circumstances; an example is the export of wood-based products, featured by a stable business during the analysed period; the availability of raw

Table 1: Summary of economic cycles features in Romania

Period 1918–1947	Contemporary period (1989–2017)
1919–1924 Main features - Diversification and increase in volume of available production factors, by joining new territories. - Economic recovery period after the Great War. - The needs of the population and domestic production were covered by imports of basic commodities. - The foreign capital was very interested in investing in Romania, especially in the processing of the primary, natural resources, available in a high degree and diversity. - Protectionism and economic stimulation (export, industry). - Diversification and increase in volume of available production factors, by joining new territories following the Great Union. Effects on external trade - Favourable development of foreign trade activity by achieving a trade surplus after 4 years after the end of the Great War and also maintaining it for another 3 years.	1990–1994 Main features - A transition period from the centralized economy to the market economy, the reorganization of the property and the reduction of the company's size by reorganization / privatization. - Increased imports of commodities of high diversity compared to the previous period (centralized economy), but not necessarily of higher quality. - The recurrence and increase of the volume of FDIs (privatizations of the large state-owned enterprises). - Reducing trade restrictions (trade barriers, customs duties), especially in relation with European countries. Effects on external trade - Intensifying the trade relations with partners in Europe through massive imports of goods. - The re-emergence in 1990 of the trade deficit and its continuous growth, by stimulating the imports for consumption and the reduction of the performant exports; this was caused by the ending of the productive activities following the short-term financial interest of the investors.
1924–1929 Main features - Intensive economic development. - Increasing activity of foreign capital in Romania; - Direct intervention of the state on the market and the limitation of the freedom to export and import goods.	1994–2008 Main features - The transition to the functional market economy facilitated the economic growth, based mainly on exports, the Romanian products, medium processed, re-entering the old markets. - The pre-accession process has opened new markets in the EU. - Increasing the volume of foreign investments and imports, determined by the substantial consumption potential of the national market. Effects on external trade

(*continued on next page*)

Table 1: Continued

Period 1918–1947	Contemporary period (1989–2017)
On the one hand, the export of primary goods[1] necessary for the survival of the population was strictly forbidden and, on the other hand, the protection of industrial activities through the customs tariff was pursued[2]. Effects on external trade - The reduction of imports and the obtaining of a commercial surplus necessary for the payment of the external debt contracted.	- Focus on trade relations with European partners. - Deepening the trade deficit.
1929–1933 Main features - A period marked by the global economic and financial crisis and the recovery of the economy. - The collapse of international commodity exchanges during the crisis. Effects on external trade - The 1929–1933 crisis characterized by the trade surplus, driven by the increase in exports of mineral products. - Traditional economic relations on both goods and partner countries.	2008–2010 Main features - Romania's accession to the EU. - A period marked by the global economic and financial crisis and the recovery of the economy. - Active participation in globalisation process. Effects on external trade - Maximum intensification of economic exchanges of goods with countries in this area. - Maintaining traditional trade relations. - The increase in the trade deficit, especially on the intra-EU, but also based on the weak performance on extra-EU markets. - The collapse of international goods exchanges. - The 2008–2009 crisis characterized by the deepening of the trade deficit, although Romania's outflow of the crisis was driven by the exports of goods performed by foreign companies. Export was the first indicator signalising the exit from the crisis (in 2010 the export exceeded already the level reached in 2008).

1 By the 1923 Constitution there were applied the agrarian reform and landowning of a massive number of peasants; this has led to a more efficient use of the land through the direct involvement of the population. At that time the population was mainly rural, 78.2 % of the active population being employed in agriculture and only 7.2 % in the industrial activity, these two being the most developed branches of the economy

2 The customs protection policy has resulted in the limitation of the quantities of foreign goods on the national market and the additional stimulation of the national goods production (Paţac, 2009).

Table 1: Continued

Period 1918–1947	Contemporary period (1989–2017)
	- The economic crisis of 2008–2009 had different effects on economic activity, but exports of goods were characterized by a positive evolution; this was mainly due to the activity of foreign-owned companies which have intensified their exports from Romania, in particular high-tech goods.
1933–1939 Main features - Economic recovery period. - State intervention in the economy. - Protectionist policy applied. Effects on external trade - Trade surplus.	2011–2017 Main features - The resumption of economic growth. - Stagnation of FDIs dynamics. Effects on external trade - Deepening of the trade deficit.
- The export dynamics was superior to the dynamics of imports. - Intensified exchanges of goods in order to satisfy the need for warfare in the future belligerent states, especially Germany. - The need to protect the population to ensure its basic needs.	- The import of goods is disorganized in terms of strategies for development and the existing industrial capabilities. - Increasing dependence on intra-EU trade (over 75 % of exports and imports are carried out with EU partners).

Source: Concept of authors.

material (wood) is a factor allowing microeconomic development, which foreign companies have not delayed benefiting from.

Imports made after 1989 were supported, as in the interwar period, by the need to re-industrialize the country on the most technologically advanced basis but also by the strong increase in demand and consumption of imported finished products including foodstuffs (Annex 4). The share of ICT products in total imports, electrical equipment and transport vehicles as well as food and textile products has increased. The shortage of basic goods on the Romanian market during the centralized economy led to a huge demand for such imported goods immediately after 1989; this was mainly a psychological reaction of the population. But all this, together with the privatization of large factories, has concluded in a weak competitiveness, loss of employees and a reduction in the production of national goods. The supply of domestic goods (food and textiles) could not

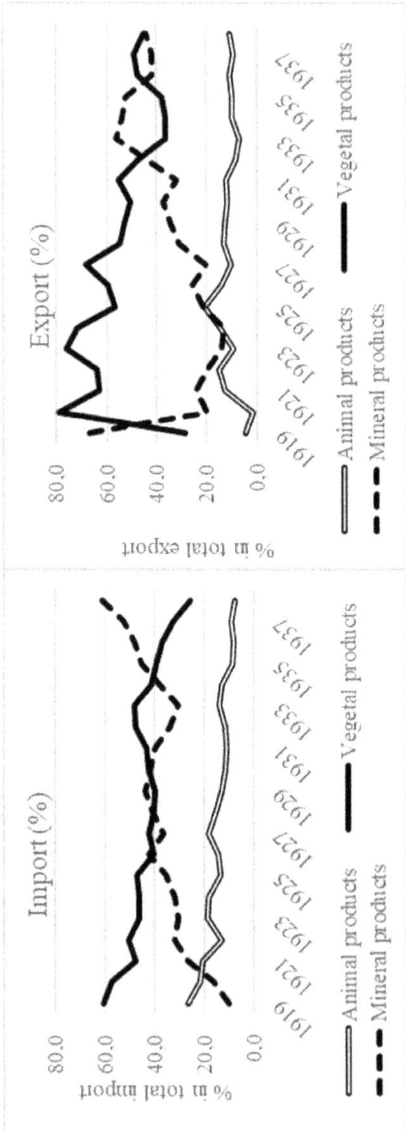

Figure 3: Romania's external trade, by main groups of goods, during 1919–1938 (%in total import and export)

Data source: Romanian Statistical Yearbook, Edition 1939.

meet the demand of consumers in terms of quality and price. Over time, national factories have disappeared or have been integrated into the structures of foreign companies.

2. Partner countries of Romania in external trade with goods

After the First World War, the resumption of Romania's external trade with goods and the restoration of the national currency equilibrium was very difficult. Economic branches were supposed to support the country's high recovery and consolidation expenditures, as well as its post-war obligations. In 1919, the top 10 trading partners accounted for 65 % of the exports of goods, with Hungary targeting 24 % of them (Table 2). Trade relations with traditional partners took off; the end of the period under review indicate the intensification of trade with Germany on the background of its war preparations.

In 1938, the developed countries dominated Romania's exports of fuels, cereals, food products of animal origin (Germany with 19 %, England with 12 %, Italy with 8 %).

The structure of imports during the interwar period has changed substantially from the point of view of the trading partners. United Kingdom, France, Italy and the USA were the main countries of origin of national imports in 1919, but in 1938 Germany and Czechoslovakia held 50 % of Romania's imports (Table 3).

Table 2: Top 10 partner countries of Romania for export, during 1919–1938 (%in total export)

	1919	**1920**	**1925**	**1930**	**1931**	**1932**	**1933**	**1934**	**1935**	**1936**	**1937**	**1938**
United Kingdom	0.1	6.0	7.5	10.8	11.8	13.9	14.7	10.6	9.9	13.3	8.7	11.9
Austria	2.3	5.9	4.6	4.6	6.9	4.4	5.2	6.6	8.5	6.6	4.4	*)
Belgium and Luxembourg	-	8.3	1.8	3.1	7.2	3.1	4.3	2.5	0.7	2.7	3.4	3.1
Bulgaria	9.3	0.7	3.2	1.5	1.2	1.0	0.8	0.9	1.0	0.8	1.0	1.4
Czechoslovakia	12.9	4.3	2.9	3.3	5.0	5.0	3.2	3.5	3.6	4.6	6.2	6.9
Egypt	-	7.3	6.2	5.9	6.7	6.3	7.7	7.4	5.4	3.8	4.0	5.1
France	10.7	3.9	4.9	6.6	10.3	12.0	11.1	9.4	4.2	9.8	7.0	4.8
Germany	-	0.8	4.0	15.6	7.3	7.6	6.2	8.9	12.4	14.6	14.0	18.7
Italy	5.9	19.8	4.3	13.7	10.3	12.8	12.7	11.9	20.5	7.9	8.1	8.5
Hungary	24.0	2.7	33.2	12.9	13.3	7.4	4.6	6.7	8.4	7.3	7.6	8.5
Top 10 partners countries	65.2	59.7	72.6	78.0	80.0	73.5	70.5	68.4	74.6	71.4	64.4	68.9

Data source: Romanian Statistical Yearbook, Edition 1939.

Table 3: Top 10 partner countries of Romania for import, during 1919–1938 (%in total import)

	1919	1920	1925	1930	1931	1932	1933	1934	1935	1936	1937	1938
United Kingdom	14.1	20.0	10.5	8.1	8.3	10.8	14.9	16.3	9.8	7.3	9.4	8.1
Austria	4.5	11.0	16.5	11.6	8.9	4.8	9.2	9.9	10.8	13.4	8.5	*)
Czechoslovakia	0.9	3.6	14.3	14.6	12.2	12.3	9.8	9.9	13.0	11.5	16.1	13.1
France	11.6	13.9	7.8	7.4	7.9	13.6	10.5	11.1	7.2	5.9	6.1	7.7
Germany	0.1	1.9	16.7	25.1	29.1	23.6	18.6	15.5	23.8	36.1	28.9	36.8
Italy	19.9	24.6	11.0	7.9	9.8	11.3	10.5	7.3	7.7	1.5	4.3	5.0
Poland	0.2	0.9	5.6	4.3	4.5	4.9	3.2	3.2	1.8	0.9	1.7	1.0
USA	14.8	5.6	1.9	5.4	3.7	3.3	3.0	4.2	3.0	3.6	3.9	4.9
Turkey	9.0	6.4	1.0	0.8	1.0	0.9	0.8	0.6	0.2	0.4	0.5	1.3
Hungary	1.9	1.1	4.0	3.9	3.7	2.3	3.0	4.1	6.5	6.1	4.1	3.6
Top 10 partner countries	77.0	89.0	89.3	89.1	89.1	87.8	83.5	82.1	83.8	86.7	83.5	81.5

Note: *) included in Germany.

Data source: Romanian Statistical Yearbook, Edition 1939

The year 1989 marks the beginning of a new stage in Romania's economic development and foreign trade relations. The last 29 years have been featured by the shift from the centralized economy to a market economy, the gradual opening of trade relations mainly with the European states, the accession to the EU and the high share of other EU Member States in external trade (about 75 % in 2016). The elimination of customs barriers and the free movement of goods, people and capital were the premises for intensifying not only the economic activity, but also the cultural and social life, as well as the cooperation on various issues of common interest between Member States[3].

For over 20 years, Romania's exports are destined to markets in Germany, Italy, France, Hungary and the United Kingdom (Figure 7). In 1989, these partners accounted for 30 % of total exports, while in 2016 they reached 50 %.

3 During the centralized economy, Romania carried out exports and imports mainly with the European countries; the countries from CAER (Mutual Aid Council) had the most important share in the foreign trade of our country. The USSR (Union of the Soviet Socialist Republics) accounted for the largest share of both total exports and total imports during the period 1950–1989 (61 % in 1950 and 23 % in 1989 for exports), while imports accounted for 43 % in 1950 and 32 % in 1989. The rest of the trade was mainly perform with Czechoslovakia, Hungary and the Germany (Democrativ Republic).

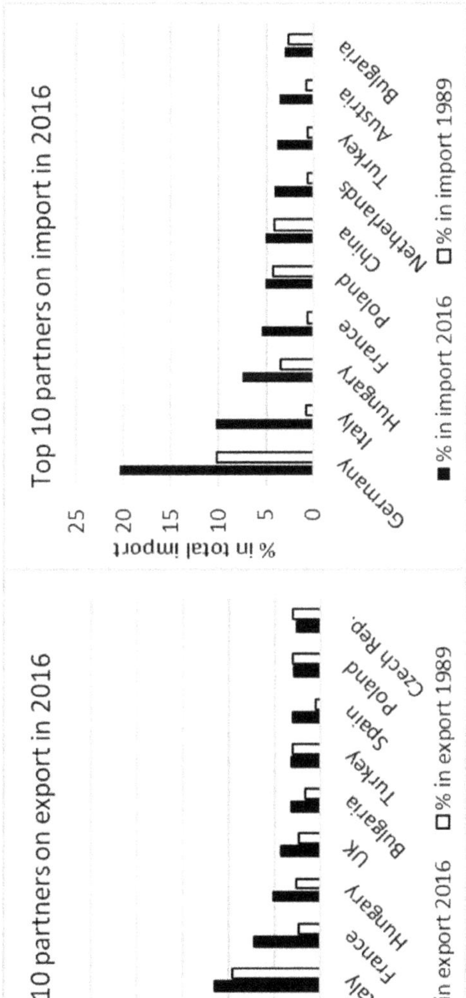

Figure 4: Top 10 partner countries of Romania in 2016 as against 1989 (%in total export and import)
Data source: TEMPO Online database, National Institute of Statistics, authors' calculations.

As for exports to the extra-EU countries, there is a relative stability of trade relations with Turkey, the Russian Federation, the USA, Serbia and China; these countries are important partners throughout 1989–2016. However, the share of these countries in total exports has reduced from 36 % in 1989 to 9 % in 2016. This happened under a general trend of falling down of exports to extra-EU countries from 55 % in 1989 to 25 % in 2016.

An important deterioration in trade relations was registered in the case of the Russian Federation; the share of imports has reduced from 34 % in 1989 to 3 % in 2016. During this period Romania significantly reduced imports from countries like Iran (from 13 % of imports in 1989 to 0.2 % in 2016) and has developed strong relations with European partners. Trade with EU Member States has increased especially since 2007, accounting for 77 % of imports in 2016, from 30 % in 1989.

3. Foreign capital in Romania

The economic development of Romania after the Great Union was achieved primarily based on industry, by encouraging the exploitation of raw national resources. An example in this direction is mineral oil extraction. Romania was among the first countries with the largest mineral oil production (in 1875 it has the greatest production of mineral oil in the world), but with a ratio between domestic consumption and production of only 22.5 %. The rest of mineral oil was exported. (Romanian Encyclopaedia, 1938). Thus, although it was the leading producer, Romania was only a supplier of raw materials and fuels for the capitalist countries; at national level the chemical industry failed to grow as expected on the base of the availability of the primary resource (Lupu et al., 1974).

The development of the Romanian industry based on the involvement of foreign capital took place especially in the areas of exploitation of natural resources. Petroleum exploitation was a monopoly field for foreign firms, given the importance of this product worldwide. The tendency to use national resources for the benefit of the country of origin of the capital rather than the country that holds them has resulted in a deepening of Romania's dependence on developed, capitalist countries.

Over 90 % of the enterprises were controlled by foreign capital while the labour force was mainly Romanian (Romanian Encyclopaedia, 1938). Although in the statistical data sources there is no information on employment in foreign-owned enterprises for the interwar period, in the graph below it is presented as example, the proportion of Romanian and foreign personnel in the 1921–1938 period in the extractive industry (Figure 5).

In the early 1930s, in the main industries took place an initiative to promote Romanian engineers in leadership positions and to replace minority personnel who had no interest in ensuring Romania's industrial development, economic and political. Nevertheless, through the still dominant positions of foreign capital in the main industrial branches and against the backdrop of protectionist laws, Romania's economic development was far from real potential. These realities have decisively influenced the structure and economic potential of Romania on property forms, with direct impact on the involved workforce.

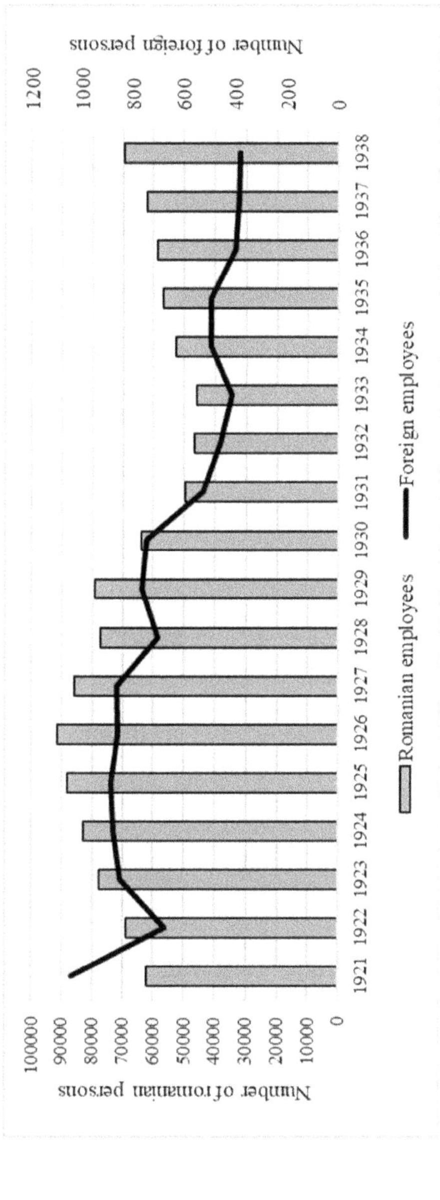

Figure 5: Romanian and foreign personnel in the extractive industry, during 1921–1938 (number of persons)
Data source: Authors' calculations based on Romanian Statistical Yearbook, Edition 1939–1940, pp. 476–477.

In the 20's there were major changes in the Romanian labour market, the new systems were implemented, including the establishment of employment offices[4] and the legislation of collective labour agreements. At the same time, because of the recommendations of the International Labour Organization, the prevention of unemployment was also under discussion.

The number of industrial enterprises and human resources involved has increased on the background of improved technology, mainly through imports, foreign capital investment, and the adoption of laws favouring the development of strategic areas where there is real development potential based on national capacities. The "by ourselves" principle (Lupu et al., 1974) applies, namely the rebuilding and relaunching of the Romanian economy through national productive forces. The taking over by Romanian productive forces of some of the foreign capital companies, was part of Romania's development and recovery strategy. The participation of foreign capital in the economic and social life of the country was not excluded, but it was no longer allowed to use the results of the exploitation of natural resources, including labour, only in the interest of enterprises controlled by foreign capital; this activity should contribute to the domestic development of the country through the economic results obtained.

After 1989, foreign capital entered again in Romania's economic life. The benefits for our economy are numerous, the most important being:

- Creating new jobs.
- Facilitating the flow of modern manufacturing technologies and knowledge from countries of origin of capital to countries of destination of investments.
- Completing the national financing sources of the economy, public and private.

From the point of view of employment, Table 4 below shows the indicators regarding the number of employees and the average salary in the companies with foreign capital compared to the companies with Romanian capital for the period 2008–2016.

Romania's foreign trade activity is mainly based on foreign-owned companies. In 2016, these firms performed over 85 % of exports and over 77 % of imports. The number of foreign-owned firms represents less than 20 % of the total number of companies involved in international transactions. There is no big difference in wage levels between domestic and foreign companies. In 2016, the average annual salary / employee was 52 thousand euro in foreign companies, while Romanian companies registered 35 thousand euro / employee.

When a company is involved in export of goods activities, most likely will benefit from the new generations of technology needed in productive activity, since goods destined for foreign markets have to meet higher quality standards; they must also be competitive in terms of price compared to similar goods. Some of the Romanian companies' problems relate to their small size, to the low level of export

4 On June 13, 1921, Convention no. 2 on unemployment of the International Labor Organization has been approved.

Table 4: Number of foreign trade companies, number of employees, the average salary and companies' size, by type of capital, during 2008–2016

	FOREIGN CAPITAL				ROMANIAN CAPITAL				
	No. of companies	No. of employees	Average salary (thou. euro / employee)	Company's size (no. of employees)	No. of companies	No. of employees	Average salary (thou. euro / employee)	Company's size (no. of employees)	
2008	18,791	1,139,267	28.8	60.6		65,294	1,539,299	25.1	23.6
2009	18,360	1,022,163	32.6	55.7		52,827	1,314,264	25.6	24.9
2010	16,540	998,998	35.8	60.4		49,834	1,178,428	27.4	23.6
2011	17,173	1,103,920	35.8	64.3		52,385	1,255,609	26.6	24.0
2012	17,493	1,072,226	38.3	61.3		56,335	1,245,521	28.2	22.1
2013	17,518	1,101,274	41.1	62.9		58,290	1,255,955	28.0	21.5
2014	17,578	1,139,979	42.2	64.9		62,531	1,274,945	30.3	20.4
2015	17,099	1,163,159	44.2	68.0		65,196	1,279,152	33.0	19.6
2016	16,407	1,207,464	51.6	73.6		64,919	1,288,831	34.6	19.9

Data sources: Authors' calculation based on NIS data.

intensity (about 8 % compared to 25 % in the case of foreign companies) and hence to a high vulnerability to market shifts / shocks. Most domestic firms belong to the category of SMEs (small and medium-sized enterprises): the average number of employees was 20 in 2016 compared to 74 in foreign companies.

Figure 6 shows the evolution of exports, imports, total turnover and total number of employees on national level and in foreign companies.

Export of goods was the macroeconomic indicator that experienced the fastest recovery after the 2008–2009 crisis. In 2010, it had already exceeded the level recorded in 2008. This was made based on foreign-owned companies, which exported larger volumes of Romanian goods, where they had comparative advantages, to the countries of origin of the capital, in order to cover or reduce the registered losses.

The export of foreign-owned companies was represented by high-tech goods in the automotive, IT, and mobile industries. Compared to 2008, in 2016 the product structure of these companies did not change significantly, as shown by the data in Table 5.

Highlighting the structure of exports and imports of foreign companies by categories of goods, reveals the low added value in Romania on the international productive chain; the main goods exported and imported by the foreign capital belong to the same industrial branches. It indicates that the activity of foreign capital in Romania do not stimulate the development of new areas, but only the low-tech industries based on the existing raw resources, similar to the interwar period. The reduced importance of Romanian capital on foreign markets and the non-stimulating environment for the small and medium enterprises, have led to the economic development of Romania mainly based on import consumption. This conclusion is also based on the increase share of food products in the foreign companies' imports for the Romanian market. Import consumption cannot lead to the development of new industrial branches or to companies' expanding on the international markets, but only to increase the vulnerability of the national economy by increasing its dependence on foreign capital from the point of view of production, export and consumption.

4. Conclusions

The development of Romania's foreign trade has experienced significant fluctuations, being strongly influenced by a multitude of national and international factors. There is a close correlation between national policies and the evolution of trade.

During the last century, Romania has gone through major political and economic international events: two world wars and two major economic crises. Other events were specific to national development: the union and creation of modern Romania, two major changes of the economic and social regime: from capitalism to socialism (after the Second World War) and the re-emergence of the market economy after the Revolution of December 1989. To all this, it should be added the policy of integration into regional structures of political and economic influence - CAER in the communist period and EU after 2007. Being a

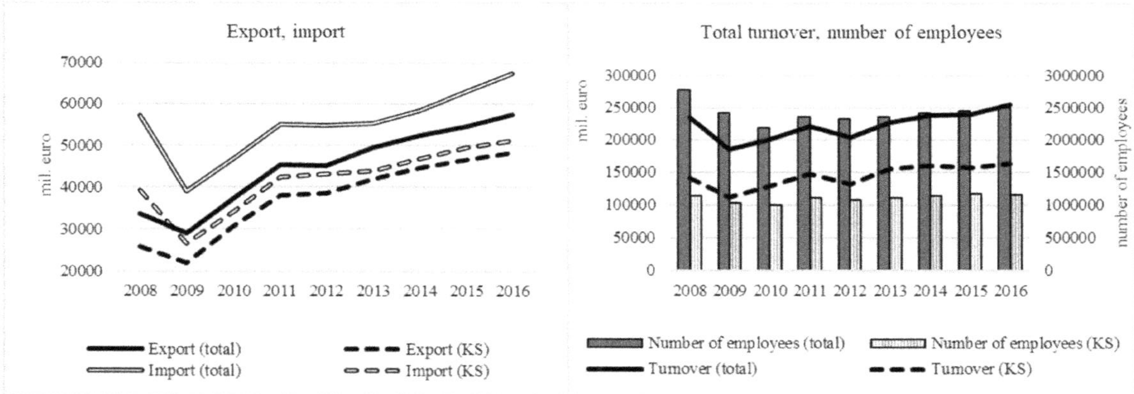

Figure 6: External trade activity of foreign companies in Romania, during 2008–2016

Data source: Authors' calculations based on NIS data

*Note: KS=foreign capital; *) Total turnover and number of employees – calculated for companies involved in external trade with goods transactions*

Table 5: Foreign companies export of high-tech goods in 2008 and 2016 (%in total export)

CPA code and description		% in total export of KS in 2008	% in total export of KS in 2016
29	Road transport vehicles	20.6	17.1
27	Electric devices	8.3	13.4
28	Machinery and electrical equipment	6.9	12.2
22	Rubber and plastic products	7.6	
26	Computers, electronic and optical products	7.1	7.6
14	Clothing articles	9.2	4.0
01	Agricultural and hunting products	6.7	6.2
16	Products from wood processing (excluding furniture)		3.9
24	Products of the metallurgical industry		3.8
25	Products of metal products industry	3.7	3.3
Top 10 CPA sections		80.7	80.0

Note: CPA=Classification of products by activities, KS=foreign capital

Data source: Authors' calculations based on NIS data

less developed economy, rich in natural resources but with insufficient financial resources, foreign investments have played an important role both in the economic development and in the results of the foreign trade activity. Overall, from the perspective of the last century of development of the Romanian economy, we can appreciate that FDIs have generated both positive and negative externalities:

a) Among the positive effects we mention:
   - Capitalizing on natural resources.
   - Increasing production in some branches of the economy.
   - Increasing employment and a relatively better wage policy, but without leading to major labour productivity developments because occupation areas in FDIs were for poor and medium-qualified work.
   - Modernizing some economic branches but without developing first-generation technologies.
   - Increasing trade in goods.
b) Among negative effects the following can be emphasised:
   - Capital placement has been made preferentially, only in certain branches, especially where raw materials were available and their processing was relatively modest; the obtained goods have reduced added-value; this situation

has led to the uneven development of some economic branches, pervading the investor's interest and not the national complementarity.
- The obtained products were integrated into the value chain of the big international companies in the initial phases, their transfer value being well below the final market price, although the subsequent processing did not exist or were very brief.
- The dependence of the country's economic development on foreign capital has deepened.
- The extra profit obtained through relatively lower costs of the production factors (material and / or human) has mostly been transferred to the countries of origin of foreign capital, without creating business sustainability through investment and employment in our country.
- It was maintained the demand for middle-qualified staff, with specializations strictly dependent on the needs of foreign capital; the relative wage benefits did not attract young people who have chosen the external mobility for work.

The effects on trade were:

- The export increase but the added value is low.
- The products of foreign companies, as well as the geographical distribution of the outlets dominate the structure of exports.
- The economic and social development by capital internalisation is difficult because of the leakage of raw materials and capital over borders.
- Imports of highly processed goods cover the deficit of domestic productive potential - foreign firms are oriented towards mass production with relatively higher profitability while the Romanian companies do not have the necessary technological and financial force.

Balance of payments deficit has become a permanent variable in the analysis of macroeconomic balances, sources of improvement / rebalancing being rather external to the business environment, i.e. remittances and external credits.

From the analyses carried out, between the two periods of the market economy in Romania, a series of similarities occurred in the evolution of exports and imports as well as in the behaviour of Romanian and foreign economic firms. The differences between the two periods are based on the impact of technologies, especially those in the communications field, which have substantially changed the way in which international business and trade are achieved.

Among the similarities of the two periods, the following can be stated:

- Increasing the importance of the private social capital and of the foreign trade that it carries out.
- The presence of foreign capital in the economic activity of Romania with positive and negative influence on employment, labour training, import of technology, the development of economic domains primarily based on the natural resources existing on the territory of Romania.
- Foreign capital has become only to a very law extent a driving factor for development, being especially focused on ensuring an overall efficiency on the value

chain of its own products, which also involved a certain increase in foreign trade - expensive import and cheap export.

- Reinvesting profit is at the limit of business survival, generated by the need to maintain the competitiveness of the products and services provided; most of the goods produced in Romania by foreign capital are present on foreign markets through export activity; otherwise they remain on the domestic market to be capitalized with relatively higher profitability rates.
- Repatriation of profits obtained in Romania, in significant proportions.

Foreign capital is a component of the development of the business environment in any modern country subject to the processes of globalization of markets and the freedom of capital movement. Foreign capital in the Romanian economy is necessary, both from the perspective of complementarity and competitiveness. Domestic capital develops better in economic sectors where foreign firms are present; it is needed the fiscal consolidation among companies in an international holding as well as a state aid to firms that may become suppliers of foreign companies. Foreign firms need Romanian workers, given the good prices on our market, and Romania needs foreign companies that have a sales market and financial strength (Pârvan, 2018).

To sustainable develop the economy in the context of increased international relations, a series of actions are needed, including:

- Increasing the added value of goods produced and exported, together with a corresponding reduction in imports, especially for goods for which national production can be assured.
- At global level, there is a tendency to protect national industries by imposing prohibitions and customs restrictions (e.g. restrictions imposed by Russia for food imported from the European Union and, as novelty, USA by imposing increased import tariffs for steel and aluminium products). These barriers to free trade produce continuous effects, while partner countries are forced take measures to reduce the vulnerability of their economies. In the context of a strong interdependence between the countries of the world, these protectionist measures appear to be disruptive, generating tensions and possible conflicts. On individual country's level, such measures might be justified, where the intensification of international trade has led to the degradation of certain indigenous industries. But on the global level a balance must be assured between the need for competitiveness on the foreign markets of goods, the increased activity and role of multinational companies and domestic industrial development. Economic policy must constantly adapt to global evolution.

These developments are well known in Romania, as in 1933, the historian Alexandru Topliceanu stressed that "defending and preserving the national heritage to be appreciated by us and with the decisive participation of the national production system" is essential for obtaining the highest profits.

Annex 1: Import, export and balance trade, during 1919–2016

	mil. USD				mil. USD				mil. USD		
	Export	Import	Balance		Export	Import	Balance		Export	Import	Balance
1919	8	285	-277	1960	717	702	15	2001	11385	15552	-4167
1920	64	129	-65	1961	793	883	-90	2002	13876	17862	-3986
1921	106	156	-50	1962	818	1019	-201	2003	17618	24003	-6385
1922	97	86	11	1963	915	1107	-192	2004	23485	32664	-9179
1923	116	92	24	1964	1000	1266	-266	2005	27730	40463	-12733
1924	145	134	11	1965	1102	1167	-65	2006	32336	51106	-18770
1925	139	143	-4	1966	1186	1314	-128	2007	40471	70414	-29943
1926	169	165	4	1967	1395	1675	-280	2008	49674	84286	-34612
1927	221	196	25	1968	1469	1743	-274	2009	40579	54344	-13765
1928	166	195	-29	1969	1633	1886	-253	2010	49494	62098	-12604
1929	173	177	-4	1970	1851	2124	-273	2011	63042	76540	-13498
1930	171	138	33	1971	2101	2278	-177	2012	57921	70285	-12364
1931	133	94	39	1972	2599	2834	-235	2013	65879	73519	-7640
1932	100	72	28	1973	3738	3797	-59	2014	69886	77907	-8021
1933	85	70	15	1974	4874	5573	-699	2015	60603	69852	-9249
1934	82	79	3	1975	5341	5787	-446	2016	63582	74605	-11023
1935	123	80	43	1976	6138	6604	-466				
1936	159	93	66	1977	6979	7603	-624				
1937	232	149	83	1978	8237	9845	-1608				
1938	158	138	20	1979	9724	11826	-2102				

(*continued on next page*)

Annex 1: Continued

			mil. USD				mil. USD				mil. USD
1939	197	168	29	1980	11401	14301	-2900				
1940	180	134	46	1981	11180	10978	202				
1941	220	163	57	1982	9848	8323	1525				
1942	282	239	43	1983	9847	7648	2199				
1943	379	506	-127	1984	9899	7731	2168				
1944	283	226	57	1985	10173	8401	1772				
1945	16	23	-7	1986	9761	8082	1679				
1946	397	628	-231	1987	10491	8312	2179				
1947	38	68	-30	1988	11391	7641	3750				
1948	149	136	13	1989	10486	8436	2050				
1949	193	210	-17	1990	5775	9202	-3427				
1950	212	264	-52	1991	4266	5793	-1527				
1951	263	295	-32	1992	4363	6260	-1897				
1952	304	394	-90	1993	4892	6522	-1630				
1953	366	501	-135	1994	6151	7109	-958				
1954	369	420	-51	1995	7910	10278	-2368				
1955	422	500	-78	1996	8084	11435	-3351				
1956	444	436	8	1997	8431	11280	-2849				
1957	411	533	-122	1998	8302	11838	-3536				
1958	468	522	-54	1999	8487	10557	-2070				
1959	522	544	-22	2000	10367	13055	-2688				

Data source: Romanian Statistical Yearbook, editions 1939, 1990, TEMPO Online database (www.insse.ro)

Annex 2: External trade with goods, total turnover, number of employees, number of companies and salary level, by type of companies

Foreign companies						
	Export (mil. euro)	Import (mil. euro)	Turnover (mil. euro)	No. of employees	Wages fund (mil. euro)	No. of companies
2008	25759.9	39329.8	141578.8	1139267	32841.5	18791
2009	22025.0	26529.3	111981.3	1022163	33333.0	18360
2010	30795.6	34149.8	128493.3	998998	35731.2	16540
2011	37960.1	42299.0	147344.1	1103920	39516.1	17173
2012	38478.2	43142.3	132457.7	1072226	41081.2	17493
2013	41891.2	43963.3	155122.9	1101274	45287.7	17518
2014	44648.3	46665.5	160425.3	1139979	48119.1	17578
2015	46468.0	49449.2	156373.4	1163159	51371.8	17099
2016	48939.0	52200.7	169613.4	1207464	62286.1	16407
Romanian companies						
	Export (mil. euro)	Import (mil. euro)	Turnover (mil. euro)	No. of employees	Wages fund (mil. euro)	No. of companies
2008	4922.1	14968.1	88367.6	1539299	38608.4	65294
2009	4280.1	9523.0	68367.6	1314264	33688.8	52827
2010	5519.8	11689.8	70421.4	1178428	32258.6	49834
2011	7132.7	12532.2	73244.2	1255609	33443.2	52385
2012	6289.4	11432.8	71020.2	1245521	35067.5	56335
2013	7232.4	11155.6	71812.1	1255955	35171.9	58290
2014	6931.8	11612.6	75867.6	1274945	38600.7	62531
2015	7034.3	13159.1	82138.5	1279152	42258.1	65196
2016	7056.6	14319.1	83620.5	1288831	44610.9	64919

Data source: NSI, authors' calculations

Annex 3: Main groups of goods exported during 1989–2016 (%in total exports)

CPA code	Description of CPA code	1989	1990	1995	2000	2006	2007	2008	2009	2011	2013	2015	2016
16	Products from wood processing (excluding furniture)	2.7	3.1	3.3	5.1	3.7	3.4	2.8	3.2	3.0	3.5	3.2	2,7
19	Coke oven products; products obtained from the processing of crude oil	17.7	18.0	7.8	6.7	9.4	7.0	8.2	5.5	5.3	4.6	3.7	3,1
20	Chemical products	10.4	7.5	11.9	6.1	5.5	5.6	5.5	3.6	4.5	3.9	3.1	2,8
24	Products of the metallurgical industry	13.4	14.3	16.6	15.3	12.8	13.5	9.5	5.5	7.4	5.6	5.4	4,7
28	Machines, machinery and equipment not elsewhere classified	13.2	14.6	6.2	5.0	7.7	8.6	7.7	7.4	7.5	8.0	8.7	9,0
26	Computers, electronic and optical products	0.3	0.2	0.1	1.3	1.0	1.0	5.2	8.2	8.9	5.2	5.3	5,5
27	Electric devices	1.9	2.4	2.8	3.6	9.3	10.2	6.8	7.2	7.3	7.7	9.9	11,2
29	Road transport vehicles, trailers and semi-trailers	7.0	7.3	2.2	2.2	6.8	9.0	12.8	16.3	15.7	19.1	19.4	20,6
Share of the main exported products in national export		66,5	67.4	51.0	45.3	56.1	58.3	58.5	56.8	59.6	57.6	58.7	59.6

Note: CPA=Classification of Products by Activities

Data source: Author's calculations based on NIS data.

Annex 4: Main groups of goods imported during 1989–2016 (%in total imports)

CPA code	Description of CPA code	1989	1990	1995	2000	2006	2007	2008	2009	2011	2013	2015	2016
06	Crude oil and natural gas	37.0	30.2	14.9	8.8	11.1	8.4	9.3	7.0	7.5	6.5	3.7	3,5
10	Food and beverages	4.2	9.3	7.0	4.7	4.3	4.4	5.3	6.9	5.5	5.9	6.1	6,4
13	Textile products	0.7	0.9	9.2	13.4	6.8	5.6	4.3	4.9	4.5	4.6	4.7	4,6
20	Chemical products	7.1	8.4	10.5	9.7	9.7	9.3	6.5	8.1	8.2	8.5	8.6	8,4
28	Machines, machinery and equipment not elsewhere classified	11.2	9.9	12.6	9.2	10.9	11.7	10.6	10.0	10.3	10.4	10.9	10,2
26	Computers, electronic and optical products	1.2	0.7	1.8	2.3	2.4	2.3	7.9	9.6	9.4	8.7	9.2	9,1
27	Electric devices	1.1	1.3	2.6	4.7	5.5	5.3	6.3	7.6	7.8	8.5	8.6	8,9
29	Road transport vehicles, trailers and semi-trailers	5.2	5.3	3.2	3.9	11.1	13.4	11.6	7.1	7.9	8.4	9.9	10,6
Share of the main imported products in national import		67.7	66.1	61.9	56.6	61.8	60.4	61.9	61.1	61.2	61.5	61.6	61.6

Note: CPA=Classification of Products by Activities.

Data source: Author's calculations based on NIS data

References:

Arcadian, N.P., Industrializarea României, Studiu evolutive-istoric, economic şi juridic, Ed. II, Bucureşti, 1936.

Banu, Florian, Asalt asupra economiei României - De la Solagra la Sovrom (1936–1956), Editura Nemira, 2004 ISBN 973-569-652-5.

Gusti, D. (coord.), Romanian Encyclopaedia, 1938.

Lupu, M.A./Tudor, P./Bozga, V./Marcu, N./Puia, I./Cherciu, A., Istoria Economiei Naţionale a României, Editura Didactică şi Pedagogică, Bucureşti, 1974.

Manoilescu M., Importanţa şi perspectivele industriei în noua Românie. Expunere din data de 24 ianuarie 1921 la Congresul industriei.

Paţac F., Istoria Comerţului şi Turismului, Editura Eurostampa, Timişoara, 2009.

Pârvan C., PIAROM, https://www.piarom.ro/cristian-parvan-presedintele-piarom-capitalul-autohton-se-dezvolta-mai-bine-acolo-unde-sunt-firme-straine/

Scărlătescu V., Aspecte ale economiei româneşti, Material documentar pentru cunoaşterea unor probleme în cadrul planului economic, Consiliul Superior Economic, 1939.

Topliceanu, A., Politica industrială, Bucureşti, 1933.

Vasile V./Ciuhu A.M./Bănică E., Human capital in Romania – between capitalization amd dissipation – a retrospective approach over the last century, http://cks.univnt.ro/cks_2018_archive.html.

National Institute of Statistics, Romanian Statistical Yearbook, editions 1925, 1939, 1970, 1977, 1990.

National Institute of Statistics, TEMPO Online database (www.insse.ro)

Gheorghe ZAMAN[1], *Iulia Monica OEHLER-ŞINCAI*[2]

[1] Corresponding Member of the Romanian Academy, Senior Researcher, Institute of National Economy, Email: gheorghezaman@ien.ro

[2] Institute for World Economy (IWE), Romanian Academy, Email: monica.oehler@iem.ro

Romanian Trade Performance after 2001 as Compared to Poland in Terms of Neighbourhood Export Competitiveness

Abstract *The objective of the research is to identify Romania's "neighbourhood export competitiveness", not geographically, but in terms of the shares in international trade. For each of the 96 chapters of HS-2 Harmonized System during 2001–2016, we analyze in which exporter group Romania falls by product categories and, at the same time, we calculate the number of positions lost/won by Romania as compared to Poland, the most competitive export country in Central and Eastern Europe. In terms of lost/won positions, one can compare the CEE countries as their shares are similar but any comparison between them and world export leaders is irrelevant.*

Keywords: *Romania, Poland, competitiveness, export, neighbourhood competitiveness*

1. Introduction

In this paper we try to answer the following questions: (1) Which is the total number of positions won/lost by Romania as compared to the most active trader in Central and Eastern Europe, namely Poland within world exports hierarchy by the main 96 chapters of the HS-2 (2 digit harmonized system) in 2005, 2010, 2015, 2016 relatively to 2001? (2) For how many chapters do Romania and Poland belong to the top 10 exporters and how many of these include high-technology products? (3) Which should be Romania's priorities in order to catch up with active traders in Central and Eastern Europe (CEE)?

We resort to a concept defined in a previous paper (Zaman, Oehler-Şincai, 2018), specifically neighbourhood export competitiveness. It refers to competitors with similar export competitive capacity as reflected by world export shares. From this viewpoint, the Central and Eastern European countries display a neighbourhood export competition, as their shares in world exports are lower than 1.5 % (Poland, the 24th world largest exporter has a market share of 1.2 %, Czech Republic, the 28th, 1 %, Hungary, the 34th, 0.6 %, Slovakia, the 38th, 0.5 % and Romania, the 40th, 0.4 %). Neighbourhood export competitiveness may be defined in terms of smaller of larger intervals.

In our analysis we will define intervals expressed in % as follows: (0; 2], (2; 4], (4; 6] etc. For instance, if there are several large competitors with shares in world exports close to 15 % and the others have shares lower than 10 %, the leaders show a neighbourhood export competitiveness reflected by the interval (14; 16], while the others are grouped around the following five intervals: (0; 2], (2; 4], (4; 6], (6; 8], (8; 10], with most of exporters concentrated in the lowest interval (0; 2]. As indicated by the International Trade Centre data, Romania is positioned in this interval for most of its exports. The size of Romania's export shares raises the problem of the relationship between price-makers and price-takers, as Romania is obviously a price-taker.

2. Literature review

The World Economic Forum (2017, p. 11) defines competitiveness as "the set of institutions, policies, and factors that determine the level of productivity of an economy, which in turn sets the level of prosperity that the economy can achieve". It is reflected by the Global Competitiveness Index (GCI) based on 114 indicators grouped into the following 12 pillars: institutions, infrastructure, macroeconomic environment, health and primary education, higher education and training, goods market efficiency, labor market efficiency, financial market development, technological readiness, market size, business sophistication, and innovation. Poland is ahead Romania at most of the aforementioned pillars, such as infrastructure (Poland 44th, Romania 83rd), goods market efficiency (Poland 45th, Romania 92nd), innovation (Poland 59th, Romania 96th) or business sophistication (Poland 57th, Romania 116th).

These factors influence also the export competitiveness, mirrored by a country's "ability to sell domestically produced goods and services on global markets" (Ketels, 2010). Porter (2004, p. 30) considers that "the most intuitive definition of competitiveness is a country's share of world markets for its products".

Definitely there is a strong relationship between the competitiveness of manufacturing industry and export competitiveness. As shifts in the relative position of economies in manufacturing value added (MVA) and industrial exports are, to a large extent, attributable to changes in individual countries' industrial competitiveness (UNIDO, 2017), we assume that shares in international trade reflect trade performance from efficiency viewpoints.

According to the United Nations Industrial Development Organization (UNIDO) and its competitive industrial performance (CIP) index (taking into account MVA per capita, manufactured exports per capita, medium-high and high-tech MVA share in total manufacturing, share of MVA in GDP, medium- and high-tech manufactured exports share in total manufactured exports, manufactured exports share in total exports, impact on world MVA and influence on world manufactures trade), in 2015 Poland was ranked the 23rd (CIP 0.168), after Czech Republic (17th, 0.218), but ahead of Slovakia (26th, 0.155), Hungary (27th, 0.150), Slovenia (33rd, 0.110) and Romania (34th, 0.105). It is worth noting that Poland enjoyed the biggest changes in rankings on par with China, each moving up 29 positions between 1990 and 2015 and its impact on world MVA and manufactures trade was much larger than the other CEE countries (UNIDO, 2017, p. 190).

Based on surveys among business leaders, the 2016 global manufacturing competitiveness index (Deloitte, 2016) reveals Poland on the 15th place, followed by Czech Republic (23rd) and Romania (33rd), with no other CEE country in the top 40. However the international export statistics shows Poland the 24th, Czech Republic 28th, Hungary 34th, Slovakia 38th and Romania 40th. According to our assumption that shares in international trade reflect trade performance, on the whole Poland is the most competitive export country of CEE, while Romania is the fifth (Chart 1).

Most of the CEE countries, including Romania and Poland remain highly dependent of EU trade. For instance, the following CEE countries had in 2016 shares of intra-EU trade larger than 70 %: Slovakia (83 %), Czech Republic (81.7 %), Hungary (79.6 %), Estonia (78 %), Romania (76.2 %), Poland (75.9 %), Latvia (75.8 %), Slovenia (73.2 %) and Croatia (72.5 %). In the last decade, the dependence on the intra-EU trade increased in Romania, but decreased in other countries such as Poland (Eurostat, 2017).

For countries such as Visegrád group (Poland, Czech Republic, Slovak Republic, Hungary), Baltic States (Latvia, Lithuania, Estonia) and Slovenia, their proximity to large Western European markets and technology sources and also the adequate infrastructure offer a strong base for agglomeration effects (Szunomár, Biedermann, 2014), to the detriment of Romania.

A country report by the International Monetary Fund (IMF, 2015, pp. 40–41) underlines that: (1) In Romania's case, infrastructure stands out as an important factor for export growth; (2) A real exchange rate appreciation has a significant and negative effect on the export market share growth; (3) Romania's export growth performed well during the past years, however it revealed a comparative advantage concentrated in labour intensive goods and low and medium skill manufactures; (4) The quality of Romania's export is relatively low in comparison

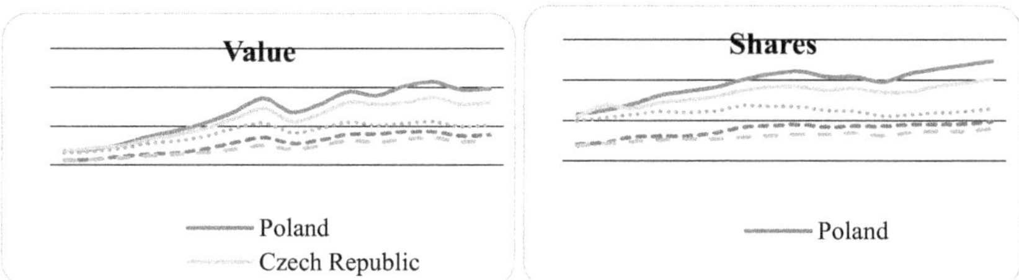

Figure 1: Poland, Czech Republic, Hungary, Slovakia and Romania – Export value and shares of the world exports during 2001–2016 (billion dollar and %)

Source: Own representation and calculations based on ITC (2018).

with regional peers; (5) The activity of foreign direct investment (FDI) is generally export oriented and the foreign investors have a large contribution to total exports (estimated at more than 70 % in 2013); (6) Therefore it is necessary that Romania promotes export diversification, a favourable business environment, greater integration in global value chains, quality improvement and repositioning towards high-skill exports.

Regarding the depreciation of the national currency as a way to stimulate exports, the experience of several countries has shown that this measure is only valid under the following conditions: Depreciation should be done in small and limited doses; There is a need for a sufficient demand on the world market for the country's export products; There is the possibility of developing additional production capacities in the country in order to meet a potential increase in external demand for export products; Take into account that a large part of the export products can have a high content of imports, so that devaluation as a factor in stimulating export competitiveness might not become an impediment for imports.

Concerning Poland, Michalski (2014) underlines that the "overall evaluation of the competitiveness of Polish mid-tech and high-tech exports still remains ambiguous". Even if there are "clear positive changes" represented by the growing technological intensity, it would not have been possible without the inflow of foreign capital. The number of Polish-owned companies which created technologically sophisticated modes of the business and successfully entered foreign markets remains relatively small and the scale of own, not easily imitated competitive advantages is swallow, which diminishes the prospects of a dynamic and effective structural catching-up. Gawlikowska-Hueckel, Śledziewska (2016, p. 72) emphasize slow but positive change at the level of high-technology trade in goods.

The shares of different groups of high-tech products among Poland's exports are not found to be stable, while the balance of trade in high-technology is negative. But even if medium or low technologies still prevail among exports, the share of goods with a high share of technological components has increased. Brodzicki (2016, p. 103) confirms the "new new trade theory" (NNTT) as regards Polish trade. This new trend in the empirical and theoretical trade literature explains the unique role of firms for the intensity and structure of international trade. According to Brodzicki (2016, p. 106), for Poland and other countries, the probability of engaging in exports increases with the size and age of the firm, the productivity of labour and the share of foreign ownership. The largest exporters (or the so-called superstar firms) in terms of employment and sales have access to more capital, generate higher added value and pay higher wages per worker owing to their higher productivity. Poland has five companies in the list of world's biggest companies (Forbes, 2017), while Romania has no one. Gawlikowska-Hueckel and Umiński (2016, p. 110) conclude that the case study of Poland as regards intra-industry trade, its intensity and determinants is of pivotal significance mainly because of the country's EU membership, its closing the (developmental) gap to the "old" EU Member States and a vital role of entities with foreign shareholdings, especially in the country's trade. FDI continues to be the driving force behind the export activity and it is considered the main determinant of actual export competitiveness.

Therefore the investment incentives represent a priority for the Polish government and these are dedicated to specific priority sectors: automotive, aviation, electronics and household appliances, food processing, biotechnology, nanotechnology, research and development and business process outsourcing, shared service centres and information and communication technology. Incentives depend on the number of new jobs created, investment per employee and location, according to the 14 special economic zones (Polish Information and Foreign Investment Agency, 2015; 2016).

Romania has six free zones (assimilated to the special economic zones, namely Sulina, Constanta-Basarabi, Galati, Braila, Giurgiu, Curtici-Arad) however they need a better visibility and systematisation of specialisation domains and opportunities offered to investors, according to the economic, social and technological vocation of the region. By contrast, in Poland the promotion strategy is dynamic and the incentives are differentiated according to the regional priorities. Moreover, clusters and their international networks – significant competitiveness incentives through linkages and spillovers of knowledge, skills and technology across companies and industries (Zmuda, 2017) – are much more developed in Poland than in Romania (European Commission, 2018).

3. Interpretation of results from the standpoints of leaders and laggards

Previous researches underline that on the competitive scale the higher a competitor advances in the hierarchy, the more difficult is to gain a position and the easier is to lose it (Zaman, Oehler-Şincai, 2018). For laggards, moving up in the hierarchy is much easier than in the case of leaders however it does not mean automatically a neighbourhood export competitiveness reflected by superior intervals.

For each of the 96 chapters of HS-2 Harmonized System, according to the International Trade Centre data, one can draw the following conclusions. As of 2016, Romania:

- Belonged to the group of top ten exporters only at one chapter, namely 50 Silk. By analogy, Poland was among the largest 10 exporters at 20 chapters.
- Lost positions at 35 chapters as compared to 2001, the largest loss was recorded at 46 Manufactures of straw, of esparto or of other plaiting materials; basketware and wickerwork (47 positions). By comparison, Poland lost positions at only 11 chapters, the largest loss was recorded at 14 Vegetable plaiting materials; vegetable products not elsewhere specified or included (17 positions).
- Won positions at 60 chapters in comparison with 2001, the most significant gains were at Section IV (prepared foodstuffs; beverages, spirits and vinegar; tobacco and manufactured tobacco substitutes): 24 Tobacco and manufactured tobacco substitutes +65 positions, 21 Miscellaneous edible preparations +44

positions and 18 Cocoa and cocoa preparations +42 positions, however from very low rankings in 2001–2005. Poland won positions at 83 chapters and kept the same position at 2 chapters.

- At 78 Lead and articles thereof, it returned to the same position of 2001 (27th).
- Continued to have shares lower that 1 % in the world exports at most of the export chapters.
- Even if it won 619 positions on the whole over 2001–2016 (more than the double of the leader – China – during the same timeframe) (Table 1), it is ranked 30–40 positions lower than the leaders at the most chapters. From this situation one can draw the first lemma: one can compare competitors from the standpoint of lost/won positions only if they are similar with respect to their world export shares (i.e. if they belong to the same group of countries as regards the neighbourhood export competitiveness). For instance, one can compare the Central and Eastern European countries as their shares are similar (Figure 1) but not these countries and world export leaders.
- It showed an evident ranking increase at 20 chapters, namely: 1, 19, 21, 33, 34, 35, 40, 50, 51, 52, 54, 55, 58, 68, 76, 84, 85, 87, 90 and 94. Most are resource or material based products, but there are also four chapters including products of medium and high technology: 84 Nuclear reactors, boilers, machinery and mechanical appliances; parts thereof, 85 Electrical machinery and equipment and parts thereof; sound recorders and reproducers, television image and sound recorders and reproducers, and parts and accessories of such articles, 87 Vehicles other than railway or tramway rolling-stock, and parts and accessories thereof, 90 Optical, photographic, cinematographic, measuring, checking, precision, medical or surgical instruments and apparatus; parts and accessories thereof. By comparison, Poland recorded significant increases at 32 chapters: 2, 3, 5, 10, 15, 16, 21, 30, 32, 34, 38, 39, 40, 41, 47, 48, 49, 56, 62, 64, 66, 69, 70, 72, 73, 80, 82, 84, 85, 90, 94 and 96. Only seven chapters are the same: 21, 34, 40, 84, 85, 90 and 94, however Romania lags behind Poland (47–11, 39–10, 25–11, 35–19, 28–19, 36–28 and 16–4 respectively).
- Romania was better positioned than Poland at ten chapters belonging to live animals, vegetable products, textiles and textile articles and footwear: 01 Live animals, 10 Cereals, 12 Oil seeds and oleaginous fruits; miscellaneous grains, seeds and fruit; industrial or medicinal plants; straw and fodder, 14 Vegetable plaiting materials; vegetable products not elsewhere specified or included, 50 Silk, 51 Wool, fine or coarse animal hair; horsehair yarn and woven fabric, 52 Cotton, 55 Man-made staple fibres, 58 Special woven fabrics; tufted textile fabrics; lace; tapestries; trimmings; embroidery, 64 Footwear, gaiters and the like; parts of such articles. However most of exported categories are concentrated in the lowest interval of neighbourhood competitiveness (0; 2].

In terms of neighbourhood export competitiveness, Romania is best positioned at chapter *50 Silk*, leading the fourth group (interval (2; 4], made of Romania 4 % of total exports, France 3.7 %, Vietnam 3 %, South Korea 2.7 %, Japan 2.7 %, Germany 2.4 % and Hong Kong-China 2.2 %) (Figure 2).

Table 1: The total number of positions won/lost by Romania and Poland – for comparison also China, US, Germany and Japan – within world exports hierarchy by the main HS-2 chapters in 2005, 2010, 2015 and 2016

Period	Romania	Poland	China	US	Germany	Japan
2005/2001	209	530	210	-111	39	-232
2010/2005	428	144	60	9	-24	-4
2015/2010	7	195	55	20	-51	-220
2016/2015	-25	25	-25	-24	21	84
2016/2001	619	894	300	-106	-15	-372

Source: Own representation and calculations based on ITC (2018).

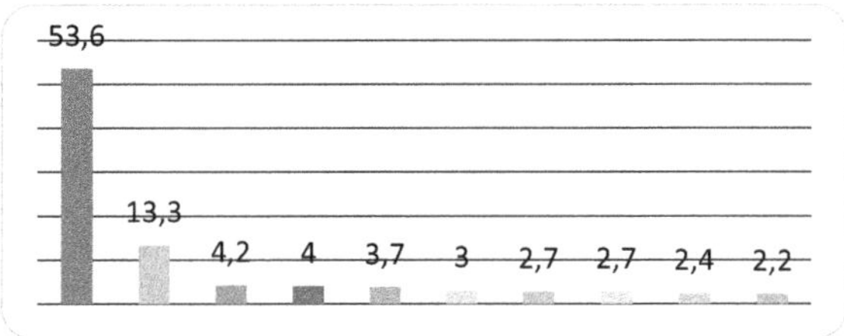

Figure 2: Top ten exporters of 50 Silk in 2016 – shares of the world exports (%)
Source: Own representation and calculations based on ITC (2018).

The leader is China (53.6 % of world exports), while the second and the third groups are made also of only one country (Italy, 13.3 % and India, 4.2 %, respectively).

For Romania, with a few exceptions (for instance 10 Cereals, with a share of 2.4 % in world exports), most of exported categories are concentrated in the lowest interval (0; 2]. By contrast, Poland is among the most active ten exporters at 20 chapters. In two cases (24 Tobacco and manufactured tobacco substitutes and 94 Furniture; bedding, mattresses, mattress supports, cushions and similar stuffed furnishings; lamps and lighting fittings, not elsewhere specified or included; illuminated signs, illuminated name-plates and the like; prefabricated buildings) Poland belongs to the interval (4; 6], in other two cases (66 Umbrellas, sun umbrellas, walking-sticks, seat-sticks, whips, riding-crops and parts thereof, 46 Manufactures of straw, of esparto or of other plaiting materials; basketware and wickerwork) to the interval (0; 2] (where are included almost all the other categories exported), and in 16 cases to the interval (2; 4]. It should be mentioned that among the 16 categories belonging to the interval (2; 4], most are primary products, products based on resources or low technology products, only five incorporate medium technology (34, 78, 82, 83, 89) and there are no products belonging to chapters of high technology.

Conclusions

Competitiveness is an extremely dynamic field under the impact of a growing number of complex factors, where the technological progress and innovation have the decisive role. In addition to these determinants should be also taken into account traditional brands whose quality and visibility can be important sources of revenue for exporters.

In a century when indicators such as infrastructure, macroeconomic environment, and goods market efficiency, technological readiness, business sophistication, and innovation are more and more relevant, Romania does not belong to the leading countries in CEE as regards export competitiveness. Poland is much better positioned than Romania in terms of shares of world exports and in for 20 export chapters it belongs to the most active ten exporters. FDI continues to be the driving force behind the export activity for both Poland and Romania and also of actual export competitiveness. Nevertheless, Romania does not modulate its FDI strategy according to regional and national objectives, as it the case of Poland. Definitely Poland is better positioned than Romania as regards its export competitiveness however it still cannot compete with the most active traders of high-technology products.

In the case of Romania, FDI, which is generally considered to be a sustainable growth factor in emerging economies, can make a greater contribution to this strategic objective of Romania by: Promoting vertical investments to a greater extent, with a propagation effect for the national economy both upstream and downstream; Focusing on the selectivity of FDI by decision-makers in Romania in order to stimulate more tradable FDI and less non-tradable FDI; Attracting FDI in the public-private, private-private and public-public partnership schemes in Romania, paying particular attention to the principle of equivalence of benefits in the fields of international trade and cooperation; Stimulating reinvestment of profits by companies with foreign equity participation, taking into account the additional opportunities that can be created for future profits both domestically and abroad.

A specific chapter for increasing the exports competitiveness is reflected by Romania's attempt to promote technological transfer with the assimilation (and even surpassing its performance) and substitution of competitive imports under similar conditions of competitiveness, but in compliance with the World Trade Organization's regulatory system.

Even if it is a price-taker, Romania shows an underutilized potential in many sectors; in our view, one of them is given by the export of organic products, knowing, on the one hand, the relative advantage of using lower amounts of fertilizers per hectare, as well as that of avoiding the genetically modified organisms or products with doubtful nutritional value, even if from the stance of their appearance and presentation they seem to outweigh the Romanian ones.

From the standpoint of the number of lost/won positions in world exports during 2001–2016, Romania is worse positioned than Poland but better than most active traders. We conclude that one can compare competitors from the viewpoint of lost/won positions only if they are similar with respect to their world export shares (i.e. if they belong to the same group of countries as regards the neighbourhood export competitiveness). In terms of lost/won positions, one can compare the Central and Eastern European countries as their shares are similar but any comparison between them and world export leaders is irrelevant.

References

Brodzicki, T. (2016), New new trade theory, in: An Analysis of Poland's Foreign Trade in the Light of the Latest Theoretical Concepts, Institute for Development, Scholar Publishing House, Warsaw, pp. 103–107.

Deloitte (2016), Global Manufacturing Competitiveness Index.

European Commission (2018), Cluster Mapping Tool, European Cluster Observatory.

Eurostat (2017), International trade in goods, database available at: http://ec.europa.eu/eurostat/web/international-trade-in-goods/data/database.

Forbes (2017), The World's Biggest Companies List, available at: https://www.forbes.com/global2000/list/23/#header:country.

ITC (2018), International Trade in Goods, Database available at: http://www.intracen.org/itc/market-info-tools/statistics-export-product-country/.

Gawlikowska-Hueckel, K., Śledziewska, K. (2016), Poland's trade following the country's EU accession with particular emphasis on high-technology goods, in: Gawlikowska-Hueckel, K. and Umiński, S. (editors) (2016), An Analysis of Poland's Foreign Trade in the Light of the Latest Theoretical Concepts, Institute for Development, Scholar Publishing House, Warsaw, pp. 43–72.

Gawlikowska-Hueckel, K. and Umiński, S. (editors) (2016), An Analysis of Poland's Foreign Trade in the Light of the Latest Theoretical Concepts, Institute for Development, Scholar Publishing House, Warsaw.

International Monetary Fund (IMF) (2015), Romania: Selected Issues, Country Report 15/80, March.

Ketels, C. (2010), Export Competitiveness: Reversing the Logic, Harvard Business School.

Michalski, B. (2014), Competitiveness of Polish mid-tech and high-tech exports to the EU-27 in the first decade of the 21st century, Poznań University of Economics Review, volume 14, no. 4, pp. 54–70.

Polish Information and Foreign Investment Agency (2016), Investor's Guide – Poland, How to do business, Ministry of Economy of the Republic of Poland.

Polish Information and Foreign Investment Agency (2015), Why Poland? Ministry of Economy of the Republic of Poland.

Porter, M. E. (2004), Building the Microeconomic Foundations of Prosperity: Findings from the Business Competitiveness Index, in The Global Competitiveness Report 2003–2004, edited by Michael E. Porter, Klaus Schwab, and Xavier Sala-i-Martin, pp. 29–56, Oxford University Press.

Szunomár, A., Biedermann, Z. (2014). Chinese OFDI in Europe and the Central and Eastern European region in a global context, in: Szunomar, A. (editor), Chinese Investments and Financial Engagement in Visegrád Countries: Myth or Reality?, Institute of World Economics, Centre for Economic and Regional Studies of the Hungarian Academy of Sciences, Visegrád Fund, Budapest.

United Nations Industrial Development Organization (UNIDO) (2017), Industrial Development Report: Demand for Manufacturing, Driving Inclusive and Sustainable Industrial Development, Vienna.

Zaman, G., Oehler-Şincai, I.M. (2018), Calculation of China's Gains/Losses in Terms of Trade Performance after 2001 as compared to Active Traders, forthcoming.

Zmuda, M. (2017), Towards a Taxonomy of International Competitiveness, Journal of Management and Business Administration. Central Europe, vol. 25, no. 3, pp. 97–116.

Mirela-Adriana RUSALI[1]

[1] Institute of Agricultural Economics, Romanian Academy, Email: m.rusali@yahoo.com

Evaluations of Growth in the Foreign Trade with Food Products and Post-Accession Comparisons

Abstract *Starting from the idea that Romania's accession to the EU is per se a process of growth, the research aims at identifying the structural changes in the increase of the commercial opening of the EU28 countries, explaining the post-accession tendencies by empirical analyzes by using recent available statistical data from Eurostat. The relationship between increasing of the agri-food foreign trade and economic growth of the processing sector has been analyzed in light of the effects of export and import dynamics and the distribution of relevant indicators in the context of the post-accession process of gap reduction between Member States.*

Keywords: *food sector, trade openness, growth indices, post-accession*

Introduction

Research on post-accession trade performance of Romania's agri-food products and compared to Member States in the EU28 context belongs to the European interest to improve national sectoral performance and reduce disparities between states. The analysis of Romania's foreign trade flows on food products compared to the total agri-food sector and the EU28 states was approached in order to highlight the post-accession changes regarding the valorisation of agricultural products, ranking of the countries and the evaluation of the external performances.

The paper presents the main results on the structure and indices of value growth on the world and community markets of the trade flows, import, export and food trade balance for Romania, as well as comparisons between states on total foreign food trade, intra-EU and extra-EU and the correlations between the variables represented by the export-to-GDP ratios and the degree of commercial opening. The objective of the topic addressed is the national interest in increasing the valorisation of the agricultural potential in the industrial sector and increasing the added value of agri-food products.

1. Literature review

A strong agricultural sector in the EU is vital for the European food industry, in an extremely competitive international environment, to remain an important supplier of high quality and safe agricultural and food products and to contribute to global food security, supporting a sustainable agricultural sector and industry in developing countries. The CAP should promote and support a sustainable agricultural sector to participate in food security efforts in line with the EU's general priorities - mentioned in the 2010 EU Food Security Policy adopted by the Commission and supplemented by the Council conclusions (EC, 2011).

The framework of the Common Agricultural Policy document reflects a reasonable concern and strategic interest in maintaining the EU's agricultural production potential to provide food for the short and long term for the needs of humans and animals. Together with the strategic actions of sustainable development, mobilized by international and European actions related to environmental protection and natural resources and the Europe 2020 Strategy, the objectives of the EU Common Agricultural Policy aim at increasing the competitiveness of the agrifood products processing sector. The NRDP 2014–2020, (MADR, 2016), in line with the Agro-Food Strategy 2020–2030, stimulates this desideratum through support measures and prospects for the sector of processing agri-food products in Romania (MADR, 2015).

The European Commission has undertaken several studies on the competitiveness of the European food industry (2005), including the economic and legal assessment of the sector (2007). The Executive Agency for Small and Medium Enterprises has called for a further study on the competitiveness of the European food industry, taking into account recent developments and scenarios on future potential changes. The study conducted in 2016 and aimed at updating the information included an assessment of the competitive position of the European food and beverage industry, which refers to the European industry towards its main trading partners - the US, Australia, Brazil and Canada - in two periods of time, 2003–2007 and 2008–2012. The study finds that the EU food and beverage industry has gained a competitive position vis-à-vis the main trading partners in terms of international trade indicators, but performance has weakened by economic indicators. It is noted that the main European regulations that have a positive impact on the competitiveness of the sector: the harmonization of key legislation under the Food Law and the regulation of food safety. The main barriers to competitiveness have identified the inconsistent application of European regulations between EU Member States, which has led to trade barriers for the internal market.

In the economic literature, industry has always been considered as a key sector of economic development, including recent academic studies, eg.: Albu et al., 2012; Alexandri et al. 2017; Chivu et al. 2016 Rusali, 2017; Steriu & Otiman, 2013; etc., include valuable information on the historical evolution of the sectors of the national industry, analyzes that highlight the positive effects of trade on international specialization in industry and economic growth, as well as competitiveness shortcomings under the impact of liberalization of agro-food trade, strategic approaches in the perspective of sustainable development.

2. Results and discussion

The results of the recent foreign trade flows analysis carried out in Romania on agricultural and agri-food products, indicating the growth trends assessed for 2015 as compared to 2012, are summarized in tables 1, 2 and 3.

The increase of 28 % in Romania's total exports of agri-food products, higher than the increase in imports of 15 %, resulted in a 2 % decrease in the trade deficit (table 1). The value share of processed products in Romania's agro-food exports increased from 48 % to 69 %.

Intra-EU trade is predominant in all EU28 Member States; for Romania, in 2015, it represented for food, beverages and tobacco 1.7 billion Euro, respectively, 66 % of the food imports and 71 % of exports, worth almost 1.1 billion Euro, (table 2). There is also a slight decrease in imports (-5 %), but an increase of 20 % on export.

A significant increase of 152 % was achieved in the share of Romanian exports of agri-food products on the extra-EU market, from 136 million Euro to 279 million Euro, while the exports of agricultural products in these markets dropped almost by half share in Romania's total agricultural exports (table 3).

Table 1: Agro-food foreign trade of Romania - Structure and growth 2012 vs. 2015

		Total agri-food			**Agricultural products**			**Food, beverages, tobacco**		
		2012	**2015**	**Growth 2012–2015 (%)**	**2012**	**2015**	**Growth 2012–2015 (%)**	**2012**	**2015**	**Growth 2012–2015 (%)**
Import	Mill. Euro	4,676	5,376	15	2,735	3,157	15	1,941	2,219	14
	%	100	100		29	30	2	71	70	-1
Export	Mill. Euro	2,599	3,339	28	1,753	1,976	13	847	1,363	61
	%	100	100		52	31	-40	48	69	43
Balance	Mill. Euro	-2,076	-2,036	-2	-982	-1181	20	-1,094	-855	-22

Source: Data processing from Eurostat - Trade by commodity and NACE Rev. 2 activity.

Table 2: Agrifood trade - Romania - Intra-EU: Structure and growth 2012 vs. 2015

		Total agri-food			**Agricultural products**			**Food, beverages, tobacco**		
		2012	**2015**	**Growth 2012–2015 (%)**	**2012**	**2015**	**Growth 2012–2015 (%)**	**2012**	**2015**	**Growth 2012–2015 (%)**
Import Intra-UE	Mill. Euro	3740	4266	14	2211	2578	17	1529	1689	10
	%	100	100		31	34	12	69	66	-5
Export Intra-UE	Mill. Euro	1899	2602	37	1188	1517	28	710	1084	53
	%	100	100		40	29	-29	60	71	20
Balance	Mill. Euro	-1841	-1665	-10	-1023	-1060	4	-818	-605	-26

Source: Data processing from Eurostat - Trade by commodity and NACE Rev. 2 activity.

Table 3: Agri-food trade - Romania - Extra-EU: Structure and growth 2012 vs. 2015

		Total agri-food			Agricultural products			Food, beverages, tobacco		
		2012	2015	Growth 2012–2015 (%)	2012	2015	Growth 2012–2015 (%)	2012	2015	Growth 2012–2015 (%)
Import Extra-UE	Mill. Euro	936	1109	19	523	580	11	412	530	28
	%	100	100		21	9	-59	79	91	16
Export Extra-UE	Mill. Euro	701	738	5	564	459	-19	136	279	105
	%	100	100		76	39	-48	24	61	152
Balance	Mill. Euro	-235	-372	58	41	-121	-396	-276	-251	-9

Source: Data processing from Eurostat - Trade by commodity and NACE Rev. 2 activity.

At the same time, was estimated a 10 % decrease in Romania's total agri-food trade deficit on the intra-EU market, due to the decrease of the deficit of food and beverage and tobacco trade by 26 %, from -818 million Euro to -605 million Euro, but the deficit in extra-EU trade suffered a substantial increase by 58 % (table 2).

The comparative trends of the foreign food products trade growth of the EU28 countries, within the limits of the data available for 2015 as compared to 2012, is presented in table 4.

It is noticed that Romania's total exports of food products (intra-EU + extra-EU) increased by 56.9 % (from 0.6 billion Euro to more than 1 billion Euro), placed the country on the first place in the EU28, followed by UK (56.6 %), Cyprus and Bulgaria (37 %). In contrast, Latvia, France and Denmark recorded declines (between -7 % and -3.6 %).

The foreign trade balance outcomes indicate recovery trends of the trade balance in Greece, Slovenia and UK. Also, in Romania, the trade deficit has been reduced from -714 million Euro in 2012 to - 407 million Euro in 2015.

In contrast, the biggest increase in food imbalance was observed in Malta - where, however, the trade balance is among the lowest in the EU, but also in other countries, including Croatia, Spain and Bulgaria.

Countries dependent on intra-EU imports were those that had the largest share of the country's intra-EU food export in total food export, respectively, in 2015, with over 90 %, were: Slovakia (96 %), Czech Republic, Hungary and Estonia, while the countries with the smallest share of intra-EU food trade were: Spain (50 %), Denmark, Malta, the Netherlands and Italy with a weight of between 60 % and 67 %.

Romania has absorbed in the foreign trade with food products, in 2015, 73 % of imports from the intra-EU relationship, down by -1.8 % compared to 2012, while exports on the intra-EU market have cumulated 85 % of the total food exports, up 6.5 % compared to 2012.

Table 4: External food trade in EU28, total and intra-EU, 2012 vs. 2015

	Export 2015	Export Growth 2012–2015	Balance 2015	Balance Growth 2012–2015	Intra-UE Import in total 2015	Intra-UE Import Growth 2012–2015	Intra-UE Export in total 2015	Intra-UE Export Growth 2012–2015
	mill. Euro	%	mill. Euro	%	%	%	%	%
Belgium	15,964	13.9	6,077	26.7	87	5.0	88	1.2
Bulgaria	1,163	36.4	516	52.1	80	0.1	72	3.4
Czech Rep.	2,137	16.2	520	38.7	92	-1.0	89	-0.1
Denmark	9,611	-3.6	5,966	-12.0	60	-11.3	67	2.4
Germany	33,414	8.8	10,091	16.0	80	4.2	80	0.1
Estonia	524	10.5	148	5.7	90	-1.0	77	-9.1
Ireland	6,730	..	4,271	..	83	..	..	..
Greece	1,885	23.9	121	-163.3	71	-0.9	72	-4.4
Spain	15,780	17.6	4,288	61.2	50	3.8	71	2.0
France	25,963	-6.9	7,546	-20.7	77	0.2	72	2.9
Croatia	736	4.7	-246	114.5	79	20.2	48	-9.6
Italy	19,026	..	2,949	..	67	..	..	..
Cyprus	163	37.2	-50	-22.9	71	8.3	55	-8.3
Latvia	422	-7.2	115	-14.6	85	-3.6	72	-5.8
Lithuania	1,385	0.2	475	-0.1	80	-4.8	75	-11.2
Luxembourg	418	..	418	..	..	..	..	..

(*continued on next page*)

Table 4: Continued

	Export 2015	Export Growth 2012–2015	Balance 2015	Balance Growth 2012–2015	Intra-UE Import in total 2015	Intra-UE Import Growth 2012–2015	Intra-UE Export in total 2015	Intra-UE Export Growth 2012–2015
	mill. Euro	%	mill. Euro	%	%	%	%	%
Hungary	3,297	4.8	1,820	8.7	91	1.1	82	-1.1
Malta		..	-107	661.7	62	-8.2	9	..
Netherlands	25,553	..	12,169	..	63	..	..	..
Austria	5,015	15.4	1,771	16.3	87	-4.3	85	-0.4
Poland	10,749	..	4,046	..	81	..	..	..
Portugal	2,126	8.2	-954	0.4	75	4.2	74	-0.9
Romania	1,058	56.9	-407	-43.0	73	-1.8	85	6.5
Slovenia	410	16.9	-26	-53.7	87	3.5	49	-28.6
Slovakia	905	..	154	..	96	..	..	..
Finland	981	..	-366	..	70	..	..	..
Sweden	0	..	0	-100.0	73	-0.8	67	..
UK	11,427	56.6	-3,853	-46.8	73	6.4	75	44.5

Source: Authors' estimates by Eurostat statistical data.

Countries with a higher dependence of the third markets, with the smallest share of intra-EU exports, were Malta (5 %), Croatia (48 %), Slovenia (49 %) and Cyprus (55 %).

By the foreign food trade opening degree, in 2015, among the EU28 Member States with the highest values (7 % -5 %) were identified Belgium, Lithuania, the Netherlands and Denmark (table 5).

Romania achieved a slight increase in the opening of foreign food trade in 2015 vs. 2012, but it was placed among the countries with the smallest values of that indicator, for the analyzed period, respectively, Sweden, Luxembourg, UK, Finland and Malta (0.9 % - 1.4 %).

Estimates show a close correlation (0.96) between the degree of commercial opening and the share of food exports to GDP of the EU28 countries, implicitly between the growth of these indicators. There was estimated a correlation (0.84) between market share and trade balance.

As shown in the figures in Figure 1, the EU28 Member States suffered a loss of export quota for food products comparing the years 2015 and 2012.

The same situation was also observed for imports, with the exception of Cyprus and Malta, where the increases are, however, insignificant, as shown in Figure 2.

However, it was found that the countries with the highest market share during the period, both for import and for export, were: Germany, with 17 % export and 16 % import, followed by France Italy, The Netherlands, Spain, Belgium and the UK (13 % -7 %), which together accounted for 75 % of imports and respectively of total EU food exports. These countries also suffered the largest market share loss in the analyzed period.

Romania is in the group of countries with a share of less than 1 % in the EU food trade, with an export market share of 0.5 % in 2015. Imports show a decrease in the market share, from 1.4 % in 2012 to 1 % in 2015, amid a 48 % rise in EU food imports, while Romania's food imports grew by only 5 %.

Conclusions

Among the main results of the research there are underlined the following remarks:

During the analyzed period (2012–2015), Romania's food competitiveness improved, as indicated by the 57 % increase in exports; a significant increase of the share of transformed products value into Romania's agro-food exports, which rose from 48 % to 69 %.

The reducing trend of the deficit of foreign trade in food products, although the balance of food trade remained negative.

Romania ranks in the group of countries with a share of less than 1 % in the food trade of the EU28, being among the countries with the lowest values of the opening of foreign food trade between the EU28 countries.

While the EU28 Member States suffered a loss of export quota as well as import quota for food products comparing the years 2015 and 2012, there was a 152 % increase in the share of exports of Romanian food products to the extra-EU market,

Table 5: Export-to-GDP ratio and degree of openness to food foreign trade, in EU28 countries

	Food Export / GDP (%)			Trade openness degree (%)		
	2012	2015	Growth 2012–2015	2012	2015	Growth 2012–2015
Belgium	4.0	4.3	0.3	6.7	7	0.34
Netherlands	0.0	4.2	4.2	..	6.4	..
Denmark	4.6	4.2	-0.4	6	5.8	-0.27
Lithuania	4.6	4.1	-0.5	7.6	6.8	-0.75
Hungary	3.8	3.6	-0.2	5.5	5.2	-0.36
Estonia	3.0	3.0	0.0	5.2	5.1	-0.02
Bulgaria	2.3	3.0	0.6	3.8	4.6	0.86
Ireland	0.0	2.8	2.8	..	3.9	..
Poland	0.0	2.8	2.8	..	4.6	..
Croatia	1.9	2.0	0.1	4.1	4.7	0.58
Latvia	2.3	2.0	-0.4	4	3.4	-0.57
Austria	1.5	1.7	0.1	2.5	2.7	0.19
Spain	1.4	1.6	0.2	2.5	2.8	0.26
Czech Rep.	1.3	1.4	0.2	2.3	2.5	0.22
Portugal	1.3	1.4	0.02	3.3	3.3	0.01
France	1.5	1.3	-0.2	2.5	2.3	-0.19
Italy	0.0	1.3	1.3	..	2.4	..
Slovakia	0.0	1.3	1.3	..	2.3	2.33
Slovenia	1.1	1.2	0.1	2.4	2.5	0.11
Germany	1.2	1.2	-0.01	2.1	2.1	-0.05
Greece	0.9	1.2	0.3	1.9	2.4	0.44
Cyprus	0.7	1.1	0.4	1.8	2.4	0.67
Luxembourg	0.0	0.9	0.9	..	0.9	..
Romania	0.6	0.8	0.2	1.76	1.79	0.03
Finland	0.0	0.5	0.5	..	1.3	..
UK	0.4	0.5	0.1	1.2	1.2	-0.02
Sweden	0.6	0.0	-0.6	1.5	0.9	-0.57
Malta	1.3	0.0	-1.3	2.8	1.4	-1.41

Source: Authors' estimates by Eurostat statistical data.

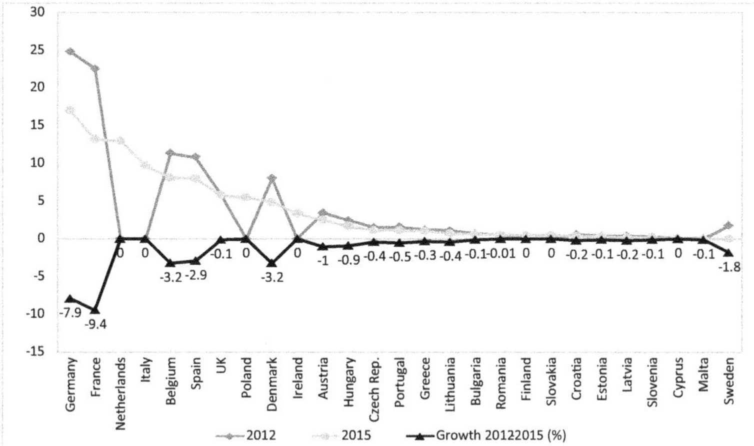

Figure 1: Market share of food exports of EU28 countries and Growth 2012 vs. 2015
Source: Author calculations by Eurostat data -Trade by commodity and NACE Rev. 2 activity.
*Note: *% in EU28 food export (intra-EU+extra-EU); **% in EU28 food import (intra-EU+extra-EU).*

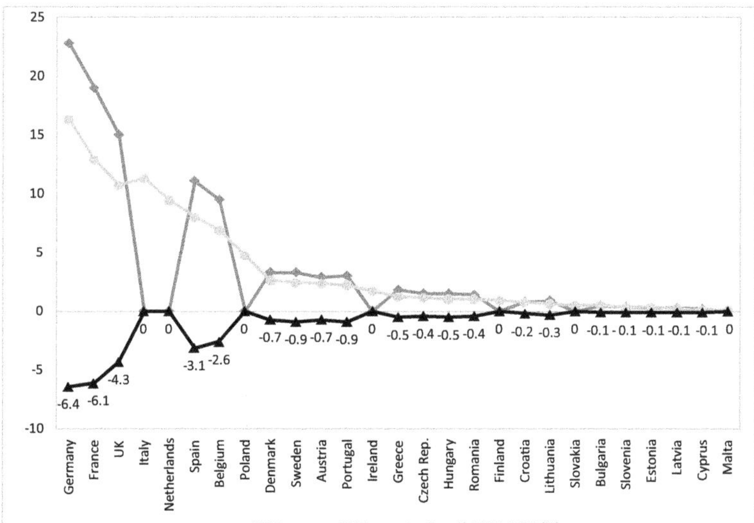

Figure 2: Market share of food imports of EU28 countries and Growth 2012 vs. 2015.
Source: Author calculations by Eurostat data -Trade by commodity and NACE Rev. 2 activity.

from 136 million Euro to 279 million Euro, while exports of agricultural products to these markets fell by almost half as a share of Romania's total agricultural exports.

Estimates show a close correlation (0.96) between the degree of commercial opening and the share of food exports to the GDP of the EU countries28, implicitly between the increases of these indicators. Also, there was a correlation (0.84) between market share and trade balance.

References

1. Albu, Lucian-Liviu (coord.): Creşterea contribuţiei comerţului exterior la realizarea convergenţei reale. Editura Economică, 2012.
2. Alexandri, Cecilia (coord.): Agricultura şi spaţiul rural – evaluări la 10 ani de la aderare. Editura Academiei Române, 2017.
3. Chivu, Luminiţa; Ciutacu, C.: About industrial structures decomposition and recomposition. 1st International Conference Economic Scientific Research - Theoretical, Empirical and Practical Approaches, ESPERA 2013, Procedia Economics and Finance 8 (2018): 157–166.
4. European Commission (EC). Common Agricultural Policy towards 2020, Brussels, Belgium, 2011.
5. Ministerul Agriculturii şi Dezvoltării Rurale (MADR): Programului Naţional de Dezvoltare Rurală (PNDR) 2014–2020, 2016.
6. Ministerul Agriculturii şi Dezvoltării Rurale (MADR): Strategia pentru dezvoltarea sectorului agroalimentar pe termen mediu şi lung orizont 2020–2030, Proiect. Bucuresti, 2015.
7. Rusali, Mirela-Adriana: Dimensiuni şi tendinţe principale privind sectorul de prelucrare a produselor agroalimentare. În: Cecilia Alexandri et al (coord.): Economie agrară şi dezvoltare rurală într-o perspectivă regională. Ed. Academiei Române, 2017.
8. Steriu, Valeriu; Otiman, Păun Ion (coord.): Cadrul strategic naţional pentru dezvoltarea durabilă a spaţiului rural în perioada 2014–2020–2030. Ed. Academiei Române, 2013.

Cristina BOBOC[1, 2], *Simona GHITA*[1], *Valentina VASILE*[2]

[1] Department of Statistics and Econometrics, Bucharest Academy of Economic Studies, Bucharest, Romania

[2] Institute of National Economy, Romanian Academy,
Email: valentinavasile2009@gmail.com

Characteristics of NEET'S in Romania

Abstract *Youth that are not in education, not employed and not in vocational training (NEETs) are at the heart of EU economic and social policies aiming at promoting inclusion and increasing prosperity. The current paper aims at characterizing the phenomenon of NEETs in Romania, compared to other EU countries, by analyzing the relationship between NEETs and other economic and social variables. The literature review allows for finding the magnitude and extent of NEETs in Romania and other EU countries. Factorial and classification methods are used on the available data provided by Eurostat to discover the relationships between NEETs, education and employment indicators. The findings are likely to provide new insights to the economic and social inclusive policies in Romania.*

Keywords: *NEET, Principal Component Analysis, Hierarchical Clustering, Non-Hierarchical Clustering, Ward Method*

Introduction

The term NEET originally appeared in the UK at the end of the 1980s, with the aim of developing an alternative classification of young people aged 16–18, a segment that was later expanded. Despite a widespread dissemination of the concept, there is a certain degree of criticism about it, due to a negative conotation based labeling of young people with different characteristics. The concept is associated with a low education level, low performance and responsibility or destructive behavior (Hutchinson & Kettlewell, 2015). However, the group of young people included in the NEET acronym presents a heterogeneity, comprising several subcategories: young people with unemployed or inactive status, who are not included in the education or training system, detailed by reasons of inactivity (Spielhofer et al., 2009).

The OECD and EUROSTAT use the NEETs acronym to identify young unemployed or inactive people (outside the labor market), not involved in the education or training process. These categories require special attention from researchers and policy-makers, as they present a high social exclusion risk. The NEETs rate expresses the proportion of NEET youngsters in an age category, out of the total number of young people in the same age group (usually 15–29 years or 15–24 years).

However, specific rates are also used for gender or age subgroups (15–19 years, 20–24 years). For European countries, the main data source is represented by EU labour force survey. According to this source, the average NEETs rate for 15–29 years age group, at EU(28) level, was 13,4 % in 2017 (a slight decrease compared to 2016). Higher values of the indicator were recorded in 2017 in South-European countries (Italy 24.1 %; Greece 21.3 %; Cyprus 17.5 %; Spain 16.4 %), but also in other developing ex-socialist countries (Bulgaria 18.9 %; Croatia 17.9 %; Romania 17.8 %). At the opposite end of the ranking - with low NEETs rates – there are some Western or Northern European countries (Netherlands 5.9 %; Luxembourg 6.6 %; Sweden 6.8 %).

According to official documents, in Romania in 2016 there were 400,000 young people in the NEETs category, the rate being one of the highest among the European countries. In Romania, the NEETs phenomenon is emphasized by the drop in the population aged 15–29, as a result of the sharp decline in birth rates compared to the pre-communist period. On the other hand, the NEET phenomenon is directly correlated with the inefficiency of the education system, on the background of minimal investments and poor educational results (the public education spending as a percentage of GDP was only 3.1 % in 2016 - among the smallest in the European Union; high discrepancy between rural and urban education, high school leaving). Under these conditions, Romania is in danger of having a mostly unskilled labor force that will seriously affect its productivity and economic progress. On the other hand, the Romanian vocational training system does not cover the requirements of the labor market.

1. Literature review

The use and spread of information and communication technology at high speed have led to an acceleration and expansion of the economy globalization (Castells, 2005; Olssen et. al., 2005). This has led to major changes in the structure and nature of employment, in employment opportunities, but also in the education system. The transition process, transforming the economies of less developed countries with a pronounced agricultural character into capitalist economies, predominantly industrial and post-industrial, has induced structural changes in the labor market. Specifically, the studies of Spielhofer et al 2009 identified a connection between the high NEETs rates in some UK regions - on one hand - and the local decline of the manufacturing industry and the reduction in the number of manual professional occupations - on the other hand.

In Scotland, Ianelli & Paterson, 2005, reported a lack of attenuation of social differences between classes, amid an increase in the level of education. Opportunities, chances of those in lower social classes to occupy top-level positions are lower than those in higher social classes. In other words, there is a direct correlation between the level of social class and the employment opportunities to top-level positions. At the same time, there is evidence that the acquired level of individuals' social class is positively influenced by the inheritance factor, more than the educational factor. Swift (2003) points to the necessity of increasing the role of choices and preferences, in changing the behavior and decisions of young people. In a study on the NEETs sector in Canada (Henderson et. al., 2017), it emerged that over 25 % of youth using the services provided by youth counseling agencies - are part of the NEETs category. This status is associated with increased risks of using prohibited substances, or with crime / violence, on the background of a predominance among young men.

The size of the NEETs sector in the UK in the fourth quarter of 2017 is given by 794,000 people aged 16–24 who were not included in the education, employment or training system, accounting for 11.2 % of the total population in the same age category (Powell, 2018). Of these, 42 % were unemployed, while the remaining 58 % were economically inactive. The phenomenon is more common among women, but gender discrepancies have been diminished in recent years. In 2010, a Report of the Audit Commission in the UK identified, among the contributing factors of the NEET status: the existence of this status in a previous period, the pregnancy, the parent status or the educational level. In a study on the NEETs sector in Mexico, Ranzani & Rosati (2013) have shown that the prior existence of NEETs status increases the likelihood of remaining at the same status by about 10 %. Also, the NEET status reduces the employment opportunities in the coming year by about 10 %. The probability of belonging to the NEET status is affected by the individual and household characteristics. Ranzani & Rosati (2013) developed a model demonstrating women's chances of becoming NEETs compared to men. The educational level is negatively correlated with the NEETs status. Thus, a young person who has graduated at least an upper secondary education level has 3 % fewer chances to become NEET. Young people living in large-sized households are more likely to get the NEET status. Also, the presence of children (0–4 years) and their belonging to the urban area increase the probability of having this status.

The two authors previously mentioned analyzed the transition paths from one status to another, identifying extensive and rapid possibilities of switching from NEET to employee status, but also possibilities for a slow transition from one NEET subcategory to another (for example, women affected by poverty and less educated). The study also analyzes the determinants of transition from one status to another. Thus, there is a significant differentiation of the gender-based transition path, young women not included in the labor force or in education system (NLFE- youth not in the labour force or education), showing a double persistence in keeping this status towards young men. Persistence in the unemployed status is low for both genders, most male unemployed (53 %) in Mexico switching to „employed" status a year later, while unemployed women (24 %) leave the workforce without re-entering the education system. The probability of transition from one status to another varies according to the education level. Thus, persistence in the NLFE status of young people decreases with the level of education.

Signe (2017) analyzed the background characteristics, specific problems and future prospects of young people disconnected from the education and labor market system, belonging to the 18–29 age group, considering them a heterogeneous group, and trying to cluster them in order to identify the ways of reconnecting young people to education and work. The youth assistance programs should be focused on the specific issues of each subgroup, thus facilitating their reintegration into work and training.

Mawn et.al (2017) analyzed the effectiveness of intervention programs for young people in the NEETs category. Some of these programs resulted in a small but significant increase in employment of 4 %. At the same time, programs involving the direct and frequent contact of young NEETs may have a potential effect in small income increases over the next two years, as well as some decreases in social benefits, especially for young women and for young people without children. No significant positive outcomes were found on the participants' health to the study, but some increases in the education level were reported. However, for most of the experiments, there haven't been reported significant decreases in youth unemployment in the NEETs category.

2. NEET's in Europe

To characterize the NEET phenomenon at European level, there are used data provided by EUROSTAT for the year 2016. For 33 European countries the following variables were analyzed:

- NEET (Not employed, education and training): youth who are not in education, not employed and not in vocational training.
- Early school leavers (18–24 years old): the percentage of people aged 18–24 who have completed lower secondary education as the last form of education.
- Young unemployed (15–29 years old): the percentage of the unemployed in the 15–29 age group.
- Young people at risk of social exclusion and poverty (15–29 years old): the percentage of young people at risk of social exclusion and poverty.
- The rate of young part-time employees (15–29 years old): percentage of young people with part-time employment.
- The rate of young temporary workers (15–29 years old): the proportion of young people working on a temporary work contract for a maximum period of 36 months.
- The rate of newly unemployed graduates: the share of young graduates who do not have a job, are available for work and looking for a job.
- The rate of participation in education and training in the last four weeks for people in the 18–24 age group.
- The share of people dropping out of education or training for family responsibilities.
- The share of people dropping out of education or training for health problems or inadequate age to follow a training program.
- The share of people dropping out of education or training for costs too high.

- The share of people dropping out of education or training for lack of employers' support.
- The share of people dropping out of education or training for no access to the Internet and computers.

First of all, it was analyzed the relationship between the factors that determine the NEET phenomenon, by using Principal Component Analysis (PCA). PCA is a technique used to reduce multidimensional data sets to lower dimensions, when all the variables used are quantitative. PCA is mathematically defined as an orthogonal linear transformation that projects the data to a new coordinate system (which is made by principal components) in order to obtain the greatest variance explained by this projection of the data.

The average NEET's rate at European level was 11.31 % in 2016. In Europe, the school drop-out rate is on average 10.47 %, while the rate of participation in education and training in the last four weeks since the analysis is 58.07 %. The unemployment rate for the age group of 15–29 years old is 15.22 % in average at European level, while the average of newly unemployed graduates is 78.05 %. Young Europeans are the adepts of part-time jobs or temporary work contracts. The first category has an average of 19.8 % and the second category has an average of 23.8 %.

Often, young people give up education or, better said, are forced to give up education for many economic and social reasons. On average, 34.5 % of young Europeans cannot study because of their family responsibilities. Although education is considered free, in most countries the costs are very high. For this reason, on average, 30 % of young people choose not to study. The lack of computers and the internet causes an average of 3.2 % of young people to drop out of studies. The need for a job is also an obstacle to education, in the sense that employers are not willing to support young people to study and 15.5 % of young people choose to work and give up studies. There is also an involuntary obstacle, namely the presence health problems. On average, 14.8 % of young Europeans cannot study because of health problems or because of their inadequate age. In 2016, in Europe, about 27.6 % of young people risk social exclusion and poverty.

By analyzing the correlation table, we can see that the NEET rate is strongly correlated with:

- Early school leavers.
- Youth unemployment rate.
- Young people at risk of social exclusion and poverty.
- Part-time young employees.
- Unemployment rate of recent graduates.
- Participation in education and training in the last 4 weeks.
- Share of people dropping out of education or training for costs too high.
- Share of people dropping out of education or training because of lack of internet access or computers.

Table 1: Descriptive statistics

Code	Variable name	Mean	Standard Deviation	N	Coefficient of Variation	Median
NEET	NEETs	11.31	5.29	33	46.77	10.50
ESL	Early school leavers	10.47	6.23	33	59.47	8.80
YUE	Youth unemployment rate	15.22	8.91	33	58.52	13.10
YPRSEP	Young people at risk of social exclusion and poverty	27.61	7.72	33	27.97	27.61
YPTE	Rate of youth part-time employees	21.14	14.29	33	67.56	19.80
YTW	Rate of youth temporary workers	27.41	15.71	33	57.29	23.80
URG	Unemployment rate of recent graduates	78.05	12.04	33	15.42	80.20
PET4W	Rate of participation in education and training in the last four weeks	58.07	8.03	33	13.83	59.10
PDETFR	Share of people dropping out of education or training for family responsibilities	34.48	7.19	33	20.85	34.48
PDETH	Share of people dropping out of education or training for health problems	14.83	3.59	33	24.21	14.83
PDETHC	Share of people dropping out of education or training for costs too high	30.04	10.19	33	33.94	30.04
PDETLES	Share of people dropping out of education or training for lack of employers' support	15.45	6.07	33	39.33	15.45
PDETNIC	Share of people dropping out of education or training for no access to the Internet and computers	3.21	1.34	33	41.67	3.21

Source: authors' calculations using SPSS software based on EUROSTAT data, 2016.

Table 2: Correlation table

Correlation coefficient	**ESL**	**YUE**	**YPRSEP**	**YPTE**	**YTW**	**URG**	**PET4W**	**PDETFR**	**PDETH**	**PDETHC**	**PDETLES**	**PDETNIC**
NEET	0,386**	0,709***	0,610***	-0,512***	-0,117	-0,861***	-0,663***	0,186	0,206	0,733***	-0,118	0,647***
ESL		0.028	0.204	-0.083	-0.209	-0.166	-0.460	0.117***	0.116	0.107	0.146	0.222
YUE			0.478***	-0.200	0.287**	-0.888***	-0.180	0.247**	0.173	0.412***	-0.093	0.327**
YPRSEP				0.046	-0.057	-0.540***	-0.012	0.014	0.360**	0.224	-0.047	0.173
YPTE					0.309*	0.342**	0.529**	0.087***	0.061	-0.273	0.179**	-0.247
YTW						-0.084*	0.381**	-0.105	-0.363**	-0.254*	0.146	-0.257*
URG							0.285	-0.111	-0.230*	-0.455***	0.101	-0.336**
PET4W								-0.282	-0.013	-0.303**	0.098	-0.298**
PDETFR									0.065**	0.069	-0.076	0.165
PDETH										0.170	-0.049	0.032
PDETHC											0.326**	0.833***
PDETLES												0.418***

Note: *** Level of significance of 0.01, ** Level of significance of 0.05, * Level of significance of 0.1

Source: author's computations on IBM SPSS Statistics 20 using EUROSTAT data, 2016

Table 3: Principal components

	Rotated Components (VARIMAX)			**Initial Components**		
	1	**2**	**3**	**1**	**2**	**3**
Unemployed rate of recent graduates	-.914	.296	-.051	.920	-.249	.131
Youth unemployment rate	.913	-.194	-.090	-.833	.385	-.193
Young people at risk of social exclusion and poverty	.763	.290	.286	-.606	.481	.388
Part-time youth employees	-.123	.901	.031	.539	.727	-.039
Participation in education and training in the last 4 weeks	-.072	.735	-.526	.489	.565	.520
Early school leavers	.063	-.085	.949	-.374	-.461	.748

Source: author's computations on IBM SPSS Statistics 20 using EUROSTAT data, 2016

Because the obstacles encountered by young people in employment have many missing answers, all these variables have been removed from the analysis. The variable Young temporary workers was also removed from the analysis.

By applying the PCA analysis, it is observed that 64 % of the information (38 % of the first axis and 26 % of the second axis) is explained by the first two main axes. The variation explained by the first three main components is 85 %. The analysis is significant with a significance level of 0.01, according to the Bartlett test.

The first principal component is positively determined by the Young Unemployed Rate and the Rate of youth at risk of social exclusion and poverty and negatively determined by unemployment rate of recent graduates. This component could be associated with young people who do not work. The second main component is positively determined by the rate of young part-time employees (15–29 years) and the rate of participation in education and training in the last four weeks. This component may be associated with young people who are in education. The third principal component is determined by the rate of early school leavers. This component can be associated with young people who are not educated.

From the analysis of the projection of the European countries on the first two principal axes it can be noticed that Greece, Spain and Italy are far from other EU countries on positive direction of first principal axis. These countries are characterized by high rates of youth unemployed and young people at risk of social exclusion and poverty and low rates of unemployed recent graduates. The Netherlands and Denmark, Norway and Ireland are projected on the positive side of Axis 2, meaning that these countries are characterized by high rates of part-time young employees and high rates of participation in education and training in the last 4 weeks.

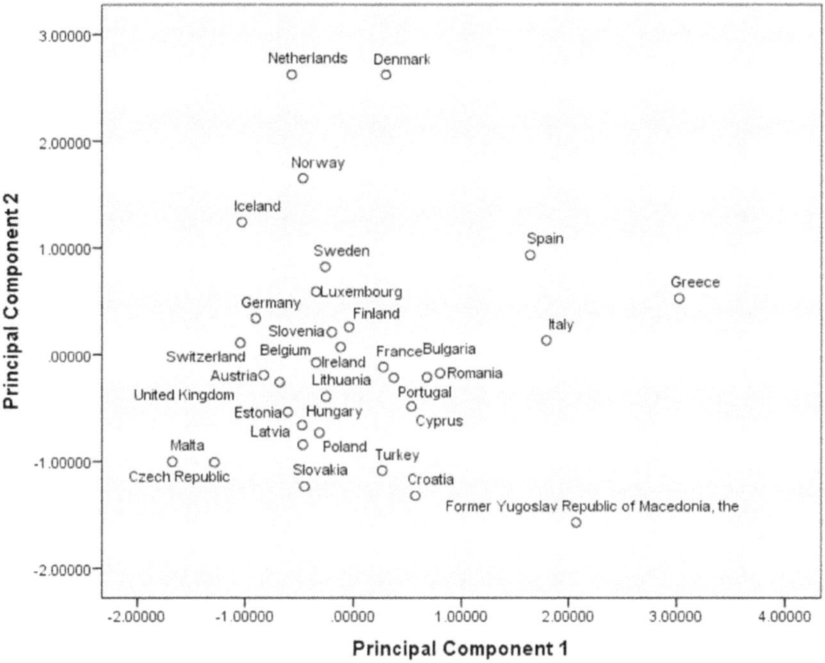

Figure 1: Country projection on the first two principal components

Source: author's computations on IBM SPSS Statistics 20 using EUROSTAT data, 2016.

Regarding Romania, it is represented on the positive side on first principal component, meaning that it is characterized by high rates of young graduates, high rates of unemployed recent graduates and of young people at risk of social exclusion and poverty compared to the others European states.

By analyzing the dependence of the NEET rate on the first three principal components, there is a strong direct relationship between first component and NEET and a strong inverse relationship between component 2 and NEET. There is no significant relationship between component 3 and NEET. By using multiple linear regression model for NEET as dependent variable and the first two principal components as independent variables, it is obtained a valid model with a significance level of 99 %, with significant parameters and with R^2 of 0.81. The first principal component has a 1.5 greater impact on NEET than the second principal component.

Romania is among the countries with the highest NEET rate in Europe. Moreover, the part-time youth employment rate and the participation in education and training in the last 4 weeks are well below the average of European countries and the youth unemployment rate, the unemployment rate of recent graduates and the rate of young people at risk of social exclusion and poverty are higher compared to the other European states included in the analysis.

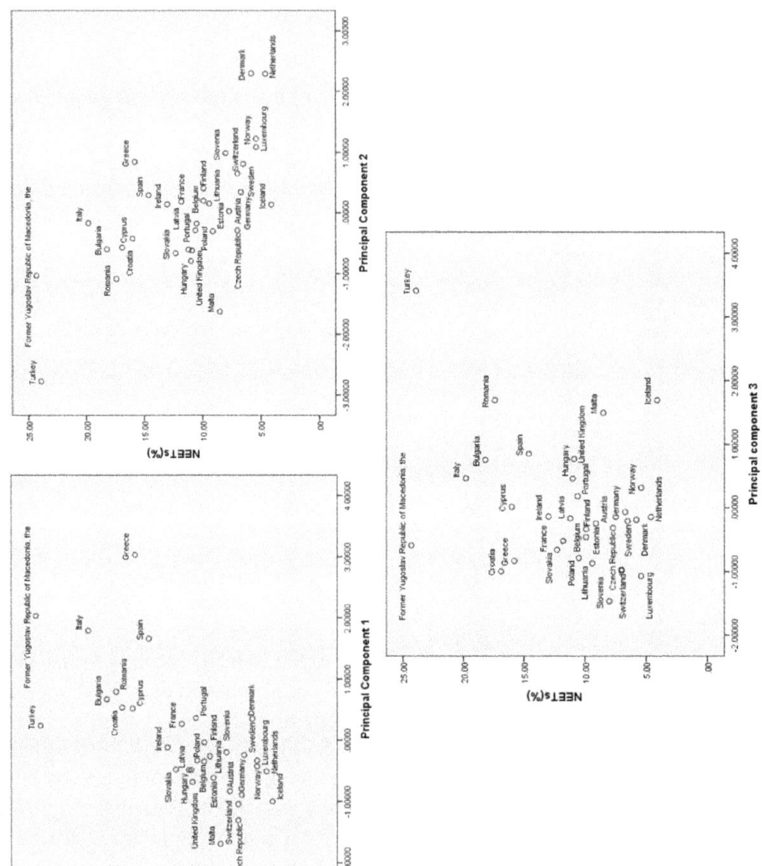

Figure 2: The relationship between NEETs and the three principal components

Source: author's computations on IBM SPSS Statistics 20 using EUROSTAT data, 2016.

Conclusions

Romania faces one of the highest NEET rate among European countries, especially in case of young women.Thus, identifying the main determinants of NEET phenomenon is of greatest importance for the policy-makers, in reducing the phenomenon level. A number of negative circumstances maintain the high level of the NEET phenomenon: the part-time youth employment rate and the participation in education and training in the last 4 weeks are below the average of European countries; the youth unemployment rate, the unemployment rate of recent graduates and the rate of young people at risk of social exclusion and poverty are higher compared to the other European states.

The results of our analysis is consistent with economic theory, Thus, NEET is the intersection of three sets. The first set consists of young people who are not employed, mainly the first principal component. The second set consists of young people who are not in education, expressed by component 2. And the third set consists of young non-educated expressed by component 3. By analyzing the position of each country in relation to these three components it could be identified the contributing factors to the formation of the NEETs. In the case of Romania, the extremely widespread NEET phenomenon is due to the large number of young people in all three categories. However, raising the level of education and participation of young people in training could be one of the main direction of action for lowering the NEET rate in Romania.

References

1. Castells, M.: The rise of the network society (vol. 1, 2nd ed.), Oxford, Blackwell, 2005.
2. Hutchinson, Jo/Kettlewell, Kelly: Education to employment: complicated transitions in a changing world. Educational Research, 57(2), 2015, pp. 113–120.
3. Ianelli, Cristina/Paterson, Lindsay: (2005) Does education promote social mobility?. CES Briefing no. 35, 2005.
4. Mawn, Lauren/Oliver, Emily/Akhter, Nasima/Bambra, Clare/Torgerson, Carole/Bridle, Chris/Stain, Helen: Are we failing young people not in employment, education or training (NEETs)? A systematic review and meta-analysis of re-engagement interventions. Systematic Reviews 6(16), 2017.
5. Olssen, M./Codd, J./O'Neill, A.: Education policy: globalisation, citizenship and democracy, London, Sage, 2005.
6. Powell, Andrew: NEET: Young People not in Education, Employment or Training, Commons Library Briefing, Number SN 06705, March, 2018, pp. 4–8, 11–12.
7. Ranzani, Marco/Rosati, Furio: The Neet Trap: a dynamic analysis for Mexico, UNICEF, Rome, 2013, pp. 11–16.

8. Signe, H.A: Disconnected youth: Past, present & future. Study Paper No. 116, The ROCKWOOL Foundation Research Unit, Copenhagen, 2017, 47 pages.
9. Spielhofer, Thomas/Benton, Tom/Evans, Kelly/Featherstone, Gill/, Golden, Sarah/Nelson, Julie/Smith, Paula: Increasing Participation: Understanding Young People Who Do Not Participate in Education or Training at 16 and 17, DCSF Research Report 072, London: DCSF, 2009.
10. Swift, A.: Seizing the opportunity: the influence of preferences and aspirations on social mobility, New Economy, 10(4), 2003, pp. 208–212.
11. OECD data, Youth not in employment, education or training (NEET), available at https://data.oecd.org/youthinac/youth-not-in-employment-education-or-training-neet.htm
12. http://ec.europa.eu/eurostat/web/youth/data/database

Ana-Maria CIUHU[1], *Valentina VASILE*[2], *Nicoleta CARAGEA*[3]

[1] PhD candidate, SCOSAAR, Romanian Academy; Expert, National Institute of Statistics, Email: dobre.anamaria@hotmail.com;

[2] Senior Researcher I, Institute of National Economy, Romanian Academy, Email: val.vasile.ien@gmail.com;

[3] Senior Expert, National Institute of Statistics; Associate Professor, PhD, Faculty of Economics, Ecological University of Bucharest, Email: nicoleta.caragea@insse.ro

The Unemployement in Romania – Evidences Based on the Philips Curve

Abstract *The main objective of the present paper is to analyze the relationship between inflation and unemployment in Romania based on the empirical evidence of Phillips curve for the reference period 1991–2017. The results confirm the theory according to that - for the long term (over 20 years) – a relationship between inflation and unemployment could be identified. The theory is not confirmed for short periods. In these circumstances, based on the empirical results, the paper proposes a new approach of the classical Phillips curve: a short term trade-off between unemployment and wages. The data analyzed in the paper are provided by National Institute of Statistics.*

Keywords: *Unemployment, Philips curve, Inflation, Wages*

1. State-of-the-art

In macroeconomic theory, the empirical model reflects the connection between inflation rate and unemployment rate or between real wages and inflation. The relationship between inflation and unemployment is known in the literature as the Phillips Curve, following the name of the one who demonstrated the existence of a reverse link between nominal wage change and the UK unemployment rate (Philips, 1958). The economist noted not only an inverse relationship between inflation and unemployment, but also the manifestation of some nonlinearities in its level, depending on the cyclical position of the economy.

Four decades later, Phelps developed the theory that states: "if the expected increase in wages is low enough (below a certain level) and if there is an illusion that the money is enough, employees would prefer to leave than to accept a reduction in nominal wages which would be under their dignity." (Phelps, 1998) In the same sense, Akerlof considered "that employees have a certain standard for wages." (Akerlof, 2007)

A study by the IMF (Hoffmann et al, 2018) concerns about salary increases and their impact on economic cyclicality. Using two series of annual data for wages - the number of weeks worked over a year and weekly wage changes, the wage gap between economic cycles is analysed.

For Romania, a study is presenting the reverse relationship between inflation and unemployment and its intensity in the post-crisis period (Iordache et al, 2015). This research proposes the estimation of a reduced shape of the Phillips curve, using the triangular model, the reference for estimating structural unemployment, being used by international institutions such as the OECD, the IMF or the European Commission. The chosen specification, which includes the unemployment gap, supply shocks and adaptive expectations, has proven appropriate to capture the inflation path in Romania. Moreover, structural unemployment, or NAIRU (Non-Accelerating Inflation Rate of Unemployment), which represents the level of consistent unemployment with price stability, is being considered in the analysis.

Other references focus on the development of econometric models. Jula (2017) produced two models for the period 1992–2017, where the inflation trend was considered a reference for its dynamics, and the unemployment gap was explained by applying the Hodrick-Prescott filter.

2. Objective of the study

By analyzing inflation and unemployment, economists have found that the reverse link between the two indicators is not always valid. The study proposes a new approach of the Phillips classic curve that highlights a short-term relationship between inflation and wage earnings. The classic Philips curve will be compared, using both registered unemployment and ILO unemployment, as well as the Philips curve in terms of the relationship between inflation and average and minimum wage earnings. The short term refers to a period of less than 20 years.

3. Philips curve – Romania's case

In Romania, the Philips curve does not confirm in the economic reality. In this study, the Philips curve will be analyzed two-fold: a) the relationship between the inflation rate and the unemployment rate (as recorded by ILO); and b) the relationship between the inflation rate and the salary (average and minimum).

In the following we will present some methodological aspects of unemployment and earnings.

The differences between the two rates of unemployment – registered and ILO unemployment - are explained by the typology. Registered unemployed represents a minor share of the total number of unemployed: those who are aware of the need to be registered and paid for. While registered unemployment includes strictly registered unemployed people, regardless of the people who left paid unemployment, or people who are temporarily out of the country to work in the short term, the data gathered from household surveys also includes people who do not work

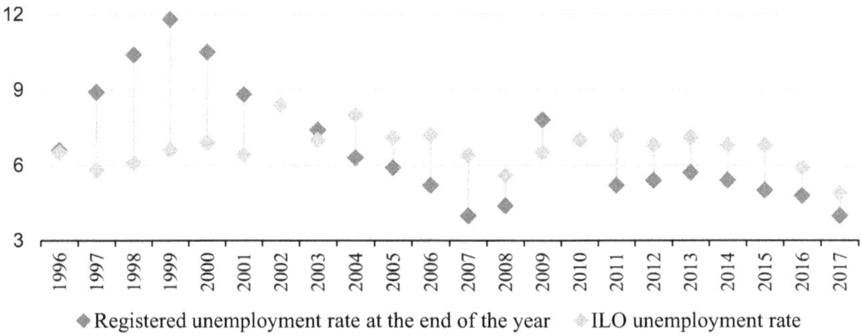

Figure 1: Registered unemployment rate and ILO unemployment rate in Romania, 1996–2017 (%)

Source: National Institute of Statistics, Tempo online database, SOM103A, AMG157B.

but who are not registered with the National Agency for Employment. Moreover, the evolution of the ILO unemployment rate seems to better capture the real developments in the labor market, including informal side. Therefore, this study will address the Philips curve considering both rates of unemployment.

Until 2003, but also in 2009, the registered unemployment rate surpassed that of ILO unemployment. The economic crisis has brought with it the need for the unemployed to register, in order to get benefits but also to find a job through the public placement service. Since 2004, Labour Force Survey (LFS) has highlighted a higher rate of ILO unemployed than those officially registered. The highest difference between the two rates was in 2007, i.e. 2.4 p.p., respectively 266.5 thousand people. There were two exceptions of this situation; in 2002 and 2010 the registered unemployment rate was at the same level as the ILO unemployment rate.

The propensity of reducing registered unemployment was due to a legislative change in the labor market, which has been applied since 2011. It brought under regulation the loss of unemployment benefit for those who refused a job offered, compatible with the level of their education. These people were removed from the National Employment Agency's records, as they did not express their will in being registered as unemployed, thus causing a drop in the unemployment rate.

The volatility of the paid and unpaid unemployed is presented in the following figure. The data show that in 1992 the share of unpaid unemployed in total registered unemployed oscillated between 9.3 % (December) and 19 % (January). In 2017, this shares were reversed, with 79.2 % unpaid not registered in December 2017. Since 2001, about one third of the registered unemployed were unpaid, and since 2002 their share has worsen, half of them not benefiting of allowances.

The wages considered for the Philips curve analysis are the net monthly and minimum monthly averages, the latter being regulated by national law.

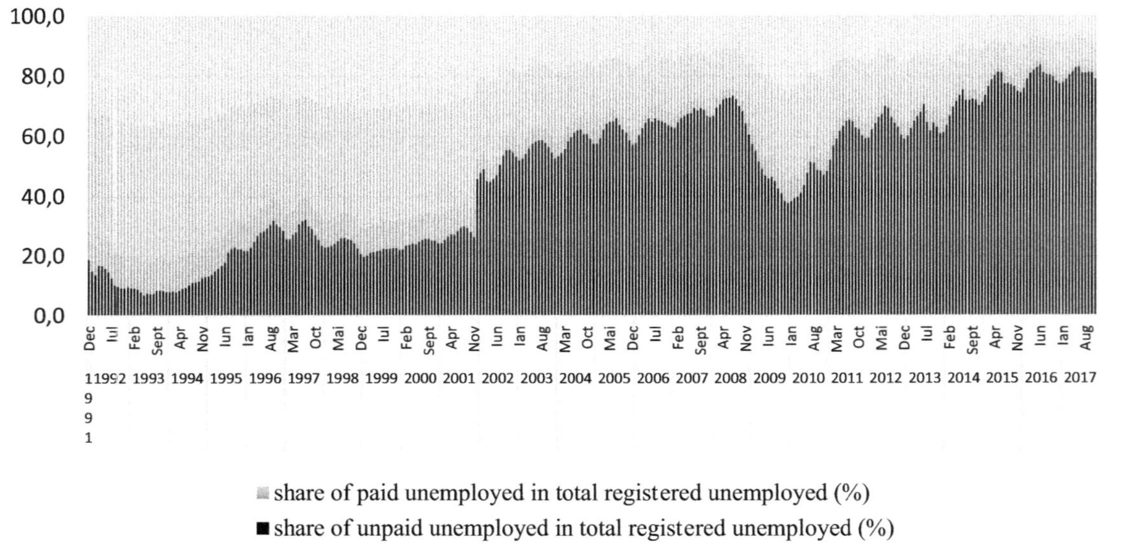

Figure 2: Monthly evolution of the share of the paid and unpaid unemployed in total registered unemployed between December 1991 and December 2017 (%)

Source: Authors' calculations, based on Romanian National Institute of Statistics, Tempo online database, SOM101A.

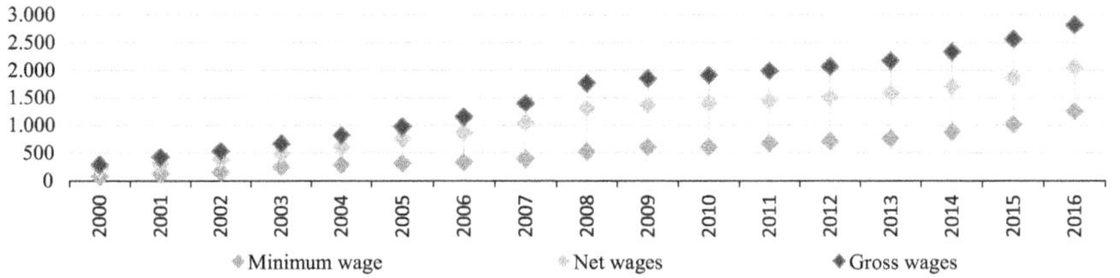

Figure 3: Evolution of minimum, net and gross wages in Romania, 2000–2016 (National currency - RON)

Source: Romanian National Institute of Statistics, Data series of wages and Ministry of Labour, Data series for minimum wages.

Note: For the period 2000–2004 the denomination of the national currency was applied.

Their progress is different between 2000 and 2016. The most significant increase in net average wages was registered in 2000 (41.1 %). The gross average salary recorded the highest growth in 2001, i.e. by 48.6 % as compared to 2000. The guaranteed minimum wage increased by 79.2 % in 2000 as compared to 1999. Official data shows that in the post-crisis period wages increased a much lower rate than in the period preceding it.

In Romania, the minimum wage was set according to the legal regulations. At the same time, the increase in income inequalities and the concentration of most individuals towards the minimum wage was supported. Thus, asymmetric polarization has developed.

According to a study which proposed a minimum wage setting mechanism for 2018 (Popescu M. et al., 2017, p. 9), the number of paid employees with a minimum wage is 1.28 million. In this research (Popescu M. et al, 2017, pp.7–8), five possible scenarios are proposed for establishing the minimum wage, of which:

- Scenario 1 – the minimum wage should be aligned with the average wage trend, to maintain a balanced average income level. In this case, the minimum wage should increase by 11.2 p.p., equal to the annual growth rate of the previous year's gross average wage. The number of employees with minimum salary would increase by 46 p.p., reaching 1.87 million people;
- Scenario 2 – the minimum wage should be aligned with GDP per capita. In this scenario, the minimum wage should increase by 6.23 p.p. The number of employees with minimum salary would increase by 28 p.p., reaching 1.65 million people;
- Scenario 3 - the minimum wage needs to be adjusted to the inflation rate and to increase by 1.7 p.p. The number of paid employees with a minimum wage would increase by 12 p.p., reaching 1.44 million people.

The conclusion of the information presented above is the following: the higher the minimum wage increases, the higher the number of people paid by the minimum wage.

The guaranteed minimum wage is an important social policy instrument that ensures equity of income at the societal level. The ratio between the minimum wage and the average wage justifies testing the Philips curve with the two types of wage earnings.

3.1 Philips Curve in Romania, as relationship between inflation and registered unemployment rates

For Romania, the Philips curve is represented throughout 1991–2017, and later for two sub-periods: 1991–2000 and 2000–2017, depending on its specificity.

The curve presents a high volatility in the 1990s. This situation arises from the fact that the relationship between the two indicators is also affected by other economic factors.

The results show that in the long run (26 years) a direct relationship between inflation and low unemployment can be identified. The regression equation between the two variables, with a correlation coefficient R^2 of 0.13, takes the following form:

$$y = -35.9 + 11.77\ x, \text{ where:}$$

$$y = \text{inflation rate}$$

$$x = \text{registered unemployment rate}$$

Interpretation of the regression equation shows that inflation, with a unit (+1 p.p.) change, will increase on average by 11.77 p.p.

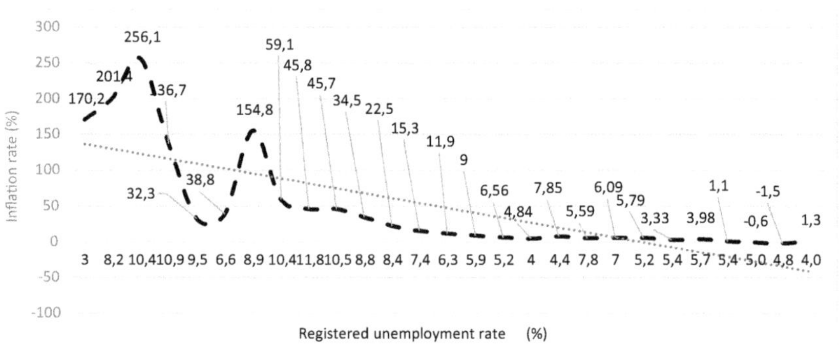

Figure 4: Philips Curve in Romania (as relationship between inflation and registered unemployment rates), 1991–2017

Source: Romanian National Institute of Statistics, Tempo online database, SOM103A and IPC data series, http://www.insse.ro/cms/ro/content/ipc-serii-de-date.

Between 1991 and 2000, the relationship between inflation and registered unemployment had medium intensity ($R^2 = 0.5146$). Between 2001 and 2017, there was a strong link between these indicators ($R^2 = 0.706$).

Since 2008, some inflection points have been identified, which can be explained by several factors that have influenced the inflation trend. The inflation has been influenced by wide supply shocks: a) changes in the VAT rate (in 2010 and 2013); b) agricultural output (below the long-term average in 2010, 2012 and record production in 2013–2014) and c) fluctuations in international oil quotas (Iordache et al, 2015, p. 15). The tendency of smoothing observed since 2007 (the year of Romania's accession to the European Union) can be explained by the influence of external developments in the pricing policy of companies, namely it can be seen because of globalization.

For a complete overview of the phenomenon, we will continue to investigate the Philips curve as a relationship between inflation and ILO unemployment. The direct relationship has an average intensity of 48 % ($R^2 = 0.4886$).

The year 1997 moves the average of the distribution of inflation and unemployment series, so comparability requires analysis in the period 2001–2017. Thus, during this period, the direct link between the inflation rate and the ILO unemployment rate is explained in a proportion of 70 % ($R^2 = 0.706$).

3.2 Philips Curve in Romania, as relationship between inflation rate and wages

In this section the relationship between inflation and average and short-term earnings will be analyzed. On the one hand, net average earnings will be considered and, on the other hand, the minimum wage.

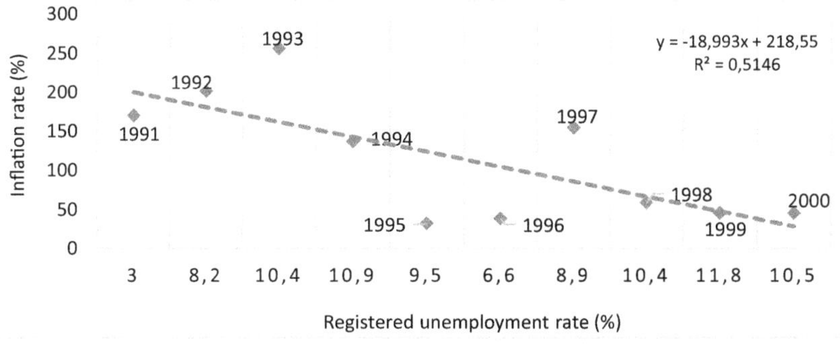

Figure 5: Philips Curve in Romania (as relationship between inflation and registered unemployment rates), 1991–2000

Source: Romanian National Institute of Statistics, Tempo online database, SOM103A and IPC data series, http://www.insse.ro/cms/ro/content/ipc-serii-de-date.

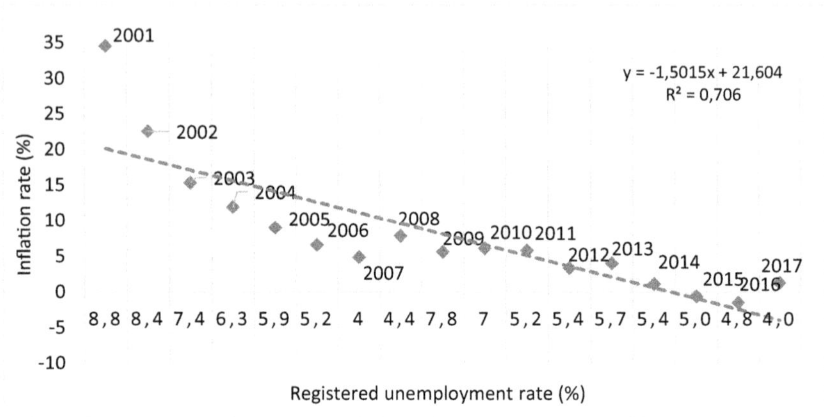

Figure 6: Philips Curve in Romania (as relationship between inflation and registered unemployment rates), 2001–2017

Source: Romanian National Institute of Statistics, Tempo online database, SOM103A and IPC data series, http://www.insse.ro/cms/ro/content/ipc-serii-de-date.

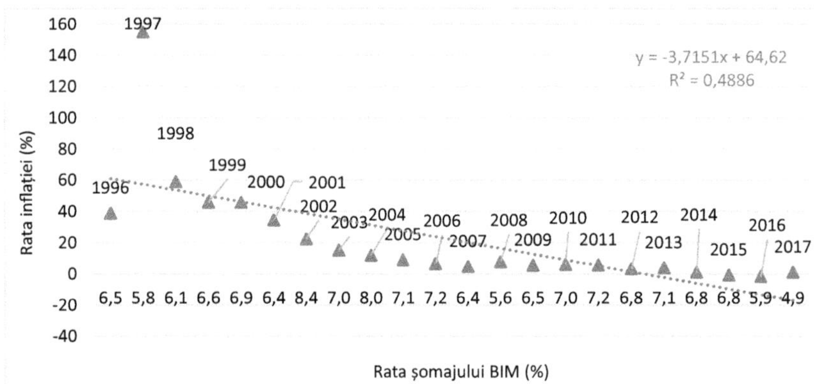

Figure 7: Philips Curve in Romania (as relationship between inflation and ILO unemployment rates), 1996–2017

Source: Romanian National Institute of Statistics, Tempo online database, AMG157B and IPC data series, http://www.insse.ro/cms/ro/content/ipc-serii-de-date

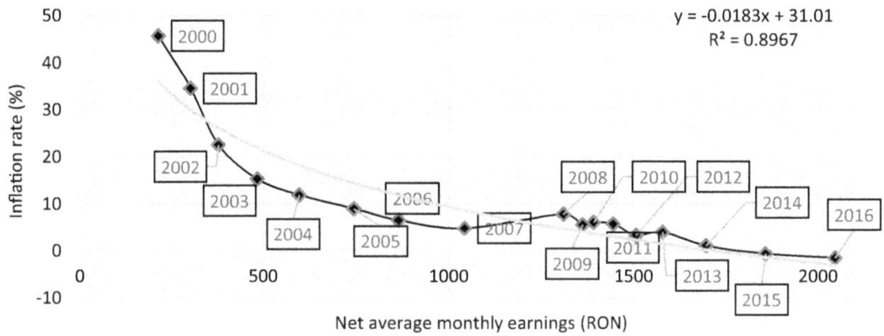

Figure 8: Relationship between inflation rate and net average monthly earnings in Romania, 2000–2016

Source: Romanian National Institute of Statistics, IPC and Wages data series

The direct link between inflation and net average monthly earnings has a strong intensity of 89 % over the period 2000–2016.

Over the same period, between the inflation rate and the minimum wage there is a strong relationship, explained 70 %.

As wages represent a significant cost to companies, their growth leads to higher prices for products and services in the economy, leading to an increase in inflation.

Conclusions

The paper proposes an analysis of the Philips curve in Romania during 1991–2017. The results validated the theory that there is a long-term relationship between inflation and unemployment. The theory has not been confirmed for short periods of time. Irrespective of the type of unemployment, the link between it and the inflation rate is direct and medium intensity in 2001–2017.

Under these circumstances, based on empirical results, the paper proposed a new approach to the Philips curve, which highlighted a short-term relationship between inflation and minimum and average wage earnings.

A possible constraint of the Philips curve is the inconsistency of the macroeconomic indicators that cannot be fully measured and aggregated: inflation can not be measured because all goods, services or assets in an economy cannot be taken into account; unemployment is impossible to be recorded in real time, and GDP does not capture intermediate goods (those included in finished goods) and, therefore, the movement of goods into the economy. All of these indicators work with approximations that in most cases can be exceeded by reality.

Thus, an economic inconsistency of the Philips curve can be discussed as it ignores the impact of inflationary policy on the capital market (with which the labor market is in a strong connection). When inflation rises, interest rises,

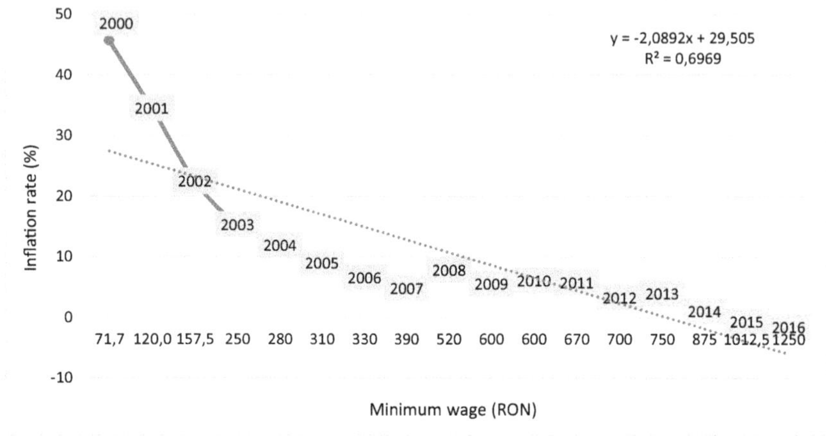

Figure 9: Relationship between inflation rate and minimum wage in Romania, 2000–2016

Source: Ministry of Labour and Romanian National Institute of Statistics, IPC data series.

investment declines because of more expensive capital, and unemployment is increasing. Therefore, between inflation and unemployment there should be a direct link - and not an inverse proportionality - as evidenced by the empirical evidence from this study.

References

Akerlof, George Arthur (2007) The Missing Motivation in Macroeconomics, American Economic Review, American Economic Association, vol. 97(1), pages 5–36.

Hoffmann, Eran B./Malacrino, Davide (2018) Employment Time and the Cyclicality of Earnings Growth, IMF Working Paper, WP/18/115

Iordache, Ştefania Cristina/Militaru, Mădălina/Pandioniu, Mihaela Luiza (2015) Relaţia inversă dintre inflaţie şi şomaj în România. Cât de puternică este în perioada postcriză?, Banca Naţională a României, Caiete de studii, nr.41, ISSN 1584-0883

Jula, Dorin/Jula, Nicoleta (2017) The Phillips Curve for the Romanian Economy, 1992–2017, Computational Methods in Social Sciences, Vol. V, Issue 1/2017, pp.36–48

Ministry of Labour, Minimum wages data series, http://www.mmuncii.ro/j33/images/Date_lunare/s1-18.pdf

National Institute of Statistics, Tempo online database

National Institute of Statistics, Wages dataseries, http://www.insse.ro/cms/ro/content/castiguri-salariale-din-1938-serie-anuala-0

National Institute of Statistics, IPC dataseries, http://www.insse.ro/cms/ro/content/ipc-serii-de-date

Phelps, Edmund S./Zoega, Gylfi (1998) Natural-rate theory and OECD unemployment, Economic Journal, 108(448), pp. 782–801.

Phillips, Alban William (1958) The Relation between Unemployment and the Rate of Change of Money Wage Rates in the United Kingdom, 1861–1957, Economica 25, No. 100 (1958): 283–299.

Popescu, Madalina Ecaterina & Militaru, Eva & Pele, Dan & Mazurencu Marinescu, Miruna & Vasile, Valentina & Ilie, Simona & Mihailescu, Adina & Serban, Adela (2017) Support for establishing a minimum wage-setting mechanism in Romania, Editura Lumen, Iași

Mimoza SERAFIMOVA[1]

[1] PhD, Asociate Professor at Faculty of Tourism, Goce Delcev University - Stip, Macedonia, mimoza.serafimova@ugd.edu.mk

Entrepreneurship and Entrepreneurial Values: Evaluation of Macedonia

Abstract *The paper elaborates the main findings of a survey conducted in the line of evaluation identifing challenges that need to be overcome for the development of entrepreneurship: low level of entrepreneurial spirit and culture. The paper intends to assess the current situation between indicators of entrepreneurial intentions and entrepreneurial activities through the perceptions and attitudes as the identification of business opportunities, business skills and perception of business. For this purpose we analyzed the results of relevant research of the Organization of Employers of Macedonia (ORM) and the Business Confederation of Macedonia (BCM) with support from the International Labour Organization (ILO). Moreover, the paper listed the specific problems that can be strengthened economic growth and national policies for entrepreneurship. The goal of research is to provide evidence for the existence of a gap between entrepreneurial intentions and entrepreneurial activity, resulting in fewer new or high growth businesses that the entrepreneurs are facing in Macedonia. The contribution of this paper consists the enrichment of the weakly developed academic work in Macedonia for resolving this issue.*

Keywords: *Entrepreneurship; SMEs; Entrepreneurial Values; Macedonia*

Introduction

Unlike the period before the transition where the most important issue was industrialization, and later the intensification of agriculture and the development of other business activities, nowadays one of the most popular questions is the one of small business that is for small and medium enterprises. Neglect of small business of the Republic of Macedonia led to serious structural imbalances that eventually seen as inefficiency and low competition in the economy (Uzunov, Georgiev, Nedanovski 2008, p.405).

Considering the negative experiences of the past, the aim should be not simply to increase the number of SMEs, but primarily made for them to show their true capabilities. Small and medium-sized enterprises (SMEs) are an important and vital part of the economy of a country. They are significant in terms of their cooperation and they represent competition from large enterprises when it comes to their participation in the creation of new jobs, products and services, and making more profits. In this context, hereafter we present the gross domestic product

Table 1: Number of active business entities in Macedonia according to the number of their employees

Year	2012	2013	2014	2015	2016	2017
Enterprises with 1–9 employees	52,910	59,398	59,276	60,620	61,053	60,599
Enterprises with 10–49 employees	3,351	3,706	4,051	4,452	4,732	4,776
Enterprises with 50–249 employees	1,177	1,159	1,211	1,187	1,280	1,291
Enterprises with more than 250 employees	189	204	203	185	201	209

Source: www.stat.gov.mk

(GDP) of the Republic of Macedonia for a period of four years, which means that we have a basis on which we should be able to further analyze the impact of SMEs on the creation of GDP, as a of the basic ways to measure performance of the economy.

The real growth rate of GDP compared to 2012 was 2.7 %. Because active business entities who act in GDP, many research papers aim at identifying which businesses according to their size have a larger or smaller share of GDP. Statistics show that in the country of micro and small enterprises are the main factors affecting the GDP growth from year to year (as shown in Table 1), and as a result a lot to contribute to real economic growth of the country.

It is obvious that the actual rates of economic growth can not be qualified as satisfactory ones to strengthen the base and the state of the domestic economy, and to increase the living standards of the population. This is supported by the fact that the average value of GDP per capita in Macedonia is still very low. For example, in 2010 this value is 3.459 € with consistent growth until 2013 when it rose to 3.930 €, and as such are still far below the level of GDP in developed countries.

1 Literature review

Taking into consideration the importance of showing the relationship between entrepreneurship and economic results, this paper provides an overview of high quality, Economics and Management Studies, focusing on different types of contributions that entrepreneurs can achieve in the economy in terms of quantitative measures and evaluating performance of entrepreneurs in the socio-economic areas.

Parker (2004) in a number of studies provide (pretty thoroughly) review of empirical studies to assess the extent of contributions to creating economic value to entrepreneurs. (Wynarczyk and Watson (2005); Maes et al. (2005), or Norton and Moore (2006); Hartarska and Gonzalez Vega (2006).)

For our theme, we reviewed five previous and recent studies that are somewhat related to each other: Acs and Audretsch (2005) entrepreneurship and innovation; Carree and Thurik (2003) entrepreneurship and economic growth from the macroeconomic perspective; Biggs (2002) analysis of small and medium enterprises (SMEs) and employment and innovation; Caves (1998) focus on entry, exit and circulation The companies and the growth and production efficiency, and finally, Sutton (1997) employment generation.

Based on a panel of 36 countries, Wennekers et al, (2005) show that correlation between the level of entrepreneurial activity and innovation capacity of a country (p. 297) was positive in more developed countries such as the US and Europe. Likewise, Acs and Varga (2005) revealed a positive relationship between entrepreneurial activity and technological change in the European Union, which confirms the foregoing.

Growth in value added was investigated at company level (Brouwer et al 2005) and more aggregate levels (Baldwin 1998; Carree 2002; Robbins et al, 2000; Carree and Thurik 2007). The results show that the growth of entrepreneurs' added value is relatively high. At company level Baldwin (2005) shows that the rate of productivity growth in terms of production and added value in terms of cost of production factors is inversely proportional to the size of the company, that is, small firms have higher growth rates productivity. Rodríguez et al. (2003, Spanish Canary Islands) use the Framework Code of Gibrat and underpin this result.

Based on pooled data, Baldwin (1998) shows an increase in the stake of the smallest classes, the cost of those larger classes. Hence, economic activity is shifting towards small companies (possibly without any real growth in the total value of the shipment, or GDP).

2 Development of SMEs in Macedonia

Macedonia, as many other former socialist countries, started with the development of SMEs in the transition process. Based on various changes in the economic and political system of the country, the process of spontaneous entrepreneurship was initiated. On the other hand, the establishment of large number of new SMEs was expected reaction of the citizens due interrupted social and economic security caused by transition, privatization and growing unemployment (Fiti et al 2007, p. 224).

The dynamic of registering new SMEs was particularly intensive in the period from 1990 until the end of 1993, followed latter on by smaller intensity (due to embargo) and gaining in force once again in 1996.

Until 2004, the share of SMEs in the trade sector was substantially reduced compared to 1993, getting to 54 % (APPRM, 2005). Concerning the regional aspect, the largest part of the SMEs is concentrated in Skopje, Bitola, Kumanovo, Prilep, Ohrid, Strumica and Tetovo.

In 2004, based on the changes within the Company Law, Macedonia adopted the methodology for classification of the enterprises based on the size, proposed by the EU Commission. According to this methodology, the enterprises are classified upon three criteria. The first criteria (number of employees) is accepted in Macedonia and consequently there are micro, small, medium and big enterprises. The other two criteria (size of the turnover and total amount of the assets) are adjusted to fit Macedonia's conditions. Hence, small enterprise in EU is an entity with yearly turnover of 10 million EUR, while in Macedonia it should have only 2 million EUR.

The State Statistical Office of the Republic of Macedonia is entitled to follow the development of the SMEs in terms of growth, sector and regional structure, demography etc.

In 2012, there were 74,424 enterprises in Macedonia, out of which 99.7 % or 74,223 are SMEs. In this line it should be noted that the SMEs are significant not only for having the dominant share of total entities in Macedonia, but for their contribution to the GDP (over 55 %) and to employment in the business sector (over 75 %). Additional conclusion arises in the line of sectorial changes in the SMEs in Macedonia. Namely the trade has decreased its share for additional 17 % compared to 2004. (Serafimova, Petrevska 2015, p. 41)

3 The impact of subcultures on the entrepreneurial economy

In Macedonia, the combination of national, ethnic, organizational, professional and other subcultures result in a unique environment. But those values have a big impact on entrepreneurial activity in its economy. According to research by the Macedonian social values (Klekovski, Krzalovski, Stoyanova 2011) Macedonian social values, the most important values for citizens: human rights (15.6 %), peace and non-violence (15.4 %), democracy (13.3 %), the rule of law (10.4 %) and respect for human life. At the bottom of the least important values for Macedonian citizens, accountability / transparency (1 %) and self-realization (1.6 %).

These indicators are important because of the emphasis on self-fulfillment as a value, which is usually attributed to entrepreneurial individuals in the country.

But there are other factors that affect entrepreneurship. How people look more and more successful entrepreneurs in their environment, so you can improve the perception of their own capabilities without increasing the actual skills. Accurate perception of the population of the success of entrepreneurs, is evident from the survey on the perceptions and attitudes towards entrepreneurs Data from Global Entrepreneurship Survey (Table 2).

According to data from Table 2, it can be concluded that there is a decline in the desire for starting a business, followed by the perception of entrepreneurship as a good career.

On the other hand, media coverage of entrepreneurs is high which is consistent with the perception of entrepreneurs as people with high status in the country. Of great importance for the generation of new businesses is that there is a decline in

Table 2: Perceptions and attitudes towards entrepreneurs in Macedonia in 2012, 2014 and 2016

Perceptions/Attitudes	**2012** %	**2014** %	**2016** %
Business opportunities	47.00	34.26	30.79
Fear of failure	35.00	30.90	44.91
Knows an entrepreneur*	46.00	41.15	38.16
Has business skills	62.20	59.72	55.11
Has desire to open a business**	39.00	26.70	29.14
Business as carrier	79.76	71.27	69.59
Media coverage	66.18	56.03	64.09
High status of entrepreneur	71.97	66.2	66.73

Notes: *Calculated from the percentage of sample at age of 18–64 population who feel that there are good business start-up opportunities;
**Calculated from the percentage of sample at age of 18–64 population not involved in entre-preneurial activities.

Source: Data from Global Entrepreneurship Survey 2012–2014–2016(p.53)

the desire to open a business, 39 % in 2012 to 29 % in 2016 What is interesting is the large gap between the desire to open a business (29.1 %) and real business to start (only 7 % of respondents are new entrepreneurs or started to organize resources for business activities).

4 Snapshot on access on entrepreneurial values in Macedonia

Compared with other countries, Macedonians are more confident that they possess the necessary skills to start a business from residents of Croatia, Slovenia and Ireland, and have more desire to engage in entrepreneurial activities. On the other hand, media coverage of entrepreneurs in Macedonia is high (see Table 3).

Respondents' domestic experts in Data from Global Entrepreneurship Survey felt that the business culture of Macedonia provides support to individual success through their own efforts, like Croatia and Slovenia.

Ireland, on the other hand, significantly supports creativity and innovation. It seems that the attitude of professionals about whether the population encourages entrepreneurial risk taking is different from the observed common values. The 4 is the average score given by the experts in Macedonia, expressed a neutral position on whether the Macedonians are encouraged to take entrepreneurial risks (see Table 4).

Table 3: Perceptions on own Skills Required for Starting Business (in %)

Self - perceptions	Macedonia	Ireland	Slovenia	Croatia
Fear of failure*	44.91	41.22	41.5	46.3
Personally knows an entrepreneur**	31.34	37.33	40.08	23.48
Has business skills	55.11	45.16	51.32	44.06
Has desire to open a business in next 3 years**	29.14	7.97	14.68	23.58
Business as carrier	69.59	45.41	52.73	64.18
Media coverage	64.09	61.45	51.08	39.72

Notes: *Calculated from the percentage of sample at age of 18–64 who feels that there are good business start-up opportunities;
**Calculated from the percentage of sample at age of 18–64 not involved in entrepreneurial activities

Source: Data from Global Entrepreneurship Survey 20012–2014–2016 (p. 55)

Table 4: Cultural and social norms

Statement	MK	IE	SI	HR
In my country, the national culture is highly supportive of individual success achieved through own personal efforts	2.86	3.43	2.22	1.98
In my country, the national culture emphasizes self-sufficiency, autonomy, and personal initiative	2.86	3.03	2.39	1.98
In my country, the national culture encourages entrepreneurial risk-taking	2.54	3.05	1.92	1.82
In my country, the national culture encourages creativity and innovativeness	3.03	3.22	2.5	2.07
In my country, the national culture emphasizes the responsibility that the individual (rather than the collective) has in managing his or her own life	2.83	2.95	2.22	2.02
Average	2.82	3.14	2.25	1.97

*The scale of possible answers is from 1 to 5 where 1 denotes completes disagreement with the statement whilst 5 signifies complete agreement with the statement.
Source: Data from Global Entrepreneurship Survey 2016

5 Methodology and research frame

The survey covers a combined methodological approach: identifying key areas for current employers in the country through focus groups on specific areas were developed questionnaires for interviews managers of 170 Macedonian companies at random. The survey results were used simultaneously with the analysis of secondary data. They included research previously available and reliable data from the World Bank, the International Monetary Fund, the International Labour Organization and other institutions.

As compared to countries based on shared history, geographical proximity and geographical size selected were: Serbia, Croatia and Slovenia, as a country with rapid economic development has been included and the Republic of Ireland. Organization of Employers of Macedonia (ORM) Business Confederation of Macedonia (BCM), favorable business environment for sustainable enterprises in Macedonia, 2013 (p. 5).

Data sets relating to the period of 2008–2013. Since quantitative analyzes provide key facts necessary for pointing out the final words about certain issues and analyzes based on qualitative approaches additionally introduced. The idea is to assess the effects of the operations of SMEs, in terms of their economic value to the economy in Macedonia.

Conclusion

In Macedonia, unlike the other countries mentioned in the survey, there is a gap between entrepreneurial intentions and entrepreneurial activity, resulting in fewer new or high growth businesses. This may also be due to entrenched values that put less emphasis on self-fulfillment, independence and creativity, which are characteristics of successful new and innovative enterprises. With the growing fear of failure in starting a business, the number of new enterprises started to decline.

Respondents to the survey of employers feel that there is entrepreneurial business culture to some extent, however, they do not point out the main obstacles to the further development of an entrepreneurial culture in the country. However, the identified challenges that need to be overcome for the development of entrepreneurship is low entrepreneurial spirit and culture as entrepreneurial values that need to pay particular attention that would significantly affect the number of new companies in the area of employment. Their contribution would increase the low level of cooperation between the business community, providers of business services and higher education institutions. To continue the intensive promotion of entrepreneurial culture, and further increase the flow of information about starting a business.

On the other hand, the authorities are fully aware that SMEs are important business segment with a significant contribution to sustainable economic development. Therefore, they identify measures and actions to support the development of SMEs and entrepreneurship in terms of institutions and instruments.

References

Acs, Zoltan J./Audretsch, David B.: Entrepreneurship, Innovation and Technological Change", Foundations and Trends in Entrepreneurship, 1 (4) 2005.

APPRM. Observatory for SMEs in the Republic of Macedonia, Report for 2004, Skopje, (2005).

Baldwin, John/Picot, Garnett: Employment Generation by Small Producers in the Canadian Manufacturing Sector, Small Business Economics, 7 (4), 1995, pp. 317–331.

Baldwin, John, R.: Were Small Producers the Engines of Growth in the Canadian Manufacturing Sector in the 1980s?, Small Business Economics, 10 (4), 1998. pp. 349–364.

Biggs, Tyler: Is Small Beautiful and Worthy of Subsidy?, International Finance Corporation, Washington, U.S.A. 2002. Available at: https://www.enterprise-development.org/wp-content/uploads/Is_Small_Beautiful_and_Worthy_of_Subsidy.pdf

Brouwer, Piter/De Kok, Jan/Fris, Pieter: Can firm age account for productivity differences?, EIM SCALES paper N200421, 2005.

Carree, Martin, A.: Industrial Restructuring and Economic Growth, Small Business Economics 18, 2002, pp. 243–255.

Carree, Martin, A./Thurik, A. Roy: The Lag Structure of the Impact of Business Ownership on Economic Performance in OECD Countries, Small Business Economics, forthcoming, 2007.

Carree, Martin, A./Thurik, A. Roy: The Impact of Entrepreneurship on Economic Growth. In: Zoltan. J. Acs/David, B. Audretsch (eds.): Handbook of Entrepreneurship Research, Boston, MA: Kluwer Academic Publishers, 2003, pp. 437–471.

Caves, Richard. E.: Industrial Organization and New Findings on the Turnover and Mobility of Firms, Journal of Economic Literature, 36 (4), 1998, pp. 1947–1982.

Economic Chamber of Macedonia. Available at: http://www.mchamber.org.mk/%28S%280rkql0qsdl5xgrm2uf01ybat%29%29/default.aspx?lId=1: [Accessed on July 2nd, 2016]

Fiti, Taki/HadziVasileva - Markovska, Verica/Bejtman, M. Entrepreneurship (in Macedonian), Faculty of Economics – Skopje, 2007, p.27.

Klekovski, Saso/Krzalovski, Aleksandar/Stojanova, Daniela: Macedonian Societal Values [Internet]. Skopje, Macedonian Center for International Cooperation (MCIC), 2011. Available at: http://www.mcms.mk/images/docs/2011/makedonski-opstestveni-vrednosti.pdf

Organization of Employers of Macedonia (OEM), Business Confederation of Macedonia (BCM), a favorable business environment for sustainable enterprises in Macedonia, 2013, p.5.

Parker, Simon. C.: The Economics of Self-Employment and Entrepreneurship, Cambridge, U.K., Cambridge University Press, 2004.

Parker, Simon. C: Learning about the Unknown: How Fast do Entrepreneurs Adjust Their Beliefs? Journal of Business Venturing, Vol. 21 No. 1, 2006, pp. 1–26.

Robbins, D. Keith, Pantuosco, Lois, J., Parker, Darell. F./Fuller, Barbara. K. An Empirical Assessment of the Contribution of Small Business Employment to U.S. State Economic Performance, Small Business Economics, 15 (4), 2000, pp. 293–302.

Rodríguez, Alicia. C., Molina, Miguei. A., Pérez, Ana.L.G./Hernández, Urbano. M. "Size, Age and Activity Sector on the Growth of the Small and Medium Firm Size", Small Business Economics, 21 (3), 2003, pp. 289–307.

Serafimova, Mimoza/Petrevska, Biljana: Entrepreneurship and financing: The evidence of Macedonia. Horisons, International Scientific Journal - Social Sciences and Humanities, (17). 2015, pp. 45–55.

Sutton, John: Gibrat's Legacy, Journal of Economic Literature, 35 (1), 1997, pp. 40–59.

Wennekers, Sander/Van Stel, Andre/Thrurik, Roy/Reynolds, Paul: Nascent Entrepreneurship and the Level of Economic Development, Small Business Economics, 24 (3), 2005. pp. 293–30.

Wynarczyk, Pooran/Watson, Robert (2005); Maes et al. (2005), or Norton, William/Moore, Stephen (2006). Nor do we assess how institutional factors affect the growth and productivity of entrepreneurial and other firms differently, i.e. Hartarska, Valentina/Gonzalez, Vega (2006).

Rodriquez et al, Rodríguez, Alicia. C., Molina, Munoz. A., Pérez, A.L.G./Hernández, U.M. (2003). Size, Age & Activity Sector on the Growth of the Small and Medium Firm Size, Small Business Economics, 21 (3), 2005, pp. 289–307.

https://docs.google.com/viewerng/viewer?url=http://orm.org.mk/images/documents/books/eses+izvestaj+ang+za+web.pdf

Cristina LINCARU[1], Speranța PÎRCIOG[2], Vasilica CIUCĂ[3], Gheorghe GHEORGHE[4]

[1] National Scientific Research Institute for Labor and Social Protection – INCSMPS, MECHATREC Cluster member, Email: cristina.lincaru@yahoo.de,

[2] National Scientific Research Institute for Labor and Social Protection – INCSMPS, INCSMPS Scientific Director, MECHATREC Cluster member, Email: pirciog@incsmps.ro,

[3] National Scientific Research Institute for Labor and Social Protection – INCSMPS, INCSMPS & General Director, MECHATREC Cluster member, Email: silviaciuca@incsmps.ro,

[4] National Institute of Research and Development for Mechatronics and Measurement Technique INCDMTM, MECHATREC Cluster Manager, Email: geocefin@yahoo.com

Tracking Human Capital thorugh Theory Based Evaluation in Mechatrec Sector

Abstract *Under the New Economic Geography and Evolutionary Economy framework we make a dynamic analysis of the main steps in the evolution of the Mechatronic domain in Romania in the last 100 years from the human capital perspective. This high tech sector presents now a competitive advantage in spatial agglomerations with high specialization profile, but not fully exploited. Tracking for the human capital in time (the last century sector's evolution) and space (the spatial snap shot in 2011 based on RPL Population Census micro data provided by National Institute for Statistics), we make an "fresh profile" for Romania under modern coordinates. The birth of Great Romania (1918) is a mile stone for radical and successive changes in the destiny of the occupations in this sector, starting from the craftsmanship specific to the rural area, making transition through the urban factory and shape shifting into our times in complex spatial structures: clusters and innovation digital hubs interconnected in European and even global networks. This hypothesis is tested through exploration of some causal chains, chains assessed thorough theory based evaluation.*

Keywords: *Human capital, 26 NACE Rev.2, agglomeration, evolution, causal chain*

Introduction

Mechanics is one of the oldest science starting with Aristotel (384–322 iChr) with the Laws of movements and the Inertia Principle and closing a loop with Albert Einstein (1879–1955) with his well-known Relativity Theory and Nature

Deterministic Theory.[1] This scientific domain, further than its theoretical dimension, grow and evolve into a multiple applications, technologies and hybrid new domains as it is the Mechatronics (interdisciplinary domain of mechanics and electronics), well reflected by NACE Rev 2 division 26 "Manufacture of computer and electronic and optical products".

The relation between man and machine was studied by many authors from various point of view: as power of human-machine collaboration (Bolton at al., 2018) or how artificial intelligence disrupts their job market (Vochozka et al., 2018), from the point of view of the expansion of the digitally mediated labor (Mitea, 2018), trying to understand if cognitive technology-driven automation lead to economic growth (Hardingham et al., 2018) or from the point of view of the future of work in relation with disruptive business practices, technology-driven economic growth, and computer-induced job displacement (Neary, 2018).

The main objective of the research is to make a "fresh profile" for the Romania's Century under modern coordinates given by the New Economic Geography and Evolutionary Economy theory, tracking the human resource with relevance for Mechatronic in time and space. This high tech sector presents important performance but not enough to brand a global "country image" for Romania as it is in Switzerland. It is ranked as the 6th sector, a priority sector, labelled as "strong point /relative strong point" in the national economy by export performance (SNER, 2014, p.10), on the background that the first 5 sectors are not high tech sectors (resource intensive sectors). The limits of this sector are given by the fact that "the most important products in this economic sector and retained the competitive advantages due to the maintenance of low labor costs. Original products developed based on native inventions are missing". (SNER, 2014, p.10)

Tracking for the human capital in time (the last century sector's evolution) and space (the spatial snap shot in 2011 based on RPL Population Census micro data provided by National Institute for Statistics), we make an "fresh profile" for Romania under modern coordinates. The birth of Great Romania (1918) is a mile stone for radical and successive changes in the destiny of the occupations in this sector, starting from the craftsmanship specific to the rural area (Criste, 2014), making transition through the urban factory and shape shifting into our times in complex spatial structures: clusters and digital hubs interconnected in European and even global networks.

This analysis is structured in causal chain (thwink.org)[2] path, penetrating the superficial symptoms layer and identifying root causes of the competitive advantage produced in spatial agglomerations by high specialization human capital.

1 http://www.nenitescu.ro/lectii/tipuri_de_miscari_mecanice/html/istoria__mecanicii.html

2 http://www.thwink.org/sustain/glossary/CausalChain.htm

1. Literature review

Krugman, Venables and Fujita (1999) in New Economy of Geography - the production is heterogeneously distributed in space, reflecting the tendency of agglomeration in highly populated locations. The success of local economies is generated by the presence of the new in both tradable and non-marketable sectors. The sectors adopting and using the new and innovation are sectors that generate new jobs in the region / location indirectly and in other sectors. In other words, high human capital agglomerations generate spill over effects called positive externalities. Moretti & Thulin (2013) found that this "multiplier effect is particularly large for jobs with high levels of human capital and for high technology industries". In other words, "the impact on a local labour market of attracting a high-technology employer to a city is three times larger than the impact of attracting a low-technology employer of similar size", (Moretti, Thulin, 2013, p.340).

Pelinescu highlighted the human capital as essential factor in "ensuring economic growth expressed as gross domestic product per capita" (Pelinescu 2015, p 189), "of competitvitiy in knowledge society"(Pelinescu, 2016, p.1) which "strongly influences the innovation level of knowledge society as well as their efficiency". (Pelinescu et.al, 2014, p. 16.). Stroe & Cojanu (2017) warns for Romania the phenomenon of increasing the in work poverty importance, fact that put in difficulty the functionality of innovation as the engine of the modern economy stress in the absence of an adequate wage policy, able to "restoring the wage-productivity correlations destroyed during the period of transition" (Pelinescu et. al. 2011, p.99).

2. Mechatronic domain in Romania – short profile

In 2015 the share of employment High-tech sectors HT (high-technology manufacturing HTM and high-tech KIS) in total employment was 2.6 % (Eurostat, NACE Rev.2, [htec_emp_reg2]) in Romania only in front of Greece EL (2.4 %) and Lithuania LT(2.3 %), while Ireland have 7.5 %.

At NUTS 2 level in Romania there are important regional disparities in HT sectors as percentage of total employmnent in 2015: the region highest is Bucharest Ilfov with 7.6 % while the Region lowest is Sud Est with 0.9 %, the 5th important disparity in EU frame work. (Eurostat, NACE Rev.2, [htec_emp_reg2])

Romania is improving its export performance, the contribution of HT sectors was doublling after the crises. High-tech products represented 7.3 % of the value of all exports from the Romania in 2015, increasing with 3.8pp compared with 2008 level, while the EU-28 tendency was slower, this share was 17 % in 2015, increasing with 0.9pp since 2008. (Eurosata, [tin00140]) Even if is export performance is improved, the HT trade balance is in deficits, the imports values are higher than exports values. As a positive tendency is visible the slower rate of imports increasing compared to rates of export increasing. The best perfomance is visible for electronics and telelcomunicaitons devices. (Eurostat, [htec_trd_group4])

The high tech manufacturing (HTM) sector, following crises increases its performance in Romania. In 2016 there were 60.6 thousand employees in HTM, representing 0.7 % from total national employment and, respectively 2.53 % from UE28 employment in HT sector. Post crises (2008–2016) decreses both total employment (with 920 thousand) and manufacturing employement (307.4 thousand) while the HTM employment increses (9.4 thousand). The EU28 tendency is reverse, for the same period even if the total employment increases (1139 thousand) the HTM employment decreases (137.3 thousands). In structural terms the share of HTM employment in total national employment is still below the UE level, incdicating an expanding potential still. The share of HTM employment in total national emplyment was 0.7 % in 2016, incresing with 0.2 pp comapered with the level from 2008, meanwhile at EU28 level was constant this share at 1.1 %. (Eurostat, NACE Rev.2, [htec_emp_nat2]).

In 2015 there were 31.8 thousand persons employed in A26 in 864 entreprises with 2.8 % the share of production value in manufacturing total, having an apparent producitvity of 15.3 thousand euros GAV/employed person. The A26 division is improving its performance post crises, in 2015 compared to 2008 in terms o increasing the employmnet, productivity and GAV. (Eurostat, NACE Rev.2, [htec_emp_nat2]).

There are remarcable two tendencies of succes:

- The diversification tendency in Manufacture of electronic components and boards (C261). In C261 there are 43.9 % employees from the C26 sector, increasing with 3 thousands during 2008–2009 period, incresing with 2.5 thousand euros GAV/employed person the apparent productivity but decreasing with 10 pp their degree of specilisation (Share of principal activity in turnover). This tendency is available especially for Manufacture of electronic components (C2611). In C2611 increases in the same time the number of employees with 3.8 thousand persons, the apparent productivity with 3.3 thousand euros GAV/employed person. This diversification tendency in the sense of decreasing the specialisation while the number of enterprises remains constant indicates the absence of spill overs and therefore we can consider that C261 firms are integrated in global chains of production, in operationalisin and execution phases of the producution processes.
- The specialisation tendency in Manufacture of instruments and appliances for measuring, testing and navigation; watches and clocks (C265). In C265 during 2008–2015, even if the number of enterprises decreases with 22 enterprise at 172 enterprise in 2015 were increasing: the number of employees increases with 2.9 thousands employees, the apparent productivity with 1.1 thousand euros GAV/employed person and also the specialisation degree with 9pp. These data could indicate an merging proceses, concentration of resources. (to be validated by literature further).

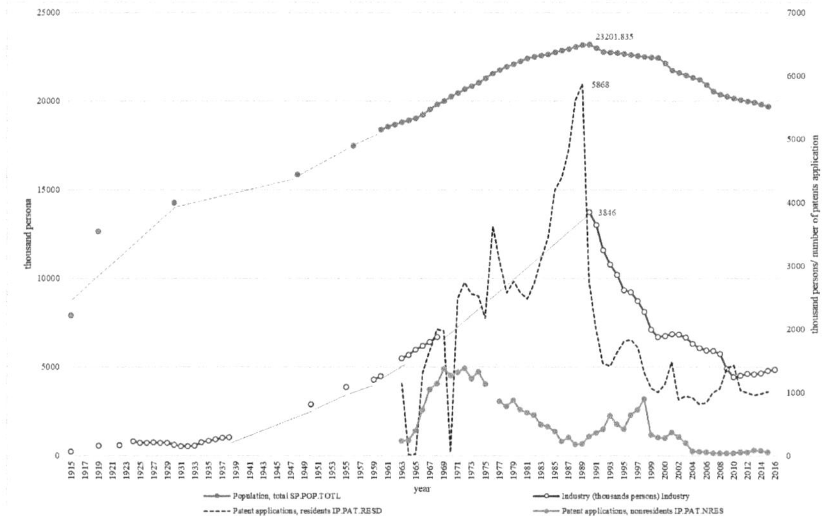

Figure 1: Total population, employees in industry and the number of (resident and non resident) application patents in Romania during 1918–2018 period

Source: all indicators for the period 1960–2016 World Bank (API_ROU_DS2_en_excel_v2, https://data.worldbank.org/country/romania) completed with For the years employees in Industry: 1915–1938 Victor Axenciuc, Evoluția economică a României, Cercetări statistico -istorice 1859–1947, vol. I. Industria, Ed. Academiei 1992, pag.486–491. For the years 1950–1969: Breviar statistic al RPR 1965–1969,: for the population 1915–1960 2.4.2 Population and population density, at territorial level, on censuses / INS Serii Statistice; Dumitrescu, I., 2018. Populația României: retrospectivă statistică - prezentare Seminarul Onicescu, INS, 15.03.2018

3. Causal Chain for the Romanian mechatronics human capital in the last century sector's evolution

Our causal chain for the Romanian mechatronics human capital in the last century sector's evolutions starts from the population trends coupled with industrialisation process. In Figure 1 is visible that the level of industry employment is dependent on the level of population. If at the begging of the century (1918), the share of industry employees were 0.7 % in 1930 this share was approximative 1.22 % reaching an intermediary level of 6.8 % in 1960, attaining the maximum level of 16.5 % in 1989. Post-1989 this share is continuing decreasing at the level of 6.14 in 2010, increasing again at 6.8 % in 2015. The same causality is visible in terms of applied patents by residents: before 1989 there were 1 patent at 1000 employees while after 1989 increases this ratio at 1.3 in approximatively terms.

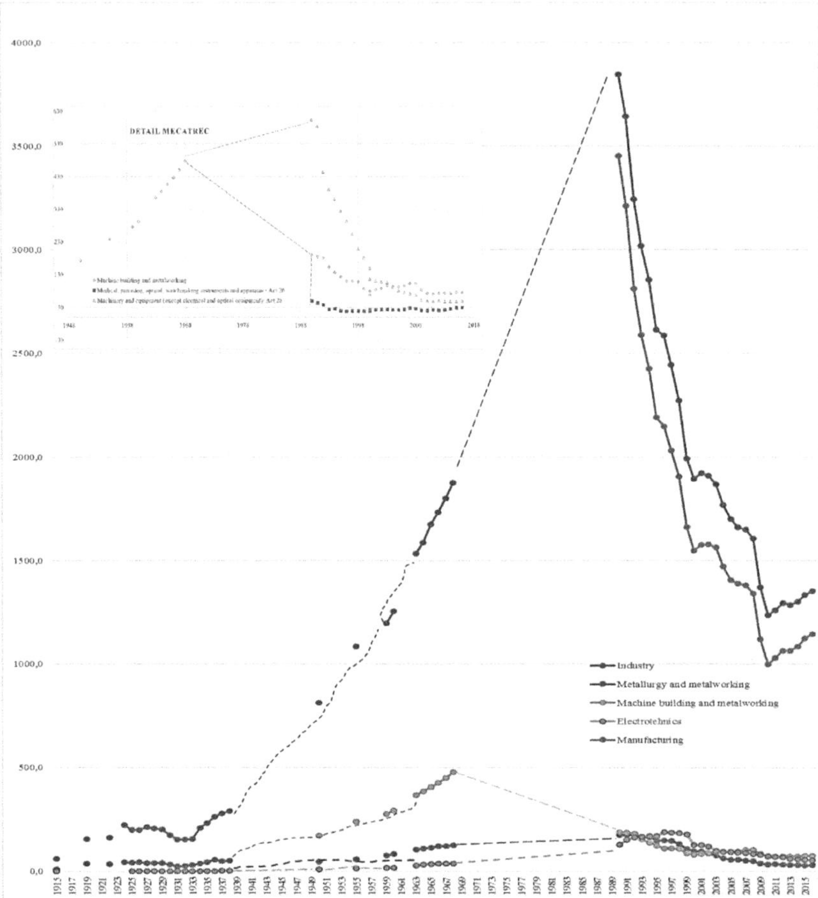

Figure 2: Tracking Romania's Industry profile in last hundred years by "ancestor sectors" for Mechatree – number of employees

Source: For the years 1915–1938 Victor Axenciuc, Evoluția economică a României, Cercetări statistico-istorice 1859–1947, vol.I. Industria, Ed.Academiei 1992, pag.486–491.

In Figure 2 is presented the path dependence of Mechatronic by its "ancestors" sectors. Following the official statistics, by tendencies, we track Romania's HTM profile by its main families of technological domains evolution: mechanical and electrical ones. Initial industry main sector was metallurgy from which mechanics was "born". Until 50's Industry includes Metallurgy and Metalworking and Electrotechnics as "parents" sectors. Following 50's, until 1989, the Metallurgy and Metalworking[3] are splitting in Metallurgy and a second, distinct sector Machine Building and Metalworking, sector which increases in diversification following 1989 from the Industry in Manufacturing. Manufacturing knows multiple splittings and reclassifications according to NACE Rev 1[4] and now, since 2008, according to NACE Rev.2. includes a new definition of high-tech industries and knowledge-intensive sectors, both definitions are available. In general, the sectoral approach uses NACE - Statistical classification of economic activities in the European Community aggregates at 2-digit level by knowledge intensity in two main families: the high tech manufacturing industries (HTMI) and knowledge-intensive services (KIS). If the HTMI are classified into "high technology, medium-high technology, medium-low technology and low technology" classes by the intensity of using technology (R&D expenditures divided by value added) the KIS is mainly "aggregated into knowledge-intensive services and less knowledge-intensive services, based on the share of employed people who have undergone tertiary education (the level of education following secondary schooling)"[5]. OECD (2011) remarks that "the technology-intensity classification is relative. Many manufacturing activities could be considered high-technology but by looking at direct R&D intensities we are classifying according to relative recent R&D performance".

In short, we identify the following causal chain: final product is decomposed step by step in history from raw materials, materials, manufacturing materials, technology, automatization (digitalisation), by the degree of novelty incorporated measured as technology intensity – strongly connected with innovation and research. Following this approach emerges as a root cause the sustainability and appropriateness of the products in the sense to respond better to the new challenges. The production of the new in terms of innovation and research just for knowing is more a superficial solution trap!

3 Main industrial sectors: Metallurgy (Ferrous metallurgy, Non Ferrous metallurgy), Machine building and metalworking and Electric and Thermic Energy

4 NACE Rev 1 explored classification items> Total – Industry / Manufacturing:Metallurgy, Metallic constr and metal products, Machinery and equipment (except electrical and optical equipment), IT and office means, Electric machinery and appliances, Radio, TV and communications equipment, Medical, precision, optical, watchmaking instruments and apparatus, Electric and thermal energy, gas and water

5 http://ec.europa.eu/eurostat/statistics-explained/index.php/High-tech_statistics_-_economic_data

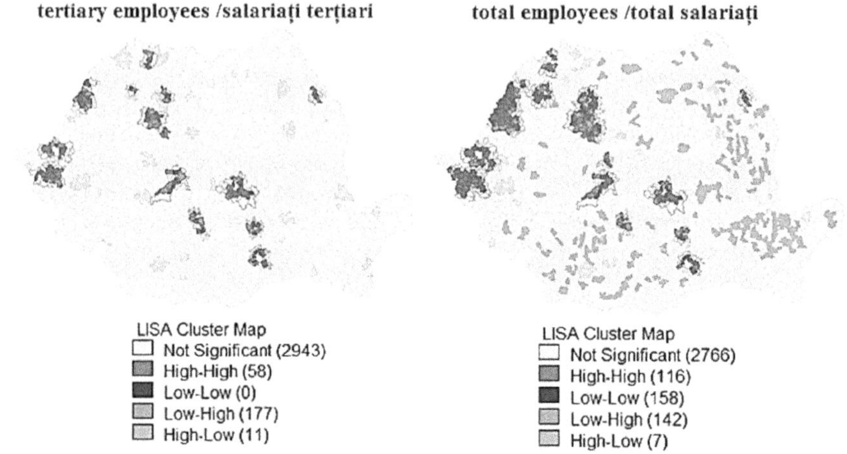

Figure 3: Spatial distribution of employees with tertiary education attained and the total number of employees in the Manufacture of computers and electronic and optical products (Act 26 CAEN Rev.2)

Source: RPL 2011

4. Theory based evaluation for the Romanian human capital - a spatial snap shot in 2011 based on RPL Population Census micro data provided by National Institute for Statistics

The interaction between space and knowledge in Mechatrec domain produce spatial patterns, located in agglomeration. The fact there are concentrated patterns reflects the accumulation processes in initial specialised locations, followed by diversification in related or unrelated domains, but exploiting the previous experiences, situation when agglomeration of HTM workers (in our case) plays the role of a memory. In relation to the new business models in spatial global networks, these agglomerations plays the role of functional "brain hubs" or "innovation clusters" in the sense of Moretti (2012) locations.

The spatial analysis (Anselin 2003, 2005, 2016) reveals for Romania a pronounced agglomeration tendency of high skilled employees from Act.26 at NUTS 5/LAU2 level, synthetically presented in Figure 3. Under the Null Hypothesis NH: complete spatial randomness (CSR), in condition Queen contiguity spatial weight rule for weighting of 1st order by SIRUTA for a number of permutation = 999, p value 0.05 with a 90 % confidence level we reject NH and make the decision of clustering tendency, there is no spatial randomness. Applying Univariate Local Moran's, calculated in GeoDa 1.10.0.8 we obtain the following results: the Moran's I is 0.0169, higher than theoretical value of -0.0003, with a pseudo p value 0.003, sd of 0.0099, z-value 1.724>1.65.

There were identified 58 LAU2 locations, following cities and their satellites, like: Timişoara, Arad, Oradea, Braşov, Ploieşti, Cluj, Bistriţa, Baia Mare, Bucureşti, şi Iaşi.

For the years 1950–1969: Breviar statistic al RPR 1965, 58 Numărul mediu scriptic al salariaţilor, din industrie pe ramuri ale economiei naţionale/ p.105; Breviar statistic al RPR 1967, 51 Numărul mediu scriptic al salariaţilor, din industrie pe ramuri ale economiei naţionale/ p.107; Breviar statistic al RPR 1969, 24 Numărul mediu scriptic al salariaţilor, pe ramuri ale economiei naţionale/ p.52; 25 Numărul mediu scriptic al salariaţilor, pe ramuri ale economiei naţionale/ p.55; Breviar statistic al RPR 1969, 51 Numărul mediu scriptic al salariaţilor, din industrie pe ramuri ale economiei naţionale/ p.117;

For the years 1990–2000: INS, serii statistice: 3.11.Average number of employees, by activity of national economy, 3.15. Average number of employees, by activity of industry, Activity (CANE Rev.2 divisions)

Series 2000–2016 TEMPO_FOM104G_16_3_2018 / INS, Average number of employees by categories of employees, types of ownership, economic activities at level of CANE Rev.2 (section and division) and by sex.

The result of spatial analysis indicating the spatial clusters for both employees and high human capital (Figure 3), registering positive spatial autocorrelation with agglomeration tendency. The functional "brain hubs" or "innovation clusters" identified by selection of LAU2 units included in HH clusters types cover 58 LAU's. In Figure 6 there were identified 17 clusters structures of tertiary employees across 17 counties, ranked by the number of HH LAU2 identified, as follows: Bucuresti (1) and Ilfov (19); Gorj (6); Iasi (5); with (3): Bihor, Braşov, Cluj, Prahova, Timiş; with (2): Arad, Dambovița, Maramureş, Sibiu and with (1): Argeş, Constanța, Dolj, Mehedinți and Mureş.

Conclusions

In a "superficial solution trap" perspective HT is regarded as a desirable objective for some / specific sectors, sectors considered able to support high exports level, mark of a competitivity in a global world. HT definition is a shape shifter in regard to sectors approach. Looking deeper in the definition of the HT and KIS becomes visible the interaction with knowledge but on short term in the intensity of technology use (mostly explicit but also tacit knowledge) and in the capacity to use knowledge (mostly tacit but in less parts also explicit knowledge), but new relatively produced knowledge. From this point forward is natural to make the next step, closer to the root cause: the knowledge use in both dimension explicit and tacit implies the capacity to access, explore and exploit full ranges of knowledge chains.

In other words, is "impossible to start a house from the roof" – used as an image for the new knowledge in the absence of its sustainable basement! High human capital agglomeration reflects the existence of long chains of knowledge in domains more or less related but in communities able to absorb, explore, exploit and develop knowledge (in all forms explicit and tacit) in new knowledge. This knew knowledge responds to needs of the people and improve their lives in a sustainable way, offering new results (id imagery application in medicine, electronics applications etc). In this logic the increase of the exports and increase in competitivity is only the superficial layer, while improving the quality of their beneficiaries life's is the fundamental layer.

In the Romanian economic activities landscape the HTM or in our terms the Mechatrec sector could become, if it is "mindfully nourished", an economic brand for Romania, taking advantage of its history, of the entire diversity of all other economic activity, spatial patterns and, in nowadays, its ability and capacity to be connected in global Mechatrec networks of Digital Innovation Hubs.

Acknowledgments

This work was supported by a grant from the Romanian Ministry of Research and Innovation, Program Nucleu - PN 18_42_0101/Contract 12N/16.03.2018. Această lucrare a fost realizată prin Programul-Nucleu, derulat cu sprijinul MCI, proiect nr. PN 18_42_0101/Contract 12N/16.03.2018, The dynamics of the labor market in Romania. Adaptive resilience and flexibility / Dinamica pieței muncii în România. Reziliență adaptivă și flexibilitate, coordinator PhD Speranța Piciog.

References

Anselin, Luc, 2016. GeoDA 1.8.1. GeoDA Workshop Part I, Center for Spatial Data Science, University of Chicago, 2016.

Anselin, Luc: Exploring Spatial Data with GeoDaTM: A Workbook, Center for Spatially Integrated Social Science, Illinois, and U.S.A, 2005 available from https://geodacenter.asu.edu/system/files/geodaworkbook.pdf.

Anselin, Luc: GeoDa™ 0.9 User's Guide, Spatial Analysis Laboratory, Department of Agricultural and Consumer Economics University of Illinois, Urbana-Champaign, Urbana, IL 61801, 2003. http://sal.agecon.uiuc.edu/ and Center for Spatially Integrated Social Science http://www.csiss.org/, Revised, June 15, 2003.

Bolton, Charlynne, Veronika Machová, Maria Kovacova, and Katarina Valaskova (2018). "The Power of Human–Machine Collaboration: Artificial Intelligence, Business Automation, and the Smart Economy," Economics, Management, and Financial Markets 13(4): 51–56.

Colescu, Leonida, Progresele economice ale României indeplinite sub domnia M.S. regelui Carol I 1866–1906: tablouri figurative şi notiţe explicative / Progrès économique de la Roumanie réalisés sous le règne de S.M. le roi Carol I: tableaux graphiques et notices explicatives /, Instit. de arte grafice „Carol Göbl", 1907

Criste, Alexandrina L. (căs. Mircea) / Conducător Ştiinţific Prof. Univ. Dr. Simona Nicoară: Meşteşugul românesc între anii 1848–1948. Bresle. Corporaţii. Meserii. Teză de Doctorat – Rezumat. Universitatea Babeş – Bolyai Facultatea de Istorie şi Filosofie Şcoala Doctorală Relaţii Internaţionale şi Studii de Securitate, 2014, p.1–25.

Dumitrescu, Ilie, 2018. Populaţia României: retrospectivă statistică - prezentare Seminarul Onicescu, INS, 15.03.2018

European Commission. Computers, electronic and optical products Comprehensive sectoral analysis of emerging competences and economic activities in the European Union, 2009, DG EMPL project VC/2007/0866

Hardingham, Eileen, Jaromír Vrbka, Tomas Kliestik, and Jana Kliestikova (2018). "Will Cognitive Technology-Driven Automation Lead to Economic Growth?," Journal of Self-Governance and Management Economics 6(4): 13–18.

Krugman, Paul/Venables, Anthony J./Fujita, Masahisa: The Spatial Economy. Cities, Regions, and International Trade, The MIT Press Cambridge, Massachusetts London, England. 1999, http://geografi.ums.ac.id/ebook/The_Spatial_Economy--Fujita__Krugman__Venables.pdf

Lincaru, Cristina: Noua geografie a locurilor de muncă. Perspective spaţiale ale pieţei muncii. / New Geography of Jobs in Romania. Spatial Perspectives of the Labour market. Editura Universitar, Bucureşti, 2017.

Mitea, Dana Raluca Elena (2018). "The Expansion of Digitally Mediated Labor: Platform-Based Economy, Technology-Driven Shifts in Employment, and the Novel Modes of Service Work," Journal of Self-Governance and Management Economics 6(4): 7–13.

Moretti, Enrico/Thulin, Per: 2013. Local Multipliers and Human Capital in the United States and Sweden, Industrial and Corporate Change, 22(1), 339–362. 2013. [Accessed 10 February 2016].

Moretti, Enrico: The New Geography of Jobs, Houghton Mifflin Harcourt, Boston, New York, 2012.

OECD 2011, ISIC REV. 3 Technology Intensity Definition, Classification of manufacturing industries into categories based on R&D intensities, OECD

Directorate for Science, Technology and Industry 7 July, 2011, Economic Analysis and Statistics Division, https://www.oecd.org/sti/ind/48350231.pdf

Neary, Breda, Jakub Horák, Maria Kovacova, and Katarina Valaskova (2018). "The Future of Work: Disruptive Business Practices, Technology-Driven Economic Growth, and Computer-Induced Job Displacement," Journal of Self-Governance and Management Economics 6(4): 19–24.

Pelinescu, Elena, Iordan, Marioara, Chilian, Mihaela-Nona, 2011. Competitiveness of the Romanian economy from European perspective. Institute for Economic Forecasting, Romanian Academy "Nicolae Titulescu" University from Bucharest, Romania 1st Workshop on Modelling and Economic Forecast New Trends in Modelling and Economic Forecast, 9–10 December 2011. https://ideas.repec.org/a/ntu/ntumef/vol1-iss1-12-086.html;

Pelinescu, Elena, 2015. The impact of human capital on economic growth, Procedia Economics and Finance 22 (2015) 184–190. http://www.sciencedirect.com/science/article/pii/S2212567115002580;

Pelinescu, Elena, coordonator, Crăciun, E., Dospinescu, Andrei Silviu, 2015b. Capitalul uman factor esential al creşterii competitivităţii în societatea cunoaşterii, Editura Universitară, 2015;

Pelinescu, Elena, Crăciun, Elisei, 2014. The human capital in the knowledge society. Theoretical and empirical approach. No. 20–2014, Manager - leadership between power temptation and effciency, 7–18. https://ideas.repec.org/a/but/manage/v20y2014i1p7-18.html;

Pelinescu, Elena, Iordan, Marioara, Chilian Mihaela-Nona, Simionescu, Mihaela, 2015c. Competitivitiate. Competitivitiatea regională în România, Editura Universitară.

Pelinescu, Elena, 2016. The human capital and development. The Romanian case study. 2nd International Conference on Recent Advances in Economic and Social Re-search May 12–13, 2016. - Conference dedicated to the 150th anniversary of the Romanian Academy - organised by Institute for Economic Forecasting. p. 1–15. https://ideas.repec.org/p/rjr/wpconf/161105.html;

SNC. Strategia Naţionala pentru Competitivitate 2015–2020, aprobată prin Hotărârea nr. 775/2015, în vigoare de la 09 octombrie 2015, formă aplicabilă de la 17.06.2014, Mof I nr. 439 din 17.06.2014. available at: https://legestart.ro/hg-nr-7752015-privind-aprobarea-strategiei-nationale-pentru-competitivitate-2015-2020/ [Accessed 13.02.2018]

SNCDI. Strategia naţională de cercetare, dezvoltare şi inovare 2014–2020, approved by HG 929/2014, published in Monitorul Oficial, Partea I nr. 785 din 28 octombrie 2014, amended by: Hotărârea nr. 81/2017 and the Ministry Order 7021/2017 of MDRAP regarding the approval of the de Minimis Aid Scheme to support the development of small and medium-sized enterprises in partnership with innovation and technology transfer entities under the 2014–2020

Regional Operational Program, available at: https://www.edu.ro/sites/default/files/_fi%C8%99iere/Minister/2016/strategii/strategia-cdi-2020_-proiect-hg.pdf [Accessed 13.02.2018]

SNER. Strategia națională de export a României pentru perioada 2014–2020, Publicat în Monitorul Oficial, Partea I nr. 439bis din 17 iunie 2014, available at: https://lege5.ro/App/Document/gm4tsnrqgy/strategia-nationala-de-export-a-romaniei-pentru-perioada-2014-2020-din-13052014 [Accessed 13.02.2018]

Stroe, C., Cojanu, S., 2017. Profiles And Dynamics of In-Work Poverty in Romania. Economic and Social Development (Book of Proceedings), 26th International Scientific Conference on Economic and Social, p.129. Available at: https://www.researchgate.net/scientific-contributions/79291127_Cristina_Stroe, [Accessed 3.20.2018]

Vochozka, Marek, Tomas Kliestik, Jana Kliestikova, and Grațiela Sion (2018). "Participating in a Highly Automated Society: How Artificial Intelligence Disrupts the Job Market," Economics, Management, and Financial Markets 13(4): 57–62.

Irina BĂNCESCU[1]

[1] School of Advanced Studies of the Romanian Academy, Department of Economic, Social and Legal Sciences, Email: irina_adrianna@yahoo.com

Analyzing Income Data Using Quantile Analogues of Gini Coefficients

Abstract *Quantile-based methods of estimating Lorenz curves and Gini coefficients are not as sensitive to outliers as moment-based indicators of income inequality, making them more appropriated to be used by economics and researchers in applications. In this paper, we review several recently introduced Lorenz curves and associated Gini measures. An extension of an estimation method is considered using the q-exponential distribution.*

Keyword: *Quantile-based estimation, Lorenz curves, Tsallis distribution*

Introduction

Analyzing income distribution of a population and its inequality has constituted over the last century the object of numerous scientific articles, which have treated the phenomenon both within a country, and also by comparison with other countries, at the regional, continental or global level. In a recent analysis made, a wide range of indicators has been utilized, with a diverse palette of their relevance and their sphere of inclusion. We are referring to the gross domestic product (GDP) per capita, total or per capita household income, mean and median gross net income, salary earnings, wages or net salaries and much more.

A recent study, supported by the European Parliament (Dreger et al, 2015), summarizing the results of the project "Wage Dispersion in the European Union", based on the analysis of earnings inequality using EU SILC microdata (2007 and 2017), emphasis among other observations that wages are very important part of income inequality.

Other numerous studies and articles are focusing on the impact of perpetuation or growth of income inequalities. In an article published in 2015 (Olivera, 2015), Javier Olivera analyzed the determinants of preferences for redistribution in 34 European countries over the period 2002–2012. This study shows that, at least in Europe, "growing income inequality leads to more individual support for redistribution".

Income inequalities have been the subject of approaches and perspectives of the ideals of economic and social cohesion at the EU level, from the perspective of inequality in household income (Chivu, Ciutacu, Georgescu, 2015a), or through the analysis of wage gaps (Chivu, Ciutacu, Georgescu, 2015b). Also, during the decades a variety of methods of constructing and estimating income inequality have been proposed. New Lorenz curves have been introduced, some based on quantile functions (unfortunately some of them are not quite Lorenz curves, meaning they do not possess the convexity property for all distributions) or hybrid Lorenz curves (Prendergast, Staudte, 2016; Wang, Smyth, 2013).

These new curves were introduced due to the necessity of having indicators less sensitive to changes in outliers. Corresponding Gini coefficients have been analyzed along with methods of estimation. A review of existing estimation methods for Gini index, with emphasis on obtaining reliable standard errors has been made by Davidson (2009), and, as far as we know, a short review of quantile-based methods for estimating Gini coefficient has been made by Zsolt Darvas in 2016 (Darvas, 2016). Darvas has compared four types of methods and concluded that each is appropriated for estimating income inequality as long as we have all the necessary data. For a review of world income distribution methods, we suggest the reader to see (Heshmati, 2006).

Section 1 presents a short review of methods of estimating income inequality both within countries and at global or regional level. Section 2 discusses an application for deriving the Gini index of a group of countries considering the Tsallis distribution. The last section concludes the paper.

1. Literature review

Estimating income inequality depends on the data available. Quantile data are one of the most common available, either as deciles or quintiles. One disadvantage of these data is their incapacity to compare between countries. Other problems can appear when there are missing values. Analyzing income data can also be made by considering grouped data which considers K groups of income. For many countries grouped data are the only ones available.

Methods of estimating income inequality and mobility are categorized as either parametric or non-parametric. Among the parametric methods we can include the fitting of income data by a distribution (for example, Beta, Dagum, Pareto, log-normal or Weibull models), and utilizing a Markov chain transition matrix (Dardanoni, 1995). Non-parametric methods are more diverse ranging from kernel density estimation to Lorenz-curve regression (Bhalla, 2002; Katwani, 1980; Sala-i-Martin, 2006).

A quantile-based method is the identical quantile income method introduced in 2002 (Milanovic, 2002). Another method for estimating income inequality at regional or global level is the two-parameter distribution method (Chotikapanich, Valenzuela, Rao, 1997).

Among various income inequality curves introduced in the specialized literature, in 2016, Prendergast and Staudte have proposed three new Lorenz curves defined as (Prendergast, Staudte, 2016).

$$L_{PS1}(p) = p\frac{Q_F(p/2)}{Q_F(1/2)}$$
$$L_{PS2}(p) = p\frac{Q_F(p/2)}{Q_F(1-p/2)} \quad (1)$$
$$L_{PS3}(p) = 2p\frac{Q_F(p/2)}{Q_F(p/2)+Q_F(1-p/2)} = \frac{2p}{1+p/L_2(p)}$$

Where $0 \leq p \leq 1$, F is the income cumulative distribution function,

And $Q_F(p) = F^{-1}(p) = \inf\{x \mid F(x) \geq p\}$ is the quantile function corresponding to F.

The associated Gini coefficients are

$$G_{PSi} = 2\int_0^1 [p - L_{PSi}(p)]dp, i = \overline{1,3}$$

One remark is that the PS Lorenz curves defined by Eq. (1) are not always convex (Prendergast, Staudte, 2016). Hence, we may want to consider other ones, for example, curves derived applying a general method for constructing Lorenz curves introduced by Wang et al. in 2011 (Wang, Ng, Smyth, 2011). For more on parametric Lorenz curves and associated Gini coefficients, we suggest the reader to see Sarabia (2008).

2. Comparison of income inequality measures

Two-parameter method is a simple method of estimating income inequality at global or regional level and it only requires information, as the name suggests, about two economic indicators of each country in the region. Based on these two values, the parameters of the distribution considered are obtained. Zsolt Darvas (Darvas, 2016) proposed simulating artificial household income data in order to be able to derive the global income inequality. By doing so, these simulated artificial data are pooled and so, the Gini coefficient of the region can be determined. One problem that arises is how many artificial data we should simulate. The answer, provided also by Darvas, was that the number of artificial data is to be proportional to the population. For example, for a country with a population of 22 million, we generate 22 000 income data. In this paper, we extend the two-parameter method by considering the q-exponential distribution which has been recently considered as an income model. Some other recently introduced statistical models based on Tsallis statistics are the q-log distributions (Băncescu, 2018).

Tsallis distribution has attracted the attention of researchers since its introduction. Its particular abnormal power decay made it suitable for many applications. In 2016, Soares et al. have estimated the whole income distribution of Brazil using this statistical model, employing the use of linear regression. Also know as the

q-exponential model, this probability law is a generalization of the well-known exponential model and it is based on deformed exponential and logarithmic functions defined as follows:

$$\log_q(x) = \begin{cases} \log(x), & if \quad x>0, \quad q=1 \\ \dfrac{x^{1-q}-1}{1-q}, & if \quad x>0, \quad q\neq 1 \end{cases} \tag{2}$$

And

$$\exp_q(x) = \begin{cases} \exp(x), & if \quad q=1 \\ [1+(1-q)x]^{1/(1-q)}, & if \quad q\neq 1, \quad 1+(1-q)x>0 \\ 0^{1/(1-q)}, & if \quad q\neq 1, \quad 1+(1-q)x\leq 0 \end{cases} \tag{3}$$

Where q is a real parameter.

Tsallis distribution is defined by the following cumulative distribution function

$$F(x) = 1-[\exp_q(-\lambda x)]^{2-q}, \quad 0<x<C_{q\lambda}(1), 0<q<2, \lambda>0$$

Where:

$$C_{q\lambda}(\rho) = \begin{cases} \dfrac{1}{\lambda(1-q)}, & q\in(0,1), \lambda>0 \\ \infty, & q\in(1,1+\dfrac{1}{\rho}) \end{cases}$$

The corresponding density function of F is:

$$f(x) = \lambda(2-q)\exp_q(-\lambda x)$$

For $q=1$, Tsallis distribution reduces to the exponential model. We employ the q-exponential distribution in order to measure regional income inequality.

Estimating regional income inequality requires having individual household data for each country, but in practice this is not possible. A solution to this problem was to find an income parametric distribution for each country, simulate artificial income data and pooled them together. The way to estimate the parameters of the distribution is with two-parameter method. For this method, we only need information about the Gini coefficient and mean income, indicators which we derive next for the q-exponential model.

The Gini coefficient for a continuous random variable X is defined as:

$$G = 1-\frac{1}{\mu}\int_0^{\infty}[1-F(x)]^2 dx$$

Where $\mu \neq 0$ is the expected or mean value of X. For $q \in (0,1.5)$ and $x \in (0, C_{q\lambda}(2))$ the expected value corresponding to Tsallis distribution is $\mu = \frac{1}{\lambda(3-2q)}$. On the other hand, the Gini coefficient of X, which is defined for $q \in (0,1.5)$, is given by: $G = \frac{2-q}{5-3q}$.

We notice that G takes values between 0.40 and 1, its minimum value is not 0 as one may expect. A value of 0 corresponds to perfect equality, while 1 represents absolute inequality. In light of this information, we may consider that q-exponential distribution is suitable for modelling the income distribution of societies having large income inequality. Therefore, we consider an application of two-parameter method for a group of countries with a Gini coefficient over 0.40, a group consisting of five countries: Argentina, Brazil, Ecuador, Mexico and Venezuela. The year to be analyzed is 2005, and for this year, Ecuador had the largest net Gini coefficient of 0.52, while Venezuela had the smallest value of 0.44.

Generating artificial income data for each country, we obtain a 0.49 value corresponding to the regional Gini coefficient. Extending the study, we employ the use of four Lorenz curves. Hence, we can compare graphically the income inequality of the countries. One of the most used graphical measures is the Lorenz curve.

The Lorenz curve associated with the q-exponential statistical model is

$$L(p) = \frac{3-2q}{q-1}\left\{\frac{2-q}{2q-3}\left[(1-p)^{\frac{3-2q}{2-q}} - 1\right] - p\right\}, 0 \leq p \leq 1$$

While the PS Lorenz curve L_{PS1} is defined by

$$L_{PS1}(p) = p\frac{\log_q\left[(1-p/2)^{1/(2-q)}\right]}{\log_q\left[(1/2)^{1/(2-q)}\right]}, 0 \leq p \leq 1$$

Its corresponding Gini coefficient is

$$G_{PS1} = 1 - \frac{1}{(1-q)\log_q\left[(1/2)^{1/(2-q)}\right]}$$
$$X\left\{\frac{4(2-q)^2}{(3-2q)(5-3q)}\left[\frac{3-2q}{2-q}(1/2)^{\frac{5-3q}{2-q}} - \frac{5-3q}{2-q}(1/2)^{\frac{3-2q}{2-q}} + 1\right] - \frac{1}{2}\right\}$$

Where $q \neq \frac{3}{2}, q \neq \frac{5}{3}, q \neq 1, q \in (0,2)$. The PS-Lorenz curve L_{PS1} in this case, it is indeed a Lorenz curve, being increasing and convex.

In Figures 1 and 2, we have displayed the two Lorenz curves for the five countries considered. The two Lorenz curves are interpreted in different manners.

The classical inequality curve Lorenz L represents the share of total income received by the poorest $100p\%$ of the population, while the measure PS Lorenz

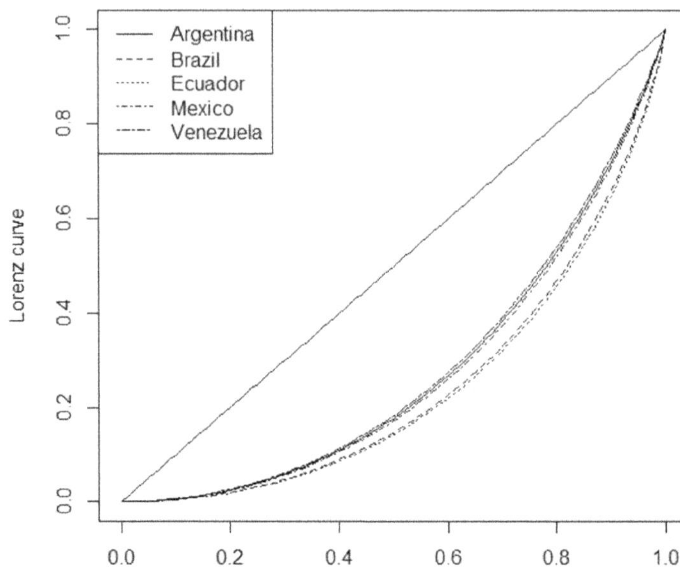

Figure 1: Lorenz curve L for Argentina, Brazil, Ecuador, Mexico and Venezuela for year 2015. Source: authors calculations based on Word Bank data

curve L_{PS1} compares the typical (median) income of the poorest proportion p with the typical (median) income of the entire population (Prendergast, Staudte, 2016). Considering both Lorenz curves in the analysis of income we have a broader image of inequality. From the two figures, we can conclude that although the Gini index tells us that some countries are more equal than others, when it comes to comparing typical income of the poorest with the median income of the whole population, the countries are not so different. This can also be seen in Table 1, where we have displayed the Gini coefficients corresponding to each curve. The Gini coefficients corresponding to curve L_{PS1} take values close to 0.40 for all the five countries.

Other PS Lorenz curves are L_{PS2} and L_{PS3} measures described in Section 2. The L_{PS2}Lorenz curve of q-exponential distribution is defined by

$$L_{PS2}(p) = p\frac{\log_q\left[(1-p/2)^{1/(2-q)}\right]}{\log_q\left[(p/2)^{1/(2-q)}\right]}, 0 \le p \le 1$$

While curve L_{PS3} is

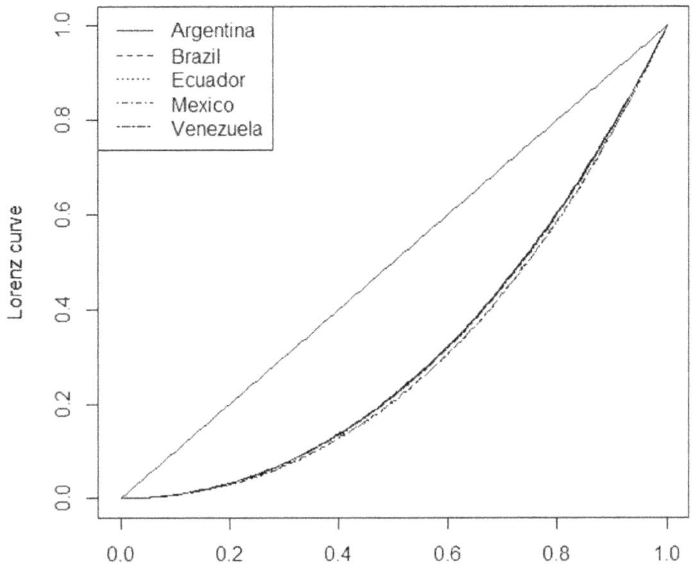

Figure 2: PS Lorenz curve L_{PS1} for Argentina, Brazil, Ecuador, Mexico and Venezuela for year 2015. Source: authors calculations based on Word Bank Data

Table 1: Gini coefficients corresponding to Lorenz curves L and L_{PS1}. Source: authors' calculations based on World Bank Data

Country	G	G_{PS1}
Argentina	0.45	0.379
Brazil	0.51	0.395
Ecuador	0.52	0.397
Mexico	0.46	0.382
Venezuela	0.44	0.376

$$L_{PS3}(p)=\frac{2p}{1+\dfrac{\log_q\left[\left(p/2\right)^{1/(2-q)}\right]}{\log_q\left[\left(1-p/2\right)^{1/(2-q)}\right]}},0\leq p\leq 1$$

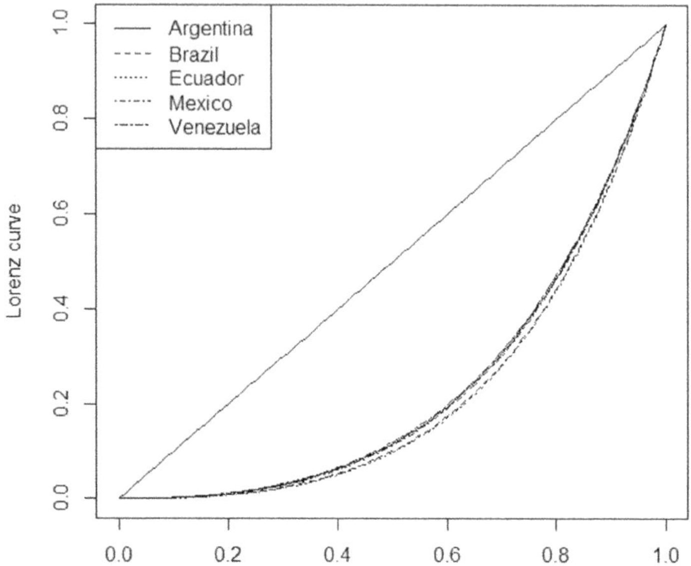

Figure 3: PS Lorenz curve L_{PS2} for Argentina, Brazil, Ecuador, Mexico and Venezuela for year 2015. Source: authors calculations based on Word Bank Data

These curves are indeed Lorenz curves being increasing and convex. In Figures 3 and 4, we have displayed the PS Lorenz curve L_{PS2} and L_{PS3} for the five Latin-American countries. Curve L_{PS2} compares the bottom median income with the top median income, while curve L_{PS3} compares the median income of the poorest$100p\%$, relative to the mid-range income of the middle $100(1-p)\%$ population. (Prendergast, Staudte, 2016)

The countries considered are similar in terms of these income inequality measures.

Conclusions

The Gini coefficient of Tsallis distribution has a minimum value of 0.40 suggesting that this statistical model is suitable for modeling the income distribution of societies having a large income inequality.

The two-parameter method is appropriate for estimating regional or global income inequality being easy to implement, while the four Lorenz curves all together give us a more complex understanding of income inequality within a society.

In the case of the region considered in this paper, composed of Argentina, Brazil, Ecuador, Mexico and Venezuela, while the usual Gini coefficient tells us

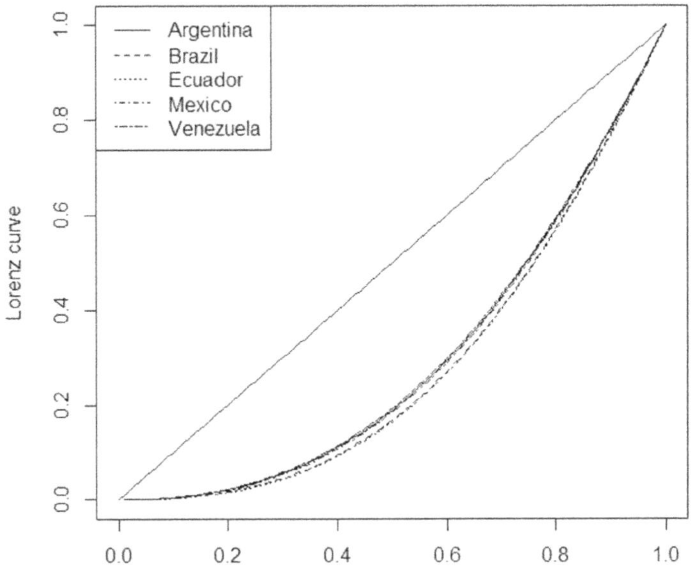

Figure 4: PS Lorenz curve L_{PS3} for Argentina, Brazil, Ecuador, Mexico and Venezuela for year 2015. Source: authors calculations based on Word Bank Data

that these countries have different income inequality ranging from 0.44 to 0.52, the other income measures suggest that these societies are similar when we compare different shares of median incomes.

References

1. Dreger, Christian / Lopez-Bazo, Enrique / Ramos, Raul / Royuela, Vicente / Surinach, Jordi: Wage and Income Inequality in the European Union. European Parliament, Directorate General for Internal Policies, IP/A/EMPL/2013-05, PE 536.294, January 2015, http://www.ub.edu/irea/european.pdf.
2. Olivera, Javier: Preferences for redistribution in Europe. IZA Journal of European Labor Studies, 4(1), 2015, pp. 14
3. Chivu, Luminiţa/Ciutacu, Constantin/Georgescu, Laurenţiu: Household Income in Romania. A Challenge to Economic and Social Cohesion. Procedia Economics and Finance 22, 2015, ISI Proceedings.
4. Chivu, Luminiţa/Ciutacu, Constantin/Georgescu, Laurenţiu: Consequences of wage gaps in the EU. Procedia Economics and Finance 22, 2015, ISI Proceedings.

5. Prendergast, Luke A./Staudte, Robert G.: Quantile versions of the Lorenz curve. 2015, Electronic Journal of Statistics 10(2), 2016, pp. 1896–1926.
6. Wang, ZuXiang/Smyth, Russell: A hybrid method for creating Lorenz Curves with an application to measuring world income inequality. Monash University Business and Economics 1, 2013, pp. 1–48.
7. Davidson, Russell: Reliable inference for the Gini index. Journal of Econometrics 150(1), 2009, pp. 30–40.
8. Darvas, Zsolt: Some are more equal than others: new estimates of global and regional inequality. Bruegel Working Papers, 2016.
9. Heshmati, Almas: The world distribution of income and income inequality: a review of the economics literature, Journal of world-systems research 12(1), 2006, pp. 61–107.
10. Dardanoni, Valentino: Income distribution dynamics: monotone Markov chains make light work. Social Choice and Welfare 12(2), 1995, pp. 181–192.
11. Bhalla, Surjit S.: Imagine There is No Country: Poverty, inequality, and growth in the era of globalization. Peterson Institute, 2002.
12. Katwani, Nanak C.: Income inequality and poverty. World Bank, New York, 1980.
13. Sala-i-Martin, Xavier: The World Distribution of Income: falling poverty and convergence, period. The Quarterly Journal of Economics 121(2), 2006, pp. 351–397.
14. Milanovic, Branko: True World Income Distribution, 1988 and 1993: First Calculation Based on Household Surveys Alone, The Economic Journal 112(476), 2002, pp. 51–92.
15. Chotikapanich, Duangkamon/Valenzuela, Rebbeca/Rao, D.S. Prasada: Global and Regional Inequality in the Distribution of Income: Estimation with Limited and Incomplete Data, Empirical Economics, 22(4), 1997, pp. 533–546.
16. Wang, ZuXiang/Ng, Yew-Kwang/Smyth, Russel: A general method for creating Lorenz curves, The review of income and wealth 57(3), 2011, pp. 561–582.
17. Sarabia, Jose María: Parametric Lorenz Curves. Models and Applications, in Chotikapanich, Duangkamon (ed.) Modeling Income Distributions and Lorenz Curves, Springer, New York, NY, 2008, pp 167–190
18. Băncescu, Irina: q-log-distributions: Log-concavity and log-convexity. The European Physical Journal Plus 133, 2018, pp. 1–18.
19. Soares, Abner D./Moura Jr, Newton J./Ribeiro, Marcelo B.: Tsallis statistics in the income distribution of Brazil. Chaos, Solitons & Fractals 88, 2016, pp. 158–171.

Marioara IORDAN[1], *Mihaela-Nona CHILIAN*[2]

[1] Senior Researcher, Institute of Economic Forecasting, Romanian Academy, Email: miordan@ipe.ro

[2] Senior Researcher, Institute of Economic Forecasting, Bucharest, Romania, Email: cnona@ipe.ro

Evolution of Economic Vulnerability of Households in Romania during the Pre-Accession and Post-Accession to the European Union Periods[1]

Abstract *Identifying the vulnerability or the exposure of countries, regions, communities, households and individuals to exogenous economic shocks has become an important issue in recent years in the economic and social research, especially in the context of research on the impact of natural disasters, poverty, food security, asset vulnerability and sustainable development. Various methods (and indicators) for assessing vulnerability and its determinants have been studied and applied across a multitude of empirical studies.Based on a multidimensional system of indicators, the paper presents a brief analysis of the economic vulnerability of households in Romania during the pre-accession and post-accession to the European Union periods. The results indicate different developments and trends of vulnerability, both between the two analyzed periods and among the household categories.*

Keywords: *economic vulnerability, poverty, incomes, households*

1. The definition of economic vulnerability and its relation to other economic concepts (welfare, poverty)

Identifying the vulnerability or the exposure of a country, region, community, households, and person to exogenous economic shocks has become an

---

1 The paper presents some results of researches on the theme "Evolutions and prospects of welfare, poverty and sustainability of population consumption patterns in Romania ten years after the accession to the European Union", coordinator Iordan M., Institute of Economic Forecasting, Bucharest, Romania, 2017.

important issue in recent years. However, vulnerability is not a simple concept, and there is no consensus among specialists about its precise meaning, but it generally refers to the potential for loss or damage due to external/exogenous shocks. In the economic field, economic vulnerability refers to the risks caused by external / exogenous shocks to the production, distribution and consumption systems.

In economic sciences, the concept of vulnerability is attributed to several areas of interest, such as natural disasters, poverty, food security, asset vulnerability and sustainable development (Noy and Yonson, 2016). In the sense of Adger et al. (2004), the vulnerability of a system, population or individual to a threat refers to his/her/its/their ability to be affected by this threat, while according to Briguglio et al. (2008) vulnerability is attributed to inherent conditions affecting the exposure of a country (or region or household) to exogenous shocks. Guillaumont (2007) argues that a country's economic vulnerability may be defined by the risk that the country will have a development hampered by the exogenous shocks it faces, with two main types of exogenous shocks or two main sources of vulnerability: environmental or "natural shocks" - natural disasters (earthquakes or volcanic eruptions) and the most frequent climatic shocks (typhoons and hurricanes, drought, floods, etc.), and external shocks (linked to trade and trade flows – decline in external demand, global price volatility of raw materials and correlated market instability), international fluctuations in interest rates, etc.

Often, vulnerability is analyzed in the context of poverty dynamics. Thus, Hoddinott and Quisumbing (2003) define vulnerability as the probability that at some time in the future (over a year, over ten years, or in old age) an individual will have a well-being below a certain norm/threshold. From an economic point of view, welfare is generally expressed through the level of consumption or income, as well as the reference standard/threshold as the poverty line. An important problem is the determination of this reference norm/threshold, which may vary depending on individuals, households, communities or regions. The two authors interpret the vulnerability as a synonym for poverty, but not as a synonym for the concept of poverty. Poverty is essentially a static concept, but vulnerability is a dynamic process, through that it captures the processes of change of people moving within and beyond the limits of poverty.

Chaudhuri et al. (2002) state that vulnerability is an ex-ante (forward-looking) concept, rather than an ex-post concept. The state of poverty may be observed over a period of time, given the welfare measure and the poverty line. Instead, household vulnerability is not directly observed, but rather may only be predicted. For example, if the financial situation of a household has deteriorated over the past 5 years, if this financial situation is considered as an indicator of vulnerability identification, then it may be said that the vulnerability level of the household has increased over the past 5 years, ceteris paribus. Therefore, for the assessment of vulnerability, data on time series is necessary to capture the long-term process of change in the vulnerability indicators. It may also be foreseen only that the financial condition of the household will deteriorate further and, thus, the household will become more vulnerable to shocks by assuming that there will be no change in other factors[2].

Vulnerability has several dimensions that need to be considered in identifying the vulnerability factors (or indicators). According to several authors, there are two dimensions of vulnerability: (1) sensitivity, i.e. the magnitude of response to a shock of individuals, households and communities, and (2) resilience, i.e. the ease and speed with which individuals, households and communities recover from a shock. Moser (1998) considers vulnerability as insecurity and sensitivity in terms of welfare or well-being (as measured by the total income or value of total assets held) of individuals, households and communities in the face of an environment undergoing a negative change (ecological, economic, social and political) and, implicitly, in this sense, the ability to react and their capacity to adapt to the risks they face during such a process.

On the other hand, Briguglio et al. (2008) associate the economic resilience with actions undertaken by policy makers and private economic agents that allow a country to withstand or recover from negative shocks (e.g. declines in production, rising poverty). Finally, Hoddinott and Quisumbing (2003) consider that vulnerability is dependent on four main factors: (1) the nature of the shock (e.g. large-scale disasters, such as drought, earthquakes, floods or landslides, global market instability, political instability), (2) the availability of additional sources of income, (3) the functioning of labor markets, of credit and insurance markets, and (4) the degree of public assistance. The second, third and fourth factors are related to the available income or money, and therefore they are linked to adaptability/resilience.

According to the above-mentioned aspects, it may be concluded that the vulnerability of, let's say, a household or region is mainly dependent on three factors: the degree of sensitivity, the degree of resilience of the household/region and the nature of the shocks. At least theoretically, it may be hypothesized that the function has a positive relationship with the first factor (more sensitive, more vulnerable); a negative relationship with the second factor (more resilient or with greater recovery capacity, less vulnerable); and a positive relationship with the third factor (greater or more serious shocks, greater vulnerability).

2. Vulnerability indicators

The vulnerability indicators are the most common methodology for vulnerability assessment. These indicators seek to capture the multidimensionality of vulnerability and/or resilience, and therefore include their economic dimensions. The most common included economic variables are production (GDP or regional production), income, employment, inflation, consumption, spending, savings, domestic and international financial transfers, public finances and trade (Noy and Yoson,

2 UK Essays, http://www.ukessays.co.uk/essays/economics/economic-vulnerability.php#ixzz4IiV9e1YG.

2016). Indicators may vary in terms of purpose (e.g. vulnerability and/or resilience assessment), spatial coverage (e.g. regional, local, global), scale of analysis (e.g. governments, local authorities, at the firm level, by households) and methodological approaches (e.g. deductive, inductive, and econometric). Also, such indicators may be aggregated into a composite index, with or without the use of weights (often based on expert advice, participatory approaches, or a combination of both, or on more systematic methods for identifying relevant variables and assignment of weights, such as Principal Component Analysis (PCA) and Factor Analysis (FA) - Noy and Yonson, 2016).

If economic vulnerability is defined in a general sense as a loss of welfare associated with poverty or shock, then, based on the above-mentioned discussion, in order to identify the vulnerability indicators the determinants (direct and indirect) of welfare or income should be first identified. For example, if employment is considered as an important source/determinant of welfare, then employment should also be considered as a vulnerability indicator.

Depending on the level of aggregation, economic vulnerability may be assessed at macro level: country, region or community, and at micro level: an individual or a household. Moreover, some of the macro-level indicators are considered as sensitivity indicators and others as resilience indicators, or both. Sensitivity indicators refer to inherent and permanent features (which cannot be subject to policy or governance) that make regions/countries prone to exogenous shocks. On the other hand, resilience indicators refer to the ability to adapt to crises. At macro level, the most commonly used indicators to assess economic vulnerability are presented in Annex 1, while at micro level, the most commonly used indicators to assess household vulnerability are the following (household characteristics): employment and professional status of the head of household, educational level of head of household, gender and age of head of household, size of household and occupational and educational structure of its members, health conditions, ownership of assets (natural, physical, financial capital and other assets of labor/financial capital), location[3].

3. Vulnerability of households in Romania

In the following, we analyzed the vulnerability of households in Romania based on the above-presented vulnerability indicators. The information was extracted from the Tempo online database of the National Institute of Statistics, based on statistical surveys on family budgets and workforce in households. Depending on the available data, both the pre-accession period to the European Union (2001–2006) and the post-accession period (2007–2016) were analyzed[4].

---

3 UK Essays, http://www.ukessays.co.uk/essays/economics/economic-vulnerability.php#ixzz4IiV9e1YG.

4 Due to limits of publishing space, the results data could not be presented in the paper and are available upon request.

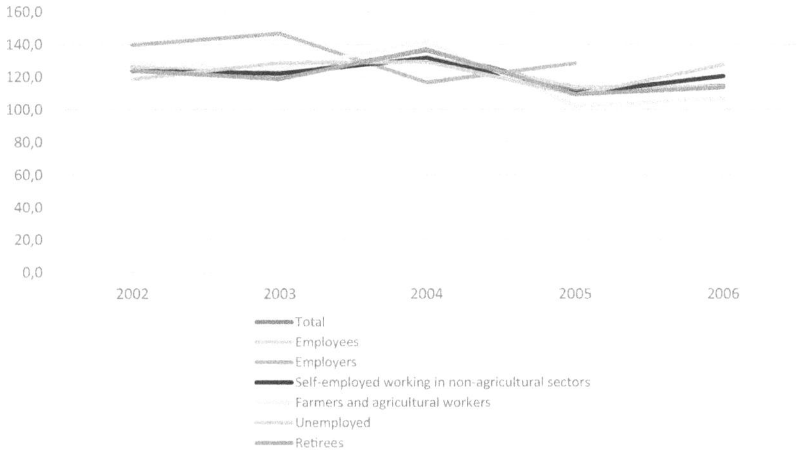

Figure 1: Annual dynamics of total monthly household income by main social categories during the pre-accession period (%)

Source: Authors' computations based on data from Tempo online, NIS.

Starting from the size of the household, it was noticed that the average number of members of a household in Romania increased in the pre-accession period to almost 3 members per household, but decreased substantially in the post-accession period, both due to the demographic decline, as well as to significant change in behaviors regarding the decision to formally or informally establish a family (less marriages, increasing the number of concubinage partnerships, increasing the number of divorces); the age of family formation (increase); the decision to have children (postponement, initial concentration on completing education and building a career) and the age at which they come to the world (increase); and the size of the family (reducing the number of children). The highest average number of members per household was recorded for households with self-employed in non-agricultural activities, farmer and unemployed heads of household, and the lowest number for households with retiree and employee heads of household, categories of households which also recorded the largest decreases in the average number of members. As the former households may be find among the ones with the lowest income per household, only in terms of size their vulnerability appears to be the lowest in the post-accession period, but the correlation with income per household and per person of the household should also be analyzed. For this purpose, the total monthly household income dynamics by the main social categories was analyzed, revealing important differences between the respective categories as well as between the pre-accession and the post-accession period (Figures 1 and 2).

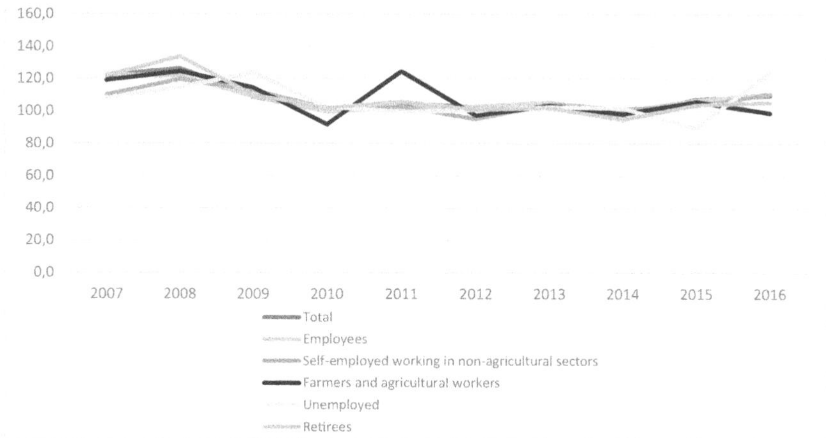

Figure 2: Annual dynamics of total monthly household incomes by main social categories during the post-accession period (%)

Source: Authors' computations based on data from Tempo online, NIS.

In the pre-accession period, significant annual increases in total monthly household income were registered by all households, with households belonging to all analyzed social categories, especially until 2004 and with a relative cap in the last years of the period. In the post-accession period, significant increases were recorded overall and for all social categories only in the first two years, while since 2009 the evolutions were oscillating, marked by the capping of growth and even decreases in the total monthly income of household for all social categories at least in one year of the period. Households with farmer or unemployed heads of household registered the highest variability in the total monthly income (which has accentuated their vulnerability), while households with employee, self-employed in non-agricultural activities and even retiree heads of household generally recorded an upward tendency also in the second part of the post-accession period, albeit lower than in the first years or during the previous period.

Total monthly household income increased (in absolute terms) in the post-accession period, on average by 90.3 lei/household at the level of the whole economy, by 133.1 lei/household in the case of households with employee heads of household, by 65.9 lei/household in the case of households with self-employed in non-agricultural activities heads of household, by 62.4 lei/household in the case of households with farmer head of households, by 68.3 lei/household in the case of households with unemployed head of households and by only 49.6 lei/household in the case of households with retiree heads of household.

Also, the analysis of evolution of total monthly household income by number of members provides important information on household vulnerability. Thus, in the post-accession period all households registered years in which income growth slowed down or even declined as compared to previous years, but the highest oscillations (the highest instability) were observed in the households with a high number of household members, 6 persons and over and the lowest in single-person households. Households with 3 and 4 members registered a relatively steady growth trend over most of the post-accession period (after 2010). In the post-accession period, the most has increased the income of households with a single member (by 453.9 lei/person) and the less has increased the income of households with 6 persons and over (by 195.9 lei/person).

From the point of view of age structure of the average number of members of a household, the economic dependency ratio is important because a lower ratio means, in theory, greater resilience and less vulnerability (but also related to the level of income and household size). In Romania, at the level of the whole economy, there is a tendency to reduce the general ratio of economic dependency (the share of members of household aged below 15 years and 65 years and over in the average number of members) in the pre-accession period and a growth trend in the last years of the post-accession period. Regarding the main social categories, in the pre-accession period there is a tendency to increase the general economic dependency ratio only in the case of households with retiree family heads, while in the post-accession period it may be noticed a downward trend in the ratio for the farmer households, a oscillating and relative stabilization trend in the case of self-employed in non-agricultural activities households and an upward tendency for most of the period in the case of unemployed and retiree households.

Other differences are revealed by the analysis of the general ratio of educational economic dependency (the share of members of households aged below 15 - mostly enrolled in a form of education - in the average number of members, which is preponderantly an "absolute" dependency, because household members of this age group are not productive and do not have income from work but indirect income from child allowances and other family benefits) and of the general ageing economic dependency ratio (the share of household members aged 65 years of age and over - in the vast majority retirees - in the average number of members, which is a "relative" dependency, because the household members of this age group, even if they are no longer productive, have direct income from pensions, and other income coming from family allowances, savings, loans, household production activities, etc.). As regards the first ratio, in the pre-accession period the observed trend was a declining one, both overall and for all analyzed social categories, while in the post-accession period per total and in the case of employee households the tendency was of relative stabilization, in the case of self-employed in non-agricultural activities, farmer and unemployed households the trend was of relative increase, but with significant annual oscillations, and in the case of retiree households the tendency was a declining one. Regarding the general ratio of ageing economic dependency, the trend of its evolution during the pre-accession period was increasing, both overall and for all social categories, while in the post-accession period the tendency was upwards overall and in the case of retiree and unemployed households, of relative stabilization in the case of households of employees and self-employed in non-agricultural activities and even of reduction in the case of farmer households.

The analysis of health status indicators highlights some differences between self-evaluation views and the situation revealed by a number of specific indicators. Thus, in the post-accession period, the opinions on the health status of members of households in Romania aged 16 and over (results from self-evaluation) indicate a relative improvement or at least a stabilization trend for both genders and all age groups and occupational categories. However, there are some differences regarding the level of appreciation, to the detriment of the female gender, of the members of the elderly households, but still possibly mostly in activity (50–64 years) and of the members of the elderly households (65 years and over), as well as of the households of farmers and retirees. The analysis of health status of the household members in Romania based on specific quantitative indicators reveals some different trends. Thus, the share in the total number of household members aged 16 and over of those suffering from a chronic illness or disability registered a relative growth tendency in the post-accession period, especially in the case of the female gender, of the elderly members of households, whether they are still active or not, and of retiree households. An even more pronounced growth trend has recorded the share in the total number of members of household aged 16 and over of those who had been affected by a health problem for a period of at least 6 months, for both genders and for all age groups and categories of occupations. There are also large differences in the respective shares, to the detriment of the female gender, of the elderly household members and of the households of retirees and farmers. Although the tendencies revealed by the two types of analyzed indicators seem to have been divergent in the post-accession period, however, from the point of view of vulnerability they are still converging, the same gender categories (female), age groups (50 years and over) and occupations (farmers and retirees) revealing the most unfavorable developments.

Finally, due to the limitations of availability of statistical data to analyze households' vulnerability from a property asset perspective, a number of indirect indicators related to physical capital, financial capital and natural capital were used. Thus, with respect to natural capital (land) correlated with physical capital (housing), the available information on household income from the sale of land, buildings and other constructions shows no clear trend either during the pre-accession period or in the post-accession one. Moreover, during the post-accession period, the statistical information is rather sporadic and does not yet allow for a thorough analysis. On the other hand, the household income from property registered a relative increase in the pre-accession period and significant annual oscillations amid a slight increase trend in the post-accession period. According to the main groups of occupations, there is an increase towards the end of the post-accession period in this income category in the case of self-employed in non-agricultural activities, farmers, unemployed and even retiree households. The largest increase in the pre-accession period (but also in the first part of the post-accession period) was registered by the income of households from the sale of assets from their patrimony, both overall and for all categories of occupations of household heads. In the rest of the post-accession period, this revenue category registered a relative decline overall and for the households of employees, while for the other households there were significant annual oscillations and increases in some sub-periods (instability). The influence of this income category on vulnerability is at least dual. On the one hand, the growth trend reveals greater availability of liquid assets to households, either occasional or systematic, which, theoretically, reduces their vulnerability in the short or medium term. In the long run or at least in the medium run, households do not have the assets they have sold and cannot earn any income either by selling them or from associated rents (rents, lease rents, etc.), which, in theory, leads to increased vulnerability. Moreover, if the amounts of the sale are used only for consumption purposes and not for saving, investment or production, the vulnerability may be even more pronounced.

On the other hand, information on the natural capital and physical capital assets of households may also be obtained by analyzing certain categories of their expenditures. Thus, the investment expenditure registered an increasing trend in the pre-accession period overall, and for all categories of households by the occupation of the head of household, but a trend of relative decrease overall and in the case of the households of employees during the post-accession period. In the case of the other categories of households by occupational status of the head of household, there were very large annual oscillations in the post-accession period, which, coupled with the instability on the revenue side, may lead to increased vulnerability, at least in terms of reduced household ability (for all occupation categories of household heads) to invest in medium or long-term assets. Production expenditures have also registered a growth trend in the pre-accession period and in certain post-accession years, but for most of this period the annual oscillations were significant for all households. Again, the influence on vulnerability may be twofold: the increase in this expenditure category may signal the increase in households' production capacity (and thus to generate income, which in theory means reducing vulnerability), but also the possible increase in self-consumption, which generally means ensuring the subsistence of the household and a slightly greater vulnerability.

Regarding indicators that relate more strictly to the physical capital, the indicator on occupancy of the main dwelling shows the predominance among households in the post-accession period of the private dwellings, the tendency to reduce the share of rented dwellings and the tendency to increase the share of occupied dwellings free of charge. A number of differences are noticed in the case of the analysis by occupational status of the household head: the largest share of the privately-owned dwellings is noticed in the case of retiree, farmers and employers households, and the lowest in the case of self-employed in non-agricultural activities, unemployed households and households with other occupational status; most of the rented dwellings were recorded in the post-accession period in the case of households with other occupational status (which includes student and pupil categories), and self-employed in non-agricultural activities and unemployed households, and the largest share of the occupied dwellings free of charge was registered in the case of unemployed, self-employed in non-agricultural activities households and households with other occupational status. In terms of household size, in the post-accession period the most vulnerable on the possession and availability of a housing appear to have been the medium-sized (3 members) and large households (6 members and more) and towards the end of the period the "standard" size households (4 members).

Analysis of households' vulnerability from the financial capital perspective shows that deposits with CEC Bank, banks and other similar institutions (which highlight both the households' saving propensity and the saving ratio) have registered a significant increase in the pre-accession period, except for the end of the period, but also large annual variations for all categories of household head occupations. The largest variations were recorded at the opposite ends of the welfare spectrum, i.e. in the case of employer households, on the one hand, and in that of self-employed in non-agricultural activities, unemployed and farmer households, on the other hand. Oscillatory trends continued during the post-accession period, with very large annual variations in the case of households with unemployed, self-employed in non-agricultural activities and farmer heads of households, and somewhat lower in the case of employee and retiree households.

In turn, household loans and credits also registered an upward trend in the pre-accession period, with the exception of the end of the period, and significant annual oscillations by occupational categories of heads of household, but lower than in the case of deposits with the banks. In the post-accession period, overall, the general trend was a decline in borrowing, but in the case of occupational categories of heads of household there were also more or less numerous annual increases. Most of these periods were recorded for the farmer households, followed by unemployed households and retiree and employee households. If in terms of debt vulnerability in the post-accession period seems to have been lowered, its instability remained at quite high levels.

Finally, the evolution of difference between the cash balance at the beginning of the period, on the household income side, and the cash balance at the end of the period, on the household expenditure side, revealed a clear negative trend in the pre-accession period (excluding employer households and, partially, unemployed households), accentuated in the post-accession period for all occupational categories of heads of household, but especially in the case of households of employees and retirees (which register relatively more stable levels of income and expenditure). From this perspective, the financial vulnerability of households seems to have increased, especially in the case of households with a more constant level of income and expenditure.

Annex 1: Indicators to assess economic vulnerability at macro level

Sensitivity indicators	Resilience indicators	Sensitivity and resilience indicators
Geographical location	Real income per capita and income distribution	Dimension – indicators used to assess the economic dimension are the GDP and population structure by gender and age
Economic openness – may be measured through the ratio of foreign trade (export plus import) to GDP	Share of population living below the poverty threshold - as alternative poverty indicator and, consequently, vulnerability indicator, may be used unemployment rate/under-employment (or employment) rate	Population density and structure by age and gender
Export dependency and concentration – the indicators that may be used are export incomes, consumption and intermediate demand and employment	Adult literacy rate and education enrollment rate	
Import dependency and concentration – the indicator used is ratio of imports to GDP	Health status	
Share of manufacturing industry/agriculture in GDP	Technological capability – at national/country level, the most used indicators are R&D investment/expenditure as share in GDP, number of scientist and engineers in R&D to 1 million inhabitants and tertiary education enrollment	
Share in total employment of employment by sectors	Social and economic infrastructure – for instance, schools, hospitals, public utilities, roads, bridges, ports, telecommunication facilities, transport facilities, water, sewerage, industrial properties, electric power, irrigated areas (for agriculturally-based regions, etc.)	

(*continued on next page*)

Annex 1: Continued

Sensitivity indicators	Resilience indicators	Sensitivity and resilience indicators
	Social capital	
	Women participation in labor/ economic activities	
	Macroeconomic stability – domestic and foreign balance	
	Efficiency of microeconomic market	

Source: Authors' adaptation after UK Essays, http://www.ukessays.co.uk/essays/economics/economic-vulnerability.php#ixzz4IiV9e1YG.

References

Adger, W.N., N. Brooks, M. Kelly, G. Bentham, M. Agnew, and S. Eriksen (2004), New Indicators of Vulnerability and Adaptive Capacity, Final Project Report, January, Oslo: Tyndall Centre for Climate Change Research

Briguglio, L., G. Cordina, N. Farrugia, and S. Vella (2008), Economic Vulnerability and Resilience. Concept and Measurements, Research Paper No.2008/55, May, Helsinki: UNU-WIDER.

Chaudhuri, S. and L. Christiaensen (2002), Assessing household vulnerability to poverty: Illustrative examples and methodologies issues, IFPRI-World Bank Conference on Risk and Vulnerability, 23–24 September, Washington, D.C.

Cutter, Susan L., Bryan J. Boruff, and W. Lynn Shirley (2003), Social Vulnerability to Environmental Hazards, Social Science Quarterly, 84(2): 242–261.

Guillaumont, Patrick (2007), Design of an Economic Vulnerability Index and its Use for International Development Policy, CERDI, CNRS and Université d'Auvergne, WIDER Conference on Fragile States-Fragile groups, 15–16 June, Helsinki.

Hoddinott, J., Agnes Quisumbing, A. (2003), Methods for Microeconometric Risk and Vulnerability Assessments, Social Protection Discussion Paper Series No.0324, December, Social Protection Unit, Human Development Network, The World Bank, Washington, D.C.

Moser, Caroline O.N. (1998), The Asset Vulnerability Framework: Reassessing Urban Poverty Reduction Strategies, World Development, 26(1): 1–19.

Noy, I., R. Yonson, R. (2016), A Survey of the Theory and Measurement of Economic Vulnerability and Resilience to Natural Hazards, Working Papers in Economics and Finance, School of Economics and Finance, Victoria Business School, Wellington, New Zealand, SEF Working Paper 03/2016.

UK Essays, http://www.ukessays.co.uk/essays/economics/economic-vulnerability.php#ixzz4IiV9e1YG.

UNCTAD (1997), The Vulnerability of Small Island Developing States in the Context of Globalisation: Common Issues and Remedies, Report prepared for the Expert Group on Vulnerability Index, UN(DESA), 17–19 December 1997.

Sorin AVRAM[1, 2], *Luminița CHIVU*[1], *Carmen Adriana GHEORGHE*[1], *Alexandru SIN*[1]

[1] National Institute of Economic Research "Costin C. Kirițescu", Email: sorin.avram@ince.ro; chivu@ince.ro; carmen.adriana@ince.ro; alexandru.sin@ince.ro

[2] The University of Craiova, Email: avram.sorin32@gmail.com

The Influence of Timisoara Urban Pole on Economic Growth and Socio-Demographic Dynamics

Abstract *During the past two years, the population of Romania decreased by about 240,000 people due to external migration. In this context, urban growth poles have not exerted a strong impact on the dynamic of demographic resources but have already become the promoters of economic growth. By addressing a research theme regarding the urban growth poles in Romania, this paper aims to investigate the possible impact of migration on the development of urban poles, economic growth, technological development, climate change as well as on the more frequent use of social networks. The main directions of the study are directed toward the analysis of the following phenomena: demographic dynamics, urban decentralization, participatory administration, urban competitiveness, as well as a series of specific socio-economic indicators for the sustainability of urban activities.*

Keywords: *Urban poles; demographic dynamics; economic growth; migration*

Introduction

During the past two years, the population of Romania decreased by about 240,000 people due to external migration. In this context, urban growth poles have not exerted a strong impact on the dynamic of demographic resources but have already become the promoters of economic growth. By addressing a research theme regarding the urban growth poles in Romania, this paper aims to investigate the possible impact of migration on the development of urban poles, economic growth, technological development, climate change as well as on the more frequent use of social networks. The main directions of the study are directed toward the analysis of the following phenomena: demographic dynamics, urban decentralization, participatory administration, urban competitiveness, as well as a series of specific socio-economic indicators for the sustainability of urban activities.

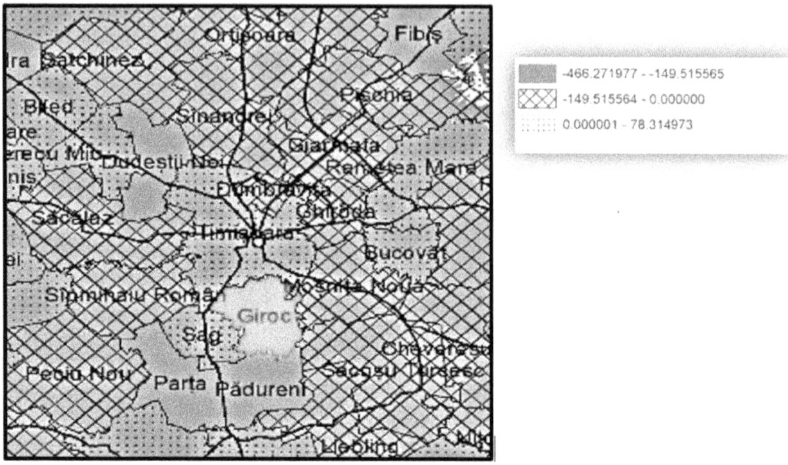

Figure 1: Spatial distribution of the demographic dynamics for the urban growth pole Timişoara during 1992–2018

Source: authors' processing.

1. The socio-demographic dynamics

The demographic dynamics and regional development are influenced by a series of factors that are not constant over time or space, such as socio-economic factors, infrastructure accessibility, land use. Their effects involve spatial expansion and vary according to population redistribution trends. The complexity of the study of population change and its relation to the factors that generated it is increased by the need to approach a space analysis, not just over time.

Most published papers on urban and regional development consider urban or metropolitan areas as a driving force, and rural areas as additional growth factors by analyzing these areas separately. Ward (2009) highlighted the fact that these areas interact with each other and together they influence regional development and population distribution change.

The progress made in spatial demographic research, access to geographic databases and the development of spatial analysis software packages allow a comprehensive and global research of influence factors and their effects on population and time evolution.

From this theme there are three questions derived: what is the relative importance of the determinants in explaining the population dynamics? Does the effect change over time and, if so, how? Do the effects vary in rural, suburban and urban areas and if so how?

This paper aims to analyze the evolution of some time series from 1992 to 2018 at the Timisoara urban pole in order to investigate the relative importance of the

Figure 2: Population dynamics of Timisoara municipality over the period 1992–2018
Source: authors' processing.

factors explaining the change of the population in the adjacent rural areas and in the center of the urban pole.

The analyzed data are provided by the National Institute of Statistics through the matrix with annual periodicity: POP107D - POPULATION BY HOUSE on 1 January by age group, sex, counties and localities; FOM104D - Average number of employees per counties and localities; LOC103B - Livelihood existing at the end of the year on property forms, counties and localities.

First, we will analyze the trend and correlation of the proposed variables for the centroid of the urban growth pole, the city of Timişoara.

The results obtained indicate that the population of Timişoara registered a decreasing trend during the period 1992–2018, revealed by the value of the negative coefficient (a = -199.04) of the linear equation which models the population dynamics, with $R^2 = 0,7679$. The linear regression equation which describes the population dynamics of the urban pole centroid during 1992–2018 can be expressed as follows: $y = -199,04x + 734135$.

For the centroid of the urban pole analyzed, namely Timişoara, we will test the existence of a correlation between the average number of employees and the total population. The results obtained are shown in Table 1. Since the value of the coefficient $R^2 = 0,026653$ is close to 0, it results that the relationship obtained does not represent a good approximation of the initial values. The Pearson correlation coefficient between the average number of employees and the population of Timisoara has a value of 0.163257, revealing a weak correlation between the two variables analyzed.

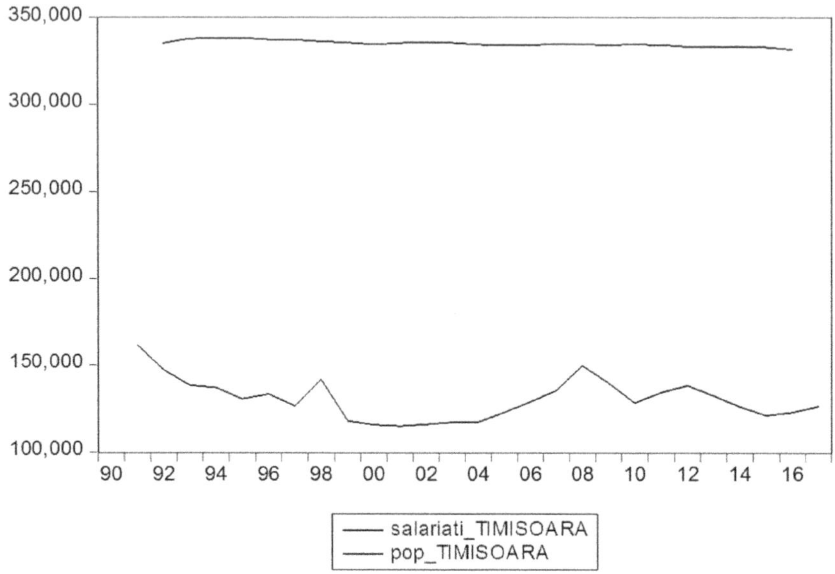

Figure 3: Population and employees of Timisoara municipality during 1992–2018
Source: authors' processing.

We will analyze the population trend for the localities adjacent to the centroid of the urban growth pole, between 1992 and 2018. The most relevant result relates to the dynamics of the population of Giroc and is presented in Table 2 and illustrated in Figure 3. This result indicates an increase of 378 % in 2018 compared to the base year 1992.

The results obtained allow to write the equation of the right which shapes the dynamics of the population of Giroc commune in the period 1992–2018, which is represented in the form y = 6.9895x-13.808. This result indicates the increasing trend of the population of this locality adjacent to the centroid over the analyzed period.

2. The contribution of the centroid of economic growth pole to the demographic dynamics of the adjacent localities

We propose the analysis of the existence of a dynamic dependency relationship between the evolution of the demographic indicator of the urban pole centroid, Timişoara Population and the evolution of the population of the localities adjacent to the centroid, as well as the modeling of this relationship.

Table 1: The results obtained by applying the correlation test between the average number of employees and the total population

Dependent Variable: POP_TIMISOARA
Method: Least Squares (Gauss-Newton / Marquardt steps)
Sample (adjusted): 1992 2018
Included observations: 25 after adjustments
POP_TIMISOARA=C(1)+C(2)*SALARIATI_TIMISOARA

	Coefficient	Std. Error	t-Statistic	Prob.
C(1)	331769.8	4407.633	75.27165	0.0000
C(2)	0.026945	0.033952	0.793601	0.4355

R-squared	0.026653	Mean dependent var	335257.5
Adjusted R-squared	-0.015667	S.D. dependent var	1671.654
S.E. of regression	1684.698	Akaike info criterion	17.77318
Sum squared resid	65278775	Schwarz criterion	17.87069
Log likelihood	-220.1647	Hannan-Quinn criter.	17.80022
F-statistic	0.629802	Durbin-Watson stat	0.309440
Prob(F-statistic)	0.435539		

Source: authors' processing.

Table 2: The dynamics of Giroc population during 1992–2018

Year	Population dynamics	Year	Population dynamics	Year	Population dynamics
1992	100.00	2001	99.77	2010	152.72
1993	98.81	2002	100.68	2011	176.97
1994	98.89	2003	101.54	2012	200.66
1995	98.06	2004	103.61	2013	220.76
1996	96.67	2005	107.47	2014	242.89
1997	96.54	2006	112.54	2015	265.26
1998	96.95	2007	119.17	2016	296.57
1999	97.65	2008	128.05	2017	332.39
2000	98.49	2009	138.98	2018	378.23

Source: authors' processing.

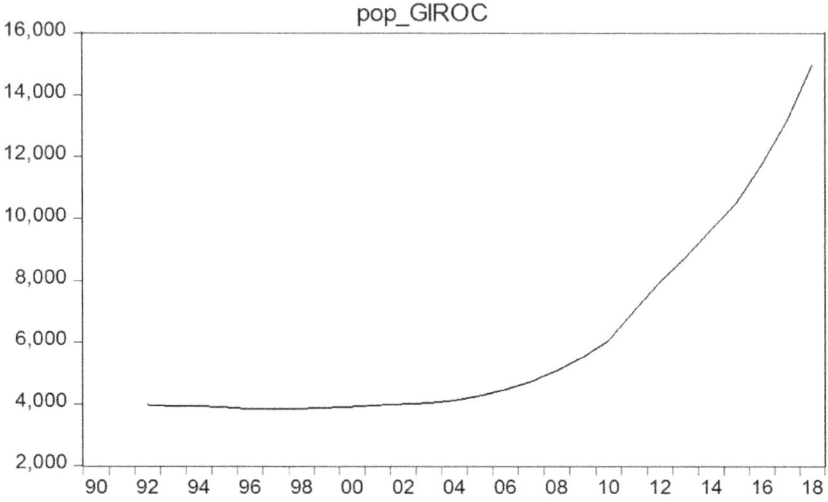

Figure 4: Population dynamics of Giroc during 1992–2018
Source: authors' processing.

We note by $(y_t)_{t\geq 0}$ the time series that model the evolution of the Population Timişoara indicator, where y_t represents the value of this indicator in year t, $t \geq 0$. We note by $(x_{it})_{t\geq 0}$, $i = \overline{1,9}$, the time series that describe the evolution of the population of localities adjacent to Timişoara (Becicherecu Mic Population, Dumbrăvita Population, Ghiroda Population, Giroc Population, Moşniţa Nouă Population, Săcălaz Population, Şag Population, Population Sînandrei, Population Sînmihaiu Român), where x_{it} represents the population of the adjacent locality i in year t, $t \geq 0$, $i = \overline{1,9}$.

In order to analyze and model the dependence relation dynamics of the general term y_t of time series population Timisoara under the terms of the previous two years, respectively y_{t-1} and y_{t-2} and in the terms x_{it}, $i = \overline{1,9}$ adjacent the localities¯ that shape population, we used a VAR (2) described by an endogenous variable (Timişoara population) and 9 exogenous variables, adjacent communities population represented by the City. Table 3 presents the results obtained for the VAR model (2) with an endogenous variable and 9 exogenous variables using the EViews.10 program. We used values of these time series for the period 1994–2017.

The obtained values of the model estimators define the following structural equation:

$$\begin{aligned} y_t = & 0.591107 y_{t-1} + 0.222068 y_{t-2} + 0.597188 x_{1t} - 1.741022 x_{2t} \\ & +15.39315 x_{3t} + 2.562767 x_{4t} - 7.809794 x_{5t} + 5.901898 x_{6t} \\ & +2.345606 x_{7t} + 0.596935 x_{8t} - 8.889387 x_{9t} \end{aligned}$$

Table 3: The results of performing the Granger causality test

VAR Granger Causality/Block Exogeneity Wald Tests			
Sample: 1992 2018			
Included observations: 23			
Dependent variable: POP_TIMISOARA			
Excluded	Chi-sq	df	Prob.
SALARIATI_TIMISOARA	1.734417	2	0.4201
SUPRAF_LOCUIBILA_TIMISOA	5.041464	2	0.0804
All	6.210505	4	0.1840
Dependent variable: SALARIATI_TIMISOARA			
Excluded	Chi-sq	df	Prob.
POP_TIMISOARA	2.663550	2	0.2640
SUPRAF_LOCUIBILA_TIMISOA	0.249651	2	0.8827
All	3.219535	4	0.5218
Dependent variable: SUPRAF_LOCUIBILA_TIMISOARA			
Excluded	Chi-sq	df	Prob.
POP_TIMISOARA	2.314202	2	0.3144
SALARIATI_TIMISOARA	1.857330	2	0.3951
All	3.479533	4	0.4810

Source: authors' processing.

We denote by $(z_t)_{t\geq 0}$ the time series which models the evolution of Timisoara Employees indicator, where z_t represents the value of this indicator in year t, $t \geq 0$ and by $(u_t)_{t\geq 0}$ the time series modeling the evolution of the Timişoara Habitable Area indicator, where u_t represents the value of this indicator in year t, $t \geq 0$.

In order to study and describe the dynamic dependency relations between the generic terms y_t, z_t and u_t of Timişoara Employees and Timişoara Living Surface respectively, according to the terms of these series from the previous two years, we used a model VAR (2) described by three endogenous variables (Timişoara Population, Timişoara Employees and Living Area Timişoara respectively). Table 4 displays the results obtained using the EViews program for the VAR model (2) with three endogenous variables. The obtained values of the model estimators allow the writing of the following structural equations that define the variables:

The R-squared value, which evaluates the performance of the model used, is the weight of the dependency-dependent dispersion explained by the independent variables. The value of this statistic is 1 if the regression model is perfectly suited to

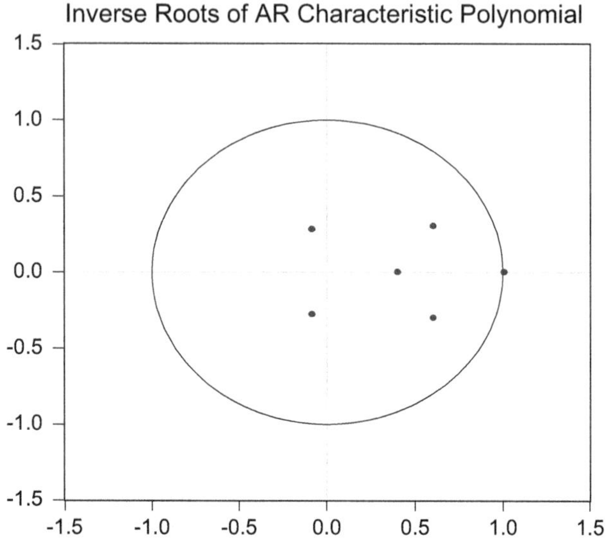

Figure 5: Inverse roots of the autoregressive characteristic polynomial associated with the model

Source: authors' processing.

the data series. In our case, the value obtained (0.897474) of the R-squared statistic indicates a good suitability of the chosen model for the description and prognosis of the dependent variable depending on the independent variables.

In order to test the suitability of using a VAR model, we will check whether the time series associated with the variables analyzed are stationary. The graph represented in Figure 1, which displayes the inverse roots of the autoregressive characteristic polynomial, indicates that only one root has the module equal to one, and the other roots have the subunit module, therefore the VAR model is stationary.

In order to test the existence of a causal relationship between the model variables, we will apply the Granger causality test. The obtained results, presented in Table 5, indicate that the Timişoara Population variable is influenced by the variables Employees Timişoara and Timişoara Residential Surface.

The graphs of the impulse / response functions, shown in Figure 6, illustrate how the Timişoara Population variable responds to a change in the Timişoara Employees variable, respectively Timişoara Residential Area.

The length of lags in the VAR is important because it has to capture the dynamics of the system without consuming too many degrees of freedom. Grades of freedom decrease rapidly by considering many lags. Also, if there are too few lags, the model is not correctly specified, and if too many, degrees of freedom are lost. So I applied the Lg Exclusion Test to check the result of the lag number. Its results indicate Order 2 through all criteria.

3. Conclusions

The lack of systematic research into interdependencies between rural and urban areas is strongly reflected in efforts to summarize previous studies. The literature on interdependencies between rural and urban areas is spread across several research areas - from studies in geography, economics, sociology and transport to the field of environmental studies.

However, in the 1990s, studies of interdependence between rural and urban environments have experienced a resurgence in research (see, for example, Barkley et al., 1996, Henry et al., 1997, Henry et al., 1999, Schmitt and Henry 2000, Henry et al., 2001, Renkow et al., 2001, Renkow 2003, Feser and Isserman, et al 2006, Partridge et al. 2007a, 2007b, 2008a, 2008b, 2010, McArthur et al. Ali et al., 2011). To a large extent, this growing interest followed after the empirical observations of the significant growth of the areas near the cities. Recent research on interdependencies between rural and urban areas has been largely devoted to population and employment interdependencies (see, for example, Barkley et al., 1996, Henry et al., 1997, Partridge et al.). Often, and reflected in previous studies, interdependencies are difficult to analyze separately as they tend to coincide. For example, Greenwood et al. (1986) found that there are population growth and employment complementarities and therefore an increase in the population of an individual generates half of the work locally.

We chose the Vector Autoregression (VAR) model because it allows the symmetric handling of all variables in the model in the sense that it does not implicitly imply the exogenousness of a certain variable (as is the case with OLS or the transfer function analysis), analyzing the existence of a relations of dynamic dependence between the evolution of the demographic indicator of the centroid of the urban pole, Timişoara Population and the evolution of the population of the localities adjacent to the centroid.

The type of rural-urban interdependence analyzed is that of labor and employment markets. Employment is a source of population growth - both at local level, as demonstrated above, and at regional level as a result of complementary growth between areas. Moving people from unemployment to jobs has long been a political objective, and allowing rural residents to get an urban job is a strategy that could counteract rural unemployment.

Increasing employment induces widespread effects on rural labor markets. We have found a significant spatial heterogeneity in terms of employment growth and distances from urban centers. Together, the findings of the data analysis for the urban growth pole Timisoara suggest that there may be benefits of urban proximity in terms of rural employment, but that these relationships differ in space.

The future directions of research refer to the analysis of other relevant indicators at territorial administrative unit level and applying the algorithm for all urban growth poles in Romania.

References

Ward, N., Brown, D. L., Placing the rural in regional development, Regional Studies, vol.43, no.10, pp.1237–1244, 2009.

Dobrescu, E., 2013. Modelling the Sectoral Structure of the Final Output, Journal for Economic Forecasting, Institute for Economic Forecasting, vol. 0(3), pages 59–89, October.

Dobrescu, E., Bianca, P., 2007. Stochastic simulations on the Romanian macroeconomic model, MPRA Paper 35723, University Library of Munich, Germany.

Dumitrescu, M., Bătătorescu, A. (2006) Applied Statistics using the R-Sytem, Editura Universitatii din Bucuresti

Jula, D. and Jula, N.M., 2009. Regional Economic Voting in Romania. Romanian Journal of Economic Forecasting, 10(1): 5–15.

Jula, D. and Jula, N.M., 2012. Prognoză economică, Editura Mustang, Bucharest.

Jula, D., 2008. Economic Impact of Political Cycles. The Relevance of European Experiences for Romania. Working Papers of Institute for Economic Forecasting (online), http://ideas.repec.org/p/rjr/wpiecf/081101.html.

Ali, K., Olfert, R., and Partridge, M. (2011). Urban footprints in rural Canada: Employment spillovers by city size. Regional Studies, vol. 45, pp. 239 260.

Barkley, D., Henry, M., and Bao, S. (1996). Identifying spread versus backwash effects in regional economic areas: A density functions approach. Land Economics, vol. 72, pp. 336 357.

Feser, E. and Isserman, A. (2006). Harnessing growth spillovers for rural development: The effects of regional spatial structure. Report to USDA Rural Development, University of Illinois at Urbana-Champaign.

Greenwood, M., Hunt, G. and McDowell, J. (1986). Migration and employment change: Empirical evidence on the spatial and temporal dimensions of the linkage. Journal of Regional Science, vol. 26, pp. 223 234.

Henry, M., Barkley, D., and Bao, S. (1997). The hinterland s stake in metropolitan growth: Evidence from selected southern regions. Journal of Regional Science, vol. 37, pp. 479 501.

Henry, M., Schmitt, B. and Piguet, V. (2001). Spatial econometric models for simultaneous systems: Application to rural community growth in France. International Regional Science Review, vol. 24, pp. 171 93.

McArthur, D., Thoresen, I. and Ubøe, J. (2010). A micro-simulation approach to modelling spatial unemployment disparities. Growth and Change, vol. 41, pp. 374 402.

Partridge, M., Bollman, R., Olfert, R., and Alasi, A. (2007a). Riding the wave of urban growth in the countryside: Spread, backwash or stagnation? Land Economics, vol. 83, pp. 128 152.

Florin-Marius PAVELESCU[1]

[1] Senior Researcher, Institute of National Economy, Romanian Academy, Email: pavelescu.florin@yahoo.com,

Evolution of Gender Gap in Romanian Educational System during 1919–2017 Period

Abstract *The paper deals with the features of the gender gap in Romania's educational system during a century after the Great Union of 1918. The respective indicator was sensibly influenced both by the economic structure and by the institutional framework of the education. The gender gap was differentiated on the components of the educational system. The gender gap in favour of men narrowed progressively from lower to higher components of the educational system. A major role in the evolution of the gender gap was also played by the massification of the education and by the implementation of the equal opportunities and non-discrimination principles in economic and social activities. This way, we can remark that during the 1919–2017 period the nature of the gender gap in the Romanian educational system dramatically changed. Sofar, during the school year 2016–2017, gender gap related to the total number of pupils in the primary and secondary education was in favour of men and non-essential, while in case of higher (tertiary) education the gender gap could be considered as excessive and in favour of women. Also, gender gap related to the teaching staff of the higher (tertiary) education was non-essential and in favour of women.*

Keywords: *education reform, massification, excessive gender gap, non-essential gender gap*

Introduction

The educational gender gap manifested in all countries during the pre-industrial era, due to the predominance of the conservative social structures and of the agrarian economy, which blocked the extension of the formal educational activities. The industrial revolution and the industrialization process and the social modernization, which accompanied the respective structural change of the economy stimulated the development of the formal education, especially the primary and secondary. The increase of the number of the pupils is obtained in almost all the developed countries in the context of the gender gap narrowing.

The transition to the post-industrial society favoured the development and massification of the higher (tertiary) education. The increase of the role of the educational system in economic and social life permitted a significant narrowing of the gender gap in favour of men. In fact, the extension of the length of the compulsory education and of the other components of the formal education contributed decisively to the elimination of the gender gap in favour of men. In this context it is important to reveal the national particularities of the process of narrowing and even the change of the nature of the educational gender gap in order to a better understanding of correlations of the economic development, social modernization and reforms of the institutional framework of formal education.

1. Theoretical-methodological aspects of the quantification of the educational gender gap

In almost all the countries, which experienced the development of the education system during the industrial era and the transition to post-industrial society the model of the transformation of the respective system was: a) the progressive extension of the number of the persons enrolled in the primary, secondary and then tertiary education. This trend was determined both by demographic dynamics and by the changes of the institutional framework; b) depending on the economic and social development the primary education and then the lower secondary education became parts of the compulsory education. In our days, in many developed countries the compulsory education includes the primary education and the whole secondary education; c) consequently, the enrollment rate of the school aged population increased, and then stabilized at relatively high levels (higher than 80 % in case of the compulsory education and higher than 30 % in case of the tertiary education). In this context, we deal with a massification of different components of the educational system[1]; d) the massification of the educational components favoured a continuous narrowing of the gender gap.

Therefore, we may speak about an excessive and a non-essential gender gap, respectively, in the educational system. Hence, it is important to define the indicators, which permit to detect the nature of the above-mentioned gap. We adopt the assumption that the gender gap refers the pupils and students enrolled, on the one hand, and the teaching staff of the different components of the formal education, on the other hand. An important feature of the gender gap is the share of the women in the total number of the pupils and students enrolled and the teaching staff. In the context of an equal rates of enrollment of the men and women in a component of formal education, the share of women takes values around 50 %. Consequently, it is important to define the limits of the respective share which permits us to detect the nature of the gender gap. We may consider a tolerance of 3 % for the deviation of the share from 50 %.

Hence, we consider that the limit of the structural gender gap is the share of 48.5 % of the feminine or masculine component in the total number of pupils or students and in the total number of teaching staff. In other words, we deal with an

---

1 In the developed european countries, the massification of the primary education is obtained before the World War One, while the massification of the secondary education can be detected during the interwar period in the context of important changes in economic and social policies. The massification of the tertiary (higher) education can be observed during the 1970"s (J. Levy-Garboa et all., 1979).

excessive gap in favour of men if the feminization degree of total number of pupils or students and total number of teaching staff is lower than 48.5 %. We register a non-essential gender gap if the feminization degree oscillates between 48.5 % and 51.5 %. We detect an excessive gap in favour of women if the feminization degree of total number of pupils or students and total number of teaching staff is higher than 51.5 %.

The evolution of the gender gap in the educational system in the long run has to consider the particular features of analyzed period. The external shocks and / or internal transformations of economic and social structure can induce contradictory trends during the different stages of a country development. Therefore, an adequate periodization and implicitly the identification of the stages of development determinate favours a good understanding of the nature of the gender gap in the educational system and the economic and social significance of the elimination or re-occurrence of the structural gender gap.

In case of Romania, a large majority of the historians agrees that the 1919–2017 period may be divided into three cycles, with sensible difference related to the economic mechanism, economic structure, social and political system and institutional framework of the formal education, namely: A) 1919–1947, B) 1948–1989 and C) 1990–2017.

2. Gender gap in educational system during the 1919–1947 period

The 1919–1947 period is in fact a reunion of three (quasi) decennial cycles, namely: a) 1919–1928, b) 1929–1939 and c) 1940–1947. The first two decennial cycles, mentioned above, form the interwar period (1919–1939), while the (quasi) decennial cycle 1940–1947 represents the period of the Second World War and of the first postwar years.

The interwar period was marked by the implementation of successful reforms in each of the three main components of the educational system. The laws, which permited the implementation of the reform of the components of the public education, were progressively adopted in an ordered manner. Therefore, a comprehensive reform of the primary education was implemented in 1924 in the context of adoption a new law for the respective component of the formal education. The respective change of the institutional-legislative framework ensured the unitary character for the training of the children of 5–14 years old age on the whole national territory and enforced the compulsory and free of charge feature of the primary education. Another target of the above-mentioned law was the creation of favourable conditions for the sensible diminish of the illiteracy degree, which was considerable higher compared with the situation registered in European developed countries[2]. In the same time, the law enforced the obligations of the parents of the

2 Therefore, the primary education included: a) the kindergartens for the children of 5–7 years old age, b) the elementary primary courses for the children of 7–12 years

children of primary school education to ensure and monitor their children presence and participation to scholar activities.

This way, the number of pupils enrolled in primary education grew at a yearly rate of 4.0 % during the 1920–1929 period and of 3.1 % during the 1928–1938 period (F. M. Pavelescu, 2016). The respective dynamics created favourable conditions for the narrowing the gender gap both from qualitative and quantitative point of view.

The number of the children of 5–7 years old enrolled in kindergarten experienced a slow growth, at a yearly rate of 0.5 % during the 1928–1938 period. The enrollment rate of the respective category of children remained low, namely 16.3 % during the school year 1931–1932, 17.1 % during the school year 1934–1935 and 15.8 % during the school year 1937–1938.

A new law for the secondary education was adopted in 1928. The respective legislative change was in line with the trends manifested in Europe and played a major role in the modernization of the Romanian educational system during the interwar period. In this context, there were clearly defined the type of schools of the secondary education. Also, the length of the lower secondary education was established at 3 years, while the length of the higher secondary education was established at 4 years. One of the most important consequence of the reform of the secondary education was the equalization of the access conditions to the respective component of public education of the boys and girls. This way, an essential premise for the elimination of the structural gender gap occurred.

The number of the pupils enrolled in the secondary education grew at a rate of 8.0 % during the 1920–1928 period and at a rate of 2.3 % during the 1928–1938 period.

The adaptation of the higher (tertiary) education to the context of interwar period was obtained through of the implementation of a law adopted in 1932. The respective normative act mentioned the higher education institutions and made provisions, which permitted the consolidation of universities and the increase of the prestige of the teaching staff.

The number of the students considerably fluctuated during the interwar period. During the 1919–1928 decade the number of the students grew at a yearly rate of 13.8 %, while the 1927–1938 was characterized by unstable dynamics, the yearly rate being negative (-0,5 %).

The trend of increase of the school population during the interwar period took place in the context of excessive gender gap in favour of men. The exception may be identified in case of the pre-school education, where the gender gap may be appreciated as non-essential one (table 1). In case of primary and secondary education the gender gap remained structural during the analysed period but tended

old age, c) the higher primary courses for the young persons of 12–16 years old age, c) the schools for the adults older than 18 years age which has not yet finished the primary courses, e) the schools for children with disabilities.

Table 1: Feminization degree of the pupils and students enrolled in the components of the educational system during 1913–1939 period (%)

School year	Pre-school education	Primary education	Secondary education	Tertiary education
1913–1914	50.6	36.3	...	9.4
1919–1920	...	37.3	28.3	12.6
1928–1929	49.8	45.2	34.8	27.1
1933–1934	49.8	45.7	34.3	31.0
1938–1939	48,0	45.7	44.9	26.0

Source: author based on Romania's Statistical Yearbook

to narrow sensibly, especially in secondary education. Therefore, the feminization degree of the number of the pupils enrolled in primary education increased from 36.3 % during the school year 1919–1920 to 45.7 % during the 1938–1939 school year. In case of the secondary education the respective indicator grew from 28.3 % during the 1919–1920 school year to 44.9 % during the school year 1938–1939.

The gender gap in favour of men also tended to narrow in the tertiary education. The feminization degree of the number of students enrolled at the higher education institutions grew from 12.6 % during the 1919–1920 university year to 26.0 % during the 1938–1939 university year. The narrowing of the gender gap is mainly associated with the increase of the total number of the enrolled students. Therefore, the respective indicator grew at 31 % during the 1933–1934 university year in the same time with the continuous increase of the total number of the enrolled students and then decreased at 26.0 % during the 1938–1939 university year in the context of the diminish of the total number of the enrolled students.

The analysis of the gender gap during the 1940–1947 is influenced by the lack of statistical data. In this context, we may remark the forced narrowing of the gender gap in the tertiary education caused by the mobilization to the army of an important of male persons of 20–25 years old age and by the increase of the women admitted to university courses. Therefore, the feminization degree of the total number of enrolled students grew from 26.0 % during the 1938–1939 university year to 34.1 % during the 1943–1944 university year.

3. The gender gap during the 1948–1989 period

The period 1948–1989 is marked by the existence of the command economy and by single Marxist-Leninist party political system. During the respective four decades, the public educational system faced three contradictory reforms. Therefore, the reform adopted in 1948, imposed in the context of the nationalization of the most important part of private properties, statuted that the educational activities were secular and could be exclusively organized by public authorities. One of the declared objective of the above-mentionated reform were the elimination of the iliteracy. The changes induced by the changes made in the institutional framework caused a brutal break with the tradition of the public education, consolidated or created during the interwar period. The length of the compulsory education was the same with the primary education, namely 4 years. The length of the lower secondary education was established at 3 years, while the length of the higher secondary education was established at 4 years. The higher education was stricly controled from ideological point of view. In 1955, the length of compulsory education was extended at 7 years, including the primary and the lower secondary education. The institutional framework created in 1948 generated negative results in the education and training, especially from the qualitative point of view.

In 1961, the public authorities initiated a series of measures in order to increase the quality of education. Sofar, the length of the lower secondary education was extended at 4 years and, implicitly the length of the compulsory education was estasblished at 8 years. Also, the barriers to the admission in higher education related to the social origin of the candidats were withdrawn. The curricula of the all the components of the education system were revised and some of the valuable interwar period traditions were re-established.

In school year 1973–1974 a new reform of the educational system was implemented. The length of the compulsory education was extended at 10 years, in the context of an excessive role granted to the industrial high schools. Consequently, the study of social and cultural disciplines was neglected. A new law of the education adopted in 1978 statuated the importance of the study in the secondary education of the mathematics, physics and biology. A trend of excesive technicization can be also detected in tertiary education.

Having in view the major impact generated by the three above-mentioned reforms we may use the following periodization of the evolution of educational system during the existence of command economy: a) 1948–1962, b) 1961–1974 and c) 1973–1989

All of the three major reform of the education implemented during the 1948–1989 period stimulted the increase of the school population and the narrowing of the gender gap. Therefore, during the 1948–1989 period the school population increased 2.41 times, at a yearly rate of 2,2 %. The trajectory of the dynamics of the rspective indicator was a concave one. The yearly rate of growth was 3,3 % during the 1948–1962 period, 2,1 % during 1961–1974 period and 1,3 % during the 1973–1989 period (table 2). The concave trajectory is observed also in case of the major components of the school population. The respective form of the growth trajectory of school population is determinated both by the demogragraphic evolution and by the massification features of each component of the educational system.

We may note that the higher growth rates registered in case of higher secondary education and higher (tertiary) education reveals the transition from an elitist status to an accessibility status of the respective components of the education system. In fact, the period of the command economy is one when the

Table 2: Yearly rate of growth of school population and its major components during 1948–1990 period(%)

Period	Total school population	Pre school education	Primary and lower secondary education	Higher secondary education	Higher (tertiary) education
1948–1962	3.3	6.9	2.7	13.0	4.3
1961–1974	2.1	5.4	0.6	5.8	4.6
1973–1989	1.3	1.1	0.6	4.1	0.9

Source: author based on Romania's Statistical Yearbook

Table 3: Feminization degree of the pupils enrolled in the components of the pre-universitary education during 1948–1990 period(%)

School year	Pre-school education	Primary education	Lower secondary education	Higher secondary education
1948–1949	39.1	48.2	43.9	35.2
1961–1962	51.2	48.6	45.0	37.6
1973–1974	45.5	48.7	48.7	40.1
1989–1990	49.5	48.7	48.7	47.6

Source: author based on Romania's Statistical Yearbook

massification of the pre-university education was obtained. The measures adopted during the 1980's maintained low enrollment rates for the school aged population most exposed to tertiary education. In this context, during the 1948–1989 period, the excessive gender degree in favour of men was eliminated in case of pre-school, primary and lower secondary education (table 3). Also, the gender gap in the higher secondary education maintained as an excessive one but considerably narrowed.

During the period of command economy, the feminization degree of teaching staff sensibly increased. From the beginning of the 1960's we may speak about an excessive gender gap in favour of women in case of the teaching staff of pre-university education.

In the tertiary education, the feminization degree of the total number of enrolled students sensibly increased from 31, 0 % in 1948–1949 university year to 44.4 % in 1973–1974 university year (table 4). The feminization degree continued to increase during the 1973–1989, even in spite of the excessive technicization of the respective component of education system.

The available statistical data show that the gender gap related to the teaching staff was an excessive one and in favour of men during the 1973–1989 period. The

Table 4: Feminization degree of the students enrolled and of the teaching staff of the higher (tertiary) education during 1948–1990 period (%)

University year	Students	Teaching staff
1948–1949	31.0	...
1961–1962	33.9	...
1973–1974	44.4	28.8
1989–1990	48.3	27.0

Source: author based on Romania's Statistical Yearbook

excessive technicization of the tertiary education favoured the wideninig of the respective gender gap.

3. The gender gap in the educational system during the period 1990–2017

During the 1990–2017 the institutional framework of public education registered ample changes in the context of the second transition to market economy (1990–2004) and to the process of Romania's integration in European Union. During the early 1990's the legislative changes permitted the functioning of private education institutions, especially in the tertiary component of the education system. In 1995, a new law of education was adopted, which reaffirmed the importance of education for the long run economic and social development and the principle of free of charge character of the compulsory education. The respective law and other normative acts adopted in the second part of the 1990's established the length of the courses within the different components of the educational system.

During the first decade of the XXI-st century the most important changes are related to: extension of the length of compulsory education from 8 years to 10 years, and the adoption of the Bologna system in tertiary education beginning with the university year 2005–2006. The reforms adopted during the 2000's had not generated positive results, which were expected from the above-mentioned reform measures. The adaptation of the secondary education graduates to the needs of the labour market did not improve and the quality of didactical and scientifical activities of an important number of faculties and universities did not satisfy the European requirements.

Consequently, in 2011, a new law for education was adopted by Parliament. The above-mentioned normative act maintained the length of compulsory education at 10 years and enforced the principle of the allocation to education of 6 % of gross domestic product. The provisions, which in legislators' opinion could improve the quality of higher secondary and tertiary education were controversial, being rejected by an important part of the social partners. Therefore, the law

Table 5: Yearly rate of growth of school population and its major components during 1990–2017 period(%)

Period	Total school population	Pre school education	Primary and lower secondary education	Higher secondary education	Higher (tertiary) education
1990–1999	-2.0	-3.3	-1.4	-6.0	11.9
1999–2008	-0.6	0.6	-3.9	0.8	8.0
2008–2017	-2.2	-2.0	-0.7	-3.5	-5.8

Source: author based on Romania's Statistical Yearbook

of education was modified several times. Among the legislative changes we mention the increase of the length of compulsory education at 11 years in 2013 and the support for the development of dual education in 2016 in order to improve the adaptability of the active persons to the requirements of labour market.

The dynamics and structural changes of school population was sensibly by the cyclical evolution of the economy. Hence, we may identify three (quasi) decennial cycles, namely a) 1990–1999, b) 1999–2008 and c) 2008–2017

Due to the negative demographic dynamics and of economic and social tensions the school population continuously diminished, the yearly rate oscillating between -0.6 % and 2.2 % (table 5). In fact, the respective trend is essentially caused by the dynamics registered by the pre-university education. The dynamics of number of the students enrolled in tertiary education grew sensibly during the 1990–2008 period, due to particular conditions, such as: a) the existence of a demand for respective type of education which was postponed in the 1980"; b) the occurrence and the development of the private universities; c) the practice of graduation of a second faculty, especially from economic and social studies field in the context of the massive restructuring of the economy; d) the lowering of the barriers to the admission to university courses determinate by the extension of the distance open courses.

The 2009–2010 recession caused the reversal of the positive dynamics of the number of the enrolled students, because, the training received especially from private universities was either of poor quality or were not concordant with the requirements of the labour market. The number of enrolled students diminished during the 2008–2017 at a yearly rate of -5.8 %.

As a rule, the above-mentioned dynamics of the school population took place in the context of non-essential gender gap in favour of men in case of all the components of the pre-university education. The respective evolution is a consequence of the extension of the length of compulsory education and implicitly of the consolidation of the massification processes. The exception from the rule was registered in case of the lower secondary education during the 2008–2017 period,

Table 6: Feminization degree of the pupils enrolled in the components of the pre-university education during 1990–2017 period (%)

School year	Pre-school education	Primary education	Lower secondary education	Higher secondary education
1990–1991	49.9	48.6	48.7	49.1
1998–1999	49.4	48.5	48.9	50.0
2007–2008	48.8	48.3	48.4	48.7
2016–2017	48.6	49.5	47.0	49.3

Source: author based on Romania's Statistical Yearbook

Table 7: Feminization degree of the students enrolled and of the teaching staff of the universitary education during 1990–2017 period (%)

University year	Students	Teaching staff
1990–1991	47.2	28.0
1998–1999	51.0	36.9
2007–2008	56.7	43.3
2016–2017	53.7	50.8

Source: author based on Romania's Statistical Yearbook

where the gender gap widened and transformed in an excessive one. In fact, this negative evolution is the outcome of the increase of the abandon rate had higher incidence within female segment of 11–14 years old.

The sensible increase of the number of the enrolled students in the tertiary education was obtained in the context of the modification of the nature of the gender gap. Sofar, during the 1990's, we may identify a non-essential gender gap (table 7). During the period 1999–2017 the gender gap was in favour of women. Under the conditions of the impetuous growth of the number of enrolled students during the 2000–2008 boom the respective gap became an excessive one. During the 2007–2017 period in spite of the sharp decrease of the demand for tertiary education, the gender gap continued to be an excessive one in favour of women.

The growth of the demand for tertiary education estimated not only the increase of the number of the teaching staff, but also the narrowing of the gender gap. The nature of gender gap was an excessive one in favour of men during the 1990–2008 period. The feminization degree of the teaching staff increased even in the context of the decrease of the demand for tertiary education during the 2008–2017 period. This way, the nature of the gender gap significantly changed. In 2016–2017 university year we may identify a non-essential gender gap in favour of women related to the teaching staff.

Conclusion

The development of the Romania's educational system during the 1919–2017 period was marked by important changes related to the gender gap. We identify a continuous narrowing of the gender gap, essentially generated by the extension and afterwards massification of the different components of the formal education. The massification of the education may be considered as the main factor of the narrowing of the gender gap and the implementation of the principle of equal opportunities aand non-gender discrimination. Therefore, the above-mentioned trend manifested even in the context of the technicization of the education during command economy. During the transition to market economy and integration in European Union the educational gender gap was a non-essential one, revealing a synchronism of Romania's social modernization with the European trends.

References

Botkin, J. W., Elmanjara, M., Maliţa M., - Orizontul fără limite al învăţării, Colecţia Idei Contemporane Editura Politică, Bucureşti, 1981

Eicher J.C., Levy-Garboa L. et all – L' economique de l'education, Economica, Paris, 1979

Gusti D. (coord.)- Enciclopedia României, Vol.I, Imprimeria Naţională, 1938

Majuru A. – Egalitatea de şanse şi perfecţionarea continuă în educaţia românească (1850–1950). Proiect POSDRU /89/1.5/S/59758 Valorificarea identităţilor culturale în proiectele globale

Pavelescu F. M.: Some considerations regarding the economic cycles in Romania during the period 1859–2010. Romanian Journal of Economics, 2013(XXIII), Volume 36, Issue 1(45)

Pavelescu F. M. - Evoluţia cadrului instituţional şi dinamica sistemului educaţional al României în secolul al XX-lea, Editura Expert, Bucureşti, 2016

Postolache, T.: Vers un idéal practicable. Notes et réflexions. Editura Academiei Române, Bucureşti, 2007, p. 72–74.

Tsantis A., Pepper R.: Romania- The industrialization of an agrarian country under socialist planning. World Bank, Washington, 1979

Wosman L.: Schooling and the quality of human capital, Springer Verlag, Berlin, 2002

Bianca BULIGESCU[1]

[1] Research Institute for Quality of Life, Romanian Academy; UNU-MERIT, Maastricht University Email: bianca.buligescu@iccv.ro,

Atypical Employment for Young Graduates: Does it represent a Stepping Stone or a Trap?

Abstract *The main aim of the current paper is to investigate to what extent atypical employment is a stepping stone for a career. Using a rich retrospective dataset on graduates across 13 European Union countries, REFLEX 2005/2006, the paper tests five hypotheses concerning atypical employment. The main hypothesis tested is whether having a first flexible job increases the chances of being trapped in a secondary labour market as predicted by the labour market segmentation theory. The paper finds that having a first atypical job increases the likelihood of having an atypical job five years later, having a PhD and a self employment first job increases the likelihood of having an atypical job five years later. If the firm faces strong competition or the firm is at the forefront of innovation that decreases the relative risk to have an atypical job, however, if the firm faces uncertain demand that increases the odds to have an atypical job five years later. More innovative firms or firms facing strong competition have personnel policies to retain their highly skilled workers, whereas firms facing uncertain demand use atypical contracts as a buffer. Changing sectors increases the chances of being in an atypical job five years later.*

Keywords: *graduate youth employment, atypical employment, flexicurity*

Introduction

Despite of the comparative advantage of a higher receptivity to change, youth are a vulnerable group on the labour market. Young people have been particularly hit by the economic crisis. Overall employment among tertiary graduates in 2015 compared to 2000 has decreased in most European Union states (youth aged 25–34 years). Even among youth that are employed in the labour market, they are more likely to be employed in atypical employment.

Atypical (or non-standard) work refers to work relationships beyond full-time and permanent employment with full social insurance coverage. The term usually includes part-time work, marginal work, temporary work, agency work and dependent forms of self-employment (Eichhorst et al. 2013). Atypical work covers employment forms on a wide range from formal jobs to informal forms uncovered by social security and of debatable working conditions. The present paper investigates temporary and part-time contracts as atypical flexible jobs.

On one hand it has been argued that atypical work often refers to precarious work[1] or a form of under-employment[2], that atypical positions are associated with detrimental effects on wage growth, on employment prospects and on individual well-being in terms of job satisfaction and health. Studies on human resources draw attention to the fact that workers in formal atypical positions have less financial and fringe benefits and less power of negociation compared to their colleagues in standard employment positions.

On the other hand the higher demand for atypical employment could be due to economic restructuring, a modernization effect of labour markets in a competitive global knowledge economy, atypical employment can be beneficial in creating more flexibility for firms and in helping to overcome crises without massive employment losses. However, little is known about the consequences of atypical employment on the individual level. Youth might be more prone to be employed in atypical jobs due to various reasons such as their lack of work experience and rutine, education-labour market mismatch, unrealistic or inadequate expectancies with respect to the labour market, personal or cultural preferences. The key issue is whether encouraging atypical employment is beneficial or not for the workers in building a career or whether they are trapped in second-best jobs compared to regular employment. In this context, the current paper asks the question whether atypical jobs are beneficial for young workers or whether they are a form of under-employment. Under-employment refers to under-utilization of productive capacity of the employed population, or under-utilization of labour resources to their full potential through situations such as over-qualification, or over-education, involuntary part-time work, over-staffing or hidden unemployment (labour hoarding) (Wilkins and Wooden, 2011).

According to both Eurostat and OECD data, overall employment among tertiary graduates 2015 compared to 2000 has decreased in most European Union states with few exceptions: Bulgaria, Luxembourg, Lithuania, Poland and Sweden. Some countries experienced a dramatic decrease Cyprus (16.5 %), Portugal, (14.7 %), Slovenia (14 %), Greece (13.8 %), Ireland (10.8 %). The southern states, Spain, Italy, Greece, Cyprus and Portugal are more likely to exhibit atypical employment as a result of under-employment since involuntary employment is half or higher of the overall percentage of atypical employment. Netherlands,

1 Precarious work refers to employment that involves instability, a lack of labour protection, insecurity, and social and economic vulnerability (Eichorst et al. 2013).

2 Under-employment refers under-utilization of labour resources to their full potential through situations such as over-qualification, or over-education, involuntary part-time work, over-staffing or hidden unemployment (labour hoarding) (Wilkins&Wooden, 2011).

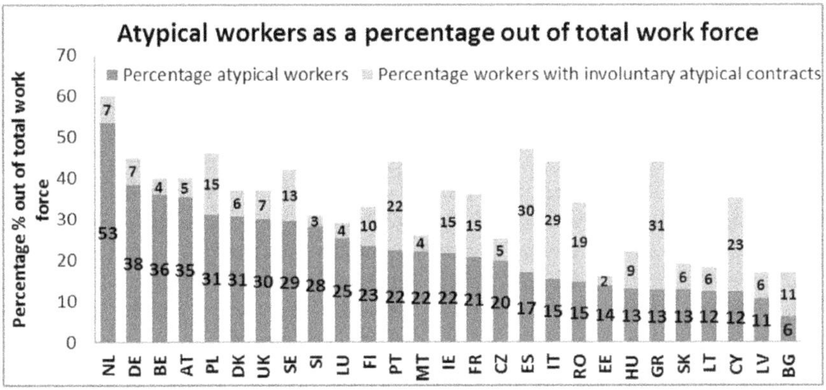

Figure 1: Atypical workers as a percentage out of total workforce
Source: Tangian (2010), extraction out of LFS, data for 2008, Eurostat database.

Germany, Belgium, Austria, the UK, Slovenia, Luxembourg although have above 30 % of their work-force in atypical contracts most are in such arrangements because they prefer them. Poland, Sweden, Ireland, France, Hungary, Slovakia, Lithuania and Latvia have more than 1/3 of the workers in atypical contracts on an involuntary basis.

Although temporary employment is below 40 % in Europe, there has been an upward trend in both temporary and part-time contracts (Hevenstone, 2008, Eichhorst 2015). Temporary contracts are hardly used at all in the UK, where the strictness of employment protection regulation is very low, compared to their prevalent usage in Spain with a very strict emploment preotection regulation. The lowest numbers of fixed-terms employees are observed in countries with liberal labour market regulation where employers have less incentives to use fixed-term contracts to increase flexibility.

Eichorst (2015) finds that temporary contracts have been decreasing in Spain as a result of the crisis, whereas France, Germany, Italy and Sweden experienced an increase in temporary contracts. In Southern Europe and many East European countries almost everywhere there is a prevalence of under-employment since many of the contracts are involuntary (Eichorst, 2015). In Italy, Cyprus, Sweden, Finland, Norway, Slovenia, Portugal, Greece, Denmak and Belgium there are more women in temporary employment than men. Although the rate of part-time is low in Romania, the risk of poverty for part-timers is the highest in Europe, the lowest risk of poverty among part-timers is in Belgium. There are considerable gender differences in part-time employment, with a higher takeup by women across the European Union. In Germany, Switzerland and Austria the rate of part-time among women is increasing with age, whereas in the rest of the countries the rate of part-time for the age category 25–49 is lower compared to the rate of part-time among 15–24 old women[3].

The current paper uses the REFLEX 2005/2006 dataset from ROA, Maastricht University on graduates from tertiary employment in 1999/2000 to test five determinants of atypical employment. The database collected retrospective information on their first job as well as information related to mismatches between education and work. In addition the database is extremely rich in private investment in education and work experience of graduates and collected information as well about their firms, their tasks, and their type of job characteristics.

The main hypothesis being tested is whether having as a first job an atypical contract increases the chances of being trapped in an atypical job five years later. The second hypothesis being tested is whether being employed in a more innovative firm increases the chances of flexible employment. The third hypothesis being tested is whether being employed in a firm facing strong competition and unstable demand increases the chances to be a flexible worker controlling for industry among other variables. The fourth hypothesis being tested is whether investments in human capital either through formal courses during the first job or whether the person graduated from a PhD decrease the probability of having a flexible job five years later. The fifth hypothesis being tested is whether mismatch of labour such as reallocation of work, changing sectors, changing occupations will have a higher impact on having a flexible job five years later. The following countries are included in the analysis: Italy, Spain, France, Austria, Germany, United Kingdom, Finland, Norway, Czech Republic, Portugal, Belgium and Estonia.

The paper is structured as follows: the first section presents a brief literature review, the second section the main findings and the last section concludes.

Literature review

There are considerable benefits of atypical employment in the sense that it has been shown that temporary contracts can avoid labour market inflexibilities (Bentolila and Bertola, 1990; Bentolila and Saint-Paul, 1994; Booth 1997). However, it might be of issue of concern if flexible jobs lead to lower quality of jobs, lack of opportunities for career advancement or lower motivation (Farber, 1999; Arulampalam and Booth, 1998, Maynard, Joseph and Maynard, 2006). On the one hand atypical employment may lead to less desirable jobs compared to standard employment. On the other hand, economic theories point to possible explanations about how atypical employment could represent a stepping stone to a permanent/full-time job, and therefore a transitory state.

Atypical employment could decrease human capital depreciation and obsolescence that would occur if the workers would have been instead unemployed

3 Data source: Eurostat, Employment Indicators and Eurostat Eurostat Statistics Explained.

and moreover it can be a way to increase human capital through experience (De Grip, A. & J. van Loo, 2002; de Grip, 2004). Alternative explanations are the signaling theory (Spence, 1973) and the screening theory (Stiglitz, 1975). Atypical contracts could be a signal of the willingness to work or motivation. Whereas the screening theory argues that employers could use atypical contracts to gain insight in the productivity of the worker. Another possible explanation is the Doerindger and Piore (1971) theory of dual labour markets. Jobs fall into either the primary or the secondary sector. Jobs in the primary sector are "good jobs" characterized by high wages, job security, substantial responsibility, and ladders where internal promotion is possible. Jobs in the secondary sector are characterized by low wages and casual attachments between workers and firms and are menial.

Francesconi and Frank (2002) using the British Household Panel data find evidence that temporary workers have lower levels of job satisfaction, receive less training and are less well-paid. They also find some evidence that temporary work might serve as a stepping stone for women who start in fixed-term employment and move to permanent jobs fully catching up to those who started in permanent jobs. Göbel and Verhofstadt (2008) using SONAR data on school leavers in Belgium find a stepping stone effect especially for vulnerable groups such as low educated school-leavers, school-leavers with a non-Belgian grandmother and with a smaller social network with respect to unemployment[4]. Calmand, Frontini and Rostand (2007) using the REFLEX database find that having a temporary job increases the probability of having a temporary job five years later.

The logistic regression finds potentially two groups of graduates more prone to temporary employment: the first group is made of graduates who attended a vocationally oriented study programme, and are holding only a first degree not giving access to doctoral or other advanced studies, they work in the private sector, especially in manufacturing and other productive activities and are refered by the authors as first-comers to a rather stable work situation; the second group hold a degree giving access to advanced studies but also gained some additional qualification such as a doctorate or a specialist degree, work in the public sector, especially in education, health, and social work, and are refered by the authors as being at the beggining of their career requiring longer preparation and/or resort to fixed-term contracts as a gateway.

4 Another school leaver survey is the Dutch DANS data (Data Archiving and Networked Services), collected by the institute of the Royal Netherlands Academy of Arts and Sciences (KNAW). The REFLEX dataset is an international survey on recent graduates in 15 countries carried on in 2005 to test whether recent graduates have a higher probability to have higher professional expertise, functional flexibility, innovation and knowledge management and mobilisation of human resources.

Results

This paper uses the RELFLEX micro-data, a survey on graduates from tertiary education in 13 European Union countries to investigate to what extent having a first atypical job influences the probability to have an atypical job five years later. The REFLEX data was provided by Maastricht University, Center of Research for Education and the Labour Market and it collected in the year 2005/2006 retrospective information from tertiary studies graduates in 1999/2000. Samples vary in sizes from 645 (Portugal) to 6794 (Czech Republic). All country samples have been weighted to 2000 observations for the analysis. The percentage of student population varies by country. The following countries are included in the analysis: Italy, Spain, France, Austria, Germany, United Kingdom, Finland, Norway, Czech Republic, Portugal, Belgium and Estonia. We excluded from analysis Japan.

The following hypotheses will be tested:

H1. Having a first flexible job increases the chances of being trapped in a secondary labour market as predicted by the labour market segmentation theory.
H2. Being employed in a more innovative firm increases the chances of flexible employment.
H3. Being employed in a firm facing strong competition and unstable demand increases the chances to be a flexible worker controlling for industry among other variables.
H4. Investments in human capital either formal courses during the first job or graduation from a PhD decrease the probability of having a flexible job five years later.
H5. Mismatch of labour such as reallocation of work, changing sectors, changing occupations will have a higher impact on having a flexible job five years later.

The following variables will be used to characterize jobs and transition: type of contractual arrangements in 2005 and in 2000. To test these hypotheses the following methods are used: multinomial regression analysis to investigate the transition from atypical jobs in the aftermath of the graduation to employment five years later.

As can be seen from Figure 2, employment in atypical jobs right after finishing the studies among graduate youth varies from 77 % in Spain to 26 % in Estonia. Graph 3 shows that the employment rate of tertiary graduates five years after finishing their studies ranges from 51 % in Spain to 17 % Czech Republic. Although the non-standard rate of atypical employment is reduced after five years, Graph 4 shows that there is considerable path dependency and once you start in an atypical job you have a higher chance to end up in an atypical job five years after in about half of the countries studied.

The multinomial logistic regression in Table 1 shows that having an atypical job increases the chances of having a non-standard job five years later controlling for country effects and other confounders. Having a first atypical job increases the odds 3.89 times to have an atypical job five years later. Being self-employed

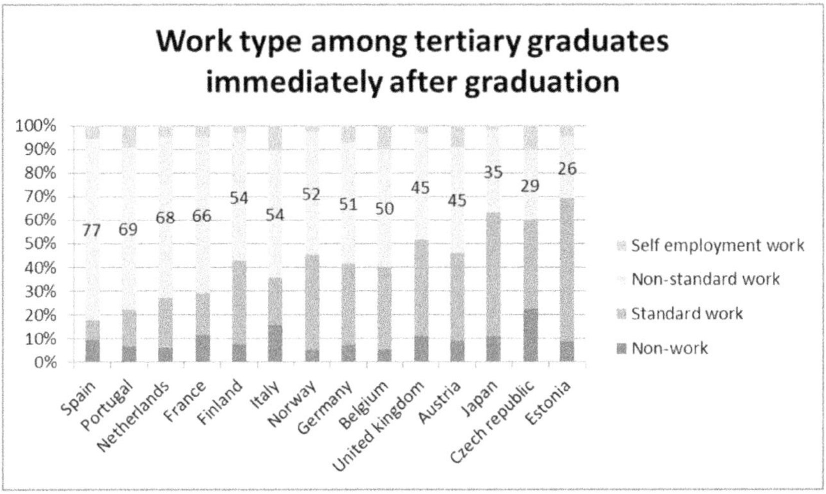

Figure 2: Employment among graduate youth by type of contractual arrangements in the first job

Source: REFLEX database, 2005/2006. Own calculations.

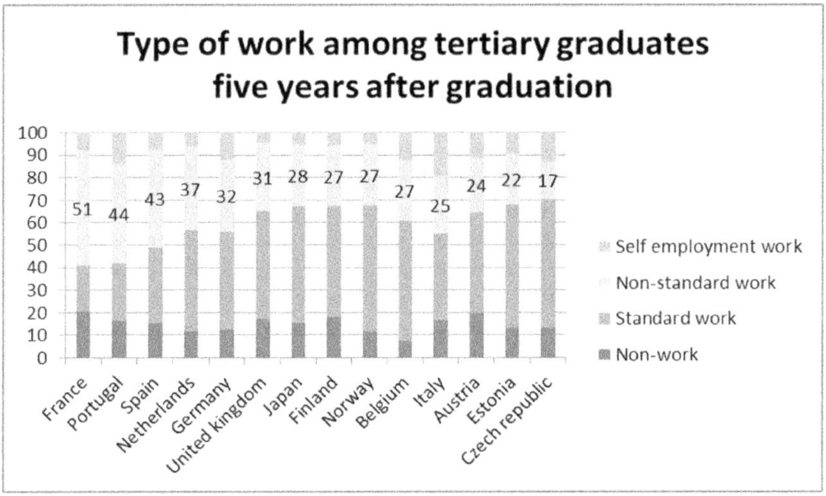

Figure 3: Employment among youth by type of contractual arrangements five years later

Source: REFLEX database, 2005/2006. Own calculations.

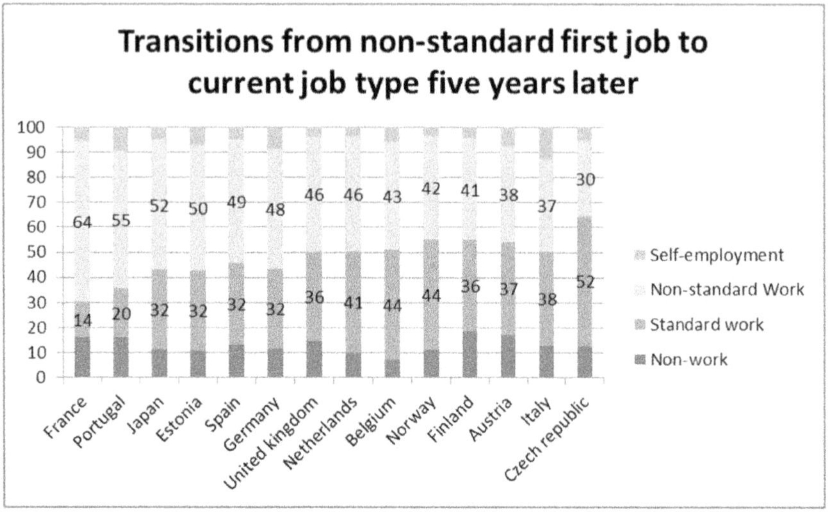

Figure 4: Transitions from non-standard first job to current job type five years later
Source: REFLEX database, 2005/2006. Own calculations.

increases the chances up to 2.43 times to have an atypical job five years later. Having training on the first job has no effect on the current job five years later. Being a woman increases the chances to have an atypical job five years later up to 1.49 times. Having kids younger than 7 years also increases the chances of having a flexible job five years later. Being still enrolled in a programme five years later increases the chances of having a flexible job up to 2.13 times. The interaction effect with the first job is not statistically significant. Those who graduated from additional programmes have equal chances of being in a flexible job compared to those who left the programme without completion. Those who graduated from a Phd and had as a first job self-employment have up to 1.60 higher chances to have an atypical job five years later. Having more labour market experience decreases the relative risk to have an atypical job five years later by a factor of 0.98. Those who graduated from the field of studies humanities and arts, and math and computing, and those from health and welfare have higher chances to have an atypical job five years later. Health and welfare professionals need to invest more in their training before they can have their own practice.

Those who work in the manufacturing sector, trade transport and traditional services, business, financial and communication services are less likely to have a flexible job in 2005 those who work in the education sector and those who work in health and social work are 2.78 times more likely, and 1.29 respectively more likely to have an atypical job five years later. Clerks on the other hand are have the

Table 1: Multinomial logistic regression: choosing between a standard job, atypical job and self employment five years later

Multinomial logistic regression	Number of obs	=	15103				
	LR chi2(108)	=	8441.57				
	Prob > chi2	=	0				
Log likelihood = -9832.9279	Pseudo R2	=	0.3003				
Standard job (base outcome)							
Atypical job 2005							

Atypical job	Relative risk ratio	Std. Err.	z	P>|z|	[95 % Conf Interval]	
Atypical job 2000	3.89	0.34	15.3	0	3.27	4.63
Self-employment 2000	2.43	0.57	3.79	0	1.54	3.85
Additional qualification no, still enroled (ref: left without completion)	2.13	0.32	4.96	0	1.58	2.87
Additional qualification yes graduated	1.12	0.12	1.07	0.286	0.91	1.39
Atypicaljob2000Xstill enroled in a graduate programe	0.85	0.15	-0.9	0.366	0.60	1.21
Self employment2000Xstill enroled	1.07	0.13	0.52	0.605	0.84	1.35
Atypicaljob2000Xgraduated from a programme	0.61	0.30	-1	0.319	0.23	1.62
Self employment2000Xgraduated from a programme	1.30	0.38	0.89	0.371	0.73	2.30
Graduated from phd programe	0.90	0.09	-1.11	0.266	0.74	1.09
Atypical job 2000Xgraduated from a phd programme	1.04	0.11	0.36	0.722	0.84	1.28
Self employment 2000Xgraduated from a phd programme	1.70	0.45	2.03	0.043	1.02	2.85
Had training on the first job	1.02	0.06	0.26	0.792	0.90	1.15
Strived for best results during studies	0.97	0.04	-0.69	0.491	0.89	1.06
Job needed more skills than the person had	0.98	0.04	-0.35	0.725	0.90	1.08
The current job underutilizes own skills	1.02	0.05	0.3	0.762	0.92	1.12
Woman	1.49	0.07	8.2	0	1.36	1.64

(*continued on next page*)

Table 1: Continued

Age below 30	0.93	0.10	-0.69	0.49	0.75	1.15
Age 30 to 40	1.09	0.12	0.8	0.423	0.88	1.36
Youngest kid less than 7	1.66	0.10	8.33	0	1.47	1.87
No. of months of employment since graduation (experience)	0.98	0.00	-13.68	0	0.97	0.98
Field of studies: education	1.05	0.10	0.52	0.604	0.88	1.26
Field of studies: humanities and arts	1.34	0.11	3.47	0.001	1.14	1.58
Field of studies: science math computing	1.18	0.10	2.11	0.035	1.01	1.39
Field of studies: engineering manuf constr	0.99	0.07	-0.11	0.913	0.86	1.14
Field of studies: agriculture veterinary	1.19	0.18	1.17	0.243	0.89	1.59
Field of studies: health welfare	1.57	0.14	4.92	0	1.31	1.88
Field of studies: services	0.88	0.13	-0.91	0.365	0.66	1.16
Manufacturing and other productive activities (ref: public adm)	0.41	0.04	-8.85	0	0.33	0.50
Trade, transport and other traditional services	0.45	0.04	-8.12	0	0.37	0.54
Business and financial services, and communication	0.49	0.04	-7.77	0	0.41	0.59
Education	2.78	0.28	10.23	0	2.29	3.38
Health and social work	1.29	0.14	2.33	0.02	1.04	1.60
Ocupation: professionals (ref: armed forces, legislators, senior officials and managers	1.03	0.06	0.47	0.638	0.92	1.15
Ocupation: Technicians and associate professionals	1.16	0.11	1.58	0.115	0.96	1.41
Ocupation: clerks	2.19	0.29	5.84	0	1.68	2.84
Person changed occupations	1.07	0.05	1.31	0.19	0.97	1.18
Person changed sectors	1.19	0.06	3.24	0.001	1.07	1.32
Firm faces strong competition	0.89	0.05	-2.21	0.027	0.81	0.99
Firm faces uncertain demand	1.13	0.06	2.24	0.025	1.01	1.25
Firm at the forefront of innovation	0.91	0.04	-2.03	0.042	0.83	1.00
Large firm size	0.97	0.05	-0.59	0.558	0.87	1.08
Small firm size	1.11	0.07	1.64	0.1	0.98	1.25
Spain	1.30	0.13	2.6	0.009	1.07	1.57

Table 1: Continued

France	5.18	0.69	12.33	0	3.99	6.73
Austria	0.85	0.10	-1.36	0.173	0.67	1.08
Germany	1.52	0.18	3.42	0.001	1.19	1.93
The Netherlands	1.41	0.14	3.34	0.001	1.15	1.72
United Kingdom	1.39	0.18	2.5	0.012	1.07	1.80
Finland	0.57	0.07	-4.77	0	0.46	0.72
Norway	0.58	0.07	-4.4	0	0.46	0.74
Czech Republic	0.44	0.05	-7.5	0	0.36	0.55
Portugal	2.53	0.43	5.45	0	1.81	3.53
Belgium	0.78	0.11	-1.76	0.078	0.59	1.03
Estonia	1.06	0.17	0.38	0.706	0.77	1.47
_cons	0.51	0.11	-3.27	0.001	0.34	0.76
Self-employment 2005						
Atypical job 2000	1.73	0.25	3.78	0	1.30	2.31
Self-employment 2000	33.90	6.64	17.98	0	23.09	49.77
Additional qualification no, still enroled (ref: left without completion)	0.85	0.23	-0.61	0.545	0.50	1.44
Additional_qualification yes graduated	1.15	0.16	1	0.318	0.87	1.51
Atypicaljob2000Xstill enroled in a graduate programe	1.82	0.57	1.91	0.057	0.98	3.37
Self employment2000Xstill enroled	0.87	0.15	-0.8	0.421	0.62	1.22
Atypicaljob2000Xgraduated from a programme	2.06	0.92	1.61	0.106	0.86	4.95
Self employment2000Xgraduated from a programme	1.20	0.30	0.74	0.46	0.74	1.97
Graduated from phd programe	1.12	0.15	0.83	0.406	0.86	1.45
Atypical job 2000Xgraduated from a phd programme	1.09	0.18	0.52	0.603	0.79	1.50
Self employment 2000Xgraduated from a phd programme	1.18	0.26	0.76	0.446	0.77	1.82
Had training on the first job	0.99	0.10	-0.07	0.943	0.82	1.20
Strived for best results during studies	0.94	0.06	-0.96	0.335	0.82	1.07
Job needed more skills than the person had	1.10	0.07	1.47	0.142	0.97	1.26
The current job underutilizes own skills	0.71	0.06	-4.29	0	0.61	0.83

(*continuedon next page*)

Table 1: Continued

Woman	0.79	0.06	-3.29	0.001	0.69	0.91
Age below 30	0.57	0.09	-3.74	0	0.42	0.76
Age 30 to 40	0.88	0.14	-0.83	0.407	0.65	1.19
Youngest kid less than 7	1.53	0.13	4.97	0	1.29	1.80
No. of months of employment since graduation (experience)	0.99	0.00	-5.82	0	0.98	0.99
Field of studies: education	0.84	0.12	-1.19	0.235	0.64	1.12
Field of studies: humanities and arts	1.68	0.20	4.37	0	1.33	2.11
Field of studies: science math computing	0.73	0.10	-2.41	0.016	0.56	0.94
Field of studies: engineering manuf constr	0.98	0.09	-0.16	0.871	0.81	1.19
Field of studies: agriculture veterinary	1.35	0.25	1.63	0.104	0.94	1.92
Field of studies: health welfare	1.39	0.20	2.34	0.02	1.05	1.84
Field of studies: services	0.98	0.21	-0.11	0.912	0.63	1.50
Manufacturing and other productive activities (ref: public adm)	0.34	0.05	-6.84	0	0.25	0.46
Trade, transport and other traditional services	0.60	0.08	-3.62	0	0.46	0.79
Business and financial services, and communication	0.76	0.10	-2.13	0.033	0.59	0.98
Education	1.28	0.19	1.66	0.096	0.96	1.72
Health and social work	1.22	0.20	1.23	0.218	0.89	1.69
Ocupation: professionals (ref: armed forces, legislators, senior officials and managers	0.66	0.06	-4.48	0	0.55	0.79
Ocupation: Technicians and associate professionals	0.31	0.07	-5.19	0	0.20	0.48
Ocupation: clerks	1.89	0.38	3.12	0.002	1.27	2.81
Person changed occupations	1.06	0.08	0.75	0.454	0.91	1.23
Person changed sectors	1.30	0.10	3.31	0.001	1.11	1.52
Firm faces strong competition	1.09	0.08	1.19	0.235	0.94	1.27
Firm faces uncertain demand	1.30	0.10	3.45	0.001	1.12	1.50
Firm at the forefront of innovation	0.98	0.07	-0.26	0.798	0.86	1.12
Large firm size	0.40	0.04	-9.25	0	0.33	0.49
Small firm size	3.18	0.26	14.24	0	2.72	3.74
Spain	0.65	0.09	-3.15	0.002	0.49	0.85

Table 1: Continued

France	1.47	0.31	1.84	0.066	0.98	2.21
Austria	0.44	0.07	-5.38	0	0.33	0.59
Germany	0.64	0.10	-2.82	0.005	0.46	0.87
The Netherlands	0.40	0.06	-6.05	0	0.30	0.54
United Kingdom	0.47	0.10	-3.49	0	0.31	0.72
Finland	0.32	0.05	-7.12	0	0.23	0.44
Norway	0.28	0.05	-7.24	0	0.20	0.40
Czech Republic	0.39	0.05	-6.93	0	0.30	0.51
Portugal	0.89	0.21	-0.48	0.628	0.57	1.41
Belgium	0.83	0.15	-1.04	0.298	0.59	1.18
Estonia	0.64	0.14	-2.12	0.034	0.42	0.97
_cons	0.42	0.12	-2.98	0.003	0.24	0.74

Source: REFLEX database, 2005/2006. Own calculations.

relative risk twice more likely to have an atypical job five years after graduation. If the person changes sectors her odds are 1.19 higher to have an atypical job. If the firm faces strong competition or the firm is at the forefront of innovation that decreases the relative risk to have an atypical job by a factor of 0.89 and respectively 0.91. However, if the firm faces uncertain demand that increases the relative risk to have an atypical job five years later by 1.13. Young tertiary graduates from Spain, France, Germany, The Netherlands, United Kingdom and Portugal are more likely to have a flexible job five years after graduation. Tertiary graduates from Finland, Norway and Czech Republic are less likely to have an atypical job five years later.

Conclusions and limitations

The current paper used a multinomial logistic regression to test five hypotheses. Our results show that having a first atypical job increases the chances of being trapped in a secondary labour market as predicted by the labour segmentation theory. If the firm faces strong competition or the firm is at the forefront of innovation that decreases the relative risk to have an atypical job, however, if the firm faces uncertain demand that increases the odds to have an atypical job five years later.

More innovative firms or firms facing strong competition have personnel policies to retain their highly skilled workers, whereas firms facing uncertain demand use atypical contracts as a buffer in hard economic times. Those who graduated from a Phd and had as a first job self-employment have up to 1.60 higher chances to have an atypical job five years later. The interaction between having training on the first job and being in atypical first job is not statistically significant. Mismatch of labour such as changing sectors increases the chances of being in an atypical job five years later.

References

Arulampalam, Wiji and Booth, Alison L. (1998). Training and labour market flexibility: is there a trade-off? The British Journal of Industrial Relations, December, vol. 36(4) pp. 521–36.

Bentolila, Samuel and Giuseppe Bertola (1990). Firing Cost and Labor Demand: How Bad is Eurosclerosis? Review of Economic Studies, 57, 381–402.

Bentolila, Samuel and Saint-Paul, Gilles (1994). A model of labour demand with linear adjustment costs, Labour Economics, vol. 1, pp. 303–26.

Booth, A. L., Francesconi, M., & Frank, J. (2002). Temporary jobs: stepping stones or dead ends?, The Economic Journal, 112(480), F189–F213.

Booth, Alison L. (1997). An analysis of firing costs and their implications for unemployment policy, in (D. Snower and G. de la Dehesa, eds) Unemployment Policy, Cambridge: Cambridge University Press, pp. 359–88.

Calmand, J.,Frontini M. & Rostan M., (2007) Being Flexible: Graduates Facing Changes in Their Work Environment in Allen, J., & van der Velden, R. (eds.) (2007). The Flexible Professional in the Knowledge Society: General Results of the REFLEX Project.

De Grip, A. & J. van Loo (2002). The Economics of Skills Obsolescence: A Review, in: A. de Grip, J. van Loo and K. Mayhew (Eds.), The Economics of Skills Obsolescence, Research in Labor Economics, vol. 21, JAI Press, 2002, 1–26.

De Grip, A., (2004) Evaluating human capital obsolensence, Paper prepared for the joint EC-OECD Seminar on Human Capital and Labour Market Performance, held in Brussels on Dec 8, 2004.

Doeringer, P., & Piore, M. (1971). Internal labor markets and manpower analysis. Heath, Lexington: Lexington Books.

Eichhorst, W. (2015). Low pay as an alternative to public direct job creation? Lessons from the German case IZA Policy Paper, 99(99).

Eichhorst, W., Hinte, H., & Rinne, U. (2013). Youth Unemployment in Europe: What to Do about It ?, IZA Policy paper no. 65.

Farber, Henry S. (1999). Alternative and part-time employment arrangements as a response to job loss", Journal of Labor Economics, vol. 17(4, pt. 2), S142–69.

Maynard D.C., Joseph T. A., Maynard A., (2006), Underemployent, job attitudes and turnover intentions, Journal of Organizational Behaviour, 27, 509–536.

Spence, M. (1973). Job market signaling, Quarterly Journal of Economics, 87, 355–374.

Stiglitz, J., (1975), The Theory of Screening, Education, and the Distribution of Income, American Economic Review, 65(3), 283–300.

Tangian, A. (2010). Not for bad weather: macroanalysis of flexicurity with regard to the crisis, ETUI Working Paper, No. 2010.06.

Wilkins, R., & Wooden, M. (2011). Underemployment. In D. C. Maynard & D. C. Feldman (Eds.), Underemployment: Psychological, Economic, and Social Challenges (pp. 13–35).

Cătălin ZAMFIR[1], *Virgil MUȘATESCU*[2], *Adina MIHĂILESCU*[3]

[1, 2, 3] Senior Researcher, Research Institute for Quality of Life, Romanian Academy, Email: catalin.basarab@gmail.com

On the Residential Energy Consumers Vulnerability

Abstract *When countries are forced to use a poverty line assume that such a decision combines the lack of resources of individuals and the financial capacity of the state to grant aid. It is not claimed that such a support is addressed to all the poor, nor that he pulls all out of poverty. There is no sufficiently grounded methodology to set the threshold of "the poorest of the poor." In addition to raising prices, the European directives included some social policy recommendations to protect vulnerable household consumers, the poorest of the poor, by asking Member States to define this social category and to establish clearly the laws national social support. Romania uses a procedural methodology established for the provision of heating aid by a policy decision: a grid based on a poverty line set by the government (615 lei / person in 2013) and a procedure for testing the costs.*

Keywords: *electricity, gas, energy consumers, vulnerability, prices, standard of living, prognoses*

1. Introduction

Establishing a threshold for energy poverty through a political decision and in relation to it determines who is poor and to what degree. To this is added the test of the property of other goods that can be used to produce income or can be sold, not offering the necessary conditions for a minimal decent standard of living. It is significant that in all countries the official adoption of a poverty line, including a threshold for energy poverty, is avoided. International institutions use some poverty thresholds: 1 dollar per person / day or 3 dollars, but they are used only to compare countries and classify them, less to be the basis for political measures. The method developed in the RIQL (the threshold of a decent living standard and the survival threshold) allows a more accurate estimation of poverty. At present, if we take into account the threshold of decent living, the proportion of people who fall below this threshold could be around 50 %.

When countries are forced to use a poverty line, they politically adopt a procedural threshold without substantial justification, assume that such a decision combines the lack of resources of individuals (obvious factor) and the financial capacity of the state to grant aid. It is not claimed that such a support is addressed to all the poor, nor that he pulls all out of poverty. It often uses the wording that the system addresses "the poorest of the poor," not to all the poor, but also aims to improve the situation of the poorest, which is in fact correct, only insufficient. There is no sufficiently grounded methodology to set the threshold of "the poorest of the poor." In addition to raising prices, the European directives included some social policy recommendations to protect vulnerable household consumers, the poorest of the poor, by asking Member States to define this social category and to establish clearly the laws national social support. These directives represent a change in energy policy. Romania uses a procedural methodology established for the provision of heating aid by a policy decision: a grid based on a poverty line set by the government (615 lei / person in 2013) and a procedure for testing the costs.

Initially, estimates of the number of vulnerable consumers in Romania amounted to 4 million households, accounting for almost 50 % of the population. The introduction of the testing of means, namely property, the number of vulnerable households has been reduced to 0.8 million of 8.36 million households of electricity and gas, i.e. 10 % of the country's population. Therefore, the rest of consumers, over 7 million, will have to adapt to the new prices. We can wonder if there is a mere coincidence that even today, heating aid, after a huge administrative effort, manages to identify about 10 % of heating aid beneficiaries, a fatidic figure for social support in all European countries, including Romania. The huge variation in the number of beneficiaries of heating aid is due to the introduction of "means testing", like property (housing, land, car, tractors, etc.). Heating aid is more generous than social aid for "the poorest of the poor". In 2013, the poverty per capita (minimum guaranteed income) was 137 lei / month, while the first decile of income per person in the same year was below 268 lei / month. It qualifies for receiving social assistance, considering only the current income, without taking into account the property, only between 5 % - 7 % of the beneficiaries.

Schedule for the elimination of regulated gas prices for household customers: 1 July 2013: domestic production price 49.8 lei / MWh; 1 October 2018: domestic production price 119 lei / MWh.

The timetable for phasing out regulated electricity tariffs for household customers: July 01, 2013: 10 %; December 31, 2017: 100 %.

Under these conditions, a possible scenario for energy prices in Romania in 2017/18 will be approximately those of the European average likely: 0.227 Euros for electricity and 0.076 for gas.

The timetable for the phasing out of regulated prices for final customers is presented in Law no. 123/2012 on Electricity and Natural Gas, a law transposing into the national legislation the European Directives 72/2009 and 73/2009 on the Single Energy Market. To reach these new prices, if we calculate our prices correctly, they will have to increase by 210 % and 280 % for gas. There will be more than double increases, a real shock for the population.

Table 1: Scenario of what can happen by aligning prices at European level: electricity and gas

	Electricity			Gas		
	2012	2017*	Increase 2012–2017	2012	2018***	Increase 2012–2017
EU 28	0.195	0.227	116.4 %	0.070	0.076	108.6 %
Romania	0.108	0.227**	210.2 %	0.027	0.076	281.5 %
% Romania level in EU	55.4 %			48.6 %		

Note: * A yearly increase of 3.1 % compared to 2012–2014; ** Assuming that the consumer price will be equal to the EU average of 28, equalized in a European market; *** Annual growth of 1.1 %, as in 2012–2014.

As you can see, in a short period of time (2015–2017/18) there is a shock of rising energy prices, perhaps the last increase by political price policy. The shock of prices will be borne by the economy, but also by family budgets. The impact on the poor segment of the population will be very difficult to bear. So, we can estimate that almost a third of the population is in poverty and another third is in a precarious situation, facing a high risk of impoverishment.

Impact of rising energy prices on the standard of living.

The effect of rising energy prices on real poverty, determined by minimal consumption, decent baskets and survival, becomes very visible. We will use the minimal consumption, decent and surviving baskets developed at RIQL (Adina Mihăilescu), differentiated on urban and rural areas. We kept the same prices for other goods and services, introducing only rising energy prices. In fact, the impact of rising energy prices is higher, direct costs are added to indirect costs by virtually increasing all products, incorporating new energy costs.

Consumer spending on chapters, including housekeeping expenses, was assessed at December 2016 level. Energy prices for 2017/18 were estimated as follows:

- The increase of the electricity price from 0.125 Euro in the beginning of 2014, the price on the Romanian market, to 0.227 Euro the price we suppose to reach the electricity in 2017 on the European market.
- The increase in the price of natural gas from 0,034 Euro in the beginning of 2014 on the Romanian market, to 0.076 Euro assumed to reach 2018.
- The above prices expressed in Euro were converted into lei at the exchange rate of the day 1 Euro = 4.5 lei.

I took as a typical example the family of two employees with two children. The analysis is based on two types of family, urban and rural, with substantial differences now.

Table 2: Urban - Consumer basket structure for the decent living and subsistence minimum for the two-parent family with two dependent children in December 2016, the 2018 forecast

		Decent Minimum	**Subsistence Minimum**	**Decent Minimum**	**Subsistence Minimum**
Nr. cr.	Specification	For a family of two employees with two children	For a family of two employees with two children	For a family of two employees with two children	For a family of two employees with two children
		% and value in lei	% and value in lei	% and value in lei	% and value in lei
1	Food	48.0–1,102.0	52.7–980.8	40.7–1,106.0	43,8–984,4
2	Clothing	6.6–151.4	5.5–102.4	5.6–152.0	4,6–102,7
3	The furnishing of the dwelling	3.4–78.0	3.1–57.7	2.9–78.3	2,6–57,9
4	Transport	7.7–176.8	9.4–174.9	6.5–177.4	7,8–175,5
5	Cultural services	2.6–59.7	3.1–57.7	2.2–59.9	2,6–58,0
6	Personal hygiene	3.1–71.2	3.8–70.7	2.6–71.4	3,2–70,9
7	Repair and maintenance services of clothing / footwear	0.7–16.0	0.9–16.7	0.6–16.1	0,7–16,8
8	Household expenses*	17.5–401.8	19.8–368.5	30.0–814.5	33,3–747,4
9	Drug expenses	1.4–32.1	1.7–31.6	1.2–32.3	1,4–31,8
10	Safety fund	9.0–207.0	0	7.7–207.4	0
Total		100.0–2,296	100.0–1,861	100.0–2,715	100.0–2,245

Note: * Expenditure on housing included postal and telecommunication expenses, namely stationery expenses.

The projected increase in energy prices from 2016 to 2018, as prices of other goods and services remain constant, makes structural changes in the minimum consumption baskets.

1. Poverty thresholds increase substantially due to rising energy prices: the decent threshold, with 118.2 % in urban and 118.3 % in rural areas; Survival threshold: 120.6 % in urban and 113.0 % in rural areas. An important segment of people are thrown into poverty.

Table 3: Rural: Consumer basket structure for the decent living and subsistence minimum for the two-parent family with two dependent children in December 2016, the 2018 forecast

		Decent Minimum	**Subsistence Minimum**	**Decent Minimum**	**Subsistence Minimum**
Nr. cr.	Specification	For a family of two employees with two children	For a family of two employees with two children	For a family of two employees with two children	For a family of two employees with two children
		% and value in lei	% and value in lei	% and value in lei	% and value in lei
1	Total food consumption, of which:	48.0–888.0	65.8–1,063.4	40.7–891.3	58.4–1,067.3
	- purchased food	17.6–325.6	19.1–308.7	14.9–326.8	17.0–309.8
	- food from self-consumption	30.4–562.4	46.7–754.7	25.8–564.5	41.4–757.5
2	Clothing	6.6–122.1	2.1–33.9	5.6–122.6	1.9–34.1
3	The furnishing of the dwelling	3.4–62.9	2.1–33.9	2.9–63.1	1.9–34.1
4	Transport	7.7–142.4	9.4–151.9	6.5–143.0	8.4–152.5
5	Cultural services	2.6–48.1	1.9–30.7	2.2–48.3	1.7–30.8
6	Personal hygiene	3.1–57.4	3.8–61.4	2.6–57.5	3.4–61.6
7	Repair and maintenance services of clothing / footwear	0.7–12.9	0.9–14.5	0.6–13.0	0.8–14.6
8	Household expenses*	17.5–323.8	12.3–198.8	30.0–656.5	22.0–403.0
9	Drug expenses	1.4–25.9	1.7–27.5	1.2–26.0	1.5–27.5
10	Safety fund	9.0–166.5	0	7.7–167.1	0
Total		100,0–1,850	100.0–1,616	100.0–2,188	100.0–1,826

Note: *Expenditure on housing included postal and telecommunication expenses, namely stationery expenses.

Table 4: The impact of rising energy prices on poverty thresholds and the cost of housing maintenance: Urban

	Decent minimum threshold			**Subsistence minimum threshold**		
	2016	**2018**	**2018/ 2016**	**2016**	**2018**	**2018/ 2016**
Poverty threshold	2,296	2,715	118.2 %	1, 861	2, 245	120.6 %
Maintenance costs / total	401,8= 17.5 %	814.5= 30.0 %	202.7 %	368.5= 19.8 %	747.4= 33.3 %	202.8 %

Table 5: The impact of rising energy prices on poverty thresholds and the cost of housing maintenance: Rural

	Decent minimum threshold			**Subsistence minimum threshold**		
	2016	**2018**	**2018/ 2016**	**2016**	**2018**	**2018/ 2016**
Poverty threshold	1,850	2,188	118.3 %	1,616	1,826	113.0 %
Maintenance costs / total	323.8= 17.5 %	656.5= 30.0 %	202.8 %	198.8= 12.3 %	403= 22.1	202.7 %

2. The share of maintenance expenditures in total household expenditure increases substantially. In the standard family considered by us, a family of two adults with two children:
   a. Urban: The minimum decent basket increases from 17.5 % to 30.0 %; in the minimum subsistence basket from 12.3 % to 22.0 %.
   b. Rural: the minimum decent basket, the share of maintenance costs of the dwelling increases from 17.5 % to 30.0 %; in the minimum subsistence basket, from 12.3 % to 22.1 %.
3. The structure of family budgets will change, pushing it toward an even poorer model of poor structure. Only revenue growth (primarily salaries) could offset, it will see to what extent the effect of energy prices.

Conclusions

The energy transition in Romania, which will be accompanied by a sharp increase in energy prices and probably indirectly, and others, generates a massive process of impoverishment. The impedimentary impact of rising energy prices can be clarified by comparing the normative consumption structures developed by the RIQL with the average real family structure calculated by the NIS. The structure of actual consumption identified by the NIS actually reproduces the structure of the minimal decent living set by RIQL.

This overlap suggests that more than half of the population is placed below the minimum decent living standard in 2016. The significant unbalanced rise in energy prices is likely to impoverish the population, push a significant part of the population into poverty. The typical family of employees is already at 90 % of the decent minimum living threshold, farmers at 70 %. While the average pensioners to the minimum decent level.

References

Mihăilescu, A., Coşul de consum al populaţiei României, Bucureşti, Editura Expert, 2012.

Mihăilescu, A., Minimul de trai, instrument în politicile sociale, Bucureşti, Editura Academiei Române, 2014.

Muşatescu, V., (f.a.), Posibilele recomandări către GLI pentru reducerea "sărăciei energetice", disponibil online la http://www.undp.ro/libraries/projects/EE/Recommendations%20for%20 Reducing%20Fuel%20Poverty_RO.pdf, p. 54, accesat în 15.06.2015.

Vasile AVĂDĂNEI[1], *Ioan SURDU*[2], *Iulia MEDVESCHI*[3], *Emanuela-Adina COCIŞ*[1], *Bogdan-Nicolae PĂCURAR*[4], *Alexandru-Sabin NICULA*[1, 3, 4]

[1] Centre of Mountain Economy CE-MONT, Vatra Dornei, Romanian Academy, Email: sabin.nicula@gmail.com

[2] Faculty of Political, Administrative and Communication Sciences, Department of Communication, Public Relations and Advertising, Babeş-Bolyai University, Cluj-Napoca, Romania

[3] Faculty of Geography, Babeş-Bolyai University, Cluj-Napoca, Romania

[4] Centre for Research on Settlements and Urbanism, Faculty of Geography, Babeş-Bolyai University, Cluj-Napoca, Romania

Analysis of Discording Geodemographic Structures and Space Polarization in Regional Context Using GIS Technology

Case Study: Apuseni Mountains Romania

Abstract *The Apuseni Mountains is the most populous mountain range in the Romanian Carpathians chain, but also the most vulnerable to demographic depopulation and urban polarization. From a methodological perspective, data structures were collected from the National Institute of Statistics, and after, its will be analyzed and processed using GIS. The analysis and mapping of research were done using QGIS 3.0 Girona and Microsoft Excel 2016. After using the Hot Spot Analysis (Getis-Ord Gi*) and Kriging tools, we created the theme maps. Research results reveal tremendous disparities in terms of population distribution in the mountain area, demographic pressure being exacerbated by the proximity to urban centers. The total population is 262,220 inhabitants, in 4,177 grids with a surface area of 1 km*^{2}*. The most populated cell numbers 5048 people while the least populated only one. General density reaches 23 inhabitants/km*^{2}*. There are 129,792 males, while females 132,428. Territorial polarization is weak and inefficient, unable to cover the area. The urban centers have been in full decline for the last 25 years, unable to economically recover. This is the main cause of their ever-increasing demographic decline.*

Keywords: *population decline, urban polarization, Grid population, GIS, Apuseni Mountains*

Introduction

Population is one of the core elements of sustainable development (Bai et al., 2018, p. 9). The main objective of this study is merely focused on providing a theoretical and methodological geographic corpus in relation to the applicability of the rural/urban interface, by defining the ways of determining the mal-functionalities in the evolution and population structure. In order to point out these disparities, analyses were performed upon the territorial articulation of the Apuseni Mountains (seen as a critical region from a geo-demographic viewpoint), due to two major geo-demographic risks, particularly the massive migration of youth population and a keen decrease of birth rates, also as a consequence of migration flows. These two mechanisms determine at least two geo-demographic perils. First and foremost, we witness the depopulation and, implicitly the geo-demographic decline of mountainous settlements (Tamás et. al., 2016, p. 1675), as well as population ageing and unbalanced socio-economic situations.

Knowledge of the evolution of working resources and of the active population is necessary for the framing-process of specific strategies for the social and territorial cohesion of the mountains. Within the great variety of subjects that must enter in the previous objective a basic aspect has been selected for this article and prior to the study of any socio-territorial transformation: the mountainous spaces and polarization potential of central places. Incontestable, mountains have an own specificity that differentiates them from other geographical spaces and that specificity does not equalise homogeneity. Mountains share similar characteristics, but at the same time offer considerable internal diversity. Analyzing, highlighting and valuing their diversity is a task of geographical high interest. Therefore, the subsequent objective of this study is to evaluate the validity and characteristics of geo-demographic diversity of mountain areas and establish the levels of populated and unpopulated areas.

Geo-demography

To place itself disciplinarily in geo-demography, geographic demography or the geography of the population, that is, between the population and the territory, has always offered epistemological challenges. Currently we assume that two stages are relevant: 1. The differentiation between urban and rural populations, by the processes of metropolization and the greater weight of criteria such as accessibility; 2. the territorial ascription of the inhabitants used in the construction of local and regional populations, questioned for the expansion of individual mobility. In the attempt to explore the socio-spatial pattern through a geo-demographic lens, we assume that "geo-demographics must be understood as a field of quantitative geography that engages in the analysis and classifications of populations into discrete classes based on socio-economic and built environment characteristics of small-area geography" (Alexiou et. al., 2016, p.382).

The new stream of studies brings to light more certain proposals, the "geo-demographic development process being perceived from the national to the regional/local level - with emphasis upon the role of each urban center as development pole." (Hincks, et. al., 2018, p. 665). In some specific contexts, the processes that generate the urban web involve nodes, connections and different hierarchical levels. However, the avoidance of over-concentrating nodes should be practiced as a form to avoid "urban hypertrophy", making the additional point that overloading any given urban centre tends to prevent the organic development of new healthy urban fabric anywhere beyond the city (Crier, 1984).

Following this scheme, it must be noted that "the monofunctional city does not only determine the directions of the city development, but also modifies the structure of all city subsystems forming the special integral generality of the community with the specific type of social organization connected with implementation of a definite socially meaningful function" (Kuzmenko, Soldak, 2010, p. 83). In extenso, the geo-demographic phenomena leave its universalistic framework, from the "off-the-shelf" to a new "one-size-fits-all" pattern. Initially, the concept was developed as a strategy in order to systematically document socio-spatial segregation, "the conceptual background of geo-demographics is still linked to the principle that people tend to align themselves with the behavior and aspirations of the local communities in which they live" (Alexiou et. al., 2016, p. 383). Years ago, when there was no statistical information adequate on spatial mobility, there was a certain difference between the expert observation, which confirmed the growing fluidity of the population in the territory, and the genetic knowledge generated in geo-demography, that was still based on a stable inhabitant model.

Now it's possible to overcome that dissimilarity by careful analysis of the growing statistical information on spatial mobility. The generalization and improvement in the last population census of the questions on spatial mobility (González et al., 2008) and institutionalization of certain official surveys on habitual mobility have expanded decidedly the potential of scientific analysis of that intuited reality. Nowadays, the demographic concept is between the accessibility and urban development binom (land use-transportation interaction, healthcare facilities, central services).

In our study we propose the following delimitation of geo-demographic in relation with adjoining concepts. First of all, we highlight the existence of geo-demographic decline interrelated to precarious territorial development. In the second place, we associate geo-demography with GIS mapping technology and Self-Organizing Maps in accordance with spatial and temporal heterogeneity of rural depopulation as confined in the studies of (Antipova et. al., 2012, p. 219, Alexiou et. al., 2016, p. 385). Thirdly, we emphasize upon the geo-demographic concept developed within mountainous areas as portrayed in the analyses of (Matiucci 2015, p. 103) which states that "the economic, political and cultural weight of urban centers has become so important that rural regions more than ever are subject to the influence of the urban concentrations. Therefore, the nonexistent urbanization of one region also tells us something of the conditions under which this historical process took place in another region. Only comparison reveals what led to the divergent development." (p.110).

Urban-Rural Interface

From a geographical perspective this urban-rural interface can be conceptualized and studied as a complex system, that is, as a cut-out of reality where the different elements that make it up are related, forming a possible complex of modeling in search of configurations to understand and explain its spatial-territorial organization. The geographical space is characterized by presenting heterogeneities, strong contrasts, discontinuities, fragmentations, dynamic changes and strong tensions and conflicts. This characterization arises both at the time of studying structural and functional aspects, such as land uses, economic activities, size of plots, accessibility to communication routes, supply and accessibility to urban services-public resources. The natural environment often contains some type of risk, such as floods or landslides depending on whether it is the edge of an agglomeration located in a flat or mountainous area. Any natural risk can become a catastrophe in the face of a lack of foresight affecting the population, its built environment and the supply of natural resources.

The lack of certain urban services in some areas of the interface leads to the presence of other problems that make life difficult for their residents as water courses and groundwater deteriorate or become contaminated by unregulated industrial activities, exposure to blind wells or sewage directly discharged into them. Erosion, deterioration and depletion of soils are added to the loss of productive soils caused by the growth without planning or control of the agglomerations -defined as the built-up continuum or "urban sprawl". (Grigorescu et. al., 2012, p. 44.)

Grid population

Population grid statistics is an alternative to population statistics for administrative areas. Population grids are a powerful tool to describe our society and to study the interrelationships between human activities and the environment. They are particularly useful for analysing phenomena, and their causes, which are independent of administrative boundaries, such as flooding, commuting and urban sprawl, to name but a few (http://ec.europa.eu/eurostat/statistics-explained/index.php/Population_grids).

Interest for the analysis of the spatial distribution of population based on grids increased significantly, with research by Lloyd et Nejad, 2014; Lloyd et al., 2017; Martin et al., 2011; Lwin et al., 2016, contributing to the theoretical and methodological background of interdisciplinary approachess to geodemogrophics. In many European states, population data is centralized at LAU level. This spatial reference point is not suitable for mapping population distribution at a high resolution (Batista e Silva et. al. 2013), regardless of the scalar reference level (regional or global), being conditioned by land usage and and specificity of their cover. Population analysis, alongside GIS, provides favorable premises for a grid - based representation of population pressure (Yang et. al, 2009). Ther importance of geospacial techniques is emphasized by Goerlich et Cantarino, 2013; Batista e Silva et al., 2013; Jia et al., 2014, which used the dasymetric modelling of demographic data in their research.

Study area

The Apuseni Mountains are the largest and highest mountain unit (11635 km^2 and with three peaks above 1800 m) in the Western Carpathians, reaching Barcău Valley to the north (47^0 14' 0.68'' N/22^0 31' 40.76'' E), boprdering the Transylvanian Depression to the east (46^0 34' 8.03'' N/23^0 45' 47.01'' E), Mureş Valley to the south (45^0 51' 10.79'' N/23^0 2' 53.93'' E) and Western Hills to the west (46^0 9' 41.97'' N/21^0 35' 30.50'' E), as a winding line created by the existence of "gulf depressions" located on the rivers Someş, Crasna, Barcău, Crişul Repede, Crişul Negru, and Crişul Alb (Pop, P., 2006, p. 170; Surd et al., 2016).

Data and Methods

The data base containing the total population and the population structured on age groups (0–14; 15–64; > 64) and gender (male and female), from the 2011 Population and Household Census, was downloaded from the website of the Romanian National Institute of Statistics and later integrated in the 1 km^2 grid, provided by the European Forum for Geography and Statistics (https://www.efgs.info/data/, accessed on 14.06.2018). GIS 3.0. Girona software was then used to convert the grid to the European Terrestrial Reference System 1989 (ETRS89) in Stereographic 1970 (Stereo70). The next step was to cut the grid according to the morphological line of the Apuseni Mountains, determined by Surd et. al., 2016. The total number of quantified cells was 4177. With the aid of the same software (QGIS 3.0. Girona), we created 9 thematic maps, while the graphs were constructed using Microsoft Office Excel 2016.

As the statistics regarding population dynamics is centralized at LAU level, we mapped the population distribution as a grid with km^2 cells. The advantages for such a method are an increase in accuracy when it comes to the analysis and cartographic depiction of the populace and its density, as well as a population spatial distribution at a suitable operational scale that adheres to interdisciplinary approaches. Furthermore, such a method offers a perspective that is closer to the reality on the ground, unlike the classical method of mapping population dynamics at LAU level.

The work flow was as follows:

- Converting the grid to a point type shapefile. Each point kept the value of the total population it represented.

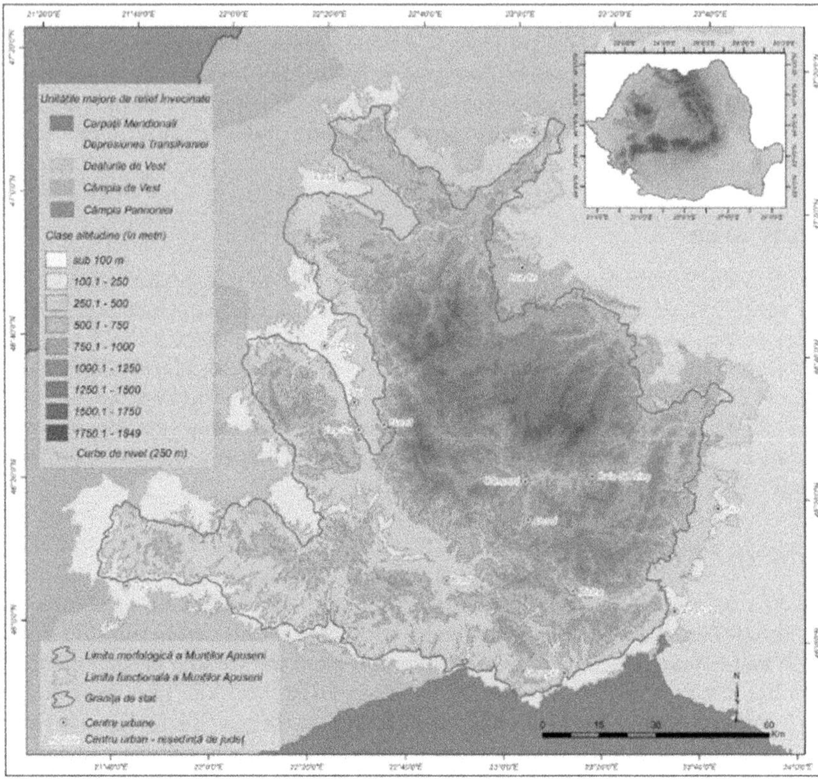

Figure 1: Study area

(Source: Surd et al, 2016)

- Analysis data structures with Geostatistical Analyst in order to identify the best interpolation method.
- In order to identify population distribution hot spots and cold spots, we employed the Hot Spot Analysis tool (Getis-Ord G*).
- Based on the Hot Spot analysis, we then utilized Kriging.
- The result were finally maped with QGIS 3.0. Girona.

Results

The cut grid according the limit of the Apuseni Mountains includes 4177 raster cells with a surface area of 1 km^2 and total population of 262220 people. The cell with the highest concentration of inhabitants counts 5048 while the smallest only one inhabitant. Population average is 62.77 inhabitants, while the general density is 23 inhabitants/km^2.

The high population density is reflected in cell groups that coincide with urban areas while the cells with a scattered density with the rural, many rural; settlements being found along rivers and/or communication routes.

The total male population is 129792 (49.5 % of the total population) and the ninimum value is 1 inhabitant. The average per raster cell 1km^2 is 31.07 while the general density is 11.15 men/1 km^2. Females number 132428 (50.5 %) of the total population. The average per raster cell is 31.7 and the general density is 11.38 women/km^2.

The grid based methods highlights the fact that in this area, households are extremely scaterred on slopes and valleys, far apart from each other, due to the specific spatial anisotropy and the terrain. Most settlements are between 200–600 m, while the permanently inhabited settlement is located on average between 1200 and 1300 m (Surd et al., 2016, pp. 55). At altitudes above 1300 m, the Apuseni Mountains thus incorporates only hamlets, isolated households and tourist accommodation units (chalets, pensions, bungalows etc.).

The spatial polarization is influenced by the towns and cities with a local reach: Câmpeni, Brad, Abrud, Baia de Arieş, Zlatna, Vaşcău, Nucet, and Ştei. Unfortunately, these urban centres have continuously decreased in size during the last quarter century, functionally, economically as well as demographically (see fig. x). Population loss is higher in rural areas, as people are drawn to urban centres located outside the mountain area: Cluj-Napoca, Alba Iulia and even Timişoara.

Spatial polarization is mostly diffuse in the mountain areas and more concentrated in the vicinity of the eight previously mentioned urban areas.

Conclusions

The studied area is defined by strong differences in terms of population spatial distribution and urban polarization. Most rural settlements are found between 200–600 m and are scattered, either on slopes or along valleys. As the highest settlement is located below 1300 m, the rest are solely temporary. The total population is 262220, 49.5 % being men, thefeore a relative balance has set in.

The spatial polarization exercised by the urban areas from within the area (Câmpeni, Brad, Abrud, Baia de Arieş, Zlatna, Vaşcău, Nucet and Ştei) projects în several weak local and zonal influence areas. It is therefore clear that large areas are only administratively polarized, while any functional polarization is lacking. Poor access to central services is caused by improper infrastructure, without any functional connectivity which could provide an optimal flow of people, goods and services to and from the area. The morphology and the unsustainable management of human and natural resources highlight, at least for now, a skeptical and non-resilient view of the population of the Apuseni mountain range.

The current approaches to population research based on 1 km^2 grids are, without a doubt, an alternative to classsical methods used by national statistical

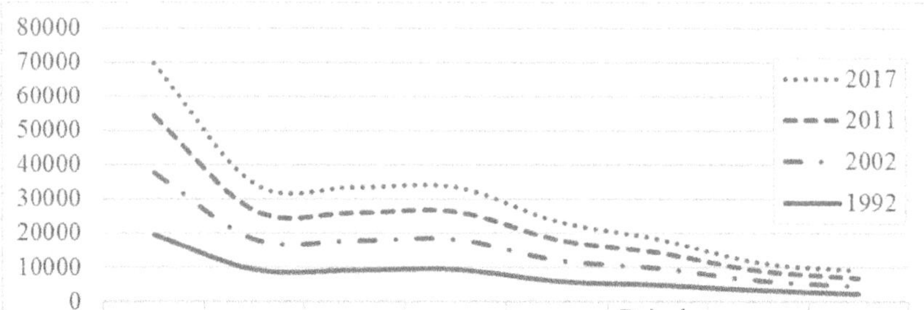

	Brad	Cîmpeni	Ştei	Zlatna	Abrud	Baia de Arieş	Vaşcău	Nucet
2017	15637	7928	7537	7299	5429	3985	2375	2137
2011	16708	8314	8038	8008	5832	4402	2624	2134
2002	18078	8940	8757	8868	6198	4956	2932	2235
1992	19473	9330	9125	9342	5952	4847	3338	2316

Figure 2: Evolution of urban population

Data source: National Institute of Statistics

departments, which operate with data structures solely at LAU level. Another advantage is that it allows for a contextualized analysis and in territorial contiguity of all the data, without being segmented by administrative boundaries.

Our future aims include the development of a methodology to depict population dynamics based on 0.5 km^2 and 0.25 km^2 grids, extremely useful in interdisciplinary approaches, uniting urbanists, planners, geographers, sociologists etc.

When it comes to spatial polarization, future measures should include the development of an interactive online website, which should allow updating data structures and information. This could help demarcate empirical polarization areas, based on the integrated analysis of population, economic, cultural, educational, medical data.

Settlement depopulation in the Apuseni Mountain range is not a singular case, as the entire Carpathian range experiences the same problem. Unfortunately, the authorities failed to implement any sort of coherent and pragmatic strategy to halt this phenomenon. One solution could be to design three types of scenarios regarding depopulation: positive, meta-stable (neutral) and negative. Based on said scenarios and demographic data modeling, authorities can make efficient rehabilitation or risk mitigation decisions.

The relational research of the population and settlements from mountain areas still remains a fertile ground for interdiciplinary study and requires a more in-depth look. The consequences of not grasping the human and habitat components of mountain ranges can lead to further depopulation crises and insurmountable social-economic convulsions.

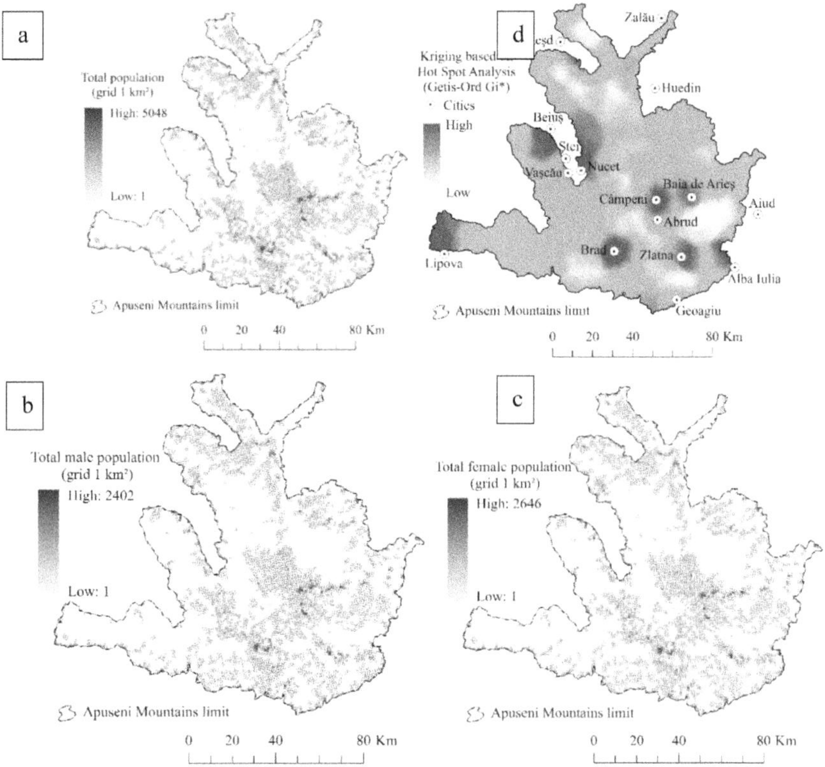

Figure 3: Distribution of total population (a), a gender base structure (b and c) and spatial polarization (d)

Data source: National Institute of Statistics.

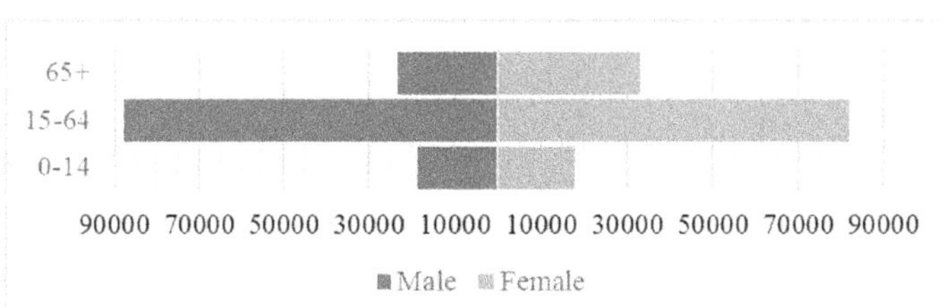

Figure 4: Population pyramid for the studied area

Source: own calculations based on National Institute of Statistics data

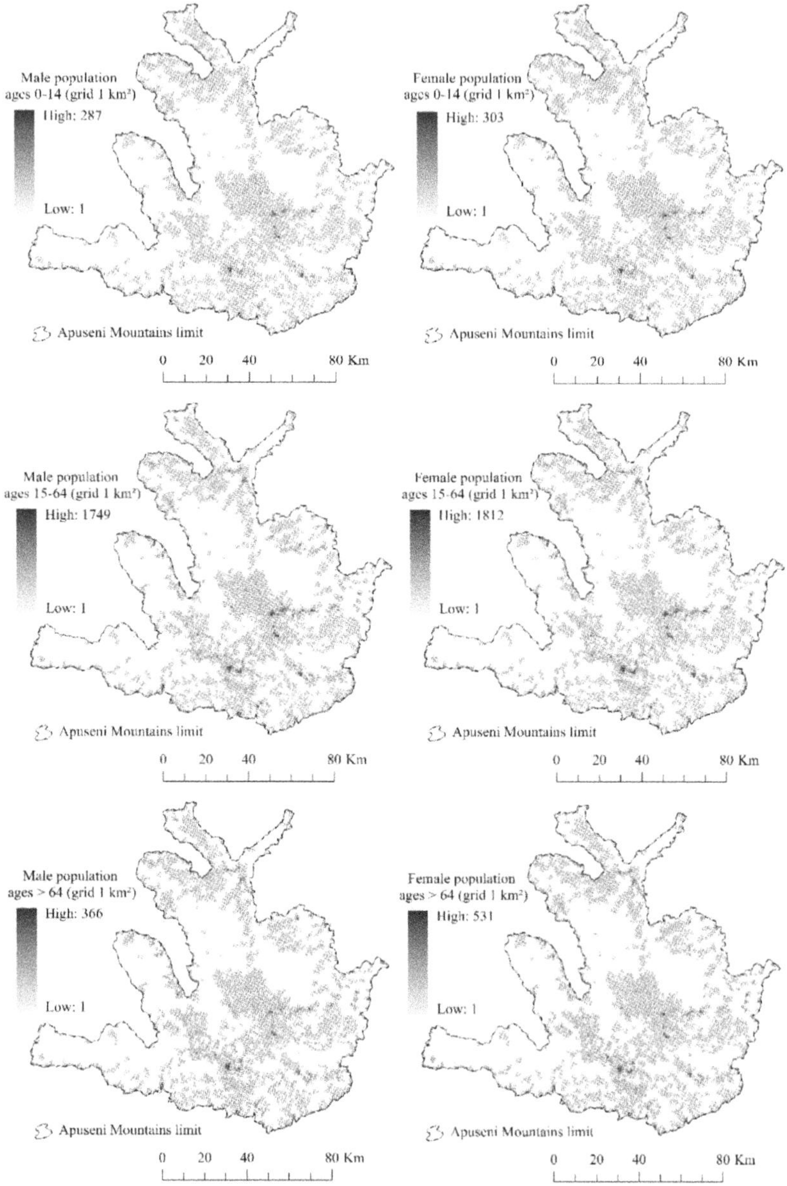

Figure 5: Spatial distribution of population per age groups, using the 1 km^2 grid
Data source: National Institute of Statistics.

References

Alexiou, Alexandros/Singleton, Alex/Paul, Longley: A classification of Multidimensional Open Data for Urban Morphology, Built Environment, 42 (3), Autumn, 2016, pp. 382–395.

Antipova, Ekaterina/Fakeyeva, Liudmila/Karobkin, Aliaksandr: GIS mapping in the geodemographic studies (Case study of the Republic of Belarus), Hungarian Geographical Bulletin, 61 (3), 2012, pp. 219–236.

Bai Zhongqiang, Wang, Juanle/Wang, Mingming/Gao, Mengxu/Sun, Jiulin: Accuracy Assessment of Multi-Source Gridded Population Distribution Datasets in China, Sustainability, 10 (5), 2018, pp. 1–15.

Batista e Silva, Filipe/Gallego, Javier/Lavalle, Carlo: A high-resolution population grid map for Europe, 9 (1), 2013, pp. 16–28.

Dmowska, Anna/Stepinski, Tomasz: A high resolution population grid for the conterminous United States: The 2010 edition, Computers Environment and Urban Systems, 6, 2017, pp. 13–23.

Goerlich, Francisco/Cantarino, Isidro: A population density grid for Spain, International Journal of Geographical Science, 27 (12), 2013, pp. 2247–2263.

González, C. Marta/Hidalgo, A. César/Barabási, Albert-László: Understanding individual human mobility patterns, Nature, 453, 2008, pp. 779–782.

Grigorescu, Ines/Mitrică, Bianca/Mocanu, Irena/Ticană, Nicoleta: Urban sprawl and residential development in the Romanian Metropolitan Areas, Revue Roumaine de Géographie/Rom. Journ. Geogr., 2012, 56 (1), pp. 43–59.

Hincks, Stephen/Kingston, Richard/Webb, Brian/Wong, Cecilia: A new geodemographic classification of commuting flows for England and Wales, International Journal of Geographical Information Science, 32:4, 2018, pp. 663–684, DOI: 10.1080/13658816.2017.1407416, Leon Crier, Houses, Palaces, Cities, New York: St. Martin's Press, 1984.

Jia, Peng/Qiu, Youliang/Gaughan, Andrea: A fine-scale spatial population distribution on the High-resolution Gridded Population Surface and application in Alachua County, Florida, Applied Geography, 50, 2014, pp. 99–107.

Kuzmenko, L.M./Soldak, M.O.: Monofunctional Cities: Problems, Support Provision and Development, Економічний вісник Донбасу № 4 (22), 2010.

Lloyd, Cristopher/Nejad, Behnam Firoozi: Surface models and the spatial structure of population variables: Exploring smoothing effects using Northern Ireland grid square data, Computers Environment and Urban Systems, 48, 2014, pp. 64–72.

Lloyd, Christopher/Sorichetta, Alessandro/Tatem, Andrew: High resolution global gridded data for use in population, Scientific Data, 4 (170001), 2017, pp. 1–17.

Lwin, Ko Ko/Sugiura, Komei/Zettsu, Koji: Space-time multiple regression model for grid-based population estimation in urban areas, International Journal of Geographical Information Science, 30 (8), 2016, pp. 1579–1593.

Martin, David/Lloyd, Chris/Shuttleworth, Ian: Evaluation of gridded population models using 2001 Northern Ireland Census data, Environment and Planning A, 43 (8), 2011, pp. 1965–1980.

Mattiucci, Cristina: Mountain Condominiums. A Discussing of Settlement and Dwelling on the Outskirts of an Alpine City, Journal of Alpine Research | Revue de géographie alpine [Online], 103–3, 2015.

Surd, Vasile/Constantin, Veronica/Nicula, Alexandru-Sabin: Aşezările din Munţii Apuseni, Presa Universitară Clujeană, 2016, p. 55.

Tamás, Telbisz/Imecs, Zoltán/Mari, László/Bottlik, Zsolt: Changing human-environment interactions in medium mountains: the Apuseni Mts (Romania) as a case study, in Journal of mountain science, 13 (9), 2016, 1675–1687.

Yang, Xiaohuan/Huang, Yaohuan/Dong, Pinliang/Jiang, Dong/Liu, Honghui: An Updating System for the Gridded Population Database of China Based on Remote Sensing, GIS and Spatial Database Technologies, Sensors, 9 (02), pp. 1128–1140.

http://statistici.insse.ro/shop/, accessed in 27.05.2018.

https://www.efgs.info/data/, accessed in 14.06.2018.

Mihnea PREOTESI[1]

[1] Senior Researcher, Research Institute for Quality of Life, Romanian Academy, Email: mihneapre1@yahoo.com

Precarious Employment-Poverty-In Work Poverty in Local Contexts of Social Underdevelopment

Abstract *This analysis uses the results of the project SIPOCA 4 "Implementation of a public policy design system in the field of social inclusion for the Romanian Ministry of Labour and Social Justice", selected on Operational Programme Administrative Capacity, co-financed by the European Union from European Social Fund. Based on the data referring to poverty rate and the poverty in work on local, county and regional levels, this analysis model identifies structural and contextual factors and the mechanisms used by these to influence the social development.Within this analysis model the key variable is the occupation. This concept is operationalized by quantitative aspects, like the employment rate, and qualitative aspects, like the type of employment, focusing on the precarious employment. The high rate of precarious work in Romania represents one of the main factors leading to a significant high rate of poverty in work comparing to EU, but also to former socialist countries in EU.*

Keywords: *in-work poverty, social underdevelopment, precarious work*

Introduction

Even though in the past years Romania made significant steps in reducing the economic differences compared to the European average, the differences are still visible from a social perspective. The comparing analysis of the socio-economic indicators (made by the Romanian Academy in the Socio-Economic Development Strategy 2015–2035) shows that Romania continues to register significant differences regarding the poverty rate, mainly in the cases of children and families with children when it comes to reduced budget percentage from the GDP, the budgetary effort for healthcare and education, and the efficiency of the social protection system in combating poverty.

Also, the poverty in work rate is almost double the European average and significantly higher than in the former socialist EU members.

While the classical employment rate is significant lower in Romania, the atypical employment is developing and diversifying in modern forms of employment in EU, in Romania is rather traditional. The subsistence and under subsistence agriculture has a significant larger importance than any other EU country; it is economical inefficient and has the characteristics of precarious work.

The differences are rather small regarding the pre-transfer poverty rate, but they grow significantly in the case of post-transfer poverty (including all social transfers other than pensions) and in work poverty.

Based on the data from the project SIPOCA 4 "Implementation of a public policy design system in the field of social inclusion for the Romanian Ministry of Labour and Social Justice", selected on Operational Programme Administrative Capacity, co-financed by the European Union from European Social Fund, implemented by Ministry of Labour and Social Justice (MMJS) as beneficiary and National Institute for Economic Research "Costin C. Kirițescu" of the Romanian Academy (INCE) as partener, during the period 2016–2018, regarding the poverty rate and the poverty in work on local, county and regional level, the model of analysis identifies structural and contextual factors and the mechanisms they influence the social development. The key variable is occupation, a concept that will be operationalized quantitatively like the rate of occupation or the number of occupied people, and qualitatively, using the type of occupation, focusing especially on jobs with high turnover rates.

This article aims to explore the relationship between the type of employment and in-work poverty, and the mechanisms through which some socioeconomic aspects influence this relationship on a local level and potentate the dynamic of social development. The analysis model includes predictors of underdevelopment, like the percentage of the population working in agriculture, reduced percentage of employees in the total employed population and aspects related to the size of the households and the geographical marginalization level of the town.

The scarcity of employment opportunities and community level poverty are factors which potentiate the development of some mechanisms which generate and maintain social underdevelopment. On the other hand, the lack of employment opportunities is compensated by practicing subsistence farming and semi-subsistence farming and local activities, these precarious activities generating work poverty.

In this theoretical and methodological context, several key variables were identified, which were used in the proposed measuring model. Among these are such concepts as vulnerable groups, main income sources in the town and their percentages, salaries, agriculture-related incomes and incomes from social transfers/services other than pensions.

Vulnerable groups identified at a local level represent one of these variables, although it is important to mention that these were also analyzed in the larger context of identifying social problems on a local level. Among the data collected at a local level through the project mentioned earlier, poverty is identified as a main social problem in most of the answers.

While poverty is identified as the second largest issue, by far the most important problem according to the representatives of local institutions is the lack of employment opportunities. This precarious employment-poverty binomial potentates the creation of certain mechanisms that generate and sustain social underdevelopment.

1. Theoretical and Conceptual Framework. Methodology. Data Sources.

The In-work poverty category includes those individuals who are employed but have a disposable income of below than 60 % of the median equivalent income of their own country.

In order to maintain the possibility of comparisons in European context "in-work poverty" is referred to in the official data reported to Eurostat as income in-work poverty. In-work poverty is generally measured using surveys dedicated to the investigation of incomes and living conditions of households/families. At European Union level, Eurostat uses the Survey of Incomes and Living Condition) investigation, which also includes data collected from Romanian National Institute of Statistics (INS).

Besides the officially agreed upon methodology using EU-SILC data, at a national level the National Institute of Statistics, in order to analyze the categories vulnerable to the risk of in-work poverty, also uses the ABF (Ancheta Bugetelor de Familie/Survey on Family Budgets) investigation.

Concepts as precarious prosperity and precarious work was developed relatively recently (Hübinger, 1996, Budowski et al. 2010; Bankoff 2001; Whelan – Maître 2007 Paugam 2000).

In Romania these preoccupations address, under the umbrella of this concepts, the relationship between atypical occupation and social vulnerability. Authors like Anita Preoteasa (2013, 2015), and Iuliana Precupeţu (2015, 2016, 2017) refine the analysis of this relationship.

In defining the concept of atypical occupation, the main characteristic is the type of employment, different from the the classic form of employees with work contracts on an undetermined period and full time payment: part time, occasional or seasonal employment; long distance employment.

Precarious occupation as a concept is relevant to the content of the employee-employer dynamic. A necessary distinction needs to be made between precarious employment and precarious jobs. (Precupeţu, 2016, Preoteasa, Ilie, 2017). Precarious employment is defined by vulnerability of the employee, high turnover jobs, limited employee rights and lack of predictability. Precarious jobs are those that are inadequately paid, monotonous and offer poor professional satisfaction. In Romania, the most ponderous form of atypical occupation is precarious occupation.

While the amount of part time jobs is low compared to the EU average, the forms of atypical occupation that are most frequently seen in Romania are those related to fields such as construction and agriculture and include occasional/ seasonal work and day labour, sustenance and semi-sustenance agriculture accounting for a rather large percentage in an European context-over 20 % of employed population.

Table 1: Comparing poverty and deprivation rate Romania –European Union for employed and outside labour force

Country	Estimated % of people below poverty line		Estimated % of people experiencing material deprivation	
	Employed	**Outside labour force**	**Employed**	**Outside labour force**
Romania	19.7 %	32.7 %	35.5 %	49 %
EU 28	9.6 %	30.5 %	12.8 %	29 %

Source: Eurofound, 2017.

Other forms of precarious occupations are very badly paid (lower than minimum) income black market jobs. Precarious employment generates the conditions for in work poverty, a situation which also depends on other aspects such as family size and how much the family depends economically the income of the employed member or members.

This analysis utilizes the results of the SIPOCA 4 project, in which I took part in 2017–2018, conducted by INCE for MMJS. The project methodology requires an indirect measure of the poverty and work poverty rates, starting with the beneficiaries of social services, identified on a local level and also from the perspective of the income bracket that the beneficiary family is in.

Complementary data sources were also integrated into the analysis, including data from INS, and research reports form MMJS and National Agency for Payments and Social Inspection (ANPIS). For the external sources of data validation, we used information collected by INS for ABS, EUSILC and AMIGO (Intergrated Survey on Population Households) in the 2016–2017 period.

Precarious occupation generates the premises for poverty in work, but this is also related to other aspects like the size of the family and the degree of economic dependence of the family upon the income of the working person/s.

The low level of the wages and the inefficiency of the social transfers other than pensions in reducing poverty are factors leading to a situation where the differences between the poverty and deprivation rate are significantly high in Romania comparing to the EU average in the case of occupied persons than in the case of unoccupied persons.

Relative poverty rate on localities, counties and regions. Relation with the poverty in work rate

In work poverty rate represents the relation in percentage between the number of occupied persons in a household whose income available on adult-equivalent (including the cost of consumption from inner resources) is inferior to the poverty limit and the total of occupied persons.

Table 2: Comparing poverty rate –in work poverty at regional level (%)

Region	Relative poverty rate	In work poverty rate
Bucuresti-Ilfov	9.3	7.3
Vest	17	14.0
Centru	19.7	14.4
Nord-Vest	18.5	16.8
Sud-Muntenia	22.7	17.1
Sud-Est	21.7	18.9
Sud-Vest Oltenia	26.5	21.1

Source: Database SIPOCA 4.

On regional level the magnitude of poverty is reflected in similar levels of poverty in work.

On county level, the compared analysis of data shows that the high values of poverty in a county are usually associated with high values of poverty in work in the respective counties, while in the counties with a high number of localities with poverty rate under the national average, the distribution of territorial administrative units (UATs) with low rates of poverty in work is not necessary similar.

In the first case, from the first 10 counties with the highest number of localities with high rate of poverty, 7 are also among the counties with the highest number of localities with highest rate of poverty in work. In the second case, only half of the counties from the first category are also in the second category.

The dispensation of poverty on UATs level is higher than on county level, confirming the hypothesis of the importance of some local, contextual factors in shaping the configuration and magnitude of the communitarian poverty.

The Nord-Est, South West Oltenia and South- East are rather homogeneous in the distribution of the localities with high poverty in work rate, and in over two thirds of the region Bucharest are localities with low rates of poverty in work.

Even though the differences rural-urban can be found also in the poverty in work rate, they are much smaller than for the poverty rate. Almost a third of the rural localities are under or near the national average of poverty in work, while over a third have a rate of poverty in work at least double than the national average.

As regards the poverty, and the poverty in work, the profiles on categories of localities are clear individualised according to their size.

The localities with a poverty rate at least double than the national average are, almost all of them, in the category of under 10.000 inhabitants, two third of the localities with over 30.000 inhabitants have a poverty rate under 10 %, and the poverty in work for almost all localities over 30.000 inhabitants and all localities over 60.000 inhabitants have a poverty rate under 10 %.

4. The analysis of the main income sources on local level from the perspective of the relation local underdevelopment- poverty in work

The analysis in this section is based on the responses to an open question from the questionnaire addressed to UATs, which intended to identify the three main sources of income on local level.

Among first 3 income sources are in similar percentage the salaries and the incomes from agriculture (both identified as main income source for almost a third of UAT). The pensions represent also one of the three income sources. The next category of sources of income hierarchy are the incomes from social transfers, other than pensions. The fact that for more than a quarter the social transfers are among the main 3 income sources represents an indicator of the magnitude of the communitarian poverty and of the high social underdevelopment on local level.

Occasional work represents the fifth most important income source; one locality in 20 identifies this source as the most important on local level.

The work abroad was identify as the most important income source in 28 UAT, and the second most important income source in other 27 localities and the third income source in 30 UAT (in total in 85 UAT the work abroad is identify as important income source).

The tourism generates incomes considered important in 40 localities.

Developed counties like Timiş, Cluj, Ilfov, and Prahova have a low percentage in incomes from agriculture.

The poorest counties like Vaslui, Teleorman, Mehedinţi, are among those with a high income from agriculture and social transfers, other than pensions.

The analysis reveal the relation between the prevalence of some income sources and poverty, respectively in work poverty.In the poorest counties the lack of employment opportunities is compensated by practicing subsistence farming and semi-subsistence farming and local activities, these precarious activities generating work poverty

Conclusions

This article explore the relationship between some characteristics of local employment oportunities, the rate of in work poverty, at the local level, and the mechanisms through which some socioeconomic aspects influence this relationship on a local level and potentate the dynamic of social development. The analysis model includes predictors of underdevelopment, like the percentage of the population working in agriculture, reduced percentage of employees in the employed population, aspects related to the size of the households and the geographical marginalization level of the town.

The scarcity of employment opportunities and community level poverty are factors which potentiate the development of some mechanisms which generate and maintain social underdevelopment.

Within this analysis model the key variable is employment. This concept is operationalized by quantitative aspects, like the occupation rate, the number of occupied persons, and qualitative aspects, like the type of occupation, focusing on the precarious work.

The high rate of precarious employment in Romania represents one of the main factors leading to a significant high rate of poverty in work comparing to EU, but also to former socialist countries in EU.

References

Ahrendt, D./Sandor, E./Jungblut, J.-M./Anderson, R./Revello, A./Schwiertz, S.: Policies addressing in-work poverty in the EU, Eurofound, 2017

Vlad, I. V., (coordinator): Strategia de dezvoltare a României în următorii 20 de ani, vol 1–3, Editura Academiei Române, 2016.

Budowski, M./Tillmann, R./Keim, W./Amacker, M.: Conceptualizing Precarious Prosperity: Empirical and Theoretical Elements for Debate, International Journal of Comparative Sociology 51 (4), 2016, p. 268–288.

Paugam, S.: Le salarié de la précarité.Presses Universitaires de France, Paris, 2000.

Precupeţu, Iuliana: Strenuous objective life circumstances and subjective responses: perceptions of well-being when living in poverty and precarious prosperity in Romania, CalitateaVieţii, no. 2/2016, p. 99–117.

Precupeţu, Iuliana/Vlase, Ionela/Preoteasa Ana Maria, Beyond Poverty in Romania: An Analysis of Household-Level Factors of Poverty and Precarious Prosperity, Sociológia 47/2015, no. 3.

Preoteasa, Ana Maria., 2013: Atypical Occupations between Conjuncture and Flexibility. In: Mărginean, Ioan (coord.): Territorial Profiles of Life Quality in Romania, Bucharest, Romanian Academy Publishing House, pp. 139–149.

Preoteasa, Ana Maria., 2015: Precarious Work, Solution for Vulnerable Population in Rural Area. Evidence for a Qualitative Survey, Calitatea Vietii no.1/2015.

Preoteasa, A, M/Sieber, R/Budowski, M/Suter C: Household Role in Coping with Precarious Work.Evidence from Qualitative Research in Urban Romania and Switzerland, Social Change Review vol. 14(2): 177–201, 2016;

Preoteasa, Ana Maria: Munca precară, soluţie pentru populaƚia vulnerabilă din mediul rural rezultate dintr-o cercetare calitativă, Calitatea Vieţii, nr. 1/2015, p. 36–59

Preoteasa, Ana Maria/Ilie, Simona: O perspectivă asupra ocupării atipice: România în comparaţie europeană, Calitatea Vieţii, nr. 3/2017, p. 243–266

Whelan, C. T./Maître, B., 2013: Material Deprivation, Economic Stress, and Reference Groups in Europe: An Analysis of EU-SILC. European Sociological Review 29 (6), 1162–1174.

Whelan, C. T. – Maître, B., 2010: Comparing Poverty Indicators in an Enlarged EU. European Sociological Review 26 (6), 713–730.

Data Sources

INS: Baze de date ABF, EUSILC.

Ministry of Labour and Social Justice (MMJS) – Database collected during the project "Implementation of a public policy design system in the field of social inclusion for the Romanian Ministry of Labour and Social Justice" / "Implementarea unui sistem de elaborare de politici publice în domeniul incluziunii sociale la nivelul MMJS", cod SIPOCA 4, selected on Operational Programme Administrative Capacity, co-financed by the European Union from European Social Fund, MMJS-INCE, 2016–2018.

Maria Livia ȘTEFĂNESCU[1], *Stefan ȘTEFĂNESCU*[2]

[1] Senior Researcher, Research Institute for Quality of Life, Romanian Academy, Email: livia.stefanescu@gmail.com

[2] Senior Researcher, Research Institute for Quality of Life, Romanian Academy, Email: stefanst@fmi.unibuc.ro

Romania and Republic of Moldavia – Differences and Similarities between Some Socio-Human Values Accepted by their Respective Populations

Abstract *In the present study are analyzed the opinions of the Romanian and Moldavian people concerning the importance in real life of several socio-human values V1-V6 as: family, friends, leisure time, politics, work or religion. The research is based on an interview applied to both populations, the resulted surveys being statistically significant at the national level.The studied variables V1-V6 are categorical ordinal ones. For this reason the statistical models must be in concordance with the type of the used variables. So, to discriminate between the opinions of the people from the two countries we applied the classical stochastic relation of order. We also used an agglomerative hierarchical procedure for grouping the variables V1-V6 in clusters. Finally is emphasized qualitatively the responses structure of the individuals from Romania and Republic of Moldavia. Concluding, we do not have major structural dissimilarities between the Romanian and Moldavian systems with the variables V1-V6 as components.*

Keywords: *Life values, survey, statistical model, Romania, Moldavia*

Introduction

The major objective of the present research is to do comparisons between the opinions of Romanian and Moldavian peoples concerning six life values V1-V6 and lastly to emphasize possible similarities between both countries. We took into consideration the following variables V1-V6: Family (F), friends (M, mates), leisure Time (T), Politics (P), Work (W) and Religion (R).

Concretely, this study is based on the application of an identical questionnaire to evaluate the opinions of Moldavian and Romanian individuals in the same period of time. The data were obtained from the international research World Values Survey (WVS, http: www.worldvaluessurvey.org) applied in 2005 and 2006. To discover the internal structure of the system {V1-V6} we proposed two statistical procedures which use a stochastic relation of order between distributions of the variables V1-V6 and also the application of an agglomerative hierarchical procedure for clustering the objects V1-V6.

1. Literature review

A lot of things are considered very important for the world people (Sayer 2011, Yorke 2010). But it is not so easy to join together all the life values accepted by different populations. More difficult seems to establish a pecking order of the items selected from such a given list. In general the hierarchization process based on multiple criteria is very complex since we must bear in mind a lot of things and principles which are often interpretable. After that, the life values vary in time, depend on the selected population, the specific group taken into consideration, the domain of activity of the persons, the concrete environment or on the cultural knowledges of the individuals.

Pursuing the opinions of different populations, a lot of sociological studies consider the family and the religion on the first places in the list of life values. But the family (Jagger & Wright 1999) and also the religion values (Gerten & Bergmann 2012) suffered multiple changes during the time. For example, in the last time for family are imposed new laws and are discussed many ethics problems (Brighouse & Swift 2014; Jagger & Wright 1999).

From these huge number of options, in our current study we operated only with the variables V1-V6 defined previously. We mentioned here that the entities V1-V6 are categorical ordinal variables. Having in mind this last aspect, to avoid interpretation errors, we must choose adequate statistical procedures for a high-quality evaluation of the real process (Agresti 2010). In the literature, for the statistical studies are used very often only direct interpretations of the raw frequencies for V1-V6. In our present study we proposed two statistical models adapted to categorical ordinal variables. Firstly we promoted the standard stochastic relation of order between the distributions of ordinal data (Le Breton & Peluso 2009). Moreover, we grouped the variables V1-V6 by using the Euclidean dissimilarities between their distributions (Everitt et al. 2011; Xu & Wunsch 2009).

Concluding, we will not treat the variables V1-V6 as independent entities. Our study will be oriented to discover the inner structure of the system *S* having the variables V1-V6 as components. The main result which was obtained asserts that the system {V1-V6} is similar enough for Romania and Republic of Moldavia.

2. The primary data

The data used in this analysis were taken from the international research WVS (World Values Survey) which was promoted in 1981. Up to 2014 there were developed many WVS research activities belonging to the waves 1–6. In the years 2017–2018 is initiated the procedure to collect data for the last wave 7 of this ambitious study (http: www.worldvaluessurvey.org). To compare efficiently the opinions of Romanian and Moldavian populations about life values V1-V6 we must

Table 1: Frequencies of the respondents from Romania in the wave 5

Var.	Country	Not at all important (code 1)	Not very important (code 2)	Rather important (code 3)	Very important (code 4)	Total	DK + NA	Total
F	RO	5	12	219	1509	1745	31	1776
M	RO	71	402	829	428	1730	46	1776
T	RO	87	400	761	464	1712	64	1776
P	RO	644	703	308	72	1727	49	1776
W	RO	50	111	619	950	1730	46	1776
R	RO	42	125	568	1013	1748	28	1776

Source: file: F00002805-WV5_Data_Romania_2005_spss_v_2015_04_18.zip, Word Values Survey Database, wave 5 (2005–2006), Romania, http: www.worldvaluessurvey.org

select those WVS surveys applied in close years. More precisely, for the years 2005 and 2006 we will operate with the following two files: RO_2005 (Romania, wave 5, 1776 respondents, year 2005), MD_2006 (Republic of Moldavia, wave 5, 1046 respondents, year 2006). We mention that WVS research has complete information regardin-g wave 6 for Romania but does not contain any information about the same wave 6 in Moldavia.

Positively, the whole WVS research is based on the same questionnaire. Concretely, in the subsequent we will analyze the following question of this common questionnaire: "For each of the following, indicate how important it is in your life: Family (F), Friends (M – Mates), Leisure time (T), Politics (P), Work (W), Religion (R)". Every questioned person from the surveys has six variants to choose from, that are: Not at all important (code 1), Not very important (code 2), Rather important (code 3), Very important (code 4), Don't know (DK), No answer (NA). Our statistical models will use effectively only the individual opinions (response codes 1–4).

Tables 1 and 2 present the frequencies computed in wave 5 for Romanian and Moldavian response codes 1–4.

It is difficult to make comparisons between Romania and Moldavia when are used only the non-normalized numerical frequencies from Tables 1–2. For this reason it is necessary to work with percentages. So, in the subsequent we will interpret all the percentages of the effective response codes 1–4. We intend to compare both these countries taking into consideration just the life values V1-V6. Figure 1 and Figure 2 illustrate the distributions of the categorical ordinal variables V1-V6 defined for Romania and Moldavia.

After a quick interpretation of the bar lengths in the graphics from Figure 3 and Figure 4 we remark the following aspects:

Table 2: Frequencies of respondents from Republic of Moldavia in wave 5

Var.	Country	Not at all important (code 1)	Not very important (code 2)	Rather important (code 3)	Very important (code 4)	Total	DK + NA	Total
F	MD	3	10	163	869	1045	1	1046
M	MD	26	227	549	242	1044	2	1046
T	MD	48	289	483	218	1038	8	1046
P	MD	290	485	220	48	1043	3	1046
W	MD	15	87	488	454	1044	2	1046
R	MD	69	213	430	332	1044	2	1046

Source: file: F00002800-WV5_Data_Moldova_2006_spss_v_2015_04_18.zip, Word Values Survey Database, wave 5 (2005–2006), Moldova, http: www.worldvaluessurvey.org

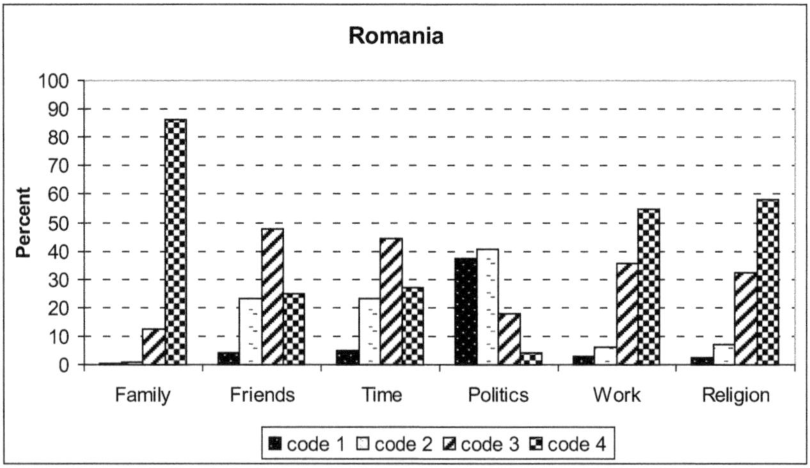

Figure 1: The distributions of the variables V1-V6 for Romanian respondents

- The Family is extremely appreciated in the opinions of Romanian and Moldavian peoples (to see the largest percent values in Figures 3–4 for the code 4, that is a "very important" positive evaluation).
- Contrasting, the lowest values belong to Politics. More exactly, in Figures 3 and 4 Politics has the greatest percentages at the codes 1 and 2 of both interviewed populations. These codes characterize "not at all important" and respectively "not very important" opinions.

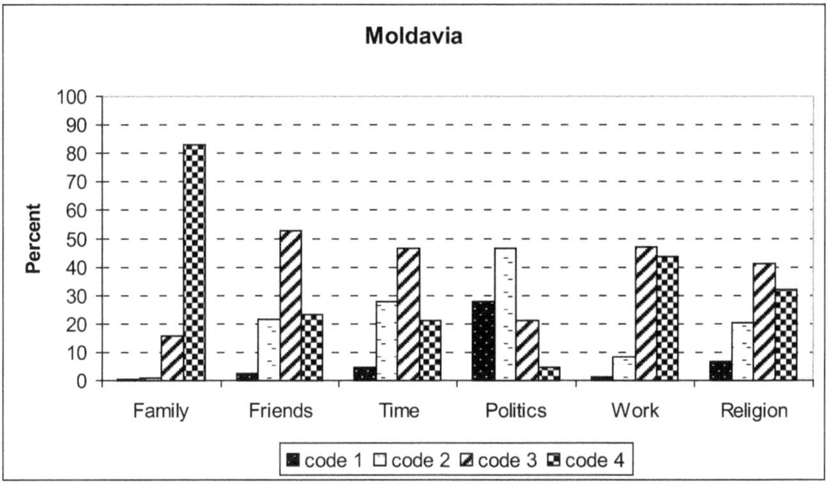

Figure 2: The distributions of the variables V1-V6 for Moldavian respondents

- If we compare the general aspect for the images of all distributions from Figure 3 and Figure 4 we observe straight away that the shapes of the corresponding distributions for all life values V1-V6 are not so different. So, we can assert that Romanians and Moldavians have similar opinions about these six studied life values.

This kind of approach, based often exclusively on percentages and on diverse graphics attached to these percentages, is customarily used in many technical papers. We intend to extend this simplified approach by proposing different statistical models to validate without doubt some work assumptions. For example, to compare rigorously the distributions of the categorical ordinal variables V1-V6 we can select one metric from many other dissimilarity measures which are known in the literature (for example, city block metric, Euclidean dissimilarity, angular separation measure, chi-square metric, etc., Everitt et al, 2011). In the subsequent, for discovering the internal structure of the system {V1-V6} we will use the customary stochastic relation of order "<" between any two distributions of categorical ordinal variables V1-V6. A classification procedure will also be applied.

3. The structure of the system {V1-V6}

Analyzing the possibility to have a stochastic relation "<" of order (Le Breton & Peluso 2009) between two distributions of the categorical ordinal variables V1-V6 we obtain the results mentioned in Table 3 for Romania. Besides the "<" symbol we used supplementary more notations: X # Y means that the variables X and Y are not comparable; by X > Y we also designate the case Y < X.

Taking into consideration all the dependence relations “<“ which can exist between the components V1-V6 of Table 3, we build in Figure 3 the graph which characterizes the structure of the system {V1-V6} for Romania.

After a similar approach, but using the data collected from Republic of Moldavia, we build Table 4 and Figure 4. Comparing Figure 6 with Figure 8 we call the attention to the subsequent aspects:

- In Romania and as well as in Moldavia the most favorable opinions of the individuals regard Family.
- For both studied countries Politics has the lowest evaluation received from the corresponding populations.
- Only for Romania, the distributions of the variables Friends and Leisure time cannot be comparable.
- In Moldavia the situation is a little different. More exactly, the distribution which evaluates the Moldavians ‘opinions about Religion cannot be compared with the distribution of Friends or with the variable Leisure time.
- Contrary to Romania, in Republic of Moldavia the Religion is less appreciated then Work. A new statistical model could achieve a better distinction between the Work and Religion in both studied countries.
- We have to remark the special position of Religion in Moldovia. New investigations are absolutely necessary regarding the role of the Church in the two countries.

Table 3: The stochastic relation of order between the variables V1-V6 in Romania

F = F	F > M	F > T	F > P	F > W	F > R
M < F	M = M	M # T	M > P	M < W	M < R
T < F	T # M	T= T	T > P	T < W	T < R
P < F	P < M	P < T	P = P	P < W	P < R
W < F	W > M	W > T	W > P	W = W	W < R
R < F	R > M	R > T	R > P	R > W	R = R

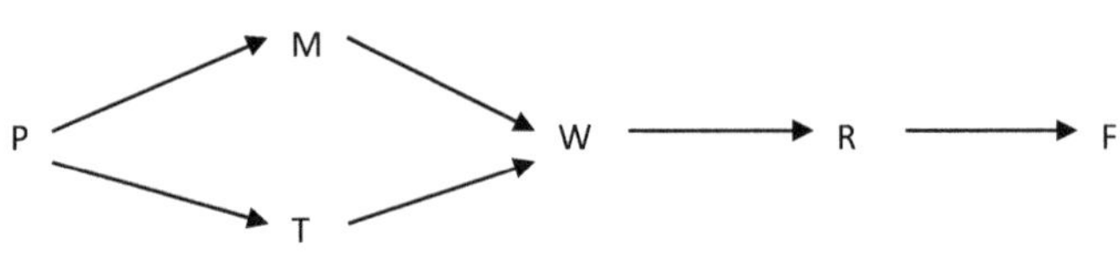

Figure 3: The structure of V1-V6 system in Romania

Table 4: The stochastic relation of order between the variables V1-V6 in Republic of Moldavia

F = F	F > M	F > T	F > P	F > W	F > R
M < F	M = M	M > T	M > P	M < W	M # R
T < F	T < M	T= T	T > P	T < W	T # R
P < F	P < M	P < T	P = P	P < W	P < R
W < F	W > M	W > T	W > P	W = W	W > R
R < F	R # M	R # T	R > P	R < W	R = R

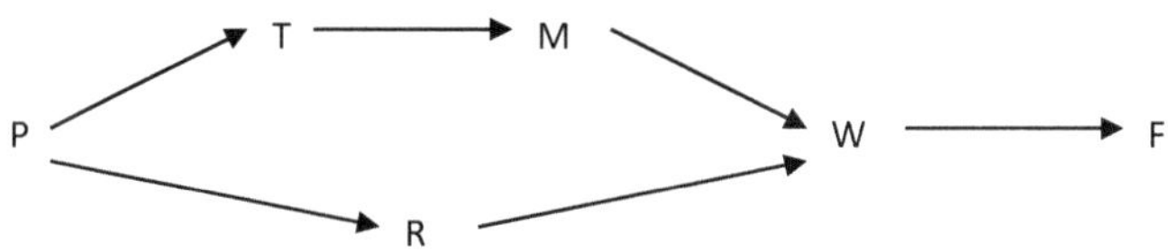

Figure 4: The structure of V1-V6 system in Republic of Moldavia

4. Grouping the variables V1-V6

Using the hierarchical agglomerative procedure of classification based on the Euclidean distances between the objects V1-V6 (Everitt et al. 2011, Xu & Wunsch 2009) we deduce the dendrograms shown in Figure 5 (for Romania) and in Figure 6 (for Republic of Moldavia). Interpreting the two dendrograms we will stipulate how are chosen the objects V1-V6 when we want to operate with two, three or four number of clusters. For the following comparisons, we will denote by R or M the Romanian clusters, respectively the Moldavian groups.

Concretely, for Romania we have the following variants of classifications for the objects V1-V6:

- The case of two clusters R_{21}, R_{22}:

R_{21} = {Politics}; R_{22} = {Family, Friends, Leisure time, Work, Religion}.

- The case of three clusters R_{31}, R_{32}, R_{33}:

R_{31} = {Politics}; R_{32} = {Family}; R_{33} = {Friends, Leisure time, Work, Religion}.

- The case of four clusters $R_{41}, R_{42}, R_{43}, R_{44}$:

R_{41} = {Politics}, R_{42} = {Family}, R_{43} = {Friends, Leisure time}, R_{44} = {Work, Religion}.

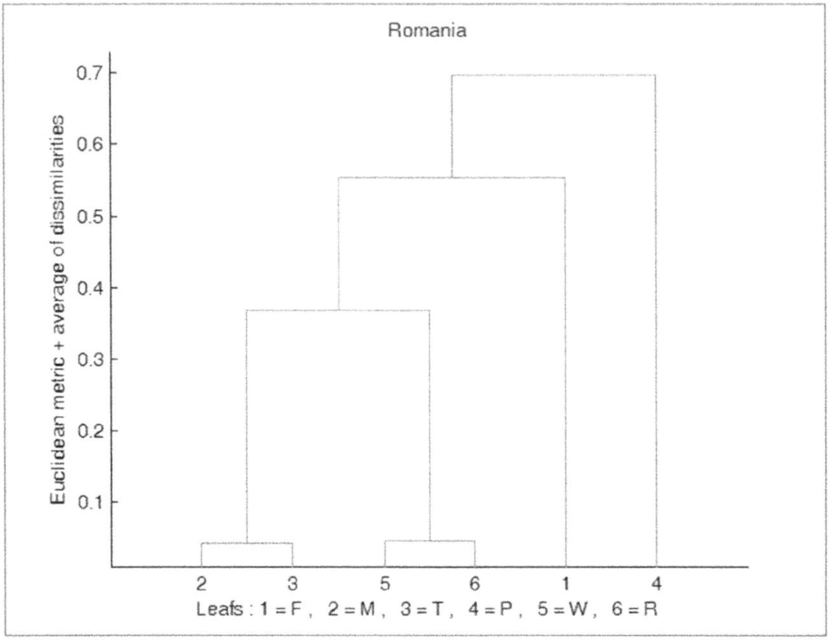

Figure 5: The dendrogram of the objects V1-V6 for Romania

For Republic of Moldavia the previous classifications are not always the same. More exactly:

- The case of two clusters M_{21}, M_{22}:

  M_{21} = {Family}; R_{22} = {Friends, Leisure time, Politics, Work, Religion}.

- The case of three clusters M_{31}, M_{32}, M_{33}:

  M_{31} = {Politics}; M_{32} = {Family}; M_{33} = {Friends, Leisure time, Work, Religion}.

- The case of four clusters M_{41}, M_{42}, M_{43}, M_{44}:

  M_{41} = {Politics}, M_{42} = {Family}, M_{43} = {Work}, M_{44} = {Friends, Leisure time, Religion}.

By interpreting Figure 5 and Figure 6 we remark:

- Observing the preceding clusters obtained for Romania and for Moldavia we remark the special role played by the variables Family and Politics. A discrepancy between these two variables was already underlined by the previous statistical model based on a stochastic order.

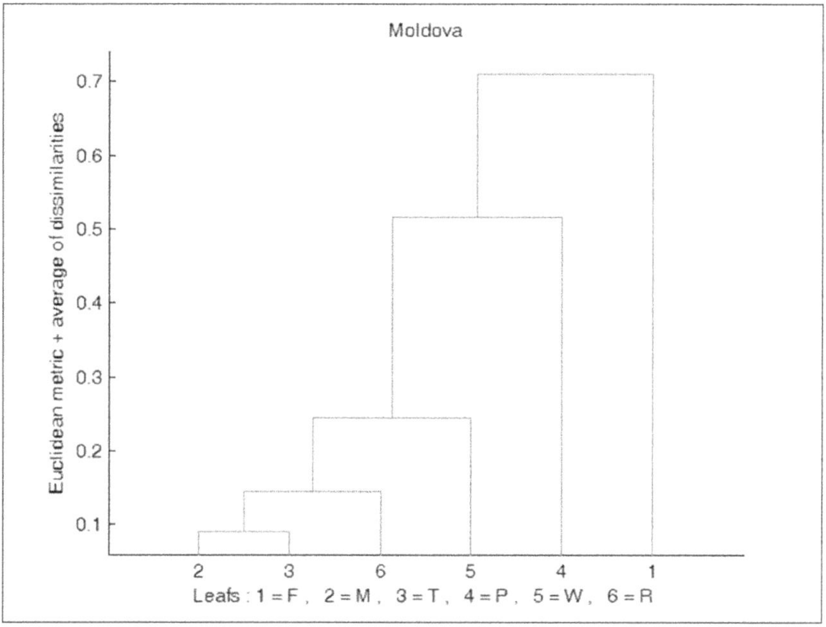

Figure 6: The dendrogram of the objects V1-V6 for Republic of Moldavia

- Work has a different evaluation in Romania compared with Moldavia. This situation changes indirectly the perception about Religion in Republic of Moldavia. A new statistical model will establish the ratio between Work and Religion in Romania and Moldavia.
- Compared with Romanians, the Moldavian respondents have similar opinions about Friends, Leisure time and Religion.
- We deduce the same classification for Romania and Republic of Moldavia if we consider only three clusters (to compare the elements of the clusters R_{31}, R_{32}, R_{33} with the corresponding groups M_{31}, M_{32}, M_{33}).

Conclusions

The opinions of the Romanian people are very similar with the attitudes of Moldavians about these six life values V1-V6 (Family, Friends, Leisure time, Politics, Work, Religion. The two proposed statistical models, which are based on the stochastic order relation (Figure 6 and 8) and respectively on usual classification procedures (Figure 9–10), confirm this idea. The structure of the system {V1-V6} is similar in Romania and Republic of Moldavia. Moreover, we obtained in Romania and also in Moldavia the same three clusters R_{31}, R_{32}, R_{33} of the objects V1-V6. This classification emphasizes the special antagonist role of Family versus Politics.

For the future we intend to extend these types of results by considering different groups selected from the two populations (for example: men / women, the size of the town of residence or poor versus rich persons).

References

Agresti, Alan: Analysis of ordinal categorical data. John Wiley & Sons: New Jersey, 2010, second edition.

Brighouse, Harry/Swift, Adam: Family values - The ethics of parent-child relationships. Princeton University Press: New Jersey, 2014.

Everitt, Brian S./Landau, Sabine/Leese, Morven/Stahl, Daniel: Cluster analysis. John Wiley and Sons: London, 2011, fifth edition.

Gerten, Dieter/Bergmann, Sigurd (Eds.): Religion in environmental and climate change - Suffering, values, lifestyles. Continuum: Londom, 2012.

Jagger, Gill/Wright, Caroline (eds): Changing family values. Routledge: London, 1999.

Le Breton/Michel/Peluso, Eugenio (2009): "Third-degree stochastic dominance and inequality measurement". J. Econ. Inequal, 7, pp.249–268.

Sayer, Andrew: Why things matter to people - Social science, values and ethical life. Cambridge University Press: New York, 2011.

Yorke, Jon (Ed): The right to life and the value of life - Orientations in law, politics and ethics. Ashgate: Birmingham City University, 2010.

Xu, Rui, Wunsch, Donald C.II.: Clustering. John Wiley & Sons: New Jersey, 2009.

Gabriela-Mariana IONESCU[1]

[1] PhD student at The School of Advanced Studies of the Romanian Academy, SCOSAAR, Email: gabrielaionescu13@gmail.com

The Economic Polarization

Abstract *Generally, social justice has a sphere of interest that goes beyond the economy, acquiring vocation and moral connotations, or related to the aspects of the freely and democratic functioning of society. The present paper focuses on the economic area only and, even less, on the economic polarization. In this perspective, the aim of the paper is to put into logical, institutional and functional relationships the concept of social justice and the concept of economic polarization. In the first part, the paper examines the two concepts defining their main definitions and attributes, and in the second part examines how the economic polarization of society influences the model of social justice, on the one hand, and on the other hand, the model of social justice influences the economic polarization evolution. The research methodology is a logical and institutional type, addressing exclusively the qualitative aspects of the two concepts and institutions. In conclusion, the paper finds that the two phenomena (social justice and economic polarization) are found on what is called a coevolutive relationship (mutual causal determination).*

Keywords: *social justice, economic polarization, coevolutive relationship*

Introduction

Social justice treats aspects of the influence of social inequalities on individual well-being arising from the effects of changes in society (e.g.: effects of the new wage law, effects of pension law, diminishing child-raising allowance, transfer of social contributions from employed to the employer, etc.).

The increase in economic inequalities, the economic polarization of society, which refers to the asymmetric distribution of current income, requires that the distribution of the economic product inside society should get a balance between needs and merit.

Social justice (through its two categories commutative justice and distributive justice, (Hayek 1998, p. 247) provides an institutional and normative framework for monitoring and controlling social inequalities felt by individuals. This paper aims to study some qualitative aspects of economic polarity from the perspective of the model of social justice.

1. Literature review

The literature in this field does not use abstract theoretical and conceptual approaches, but only empirical, local and factual approaches. Our work, however, aspires to carry out a non-contextual examination of the problem of economic polarization.

2. Conceptual delimitations

The concept of social justice (defined on the basis of sufficient predicates that the author has identified in his research so far) is a distributive artifact that verifies the criterion of equity. The three predicates of sufficiency[1] are as follows:

- P1 - institutional origin - is of a normative nature, the character of the norm gives it the conservative capacity of maintaining, of permanence.
- P2 - distributive device of the economic product - part of the individuals or homogeneous categories of individuals based on the intrinsic quality of human beings protected by the state through the implicit conditions of the social contract.
- P3 - fair distribution - proper distribution of the economic product to society.

The pursuit of social justice has a dual purpose:

- Social - seeks to ensure reparatory measures until the social demotivation threshold appears.
- Economic - distribution of the economic product on the basis of distributional procedures.

The concept of economic polarization is a dichotomous concept. This concept works not only in the economic field (when it comes to income or wealth) but also in other social areas (when it comes to the center, periphery, urbanization, trained and non-trained in the field of education, polarization of centers of political and military power) and even in the field of natural sciences (polarization of light).

Economic polarization refers to an asymmetric distribution of either current income (salary, profit, etc.) and / or wealth. In the literature, the relevance of economic polarization based on current income in relation to its relevance on the basis of wealth has not yet been resolved. In our opinion, the criterion of choosing between economic polarization based on current income and economic polarization based on wealth should be the persistence of economic polarization. By persistent economic polarization we understand that polarization that does not have significant oscillations over a time horizon of scientific interest or public policy interest. However, economic polarization based on wealth is by far the right one

1 Predicates of sufficiency are attributes, characteristics of a concept.

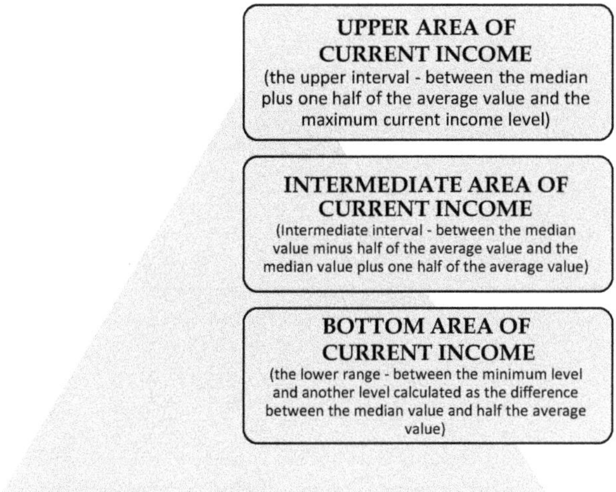

Figure 1: The hierarchy of current income in society
Source: author's work.

to meet this criterion. However, a softer concept of economic polarization, namely that based on current income, will be discussed in this paper. The concept of economic polarization based on current income will be mentioned, throughout the paper, abbreviated, using the EPCI[2] abbreviation.

In relation to the EPCI, we need to look for the following questions:

a) From what degree of current income asymmetry we are talking about the EPCI?
b) Is there a persistence duration that is significant in the case of the EPCI?
c) Is there a typology of the EPCI that is theoretically relevant, i.e. relevance from the perspective of public policies?

Some conceptual clarifications in response to the above questions:

a) Theoretically we consider that the hierarchy of current income in society contains three areas (numerical intervals) of scientific interest and public policies, as followings:

b) As regards the calculation of the degree of asymmetry of economic polarization in principle, three calculation methods can be used:

   I. By reporting the average value of the upper area to the mean value of the lower area.

2 EPCI - the concept of economic polarization based on current income.

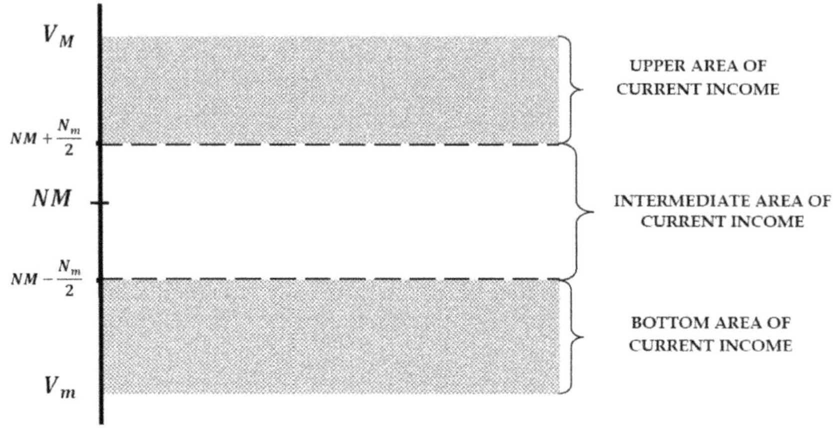

Figure 2: The graph of the numerical ranges of current revenue - the method based on the median

Source: author's work.

II. By reporting the median value of the upper zone to the median value of the lower zone.
III. By reporting the minimum level of the upper zone to the minimum level of the lower zone, respectively by reporting the maximum level of the upper zone to the maximum level of the lower zone (in this case there is not a degree of asymmetry but an interval that contains the degree of asymmetry)

We propose that from the three methods to choose the method based on the median, taking in the consideration that the concept of economic polarization is rather a positional concept (similar to the concept of median) than dimensional one (analogous to the average). It remains to be elucidated the issue of the numerical value of the degree of asymmetry over which we consider that we are dealing with economic polarization. As this issue is not a theoretical but an empirical one, it will not be addressed in this work. The following figure shows the numerical ranges of numerical income using the median-based method.

According to the above graph, the lower area of the current income is between:

$$Z_{Inf} : \left[V_m, NM - \frac{N_m}{2} \right] \tag{1}$$

where: Z_{Inf} = the lower area of the current income, V_m= the minimum value, NM = the median level, N_m = the average level

The current income intermediate zone (Z_{Intrm}) is in the range:

SOCIAL POSITIONING / INTELLECTUAL POSITIONING	FAVORED (F)	UNFAVORED ($\bar{F}$)
MERITED (commutative justice)	JFSQ	$J\bar{F}SQ$
DUE (distributive justice)	$J\bar{F}SQ$	$J\bar{F}SQ$

Figure 3: The logical "square" of social justice[3]
Source: author's work.

$$Z_{\text{Intrm}} : \left[NM - \frac{N_m}{2}, NM + \frac{N_m}{2} \right] \tag{2}$$

The upper current income area (Z_{Sup}) as shown in figure 3, is in the range:

$$Z_{\text{Sup}} : \left[NM + \frac{N_m}{2}, V_M \right] \tag{3}$$

where V_M= the upper value of the range

In order to discuss about the duration of persistence, which allows us to qualify the phenomenon of economic polarization, we will have to identify a duration in which a certain degree of asymmetry (i.e. a certain economic polarity) is preserved, it has not varied (i.e. it is irreversible). Although this issue can be dealt also theoretically, in the present paper we will not address this issue, we propose a duration of this irreversibility from an empirical perspective, namely a 6-month period, taking into account that in the economy there are phenomena whose stability / irreversibility is also considered for a 6-month period (coverage of imports through exports, granting of unemployment benefit for the smallest period of contribution to social contributions). Thus, if the degree of asymmetry calculated for a state of economic polarity increases and comes back to the initial value within the 6-month period, we will have to consider that the economic polarity has not changed.

3 This author's scheme is part of the scientific communication titled „The Relationship of complexity, sustainability, diversity in social justice", supported at the International Scientific Conference "
„Accounting and Finance - Universal Business Languages", 3rd edition, organized by University „Constantin Brâncoveanu", Piteşti, March this year.

c) From the perspective of general, non-contextual typologies, we propose the following typologies of economic polarity and economic polarization:
   - According to the intensity of economic polarity we can have:
   1) Severe economic polarity - where the degree of asymmetry exceeds a threshold considered socially sustainable.
   2) Neutral economic polarity - where the degree of asymmetry is approximately equal to the degree of asymmetry that ensures sustainability.
   3) Ambiguous economic polarity - where the degree of asymmetry that ensures sustainability is below a certain threshold.

In connection with this typology we can say that from a functional point of view, the neutral economic polarity is the desirable one, and from the moral point of view, the ambiguous economic polarity is the desirable one.

- By the intensity of economic polarization:
  1) Genuin economic polarization - refers to the case where the degree of asymmetry increases.
  2) Economic depolarization (reverse polarization) - where the degree of asymmetry decreases.
  3) Invariant economic polarization - if the degree of asymmetry does not change.

In conclusion, it can be said that the economic polarity measures a state of an analyzed system and the economic polarization refers to the process of reaching the state of economic polarity. For example: an increase in economic polarity is generated by an economic polarization process, while a decrease in economic polarity is generated by a process of economic depolarisation.

3. Social justice and economic polarization

Is social justice the only tool to deal with economic polarization?

Economic polarization can also be "administered" outside a model of social justice, namely through economic or social public policy measures that are not subsumed under an ideal or objective of social justice. For example, under the pressure of trade unions, measures can be taken to raise income, or to modify taxation, independently of the pursuit of a certain degree of asymmetry in economic polarity. This situation can be termed "social competition" between different socio-professional categories or sectoral categories (Elster 2013, p. 83). However, the absence of an ideal of social justice in dealing with economic polarization may introduce vulnerabilities and unsustainability in the medium and long term as a result of ignoring the economic fundamentals (Rawls 2011, p.255–263) of changes in current income in society.

Regarding the virtues of treating economic polarization from the perspective of social justice, both types of social justice (commutative justice and distributive justice) must contribute to maintaining economic polarity in its neutral category.

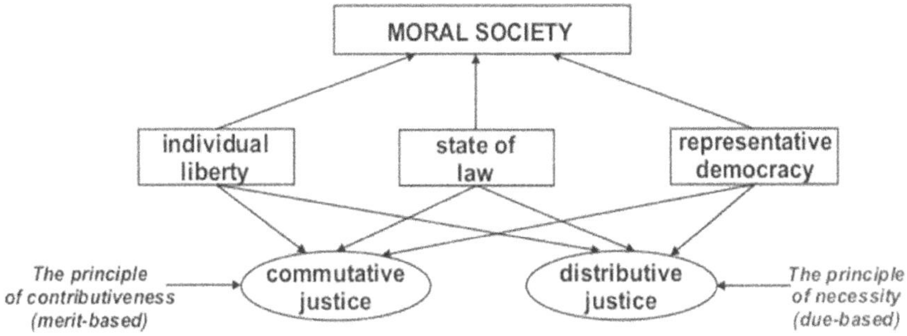

Figure 4: Algorithm for the establishment of social justice
Source: author's work.

Thus, commutative justice must ensure the meritocratic distribution of the economic product so as to ensure the economic sustainability of society, and distributive justice must ensure a due redistribution (not based on merit), thereby ensuring social sustainability. These considerations can be organized into a "logical square" (figure 3).

The "logical square" refers to the logical formulas, which are applicable to the four cases resulting from the combination of two types of social justice (commutative justice, respectively distributive justice) with two categories of persons (favored or unfavored from the economic point of view). What is noteworthy is that in the case of distributive justice, the two categories of people are subject to the same logical formula, because what they receive as redistribution, the disadvantaged are to be collected from the favored persons.

The structure and ways through which social justice is designed and on the other hand is implemented is based on the algorithm shown in Figure 4. Social justice has as a last resort (i.e.: endness) the realization of a moral society. But a moral society is based on three pillars: individual freedom, representative and constitutional democracy, and the rule of law.

On the basis of these pillars, social justice will be able to ensure, guarantee, and defend the principle of contributory participation in the distribution of the economic product of society. From a graphical point of view, this algorithm for the establishment of social justice is as follows:

Conclusions

Although economic polarization is also treatable by public policies that do not appeal to distributive justice, that is, it is treatable by public policies which, through norms (Hollis 2001, pp. 171–172), require the observance of the meritocratic principle in distributing the economic product of society, inherently more or less extensive situations arise, where a certain redistribution is necessary to maintain economic polarity within economically and socially sustainable limits. In this context, however, the work advocates for framing the effect of applying the two components of social justice to a "mix" that places economic polarity within what has been called in this work of neutral economic polarity.

From the conceptual point of view, we consider that the quantitative areas of economic polarity must be delimited simultaneously from the point of view of position (by taking into account the average of the current income at the society level) and dimensionally (by taking into account the average current income at the level of society).

The next step in research on this issue will be that, in an abstract (not based on empirical) basis, an exclusive quantitative interval of neutral economic polarity would be set, which would be the main benchmark for economic policies aimed at manage the phenomenon of economic polarity (and polarization).

References

Elster, J. – Social behavior. Fundamentals of explanation in social sciences, All Publishing House, Bucharest, 2013.

Hayek, F. – Constitution of Freedom, European Institute Publishing House, Bucharest, 1998.

Hollis, M. – Introduction to the Philosophy of Social Sciences, Trei Publishing House, Bucharest, 2001.

Rawls, J. – A Theory of Justice, Publishing House Alexandru Ioan Cuza, Iaşi, 2011.

Cătălin BERESCU[1]

[1] Research Institute for Quality of Life, Email: catalinberescu@gmail.com

Living Tomorrow. Housing in Romania in the Next 100 Years

Abstract *The paper provides an analysis of the housing stock of Romania, its structure and current problems then, drawing on the current state of affairs, aims to formulate a number of tenets that could serve as a starting point in addressing some of the issues that were identified in regards with the current state of affairs through a policy design process.*

Keywords: *Housing, urban policies, planning*

Introduction

Despite being regarded as a key domain and almost always being mentioned in major research reports and policy documents, housing is not the subject of intense research in Romania, nor of explicit policies. The first housing strategy of Romania was only put together as a draft proposal at the end of 2016 and it is still in the process of being adopted. In the meantime, in most reports and documents that aspire to build a comprehensive view about the field, housing is often reduced to "houses", and quite as often to „new houses". Constructions and infrastructure, as major investment domains, tend to focus the attention of the public to the market value of the houses and that of the policy makers to the industry that produces them, leaving less space for debate for the issues related to the management of the existing housing stock.

Actually, this problem appears to be wiped off the public agenda following the mass privatization of the public housing stock in the early '90s and the abandonment of the rent control policies in the early 2000s. The plethora of data referring to the variation of price, either on the real estate market or the rental market tells us an important thing about a particular piece of property and its relationship with all the others but does not tell enough about the quality of life in particular areas of our cities and almost nothing about what kind of policies would be needed to improve it. Actually, throughout history, the major decisions that changed housing had less to do with financial issues and more to do with major political decisions, revolutionary health policy changes or major infrastructural operations.

Romania managed to produce close to 1.263.000 housing units after the revolution of 1989, yet the situation of housing is far from ideal. Smaller cities and rural settlements are collapsing, major cities are struggling with congestion and lack of affordable housing, the architectural patrimony is neglected, slums and ghettos are on the rise. Most of the problems arise from the lack of public policies, or from their incomplete design and from the undisturbed faith of most policy makers in the power of the free market to also regulate the housing market. Any comparison with any industrialized nation shows that the housing market is heavily regulated by the state and that many of the problems that we have are related with the management of the communalities that are featured in any housing unit, in any housing area and in every settlement. My analysis tries to put together a set of problems that were identified by different authors and by the authorities in regards with the housing situation in Romania and to add brief remarks on what kind of approaches are needed in order to deal with those issues.

Most of the data is drawn from the National Institute for Statistics report on housing from 2016, from the Ministry of Regional Development and Public Administration documents but also from a variety of European documents that pertain to housing policies.

1. Literature review

It is only natural that various disciplines would tackle housing by favouring a particular point of view, sometimes narrowing the area, other times widening the perspective. Economists tend to favour the real estate perspective, sociologists draw on household inventories and lifestyle, geographers on residential mobility and regional variety while architects, as it is to be expected from the designers of the houses, tend to consider most of the aspects of everyday life as part of housing. A complete ethnography of what people do based on the fact that they live in a house is quite impossible, still, we can collect a variety of topics that are of relevance for contemporary Romania and place them in a larger context.

According to one study that aimed to rank the issues associated with the quality of life in Britain (Phillips, 2006, p. 34) the cost of owner-occupied and rented housing and quality of public rented housing was on the fourth position after crime, health and environment and above education, employment and cost of living. This self-defined scale might be subjective and local but it first tells us that all of the above are interconnected and that, in a society with a higher economic level, where the cost of living represents a much smaller share of the income, housing is more important than in Romania. In this respect, the huge ownership rate in Romania is a critical asset for low income families and creates a form of social protection. Not being exposed to high rents, like in most of the developed economies, is a key factor that can explain how so many Romanians can survive with such low incomes. The downfalls of this situation reside in the lack of capacity to maintain the quality of the housing unit, visible at first sight in the way so many houses look, but deeper, in their structural and technical state that is steadily advancing to dilapidation. For a lot of the poorest families of Romania, the status of ownership is not an economic achievement but a form through which the state got rid of underperforming assets.

Another major problem associated with the huge ownership rate in Romania is the actual very low level of residential mobility. Even though this has a historic explanation and, for specific social categories is within normal parameters (Suditu, 2011), its current state has a strong impact on the economy. Long commutes and lack of workforce are directly linked with the imperative to buy a house and the poor alternatives that are offered by the rent market. The very idea that residential mobility affects traffic is not really considered in planning documents, most of them still rely on functional zoning schemes that imagine residential areas connected through various forms of transportation with technological parks.

Mobility is another key political and planning issue. As Jaime Lerner, the famous architect and mayor of Curitiba, Brazil, one of the best managed cities of the planet and a favourite example of a successful public transportation revolution says "Every child needs to know the design of his or her own city". He further mentions that "the mobility system, which is not only a system of transport; it's the whole understanding of the city" (Mau, 2004, p.59). Obviously, this cannot be done without a basic understanding of the basic premises of commonality.

There is a visible decline in small cities, particularly severe in mono-industrial ones that is dramatically emphasised by the decrease of the Romanian population. "Shrinking cities" is the concept that was extensively covered by research in Germany and worldwide (Oswalt, 2004) and in the US (Weaver et. al, 2017), and this shows not only a global phenomena that takes the same form in various economic environments but one that has a specific impact in post-socialist countries. Largely ignored by the Romanian authorities because of its lack of political value, shrinking is not addressed by any current policy. During the last years, research was also conducted in Romania and one of the findings is that, out of the 320 Romanian cities, 161 of them lost at least 20 % of the population and some of them even as much as 59 % (Constantinescu, pp.26).

2. Housing in Romania

According to the analysis provided by the National Housing Strategy, housing in Romania is affected by the following processes:

a) One of the fastest population decrease rates in the world – as a result, the proportion of empty houses is on the rise. What is less visible and possibly not well reflected in statistics is the abandonment of individual construction projects. The building sites spread all over the peri-urban areas of our cities and villages, in areas with little or no infrastructure, started by families that are at work abroad and that have little perspectives of coming back are a vivid depiction of bad investment and population decrease. The small cities are drastically affected. In spite of the hegemonic discourse of development and of the over-optimistic local strategies that were produced by every municipality in the last decade, the reality is that we are now facing a major shrinking cities process. Even Bucharest, a city that is not affected by shrinkage and that looks more and more congested every day has a 0 % population growing perspective, after loosing around 10 % of the population in favour of Ilfov.

b) A strong degradation of the housing stock – this affects primarily the multi-storey buildings, with a major seismic threat for the buildings built before 1977 but also the socialist era collective dwellings that do not reach current standards. It is also very visible in what regards the architectural patrimony, the post-industrial landscape (Chelcea, 2008), and the dereliction of retrocessed buildings (Chelcea, 2002).
c) A lack of public housing – Romania is one of the champions of privatization and, as a result has nowadays no means to deal with vulnerable groups, being them evicted people, victims of natural disasters or economically excluded categories.
d) An unofficial (grey) and unregulated rental market.
e) A volatile construction market that was heavily affected by the financial crisis.
f) A rapid and unregulated expansion of the territory of the cities with a highly negative impact on the environment, lack of resilience and traffic issues.

All there require a reform of the housing policy in Romania and represent a possible opportunity for a better allocation of resources, a more solid policy of investments, more safety and resilience and, last but not least, providing housing for the population of Romania.

The last three national censuses shows us an increase in the number of dwellings, this growth, combined with the decrease of the population led to a general improvement of the aggregated indicators of housing quality. Nevertheless, the distribution of the growth tells a different story, nothing changed for the poor people significantly, all the growth was confiscated by the upper-middle class.

A third of the urban population lives now in cities that have under 50,000 inhabitants, places that are not well equipped for urban life, have little economic activities and in which there is no perspective for improvement. These are the reservoirs of external migration from which the fertile, better educated population of Romania leaves towards the West.

3. Living Tomorrow in Romania

During the nineteenth century, the major epidemics showed that poor housing, rudimentary sewage and lack of clean drinking water required communities to act collectively (Phillips, 2006, p.55). This idea was not lost but it underwent a significant ideological split. The massive and radical infrastructure improvements and the innovations in public health lead to two, apparently opposite, actually complementary phenomena. One is the extraordinary aggregation of houses in the contemporary city. In any aspect: personal security, food security, access to any kind of services, culture and welfare, etc. a high density city provides a better quality of life then a low density one and it is better equipped and functionally superior to any other form of human settlement.

Despite the collective imaginary and the popular culture depictions of the big city as a place ruled by gangs and dirty politicians, it is nowadays safer to live in the centre of New York or Bucharest then in an American suburbia or in a peri-urban Romanian zone. There is a lot a lot of concern from the part of city dwellers in regards with the air quality, noise level or pollution and a constant, if not rising, high level of anger however, the very reason of why they live in the city is the obviously higher quality of life that most contemporary cities offer. This is the main reason why urbanization is the growing trend.

The opposite view that animates the current urban imaginary is the suburban sight. Contemporary urban centres function today in migration terms in a similar way in which rich countries attract, reject and select migrants from poor countries. Push and pull factors can be observed and measured in their complex mechanic that makes cities like Lyon or Naples function so well. At a smaller scale, Timişoara and Cluj operate in the same manner. A problem that can be foreseen is one that arrives from the reading of the local planning documents for cities like Tîrgu Mureş or Călăraşi, that imagine themselves as working in the same manner. Commuters have a poor life quality and they make the life of the other inhabitants miserable. Still, the dream of a house on the ground, with a barbecue and a dog is the most powerful incentive for the contemporary middle class. Its impact on the environment, urban life and economy will continue to be huge.

Alternative models of housing are not here yet but we should look at what is going on more mature markets and in societies that had enough time to test them. One is that of the micro-apartments, and anyone can see Romanian entrepreneurs trying to build smaller apartments. The trend is correct, the implementation is just wrong, again, the need to properly define the minimal needs and standards is a collective and a professional business, not an economic game. Another one is cohousing, a model developed by various communities around Europe that provides an alternative to market led development and offers a model of self management and cooperation and a sense of living together that can bring together people with common interests and a similar philosophy of life. What is really interesting about this cooperative housing is that it can be seen in both rural and urban areas and was adopted by rich and by not so rich groups.

A third alternative is that of The Tiny House Movement, an American trend for independent, off the grid, sustainable housing, extremely small housing units, minimalistic, often on wheels that are adopted by a large number of US citizens in their struggle to secure themselves a decent and very affordable shelter and to secure their independence. Alternative models are not suitable for everybody. It is obvious that we need first to have the major policies put in place. But it worth a try to have a bit of diversity in our options.

Conclusions

Romania has major structural problems in what regards the housing stock. The first one is the lack of public housing. Social housing almost disappeared and this led to the creation of a large number of slums and informal settlements. People living in extreme poverty are non-productive members of the society and the general view and political preference to address poverty through education or vocational training or other soft measures has almost no impact on the integration of the poor into society.

A second one is the one of the rent market. Unregulated rental market keeps renting in the grey area and has an impact on: a) local taxes; b) both landlords and tenants protection; c) vulnerable families. One solution could be the establishment of social rental agencies, bodies that could intermediate between landlords and tenants.

A much more complex one is that of the territorial management. Investments in unsustainable housing units (poorly built, oversized, disconnected from infrastructure, placed in flooding areas, inneficient in energetic terms, placed in remote areas etc.) are a sign of bad economic decisions for which not only the families are to blame but mostly the authorities that promote mediocre development models.

References

1. Chelcea, Liviu. Grupuri marginale în zone centrale: gentrificare, drepturi de proprietate și acumulare primitivă post-socialistă în București. Romanian Sociology, XI new series no. 3–4/2000, pp. 51–67. accesed 25.03.2018, retrieved from http://www.arsociologie.ro/images/stories/sr/articles/sr_2000_3–4/SR_2000[III]2(3-4)_51-67_Chelcea.pdf
2. Chelcea, Liviu. Bucureştiul postindustrial. Memorie, dezindustrializare şi regenerare urbană. Polirom, Iaşi, 2008.
3. Cities of Tomorrow (DG Regio report). Accesed 25.03.2018, retrieved from http://ec.europa.eu/regional_policy/archive/conferences/urban2014/doc/report_cities_of_tomorrow_2014.pdf.
4. Cities of tomorrow - Challenges, visions, dys-visions as seen by cities (Institute Destree report). Accessed on 25.03.2018, retrieved from http://ec.europa.eu/regional_policy/sources/docgener/studies/pdf/citiesoftomorrow/citiesoftomorrow_foresight.pdf.
5. Decizia etapei de încadrare a Strategiei Naţionale a Locuirii a Ministerului Mediului din 08/01/2018, accessed 25.03.2018, retrieved from http://www.mdrap.ro/userfiles/decizie_10011.pdf
6. Hall, Peter: Great Planning Disasters. University of California Press, Berkley, 1982.
7. Hamdi, Nabeel. The Placemaker's Guide to Building Community. Earthscan, London, 2010.
8. Iagăr, Elena Mihaela (ed). Fondul de locuinţe. Anul 2016. Institutul Naţional de Statistică, Bucureşti, 2017.
9. Lerner, Jaime: On public transport. In: Mau, Bruce (ed). Massive Change. Phaidon Press, London, 2004.

10. Păun Constantinescu, Ilinca. Shrinking cities în România. O abordare contemporană a contracției și declinului urban, PhD thesis, University of Urbanism and Architecture Ion Mincu, Bucharest, 2013.
11. Phillips, David. Quality of Life. Concept, Policy and Practice. Routledge, London, 2006.
12. Roberts, Peter/Sykes, Hugh. Urban Regeneration. Sage, London, 2008.
13. Suditu, Bogdan. Mobilități și strategii rezidențiale urbane și periurbane. Studiu de caz – București. Editura Universității din București, București, 2011.
14. Strategia Națională a Locuirii (proiect). Accesed 25.03.2018, retrieved from http://www.mmediu.ro/app/webroot/uploads/files/2017-01-13_Strategia_Nationala_a_Locuirii_2016-2030.pdf
15. Tosics, Ivan. Governance challenges and models for the cities of tomorrow. Accesed 25.03.2018, retrieved from http://ec.europa.eu/regional_policy/sources/docgener/studies/pdf/citiesoftomorrow/citiesoftomorrow_governance.pdf
16. Vranken, Jan. Social Challenges of Cities of Tomorrow. Accesed 25.03.2018, retrieved from http://ec.europa.eu/regional_policy/sources/docgener/studies/pdf/citiesoftomorrow/citiesoftomorrow_social.pdf
17. Weaver, Russel/Baghchi-Sen, Sharmista/Knight, Jason/Frazier, Amy. Shrinking Cities. Understanding urban decline in the US. Routledge, New York, 2017.

Cristina DEL-CASTILLO[1], *Encarnación GONZÁLEZ-VÁZQUEZ*[2], *Jaime GIL-LAFUENTE*[3], *Alicia BLANCO-GONZÁLEZ*[4]

[1] Professor, University Rey Juan Carlos, Email: cristina.delcastillo@urjc

[2] Professor, European Academy Of Management And Business Economics, Email:egzlez@uvigo.es

[3] Professor, University of Barcelona, Email:j.gil@ub.edu

[4] Professor, University Rey Juan Carlos, Email: alicia.blanco@urjc.es

Spanish Universities' Reputation as a Determinant of the Country´s Competitiveness

Abstract *Reputation has been considered as a crucial intangible asset for organizations´ success and survival. Well-reputed institutions will benefit from having better access to resources, competitive advantages and strong relationships with stakeholders, as well as from being more protected when facing a crisis. Spanish Public Universities operate in a highly competitive sector where factors such as globalization has extended this competition to international levels. Therefore, managing their reputation is a crucial matter. Higher Education Rankings have been considered as a tool to increase reputation due to stakeholders´ expectations on the positions occupied by universities. However, apart from the benefits that good positions in rankings can offer higher education institutions, there are many critics and other aspects to take into consideration when managing reputation. The aim of this paper is to understand the relevance of managing reputation for higher education institutions and to analyze the outputs of being present in higher education rankings. To follow this purpose, a review of the literature on the field will be carried out and a descriptive analysis of the effect of appearing in three international higher education rankings will be developed.*

Keywords: *Reputation, Universities, Rankings*

Introduction

Competition in the Higher Education sector has been increasing over the last years. Nowadays, new global trends have forced universities to compete at national and international levels to attract top students and professors. (Plewa, Ho, Conduit, & Karpen, 2016; Christensen and Gonitzka, 2017; Hemsley-Brown, Melewar, Nguyen & Wilson, 2016) In addition, governments funding has decreased, what has motivated that most Spanish Public Universities are losing students in favor of private universities. Furthermore, despite the existing criticism (Barron, 2017), stakeholder´s and society expectations regarding the scores hold by Universities in quality and employability rankings are increasing, augmenting the pressure for these organizations.

Reputation has been considered as a crucial intangible asset for organizations´ success and survival. Well-reputed institutions will benefit from having better access to resources, competitive advantages and strong relationships with stakeholders, as well as from being more protected when facing a crisis. (Fombrun, 1996; Turban & Greening, 1997; Deephouse, 2000; Milgrom &Roberts, 1982) Under this current scenario faced by higher education institutions, the correct management of reputation can be a crucial element for Spanish Public Universities in order to survive and succeed in the market, as well as to obtain a more competitive position (Hemsley-Brown et al., 2016; Plewa et al., 2016; Christensen & Gornitzka, 2017; Farrugia & Lane, 2013).

Within some of the tools used by universities to increase their reputation level and, as a result, attract more talented students and professors, higher education rankings can be highlighted. They are of vital importance in higher education sector. (Wilson & Thomas, 2012; Martensson & Richtner, 2015) Rankings are a technology of visibility and simplification, their main purpose is to aid decision making for stakeholders. (Barron, 2017) They serve as guarantees of the quality and prestige of the institutions, and they are considered as one of the most important sources of legitimacy from the stakeholders' point of view. (Wedlin, 2011; Gioia & Corley, 2002; MArtensson & Richtner, 2015) However, other relevant factors should be taken into consideration when managing reputation, since other elements can also affect stakeholders' decision towards one university.

The objective of this research is to explain the relevance of managing reputation for higher education institutions given the high competitive environment in which they operate as well as to analyze the outputs that Spanish Public Universities obtain by being present in international higher education rankings. In order to do so, a review of the literature on reputation and higher education sector will be carried out, followed by a descriptive analysis of the effect of appearing in three international higher education rankings will be developed, and finally the main conclusions will be presented.

1. Literature review

1.1 Reputation in the Higher Education Sector

Corporate reputation has been considered as a valuable intangible asset for organizations´ survival and success due to its relationship with positive performance in the market. (Rindova, Williamson & Petkova, 2015) Well-reputed institutions will have a competitive advantage compared to those that do not within their industries (Fombrun & Shanley, 1990) due to its unique and difficult to imitate characteristics (Fombrun & Van Riel, 1997; Roberts & Dowling, 2002) that differentiate them and create entry barriers for future competitors. (Feldman, Bahamonde & Velasquez Bellido, 2014)

Organizations with good reputation levels could benefit from a great variety of aspects. Within the literature, some of the identified benefits of having a good reputation relate to aspects such as being able to lower the company´s costs (Deephouse, 2000; Fombrun, 1996), benefiting from the possibility of charging higher prices (Deephouse, 2000; Fombrun & Shanley, 1990; Fombrun, 1996; Rindova et al, 2005), attracting better employees (Fombrun, 1996; Turban & Greening, 1997) as well as investors (Srivastava, McInish, Wood & Capraro, 1997) or having better access to capital markets. (Fombrun & Shanley, 1990)

In relation to the concept of reputation, scholars highlight the issue of the inexistence of a unified definition. One of the most common reputation definitions is the one provided by Fombrun (1996), who defined reputation as "the perceptual representation of past actions and future expectations of a company that describes the firm´s overall appeal to all its key constituents when compared with other rivals. It is the stakeholder´s perceptions about the ability that an entity has to create value in comparison to its competitors. (Deephouse, 2000; Elsbach & Kramer, 1996; Fombrun & Shanley, 1990; Fombrun, 1996; Rindova et al, 2005) Analysing a firm´s past actions is a key element for the reputation judgment, since history has been used many times to predict the way organizations might behave in the future. (Bitektine, 2011)

The competition level in the higher education sector has been experimenting important increases over the years. Globalization, internationalization, changes in the market as well as reduction in government funding have increased the pressure for the institutions in the sector. (Hemsley-Brown et al 2016; Verčič, Verčič, & Znidar, 2016) Moreover, global trends have increased the pressure for universities regarding the positions that they hold in national and international rankings in their aim to attract international students and professors.

Under this scenario, institutions in the HE sector have been adopting more business-like practice in their management. (Veloutsou, Paton, & Lewis, 2005) Universities understood that the correct management of intangible assets such as reputation is a key element for attracting and retaining stakeholders such as students, professors, economic resources etc (Hemsley-Brown, 2016; Plewa, et al, 2016).

In the higher education context, the benefits of having a good reputation due to its intangible character can became even more relevant. (Suomi, 2014; Jevons, 2006) Reputation could serve as a quality sign as well as an indicative of the institution's capacity to respond to customer´s needs in the correct manner (Nguyen & LeBlanc, 2001) and, as a result, will reduce uncertainty (Rindova et al., 2005) for stakeholders in their decision-making processes (Hemsley-Brown, 2016). Therefore, obtaining a positive reputation will determine the university´s survival given the competition in the sector. (Aula & Tienari, 2011; Alves & Raposo, 2010)

When managing reputation, researchers have highlighted the importance of rankings in the higher education sector. (Wilson & Thomas, 2012; Mårtensson & Richtnér, 2015) For stakeholders, rankings serve as a technology of visibility and simplification, their main purpose is to aid decision making processes when selecting a university to engage with (Barron, 2017). They serve as guarantees of the quality and prestige of the institutions, and they are considered as one of the most important sources of legitimacy from the stakeholders' point of view. ((Wedlin, 2011; Gioia & Corley, 2002; Mårtensson & Richtnér, 2015) On the other hand, many critics to rankings exist in the literature due to the complicated environment they create for universities, the methods they use or their preferences towards some disciplines over others. (Barron, 2017; Amsler & Bolsmann, 2012; Hazelkorn, 2011)

2. Sample, Methodology and Results

This research is developed through a descriptive analysis of the position hold by Spanish Public Universities in three international higher education rankings. The selected rankings where those considered more relevant and prestigious within the field: Times Higher Education Ranking (THE), Shanghai ARWU and QS Ranking.

As it has been previously stated, nowadays, higher education rankings represent a relevant tool for the reputation of universities. Stakeholders´ decisions towards universities are determined by the positions that the institutions hold in rankings. Therefore, despite the existing criticism in terms of the risk of promoting stereotypes as well as using limited criteria for their definition, universities need to consider them as important elements. In Table 1 the list of Spanish Public Universities is presented with the position that they hold on the THE Ranking, Shanghai Arwu Rankings and the QS Ranking.

From all the Spanish Public Universities only eighteen are present in the three selected international higher education rankings. Seven universities appear at least in two of the three international rankings. Eight universities have presence in only one ranking and the rest of them, eighteen universities, do not appear in any of the selected rankings.

Furthermore, the university holding the best position in the The Ranking is University Autónoma of Barcelona, which appears in position 117, followed by University Pompeu Fabra in position number 140. In the Shanghai Arwu Ranking, University of Barcelona, University Pompeu Fabra and University of Granada appear ranked between the 201–300 positions. Finally, if analyzing QS Ranking, University of Barcelona in position 156, followed by University Autónoma of Madrid ranked in the 187 position. The rest of the Spanish Public Universities appear on relatively low positions.

In addition, as part of the descriptive analysis of the selected Spanish Public Universities, an analysis of the degree of internationalization has been carried out. First of all, this analysis was developed by identifying the number of international students and faculty members that came to Spanish Public Universities over the last years. Figure 1 shows the evolution of the international students and Figure 2 represents the international faculty members.

Table 1: Spanish Public Universities in International Rankings

Spanish Public Universities	The Ranking	Shanghai Arwu	QS Ranking
University Autónoma of Barcelona	117	301–400	195
University Autónoma of Madrid	351–400	301–400	187
University Carlos III of Madrid	601–800		281
University Complutense of Madrid	501–600	301–400	233
University of A Coruña	801–1000	601–700	801–1000
University of Alcalá	601–800		551–600
University of Alicante	801–1000		
University of Almería	801–1000		
University of Barcelona	201–250	201–300	156
University of Burgos			
University of Cádiz			
University of Cantabria			
University of Castilla-La Mancha	801–1000		801–1000
University of Córdoba		701–800	
University of Extremadura			
University of Girona			
University of Granada	501–600	201–300	501–550
University of Huelva			
University of Jaén	601–800		
University of La Laguna	601–800	601–700	
University of La Rioja			
University of Las Palmas de Gran Canaria			
University of León			
University of Lleida			
University of Málaga			
University of Murcia	601–800	701–800	801–1000
University of Oviedo	601–800	501–600	801–1000
University of Salamanca	601–800	701–800	601–650
University of Santiago de Compostela	601–800	301–400	601–650
University of Sevilla	601–800	501–600	601–650

(*continued on next page*)

Table 1: Continued

Spanish Public Universities	The Ranking	Shanghai Arwu	QS Ranking
University of Valladolid			
University of Vigo	601–800	501–600	
University of Zaragoza	601–800	501–600	461–470
University of País Vasco	601–800	401–500	651–700
International University of Andalucía			
International University Menéndez Pelayo UIMP			
University Miguel Hernández of Elche		601–700	
U.N.E.D			
University Pablo de Olavide			
University Politécnica of Cartagena			
University Politécnica of Cataluña	401–500	601–700	275
University Politécnica of Madrid	601–800	601–700	491–500
University Politécnica of Valencia	501–600	401–500	373
University Pompeu Fabra	140	201–300	296
Public University of Navarra			
University Rey Juan Carlos	601–800		801–1000
University Rovira i Virgili	401–500	601–700	
University of Illes Balears		501–600	
University of Valencia	501–600	401–500	551–600
University Jaume I de Castellón		401–500	

Source: Own elaboration

As it can be perceived in Figure 1 the number of international students has increased by 25 % and the percentage that international students represent over the total students in Spanish Public Universities has increased from 5.07 % to 6.17 %. In Figure 2, the number of international faculty members has also increased, and the percentage that they represent compared to the total faculty members in Spanish Public Universities remains almost the same, representing a 1.98 %.

Furthermore, the distribution of the international students in Spanish Public Universities by Autonomous Community is presented in Figure 3. The Autonomous Community that attracts a higher number of students is Cataluña with 27.7 % of the international students, followed by the Community of Madrid with

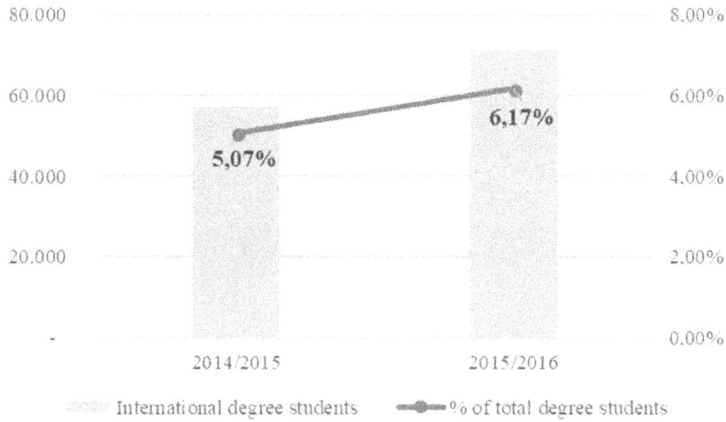

Figure 1: International students and percentage of international students over total students in Spanish Public Universities

Source: Ministerio de Educación, Cultura y Deporte.

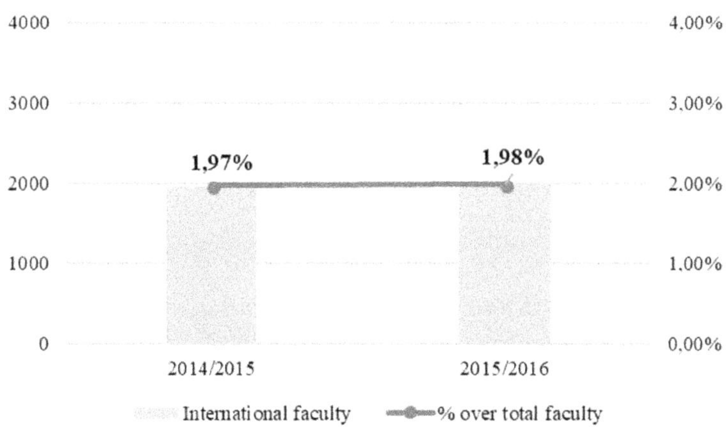

Figure 2: International faculty members and percentage of international faculty members over total faculty members in Spanish Public Universities

Source: Ministerio de Educación, Cultura y Deporte

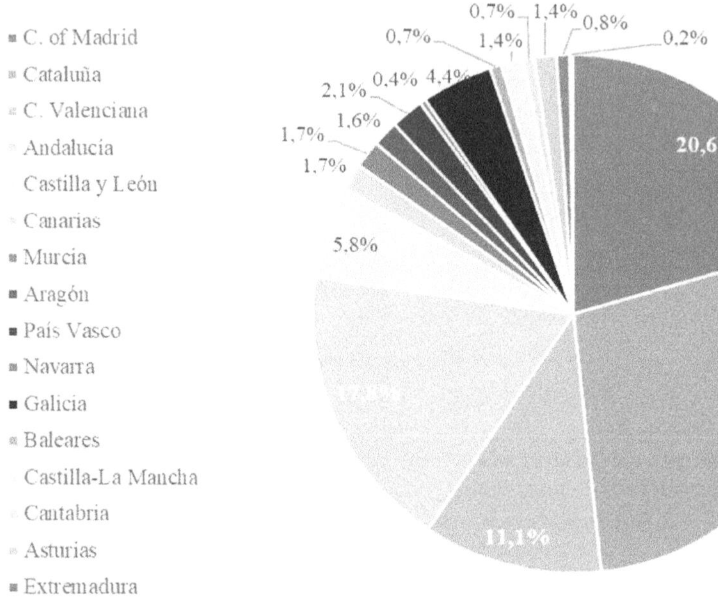

Figure 3: International students' distribution by Autonomous Community
Source: Ministerio de Educación, Cultura y Deporte.

20.6 %. The third and fourth position is occupied by Andalucía with 17.8 % and Community of Valencia with 11.1 % respectively.

3. Conclusions

Competition in the higher education sector has increased over the last years. Spanish Public Universities need to compete at national and international levels to attract talented students and professors. Under these circumstances, managing reputation can be a crucial element for public universities´ success in their markets. Within the tools used in the higher education sector to gain reputation, rankings can be highlighted. Stakeholders use the information included in rankings to make their decision regarding which university to attend. Despite de existing criticism (Barron, 2016) in terms of the criteria to rank universities, their effect on universities by promoting inequality and exclusion (Amsler and Bolsmann, 2012; Hazelcorn, 2011; West 2009), it is a fact that universities holding high positions in them can benefit from several positive aspects.

After analyzing Spanish Public Universities´ presence in THE Rankings, Shanghai Arwu Ranking and QS Ranking, it can be concluded that the positions hold by them are not very positive. Only eighteen are present in the three selected international higher education rankings and other 18 are not even present in one of the rankings. However, even though the positions occupied by Spanish Public Universities in international rankings are not high, the level of international students and faculty members they attract has been increasing over the years. In the case of international students, this increase can be reflected in the number students studying in Spanish Public Universities, but also in the percentage that international students represent form the total students in these universities. Based on this analysis it could be said that stakeholders consider other factors apart from position in rankings when selecting a university and destination to study aboard.

On the other hand, when analyzing the international students′ distribution by Autonomous Community there is a positive relationship between the number of universities from each Autonomous Community present in the selected rankings and the percentage that they hold from the total of international students studying in Spanish Public Universities. In the case of Cataluña, the relationship appears in a clear manner, since it is the community with more universities ranked in the three rankings, as well as the one whose universities′ hold the best positions, and they represent the highest percentage of international students from the total studying in Spanish Public Universities (27,7 %). The Community of Madrid represents 20,6 % of the international students and it counts with 3 universities ranked in the three international rankings. A similar situation happens with Andalucía and the Community of Valencia, that represent 17,8 % and 11,1 % of the students respectively and count with 2 universities in the three rankings each one of them. Under this scenario, the positive effect that rankings can have on a university′s attractiveness towards its stakeholders and as a result on its reputation appears clearly. All together, the four main Autonomous Communities in Spain in terms of attracting international students to their public universities represent 77,2 % of the total students coming to Spanish public universities, and they count with 11 of the 18 universities listed in the three international rankings.

In conclusion, due to the existing competition, higher education institutions need to manage their reputation in order to obtain more competitive positions in the market. Rankings might serve as an efficient tool to attract stakeholders and to increase its reputation level, however, it is important to consider and to identify which other factors are determinant in stakeholder′s decision processes when selecting a university to engage with, since, as in the case of Spanish Public Universities their level of attractiveness for international students and professors was positive despite the diverse positions that they held in international rankings.

References

Alves, Helena, and Mário Raposo. The Influence of University Image on Student Behaviour. International Journal of Educational Management, vol. 24, no. 1, 2010, pp. 73–85, doi:10.1108/09513541011013060.

Amsler, Sarah S., and Chris Bolsmann. University Ranking as Social Exclusion. British Journal of Sociology of Education, vol. 33, no. 2, 2012, pp. 283–301, doi:10.1080/01425692.2011.649835.

Aula, Hanna-Mari, and Janne Tienari. Becoming World-class? Reputation-building in a University Merger. Critical Perspectives on International Business, vol. 7, no. 1, 2011, pp. 7–29, doi:10.1108/17422041111103813

Barron, Gary R. S. The Berlin Principles on Ranking Higher Education Institutions: Limitations, Legitimacy, and Value Conflict. Higher Education, vol. 73, no. 2, 2017, pp. 317–33, doi:10.1007/s10734-016-0022-z.

Bitektine, Alex. Toward a Theory of Social Judgments of Organisations: The Case of Legilimacy, Reputation, and Status. Academy of Management Review, vol. 36, no. 1, 2011, pp. 151–79, doi:10.5465/amr.2009.0382.

Christensen, Tom, and Åse Gornitzka. Reputation Management in Complex Environments—A Comparative Study of University Organizations. Higher Education Policy, vol. 30, no. 1, 2017, pp. 123–40, doi:10.1057/s41307-016-0010-z.

Deephouse, David L. Media Reputation as a Strategic Resource: An Integration of Mass Communication and Resource-Based Theories. Journal of Management, vol. 26, no. 6, 2000, pp. 1091–112.

Elsbach, Kimberly D., and Roderick M. Kramer. Members' Responses to Organizational Identity Threats: Encounterin.g and Countering the Business Week Rankings. Administrative Science Quarterly, vol. 41, no. 3, 1996, p. 442, doi:10.2307/2393938.

Farrugia, Christine A., and Jason E. Lane. Legitimacy in Cross-Border Higher Education: Identifying Stakeholders of International Branch Campuses. Journal of Studies in International Education, vol. 17, no. 4, 2013, pp. 414–32, doi:10.1177/1028315312464379.

Feldman, Percy Marquina, et al. A New Approach for Measuring Corporate Reputation. Revista de Administração de Empresas, vol. 54, no. 1, 2014, pp. 53–66, doi:10.1590/S0034-759020140102.

Fombrun, C. J., & Van Riel, C. B. The Reputational Landscape. Corporate Reputation Review, vol. 1, no. 1, 1997, pp. 5–13, doi:10.1057/palgrave.crr.1540008.

Fombrun, C. Reputation. 1996

Fombrun, C., and M. Shanley. What'S in a Name? Reputation Building and Corporate Strategy. Academy of Management Journal, vol. 33, no. 2, 1990, pp. 233–58, doi:10.2307/256324.

Gioia, Dennis A., and Kevin G. Corley. "Being Good versus Looking Good: Business School Rankings and the Circean Transformation from Substance to Image." Academy of Management Learning & Education, vol. 1, no. 1, 2002, pp. 107–20.

Hazelkorn, Ellen. 29 Measuring World- Class Excellence and the Global Obsession with Rankings 1. Handbook on Globalization and Higher Education, vol. 2050, 2011, pp. 497–516.

Hemsley-Brown, Jane, et al. Exploring Brand Identity, Meaning, Image, and Reputation (BIMIR) in Higher Education: A Special Section. Journal of Business Research, vol. 69, no. 8, 2016, pp. 3019–22, doi:10.1016/j.jbusres.2016.01.016.

Jevons, C. Universities: A Prime Example of Branding Going Wrong.Journal of Product & Brand Management, vol. 15, no. 7, 2006, pp. 466–67.

Mårtensson, Pär, and Anders Richtnér. What Parameters Do Students Value in Business School Rankings? Journal of Higher Education Policy & Management, vol. 37, no. 6, 2015, pp. 646–58, doi:10.1080/1360080X.2015.1102821.

Milgrom, Paul, and John Roberts. And Entry Deterrence. Journal of Economic Theory, vol. 312, no. 2, 1982, pp. 280–312.

Nguyen, Nha, and Gaston LeBlanc. Image and Reputation of Higher Education Institutions in Students' Retention Decisions. International Journal of Educational Management, vol. 15, no. 6, 2001, pp. 303–11, doi:10.1108/EUM0000000005909.

Plewa, C., et al. Reputation in Higher Education: A Fuzzy Set Analysis of Resource Configurations. Journal of Business Research, vol. 69, no. 8, 2016, pp. 3087–95.

Rindova, Violina P., et al. Being Good or Being Known : An Empirical Examination of the Reputation. The Academy of Management Journal, vol. 48, no. 6, 2005, pp. 1033–49, doi:10.5465/AMJ.2005.19573108.

Roberts, Peter W., and Grahame R. Dowling. Corporate Reputation and Sustained Superior Financial Performance. Strategic Management Journal, vol. 23, no. 12, 2002, pp. 1077–93, doi:10.1002/smj.274.

Srivastava, Rajendra K., et al. Part IV: How Do Reputations Affect Corporate Performance?: The Value of Corporate Reputation: Evidence from the Equity Markets. Corporate Reputation Review, vol. 1, no. 1, 1997, pp. 61–68, doi:10.1057/palgrave.crr.1540018.

Suomi, Kati. Exploring the Dimensions of Brand Reputation in Higher Education – a Case Study of a Finnish Master's Degree Programme. Journal of Higher Education Policy and Management, vol. 36, no. October, 2014, pp. 646–60, doi:10.1080/1360080X.2014.957893.

Turban, D. B., and D. W. Greening. Corporate Social Performance and Organizational Attractiveness To Prospective Employees. Academy of Management Journal, vol. 40, no. 3, 1997, pp. 658–72, doi:10.2307/257057.

Veloutsou, Cleopatra, et al. Consultation and Reliability of Information Sources Pertaining to University Selection. International Journal of Educational Management, vol. 19, no. 4, 2005, pp. 279–91, doi:10.1108/09513540510599617.

Verčič, Ana Tkalac, et al. Exploring Academic Reputation – Is It a Multidimensional Construct? Corporate Communications: An International Journal, vol. 21, no. 2, 2016, pp. 160–76, doi:10.1108/CCIJ-01-2015-0003.

Wedlin, Linda. Going Global: Rankings as Rhetorical Devices to Construct an International Field of Management Education. Management Learning, vol. 42, no. 2, 2011, pp. 199–218, doi:10.1177/1350507610389683.

Wilson, David C., and Howard Thomas. The Legitimacy of the Business of Business Schools : What's the Future? Journal of Management Development, vol. 31, no. 4, 2012, pp. 368–76, doi:10.1108/02621711211219040

Marta-Christina SUCIU[1], *Mina FANEA-IVANOVICI*[2]

[1] Professor, Bucharest University of Economic Studies, Email: christina.suciu@economie.ase.ro.

[2] Bucharest University of Economic Studies, Email: mina.ivanovici@economie.ase.ro

The Role of Sponsorship, Patronage and Philanthropy for Supporting the Cultural & Creative Industries

Abstract *All over the world there are a multitude and diverse sources of financing creative and cultural activities. Certain creative-cultural activities generate positive externalities, which have to be next internalised by the state as the socially desirable level of the cultural- creative products is usually well above the level provided by and on the market. In such cases, public financing is required in order both to provide a larger amount of creative-cultural products and services, and to support also cultural operators. According to some authors, cultural and creative activities are affected by the Baumol-Bowen cost-disease. Other creative-cultural actors are aligned to market rules and do not require public financing (as is the case of architecture design). The paper aims to explain the importance of alternative financing sources designed such as to support the cultural and creative activities, such as sponsorship, patronage and philanthropy. The paper is also intending to assess the dimension and scale of giving for cultural-creative activities. The paper includes also the presentation of several examples of good practice from Europe.*

Keywords: *Creative & cultural industries, creative economy, sponsorship, patronage, philanthropy*

Introduction

At times of economic downturn, it has been noted that public expenditure is usually kept at a minimum and the amounts aimed at financing creative-cultural industries drop. Such austerity policy has not long ago affected those industries that mostly depend on public financing, especially cultural activities. To exemplify, during 2008–2010, arts, recreational and entertainment services fell by much more than information and communication activities (Reid, B., Albert, A. et al., 2010).

Under such recent economic developments it becomes more and more clear the necessity to find alternative financing sources for supporting the creative and cultural industries in order to supplement, and not replace, public financing. Moreover, the Work Plan for Culture (2015–2018) of the Council of the European Union considers that access to finance is critical for this sector. Thus, one of the topics of the plan is to analyse all financing alternatives for the cultural-creative industries, which involve financial instruments, such as equity investment and bank loans. Besides the traditional financing, the Council of the European Union recommends other sources of finance, such as: public-private funds, business angels, venture capital, crowdfunding, sponsorship, patronage and philanthropy (Council of the European Union, 2014).

Attracting private investment and giving in culture and creative activities is a major objective for many countries, including for Romania. For instance, only 1 % of the British sponsorship is directed towards creative and cultural industries all the more so as the UK level of awareness insofar as the contribution of the creative-cultural sectors to the economy is higher than the one in Romania (Corporate Finance Faculty, ICAEW 2015).

The main objective of the paper is to illustrate the role of philanthropy in cultural-creative activities, to explain this behaviour and to present the main achievements at European level in terms of philanthropy in culture.

1. Literature review

Giving to Culture in Europe-A survey of methodologies for the study of corporate giving in Europe, prepared by Kömhoff, Heinsius and van Dorssen (Kömhoff, H, van Dorssen, J, 2015) recommends that the EU should strengthen the culture of asking and the culture of giving. Specifically, we consider that the EU should strengthen the culture of asking by building capacity for providers of creative-cultural output and services in making proposals for sponsorship and donation. Additionally, the EU should strengthen the culture of giving by enforcing tax reliefs to those entities giving or arranging sponsorship deals; by promoting goods practices and examples of sponsorship; by providing solid and comparable data on giving to culture; by supporting cooperation between the cultural organisations and businesses for matchmaking, training and research purposes.

The same study sets out several recommendations for national governments in their endeavour to stimulate the culture of asking and the culture of giving. Among the recommendations, we consider mostly important the following: fostering a better relationship between businesses and the creative-cultural industries, implementing tax reliefs for those giving to culture (donors, sponsors, natural and legal persons alike), helping improve the skills related to asking for donations (applying for sponsorship) and increasing public awareness about this need. Last but not least, equally important is the participation in research collecting data on cultural sponsorship.

Heather Tunis (Tunis, H., 2015, p. 4) highlights the importance of a culture of philanthropy, which is defined as "a set of organisational values and practices that support and nurture fund development within a non-profit organisation". Further on, the author proposes a set of indicators in this respect take into account mainly:

- "Philanthropy and resource (fund) development have to be well understood, viewed and valued as mission-aligned by all – board, management and staff.
- The chief executive and board are actively involved in fund development.
- Everyone is trained and supported in their role(s) in philanthropy.
- Everyone involved with the organisation can articulate the case for giving, serve as ambassadors, engage in relationship building and promote philanthropy.
- Every interaction is a respectful cultivation.
- Organisations systems are in place to support all aspects of cultivation and stewardship" (Tunis, H., 2015, p. 4).

But what is actually the reason why a corporation or an individual would be willing to donate to culture? It could be that they want their image to be associated to charity or because they believe in a cause, be it religious, social, moral or intellectual. The cause may be social inclusion and cohesion, regeneration or revitalisation of places and regions, etc. In other words, causes should be visible, and cultural actors able and willing to express and advance their needs for financial assistance.

2. Various approaches concerning non-profit support and private support for creative and cultural industries

Before analysing the stakes of support for the CCI (creative and cultural industries), it is critical to clearly refer to the main approaches regarding the alternative financing of CCI (Directorate General Internal Policies of the Union, 2006):

- Sponsorship is the act of giving with an aim to derive a direct benefit (sales, image, etc.). Thus, sponsorship is support with returns, either direct or indirect.
- Patronage (maecenatism) implies support with some return. Patronage is financial, material or moral assistance, which is of no direct benefit to the patron's activities, but it contributes to its reputation and honour.
- Philanthropy (donation) is support without returns.

The European recommendation in terms of the concepts and approaches related to alternative financing is to use the concepts of non-profit support and business support.

3. Rationale for giving to and supporting the creative and cultural industries

Philanthropy may come under different forms for the creative and cultural industries. The first and most obvious one is financial support. A second contribution could be under the form of consultancy or expertise services, which can consolidate the business and lay the foundations for business sustainability of entrepreneurs in the arts.

Next, one should analyse the reasons for the low level of sponsorship, patronage and philanthropy in the cultural and creative sector. The most important reason for not giving money to the CCI is the lack or insufficient level of tax exempts (tax incentives) that the private entity could benefit from following the donation. Besides tax reliefs, such persons or companies with the ability and willingness to finance could seek to improve their image, to grow and develop their business, PR, corporate social responsibility, etc.

Marketing reasons for donating is one factor that determines creative and cultural actors to be present into the new media. By improving their online presence, such actors become potential recipients of donations, as donors can benefit the online marketing. Not only do donors benefit, but such creative and cultural companies may attract public and audience through such media.

For any donor and not only, is it extremely important that the ties between the giver and the recipient be very strong: the motivation of the donors and sponsors should rhyme with the goals of the creative-cultural actor. Important donors usually have positions in the board of the cultural-creative company or is involved in various events. Also, when large contributions are offered, the donor may want to interfere with the use of the money.

4. Giving in the Romanian creative and cultural industries

In Romania, giving in general could be under the form of a grant (which can be offered under the conditions of the Law of sponsorship/patronage – Law no. 32/1994) or as a reimbursable fund, as an investment or participation. In the latter case, the financing is made in order to obtain a profit. For cultural activities, however, grants can be offered as per Government Ordinance no. 51 dated August 11th, 1998. The ordinance determines and regulates the general framework, principles and procedures of the grant system from the state budget or local budgets for cultural programmes, projects and actions. Grants are awarded as long as there are other financing sources, either owned by the beneficiary or attracted and for non-profit activities.

Private financing for various types of activities is usually made towards the end of the year, when managers have a clearer image of the turnover, profit, profit tax, and cash. Such information is necessary to determine the amount directed towards the financing of CCI. In order words, the amount invested or donated to CCI largely depends on the financial performance of private companies.

Up until 2016, tax reliefs for philanthropic companies meant the possibility to deduct from the profit tax the amounts given as sponsorship, should the two conditions were met at the same time: a) they did not exceed 0.3 % of the turnover and b) they did not exceed 20 % of the profit tax due.

According to the Tax Code enforced in 2016, the amounts given as sponsorship could not exceed 0.5 % of the turnover (an improvement of the former provision), while the second condition remained unchanged. The New Tax Code enforced in 2018 has not changed any of these limits.

5. European sponsorship in culture and the supporting legal provisions

Most of the countries included in the Compendium – Cultural Policies and Trends in Europe (Council of Europe, 2014) have designed specific legal provisions to encourage sponsorship in culture. Obviously, there are very few European countries without such legislation. For instance, that is the case of: Belgium, where there are no legal provisions for corporate tax deductions for investment in culture; Norway, where there are no specific incentives for private sector investment in culture; Sweden – where there is no law to encourage private sponsorship of culture and the arts.

Certain countries have designed special laws on Sponsorship. Thus, in Austria: the Sponsors' Ordinance (1987); in France: the Law on Development of Sponsorship (1987) and the Mécenat Law (2003); in Germany: the Directive of the Ministry of Finance (BMF-Sponsoring-Erlass 1998); in Lithuania: the Law on Charities and Promotion (1993 amended in 2011); in Portugal: the Statute of Patronage (Law 74/99); in Spain: Tax Exemptions Act for Non-profit Organisations and on Sponsorship (2002); in the UK: the Charity Tax Law.

Most of the countries have specific provisions included in the Tax Law that refer to sponsorship, patronage and donations, including in the field of culture. That is the case of: Bulgaria, Croatia, the Czech Republic, Denmark, Estonia, Finland, Greece, Hungary, Ireland, Italy, Latvia, Luxembourg, Malta, the Netherlands, Poland, Slovakia, Slovenia, Switzerland, to name a few.

6. Estimating the value of private sponsorship in culture across Europe

It is very difficult to aggregate and report the level of sponsorship in culture. Very often, official statistics do not break down the level of sponsorship into categories. Consequently, scarce information is available.

For instance: in Austria, the level of sponsorship in 2013 was of 50 million euros, which represents a little less than 2 % of the total public financing in culture; in Belgium (Flanders), the level of private sponsorship was 89 million euros in 2011; in Croatia, the level of sponsorship was roughly 4 million euros in 2013; in Estonia, the level of private sponsorship in the field of culture was 0.13 million euros in 2012; in Finland, total sponsorship in culture was 17.4 million euros in 2008; in France, corporate cultural investments reach 494 million euros per year; in Germany, private sponsorship was 350 million euros in 2010; in Hungary, the level of sponsorship is around 16.5 million euros per year; in Ireland, the total sponsorship in culture was 3.9 million euros in 2010; in Italy, total sponsorship reached 391 million euros in 2011; in Netherlands, total sponsorship in culture was 287 million euros in 2011; in Norway, the total amount of sponsorship in the field of culture was 65.78 million euros in 2006; in Spain, cultural sponsorship reaches 45.1 million euros per year; in the UK, the level of sponsorship in culture was 816 million euros in 2009.

The first conclusion is that information on the level of sponsorship is not available for recent years in most countries and that the level of this type of financing varies to a large extent from country to country, depending on the legislation in force and on the government schemes at work to promote business sponsorship in the arts and culture.

In addition, many countries included in the Compendium do not have information available on the sponsorship in culture at all. This is the case of Bulgaria, the Czech Republic, Denmark, Greece, Latvia, Lithuania, Luxembourg, Malta, Monaco, Poland, Portugal, Romania, Slovakia, and Slovenia.

7. Cultural sponsorship – a case study on the UK

The level of giving in culture was worth 660.5 GBP in 2011/2012 according to the latest figures reported (Business in Community, 2012). The level of giving, as previously stated, largely depends on the relationships with donors and partners, because it is due to such contributions that companies thrive and creative industries grow.

Giving could be specifically done by charitable organisations, which is a more appropriate legal form. Some of the benefits of establishing a charity are: the existence of various funding opportunities as well as tax reliefs. The inconvenient of charities is that they are limited in their scope and activities, and additional legislation should be complied with. Also, its assets cannot be used but for the charitable scope.

According to Creative industries – routes to finance. A guide to sources of funding and investment for arts, cultural and creative organisations, the main advantages of setting up charities are:

- Income tax exemption on amounts directed towards charitable purposes.
- Tax reliefs on trading profits of a subsidiary company donated to the parent charity.
- Rate reliefs for buildings used on charitable purposes.
- Specific VAT reliefs and exemptions.

Other legal forms used to facilitate donations, sponsorship or patronage are: charitable trusts, corporate partnerships, reward-based crowdfunding. Social enterprises do not have a specific legal status, but they may be any of the above organisations.

Despite the multitude of legal forms established to support charity, the main contributor to cultural and creative industries remains the individual. Individual giving accounted for 56 % of philanthropic income, while trusts/foundations donated 26 % and businesses 17 % (Business in Community, 2012). Technology too plays an important role in donations, e-giving becoming more popular and efficient in recent years. Philanthropy may come under other forms too, such as legacies or endowments.

Conclusions

Given the increasing role of creative-cultural industries (CCI) for achieving smart sustainable development as well as their impact on social inclusion, urban revitalisation and regeneration, it has become extremely important to encourage and promote giving to this sector, in order to supplement existing public finance. The main difficulties identified are the lack or insufficient tax reliefs for donors, the lack of a culture of asking and the lack of a culture of giving, especially in countries where such an objective has no tradition. On the other hand, statistics in cultural sponsorship and philanthropy are discontinuous and sometimes not reported at all.

The paper is both an analysis of the current state of facts in matters concerning cultural philanthropy, but also a starting point for future research.

Among the topics suggested for future research we name: analysing the means of increasing public awareness about the necessity to donate for the culture, identifying the main would-be categories of contributors or donors, proposing a public policy document for encouraging donations in culture, collecting relevant and updated data on cultural sponsorship.

References

Business in the Community, Arts & Business: Private Investment in Culture Survey, 2011/12. Internet source: https://artsandbusiness.bitc.org.uk/sites/default/files/kcfinder/files/artsandbusiness/artsandbusiness-pics-2011–12.pdf (accessed on January 18, 2018).

Corporate Finance Faculty: Creative industries – routes to finance. A guide to sources of funding and investment for arts, cultural and creative organisations. ICAEW: 2015. Internet source: http://www.thecreativeindustries.co.uk/media/322389/creative-industries-routes-to-finance.pdf (accessed on January 18, 2018).

Council of Europe: Compendium Cultural Policies and Trends in Europe. Internet source: http://www.culturalpolicies.net/web/comparisons-tables.php?aid=41&cid=46&lid=en (accessed on March 2, 2018).

Council of the European Union: Draft Conclusions of the Council and of the Representatives of the Governments of the Member States, meeting within the Council, on a Work Plan for Culture (2015–2018). Internet source: http://data.consilium.europa.eu/doc/document/ST-16094-2014-INIT/en/pdf (accessed on March 11, 2018).

Directorate General Internal Policies of the Union: Financing the Arts and Culture in the European Union, Study. Policy Department Structural and Cohesion Policies: 2006, Internet source: http://www.culturalpolicies.net/web/files/134/en/Financing_the_Arts_and_Culture_in_the_EU.pdf (accessed on February 3, 2018).

Kömhoff, Well, Heinsius, Joost, van Dorssen, Antoinette: Giving to Culture in Europe, A survey of methodologies for the study of corporate giving in Europe. 2015. Internet source: http://www.connectingartsandbusiness.eu/wp-content/uploads/2013/09/Giving-to-Culture-report-ConnectingAB-final-10–2.pdf (accessed on March, 20 2018).

Reid, B., Albert, A., Hopkins, L.: A Creative Block? The Future of the UK Creative Industries. A Knowledge Economy & Creative Industries report. 2010. Internet source: http://www.theworkfoundation.com/assets/docs/publications/277_a%20creative%20block.pdf (accessed on September 16, 2017).

Tunis, Heather: Creating a Culture of Philanthropy: A Great Adventure. Center for Nonprofit Management: 2015, Internet source: https://cnmsocal.org/wp-content/uploads/2014/06/CultureofPhilanthropyPPTFinal.pdf (accessed on March 24, 2018).

Ion STANCU[1], *Georgeta- Mădălina MEGHIȘAN- TOMA*[2]

[1] University of Craiova, Faculty of Economics and Business Administration, Craiova, Romania, Email: ioncstancu@gmail.com

[2] The Bucharest University of Economic Studies, Faculty of Business Administration in foreign languages, Romania; National Institute for Economic Research "Costin C. Kiritescu", Romanian Academy, Email: madalina_meghisan@yahoo.com

Sustainable Development Indicators for Education and Professional Training

Abstract *The main aim of the research article is to underline the connection between early school leavers, persons with low educational attainment (25–64 years old), individuals' low level of computer skills, public expenditure on education, total employed population. Descriptive statistics and correlation was used to analyze the data. The main findings revealed important correlations between three indicators: early school leavers, persons with low educational attainment (25–64 years old) and individuals' low level of computer skills. Eventhough there is no connection between all the elements, the two variables: public expenditure on education and total employed population have an important influence, form the point of view of their focus: more on modernization of educational and professional training systems through technology.*

Keywords: *Education and professional training, sustainable development, early school leavers, low educational attainment, level of computer skills, public expenditure on education*

Introduction

Education is an important pillar of development for a society. This research article emphasis the link between: early school leavers, persons with low educational attainment and individuals 'level of computer skills, at a macroeconomic level. Romania is a country for which education has lost important steps in the development, eventhough the country takes effort to increase the performance of education related indicators.

1. Literature review

There are several research articles that focus on education in Romania. Costea et al. (2012, p. 3582) underlines the role of education as a "supplier of labour". However, the labour market is also influenced by the "business climate". (Dascalu

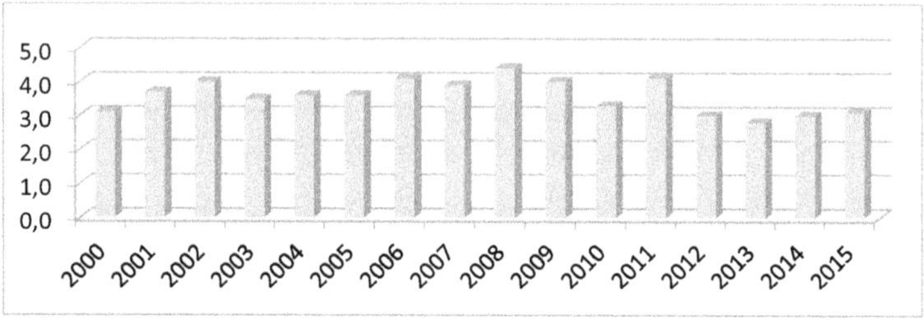

Figure 1: Public expenditure on education in Romania (2000–2015)
Source: www.insse.ro, accessed 03.03.2018.

et al., 2016, p. 138) The demographic trend is also considered an important factor that was further analysed, because "the countries are facing major problems like declining of the birth rate and the rising of life expectancy". (Cristea et al., 2016, p. 28) Education is considered to have an important influence to the development of "a country's economy and society". (Fazilah et al., 2011, p. 443)

The current situation of the educational system from Romania can be revealed by the percentage of the public expenditure on education in GDP. According to the data provided by the Figure 1, the Romanian Government allocated a percentage of 3.1 % of the national financial income to public expenses for education. The highest value was registered in 2008 (4.4 %).

The growth of the total occupied population (15–65 years old and over) underlines the evolution of the total occupied population aged between 15–65 years old and over. The occupied population can be defined as all the persons that undertake a productive work for the market. According to the data from the Figure 2, the percentage of the total employed population undertook a decrease of -0.9 %, within the current period compared to the previous period. The highest decrease was registered in the years 2002 (-10.2 %) and 2012 (-4.8 %). On the other hand, the highest growth was registered in the years 2006 (+0.7 %) and 2014 (+0.8 %).

The indicator Early school leavers is calculated as the ratio between the population aged between 18–24 years old with a low level of education, that is not enrolled in any form of training (formal or non-formal), and the total population aged between 18–24 years old. However, the percentage of early school leavers was 18,5 at the level of the year 2016. The highest value of this indicator was registered in the year 2004 (23 %). (Figure 3)

The indicator Persons with low education attainment by age group (25–64 years old) measures the level of education of the persons aged between 25–64 years. The level of education is considered to be low for the persons that graduated secondary school, primary school or no school. The percentage of Persons with low education attainment by age group (25–64 years old) was 23,3 for the year 2016. (Figure 4)

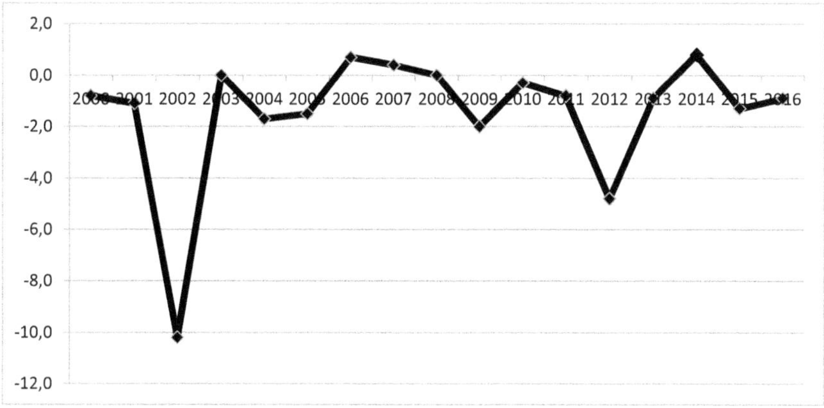

Figure 2: Total employed population growth (aged 15–65 and over) in Romania (2000–2016)

Source: www.insse.ro, accessed 03.03.2018.

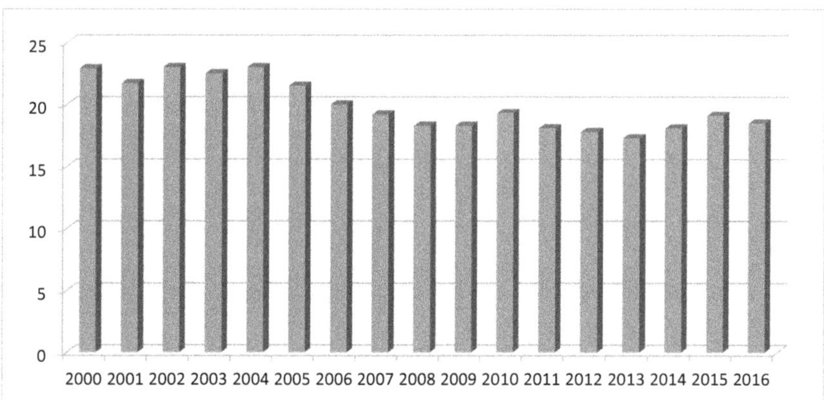

Figure 3: Early school leavers in Romania (2000–2016)

Source: www.insse.ro, accessed 03.03.2018.

Individuals' level of computer skills is considered to be low if the persons had one or two activities related to computers (copying or moving files; copying/moving texts; usage of mathematical formulas for calculation; compressing files; installing new devices; writing computing programs through specialised programming languages). At the level of the year 2014, the value of the indicator Individuals' level of computer skills (low) was the highest (18 %). (Figure 5)

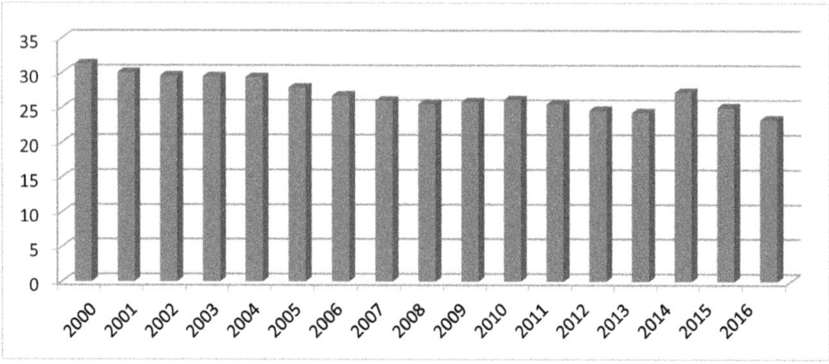

Figure 4: Persons with low education attainment by age group (25–64 years old) in Romania (2000–2016)

Source: www.insse.ro, accessed 03.03.2018

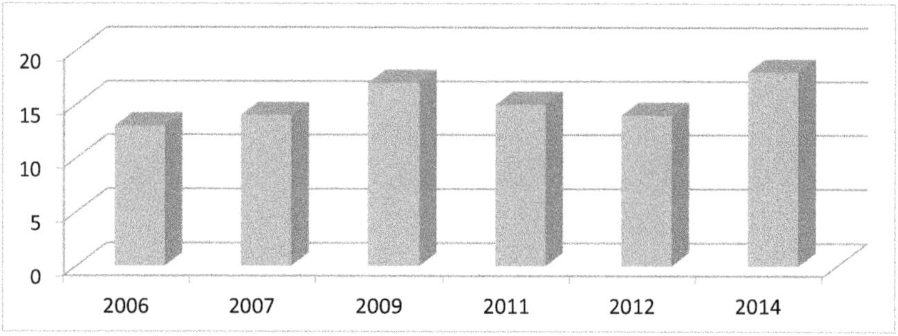

Figure 5: Individuals' level of computer skills (low) in Romania (2000–2016)

Source: www.insse.ro, accessed 03.03.2018

2. Research methodology

In order to analyze the current situation of the Romanian national education and training system, we chose a series of variables, representative for the Objective 9. Education and Professional Training, part of the National Strategy for Sustainable Development. (Table 1)

The correlation matrix is used to determine the connection between variables. The Pearson correlation coefficient indicates if two measured variables have an analoguous variation or not.

The results indicate the correlation coefficient and the significance (Sig.). If Sig. < 0,05, we can affirm that there is a correlation between the two variables

Table 1: Sustainable development indicators for Education and professional training (2000–2016)

Variables	Code
Early school leavers (by youngsters)	(1)
Persons with low education attainment by age group (25–64 years old)	(2)
Individuals' level of computer skills (low)	(3)
Public expenditure on education	(4)
Total employed population	(5)

Source: Authors' own processing data.

at the level of 0,05. The sign ** indicates that the correlation is significant at the level of 0,01.

According to the data from the Table 1, the most significant results are:

- There is a positive correlation (Pearson coefficient= 0,903) between Early school leavers and Persons with low education attainment by age group (25–64 years old).
- There is a negative correlation (Pearson coefficient= -0,970) between Early school leavers and Individuals' level of computer skills (low).
- There is a negative correlation (Pearson coefficient= -0,977) between Persons with low education attainment by age group (25–64 years old) and Individuals' level of computer skills (low).

However, the variable Public expenditure on education does not have an influence on: Early school leavers; Persons with low educational attainment (25–64 years old); Individuals' level of computer skills (low) and Total employed population.

The variable Total employed population does not have an influence on: Early school leavers; Persons with low educational attainment (25–64 years old); Individuals' level of computer skills (low) and Public expenditure on education.

Conclusions

Education can be considered a tool to attain the sustainable development of a country. The main purpose for the governmental policies should be to create a legal frame in order to diminish the percentages of the Early school leavers and the Persons with low education attainment by age group (24–64 years old) and increase the percentage of Individuals' level of computer skills. Thus, Public expenditure on education should focus more on accelerate modernization of educational and professional training systems through technology.

Table 2: Pearson correlation coefficient

		Early school leavers	Persons with low educational attainment (25–64 years old)	Individuals' level of computer skills (low)	Public expenditure on education	Total employed population
Early school leavers	Pearson Correlation	1	,903**	-,970**	,114	-,297
	Sig. (2-tailed)		,000	,000	,674	,246
Persons with low educational attainment (25–64 years old)	Pearson Correlation	,903**	1	-,977**	,055	-,178
	Sig. (2-tailed)	,000		,000	,838	,494
Individuals' level of computer skills (low)	Pearson Correlation	-,970**	-,977**	1	,503	,526
	Sig. (2-tailed)	,000	,000		,167	,146
Public expenditure on education	Pearson Correlation	,114	,055	,503	1	-,064
	Sig. (2-tailed)	,674	,838	,167		,814
Total employed population	Pearson Correlation	-,297	-,178	,526	-,064	1
	Sig. (2-tailed)	,246	,494	,146	,814	

**. Correlation is significant at the 0.01 level (2-tailed).

Source: Authors' own processing data using SPSS 20.0 statistics software for Windows.

References

Costea, Carmen/Cismas, Laura/Libardea- Vladuca, Laura: The relevance of education as a capital asset for economic development: references to the Romanian situation. Procedia- Social and Behavioral Sciences, 46, 2012, pp. 3582–3587.

Cristea, Mirela/Marcu, Nicu/Cercelaru Oana-Valentina: Longer life with worsening pension system? Aging population impact on the pension system in two countries: Romania and Croatia. Economic and Social Development: Book of Proceedings, 2016, pp. 28.

Dascălu, Elena Doina/Marcu, Nicu/Pete, Ştefan/Ulici, Maria- Lenuta/Dumitraşcu, Vadim: Dependent business climate. A network-based analysis. Romanian journal of economic forecasting, 19(1), 2016, pp. 138–152.

Fazilah Idris/Zaharah Hassan/Azizah Ya'acob/Saran Kaur Gill/Noor Aziah Mohd Awal: The Role of Education in Shaping Youth's National Identity. Procedia - Social and Behavioral Sciences, Volume 59, 2012, pp. 443–450, ISSN 1877-0428, https://doi.org/10.1016/j.sbspro.2012.09.299.

Ministery of Environment and Climatic change, http://www.mmediu.ro/beta/domenii/dezvoltare-durabila/strategia-nationala-a-romaniei-2013-2020-2030/, accessed 10.03.2018;

National Institute of Statistics, http://www.insse.ro/cms/files/Web_IDD_BD_ro/index.htm, accessed 03.03.2018.

Cosmin ȘERBĂNESCU[1], *Adrian VINTILESCU*[2]

[1] PhD, National Institute of Internal Control, Bucharest, Romania,
Email: cosmin.serbanescu@incir.ro

[2] PhD, National Institute of Internal Control, Bucharest, Romania,
Email: adrian.vintilescu@incir.ro

Optimal Strategies for Organizing Public Internal Audit Departments

Abstract *The planning activity in public internal audit includes the auditing resources represented mainly by the number of auditors and other aspects of the audit organization itself (entity or hierarchical entity level). The proper organization can be mainly analyzed based on the associated risks, the assessment of their impact and their probability, but also on taking into account other relevant elements, too. Often, this analysis, besides being very elaborate, does not capture all important aspects, namely those that derive from the assessment of information asymmetry. The study aims to create a model for preliminary analysis of the optimal decision to organize public internal audit either at the level of the public entity or at the level of a higher entity that can be quickly used by decision-makers.*

The paper addresses the issue of the internal audit in the context of a mandate contract with the head of the public entity on the one hand and with the state itself on the other hand and complying with the requirements of an optimal mechanism. The objective of the study is the preliminary design of a mechanism to ensure optimal mandate contracts that the audit has with both the head of the unit and the state, obviously in imperfect information conditions. Thus, the quantitative model used aims to aggregate in a scorecard the optimality requisites specific to the theory of mechanism design in a tool for rapid and formal analysis decisions to exercise public internal audit at the level of the hierarchically superior entity.

Furthermore, the research provides a formal preliminary tool for analyzing the decision in the public sector internal audit and offers the possibility of identifying some directions of action that provide the basis for the decision to perform the audit from the hierarchical entity level, which also takes into account the information asymmetry theory and mechanism design.

Keywords: public sector internal audit, asymmetric and private information, mechanism design, criteria for decision-making under risk and uncertainty

Introduction

An effective policy in the field of public internal audit can not disregard a corresponding mechanism that includes well-defined processes and institutions capable of adequately managing them. The organization of public internal audit in Romania requires a well-founded, transparent and appropriate, but mostly formalized analysis of the audit organization's decision at the entity level or at higher hierarchical entity level. Therefore, it is necessary to define suitable instruments, such as quantitative analysis or appropriate impact studies.

The public internal audit in Romania is regulated by Law no. 672/2002 on the organization and exercise of internal audit in public entities, with subsequent amendments. Regarding the organization of public internal audit departments there are two important aspects of the managerial decision: (1) whether the audit should be exercised from the hierarchical level and (2) which would be the optimal number of auditors to be part of an internal audit structure.

Article 12, paragraph 4) of the law stipulates the necessity of a proper dimensioning, depending on the volume of activity and the level of associated risks, based on a formal document. In order to define the existing context, we will formulate some assertions regarding the meaning of some precepts, as they are provided in the Romanian legislation.

The public entity is defined in art. 2, letter n) of the abovementioned law as: "the public authority, the public institution, the company / national company, the autonomous institution, the commercial company to which the state or an administrative-territorial unit is a majority shareholder and which has legal personality and the entity funded more than 50 % of public funds".

Public authorities are defined in art. 2, point b) as: "any state body or administrative-territorial unit acting under a public power regime for the purpose of satisfying a legitimate public interest; the associative structures of the local public authorities and other private legal entities are assimilated to the public authorities which have acquired, according to the law, public utility status and are authorized to provide a public service under a public power regime".

The term "public institution" according to the legislation is defined as a "generic name including the parliament, the presidential administration, the ministries, the other specialized bodies of the public administration, other public authorities, the autonomous public institutions, the administrative-territorial units, cities, municipalities, counties, districts and the municipality of Bucharest, subordinated central and local public institutions, under the coordination or under the authority of other public entities, regardless of how they finance their own activity".

Regarding the organization of the public internal audit department, Law no. 672/2002 stipulates, at art. 11 that it falls within the competence of the head of the public institution or, as the case may be, the collective management body has the obligation to ensure the organizational and functional framework necessary for carrying out the public internal audit activity. The decision about organization and sizing presupposes a foundation that is difficult in the absence of an appropriate analysis tool.

From the analysis of the normative framework in force, there is the possibility of exercising the public internal audit function either within a public entity (subordinated to a higher level entity) or even by the higher hierarchical institution. The rules in force stipulate that the manager of the subordinated public entity, who is under the coordination or under the authority of another public entity, establishes and maintains a functional public internal audit department with the consent of the higher public entity; if this agreement is not given, the entity's audit is performed by the internal audit department of the public entity that has decided it.

Thus, for subordinate entities, it is necessary that the audit be carried out either at their level on the basis of the agreement given by the principal authorizing entity, or that the public internal audit is conducted at the department level. The decision involves an opportunity analysis, for which should be implemented a formalized assessment tool. In order to ensure the supervisory requirements, it is mandatory according to the regulation in force that each public internal audit department to be comprised of at least 2 auditors.

International Standards for the Professional Practice of Internal Auditing issued by the Institute of Internal Auditors (IIA, 2016) recommend general principles of good practice but do not establish any quantitative model to be considered in addressing one or other of the alternatives. Standard 2030 specifies that the Chief Audit Executive must ensure that the internal audit has adequate, sufficient resources and effectively allocated to the implementation of the approved plan. Standard 2010 requires that the Chief Audit Executive should establish a risk-based plan to determine the priorities of the internal audit activity that are in line with the organization's objectives.

The quality and relevance of the audit tests performed is another factor that must be taken into account in establishing the audit plan. The need for reasonable assurance provided by the audit also affects the decision to perform the audit at the higher level or at the level of each subsidiary. An opinion on the decision to organize the audit from a hierarchical level was probably considered in the model of Jacques Renard (Renard, 2004), which states that the most important factor in dimensioning the internal audit is the size of the organization. Renard divides the number of auditors into two possibilities: small institutions will have between 1 and 3 auditors, while the internal audit department of a large corporation that also performs the audit at the subordinate entities may have between 20 and 100 internal auditors.

Currently, art. 12, par. 4) of Law no. 672/2002 on the public internal audit stipulates that the internal audit department's dimensioning is performed based on the volume of activity and the associated risk size so as to ensure the auditing of the activities within the scope of the public internal audit.

With regard to sizing, the general rules for the exercise of the public internal audit activity approved by the Government Decision no. 1086/2013 stipulates that the number of internal auditor jobs shall be determined according to the following steps:

a) Identification of all activities carried out both within the public entity and within the subordinated / coordinated entities, in which the superior hierarchical entity directly performs public internal audit engagements.
b) Identifying the risks associated with the activities.
c) Identifying the internal controls associated to each activity.
d) Establishing the residual risks as a result of exercising the control forms.
e) Establishing the necessary time for carrying out the public internal audit assessments, taking into account the following factors: the entity's budget; the number of subordinated / coordinated entities; the number of employees; the specific nature of the public entity; the complexity and social importance of the activities; compliance with periodicity in auditing; high / medium risk activities.

From the analysis of the above-mentioned text, it follows that certain stages defined by the legislator must be taken into consideration for the optimal size of auditors' number. First of all, it should be mentioned that although the stages in the normative act are presented, they are not accompanied by a support that provides an adequate quantitative model. The creation of a quantitative method of analysis regarding the decision to exercise the audit, either from higher-level public funds authorizer or from the higher-level hierarchical institution, would be a useful approach in the Romanian public internal audit.

Let us assume a hypothetical case where there is a public funds secondary authorizing entity with 52 territorial units (each with 80 employees), each of which has legal personality. If we consider that there are two auditors at each territorial structure, 104 jobs would be needed, and if the audit would be carried out centrally, it would take up to 100 jobs, according to Renard's theory, which is the maximum number. Currently there are territorial structures with more than 150 employees. In these cases, the central audit option could provide an integrated approach using representative samples or a more robust global risk management. However, centralizing the internal audit function generates inherent specific risks.

Modeling the decision and creating a quantitative tool according to the rules can be performed based on a linear optimization algorithm that takes into account the following elements:

The maximum problem can be that the sum of the residual risk exposures $\Sigma\, Exr_{ij}$ to be maximum, as long as it is $\Sigma\, T_{ij} < T_{disposable}$. Other specific restrictions may also be defined. We will not insist on this type of modeling as it is the subject of a further paper that will present the work extensively. The above model, as observed, does not take into account the informational asymmetry of a mandate contract.

Consequently, in order to obtain a suggestive image, including elements of informational asymmetry, we will proceed to the analysis of important factors in dimensioning the internal audit departments that were defined by authors such as Bal (2012). This is necessary for the aggregation of the factors defined in the literature with the economics of mechanism design. The analysis started with

Table 1: Elements of a linear optimization system

Subordinate entities	**Audit missions**	**Objectives**	**Auditable areas**	**Risks**	**Probability**	**Impact**	**Exposure**	**Residual exposure**	**Time**
E_i	M_{ij}	D_{ij}	T_{ij}	R_{ij}	P_{ij}	I_{ij}	Ex_{ij}	Exr_{ij}	T_{ij}

Source: authors own research results.

the studies of Baron and Besanko (1984) which address the theory of information asymmetry in public policy and Anderson's studies (Anderson at al, 2010), who makes specific reference to factors to be considered in the proper dimensioning of internal audit departments.

We may consider that the architecture of the Romanian public internal audit organization should take into account the mandatory phases of management that themselves contain delegation acts in risk and uncertainty conditions such as:

a) Policy development and monitoring phase (prediction) - performed by a central body like the Central Harmonization Unit for Public Internal Audit (CHUPIA).
b) Regulatory phase - carried out by a specialized structure such as the Public Internal Audit Committee (PIAC).
c) Effective implementation phase - carried out at the level of the public funds authorizing institutions where the public internal audit is actually carried out or, as the case may be, the institutions that may or may not approve to perform the internal audit at the lower-level public funds authorizers.
d) Coordination and methodological guidance phase - carried out on a delegation of CHUPIA and hierarchically to Ministry of Public Finance (MPF) or senior public funds authorizing managers.
e) Inspection and control function - carried out by delegation by CHUPIA to MPF or senior public funds authorizing supervisors (evaluation).

The factors that influence the sizing of the public internal audit departments can be described as follows:

- Particularities of the management structure of the organization

Performing centrally-controlled audits can bring added value to the possibility of unitary approaches, although there is a major threat that is given by the heterogeneous approach to risks. Regarding the mandate given by the organization's management, the independence of the internal auditor is increased in the case of the audit being carried out by the superior hierarchical institution.

- Internal audit department's mission

The scope of activities performed by the internal audit department increases with the legislative, managerial and control system changes. Organizational features, complexity and risk level, testing difficulties (cost of audit) give this component an importance that is granted by shareholders (state's role), not only by management. Therefore, the legal provision of maintaining a minimum of 2 auditors for an entity means, in fact, the need for the state to have a minimum level of insurance, regardless of the type of manager (public in this case).

In fact, a department's mission is defined on the basis of general rules set out by the Ministry of Public Finance, after which managers can define their own rules, but they enter into an endorsement process. Consequently, the legislator's intention to set a minimum number of auditors to a certain number of employees covers the state's need to receive assurance under the mandate it gave to the public institution to operate on the basis of the Regulation of organization and functioning.

- Value added by internal audit

In case of exercising the audit from the hihger-level public funds authorizing institution, risk management can be unitarily approached and good practice can be extended more easily. Testing tools may also be more relevant and samples become more representative. However, everything has a cost. The cost of conducting audit assigmnents at the higher-level public funds authorizing institution is bigger sometimes due to travel or other indirect costs, although staff costs may be reduced. If we look at the audit as a risk-based investment, it is possible to create a specific model of the portfolio theory to ensure a return on risk in relation to an allocated budget.

- Alignment between management and internal audit department

This factor can be seen in the sense of a different efficiency of the audit function of the entity, both for the management, with which the auditor has a mandate contract (via the Organization and functioning regulation and through the job description) and also for the state which delegates by means of a normative act its own competencies that it pursues through the specialized directorate from the Ministry of Public Finance. The regulatory role towards this state delegation act is given by CHUPIA, which establishes the normative regulatory framework and constantly monitors the internal auditors work.

- Internal audit department's specificity

Imperfect knowledge depends on the internal auditors experience and the techniques used in audit engagements. Within the agent theory, the principal may know more or less completely the techniques held by the auditors.

- The quality of internal audit services

The factor targets the perception of the quality of the audit act in representing the state's interests. CHUPIA, as principal, can define indicators to be tracked during a mandate contract that it has as the state's representative for internal audit. Managers, as principal, can also define indicators (which may be different) and can be tracked during a mandate contract. In view of the above analysis, we can state that the public internal audit produces added value for both the management and the regulatory body. The gap (difference) between the two values leads to the instability of the function itself, and therefore we consider that the role of CHUPIA is decisive in regulating and harmonizing the framework to ensure stability between the two values.

As such, the authors propose to develop a model of analysis in order to determine an optimal decision regarding the exercise of the audit at the higher-level public funds authorizing institution. Specifically, the authors proposed to define a formal mechanism for analyzing the decision to approach the public internal audit at the higher-level public funds authorizing institution compared to a given structural context.

A first concept from which the study starts is that public policies address the failure of markets as a consequence of the state holding more or less concrete and coherent information. The second concept used consisted in modeling the process by using the mechanism design. Theory of mechanism design involves incomplete (or asymmetric) information games characterized by a "principal" who would like to condition his actions on information specifically known to the other player (or other players) called "agents".

A mechanism is a game where the agents send messages and the principal chooses a result or allocation based on the messages received. Agents choose to accept or reject the mechanism. Agents that accept the mechanism play the game specified by the mechanism. Mechanism design theory was developed by Grossmann and Hart (1983), Khalil (2001), Laffont (1987), Maskin (2007), Holmstrom (1977), Myerson (1978), based on Hurwitz's ideas and characterizes the results of all equilibria possible games of all games that can be projected with different coordination mechanisms.

With reference to the informational asymmetry, we can specify that this is the relationship between the hidden actions given by the productive "effort" of the agents, in the context of the hidden information that they hold as agents having an informational advantage over the principal (1979). In this sense, we can define a mechanism as a procedure by which the main contracted agents properly exercise the obligations arising from the norms, regulations and specific performance criteria defined in the standards.

A third component of the model construction is the scorecard developed by Kaplan and Norton (1996).

– Using optimal mechanisms in determining public internal audit structures

The chapter deals with integrating contracts and delegation in conditions of informational asymmetry in a model to be considered in establishing a relationship between hidden actions and the "effort" of the agents (audit departments) in the context of the asymmetric information. Aggregation of a set of indicators is a difficult task if we think of Condorcet's paradox or the theory of the impossibility of aggregating the indicators. (Arrow, 1950)

Defining a mechanism as a procedure by which the principal (in this case the senior management and the state) contradicts the agents to properly exercise the obligations deriving from the specific norms, regulations and performance criteria defined in the standards. (Barron, Besanko, 1984) Creating design engineered models, analysis and simulations on them is a difficult process for decision makers. That is why it is important, at an initial stage, at least a rapid preliminary analysis based on general principles of designing such mechanisms. Next, the authors created a scorecard based model which has aggregated several principles that can be considered in organizational redesigns.

The first principle is that in a contract where there is an informational asymmetry, the efficiency of the mechanism is based on the penalty and rewards system. Thus, for example, in the case of the delegation of state power in the field of auditing to public funds authorizing institutions, the higher the penalty, the lesser the tendency for fraudulent bahaviour. The penalty may be both for the first principal or the manager who may have a penalty policy given by the status of the civil servant but also by CHUPIA who can only propose sanctioning the internal auditor. The sanction granted by the manger without the CHUPIA enforcement is difficult to achieve towards an optimal sanctions policy, imposing very high penalties implies a more difficult implementation that over time may prove to be ineffective.

Another direction in streamlining mechanisms is to provide incentives that should help make agents more efficient. Benefits may consist of rewards such as attendance at courses or other events by both principals. Obviously, the courses can be organized by both the public funds authorizing institution, the CHUPIA or the public sector internal audit department. The existence of possible overlaps can lead to a reward policy, as well as a sanction policy, which can be difficult to apply.

A second principle is that the flow of information between actors must be as fast as possible and without very high costs. In the Romanian public internal audit system, communication between audit departments and managers as well as between them and CHUPIA is done through audit reports. The reports between the audit department and the CHUPIA are generally annual and those between management and the audit department are usually monthly and in written form.

A third principle is that information asymmetry is reduced when signals from various actors are received. This principle starts from the fact that some people, including the guardians, as Juvenal said, have the ability and inclination to discourage the inappropriate behavior of lower-level guardians. This mechanism is well described by Hurwitz (2008) and may involve the development of other reporting channels, including those related to quality control in audit.

A fourth principle is the outsourcing of processes taken to control the adverse effects of the mandate contract. In the public sector, the use of external audit could be equivalent to recourse to the Court of Accounts. The outsourcing of internal audit processes may also be considered by other organizations, whether public or private. If we are referring to public organizations, this direction of action can also be assimilated in the exercise of internal audit at the higher-level public funds authorizing institution.

A fifth principle is transparency that contributes to keeping moral hazard under control. In Romania, with the exception of the Court of Accounts, there are rare cases in which the findings and recommendations form the reports are given to the public ex officio. Government Transparency Rules given by Law no. 544/2001 does not provide for any obligations regarding the existence of transparency practices that would ensure, for example, the obligation to publish certain situations ex officio.

Furthermore, we can build a multi-criteria aggregation model based on a scorecard to ensure the integration of the stated principles by giving a note and weight coefficients. For each option V_X[1] it is quantified the impact on the principles of information asymmetry described above and on other measures that may be taken into account by CHUPIA on one hand and the public entity management on the other hand. CHUPIA, as a principal, may define indicators to be followed in the course of a mandate contract that the entity has as a state representative. The sum of these three defined measures will be equal to 1 (e.g 0.4, 0.4, 0.3). Each value of an indicator is adjusted with a wieght coefficient. For each measure the coefficients are equal to 1.

The table below defines measures and coefficients by CHUPIA regulations, policies and procedures issued by management and public policy transmission mechanisms, the sum of the indicators weightings being equal to 1 within the same measure.

Table 2: Decision analysis model to perform the audit from the higher-level public funds authorizer

Measure	**Component (component coefficient)**	**Principle (P_{ix}) / Indicator I_{Jx}**	**Significance coefficient C_{ix}**	**Option 1 Exercise the audit from the central structure with a number of (x) auditors**		**Option 2 Exercise the audit from the territorial structure with a number of (y) auditors**	
			Coefficient C_k	Notes V_{ik}	Costs	Notes V_{jj}	Costs
1	**Mechanisms of public policy transmission (p_i =0.4*)**	**Penalty**	$C_p = 0.2$	V_{px}	C_i	V_{py}	C_j
		Rewards	$C_r = 0.1$	V_{rx}		V_{ry}	
		Information flow	$C_c = 0.3$	V_{cx}		V_{cy}	
		Signals from various actors	$C_s = 0.4$	V_{sx}		V_{sy}	
		Transparency	$C_t = 0.1$	V_{tx}		V_{ty}	
2	**Regulations CHUPIA (p_i =0.3*)**	**Indicator 1 CHUPIA**	$C_{11} = 0.3$	V_{11x}		V_{11y}	
		Indicator 2 CHUPIA	$C_{12} = 0.7$	V_{12x}		V_{12y}	
3	**Management regulations (p_i =0.3*)**	**Indicator 1 M**	$C_{21} = 0.8$	V_{21x}		V_{21y}	
		Indicator 2 M	$C_{22} = 0.2$	V_{22x}		V_{22x}	

Source: authors own research results.

1 In the example, two options are considered: Option 1 when the audit is performed from the central structure with a number of (x) auditors and Option 2 when the audit is carried out at the territorial structure level with a number of (y) auditors.

The model's solution will be chosen based on a linear programming algorithm in relation to the values (x) or (y) that provides the maximum solutions of the maximum equation with restrictions given by the tolerable costs of the two functions, namely:

$$f_{1(x)} = [(C_k x\ V_{ik})p_i] / C_i$$

$$C_i < C_{tolerable}$$

and

$$f_{2(y)} = [(C_k\ x\ V_{jk})p_i] / C_j$$

$$C_J < C_{tolerable}$$

Where (x) is the number of auditors carrying out the audit from the central structure and (y) the number of auditors carrying out the audit from the territorial structure.

Once the solution is identified for both $x_0(f_{1xmax})$ as well as for $y_0(f_{2ymax})$ the optimal option is obtained which is determined by the value and the total costs of implementing the option.

Conclusions

The study has created an algorithm for the rapid and formal analysis of the decision to exercise internal audit in public entities, either at the public entity's level or at the higher-level public funds authorizing institution, based on the principles of mandate theory, under asymmetric informational conditions. The definition of such a formal instrument allows further substantiation of the decision regarding the exercise of the public internal audit, contributing to the outline of the premise that the reorganizations in the public system should be accompanied by a transparent and adequate substantiation, based on a simple quantitative evaluation algorithm which can be quickly analyzed by decision-makers.

By using the mechanism design theory principles, the paper offers the possibility to identify solutions to the issues given by the fact that the public internal auditors are in the direct subordination of a public funds authorizer but have to methodologically comply to the requirements of a central harmonization unit. The limits of the study are given by the method used and by the inherent subjectivity of the decision-makers.

The analysis can be extended to other areas of redistribution policies specific to public finances and institutional reorganization if governments propose to streamline and de-bureaucratise the administrative apparatus. To futher develop the research, the authors propose to use other tools for decision modelling to perform the internal audit from the higher-level hierarchical institution.

References

1. Bal, S., (2012). How much internal audit is enough?, [pdf] Avaibale at: http://auditandrisk.org.uk/features/how-much-internal-audit-is-enough, (accessed on 10.01.2018).

2. Baron, D., Besanko, D., (1984). Regulation, Asymetric Information, and Auditing, RAND Journal of Economics, vol. 15, no. 4, pp. 447–70.
3. Anderson, U.L., Christ, M.H., Johnstone, K.M., Rittenberg, L., (2010). Effective Sizing of Internal Audit Departments, Altamonte Springs: The IIA Research Foundation.
4. Grossman, S., Hart, O., (1983). An analisis of principal agent problem, Econometrica, 53(1), 1357–1368.
5. Khalil, F., Lawarrée, J., (2001). Catching the agent on the wrong foot: ex post choice of monitoring, Journal of Public Economics, Elsevier, vol. 82(3), pp. 327–347.
6. Laffont, J.J., (1987). Incentives and the Allocation of Public Goods, in Alan J. Auerbach and Martin Feldstein, eds., Handbook of public economics, vol. 2, Amsterdam: North Holland, pp. 537–69.
7. Maskin, E.S., (2007). Prize Lecture by Eric S. Maskin, Nobel Media AB, Nobel Prize.
8. Holmstrom, B., (1977). On Incentives and Control in Organizations, Unpublished Ph.D. dissertation, Graduate School of Business, Stanford University.
9. Myerson, R., (1978). Refinements of the Nash equilibrium concept, International Journal of Game Theory, 7, 73–80.
10. Shavell, S., (1979). Risk Sharing and Incentives in the Principal and Agent Relationship, The Bell Journal of Economics, vol. 10, no. 1, pp. 55–73.
11. Kaplan, R.S., Norton, D.P., (1996). The Balanced Scorecard: Translating Strategy into Action, Boston, MA.
12. Arrow, K.J., (1950). A Difficulty in the Concept of Social Welfare, Journal of Political Economy 58 (4): 328–346.
13. Baron, D., Besanko, D., (1984). Regulation, Asymetric Information, and Auditing, RAND Journal of Economics, vol. 15, no. 4, pp. 447–70.
14. Hurwicz, L., (2008). But Who Will Guard the Guardians?, American Economic Review, American Economic Association, vol. 98(3), pp. 577–585.
15. International Standards for the Professional Practice of Internal Auditing, Institute of Internal Auditors, Florida, USA (issued October, 2016; revised January, 2017).
16. Ministry of Public Finance. Law no. 672/2002 on public internal audit, republished in the Official Gazette no. 856/05.12.2011, as subsequently amended.
17. Law no. 544/2001, on free access to public information, with subsequent amendments.

Alexandru-Sabin NICULA[1, 2], Iulia MEDVESCHI[3], Vasile AVĂDĂNEI[2], Ioan SURDU[2], Emanuela-Adina COCIŞ[2]

[1] Faculty of Geography, Babeş-Bolyai University, Cluj-Napoca, Romania, E-mail: sabin.nicula@gmail.com

[2] Centre of Mountain Economy "CE-MONT", Romanian Academy, Faculty of Political, Administrative and Communication Sciences, Department of Communication, Public Relations and Advertising, Babeş-Bolyai University, Cluj-Napoca, Romania

Accessibility and Ecclesiastic Polarization of Monastic Settlements in the Romanian Carpathians. Case Study: Monastic Settlements on the Occidental Carpathians

Abstract *The purpose of this article is to emphasis the intensity of ecclesiastical polarization reflected in mountainous territory in terms of accessibility. The research is conducted across the Western Carpathians, extending over an area of 18,650 km². We identified 65 monastic establishments of which together hold 892 accommodation places and a number of 631 dwellers.The methology consisted in identifying the coordinates of monastic establishments in Google Earth Pro and after in their conversion in a shapefile point format, using QGIS 3.0. Girona. The ecclesiastical polarization analysis was conducted using the Kernel Density tool. The accessibility of the monastic establishments to the road network (adapted after Open Street Map) was determined through Service Area tool. The main results of the paper are bringing to front three major areas regarding ecclesiastical polarization, clustered around the following most important monasteries: Râmeţ, Prislop and Nera. The accommodation capacity reveals four spatial groups in the Apuseni Mountains and three in Banatului Mountains. Regarding the accessibility, for 59.56 % (11101.76 km²) from the study area, the access is exceeding 1 hour isochrone (60.1'-90')and for30.82 % (5,749.26 km²) the cost access time is between 30.1'-60'.The optimal accessibility (0'-20' and 20.1'-30'), summarize together under 10 % (1,798.98 km²).*

Keywords: geographic accessibility, geographic connectivity, mountain accessibility, spatial polarization

Introduction

Until now, few studies have been conducted in respect to the geographic aspects of monastic places. Starting from this consideration, the present article encompasses an introductory scientific endeavour that one may need to comprehend the relational approach established between territorial accessibility and ecclesiastical polarization. Without fail, Romanian mountainous areas and their surrounding territories are spaces that still own developmental gaps concerning the accessibility and geographical connectivity of the territory. Using an appropriate range of intellectual and methodological traditions within geographical research we aim to determine the accessibility and geographical connectivity of monastic settlements located in the Occidental Carpathians.

Thus, the paper consists in two major parts, dealing with: 1. the first procedure consisted in highlighting time-based accessibility using the Service Area tool in the QGIS 3.0 software. Girona, respectively, the access roads (natural accessibility vs. territorial accessibility). 2. Interpolation based on the following data: a) the accommodation capacity of the monasteries; b) the polarization potential of the administrative territorial units. Undeniable, urban centres have even-greater impact on surrounding rural areas, especially in mountains, by being increasingly powerful sinks of resources (mineral, forests for fuel and building materials, agricultural products and of people through migration).

The integrated analysis of the territorial accessibility in relation to the socio-economic polarization expressed in the territorial profile of the monastic centres leads to the identification of the communication dysfunctions but also to the evaluation of the economic potential of the secluded centres in the conditions in which the fluency of the material and informational flows take place in the territory in a precarious way. Different regional and local players should be involved in promoting the inclusion of mountain areas in Romanian's overall development aims, enabling a more efficient and effective implementation of existing national sectoral policies to ensure growth attractiveness and sustainable development of disadvantaged rural and mountainous areas, thus enhancing the resources, stabilizing the population, reinforcing economic power conditions at local level, while preserving the ecological balance and protecting the natural environment.

Study area

With a surface area of 18650 km^2, the Western Carpathians extend southwards, from the valleys of Someş and Barcău (47^{0}14'0''N/22°31'40''E) to the Danube (44^{0}28'47''N/22°8'28''E). To the east (46^{0}34'8''N/23^{0}45'47''E), they border the Transylvanian Depression through a tectonic and lithological line, while the demarcation between them and the Southern Carpathians is given by the Strei-Bistra and Timiş-Cerna valleys. Towards west (44^{0}50'29''N/21^{0}21'15''E), the mountains border a complex and winding series of "gulf" depressions (Pop, 2006).

Literature review: Geographic accessibility and spatial polarization

A mature body of studies about accessibility and connectivity have been developed. Both concepts are included in multiple contexts, some concerns being raised in the absence of a consensual agreement among researchers regarding a set of standard definitions. Depicting a geographical perspective, Handy, convincingly argues that accessibility "involves a combination of two elements: location on a surface relative to corresponding destinations, and the characteristics of the transport network (or a network of another nature) formed between the points on that surface."(Handy 2002, p. 65). In short, this model indicates that geographic accessibility is a distance that allows understanding the proximity, separation and/or discontinuity between two or more elements in space. Spatial accessibility encompasses the access towards a territory and the various activities held there. Accessibility, related to the role of transport infrastructure networks in synchronizing and organizing social and economic activities in the territory served, signifies the greater or lesser ease with which goods or people can move from one place to another by calling at one or all of the transport modes whose connection in relation to the criterion chosen is favourable to the interests of the beneficiary of the transfer or exploitation system. Facing this realities, religious settlements were determined to obtain funds by means of trade, entry tax levy, provision of catering, guide or accommodation services. (Stănciulescu, Ţârca, 2010, p. 132)

At the same time, in terms of geographic connectivity, Brierly underlines that effective description of landscape compartments, and their spatial organization, provides a catchment-framed basis with which to appraise system dynamics and related evolutionary tendencies. (Brierly et. al, 2006, p. 166) In a broader perspective, connectivity is a property of a network to offer alternative itineraries between centres, is pivotal in explaining spatial relationships, the behaviour of biophysical fluxes and associated trajectories of adjustment. In this respect, the connectivity is the degree of cohesion between the different centres of a road network. These centres have a hierarchy that determines the connection levels. In this sense, process-response relationship must be understood as a dynamic system and not as elements without interaction defined by the spatial distribution of various components and their topological relationships (Preston et. al, 2011, p. 21). Of noteworthy importance are landscape compartments and the degree of landscape connectedness of differing parts of landscapes, associated residence times, and the frequency of events that drives change along with the spatial ramifications of those changes (Brierley, Fryirs 2011, p.27). Ultimately, connectivity contributes as an indicator to be considered for measuring local development and in the establishment of planning areas.

Going further, we propose a classification to determine the homogeneous units of geographical accessibility and mountainous exploration. Incipiently, in understanding the spaced-time accessibility authors such as: (Merciu et. et al, 2013, p. 106.), pledge for using GIS toolbox for measuring and mapping space-time accessibility. Secondly, the concept of accessibility gravitates around facilities with central role (health care services, economic facilities and supply services, transportation, cultural and educational, recreational services and networks, etc.) as distributed in studies emphasizing upon: developing a composite index of spatial accessibility across different health care sectors (Siegel, et al., 2016, p. 205), behavioural model of accessibility based on the number of available opportunities.

(Cascetta et al., 2016, p. 45) Last, we must bring to light the concept of mountainous accessibility.

In Romania, economically disadvantaged rural communities, often isolated or located in mountain regions, are very vulnerable, confronted with the phenomenon of depopulation and the lack of prospects for the future. Mountain regions differ from other regions due to "natural disadvantages (i.e., elevation, low soil fertility, reduced access to the communication routes and markets), and structural disadvantages (i.e., migration trends, restricted jobs, distances from decisional centres, and insufficiently developed infrastructure). Following this line, it is imperiously necessary to find solutions in order to connect mountainous accessibility to destination accessibility."

If we consider the perspective of Middleton, accessibility to mountainous destinations is linked to components of infrastructure (roads, airports), equipment (size, speed and range of public transport), and government regulations regarding transportation. (Middleton 2001, p. 292). Encapsulating a similar perspective, Munteanu (2010, p. 130) points out that destination accessibility should be regarded in terms of transport accessibility and must require four components: 1. spatial/territorial accessibility (involving the physical distance to the destination) 2. Economic accessibility determines the travel cost that must be paid by tourist, 3. psychological accessibility (including the effort of travel tourists are willing endure to reach the destination and 4. Social accessibility (reflected by the educational levels and personal and/or social experience).

In relation to poverty and distance to urban centres, two broad categories of rural areas can be identified (de Ferranti et al., 2005, 8), "Marginal rural areas", which are characterized by low densities, being far from markets (urban centres) and with silvo-agricultural potential not very favourable and "favourable rural areas", which are closer to the markets (urban centres) and with forest tourism potential. Any attempt to highlight the totality of rural characteristics that can synthesize and value the entire rural, complex, universal, valid and complete picture will not be enough. Gradually, Friedmann and Stöhr (1967) continued the research in the field of regional development as they apply to classical theories by issuing the theory of endogenous development. This theoretical perspective is built on the opposite scheme to the theory of poles of growth, putting the so-called development on the basic structural lenses. According to this conceptual framework, the relations between centres and peripheries are characterized by 2 features: (1) centres consolidate their domination through reinforcing mechanisms of polarization, establishing a closed spatial system. Ultimately, the so-called feedback mechanisms involve different types of effects (domination, information, psychological, modernization, linkage and production effects); (2) as a result of this domination, innovations developed in the centres will be introduced in the peripheries, where by further intensifying the information flows in the dependent areas; p. 210).

Synthesizing, accessibility "describes the positioning of a place and its qualities in relation to opportunities, activities and / or resources existing elsewhere, where a place can mean a region, a city or a corridor." (Wegener et al., 2002 quoted by Muntele et al., 2010, p. 16). The activities or opportunities to be achieved, such as effort, time, distance, cost to reach these activities or opportunities (Wegener et al., 2002 quoted by Muntele et al., 2010.)

Data and Methods

In order to perform the analysis of accessibility to monastic settlements, it was necessary first of all to prepare the data structures necessary for this approach. In this respect, we identified and mapped out all the monastic settlements in the studied territory, and subsequently corrected and verified the major road network (highways, European / national and county roads) available in the territory by the year 2017.

The coordinates for monastic settlements were identified in Google Earth Pro, based on data and information collected in (Surd et. et al., 2016; Ciocioi et al., 2016; Iraşcu, 2014); and some online sources of ecclesiastical institutions. They were saved in a.kml file format and imported into the QGIS 3.0 Girona software, where they were converted to a point-shaped file and redesigned in the 1970 Stereographic Projection. The new shape file was validated according to the reality of the territory and then added to the attribute table two other fields of interest for analysis the potential for ecclesiastical polarization: the number of monastic dwellers at each ecclesiastic settlement, respectively the number of accommodation units of the monasteries.

The road network used in accessibility analysis comes from the Open Street Map database. The entire network was corrected, verified and redesigned in the same cartographic projection with the monastic settlements (Stereographic Projection 1970) for the compatibility of the layers. Analytically, the first procedure consisted in highlighting time-based accessibility using the Service Area tool in the QGIS 3.0 software. Girona. The analysis was based on the data in the two shape files: the vector point and the road network made up of highways, European, national and county roads (vector polyline). The cost of time has been set to outline the following time intervals: 5 ', 10', 20 ', 30', 60 ', 90'.

The second accessibility analysis was to run the Multiple Ring Buffer from the same software application to make the buffer zones of 1 km, 2 km and 3 km respectively spread in the mountainous area. This analysis is particularly useful in detecting accessibility to monastic settlements reported to the access network, expressing the proximity or remoteness of a location to a major road.

In order to highlight the spatial patterns of ecclesiastical polarization, we have recourse to the calculation of Kernel density for the following parameters: the number of inhabitants, respectively the number of accommodation places of each monastic settlement. The Kernel Density tool calculates the density of features (point or polyline) in a neighbourhood around those features (Silverman, 1986). In our case, Kernel Density calculates the density of point features around each output raster cell. Conceptually, a smoothly curved surface is fitted over each

Table 1: The cost time in terms of territorial accessibility

No. crt.	Time travel (minutes)	Area (km^2)	%
1	0–5	96.74	0.51
2	5.1–10	182.26	0.97
3	10.1–15	178.26	0.95
4	15.1–20	384.57	2.06
5	20.1–30	957.15	5.13
6	30.1–60	5749.26	30.82
7	60.1–90	11101.76	59.56
=	**Total**	**18650**	**100 %**

Source: own calculations based on territorial analysis.

point. The surface value is highest at the location of the point and diminishes with increasing distance from the point, reaching zero at the Search radius distance from the point (Arc GIS 10.3. help).

Results

After the spatial analysis of the Western Carpathians in Romania, a number of 65 monastic settlements were quantified, out of which 42 (64.6 %) are monasteries and 23 (35.4 %) are hermitages. More than half of all monastic settlements, 34 (52.3 %) are nunnery and the remaining 31 (47.7 %) are monasteries. Nunnery monasteries include a staff of 463 (73.4 %) as opposed to monasteries with a much smaller number of only 168 (26.6 %). The accommodation capacity of the monasteries and hermitages does not exceed 1000 seats, being at the level of 2017 at 892 seats. Accessibility to the monastic settlements is relatively low, the most significant factors being the morphology of the mountain relief, the low connectivity of the road network as its modest yawning. It is not necessary to exclude from the equation a qualitative criterion, more difficult to quantify, namely the location of the monasteries in less populated locations, where spiritual peace is not disturbed, and monastic life blends harmoniously into communion with nature.

The spatial analysis shows that 18 of the monastic settlements have a low accessibility. Among the monasteries with low accessibility are Călugăra, Almăj-Putna, Feredeu, Sub Stone, Poiana Sohodol, Izbuc, Piatra Craiului, Stâna de Vale, Brâncoveni and Teiuş and among the herds: Semenic, Petrosniţa, Almaş, Huta, Leşu, Poiana Florilor, Poşaga (see Figures 1 and 2). The monastic settlements with high

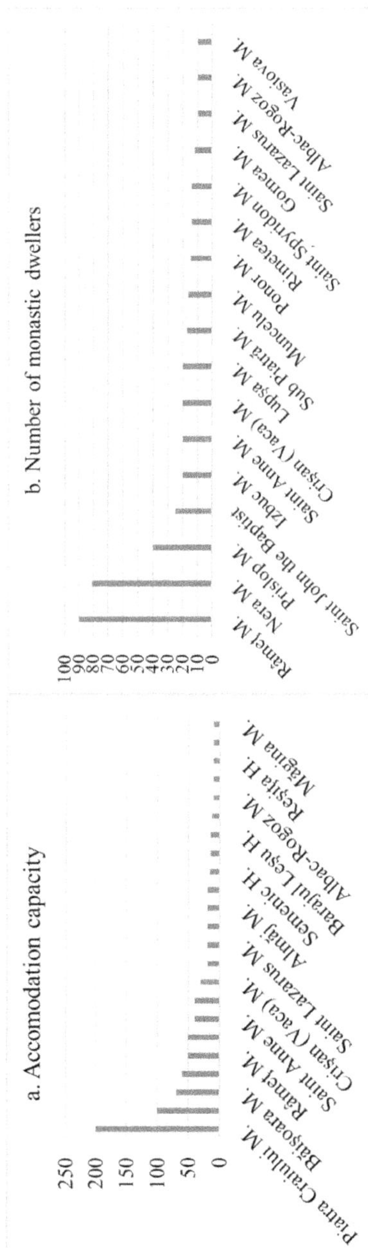

Figure 1: The size of monastic settlements after: a) accommodation capacity and b) number of dwellers

Source: own calculations based on Ciocioi et al., 2016; Iraşcu, 2014 data.

accessibility are: Râmeţ, Prislop and Nera, which are the largest monasteries as a number of inhabitants and exert a more intense ecclesiastical polarization in the territory.

The relational cost analysis of the service area in terms of territorial accessibility reveals an uneven distribution over time scrolls. For 59.56 % (11101.76 km^2) of the territory studied, access time to a monastic settlement is between 60.1'-90'while for 30.82 % (5749.26 km^2) of the same territory, access time to the monastic settlement is between 30,1'-60'. Accessibility with higher values is recorded, as we expected, in the 0'-20'(841.83 km^2, which means 4.49 % of the territory), respectively in the 20.1'-30' an area of 957.15 km^2, which means 5.13 % of the whole territory (see Table 1).

Through the connectivity perspective, we can remark (see figure 2b) the fact that the majority of monastic establishments are connected to the road network, excepting the hermitages: Huta, Almaş, and Almăj-Putna, wich are connected through forest and dirty roads. These hermitages have a peripherical position in territory, with low accessibility caused by morphological and petrographically restricted factors.

The ecclesiastical polarization of the monastic settlements was established according to two criteria, namely: the number of available places in the accommodation units and the number of monastic dwellers in each monastery. For spatial modelling, kernel density analysis was used.

The modelling of the ecclesiastical clusters according to the number of available places in the accommodation units reveals four spatial groups in the Apuseni Mountains and three in the Banatului Mountains.The highest value of Kernel density was detected in the case of Piatra Craiului monastery (0.51) and the lowest value was recorded by Huta, Almaş and Almăj-Putna hermitages (0).Other monastic establishments with significative Kernel density values are: Izbuc, Râmeţ, Ponor, and Ciucea, all with values recorded between 0.20–0.30.

The results regarding the number of monastic dwellers in each monastery, show a strong spatial cluster in the central-eastern part of the Apuseni Mountains, where there is a relatively short distance between 12 monastic establishments (Albac-Rogoz, Livezile, Lupşa, Măgina, Muncelu, Ponor, Poşaga, Râmeţ, Schimbarea la Faţă, Sfântul Spiridon, Sub Piatră, Valea Bistrei), of which the most important is Râmeţ Monastery. Another cluster was identified in the south-western part of the Banatului Mountains, where the monasteries Nera and Călugăra are the most representative. The third cluster was identified in the central part of the Western Carpathians, more precisely at the eastern border of the Poiana Ruscă Mountains, where the Prislop and Ghelari monasteries are located. The highest value of Kernel density was recorded in the case of Râmeţ, Ponor, Sub Piatră, Nera and Livezile (with values between 0.20–0.30). Prislop monastery has a value around 0.10. The lowest Kernel values (under 0.10) were recorded in the case of Sfânta. Ana, Crişan, Crişcior, Poşaga, Lupşa, Valea Bistrei etc.

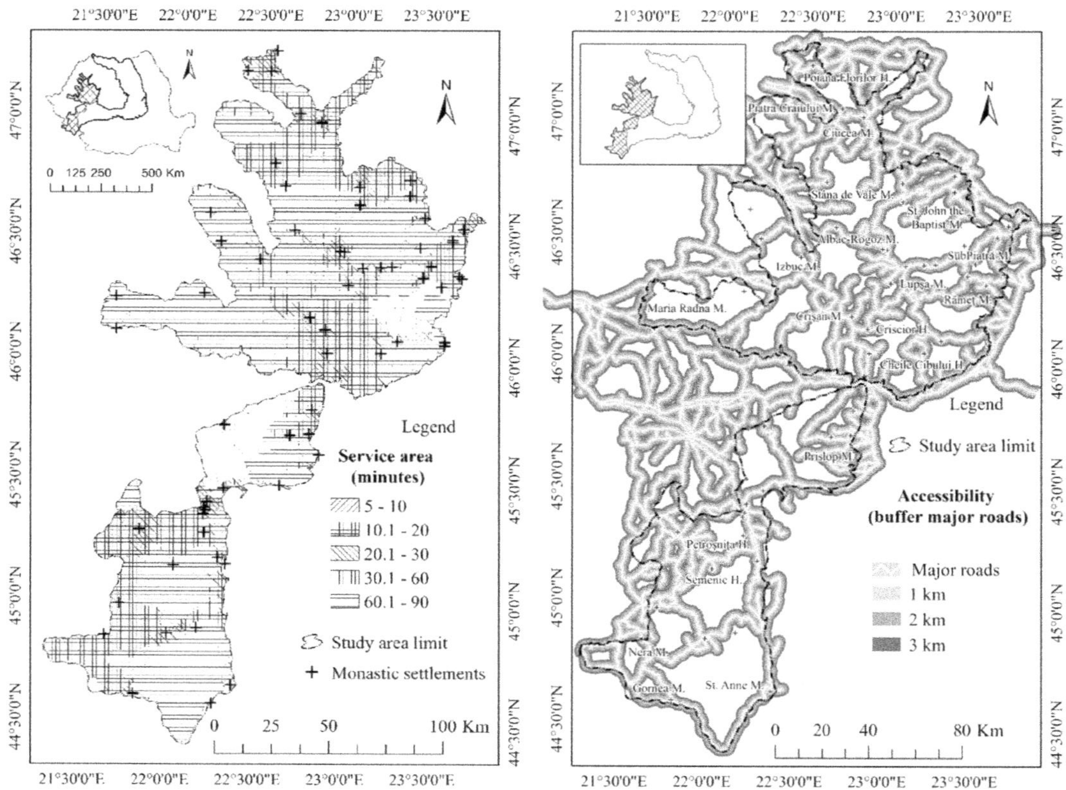

Figure 2: Accessibility in Occidental Carpathians. a. Service area (time cost) b.accessibility to the major road network

Source: own calculations based on QGIS 3.0. Girona analysis and OSM.

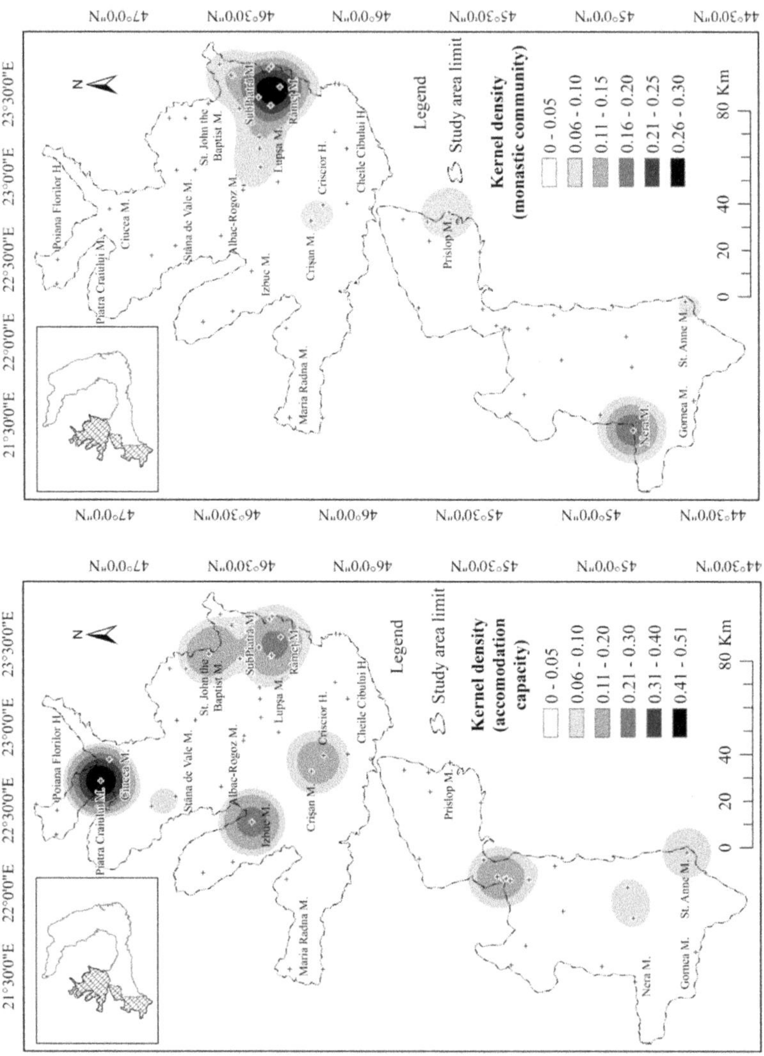

Figure 3: Kernel Density Estimation: a) after the accommodation places; b) after number of dwellers

Source: own calculations based on QGIS 3.0. Girona analysis.

Conclusions

The accessibility to the monastic settlements in the Western Romanian Carpathians is strongly conditioned by the spatial morphology, the poor connectivity of the road network and the quality of the territorial access infrastructures. The relational analysis of the accessibility and ecclesiastical polarization exercised by the monastic settlements in the territorial aspect reveals a relationship of mutual conditioning, decisively influencing the frequency and intensity of the flows of pilgrims that converge to cloistered central place. As a general rule, monastic settlements that exert more intense polarization are located in proximity to major communication routes with good connections to the regional road network. It is the case of Râmeţ monasteries (located near E81, connection made through the DJ750C), Prislop (DJ687K allows DJ 687A connection to DN68) and Nera (DJ 571). The monastic settlements with the highest accommodation capacity (Piatra Craiului, Izbuc and Băişoara) are on an upward trend with regard to the pulsating attraction of the pilgrims, having constructive prerequisites to exercise a greater ecclesiastical polarization in the future.

This study, through the methodological framework transposed in a transdisciplinary matrix, is opening new research directions regarding the relational analysis of ecclesiastical polarization exercised in the territorial profile. Also, through this research we are bringing to front the analysis of the accessibility to the monastic establishments located in a undeveloped territory such as the Western Carpathians.

The main conclusions relevate the fact that the mountain area has a lower accessibility, the landform and petrographic structure being the most important conditioning factors. In addition, the poor connectivity and low infrastructure quality of road network contribute to the dificult access in territory.

The highest ecclesiastical polarization is exercited in territory by the oldest, prestigious and largest monasteries, such as Râmeţ, Prislop and Nera. The newest hermitages, builted nowadays, have a lot of favorable premises to develop their specific activities and to fortificate the monastical functions.

References

1. Brierley, Gary/Fryirs, Kirstie/Vikrant, Jain: Landscape connectivity: the geographic basis of geomorphic applications, Area, (38)2, 2006, pp. 165–174.
2. Cascetta, Ennio/Cartenì, Armando/Montanino, Marcello: A behavioral model of accessibility based on the number of available opportunities, Journal of Transport Geography (51), 2016, pp. 45–58.
3. Ciocioi Gheorghiţă, Dragne Amalia, Vlad Diana-Cristina.,Voicu Mihaela, Ghidul mănăstirilor din România, Ed. a 4-a, Edit. Sophia, Bucureşti, 2016.
4. de Ferranti, Perry D.,G, Foster, W. Lederman D., and Valdés A, Beyond the city: The rural contribution to development. World Bank Latin American and Caribbean Studies. Washington, D.C.: World Bank, 2005.

5. Friedmann John and W. Stöhr: The Uses of Regional Science; Policy Planning in Chile, K.S A Papers XVIII, Regional Science, Volume18, Issue1, 1967, pp. 207–222.
6. Handy, Susan L/Boarnet, Marlon G/Ewing, Reid/Killingsworth Richard, E/.: How the built environment affects physical activity: views from urban planning. The American Journal of Preventive Medicine, (23), 2002, pp. 64–73.
7. Iraşcu Viorel, Ghidul mănăstirilor catolice din România: (al caselor, centrelor, oratoriilor, institutelor seculare, congregaţiilor şi ordinelor catolice, Edit. Rovimed, Bacău, 2014.
8. Merciu Cristina, Stoian George, Merciu Daniel, Saghin, Irina, Using GIS for calculating the accessibility to hospitals in the city of Bucharest and its metropolitan area (Romania), Geographica Pannonica, 17(4), 2013. pp. 106–113.
9. Middleton, Victor T. C., Clarke Jackie, (1994). Marketing in travel and tourism. Butterworth Heinemann, Oxford, 2001.
10. Munteanu, A. Conceptualizing and composing tourism accessibility. Lucrările Seminarului Geografic Dimitrie Cantemir, 30, 2010, 125–133.
11. Muntele I., Groza O., Ţurcănaşu G., Rusu A., Tudora D., Calitatea infrastructurii de transport ca premisă a diferenţierii spaţiilor rurale din Moldova. Edit. Universităţii Alexandru Ioan Cuza, Iaşi, 2010.
12. Pop, Gr., Carpaţii şi Subcarpaţii României, (2006), Ed. a 2-a, Edit. Presa Universitară Clujeană, Cluj-Napoca, 2006
13. Preston, Nicholas/Brierley, Gary/Fryirs, Kirstie, The geographic basis of geomorphic enquiry. Geography Compass. 5(1), 2011, pp. 21–34.
14. Siegel Martin, Koller Daniela, Vogt Verena, Sundmacher Leonie, Developing a composite index of spatial accessibility across different health care sectors: A German example, Health Policy, 120(2), 2016, pp. 205–212.
15. Silverman, B. W., Density Estimation for Statistics and Data Analysis. New York: Chapman and Hall, 1986.
16. Stănciulescu, Cecilia G./Ţârca, Alexandra M.: Implications of Commercial Activity within Monastic Settlements as a Way to. Maintain the Sustainable Development of Religious Tourism in Romania. Revista Amfiteatru Economic (12) 27, 2010, pp.129–144.
17. Surd Vasile, Constantin Veronica, Nicula Alexandru-Sabin, Aşezările din Munţii Apuseni, Presa Universitară Clujeană, Cluj-Napoca, 2016.
18. Wegener M., Eskelinnen H., Fürst F., Schürmann C. and Spiekermann K. (2002), Criteria for the Spatial Differentiation of the EU Territory: Geographical Position, Forschungen 102.2, Bundesamtfür Bauwesen und Raumordnung, Bonn.
19. https://download.geofabrik.de/europe/romania.html, accesed in 14.06.2017.

Paul MARINESCU[1], *Sorin-George TOMA*[2],
Gheorghe-Florentin MIULESCU[3]

[1] Faculty of Administration and Business, University of Bucharest,
Email: paulmarinescu1@gmail.com

[2] Faculty of Administration and Business, University of Bucharest,
Email: tomagsorin62@yahoo.com

[3] Faculty of Administration and Business, University of Bucharest,
Email: flo.miu17@gmail.com

Creativity and Innovation, Catalysts of Tomorrow's World

Abstract *There is currently a concern regarding the manner in which creativity stimulates innovation. The process of generating new ideas and innovative potentials does not necessarily mean that such are implemented. The role of innovation is precisely to enhance these ideas within the socio-economic environment. The current concern of society is to use innovation in a constructive manner as we are many times tempted to use innovation in a destructive sense as well. The number of patents at the level of a country demonstrates the innovative potential but if they do not reach the marketing stage, the results have no economic effect. Highly competitive companies are considering investing resources in research as well in order to ensure a competitive advantage on a market where competition is increasingly tough. Creativity and innovation become strong arguments in the world competition, and the areas in which they apply are very varied. The resources of creativity and innovation are unlimited but the biggest challenge is that they are used for the development of society. The paper aims to show areas where creativity and innovation are present and to outline some perspectives about the development of creativity and innovation in the future society.*

Keywords: creativity, innovation, growth, research and development

Introduction

It is generally known that today innovation and creativity play an important role in organizational dynamics. In our analysis, we refer to creative people, innovative solutions, to the dynamics of the working environment and, not least, to the companies investing in research and development (Glăveanu 2018).

Doing an analysis of the various areas of the world, we find that the intensity of innovation is the lowest in Africa, 20 % and at the highest level in North America,

39 % (Global Entrepreneurship Monitor 2017). Creativity and innovation play an important role in the development of society by increasing organizational performance but we must also consider competitiveness as a key factor in increasing the level of general prosperity (Garelli 2006). Nowadays it is important to ask the right questions but also to find the necessary answers. Thus, creativity will play an important role because without clear questions and without the right answers, we cannot solve the problems of the current world.

Creativity can be defined as a process of identifying some useful ideas, while innovation represents a process of designing the best ideas in reality. Specifically, we can define creativity as an individual activity in general, while innovation may represent a team effort. The innovative process starts from a necessity that requires finding a creative idea, leading to a creative product in essence (Bisadi et al 2012).

In this article the authors intend to present some aspects in relation to the influences of innovation and creativity at the level of society's evolution, but also to define some perspectives on the influences that they will have in the future in various components of reality: social, cultural, economic, technical, educational, etc. The paper aims to show areas where creativity and innovation are present and to outline some perspectives about the development of creativity and innovation in the future society. The methodology was based on researching secondary data found in electronic databases.

1. Literature review

Innovations that are potentially marketable may materialize on global markets, helping to increase productivity at the level of a technologically advanced economy. We can talk about the innovation of products or services from the perspective of their content, but we can also talk about the design of a product or service. Innovation can become an engine factor and at the level of organizational structures and at the level of institutional components as well:

"Commercially viable innovations are becoming the linchpin of success in global markets by helping to raise total productivity, and they account for a major portion of the growth in advanced and industrializing economies. Innovation can take many forms, among which product innovation is but one. Design and incremental process innovations are more common, and in recent years myriad innovations have been introduced by providers of services. Innovation is changing the structure and enhancing the capabilities of organizations. Moreover, institutional innovations are sharpening market incentives for entrepreneurial activity and technology trading, which take new ideas, products, and practices into the commercial domain." (Yusuf 2009, p. 1)

It is very important to establish as clearly as possible the role that creativity and innovation have within the development process of the economy by highlighting each component of the two processes. Creativity is influenced by individual talent, by the culture of the masses, but also by the educational system. The innovative spirit is influenced by incentives, by the resources allocated for fundamental

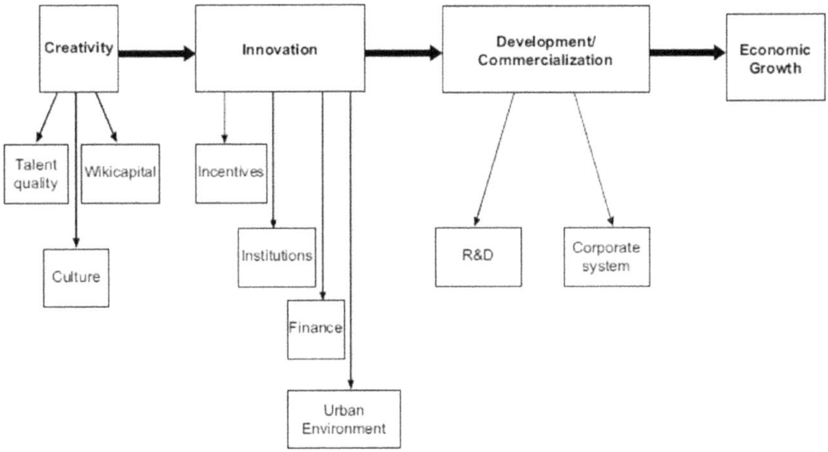

Figure 1: Creativity and economic performance

Source: Yusuf, Shadid: From creativity to innovation. Technology in Society 31, 2009

research, by the socio-economic environment, and institutions as referees in validation processes and legislative initiatives. Creativity and innovation become the motor factors of economic development if each materialized idea enters the process of research and development and, in the end, in the materialization on the markets through the marketing process. In this respect, Shadid Yusuf's model is noteworthy as there are mentioned the possible links between creativity and innovation:

The author highlights that the talent, components of culture and wikicapital developed through networks facilitate the expression of creativity at organizational level. The ways in which representative companies value the elements that facilitate the development of creativity are illustrative in this respect.

Thus, Google is concerned about the identification of talents from various areas of the world and therefore offers countless benefits (catering services, free training programs, facilities for sporting activities, etc.). Within Google Company the recruitment and selection process is permanent; there is concern to identify human potential in all areas of the world. The company is concerned with creating conditions for people selected to be placed in teams within which they can value their potential, thus the team becoming an extension of the family (Inc.). To attract valuable specialists, high-performance companies are considering synchronizing the personal values of employees with the organizational values.

In this respect, the components of the organizational culture of the company Zappos, specializing in the distribution of products online, are enlightening. Participants in internships who promote the recruitment test and who consider that the proposed job does not suit them receive a sum of money even if they are not employed (according to Entrepreneur). It thus creates the premise for people to come to companies, this way facilitating the attraction of the most competent people in different areas of the world. Thus, the wikicapital can become a catalyst for the future allowing the realization of some collaboration in the virtual environment and attracting some important resources necessary to achieve the objectives of these companies. Investors or foundations can play an important role in sustainable development because, in this way, they contribute to the concentration of financial resources and human experiences as well. The great quality of these networks is that they are dynamic and can permanently create nodes in which human experiences center in relation to the necessities that occur at some point.

In the model presented above, innovation represents an important component being often an effect of creativity. The incentives, the quality of the legislation, the capacity to attract investments, the performance of urban clusters, all contribute to the creation of an innovative spirit, but also to materialize thereof. Some examples of the application of innovation in the economic environment are suggestive. Therefore, we mention the way in which Ultimate Software offers free vacations to stimulate employees by encouraging them to participate permanently in innovative processes (according to Robinson Resource Group). Regulatory institutions can ensure the necessary legislation for the development of the innovative spirit and their activity can be also potentiated by the solutions that consultancy companies offer. We notice how Deloitte, provider of consulting services, has developed on several levels, providing solutions for developing products, services, business models or innovative management in very diverse areas of the economy. On the other hand, the need for funding requires innovative activities that can reduce the time of identifying the funding sources and the materialization thereof into the business plan (Deloitte Insights). Innovative online platforms can facilitate communication between investors and users of online platforms as beneficiaries (e.g. kickstarter). Urban concentrations have facilitated the creation of advanced technology centres in which the competences of experts and financial resources are gathered. Such centres can offer innovative solutions in relation to the needs of the companies.

Creativity and innovation decisively influence the evolution of global technology being considered as essential elements for the development of the society. Studies on the necessity of an environment based on creativity and innovation are enlightening in relation to the concern of all stakeholders (entrepreneurs, banks, beneficiaries, etc.) to create the conditions necessary for a framework in which creativity and innovation can be manifested and can contribute to the progress of the organizations:

> "So far, the effect of built environment on creativity and innovation has been studied in contexts of educational places such as kindergartens and schools (e.g. Mozaffar, 1997; Niu, 2007; Shafaie & Madani, 2010), urban and residential areas (e.g. Brodersen,

2005; Faizi et al., 2012), and workplaces (e.g. Amabile,1997; Du l& Ceylan, 2011; Martens, 2011; McCoy & Evans, 2002)." (Bisadi 2012, p. 233)

There is concern for the creation of some tools and methods that can be used in schools, communities, enterprises, industries, universities to generate conditions in which new products/services can be achieved or improve the existing ones:

> "Intelligent Fast Failure (IFF) is a tool, method and theory that may be utilized individually or in schools, communities, businesses, industry, universities and anywhere else where individuals or groups of people are trying to create something new and of value or improve something already in use. The IFF concept and acronym was coined by Jack V. Matson initially in an article titled Intelligent Fast Failure in Management Letter (March 25, 1989)" (Tahirsylaj 2012, p. 266)

2. The role of creativity and innovation in the development of companies

Starting from a statistical study on the most innovative companies conducted by The Boston Consulting Group, several suggestive situations were presented. Here we refer more precisely to the analysis of four parameters: revenue change, EBIT change - Earnings Before Interest & Tax, TSR change - Total Shareholder Return and R&D spending change - Research and Development with an important role in creating conditions for the dynamics of an innovative environment. Comparative analysis of innovative activity at BMW and Tesla companies provides interesting information about the contribution of these parameters to the evolution of performance within the two organizations. In the graphs shown below one can observe the organizational dynamics of the two companies whose innovative evolution was analyzed between 2013 and 2017.

We can see a remarkable ascent of Tesla starting with 2013 (the year starting with which the company is mentioned in the study) until 2016, and a slight decrease in the innovative trend between 2016 and 2017. The question is what the elements that led to such an evolution were. Analyzing Tesla's data we find that it has a 73 % increase in income (revenue change), a 12.7 % decrease in EBIT change-Earnings Before Interest & Tax, a decrease of 11 % on TSR change -Total Shareholder return and a 16.2 % increase in R&D spending change-research and development. Even if there is a decrease in the percentages of EBIT change and TSR change, there is concern for investments, R&D so that in the future will increase net profit and TSR. We find that Tesla ranks 6th of a total of 50 companies mentioned in the analysis of the Boston Consulting Group, the first 5 places being occupied by: Apple, Google, Microsoft, Amazon and Samsung.

In the case of BMW, the evolution is different. If in 2013 the company was ranked 9th, and in 2015 it was on the 7th place, in 2017 the company reached number 36 in this ranking (in the second half of the rankings). The percentage figures are low, more specifically: there is a 2.2 % increase in revenue change, a

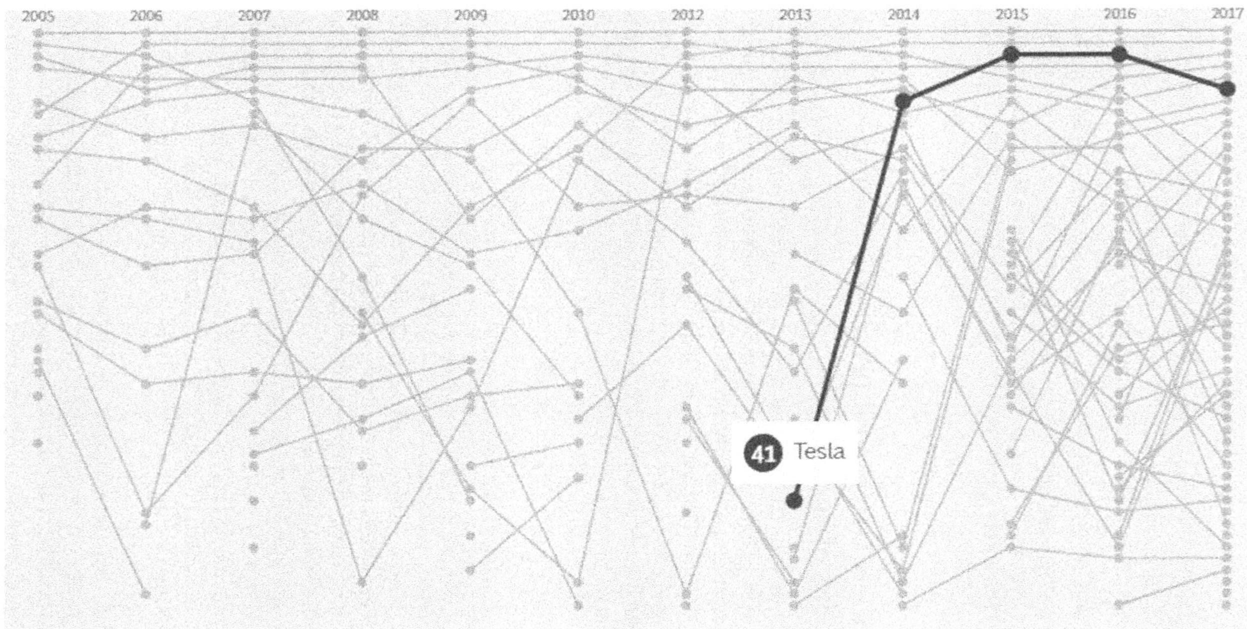

Figure 2: The most innovative companies 2018 - Tesla situation

Source: The Boston Consulting Group, The most innovative companies 2018, https://www.bcg.com/publications/collections/most-innovative-companies-2018.aspx

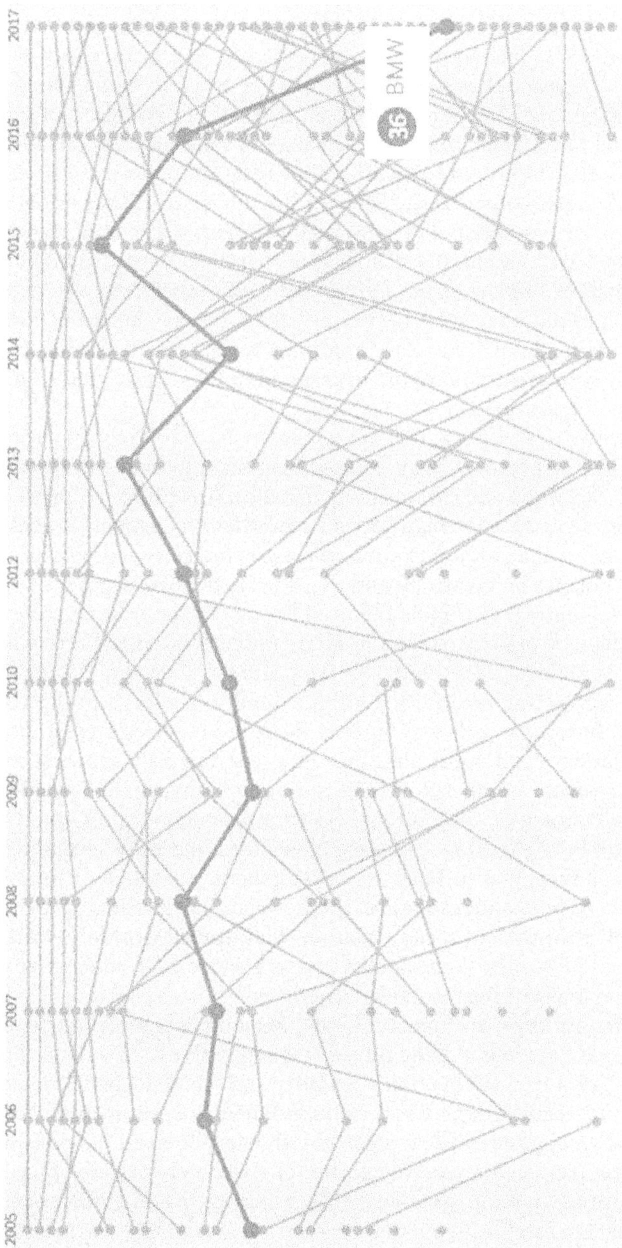

Figure 3: The most innovative companies 2018 - BMW situation

Source: The Boston Consulting Group, The most innovative companies 2018, https://www.bcg.com/publications/collections/most-innovative-companies-2018.aspx

decrease of 0.8 % of EBIT change, a 5.5 % decrease in TSR change and no increase in investments in R&D spending change in relation to the previous year.

Tesla registered 73 % income growth, respectively 16.2 % increase in R&D investments, BMW registered only 2.2 % increase in revenue while the level of R&D remained unchanged. The comparative analysis of the evolution of the two companies over the last 5 years indicates a change of ranking positions between the two companies. It is important to mention that Tesla has taken over the electric car market through innovation and the efficient use of resources thus establishing another direction of development of the automotive industry, also important in the conservation of the environment. Even though Tesla initially recorded higher negative values in terms of EBIT change (12.7 %) and TSR change (16.2 %) compared to the BMW which initially registers lower negative values (as mentioned above), yet the investments made by Tesla for important results in the future, provide the company with even greater potential to respond to the market challenges and competition with competitors.

Companies have registered a significant increase in innovative products or services portfolio, in this respect it is very enlightening a study made by United Nations Educational, Scientific and Cultural Organization (UNESCO) on products or processes of this kind, in 2015 for high-income countries on company size classes:

The study highlights that, although a job collapse is forecasted, companies have adopted coherent policies on creativity and innovation, thus ensuring the premise of sustainable development. The skills required for a creative or innovative environment are permanent preoccupations of contemporary organizations. Companies with the largest innovative potential are supported by investors that intuit the advantages of concentrating creativity and innovation knowledge in the competency centers that become in this way human focus of knowledge, creativity and innovation, facilitating avant-garde solutions on a continuously growing market where the pressure of the competition is increasingly higher. (Janků and Růžena 2015).We note the concern of decision makers from Luxembourg on investments in research and development on 92 % of large companies. There are several reasons why this country is receptive to business development, the value of innovation and the realization of public investments. These are: business-oriented legislative policy, an excellent political and social situation, well-trained workforce with proficiency in several languages, high-quality infrastructure and connectivity, tax advantages and the lowest value tax added in Europe.

Another direction of the use of creativity and innovation is social media which becomes a catalyst of the society of the future. It is suggestive to this effect the evolution of Facebook that uses innovation, creativity and social media in facilitating communication and relationships between individuals and companies. Starting from the needs of young generations regarding the development of inter-human relations, Facebook triggered a true revolution of social networks in 2004, using an extremely tempting mission statement ("To bring the world closer together") which has imposed the establishment of a creative and innovative environment for the employees and facilitated the creation of communication networks that have

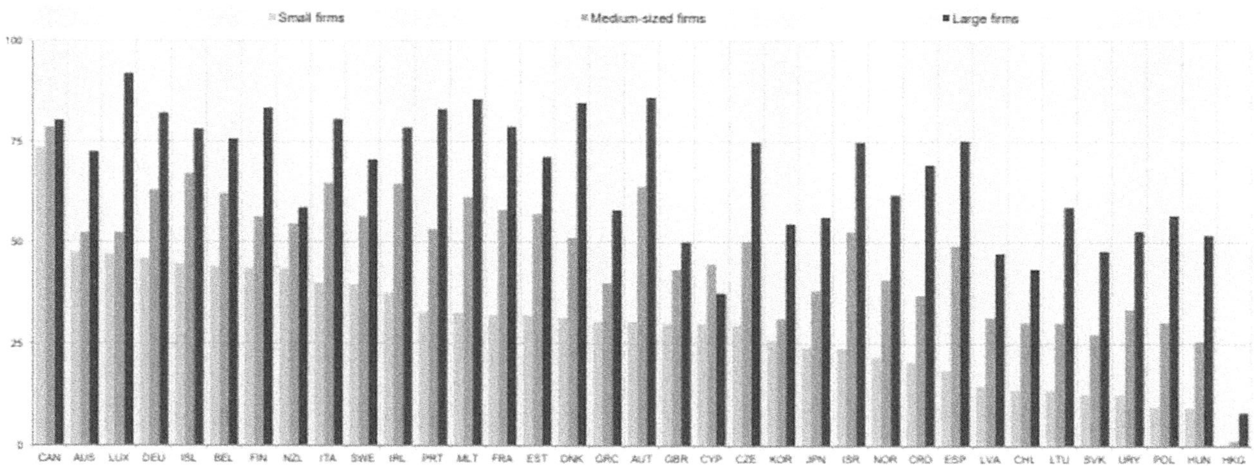

Figure 4: Product or process innovative firms in high-income countries by size class (as a percentage of manufacturing firms in each size class)

Source: UNESCO and UNESCO institute for statistics, Information Paper N. 37 March 2017, http://uis.unesco.org/sites/default/files/documents/ip37-summary-report-of-the-2015-uis-innovation-data-collection-2017-en.pdf.

become genuine information concentrators, processing nodes and even decision centres. We can say that power is actually distributed in a global network, and the decision-makers can be anywhere. Businesses will develop in virtual networks, and active customer feedback will provide creative and innovative solutions for future products and services.

A study conducted in the U.S.A. has highlighted that 69 % of people have an account in at least one social network. If we refer to people aged between 18–29, the percentage reaches up to 88 % (Pew Research Center 2018). Membership to a social network may represent an advantage, but excess use can create addictions with a negative effect in individuals' behaviour. The important thing is that creativity and innovation are used for purposes that follow the development of society because there is a risk that the uncontrolled use of innovation also to produce negative effects.

Conclusions

The analysis that we have made results in that the economy of the future will be based more and more on creativity and innovation. Educational systems will provide the human resources needed for the development of top technologies. Studies show that in the next 30 years there will be 500 million jobs, and the population will reach 12 billion people. This challenge will require the finding of employment-related solutions. The automatization of production processes and the increase of life expectancy will create a surplus of labour force that will probably have to be oriented to areas that will be developed in the future. Environmental protection will require innovative technologies and, at the same time, will impose clear regulations on how resources will be used to stop crises of overproduction, demographic problems and social tensions. Obviously, mankind will be concerned about finding a balance between the active population and the other components of the demographic structure. Creativity and innovation will also help to avoid excesses in connection with resource consumption for a sustainable economic development.

Creativity and innovation impact all components of society. Innovative solutions can occur in industry, agriculture, transport, tourism, education, etc., and the facilities they create can help lower production costs and increase the quality of life. There is a risk that the lack of proper legislation leads to the use of innovations for destructive purposes. This is the reason why there must exist a concern for ethics and moral behaviour. The institutions regulating the research activity must define, on the one hand, the way in which the research activity is financed, and on the other hand, the manner in which the results of the research are used. Human curiosity is unlimited, but the results must be used for constructive purposes. Technological solutions must provide facilities for society and, at the same time, protect the environment. Education will play an important role in the correct use of innovation results because excesses can lead to serious social and economic problems. The future will demonstrate whether the current generations are mature to think in terms of continuity because otherwise, discontinuities would endanger the evolution of human civilization.

References

Amabile, Teresa M.: Motivating creativity in organizations: On doing what you love and loving what you do. California. Management Review 4, 1996, pp. 39–58.

Bisadi, Mona/Mozaffar, Farhang/Bagher, Seyed H: Future Research Centers: The place of creativity and innovation. Procedia - Social and Behavioral Sciences 68, 2012, pp. 232–243.

Brodersen, Marc R..: Environmental effects on creative thinking and the role of affect, arousal, and person-environment fit. Ph.D. dissertation, Colorado State University, 2005.

Deloitte Insights, https://www2.deloitte.com/insights/us/en/topics/innovation/institutional-innovation.html

Dul, Jan/Ceylan, Canan: Work environments for employee creativity. Ergonomics, 54, 2011, pp. 12–20.

D'Onfro, Jillian: An Inside Look at Google's Best Employee Perks. Inc., https://www.inc.com/business-insider/best-google-benefits.html

Faizi, Mohsen/Azari, Amirreza Karimi/Maleki, Saeid Norouzian: Design Principles of Residential Spaces to Promote Children s.Creativity. Procedia - Social and Behavioral Sciences, 35, 2012, pp. 468–474.

Garelli, Stéphane: Top Class Competitors: How nations, Firms, and Individuals Succeed in the New World of Competitiveness. John Wiley & Sons: Chichester, 2006.

Glăveanu, Vlad. P.: Educating which creativity? Thinking Skills and Creativity 27, 2018, pp. 25–32.

Global Entrepreneurship Monitor: Global Report 2016/17. Global Entrepreneurship Research Association: Massachusetts 2017.

Janků Šárka/Růžena Petříková: The using of innovation and creativity is inexhaustible. Procedia Economics and Finance 34, 2015, 638–643

Yusuf, Shadid: From creativity to innovation. Technology in Society 31, 2009, pp. 1–8.

Martens, Yuri: Creative workplace: instrumental and symbolic support for creativity. Facilities, 29(1/2), 2011, pp. 63–79.

McCoy, Janetta Mitchel/Evans, Gary W.: The Potential Role of the Physical Environment in Fostering Creativity. Creativity Research Journal, 14(3/4), 2002, pp. 409–426.

Mozaffar, Farhang: A suggested approach for school design based on psychological and communication theories, for Iran. Doctoral dissertation, Sheffield University, 1997.

Niu, Weihua: Individual and Environmental Influences on Chinese Student Creativity. Journal of Creative Behavior, 41(3), 2007, pp. 151–175.

Tahirsylaj, Armend S.: Stimulating creativity and innovation through Intelligent Fast Failure, Thinking Skills and Creativity 7, 2012, pp. 265–270.

The Boston Consulting Group, https://www.bcg.com/publications/collections/most-innovative-companies-2018.aspx.

Patel, Sujan: 10 Examples of Companies with Fantastic Cultures. Entrepreneur, https://www.entrepreneur.com/article/249174

Robinson Resource Group, http://www.rrgexec.com/rewarding-your-employees-15-examples-of-successful-incentives-in-the-corporate-world/

Shafaie, Minoo/Madani, Ramin: Design of educational spaces for children according to the creativity model. Journal of Technology of Educeation, 4(3), 2010, pp. 215–222.

Sorin-George TOMA[1], Paul MARINESCU[2], Andreea SĂSEANU[3]

[1] Faculty of Administration and Business, University of Bucharest,
Email: tomagsorin62@yahoo.com

[2] Faculty of Administration and Business, University of Bucharest,
Email: paulmarinescu1@gmail.com

[3] Faculty of Business and Tourism, University of Economic Studies, Bucharest,
Email: andreea.saseanu@com.ase.ro

Smart Cities for Sustainable Development in the 21st Century

Abstract *There is an increasing concern at the global level to promote development in a comprehensive and equitable manner by taking into account several key factors such as climate change, extreme poverty and hunger, child mortality, environmental sustainability and universal primary education. This is why many stakeholders have made significant efforts to design and implement smart and sustainable development strategies in order to find smart solutions for global, regional and national problems. During the history, urbanization has represented a positive force that fostered the prosperity of human beings and contributed to the economic development. The paper aims to present the theoretical foundation of the concepts of smart city and sustainable development and to show their connection in the 21st century. To such end, the authors used a quantitative research method that explains these two concepts and seeks to validate their relationship. The concept of smart city has proved to represent both a useful tool and a successful way of thinking to address the unprecedented sustainability challenges of the 21st century. The paper shows that the connection between smart city and sustainable development has led to the emergence of a new concept: the smart and sustainable city.*

Key words: smart city, sustainable development, smart and sustainable city, urbanization, twenty-first century

Introduction

The world economy is currently going through a very dynamic era characterized by both rapid upward and downward movements. In order to cope with a turbulent environment the economies of the world are seeking ways and means to support economic development. Governments worldwide have for some time searched to achieve greater economic development in order to become more competitive. As higher competitiveness leads to a higher level of prosperity of a nation and its people (Garelli 2006), policy makers, development practitioners and researchers are continuously trying to discover the optimal development strategy. Also, there is an increasing concern at the global level to promote development in a comprehensive and equitable manner by taking into account several key factors such as climate change, extreme poverty and hunger, child mortality, environmental sustainability and universal primary education (The World Bank and ClimateWorks Foundation 2014; United Nations 2015a). This is why many stakeholders (e.g., governments, companies, citizens, think tanks, non-governmental organizations etc.) have made significant efforts to design and implement smart and sustainable development strategies in order to find smart solutions for global, regional and national problems (e.g., gender equality, human rights, sustainable lifestyles, equitable quality education, global citizenship, sustainable cities etc.) (Lomborg 2013; Copenhagen Consensus Center 2015; United Nations 2015b; PricewaterhouseCoopers 2015; United Nations 2017).

During the history, urbanization has represented a positive force that fostered the prosperity of human beings and contributed to the economic development. Since the beginning of the 21st century, urban-based economic activities have owned a major part of the gross domestic product (GDP) in all countries (United Nations Human Settlements Programme 2004). Increasing metropolitanisation has led to the growing economic influence of the cities (PricewaterhouseCoopers 2005) as the world has already entered in the urban age (United Nations Human Settlements Programme 2013). Today's cities are competing not only for residents, but also for investments, artificial intelligence (AI) technologies, knowledge, creativity, ideas and so on (KPMG 2016). Also, the expanding urban living requires progressive ideas and intelligent systems capable to deal with the complexity of urbanization. Therefore, the emergence of smart cities has proved to be an innovative solution in this context. Consequently, there is a need for smarter cities capable to transform themselves into important hubs of the global economy (Dirks, Gurdgiev and Keeling 2010) and to promote sustainable urban development in the 21st century (European Investment Bank 2016). Many contemporary cities are smart cities that articulate their vision around three pillars: culture (e.g., heritage and ancient traditions of the city etc.), cognizance (e.g., developing human capital) and creativity (e.g., ability to innovate etc.) (Rossi, Žibret and de Clercq 2011).

Urbanization represents a continuously expanding phenomenon at the global level and by the mid of this century more than 6 billion people will be living in cities (Bennett, Pérez-Bustamante and Medrano 2016; Hasbini, Eldabi and Aldallal 2018). Thus, the emergence and evolution of smart cities have become a topic of interest in the social and economic literature in the past decades. Their relationships with sustainable development have also constitutes a theme of reflection in recent years. In this respect, the paper aims to present the theoretical foundation of the concepts of smart city and sustainable development and to show their connection in the actual century. To such end, the authors used a quantitative research method that explains these two concepts and seeks to validate their relationship. The secondary data were collected through the deployment of an appreciable literature review. The sources were articles, reports and books from the domains of economics, management, entrepreneurship, urban planning and geography, and were found mainly in electronic databases and libraries.

1. Literature review

Defining the concepts of smart city and sustainable development is beneficial for explaining their connection in the following section of the paper. There is a growing body of research related to these two concepts. Since the beginning of this century the smart city topic has been increasingly debated as it proved to constitute a key element of urban life. The trilogy on intelligent cities written by Komninos (2002, 2008, 2015a) showed that a new generation of cities emerged and developed: knowledge-intensive, innovative and smart cities. The term of intelligent or smart city characterises "areas (cities, regions, district in cities, clusters) where the local system of innovation is supported by and improved via digital networks and AI applications" that "gain innovation capability, which translates into competitiveness and prosperity" (Komninos 2008, p. 19). Smart city has been defined in various ways by specialists from different fields of activity as follows:

- "connecting the physical infrastructure, the IT infrastructure, the social infrastructure, and the business infrastructure to leverage the collective intelligence of the city" (Harrison et al. 2010, p. 2).
- "a fusion of ideas about how information and communications technologies might improve the functioning of cities, enhancing their efficiency, improving their competitiveness, and providing new ways in which problems of poverty, social deprivation, and poor environment might be addressed" (Batty et al. 2012, p. 483).
- "places where information technology is combined with infrastructure, architecture, everyday objects, and even our own bodies to address social, economic and environmental problems" (Townsend 2013, p. 15).
- "a knowledge-based city that develops extraordinary capabilities to be self-aware; functions 24 hours and 7 days a week; communicates, selectively, knowledge in real time to citizens end-users for satisfactory way of life with easy public delivery of services, comfortable mobility, conservation of energy, environment and other natural resources; and creates energetic face-to-face communities and a vibrant urban economy even at a time of national economic downturns" (Vinod Kumar 2014, p. 2).
- "a smart regional ecosystem, that includes several interconnected stakeholders that develop collaborative networks (firms, citizens, public organizations, cultural, economic and social infrastructures) to create an open and creative environment useful to improve the population's life quality and to develop smart and innovative businesses and social projects" (Carvalho 2017, p. 3).
- "the utilization of ICT and innovation by cities (new, existing or districts), as a means to sustain in economic, social and environmental terms and to address several challenges dealing with six (6) dimensions (people, economy, governance, mobility, environment and living)" (Anthopolous 2017, p. 8).

The above mentioned definitions indicate that the concept of smart city is not consensual and, therefore, has different meanings for researchers. However, there are several characteristics of a smart city such as:

- The use on a large scale of information and communications technologies in order to solve the problems (e.g., social deprivation) of cities and improve their performances.
- The connection among various types of infrastructure: physical, social, business, and digital.
- The conservation of resources and the protection of the environment.
- The interconnection among numerous stakeholders (e.g., public administration, companies, citizens, non-governmental organizations etc.) that leads to the creation and development of collaborative networks.
- The creation of an open and creative environment that improves citizens' life and social inclusion of various residents, stimulates innovative businesses and facilitates the urban economic growth etc.

On its turn, the concept of sustainable development emerged when the Brundtland Commission Report stated that "humanity has the ability to make development sustainable to ensure that it meets the needs of the present without compromising the ability of future generations to meet their own needs" (United Nations 1987, p. 16). Thus, sustainable development represents a desired state of development and refers to a global perspective.

2. Linking smart cities to sustainable development

In order to address the second aim of the paper the authors adopt a multidimensional approach. The architecture of smart cities comprises three layers/building blocks and four key functions (information gathering, learning, collaborative innovation, and information dissemination) (Komninos et al. 2015b). Thus, smart cities are multi-layer ecosystems of innovation that bring together digital spaces, cooperation-based institutions and knowledge-intensive activities (Table 1).

These layers express the dimensions of intelligence (human, collective, artificial) and the expansion of innovation (Komninos 2008). In other words, there are three building blocks or layers as follows: "(i) the city, citizen, and activities block; (ii) the knowledge, intelligence, and innovation block; and (iii) the smart systems and urban technologies block" (Komninos et al. 2015b, p. 35). The first block encompasses city's resources (e.g., people, communities), the second block contains processes for knowledge creation (e.g., information gathering and management), and the third block incorporates sustainable technologies, broadband networks etc.

Today's smart cities have to face numerous provocative and ubiquitous challenges (e.g., quality of life and place). This is why their ecosystem should include the following eight components: smart infrastructure, smart transportation, smart environment, smart services, smart governance, smart people, smart living, and smart economy (Table 2).

Table 1: The layers of a smart city

Layer's number	Description
First layer	city's knowledge-intensive activities in manufacturing and services that are usually organised into clusters
Second layer	institutional mechanisms for knowledge creation and social cooperation in technology and innovation
Third layer	digital networks and e-services that make innovation achievement easier

Source: Komninos 2008

Table 2: The components of a smart city ecosystem

Component	Description
Smart infrastructure	city facilities (e.g., water and energy networks) with embedded smart technology (e.g., sensors)
Smart transportation	transportation networks with enhanced embedded real time monitoring and control systems
Smart environment	innovation and ICT incorporation for natural resource protection and management (e.g., waste management systems)
Smart services	utilization of technology and ICT for health, education, tourism, safety etc. across the entire city
Smart governance	smart government establishment in the urban space
Smart people	measures that enhance people creativity and open innovation
Smart living	innovation for enhancing quality of life in the urban space
Smart economy	technology and innovation for strengthening business development, employment and urban growth

Source: Anthopoulos 2017.

The above components allow the pinpointing of several major dimensions of a smart city. In this respect, different researchers have emphasized multiple dimensions such as:

- Economy, mobility, environment, people, living (Giffinger et al. 2007).
- Quality of life, sustainable economic development, management of natural resources through participatory policies, convergence of economic, social, and environmental goals (Thuzar 2011).

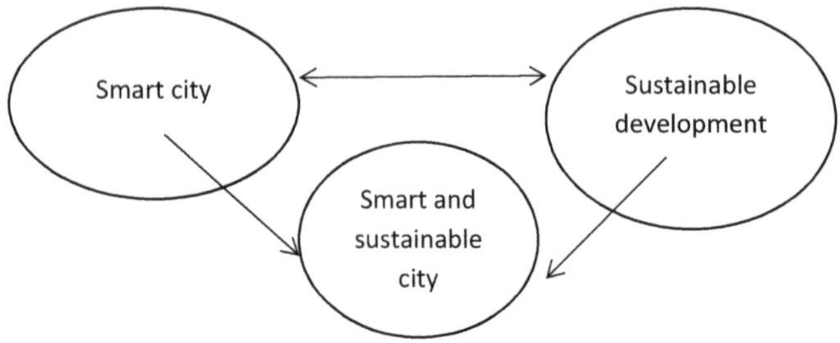

Figure 1: The relationship between smart city and sustainable development.
Source: authors' contribution

- Social, management, economy, legal, technology, sustainability (Sujata et al. 2016).
- People, economy, mobility, environment, living, governance (Vinod Kumar and Dahiya 2017).
- ICT infrastructure, energy, mobility, construction, security, metabolism, industries, economy, education, living, governance (Fromhold-Eisebith 2017).

On its turn, sustainable development refers to three specific dimensions: social, economic, and environmental. It takes into account at the same time all these three issues. Thus, smart city and sustainable development are two connected concepts as several dimensions are common for both of them. On the one hand, smart cities may contribute to sustainable development (e.g., smart infrastructure, smart living, education), and, on the other hand, sustainable development may stimulate the emergence and expansion of smart cities (e.g., air quality, water quality, noise). This relationship leads to the emergence of both a new perspective and concept: the smart and sustainable city (Figure 1).

As an interdependent construct that provides an integrated view of today's urbanization, the smart and sustainable city perspective involves a dynamic and multidisciplinary approach on a long-term horizon. However, cities can become sustainable without the use of smart technologies whereas smart cities are not necessarily sustainable cities. Therefore, a smart and sustainable city has to use smart technologies in order to ensure sustainability. In other words, a smart city can be sustainable by providing a high quality of life to its citizens and a sustainable city can be smart by utilizing ICT in order to observe, assess and monitor the use of its resources.

Conclusions

The first period of the 21st century has witnessed the rapid and dynamic growth of cities all over the world. Parallel to this growth the environmental, economic and social problems of urbanization have also expanded. Various challenges, such as climate change, economic crises, demographic explosion and migration flows, has put considerable pressure on urban systems. Consequently there appeared a need for a new urban approach in order to find solutions for a wide range of city problems.

Thus, the concept of smart city has proved to represent both a useful tool and a successful way of thinking to address the unprecedented sustainability challenges of the 21st century. During the time, the connection between smart city and sustainable development has led to the emergence of a new concept: the smart and sustainable city.

The paper contributes to the development of the scientific literature in two ways. First, it emphasizes the key dimensions and components of a smart city. Second, it shows the relationship between the concepts of smart city and sustainable development. Further researches could be carried on in order to deeply analyse this connection from other perspectives as both concepts are multidimensional.

References

Anthopoulos, Leonidas G.: Understanding Smart Cities: A Tool for Smart Government or an Industrial Trick? Public Administration and Information Technology, 22, Springer Science+ Business Media: New York 2017.

Batty, Michael et al. Smart cities of the future. The European Physical Journal Special Topics, 214(1), 2012, pp. 481–518.

Bennett, Dag R./Pérez-Bustamante, Diana/Medrano, Maria-Luisa: Challenges for Smart Cities in the UK. In: Peris-Ortiz, Marta/Bennett, Dag R./Pérez-Bustamante Yábar, Diana (eds.): Sustainable Smart Cities: Creating Spaces for Technological, Social and Business Development. Springer International Publishing: Switzerland 2016, pp. 1–14.

Carvalho, Luísa C.: Entrepreneurial Ecosystems: Lisbon as a Smart Start-Up City. In: Carvalho, Luísa C. (ed.): Handbook of Research on Entrepreneurial Development and Innovation within Smart Cities. IGI Global: Hershey 2017, pp. 1–19.

Copenhagen Consensus Center: The Smartest Targets for the World 2016–2030. Copenhagen Consensus Center, 2015. Available at: http://www.copenhagenconsensus.com/sites/default/files/post-2015_presentation_3.pdf [Accessed 12 March 2018].

Dirks, Susanne/Gurdgiev, Constantin/Keeling, Mary: Smarter cities for smarter growth. IBM Institute for Business Value: Somers 2010.

European Investment Bank: Smart development for a smart Europe. European Investment Bank: Luxembourg 2016.

Fromhold-Eisebith, Martina: Cyber-Physical Systems in Smart Cities- Mastering Technological, Economic, and Social Challenges. In: Song, Houbing/Srinivasan, Ravi/Sookoor, Tamim/Jeschke, Sabina (eds.): Smart Cities: Foundations, Principles, and Applications. Wiley: Hoboken 2017, pp. 1–22.

Garelli, Stephane: Top Class Competitors: How Nations, Firms and Individuals Succeed in the New World of Competitiveness. John Wiley & Sons: Chichester 2006.

Giffinger, Rudolf/Fertner, Christian/Kramar, Hans/Kalasek, Robert/Pichler-Milanović, Nataša/Meijers, Evert: Smart Cities: Ranking of European medium-sized cities. Centre of Regional Science: Vienna 2007.

Harrison, Colin et al. Foundations for smarter cities. IBM Journal of Research and Development, 54(4), 2010, pp. 1–16.

Hasbini, Mohamad A./Eldabi, Tillal/Aldallal, Ammar: Investigating the information security management role in smart city organisations. World Journal of Entrepreneurship, Management and Sustainable Development, 14(1), 2018, pp. 86–98.

KPMG: The future of cities: creating a vision. KPMG, 2016. Available at: https://assets.kpmg.com/content/dam/kpmg/pdf/2016/04/the-future-of-cities-creating-a-vision.pdf [Accessed 10 March 2018].

Komninos, Nicos: Intelligent Cities: Innovation, Knowledge Systems and Digital Spaces. Routledge: London 2002.

Komninos, Nicos: Intelligent Cities and Globalization of Innovation Networks. Routledge: London 2008.

Komninos, Nicos: The Age of Intelligent Cities: Smart Environments and Innovation-for-all Strategies. Routledge: London 2015a.

Komninos, Nicos/Bratsas, Charalampos/Kakderi, Christina/Tsarchopoulos, Panagiotis: "Smart City Ontologies: Improving the effectiveness of smart city applications". Journal of Smart Cities, 1(1), 2015b, pp. 31–46.

Lomborg, Bjørn: Global Problems, Smart Solutions. Cambridge University Press: Cambridge 2013.

PricewaterhouseCoopers: Cities of the future- global competition, local leadership. PricewaterhouseCoopers, 2005. Available at: https://www.pwc.com/gx/en/government-public-sector-research/pdf/cities-final.pdf [Accessed 11 March 2018].

PricewaterhouseCoopers: Make it your business: Engaging with the Sustainable Development Goals. PricewaterhouseCoopers, 2015. Available at: https://www.pwc.com/gx/en/sustainability/SDG/SDG%20Research_FINAL.pdf [Accessed 10 March 2018].

Rossi, Luca/Žibret, Branko/De Clercq, Matthieu: The City of the Future. A. T. Kearney, 2011. Available at: http://www.atkearney.co.kr/documents/10192/586874/The+City+of+the+Future.pdf/bea77d29-6359-4d53-92ff-ed7c685d5fea [Accessed 12 March 2018].

Sujata, Joshi/Saksham, Saxena/Tanvi, Godbole/Shreya: Developing Smart Cities: An Integrated Framework. Procedia Computer Science, 93, 2016, pp. 902–909.

The World Bank and ClimateWorks Foundation: Climate-Smart Development. The World Bank Group: Washington 2014.

Thuzar, Moe: Urbanization in Southeast Asia: Developing smart cities for the future? Regional Outlook, 2011/2012, pp. 96–100.

Townsend, Anthony M.: Smart Cities: Big Data, Civic Hackers, and the Quest for a New Utopia. Norton & Company: New York 2013.

United Nations: Report of the World Commission on Environment and Development: our Common Future. United Nations, 1987. Available at: http://www.un-documents.net/our-common-future.pdf [Accessed 10 March 2018].

United Nations Human Settlements Programme (UN-Habitat): The State of the World's Cities 2004/2005. Earthscan: London 2004.

United Nations Human Settlements Programme (UN-Habitat): State of the World's Cities 2012/2013. Routledge: New York 2013.

United Nations: The Millenium Development Goals Report 2015. United Nations: New York 2015a.

United Nations: Transforming Our World: The 2030 Agenda for Sustainable Development. United Nations, 2015b. Available at: https://sustainabledevelopment.un.org/content/documents/21252030%20Agenda%20for%20Sustainable%20Development%20web.pdf [Accessed 10 March 2018].

United Nations: The Sustainable Development Goals Report 2017. United Nations Publications: New York 2017.

Vinod Kumar, T. M.: Geographic information system for smart cities. In: Vinod Kumar, T. M. (ed.): Geographic Information System for Smart Cities. Copal Publishing Group: New Delhi 2014, pp. 1–25.

Vinod Kumar, T. M./Dahiya, Bharat: Smart Economy in Smart Cities. In: Vinod Kumar, T. M. (ed.): Smart Economy in Smart Cities: International Collaborative Research. Springer Nature: Singapore 2017, pp. 3–78.

Maria VIȘAN[1], *Florin Gheorghe FILIP*[2]

[1] Department of Engineering, Mechanics, Computers, Romanian Academy, School of Advanced Studies of the Romanian Academy (SCOSAAR), Email: maria.visan@ingr.ro,

[2] Romanian Academy & INCE

Knowledge, Innovation and Heritage - Cross-Sectorial Support for Smart Development and Human Capital Transformation

Abstract *The field of national heritage (natural, cultural, and industrial) heritage is subject to various threats such as deterioration, lack of funds for maintenance and conservation or deliberate destruction is, at present greater than ever. In this context, the article provides a review of several new digital technologies such as data collection through different methods and from various and multiple sources, 3D visualization, and use in augmented reality, and virtual reality, serious games, web techniques, cloud and mobile computing applicable in the field of heritage protection, preservation, documenting, analyzing and interpreting the past, publishing information focusing on the cross-sectorial impact on the intelligent development of organizations and the transformation of human capital.*

Keywords: Big Data services, heritage, innovation, knowledge, human capital, smart development

Introduction

The destruction in the field of heritage has occurred over the millennia. It has been caused either by natural disasters (earthquakes, landslides, floods, fires, and so on), or environmental changes such as droughts, sea level rise or climate change etc. In addition to those above natural causes, there are several anthropic causes related to terrorism and politics, malicious actions of deliberate destruction of the heritage due to ideological mismatches or due to the lack of cultural awareness and even the lack of financing for maintenance and preservation. Emerging technologies attempt to mitigate effects and limit losses.

1. Solutions for the Knowledge Era

Operationalization of solutions at local, national and international factors (governmental institutions, regulatory and protection organizations, NGOs, service

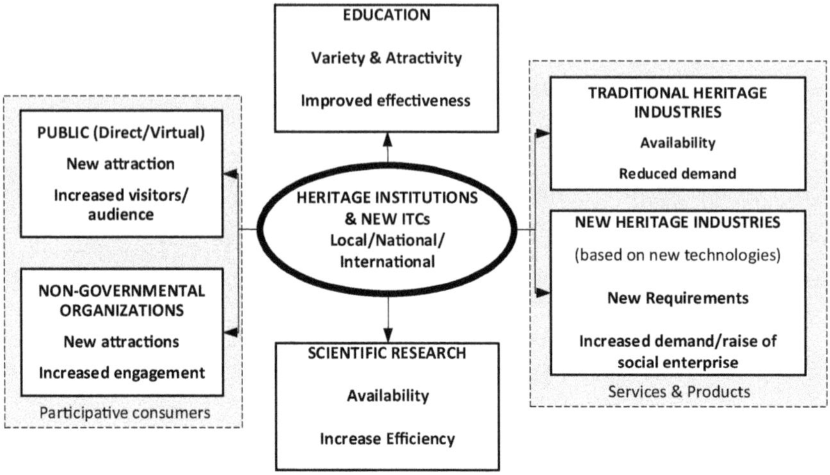

Figure 1: Cross-sectorial scheme - characteristic features of interactions and expected impact

Source: adapted after Filip et al. (Filip et al, 2015)

providers in the traditional industries and the new ones enabled by the emergence of the new technologies) involved in specific activities such as management, governance, scientific research, preservation, mapping, inventory, examination, documentation, treatment, archiving, photography, measurement, information, entertainment and education, software development, media and advertising, marketing, and so on in the field of heritage, and, not least, the public or non-profit organizations (accessing directly or virtually heritage assets) that form a class of participatory consumers, similar to Toffler's "prosumers" (Toffler, 2018), contributes to the intelligent development of communities and the strengthening of human capital through the creation of new and enhanced key competences in society (Boden, Miles, 2000).

Now, we are indisputably in the era of knowledge-based economy (Boden, Miles, 2000), which requires knowledge to generate tangible and intangible values. Because, at present, a large amount of data is currently available, it is essential to filter and quickly identify the required information, and so, the traditional methods no longer work. Therefore, more efforts is required to understand the effects of new emerging technologies in the setting entities involved in the preservation of natural, industrial and cultural heritage.

The new technologies such as augmented reality, mobile applications and platforms for citizens' information, promoting awareness and communication between visitors to the sites and museums/galleries or any other cultural institutions or sites, provide an effective opportunity to preserve and protect heritage around the world.

The usage of information technology in the field of heritage is growing rapidly, with the development of primary data sources (such as Big Data for heritage goods or sites) and the widespread expansion of heritage digitization programs. A number of new methodologies and applications for digital preservation in the field of heritage brings into practice new systems for visual analysis and visual interpretation of the past. At the same time, the heritage research itself should answering to the questions and concerns raised by general interpretation of large data volumes (Big Data), for the knowledge extraction and valorization from quantity through innovation.

2. Big Data and Decision Support Systems

The set of digital technology used to mitigate the effects of destroying the heritage includes:

- Smart collecting heritage data by remote sensing, photogrammetry, laser scanning or point cloud collection, multispectral imaging that generates large volumes of data in different formats.
- Smart and accurately collecting geolocation data.
- Creating 3D models for rebuilding/recreating the heritage through photogrammetry, the digital terrain model to show them as they were in the past.
- Creating predictive models to highlight vulnerable areas of the heritage, goods or sites, identifying priority locations and optimizing conservation spending in the context of limited funds.
- Building web-based networks for collecting, analyzing and sharing information of any type owned by the public or private collectors, from images to any other data format, including social media.
- Platforms enabling a) the awareness and participation of the general public, and b) the public monitoring of the heritage through inventory of vulnerabilities, in which case, the users can identify heritage incidents using appropriate tools such as Google Maps or other similar support platforms.
- The creation of the quantitative models for physical diagnosis and preservation by methods of a) terrestrial laser scanning to monitor material losses due to erosion of walls by comparison to cloud points, b) multispectral imaging for quantification of humidity or other parameters, c) sensors measuring for monitoring different heritage's features.
- The use of interactive technologies such as virtual reality generates new perspectives by the presence of interactivity and responds in some way to user presence, developing new perceptions and knowledge by sending information to various senses, by creating the illusion of presence in an environment that isn't really there, and fool user brains into experiencing something virtual. Just to mention a few of used equipment a) devices for implicit interaction: trackers (sensors which are in charge of capture the position and/or orientation of a real object – head, eye, face, hand, body tracking based on movement of different parts

of the body or devices tracking), data gloves, voice recognition, Kinect, b) 3D input: mousses 3–6DOF (3D mouse with 6 degrees of freedom), space balls, etc.; c) haptic devices (Input-Output) like 3D googles glasses, and even smells, tactile and kinesthetic senses d) capture (used to create virtual worlds): 3D scans. These devices for interactions allow fully immersive experiences into virtual reality.

- The enhanced reality that uses the users' mobile devices to display, zooming in or out, representing great potential as emerging technology that replaces audio guides and expensive traditional devices. In addition, the augmented reality is especially interesting because it allows people to learn through specific activities more about the location they visit, and, in the same time, can contribute by learning to the scientific initiatives, enriching the cultural perception or experience of the users.
- The site monitoring through games in augmented reality, without paying too much attention to the collected data. They are automatically transferred and recorded on a server, where they can be verified by experts, thus becoming necessary data for daily monitoring of such goods from the territory or sites/buildings over relevant periods of time using 3D modeling techniques.
- The serious games for entertainment, which gain ground as a category of emerging technology, because the game is used with a serious purpose in virtual environments, improving the educational activities, user experience (visitors) and curriculum.
- The reproduction of the scanned heritage goods to real dimensions, 1:1, for preservation, as well as to be made available to visitors, using augmented reality.
- Recognizing a target image as well as 3D goods that are scanned with interactive viewing or gamming applications.
- The goods analysis by visitors when exploring the site to discover the historical materials that were used. The target object is left on the visitor's path, they follow the instructions in a printed guide, or use the specially developed application, identifying the real-world object in the virtual world by comparison, or using application layers and, therefore, being able to plan the next gamming activity. In fact, there is a narrative part of the game developed in collaboration with historians and archaeologists, so that is more than one journey experience that can be followed.
- The creation of the video avatars that allow experimentation with digital web gaming technologies and provide free audible video tools to the public, with welcome or departure messages, imposing time limits for completing an activity, generating routes scroll through the most beautiful areas of the visited site.
- The 3D goods printing.
- Souvenirs provided in the form of photos, scanned and 3D printed, 3D models or physical badges, or downloaded images from the server for personal use.
- Identifying important site management information based on analyzing collected data to find out what's important by using a visitor-targeted application.
- The data collected during the playing on different scenarios, which are allowing the prediction of what happens during an emergency situation and how people

do react (in simulated reality), e.g., the simulation of a fire discharging according to the visitor position in the park, and the analysis of their reactions.
- Research projects, which include mixed activities such as: a) planning and data collection from the field, with UAVs (unmanned aerial vehicle) or laser scanning, or cloud points, b) 3D models based on UAV data to represent archaeological and historical sites, buildings or infrastructures in a virtual reality to interact with, c) 3D models for scanned heritage goods that can be included in the virtual reality environments to be made available to visitors for manipulation and interaction with them in dedicated applications, d) uploading all this information into augmented reality applications, e) monitoring buildings by collecting data from seasonal visitors during periods of time when specialists' teams are not present on the site, and using data collection applications that upload information to a server for later use.
- Educational projects and networking to connect universities and institutions' campuses for sharing the software and hardware resources, and real-time usage of models and a faster way of cooperation for generating 3D objects by the public.
- Verifying applications and data by improving the functionality of the heritage applications or site monitoring, which are freely available in the Google store.
- The work with the visitors in the objects collection stage that can continue with any new visitor, contributing to the expanding of the digitization activity of collections. Some of the collected, scanned / digitized items become available to the public. There are still many protected collections under glass or in warehouses that are sometimes not accessible or not easy accessible, so this could be a great way to digitize all these and make them available to the students/interested groups through web apps, sort and compare them, view 3D models, measure them, write dissertations.

Today, because of the lifestyle changes at the level of the members of the entire society, changes of processes, modes of expression, communication tools through various innovative platforms, augmented reality applications, mobile applications are required. These changes allow a wide range of new services for society. Facing the platform diversifications and unlimited web information, the user becomes incapable of handling this huge amount of information. Specifically, for example, in the tourism sector, there are numerous services and resources but few of those are customized to the particular users' preferences. Therefore, the resulting information overload affects service consumption, which makes the integration of intelligent systems an indispensable operation, applying a personalized user profile based architecture on the collaborative filtering technique and referral systems.

2. Virtual world versus Real world

By implementing emerging technologies, the real world will not be replace by the virtual one. Instead, a parallel digital one will be generate. Additional layers can be use optionally. If people are accustomed to use the phone to take pictures, why not these resulting images used for other purposes? Many visitors to the heritage sites do use the social media to chat with friends about the locations visited. What will happened if these resulted images will be used also for a more noble cause, generating a citizen's scientific initiative to create cultural awareness?

Visitors can voluntarily choose to use these technologies or not. Young people are very committed and it is important to involve them because they will be tomorrow's stakeholders who will help institutions in preserving and protecting the heritage. If they are not involved today as public, since they are tomorrow's visitors, what will happen to the heritage thirty years later? The reaction of the archaeologists to these applications is positive, holding it as a serious effort to archive or generate Big Data to which everyone contributes.

The main question is if in the virtual world the pleasure of the touch from the real world is lost. Nowadays this myth disappears due to the invention of the tactile devices or the 3D-printed objects. The replicas can be spotted by the public are made without the risk of damage to the originals, with the maximum gain in the users' experience.

As a result, dematerialization of culture does not arise due to augmented reality applications, but generates a gain factor by involving the public in the heritage conservation activities.

Another concern about the digital transformation of the heritage cover overcome by standardizing formats and metadata. If 10 years later, these formats will be changed, for example, 3D formats in holograms, and the question that arises is what should be done with the enormous volume of millions of digitized objects? In addition, what will happen to many other millions of structured and unstructured heritage records? Evolution is inherent. If these formats can change over time, we may consider it secondary to the fact that these collections are now available to the public and are not lost anymore. This representing an important value for the society and the educational environment, and increases accessibility, as some of these non-digitized collections are today closed or underground and very difficult to be accessed.

The overall impact of emerging technologies is significant. In general, there has been an annual increase in the number of visitors to cultural and historical touristic sites. Heritage conservation and promotion activities have seen a positive effect through the increased number of tourists encountered by the country's local economies, creating a direct and indirect diversification of the touristic, economic, cultural, entertainment, service and commerce activities. In addition, expanding interest in the cross-border cultural heritage it strengthens the preservation and identity of it, stimulating the expansion and consolidation. From an economic point of view, the heritage sector is an important source of prosperity and economic growth.

Just because the world is in a profound change and this mainly affects perceptions, the museum/sites confronted with the problem of transforming the old audio guides into interactive applications that allow users to experience a different museum experience. We are discussing the digital transformation of the entire collection and putting it on online environments. The systems must be of high quality to be available to everybody, to stimulate people to use technology. As a result, it does not bother if people use such applications. The digital world is not stealing the public, but it allows the expansion of physical boundaries by using the marketing techniques applicable today, from product launches, to museums, and by creating an interactive game form. In this context, games become a powerful teaching medium that reaches a very broad audience using a story that captures and receives very well.

Themes such as art, culture, and history, using augmented reality, increase the value of the observed asset and do not replace it. Even more, it can turn into a system of analysis and decision support that facilitates strategic planning. Identifying the success stories of customer-responsive strategies is critical because the customer has changed his habits, needs and behavior.

Analyzing all the available data by conducting conversational reviews using a semantic algorithm interpreting their content to understand what customers are content/dissatisfied with, it determines the visitors' segments in which they are interested and can customize the experience, it can accurately improve their points of which they complain.

There is no question of whether or not to use virtual or augmented reality. The heritage object remains in the customer's attention and the museum/galleries/sites environment becomes a distribution environment. Therefore, designers of spaces for exposure the heritage should activate more senses, not just vision.

The curators of the museums/galleries are obsessed with the words "look and do not touch". What if it would activate more senses, create a more personal world, and when we get into a museum / gallery/site, instead of looking at, without touching? Changing the approach, you can touch, without getting tired of watching, you can stimulate senses with exhibits, taste them, smell them, rest in chairs that stimulate all your senses in a very personal way. If the things that surround us would give us information, it would guide us where to go, we would perceive them differently, not just by looking. If it would encompass our whole body, stimulating all the senses, the world would certainly be different, we could create a much more interesting and accessible world for everyone. Fortunately, the road is open and it is only a matter of time before becoming to life in the real world on a large scale. Today there are already many inventions related to sounds and sensations, vibrations on the skin that activate and other senses, not just the sight, and all are just ready for use.

Conclusions

Digital transformation is an irreversible, complex and crucial process that transforms the future of the heritage into places of experience and sharing. Communicating in a new way to be closer to the user's needs, we meet expectations in terms of customer experience, which is constantly developing. In addition, the continued evolution of digital transformation will permanently generate new digital models to align the physical world with the digital world, generating challenges for all actors involved in process. "In 2018, we'll cross the significant 50 % adoption milestone, and cloud applications, platforms, and services will continue to radically change the way enterprises compete for customers" (Bartoletti, 2018).

"OECD estimates suggest that around 14 % of the workers are at high risk of automating most of their existing tasks over the next 15 years. Another 30 % will face major changes in the tasks required in their work and therefore the necessary skills. About half of all workers will face the need to adapt significantly to the new work environment." (OECD, 2018) As a result, workers will have to adapt to new technologies and work practices to harness the opportunities that arise because of digital transformation. In particular, "young people need to prepare themselves for future jobs by equipping themselves with the mix of skills needed for ever-changing workplaces rich in technology. This mix includes general cognitive skills, complementarity skills such as problem solving, creative thinking, communication, generic information technology and communication skills, and technical abilities and a strong ability to continue learning" (OECD, 2018). ..."Survival today requires the capacity for rapid change, and forward-thinking ... transforming themselves to meet the demand for evolving skills and work models". (Ignatius, 2018)

As today's organizations are increasingly valued in terms of their relationships with the workers, their customers and their communities, and their impact on the society as a whole - turning them from traditional enterprises into social enterprises, it is not possible to innovate without knowledge. In addition, not just knowledge, but also technology and innovation.

"Intelligent apps ... have the potential to transform the nature of work and the structure of the workplace". (Gartner, 2018) Technology changes all cross-sectorial domains and develops human capital.

Finally, we can state that emerging technologies offer another perspective on the future development of the heritage, innovative through knowledge, intelligent as development and with direct implications on human capital. We must, however, pay attention to select the appropriate technologies to design effective useful, usable and used information systems that enables enhancing human knowledge (Filip, 2012).

References

1. Bartoletti, Dave. Predictions 2018: Cloud Computing Accelerates Enterprise Transformation Everywhere. Forrester /Blogs/Predictions 2017 available at: https://go.forrester.com/blogs/predictions-2018-cloud-computing-accelerates-enterprise-transformation-everywhere/, accessed on 01.05.2018.
2. Boden, Mark, Miles, Ian, Services and the Knowledge-based Economy. Continuum, London, 2000.

3. Filip, Florin, Gheorghe; Ciurea, Cristian; Dragomirescu, Horaţiu & Ivan, Ion, Cultural heritage and modern information and communication technologies, Technological and Economic Development of Economy, 21:3, 441–459, 2015.
4. Filip, Florin Gheorghe, A decision-making perspective for designing and building information systems. International Journal of Computers Communications & Control,7:2, 264–272
5. Gartner, Top 10 Strategic Technology Trends for 2018 - Smarter with Gartner, available at https://www.gartner.com/smarterwithgartner/gartner-top-10-strategic-technology-trends-for-2018/, accessed on 01.05.2018.
6. Ignatius, Adi, How Tech Is Transforming HR, Harvard Business Review, March–April 2018, p.19.
7. OECD (Organization for Economic Co-operation and Development), Transformative Technologies and Jobs of the Future, Background report for the Canadian G7 Innovation Ministers' Meeting Montreal, Canada 27–28 March 2018 available at https://www.oecd.org/innovation/transformative-technologies-and-jobs-of-the-future.pdf, accessed on 01.05.2018.
8. Toffler, Alvin, The Third Wave, William Morrow, New York, 1980, available at http://calculemus.org/lect/07pol-gosp/arch/proby-dawne/materialy/waves.htm, accessed on 01.04.2018.

Zizi GOSCHIN[1], *Elena DRUICĂ*[2]

[1] Professor, University of Economic Studies, Institute of National Economy, Romanian Academy, Bucharest, Email: zizi.goschin@csie.ase.ro

[2] Professor, University of Bucharest, email: elena.druica@faa.unibuc.ro

A Composite Healthcare Index and its Relation with Romania's Regional Development

Abstract *The primary purpose of this research is to design a spatial composite indicator of medical infrastructure and to analyse its territorial distribution in Romania, in relation with regional development, a key factor for understanding the spatial healthcare setting. Such composite indicators are useful for policy makers, as they allow to benchmark and monitor regional medical endowment more clearly and can signal critical situations that need special attention. In order to provide distinct measures for the relevant material and human factors, we separated the variables included in the Composite Healthcare Index in two groups, and calculated a Synthetic Index of Physical Medical Infrastructure and a Synthetic Index of Healthcare Personnel. We computed these indices annually, covering the period 1997 to 2014, and found significant variation in time and space. Another line of our research targeted the relation between the Composite Healthcare Index and the regional development, captured by means of spatial regression models for several relevant years of the period under consideration. We found that GDP per capita, as a proxy measure of the development level, is a positive and highly significant factor of influence for the Composite Health Index in all our annual regression models.*

Keywords: Healthcare, composite index, spatial regression, regions, Romania

Introduction

Healthcare is an economic sector that calls for special attention from the policy makers in order to protect already vulnerable social groups, and prevent other groups from falling into vulnerable categories. Investment in healthcare means investment in economy, and that is for at least two reasons. On the one side, a healthy person is more productive and as a consequence affords to work for a better standard of living, and live longer. A healthier person is less exposed to extreme medical events and therefore less exposed to risks related to unaffordable (as well as unavoidable) spending for health reasons. On the other side, healthier persons claim for less public spending, as well as less medical resources of any kind.

Against the background of chronic poor healthcare provision throughout Romania, the existence of significant territorial disparities across regions means very low access to medical services in many disadvantaged zones (Vladescu et al., 2008). As in other sectors of activity, information is important for a proper benchmarking and monitoring, as well as for designing the appropriate healthcare strategies. Since this topic was insufficiently researched in Romania, in this paper we develop a new synthetic indicator of medical infrastructure that reflects both material and human conditions in the healthcare system from a spatial perspective. Our composite index draws on official health statistics available at county level and captures critical factors for the medical infrastructure.

The contribution of our work is twofold. First, we explore and summarize the main data related to regional distribution of healthcare resources at county level, covering the time span from 1997 until 2014. This provides insights not only into the absolute state of development, but also into a comparison between public and private dimensions. Second, the composite index is a novelty that may serve in further studies as a proxy that stands for healthcare development. To our knowledge, this is the only contribution in Romania that provides such a tool on healthcare data.

The paper is organized as follows: next section briefly reviews the literature related to healthcare and composite indices. Section three introduces the research method to be employed in our analysis and section four presents the main results and discussions, followed by the concluding section.

1. Literature review

For decades the Romanian healthcare system has been adversely affected by meager founding, insufficient and outdated medical equipment, and scanty medical staff, not in the least due to large emigration of physicians and medical assistants, especially after Romania's accession to EU (Boncea, 2014; Roman and Goschin, 2014). Despite many changes focused on decentralization and better management, as well as the progressive development of a new private healthcare sector, resource constraints, inefficient and non-inclusive health care services continue to be critical issues for healthcare provision in Romania. Notwithstanding recent improvement, the health status continues to be considerably lower than EU average and significant disparities in healthcare availability persist in Romania, e.g., the high rural-urban inequity (Vladescu et al., 2008 and 2016).

Most of the research in the area of Romanian healthcare (e.g., Dragoi et al, 2008; Zanfir et al., 2012; Ghita et al., 2015) have been devoted so far to overall evaluations based on single variables, and less effort have been paid to multi-factor analyses. One of the reasons may be the scarcity of regional data regarding health indicators. But if we don't look closer into relations between factors, we cannot understand too much. Regression models have been used to explain variations in results, having specific healthcare variables as predictors. In this way, each factor's contribution can be isolated, and advanced econometric techniques can be used to assess not only their relevance in explaining variability, but also to quantify their estimated impact. However, any regression model would prefer to avoid data that suffer from multicolinearity, as the estimated coefficients of the model would be biased.

Research conducted in Romania usually founds high correlations between variables. The reasons the Romanian data face this type of problem is, most likely, related to the dynamic of the public and private dimensions within the healthcare system. We claim that the private side of the Romanian medical assistance have been developed based on similar human resources employed in the public sector. But regardless the cause, the consequence is that any attempt to explain the performance of the Romanian healthcare system based on raw data should rely on a reduced number of variables, and considerably less information. Composite indices can play this part in healthcare analyses. These indices have been extensively used in other areas and their effectiveness was confirmed by a long practice (OECD 2008). They are built combining various dimensions of a phenomenon, usually as a weighted average (Saisana and Tarantola, 2002; Nguefack-Tsague et al., 2012).

An interesting summary of pros and cons of using composite indices in healthcare is provided by Metge et al. (2009). They argue that although such indices serve well the purpose of downsizing the number of indicators, facilitate performance assessment, indicate trends and are easy to use by decision-makers, they might also prompt simplistic or even incorrect policy measures if they are poorly built or used without paying attention to their component indicators as well.

Despite their limitations, we believe that such instruments can be valuable for Romanian decision-makers, given their constant need to better monitor healthcare expenditures (Vladescu et al., 2016).

2. Method

Based on the standard technique for building composite indices (OECD, 2008) we introduce a synthetic measure of health infrastructure in Romania, following a four step procedure.

1. Variable selection. The complexity of the healthcare sector would require a diversity of variables to reflect accurately the spatial inequalities in the relevant factors of influence. Unfortunately, our endeavour is limited by the information currently available in official statistics. We use 5 variables that reflect material and human resources available in the healthcare sector (see Table 1 for the description of variables). The selected variables are spatially relevant, displaying considerable variation among Romanian counties.
2. Variable standardization. The computation of a composite index requires the aggregation of heterogeneous data sets. For reasons of territorial comparability, the initial variables have been transformed through dividing each of them by total population of the county. The min-max standardisation technique was further applied, as follows:

$$y_{ij} = \frac{x_{ij} - \min(x_j)}{\max(x_j) - \min(x_j)}, \tag{1}$$

Where:

y_{ij} - standardised value of variable j for county i; i = $\overline{1,42}$, j = $\overline{1,6}$
x_{ij}- initial data.

The above formula allocates a standardised score ranging from 0 (worst) to 1 (best) for each initial value, allowing for further aggregation of the standardised variables.

3. Synthetic group indices. The variables have been assigned to groups according their different nature: material factors (hospitals, hospital beds, medical offices in schools) and human factors (physicians in public sector and in private sector, medical nurses). Two synthetic indices that highlight these two dimensions of healthcare infrastructure have been computed. Each index I_g^i was calculated as a simple arithmetic mean of the standardised values:

$$I_g^i = \frac{1}{m_g} \sum_{j=1}^{m_g} y_j^i, \tag{2}$$

Where m_g is the number of variables in group g.

4. Finally, the composite index of healthcare infrastructure (CHI) is obtained as a mean of the two synthetic indices, giving higher weigh (p_g) to the human factor, essential for the correct diagnosis and treatment of the malnutrition-related diabetes.

$$\bar{I}_i = \frac{\sum_{g=1}^{m} I_g^i \cdot p_g}{100}, \quad i = \overline{1,n}. \tag{3}$$

In theory, the value of the composite index might rank between a minimum of 0, if the same county holds the lowest performance for all variables, and a maximum of 1, if a county happens to stand on top position for all variables included in the composite index. In practice, reaching one of these two extreme values is unlikely.

Our second line of research envisages the relation between the Composite Healthcare Index (CHI) and the regional development, proxied by GDP per capita, in the framework of simple spatial regression models that account for possible spatial interactions among neighbours.

According to the standard estimation strategy, we will start from a classic regression model:

$$CHI_{i,t} = a + b \cdot GDP_{i,t} + \varepsilon. \tag{4}$$

and we will further test for spatial dependence in healthcare sector based on Moran's I measure of spatial autocorrelation (Anselin and Rey, 1991):

$$MI = \frac{n\sum_{i=1}^{n}\sum_{j=1}^{n} w_{ij}(x_i - \overline{x})(x_j - \overline{x})}{(\sum_{i=1}^{n}\sum_{j=1}^{n} w_{ij})\sum_{i=1}^{n}(x_i - \overline{x})^2}, \tag{5}$$

where x_i and x_j represent the values of the Composite Healthcare Index, i and j are neighbour regions captured by the spatial weights w_{ij} where $w_{ij} = 1$ if regions *i* and *j* share a common border and $w_{ij} = 0$ otherwise. The permutation test further checks statistical significance of the computed Moran's *I* (Anselin and Rey, 1991).

According to spatial science literature (e.g., Anselin, 2005; LeSage and Pace, 2009), spatial dependence is accounted for by using a spatial lag of the dependent variable - Composite Healthcare Index ($\rho \cdot W \cdot CHI_{i,t}$):

$$CHI_{i,t} = a + b \cdot GDP_{i,t} + \rho \cdot W \cdot CHI_{i,t} + \varepsilon \tag{6}$$

or by including it in the error term, as follows:

$$CHI_{i,t} = a + b \cdot GDP_{i,t} + (\lambda W \varepsilon + v). \tag{7}$$

The best fit for our data is indicated by the Lagrange multiplier test.

Data. We would have liked to include in our analysis a very broad range of health relevant indicators, but only a small part of the official statistical data are available at county level. The variables included in the Composite Health Index have been structured in two synthetic indices, capturing separately the relevant material and human factors. The first one is the Synthetic Index of Physical Medical Infrastructure which combines data on number of hospitals and number of hospital beds both per 10000 inhabitants. The second one is the Synthetic Index of Healthcare Personnel which incorporates the variables: number of physicians in public and in private sectors, respectively, number of dentists in public and in private sectors, physician assistants and auxiliary medical staff, all considered per 10000 inhabitants.

3. Results and discussion

Following the initial data transformation by computing relative (per capita) measures and standardizing them with the min-max procedure (as previously described in the methodology section), we calculated the two synthetic indices (for Physical Medical Infrastructure and for Healthcare Personnel), and the final Composite Healthcare Index (CHI), covering every year of the period 1997 to 2014. Within each group, the standardised variables have been allotted equal weights and the same strategy was employed for the composite index.

We also explored different weighting variants for the two synthetic indices and obtained similar final rankings of the counties. Lacking a strong motivation for any of the alternative differentiated weighting scenarios, we finally adopted the equal weighting scheme. The results for selected years, and only for top and bottom values, are displayed in Table 1, while the Annex presents the territorial variation of the composite index across all counties, in the most relevant years.

Table 1 shows that Bucharest Municipality, as well as Cluj, Timis and Iasi counties, are constantly placed on top positions for their good healthcare infrastructure. On the opposite, less developed counties such as Giurgiu, Neamt, Ialomita, Calarasi and Bacau are to be found among the least healthcare endowed.

Comparing the maps in the Appendix, one can see that Composite Healthcare Index (CHI) differences among Romanian counties tend to fade over time. The Cluster Map associated to the Local Indicators of Spatial Autocorrelation points to significant cases of local spatial dependence by type of spatial correlation (positive-similar or negative-dissimilar). These maps suggest clustering of similar values of CHI. The initial 1997 map points to a clear delimitation between the high CHI values clustered in the West and the low values in the South-Est (except for Bucharest Municipality). The clusters tend to disperse in the following maps. This suggests that spatial regression is appropriate for our data.

GDP per capita, as a proxy for regional development, was further analysed in relation to the spatial distribution of the Composite Health Index, as well as in connection with the two synthetic indices. We found that GDP per capita is a positive and highly significant factor of influence for the Composite Health Index in all our annual models (Table 2).

Aiming to select the most relevant years for our analysis, our choice was guided by data availability (restricted to the period 1997 to 2014) and the phases of the economic cycle. The years 2001 and 2008 mark the beginning and the end of a period of strong and continuous economic growth that created favourable conditions for better healthcare endowment as well.

The intensity of spatial interactions seems to change in time, spatial dependence among neighbouring counties becoming stronger since the year 2008, as indicated by the regression estimations displayed in Table 2. Consequently, the spatial error model represents a better fit for our data for the years 2008 and 2014. This means that the neighbour counties share common influence factors, other than GDP per capita, that affect their healthcare infrastructure.

Conclusions

Starting from the need to benchmark and monitor regional medical endowment more clearly, this paper developed a Composite Healthcare Index at county level. Aiming to provide distinct measures for the relevant material and human factors, we also separated this index into a Synthetic Index of Physical Medical Infrastructure and a Synthetic Index of Healthcare Personnel. Our annual computations over 1997 to 2014 indicated significant variations both in time and space.

Table 1: Top and bottom counties according to the Composite healthcare index, selected years

Bottom 5 counties				**Top 5 counties**			
County	**Material infrastructure index**	**Human capital index**	**Composite index**	**County**	**Material infrastructure index**	**Human capital index**	**Composite index**
1997							
Ilfov	0.1903	0.0859	0.1381	**Hunedoara**	0.8954	0.3823	0.6388
Neamt	0.1393	0.2086	0.1739	**Iasi**	0.9011	0.5623	0.7317
Giurgiu	0.2356	0.1882	0.2119	**Municipiul Bucuresti**	0.8461	0.6671	0.7566
Ialomita	0.2825	0.1489	0.2157	**Cluj**	0.8354	0.7103	0.7728
Bacau	0.1833	0.2511	0.2172	**Timis**	0.8634	0.7486	0.8060
2001							
Neamt	0.1235	0.1864	0.1549	**Bihor**	0.7839	0.4673	0.6256
Giurgiu	0.1976	0.1237	0.1607	**Iasi**	0.7758	0.6181	0.6970
Ialomita	0.2371	0.0984	0.1678	**Timis**	0.7331	0.7247	0.7289
Bistrita-Nasaud	0.1724	0.2342	0.2033	**Municipiul Bucuresti**	0.8374	0.9251	0.8812
Olt	0.2914	0.1188	0.2051	**Cluj**	0.9824	0.7866	0.8845
2008							
Ialomita	0.0336	0.0965	0.0651	**Covasna**	0.7724	0.2907	0.5316
Giurgiu	0.1139	0.1366	0.1252	**Timis**	0.5561	0.7065	0.6313
Calarasi	0.2065	0.0912	0.1489	**Iasi**	0.5855	0.6851	0.6353

(continued on next page)

Table 1: Continued

Bottom 5 counties				**Top 5 counties**			
Dambovita	0.1077	0.2125	0.1601	**Municipiul Bucuresti**	0.7439	0.8265	0.7852
Neamt	0.1232	0.2068	0.1650	**Cluj**	1.0000	0.7797	0.8898
2014							
Giurgiu	0.0358	0.1218	0.0788	**Mures**	0.4662	0.6006	0.5334
Ialomita	0.0663	0.1583	0.1123	**Timis**	0.4974	0.7316	0.6145
Calarasi	0.1417	0.1457	0.1437	**Iasi**	0.7330	0.6422	0.6876
Neamt	0.0807	0.2421	0.1614	**Municipiul Bucuresti**	0.8506	0.9048	0.8777
Dambovita	0.1321	0.2026	0.1673	**Cluj**	0.9457	0.8474	0.8966

Source: authors.

Table 2: Results from the regression models (dependent variable – the composite healthcare index)

1997*			
Variable	***Coefficient***	***t-Statistic***	***Probability***
GDP per capita	0.001263832	3.662416	0.00072
Constant	0.0144743	0.1316601	0.89592
Statistics		***Value***	***Probability***
R-squared		0.251123	
F-statistic		13.4133	0.000723
Breusch-Pagan test		2.1081	0.14652
Spatial dependence (Moran's I)		2.2269	0.02595
2001*			
Variable	***Coefficient***	***t-Statistic***	***Probability***
GDP per capita	0.001240352	5.456244	0.00000
Constant	-0.00023570	-0.003146	
Statistics		***Value***	***Probability***
R-squared		0.426693	0.99755
F-statistic		29.7706	0.00000
Breusch-Pagan test		2.3075	0.12875
Spatial dependence (Moran's I)		2.0666	0.03878
2008**			
Variable	***Coefficient***	***z-value***	***Probability***
GDP per capita	0.0006327129	5.884063	0.00000
Constant	0.041921	0.6974709	0.48551
Lambda (spatial error)	0.3775034	2.005418	0.04492
Statistics		***Value***	***Probability***
R-squared		0.475880	
Log likelihood		26.964874	
Breusch-Pagan test		4.2797	0.03857
Spatial dependence (Likelihood Ratio Test)		4.0647	0.04379
2014**			
Variable	***Coefficient***	***z-value***	***Probability***
GDP per capita	0.0007004657	6.936972	0.00000
Constant	0.002587186	0.0446793	0.96436
Lambda (spatial error)	0.3945665	2.127388	0.03339

(continued on next page)

Table 2: Continued

Statistics	***Value***	***Probability***
R-squared	0.516855	
Log likelihood	26.973557	
Breusch-Pagan test	2.1365	0.14383
Spatial dependence (Likelihood Ratio Test)	4.0897	0.04315

Note: * OLS model; **spatial error model.

Considering the regional development (proxied by GDP per capita) as a key factor for understanding the inequalities in spatial healthcare infrastructure, we estimated its influence on healthcare, by means of spatial regression models, for several relevant years of the period under consideration. We found that GDP per capita was a positive and highly significant factor of influence for the Composite Health Index in all our annual regression models. Given that the spatial error model is the best fit for our data in recent years, we consider that spatial dependence among neighbouring counties tends to become stronger after the crisis. Neighbour counties seem to share common influence factors, other than GDP per capita, that impact significantly on their healthcare infrastructure.

References

Anselin, L./Rey, S.: Properties of Tests for Spatial Dependence in Linear Regression Models. Geographical Analysis, 23, 1991, pp. 112–131.

Anselin, L.: Exploring Spatial Data with GeoDaTM: A Workbook, 2005, Spatial Analysis Laboratory Department of Geography University of Illinois, Urbana, available at: http://sal.agecon.uiuc.edu/

Boncea, I.: Brain drain in Romania: factors influencing physicians` emigration. Journal of Community Positive Practices, 1, 2014, pp. 64–74.

Dragoi, MC./Ionescu, E./Iamandi, IE./Chiciudean, A./Constantin, LG.: An Economic Analysis of the Romanian Healthcare System based on a European Comparative Approach. WSEAS Transactions on Business and Economics. 6, 2008, pp. 330–340.

Ghita, S./Titan, E./Boboc, C.: Effects of the Global Financial Crisis on the Resources of Health System in Romania. Ovidius University Annals, Series Economic Sciences. 2015, 15(2), pp. 98–103.

LeSage, J.P./Pace, R.K.: Introduction to Spatial Econometrics, 2009, Boca Raton, CRC Press.

LeSage, J.P.: The Theory and Practice of Spatial Econometrics. 1999, Department of Economics, University of Toledo.

Metge, C./Chateau, D./Prior, H./Soodeen, R. A./De Coster, C./Barré, L.: Composite health indices: Useful tools or more work than they're worth? Summary of report: Composite Measures. Indices of Health and Health System Performance, Manitoba centre for health policy, August 2009, available at: http://mchp-appserv.cpe.umanitoba.ca/reference/CHIP-4_Page_Summary_web.pdf

Nguefack-Tsague, G./Klasen, S./Zucchini, W.: On weighting the components of the human development index: a statistical justification. Journal of Human Development and Capabilities, 12 (2), 2011, pp. 183–202. http://www2.vwl.wiso.uni-goettingen.de/courant-papers/CRC-PEG_DP_37.pdf

OECD: Handbook on constructing Composite Indicators. Methodology and user guide. 2008, Paris: OECD Publications.

Roman M./Goschin, Z.: Return migration in an economic crisis context. A survey on Romanian healthcare professionals, Romanian Journal of Economics, 48(2), 2014, pp.100–120.

Saisana, M./Tarantola, S.: State-of-the-art report on current methodologies and practices for composite indicator development. Report EUR 20408 EN. European Commission–Joint Research Centre, Ispra; 2002.

Vlădescu C./Scîntee, G./Olsavszky V./Allin, S./Mladovsky, P.: Romania: Health system review. Health Systems in Transition, 10(3), 2008, pp. 1–172

Vlădescu C./Scîntee, G./Olsavszky V./Hernandez-Quevedo, C./Sagan, A.: Romania: Health system review. Health Systems in Transition, 18(4), 2016, pp. 1–170.

World Bank: Romania. Health sector. Policy note. Romania Human Development Program; 2007. Available at: www.worldbank.org.ro

Zanfir, A./Marinescu M./Sarbu, R.: The analysis of the current problems and drawbacks in the Romanian health system. International Journal of Academic Research in Economics and Management Sciences. 2012, 1(6), pp. 60–6.

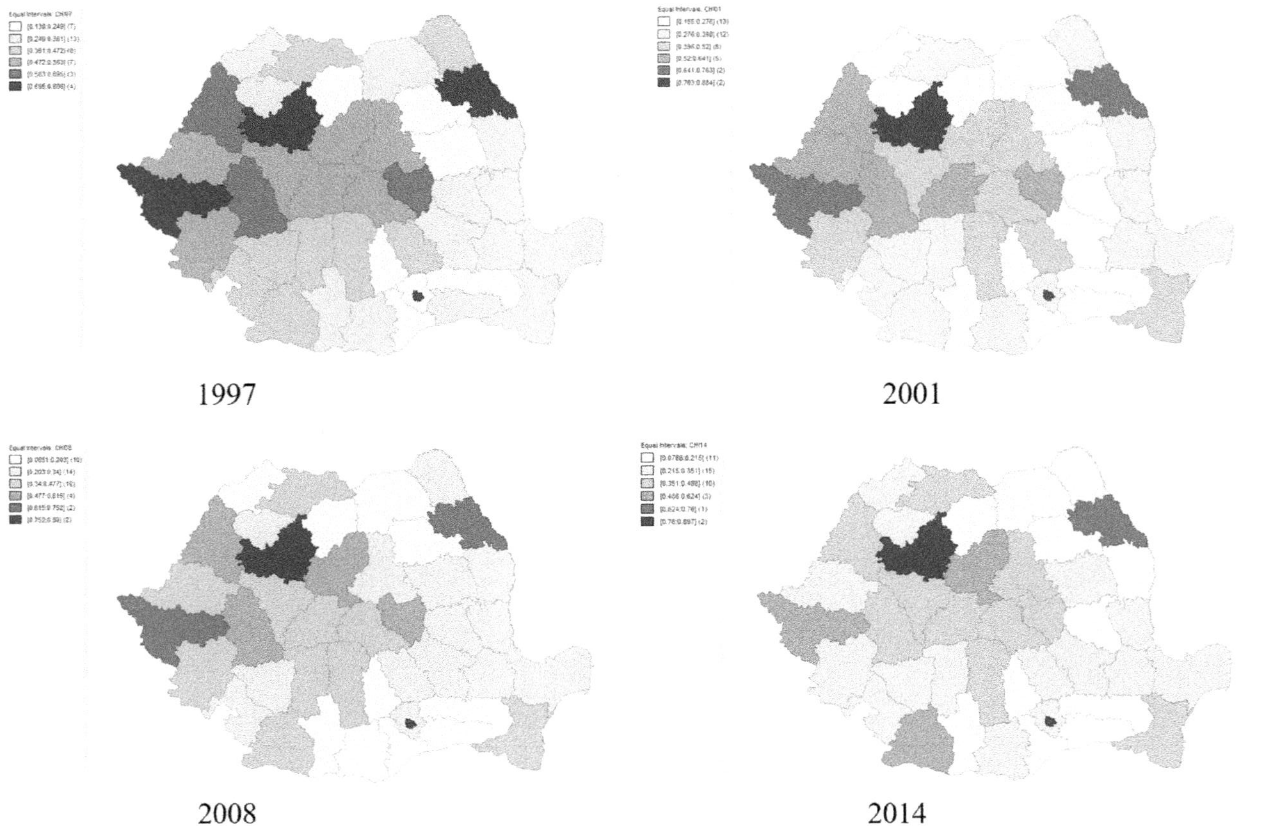

Annex: The composite healthcare index by county, selected years. Source: Authors.

Simona IVANA[1], *Nicolae STARCIUC*[2], *Cristea COSTACHE*[3], *Delia COSTACHE*[3]

[1] National Institute for Economic Research "Costin C. Kirițescu" (INCE), Romanian Academy, Email: simonaivana@yahoo.com

[2] State Agrarian University of Moldova (SAUM), Chișinău, Republic of Moldova

[3] Faculty of Medicine, Transilvania University of Brașov, Romania

Innovations in Green Nanotechnology for a Circular Economy

Abstract *Green nanotechnology play a fundamental role in bringing a key functionality across the whole value chain of a product, through the beneficial properties of nanomaterials. The unique properties of nano-scale materials have made them attractive for a number of innovative, sustainable green applications in this context, the "green economy" concept has offered the opportunity to change the way that society manages the interaction of the environmental and economic domains. Health 2020 focuses on improving health for all and reducing health inequalities through improved leadership and governance for health. This paper reports the experimental results we achieved by testing the glutaraldehyde and trichloroisocyanuric acid multi-functionalized* Fe_3O_4 *nanoparticles on Campylobacter jejuni, Listeria monocytogenes and Listeria innocua. Reticulation mixtures built up of functionalized nanoparticles and microorganisms were investigated by Scanning Electron Microscopy (SEM), Energy-dispersive X-ray spectroscopy (EDX) and IR spectroscopy. Additionally, biological viability investigations were performed in order to establish the level of biological inhibition, as well as to check the potential solutions offered by the fabricated nanoparticles in the field of biohazard limitation and prevention. We prove that functionalized nanoparticles are able to collect all types of microorganisms and residual growing protein in less than one minute. Additionally, we demonstrate that functionalized nanoparticles are able to completely inhibit biological activity of Campylobacter jejuni, coming from the volume of built-up tested mixture. Also, by remixing the tested reticulation mixtures we prove that biological functionalities of Campylobacter jejuni are inhibited only partially.*

Keywords: Campylobacter jejuni, Listeria spp., green economy, nano-scale materials, circular economy, Fe3O4 nanoparticles

Introduction

The term "circular economy" refers to the necessity of introduction. The used products in the circular flux. This model is adapted by the European Union countries follows the slogan mentioned at biomimicry: "The best solution to safeguard nature is to imitate it". In this context, the "green economy" concept has offered the opportunity to change the way that society manages the interaction of the environmental and economic domains (Ivo Iavicoli, et al., 2014).

Nanotechnology is promoted as one of the most challenging key technologies of this century. Billions of dollars have been spent on research framework programs intended to promote nanotechnology and to bring novel materials and processes to market. In Europe, nanomaterials are regulated by REACH (Registration, Evaluation, Authorization and Restriction of Chemicals) because they are covered by the REACH definition of a chemical substance.

Health 2020 is for everyone: not just politicians and experts but also civil society, communities, families and individuals. Food health is essential for economic and social development and a vital concern to the lives of very single person, all families and communities. Research priorities of Microbiology and the Food Chain Division (MICA) are: (1) microbiology for a rational approach to biotechnologies; (2) microbiology for food quality, sustainability and safety; (3) microbiology for sustained animal and human health.

Foodborne diseases are a growing public health problem, as the amount of food prepared outside the home has steeply throughout the increasingly complex food chain requires collaboration between the health sector, agriculture, food transport, food service establishments and the food industry. Food safety and security depends strongly on the availability of safe water, land use policies and the availability of technological advances for improving food production, storage, transport and preparation. Setting targets for health promote well-being, by improving performance and accountability as the Health 2020 policy is implemented.

The federal Centers for Disease, Control and Prevention estimates that each year 48 million people in the United States get sick from a foodborne illness. Researchers have identified more than 250 foodborne diseases. Most of them result in infectious, caused by variety of bacteria, viruses and parasites. *Campylobacter spp.* and *Listeria spp.* are microorganisms that are well-known to have high risk for the contamination of humans, food, environment and animals. (Nadeem O. Kaakoush, 2015).

Bacteria included in the Listeria genus may be found in the soil, vegetation, sewage, water, animal food, fresh and frozen meat, including poultry, slaughter house wastes and in the feces of healthy animals, including humans (Simon Gebretsadik, 2011). These organisms can become endemic in food processing environments.

Listeria species can contaminate foods we don't usually cook, such raw milk, pasteurized fluid milk, cheeses, ice cream, raw vegetables, fermented raw-meat sausages, raw and cooked poultry, raw and smoked fish (Dalton C.B., 1997; Miettinen M.K., 1999; Schlech W.F., 1983; Kvenberg J.E., 1988; Aureli P., 2000; Misrachi A., 1991; Farber J.M., 2000). It is resistant to the effects of drying, freezing and heat. It has the ability to grow at temperatures as low as 0^0C permits exponential multiplication in refrigerated foods. Listeriosis is a serious infection most likely to sicken pregnant women and their newborns, adults aged 65 or older, and people with weakened immune systems. An estimated 1,600 people get listeriosis each year, and about 260 die (Centers for Disease Control and Prevention, 2017).

Campylobacter jejuni is one of the most common causes of food poisoning in the world (United States and Europe). The European Food Safety Authority estimated in 2011 that there are approximately nine million cases of human campylobacteriosis per year in the European Union. Active surveillance through the Foodborne Diseases Active Surveillance Network (Food Net) indicates that about 14 cases are diagnosed each year.

Campylobacter jejuni infections are extremely common worldwide. New Zealand reported the highest national campylobacteriosis rate, which peaked in May 2006 at 400/100,000 population (Sharon V. R. Epps, 2013). Individuals with recent *Campylobacter jejuni* infections develop Guillain-Barré syndrome at a rate of 0.3/1000 infections, about 100 times more often than the general population.

Campylobacter jejuni is commonly found in animal feces.

Nowadays, the cumulated know-hows in the field of nanoscience and nanotechnologies are oriented in order to develop novel material for aseptic handling and packaging, the mechanical removal of microorganisms by washing or filtration, the destruction of microorganisms by physical or chemical sanitization, the inhibition of pathogens or saprophytes through environmental control, etc. (Davidson P. M., 2005). Life science (drug delivery, human body nanoparobes, cancer cell targeting, contrast agents for MRI investigations, nanomedicine), food conditioning and preservation, as well as the conservation and protection of environmental biodiversity require special design constraints in the processes of nano-engineering of some specific applicable nanotechnology-based solutions.

Taking into account the structural complexity and organization of the living matter, certain current opinions coming from the scientific community and society consider that interactions between nanomaterials and living mater can became uncontrollable. According to this, the fundamental structures of the living matter (such as DNA or other macromolecules with biological functions) may be irreversibly damaged.

In this context, the goal of this work was the investigation of the specific reticulation patterns established in the processes of interaction between nanoparticles and the constituents of living matter. It is well-known that each type of nanoparticles establishes a unique pattern of reticulation for each type of targeted microorganisms.

In this context, the research we present in this paper, as well as other research we have not published yet, show that the functional structure of nanoparticles is the main factor responsible for the type and interaction complexity of nanomaterials with living matter. Additionally, as we demonstrated elsewhere, we concluded that the nature of this interaction can be controlled by adequate nano-engineering of chemical functionalities that will be engrafted on the surface and in the depth of carrier nanoparticles (Iordache P. Z., 2011).

As a consequence, we believe that at the end of the nano-engineering process we will be able to control the targeted structures and the strength of biochemical interactions. Novel research activities in nanotechnology focus on improving selectivity and flux efficiently. Metal oxide nanoparticles (Al_2 O_3, TIO_2) can help to increase the mechanical and thermal stability as well as permeate flux of polymeric membranes. Magnetic nanoparticles can be injected directly into the contaminated ground, and loaded particles can be recovered simply through a magnetic field. Nano-0 valent iron can be used for remediation of groundwater contaminated with chlorinated hydrocarbon fluids and perchlorates (Iordache Petrişor Zamora, 2012). The toxicity potential of nanometal oxides is quite low (Innovations in Nanotechnology for Water Treatment, Nanotechnol. Sci. Appl. 2015. 8: 1–17). The use of magnetic nanoparticles have been established in medical applications, and are approved by the US Food and Drug Administration as a contrast agent for magnetic resonance imaging. The use of magnetic nanoparticles (magnetite Fe_3O_4) for separation of water pollutants has been established in ground water remediation.

The mobility of nanoparticles in water bodies depends on their properties (water solubility, physical binding to other components, and their chemical reactivity (for example: oxidation and reduction behavior). Nanoparticles can be altered by sunlight, induced photoreaction depending on the turbidity of the water and by biotic and abiotic degradation processes. There is a significant need for novel advanced water technologies, for ensure a high quality of drinking water, eliminate micropollutans, and intensify industrial production processes in water treatment systems.

Materials and methods

Functionalized nanoparticle fabrication.

The Fe_3O_4 nanoparticles were obtained by coprecipitation route, by using a ratio of Fe^{2+}:Fe^{3+}=1:2[10] (Hyeon T., 2003). 600 mL of ethyl alcohol and 400 mL Fe_3O_4 nanoparticle suspension were coated with organosilane by using 10 mL of (3-aminopropyl) triethoxysilane, in the presence of 60 mL ammonia (25 %).

The coating process of the Fe_3O_4 nanoparticles ended by continuing to mix for another 60 minutes. The coated nanoparticles were functionalized with glutaraldehyde, by treating them with 2 mL of $C_5H_8O_2$ at pH 11.

Subsequently, the glutaraldehyde-functionalized nanoparticles were admixed to a 6 gram-trichloroisocyanuric acid (TCCA) and 400 mL-ethyl alcohol built-up mixture.

The TCCA functionalization process ended by continuing to mix for another 90 minutes. At the end of the fabrication process, the suspension pH was about 7–7.5. The concentrations of the functionalized nanoparticle suspensions were gravimetrically determined. We found that they were about 5 mg∘mL-1.

The biological viability tests performed. We used for determining the number of microorganisms a quantitative plating method namely Standard Plate Count (SPC).

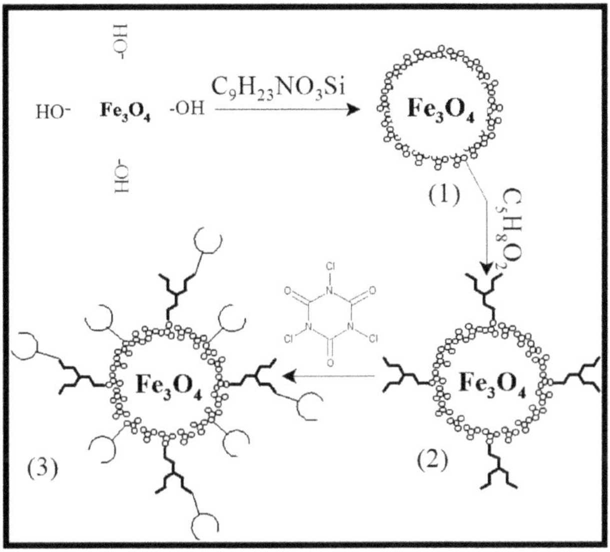

Figure 1: The main diagram of nanoparticle fabrication

Note: In the first stage, the Fe_3O_4 nanoparticles are coated mainly by ethoxysilane co-hydrolysis processes (1). The engrafted amino- functional groups can host – CHO functionalities (2). Finally, the TCCA can be reticulated by amino- or -OH functionalities, which are found in various chemically active forms (3)

This procedure consists of diluting the microorganisms with a series of sterile water blanks. By using 24-hour fresh biological cultures, we perform dilutions by factor 10−1, 10−2, 10−3, 10−4, respectively 10−5, by using 4.5 mL normal saline solution. Subsequently, 0.5 mL of functionalized suspension and 0,5 mL of freshly grown *Campylobacter jejuni* were mixed for about 30 seconds.

After 12 hours, several drops of nanoparticles and microorganisms previously built up mixture were collected and transferred into empty petri plates. Nutrient agar, cooled to 50^{0}C, and then poured into each plate. After the nutrient agar has solidified the plates are incubated for 24 hours and examined.

The results we obtained are summarized in Table 1. Following the same testing strategy we also performed viability tests in the case of *Listeria monocytogenes* and *Listeria innocua.*

The IR investigation performed. In the case of built-up reticulation mixtures we have performed IR investigations in order to observe the fluctuations in the functional structure of the microorganism surface.

For this purpose, we used reticulation mixture volumes built up by using microbiological cultures diluted by 10.

Table 1: Summary of biological viability investigations

Tested microorganism	Dilution*	Number of viable colony
Viable biological colony coming from the supernatant		
Campylobacter jejuni	10^3	0
	10^4	1
Listeria inocua	10^3	> 500
	10^5	> 500
Listeria monocytogenes	10^1	0
	10^2	0
	10^3	0
Viable biological colony coming from homogenized reticulation mixture		
Campylobacter jejuni	10^1	0
	10^2	0
	10^3	0
	10^4	180
	10^5	160
Listeria inocua	10^1	> 500
	10^2	> 500
	10^3	70
	10^4	30
	10^5	10
Listeria monocytogenes	10^1	> 500
	10^2	> 500
	10^3	> 500
	10^4	> 500
	10^5	> 500

Note: *This parameter represents the degree of the initial biological culture dilution and may be expressed in terms of microorganisms per milliliter.

We believe that the fluctuations of chemical functionalities are the consequences of interactions established between the functionalized nanoparticles and the surface of tested microorganisms in the volume of reticulation mixture.

Thus, several drops of reticulation mixture were laid down on a thin microscopy cover glass surface. Subsequently, the mixture was sealed by using another cover glass, followed by their soldering.

Results and discussions

Campylobacter is helical-shaped, non-spore-forming, Gram negative, microaerophilic, non-fermenting bacterium forming motile rods with a single polar flagellum. It is oxidase-positive and grow optimally at 37 to 42^{0}C. When exposed to atmospheric oxygen, *Campylobacter jejuni* is able to change into a coccal form. Its structure is similar to most Gram negative bacteria.

The cell contains an outer membrane and an inner membrane with periplasm in between the two membranes. The outer membrane consists of lipopolysaccharide which are endotoxic. Membrane proteins are embedded on the outer membrane surface, they are antigenic and are used for invasion of the host.

Listeria spp. is a Gram positive and rod shaped bacterium, non-spore-forming, motile, facultatively anaerobic, catalase positive. Researchers have found *Listeria monocytogenes* in at least 37 mammalian species, 17 species of birds and possibly in some species of fish and shellfish. An early study suggested that *Listeria monocytogenes* is unique among Gram positive bacteria in that it might possess lipopolysaccharide, which serves as an enterotoxin.

Listeria cell walls consistently contain lipoteichoic acids in which a glycolipid moiety, such as a galactosyl-glucosyl-diglyceride, is covalently linked to the terminal phosphomonoester of the teichoic acid. This lipid region anchors the polymer chain to the cytoplasmic membrane. These lipoteichoic acids resemble the lipopolysaccharides of Gram negative bacteria in both structure and function, being the only amphipathic polymers at the cell surface.

The main idea of our strategy was to fabricate smart, functionalized nanoparticles so that the targeted microorganism could be reticulated and biologically inhibited.

The main designated function of -CHO functionalities coming from the glutaraldehyde was to capture the microorganism by their surface reticulation. In the case of TCCA, their main function was to generate and infuse Cl- ions in the depth of microorganisms. According to this, the normal functions of biochemical molecules, as well as of other biochemical fractions of microorganisms may be irreversibly disturbed.

Finally, in terms of disturbed functions, the microorganisms can be partially affected or killed.

We believe that there are two scenarios for the inhibition of the biological activity of targeted microorganisms. In the first stage functionalized nanoparticles can reticulate specific micro-surfaces of microorganisms.

Thus, the chemical structure of microorganisms may be degraded, so that a significant fraction of nanoparticles may remain reticulated on the surface on the cell wall. Other fractions of nanoparticles may permeate the cellular wall and finally break inside microorganisms.

Most probably, another significant fraction of nanoparticles returned in the volume of the reticulation mixture as a consequence of their neutralization by depletion of chemical functionalities.

Secondly, it is most likely that the integrity of cell wall should be compromised by sequential extraction of its macromolecular constituents.

Finally, the nanoparticles that come in contact with the cell wall are charged, depleted and neutralized by the chemical constituents of cell wall.

Another way for the inhibition of biological viability of microorganisms may be supplied by the blocking of cell wall macromolecular channel. Therefore, nanoparticles may be reticulated in the interior of the channel frameworks and finally they block the access of nutrients and other vital fluids. We believe that this scenario has a limited contribution to biological inhibition, taking into account that DNA or other essential biomolecules are not directly affected.

Taking into account the previously exposed biological inhibition strategy, in Table 1 we observe that only *Campylobacter jejuni* is completely inhibited.

Moreover, we observe that the number of viable microorganisms colony increases at low tested culture dilutions. A possible explanation for this behavior may be due to the proteins coming from broth culture.

Thereby, in order to explain the biological inhibition behavior we must admit that in the first stage proteins are quickly reticulated by the functionalized nanoparticles.

We observed that each type of microorganism presents distinct agglomeration morphologies.

By lowering the dilution we increased the quantity of proteins in the volume of reticulation mixtures. Experimental evidence shows that the reticulation of microorganisms takes place at the end of protein reticulation processes. Also, differentiated reticulation behavior in the case of proteins and microorganisms was observed in all cases. Moreover, we clearly observed the formation of two distinct types of agglomeration domain (Figure 2a.2, Figure 2b.1, Figure 2b.3, Figure 2c.1): (a) an agglomeration domain type which presents a compact and irregular morphology and (b) an agglomeration domain type with regular and dendrimeric morphology. By comparing the photomicrographs in Figure 2 and Figure 3, we conclude that the dendrimeric structure is characteristic for the reticulated microorganisms (MD).

Moreover, we assigned compact agglomeration domains with proteins that were reticulated on the surface of functionalized nanoparticles. Besides, we observe that specific protein agglomeration domains (PAD) do not present favorite sites for positioning in the structure of the framework of agglomeration domains. Additionally, it can be observed that at low culture dilution PAD are the major fractions in the framework of agglomeration domains that consist of a mixture of reticulated protein and microorganism (Figure 2a.4, Figure 2a.5).

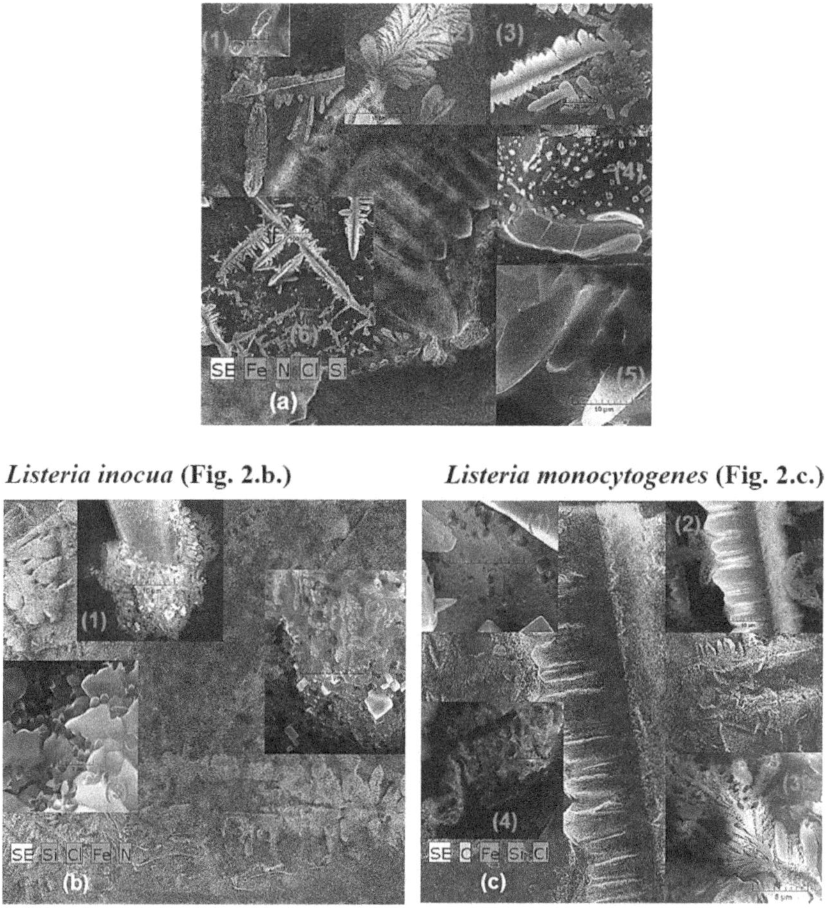

Figure 2: SEM and EDX photomicrographs of biological reticulation by-products resulted in the process of nanoparticle reticulation. For convenience purposes we present photomicrographs acquired at different magnifications in order to distinguish specific reticulation patterns in the case of Campylobacter jejuni (Fig. 2.a.) *Listeria inocua* (Fig. 2.b.) *Listeria monocytogenes* (Fig. 2.c.)

For simplicity purposes, we henceforth assign "agglomeration domains" with the "precipitate" that resulted as a consequence of the reticulation process.

Contrariwise, in the case of *Campylobacter jejuni* we did not observe such behavior regarding the presence of free viable microorganisms. Moreover, we could observe that the framework of the precipitate establishes amorph

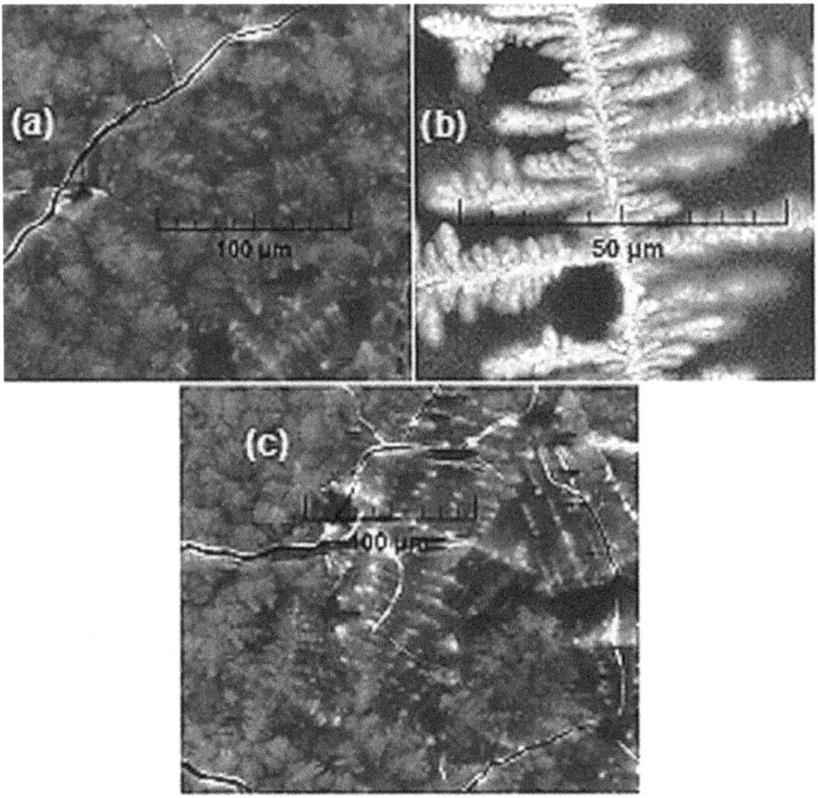

Figure 3: SEM photomicrographs of untested *Campylobacter jejuni* (a), *Listeria inocua* (b) and *Listeria monocytogenes*(c)

agglomeration domains which completely embed the microorganism colony (Figure 2a.2, Figure 2a.5, Figure 2a.6).

Additionally, the colony of isolated microorganisms is entirely covered by functionalized nanoparticles (Figure 2a.4).

Secondly, EDX photomicrographs proffer clear mapping images of the morphochemical structure that belongs to the identified agglomeration domains. Also, this investigation is in complete agreement with the formulated assumptions and SEM investigations.

Thereby, we can observe that MD contains the chemical elements Cl, Fe, Si and N, which are characteristic for Fe_3O_4 nanoparticles, TCCA, normal saline solution (which contains NaCl) and proteins (coming from broth culture).

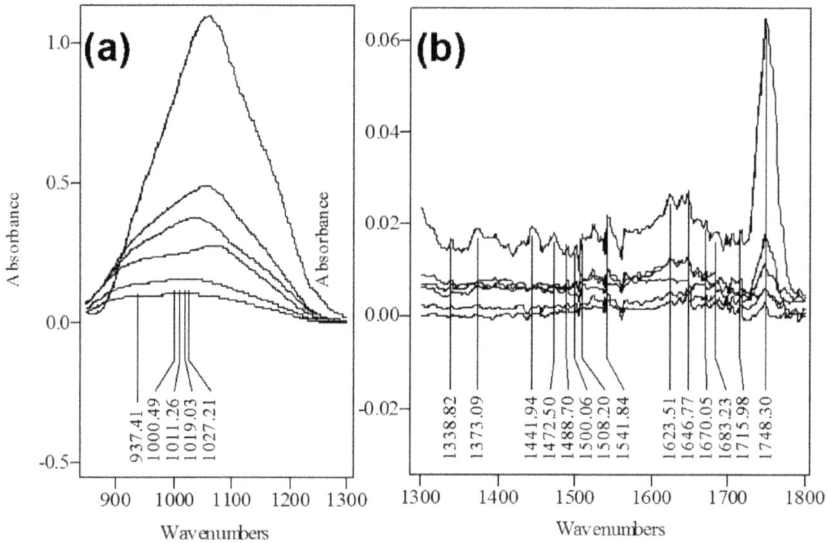

Figure 4 (a): Reference IR spectra of untested *Campylobacter jejuni, Listeria inocua, Listeria monocytogenes*, Broth culture, glass, normal saline solution; (b) IR spectra acquired at the end of biological reticulation proceses in the cases of *Campylobacter jejuni, Listeria inocua* and *Listeria monocytogenes*

We conclude that MD is built from proteins that were reticulated on the surface of nanoparticles, as well as from functionalized nanoparticles reticulated on the surface of tested microorganisms.

Also, in Figure 4a we clearly observe the IR fingerprint region of proteins coming from the structure of *Campylobacter jejuni, Listeria monocytogenes* and *Listeria innocua* and broth culture, as follows: (a) β-sheet proteins (a strong band between 1623.51÷1646.77 cm-1; a weaker band at 1683.23 cm-1; 1670 cm-1); (b) unordered or random protein structures at 1646.77 cm-1; (c) N–H bend combined with C–N stretch (known as amide bands II) at 1541.84 (β-sheet protein structures) and 1508.2 cm-1; (d) C–N stretch combined with N–H bend (known as amide bands III) at 1338.82, 1373.09 and about 1400 cm-1. Moreover, the peak at 1748.3 cm-1 was assigned for free water (in the case of glass) and for the Eigen and the Zundel forms of the hydrated proton (in the case of microorganisms and broth culture). Besides, in Figure 4b we observe that the IR fingerprint regions of protein coming from the structure of *Campylobacter jejuni, Listeria monocytogenes* and *Listeria innocua* and broth culture are preserved after the reticulation process.

This is strong experimental evidence which proves that the framework of the precipitate is mainly charged with proteins reticulated on the surfaces of the nanoparticles.

In comparison with the IR spectra of *Campylobacter jejuni*, the spectrum of *Listeria monocytogenes* and *Listeria innocua* is clearer and presents a well-delimitated shape, both before and after testing. This could be a possible explanation for the lack of biological inhibition in the case of *Listeria monocytogenes.*

In the case of reticulated microorganisms, the band centered at 753.93 cm-1 can be attributed to the Si-O stretching bonds. This additional experimental evidence proves once again that the framework of the precipitates coming from the supernatant is completely charged with organosilane Fe_3O_4 coated nanoparticles.

In Figure 3 can be observed that unreticulated *Campylobacter jejuni* form agglomeration domains which adopt a star-shaped morphology. The dimensions of the star-shaped agglomeration domains are about 50 µm (Figure 3a, Figure 3c).

Moreover, a small fraction of these microorganisms adopts an acicular-dendrimeric morphology. It can be seen that the dimensions of the acicular-dendrimeric agglomeration domains are more than 150 µm (Figure 3c). By comparison, in Figure 3b we observe that *Listeria monocytogenes* forms agglomeration domains which adopt a more pronounced acicular-dendrimeric morphology. As in the previously cases, the dimensions of the agglomeration domains are more than 150 µm.

Additionally, in Figure 2 we can see that the agglomeration domains coming from the untested microorganisms and proteins constitute the skeleton for the agglomeration domains resulted as a consequence of the nanoparticle reticulation. Most probably, the reticulated microorganisms constitute the nucleation sites for the agglomeration domains due to the micromagnetic agglomeration processes.

Micromagnetic agglomeration is induced by the magnetic moment of the Fe_3O_4 nanoparticles. Moreover, as a consequence of micromagnetic agglomeration, functionalized nanoparticles, protein-charged nanoparticles and microorganism-coated nanoparticles may establish more physico-chemical bonds (hydrogen, electrostatic, coordinative or other types of bonds) which can lead to the formation of more compact three-dimensional reticulation frameworks.

Conclusions

In summary, we have fabricated functionalized nanoparticles able to reticulate undifferentiated both microorganisms and proteins.

The nanoparticles were tested on *Campylobacter jejuni, Listeria monocytogenes* and *Listeria innocua* in order to investigate their ability for biological viability inhibition.

The by-products resulted in the volume of the reticulation mixture were investigated by SEM, EDX and IR techniques. Additional tests for biological viability checking were performed.

The following results have been found:

1. The functionalized nanoparticles can reticulate undifferentiated microorganisms, as well as proteins.

2. We proved that functionalized nanoparticles can completely inhibit the biological functions of *Campylobacter jejuni.*
   Moreover, we proved that the process of biological viability inhibition is strongly dependent on the quantity of proteins and the number of microorganisms found in the volume of reticulation.
3. We proved that the functional structure of nanoparticles we fabricated is not able to inhibit completely the biological viability of and *Listeria innocua* and *Listeria monocytogenes.*
4. IR, SEM and EDX investigations proved that the surface of microorganisms was completely charged with nanoparticles. Moreover, we proved that the agglomeration domains consist of mixtures of microorganisms and proteins that were reticulated by nanoparticles.
5. Each type of the tested microorganisms adopted specific patterns of agglomeration morphology toward the functional structure of reference functionalized nanoparticles. Additionally, we proved that the reticulation and micromagnetic agglomeration are the main processes responsible for the morphology of agglomeration domains resulted at the end of the reticulation.

Accordingly, we conclude that multiple-functionalized nanoparticles are promising solutions in the field of biohazard limitation and prevention.

Acknowledgements

We would like to thank to Dr. PhD. Iordache Petrişor Zamora by Scientific Research Center for CBRN Defense and Ecology, Radiometry Department, Bucharest.

References

Aureli P., Fiorucci G.C., Garoli D., Marchiaro G., Novara O., Leone L., Salmaso S., 2000. An outbreak of febrile gastroenteritis associated with corn contaminated by Listeria monocytogenes, New England Journal of Medicine. 2000; 342: 1236–1241.

Dalton C.B., Austin C.C., Sobel J., Hayes P.S., Bibb W.F., Graves L.M., Swaminathan B., Proctor M.E., Griffin P.M., 1997. An outbreak of gastroenteritis and fever due to Listeria monocytogenes in milk. New England Journal of Medicine. 1997; 336: 100–105.

Davidson P. M., Sofos J. N., Branen A. L., 2005. Antimicrobials in food. Boca Raton, CRC Press, 2005.

Farber J.M., Daley E.M., Mackie M.T., Limerick B., 2000. A small outbreak of listeriosis potentially linked to the consumption of imitation crab meat, Letters in Applied Microbiology. 2000; 31: 100–104.

Hyeon T., 2003. Chemical synthesis of magnetic nanoparticles. Chem. Commun. 2003; 927.

Iordache P. Z., Petrea N., Lungu R. M., Petre R., Său C., Safta I., 2011. Nanocomposite Materials with Oriented Functionalized Structure in Nanomaterials. Rijeka, Croatia, Intech Publishing.

Iordache Petrişor Zamora, Ivana Simona, Pîrvu Dinu Cristina, 2012. Material compozit polifuncţionalizat biodegradabil şi procedeu de obţinere a acestuia. RO 127 171 Romanian Patent.

Ivo Iavicoli, Veruscka Leso, Walter Ricciardi, Laura L Hodson, and Mark D Hoover, 2014. Opportunities and challenges of nanotechnology in the green economy. Environ Health. 2014; 13: 78. Published online 2014 Oct 7. doi: 10.1186/1476-069X-13-78.

Kvenberg J.E., 1988. Outbreaks of listeriosis/Listeria-contaminated foods, Microbiological Science. 1988; 5: 355–358.

Misrachi A., Watson A.J., Coleman D., 1991. Listeria in smoked mussels in Tasmania, Communicable Disease Intelligence. 1991; 15: 427.

Miettinen M.K., Siitonen A., Heiskanen P., Haajanene H., Bjorkroth K.J., Korkeala H.J., 1999. Molecular epidemiology of an outbreak of febrile gastroenteritis caused by Listeria monocytogenes in cold-smoked rainbow trout, Journal of Clinical Microbiology. 1999; 37: 2358–2360.

Nadeem O. Kaakoush, Natalia Castaño-Rodríguez, Hazel M. Mitchell, Si Ming Man, 2015. Global Epidemiology of Campylobacter Infection. Clin Microbiol Rev. 2015 Jul; 28(3): 687–720. Published online 2015 Jun 10. doi: 10.1128/CMR.00006-15

Preedy P.R., Watson R.R., 2005. Reviews in food and nutrition toxicity. vol. 4 London, Taylor & Francis. 2005; 154.

Simon Gebretsadik, Tesfu Kassa, Haile Alemayehu, Kahsay Huruy, Nigatu Kebede, 2011. Isolation and characterization of Listeria monocytogenes and other Listeria species in foods of animal origin in Addis Ababa, Ethiopia. Journal of Infection and Public Health, Volume 4, Issue 1, March 2011, Pages 22–29.

Schlech W.F., Lavigne P.M., Bortolussi R.A., Allen A.C., Haldane E.V., Wort A.J., 1983. Hightower A.W., Johnson S.E., King S.E., Nicholls E.S., Broome C.V. Epidemic listeriosis – evidence for transmission by food, New England Journal of Medicine. 1983; 308: 203–206.

Sharon V. R. Epps, Roger B. Harvey, Michael E. Hume, Timothy D. Phillips, Robin C. Anderson, David J. Nisbet, 2013. Foodborne Campylobacter: Infections, Metabolism, Pathogenesis and Reservoirs. Int J Environ Res Public Health. 2013 Dec; 10(12): 6292–6304. Published online 2013 Nov 26. doi: 10.3390/ijerph10126292.

Diana Loreta PĂUN[1], Constantin Sorin PĂUN[2], Laurențiu Alexandru CHIOTOROIU[3], Silvia CHIOTOROIU[4]

[1] Senior Lecturer, PhD in Medicine, Carol Davila University of Medicine and Pharmacy, Bucharest / Manager National Institute of Endocrinology C.I. Parhon, Email: dianaloreta_paun@yahoo.ro

[2] Lecturer, PhD in Medicine, Carol Davila University of Medicine and Pharmacy, Bucharest / Floreasca Hospital, Bucharest, Romania, Email: drspaun@yahoo.ro

[3] PhD in Medicine, Floreasca Hospital Bucharest, Romania, Email: chiotoroiu@yahoo.com

[4] PhD in Medicine, Malaxa Hospital, Bucharest, Romania, Email: chiotoroiu@yahoo.com

Exogenous-Endogenous Associative Tensions in the Multitude of Threats to Human Health: Social and Economic Consequences

Abstract *In the paper, it is appreciated that from a socio-economic perspective, the general / generic surgical act should benefit more (complementary, implicitly, intrisse, articular, etc.) of 1) reordering the psychosomatic behavior and 2) reordering the drug therapy, respectively the action on the disease using ultra-resolving drugs and the quasi-controlled induction of the psychosomatic behavior of the patient, not only as an adjuvant but as an osmotic need, fully assumed. The upper / lower order during / post-manifestation of human dysfunction, are non-endogenous and exogenous non-linearisation of causality and threats to human health, as well as the thesis of "endogenous-exogenous" associative tensions in the set of threats to human health. In this context, it is proposed to move the surgery from protocols and conventional standards to innovation under the influence of information technology mechanisms, medical engineering and, more recently, under the aegis of the medical economy, to "medical breaks", relying on the new intelligence in the field. The article presents the concept of global redevelopment of medical knowledge used in continuous / quasi-continuous feedbacks for the return of the human body to the conventional natural considered starting point, good, acceptable, reliable, feasible, sustainable health.*

Keywords: exogenous-endogenous associative tensions, human health, circular medicine, circularity of medicine, social and economic consequences

Introduction

Disease is a particular occurrence of the body as a result of the harmful action of the various environmental determinants. The disease is characterized by a complex of morphological and functional changes. The changes in question may be: 1) local; 2) general; 3) reactive; 4) lesional; 5) disturbing the adjustments and activities at different functional levels.

Disease limits the adaptive potential, reduces work capacity, affects the biological and social unity of man. (Saragea M., 1985)

The causes of the diseases are complex and the overall factors are: 1) the determinant factor - the indispensable but not sufficient etiological agent, 2) the complex of factors or favorable conditions, 3) the risk factors and 4) the terrain or specific reactions of the organism. Excessive demand for adaptive mechanisms, increasing the intensity of environmental agents, reducing adaptability, - all determine events in the current adaptation of the human body to the course of life. On the other hand, there are observed the cause beach and the action of unusual agents of traumatic, toxic, ionizing radiation and so on, causing damage, destruction or direct structural alterations.

In the face of the disease state there is a complex of reactions of the organism in relation to the causative agent. In fact, we are dealing with a functional adaptation arsenal, a compensatory generator intervention. Post-aggressive reactions are versions of associative tensions behavior of the body rolled in relation to external requests / outside the human body. Of course, a tension generated by the reactions shows the loss of the harmonic character of the complex of reactions and, incidentally, we are witnessing degenerations to deviant consequences.

The specificity of the reactive defense mechanisms originates during phylogenetic evolution, having the role of intervention against the pathogens, with the character of general or local reactions of the organism (haemostasis in the area of lesions, fibrin-leukocyte barriers, etc.).

Associative tensions also show non-specifics states (for example, the post-aggressive systemic reaction face to face with specificities such as anti-corpogenesis).

We believe that endogenous - exogenous associative tensions, in the multitude of threats to human health, play a real role in connecting or disconnecting health security mechanisms, since, from an economic, social and medical perspective. The curative concern is to maintain the body's reactions within the limits / as a source of transformations of adaptive manifestations in pathological phenomena / processes.

The disciplinary consequences, for example, in surgery, appear on the background of inadequate central coordination of associative tensions, in which case the compensatory manifestations become themselves sources of deficiencies, difficulties, barriers. If associative tensions maintain disturbances, then the potential for self-sustainability of the body worsens, leading even to critical moments, to the dissolution of normal conventional equilibrium by its own means, requiring intervention of medicine / surgery as such.

Therefore, endogenous-exogenous associative tensions should not affect adaptive reserves, not generate excessive energy consumption and low defense yields. It is, therefore, possible to see the correlation between the reduction of the compensation and adaptation capacities in the face of human pathology and the decrease of the work capacity and social integration of the people.

From the nosological point of view, anatomical, clinical, anatomo-clinical, genetic, hereditary, multifactorial diseases as well as diseases with mesological determinism all fall under the re-establishment of the functional adaptive balance of the organism under conditions in which endogenous-exogenous associative tensions are modeled, optimized, organized and managed.

1. Literature review

The topic of exogenous-endogenous associative tensions in the multitude of threats to human health, in general, is insufficiently addressed in the literature. The reason for this deficiency is related to the high resolution of the subjects to be researched, that is, the novelty hard to investigate. Mainly, getting explanations on associative tensions in the multitude of threats to human health requires the search for specific phenomena and processes by applying transdisciplinarity, invoking procedural endogenous and exogenous areas of the human body / organism, but in coherent cognoscibility articulations.

It is of particular importance that the exogenous-endogenous associative tensions in the multitude of threats to human health determine social and economic consequences by the fact that the person / patient is quasi-blocked, stopped from his / her societal functioning when diseases / diseases are established by pathogenic aggression from the inside and outside of the body / organism.

Pragmatically, the endogenous-exogenous relationship is affected, transformed from communication perspectives. For example, Lingard L., (2004), show that "Ineffective team communication is frequently at the root of medical error. (...) As observational methods become more common in patient safety research, ethical considerations arise. (...) The evidence suggests that adverse events resulting from error happen at unacceptably high rates in the inpatient setting and that ineffective or insufficient communication among team members is often a contributing factor. In fact, communication failures have been uncovered at the root of over 60 % of sentinel events reported to the Joint Commission on Accreditation of Healthcare Organizations." (Sentinel event statistics, 2003)

Furthermore, Gillespie M. Brigid, et al., (2011) [2], states that "In the operating room, factors such as interruptions, communication failures, team familiarity and the unpredictability of unplanned cases can prolong the length of an operation, and lead to inefficiency and increased costs."

Medical education of specialists and patients has a transformative role on exogenous-endogenous associative tensions. Thus, Sadideen Hazim and Kneebone Roger, (2012) [5], consider that "Several aspects of surgical education, modeling them on current educational theory, and these include the following: (1) acquisition and retention of motor skills (Miller's triangle; Fitts' and Posner's theory), (2) development of expertise after repeated practice and regular reinforcement (Ericsson's theory), (3) importance of the availability of expert assistance (Vygotsky's theory),

(4) learning within communities of practice (Lave and Wenger's theory), (5) importance of feedback in learning practical skills (Boud, Schon, and Endes' theories), and (6) affective component of learning."

Exogenous-endogenous problems are also encountered in the nosocomial operational perimeter, as noted by Stângă L., et al., (2012), when he states that "Depending on the infection source and transmission mechanisms, one can identify:

- Endogenous infections – when an endogenous pathogen which colonizes the host organism or is present in a localised infectious process becomes innoculated/ vehiculated/ transmitted in another site (usually through invasive exploratory procedures) resulting in an secondary infectious process.
- Exogenous infections – when the infection is produced by pathogens which come from another patient, from the health care personnel or from the hospital environment."

The specialized literature is enriched by the multidisciplinary and transdisciplinary approach of the resolving problem related to the exogenous-endogenous associative tensions, especially when the socio-economic aspects, which ensure the social immersion of the modern man, also come into question.

2. Research Method. Data Collection and Preparation

2.1. Basic concepts and definitions

A definition for the exogenous term shows, in connection with phenomena, processes, etc. that they originate or act from the outside and originate or materialize in peripheral elements. (DEX '09 2009, MDA2, 2010) In fact, a process / phenomenon of health damage develops outside and is due to causes outside the body. (DEX '09, 2009) Definitions of *endogenes* refer to phenomena, processes, etc. "that arise and develop within a foreign tissue that they pierce to get out."

The present study also aimed at assessing the anamnesis of the detailed and systematic interrogation and observation of the symptoms and signs, plus paraclinical investigations of the nature of the deficiency or dysfunction. On this basis, internal biological events that induce malady / disease are retained.

Explicit hypothesis highlights causal relationships, which are almost always linear between symptoms and pathophysiology, between them and the biological determinant.

"Healing" is found when the system regains its pre-pathogenic state.

We appreciate the thesis that the value of the medical model is always assumable.

2.2. Circularity of stochastic dependencies

In cyber thinking, circularity is an essential explanatory principle depicting the result of the reversibility of self-organized systems processes. Circularity shows the behavior of a system marking the reversible movement of the effects of its own behavior on the cause that triggered it, thus being able to directly influence it. Circularity originally had a predominantly negative meaning, by associating it with the ineffective vicious circles, returning to the starting point, spinning on the spot, in the circle of dependencies.

Circular explanatory models have become the most widespread scientific paradigms, and the recurrent circularity thesis has been launched in connection with the causal explanations characteristic of self-organized organisms, being an effective explanatory principle, despite simple linear causality. So, the behavior of the body targets „cybernetic examination of the adaptation of the sensory environment", and the „functional regulator circle" disorder induces psychosomatic tachyarrhythmia, conversion syndromes or signs of anatomical lesions.

That is why we are considering the somatocorporal regulatory circles and, equally, the functional or situational circles.

Through their dynamic, processual, both medical / surgical situations, states, phenomena and processes are in continuous / permanent interaction, through mutual connections, expressing stochastic dependence.

For a sufficiently specialized field of medical reality, such as surgery, strict causal links are encountered between the interaction variables.

As such, the manifestation of a cause (x_i) determines / induces the same invariably effect (y_i).

The conservative repeatability of links shows that they meet the requirements / exigencies of medical causality determinism and on this basis can be modeled by functional dependencies such as: $y_i = f(x_i)$, $i = 1,...,k,...,n$.

That's why some value x_i taken by the variable X is uniquely associated with a value y_i of Y variable.

In the terms of a conditional probability, the deterministic dependence, strictly causal, of the variables X and Y is as follows: $P(Y = y_i \mid X = x_i) = 1$

As a result of the high complexity of the links / variables and the presence of factors with ignorant or immeasurable influence, so that these are disruptive elements, the relationships between medical, surgical situations, states, phenomena and processes acquire the form of stochastic dependencies. So, they fall under a more general type of statistical determinism, assumed only from the perspective of the large numbers law.

2.3. Linearity - causative determinant of disease. Endogenous-exogenous associative tensions - assumptions in the set of threats to human health: disciplinary surgical consequences

About four decades ago, Dossey L., (1982) launched a thesis, which is also the current one, that different diseases have causal determinants in the inappropriate perception of time. In other words, assuming a linear understanding / perception of time, dragging on unidirectional temporal vectors represents endogenous psychological sources of disease among people.

We express the view that as in society it is on the way of a generalized establishment of the circular economy, it would also be possible to model the symbolic form of circular time / circularity of time in human sciences, for example in medicine and, in particular, disciplinary surgery.

In this way, a certain cyclicality detracts from the implacability of the deteriorating advance of human health towards a predictable end.

In the past-present-future linear flow, the observer (the health specialist) discovers successive sequences of events from the multidimensional general matrix of the human body. Antinomic vision, in context, highlights "resumption / reconstruction over time", but without repeating the respective sequence of events.

In fact, it is immersion in a "timeless" area of medical examination - evaluation.

Larry Dossey (1982) [1] even formalized an equation of pain sensation described by Solomon Marcus (1988) [4] as follows:

$$D = kS / T \tag{1}$$

Where: D = pain, S = pain generator (injury stimulus), k = constant proportionality factor, T = duration (time).

The common mathematical interpretation is that the sensation of pain is even lower as the term $S \rightarrow min$, respectively if $S \rightarrow max$ and concurrently $T \rightarrow min$.

As such, temporal perception of pain plays a decisive role in provoking / supporting disease states, and T time factor has decisive implications for the state / status of the process.

On the other hand, in the classical conception, it is remembered that if a disease state worsens (from preclinical / clinical findings), the time parameter influences the patient's perceptions (anxiety, consciousness, pre-intuition, etc.).

We appreciate that in general the general / generic surgical act must benefit more (complementarily, implicitly, intrisse, articular etc.) of 1) the reordering of the psychosomatic behavior and 2) the reorganization of the drug therapy, respectively the action on the disease using ultra-resolution drugs and to the quasi-controlled induction of the psychosomatic behavior of the patient, not only as adjuvants but as osmotic needs, fully assumed. (Figure 1)

On this basis, the symbolic / mathematical formalization of the domain relationship is formalized, aiming at the normality and mini-maximization (as the case may be) of the said reordinations.

$$\begin{cases} (O_r^i) \cap (O_r^s) \longrightarrow (O_r^o)_{normal} \\ (O_r^i); (O_r^s); (O_r^o) \neq \max \end{cases} \tag{2}$$

Linearity should not be "defeated" but "overcome" with new innovative concepts in medicine / surgery.

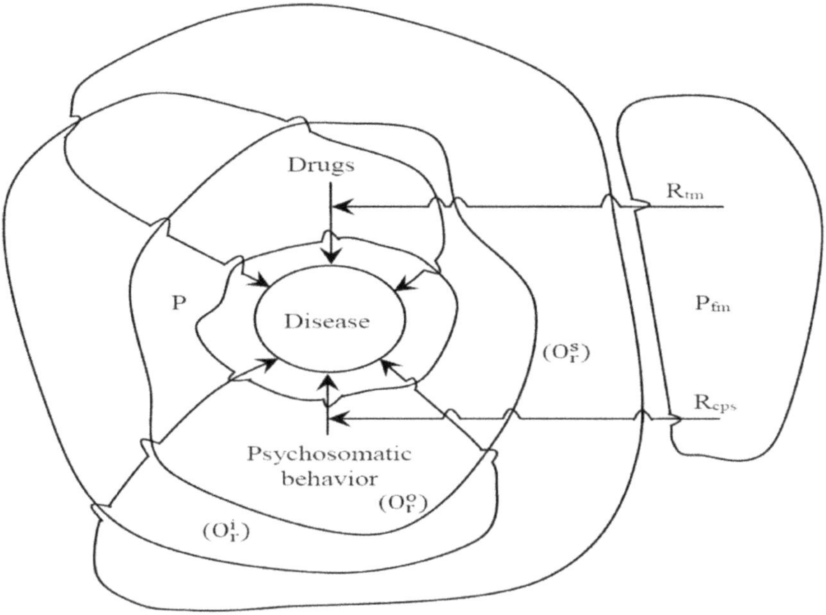

Figure 1: Upper / lower order during / post-manifestation of a dysfunction of the human body

Source: Authors, 2018.

Note: P = disruption; (O_r^o) = physio-psycho-somatic order; (O_r^i) = lower order; (O_r^s) = superior order; R_{cps} = reordering psychosomatic behavior; R_{tm} = re-ordering drug therapy; P_{fm}= medical psychophysics.

The threat to health by exogenous and endogenous factors is articulated with a general causal causality of the human body (molecular biology, neuronal, hormonal activities, etc.) generically found in the so-called predisposition, as a premise of the non-linear behavioral behavior of the human organism.

Eradications (with antibiotics, pathogenic annihilation, preventative immunization, etc.) involve activities characterized by hyper-links. (Figure 2)

From this picture, the logic of the "endogenous-exogenous" associations is pseudo-contac- torous but real tensional. That is why we can speak, in context, about the existence and manifestation of associative tensions. (Figure 3)

In order to accumulate varied and extensive information in surgery, a creative vision is needed on its disciplinary structure and functionality.

It is well-known that modernity in modern surgery is not enough to carry out only explanatory, case-specific procedures, protocols, etc., solved / results or

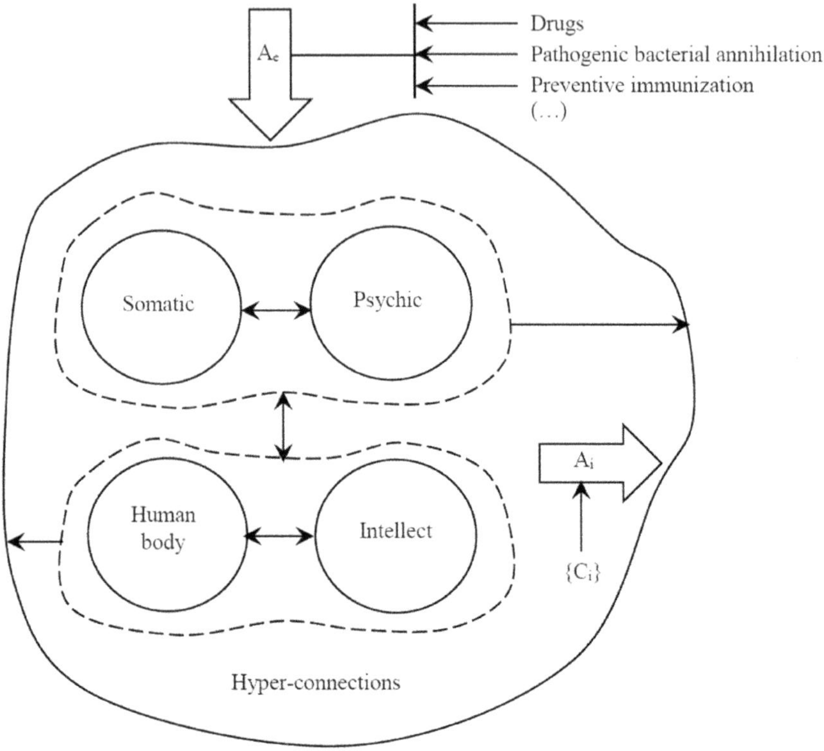

Figure 2: Endogenous-exogenous non-linearisation of causality and threats to human health

Source: Authors, 2018.

Note: A_e *= the threat of health by exogenous factors;* A_i *= the threat of health by endogenous factors;* $\{C_i\}$ *= causalities of the human body (molecular biology, neuronal activities, hormonal activities, etc.).*

statistics, but rather a strong emphasis on organizational structures and exploitation in the field.

Innovation in surgery, for example, occurs through gradual detachment of "routine", medical procedures, standardized procedures.

Thoughts and actions, fortunately, are permanently and objectively individualized by the surgeon, in that his interventionist actions are on man as "ego", each body of a person being unique in its own way.

In fact, at any level of medical science culture can be triggered, stimulated initiatives of innovative disciplinary discovery, for example, of new "surgical search". (Figure 4)

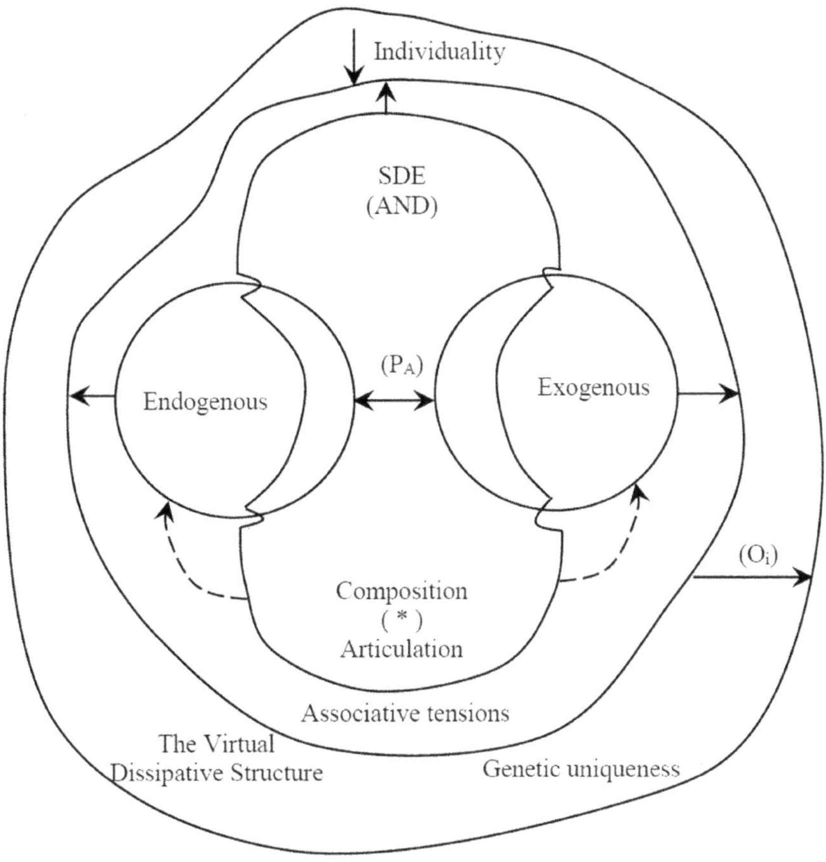

Figure 3: The thesis of the existence of "exogenous – endogenous" associative tensions in the multitude of threats to human health

Source: Authors, 2018.

Note: P_A = the association principle; SDE / (ADN) = the double helical structure of the deoxyribonucleic acids inserted (in / through) the association principle; (O_i) = medical / intuitive habits.

Information technologies, which include the disciplinary, inter- and transdisciplinary environment of knowledge and the material-practical societal, already play a role in releasing the "endogenization" of surgery between apparently its conventional limits. In fact, we are dealing with the "limitation" of surgery, marking the phenomenon of "challenge" in medical science.

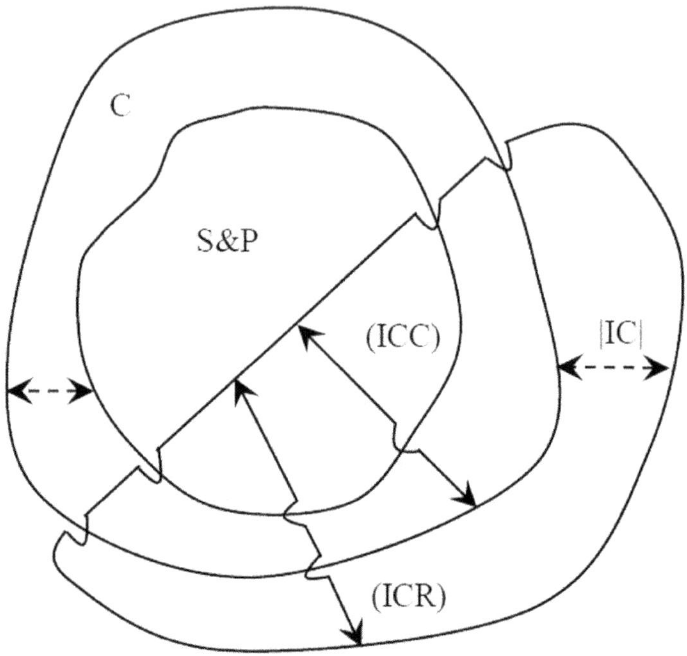

Figure 4: Movement of surgery from standard protocols and standards (induction of innovation in surgery)

Source: Authors, 2018.

Note: C = surgery (disciplinary system); S&P = standards and protocols; (ICC) = conventional surgery; ICI = innovative surgery, in absolute value; (ICR) = innovative surgery, in relative value.

Surgery is no longer just incision / cutting, extirpation / detachment but, on the contrary, it is minimally invasive, additional (add-on) organo-biological sub-systems that replace or develop functions / functionalities in the human body. Surgery records advancement and unprecedented implications in "health" (its sustainable assurance).

Our finding is that to date (2018), information technology is still not "interfering" in surgery but, on the contrary, there is a fierce struggle by the medical world to attract them. So, information technologies "are not yet in surgery", but the undeniable effort is that they are attracted to this field.

Medical / surgical thinking (in the field of surgery) has not changed and will not soon be changed into / in any relationship of obedience to informational thinking, based on the dominance of technologies. Informational scientific / technological advances do not in any way determine the destruction of the surgery, but rather assist in the reinforcement of it. Without proper progress and dense application of intrisse / implicit and osmotic information technology in medicine, knowledge and surgical practice remain behind, and the gap (any undetermined intervals) is almost impossible to overcome, at least for alignment.

We note that the style of developing surgery under the influence of information technology mechanisms, medical engineering, and, more recently, under the aegis of the medical economy, is not an ostentatious, "free rupture", but an expansive pattern in an "accelerated calm" new intelligence in the field.

Major hazards may arise in specialized human resources (the lack of "computer surgeons") and in the outdated field of education / medical education. Surgery is much "more complex" today than it has been several decades ago.

For the first time in the literature, we are launching the original concept of "circular medicine / circularity of medicine" by extension. In fact, paradigmatically, this concept is the global re-use of medical knowledge used in continuous / quasi-continuous feed-backs for the return of the human body to the starting point considered conventional, good health, accepted, reliable, feasible and sustainable.

Essentially, we are talking about the introduction of sustainability in medicine, which is the quasi-infinitesimal methodological, procedural and operational parameterization of intervention and modeling to ensure the healthy functioning of the human body.

Conclusions

The paper is issued conception that as the company is about-building general circular economy, so it is possible to formalize modellers-symbolic time circular / a circularity of time in human sciences, for example, in medicine and in particularly in surgical disciplinary areas.

For the first time, the original concept of "circular medicine / circularity of medicine" is launched in the literature by extension.

The link between reducing compensation and adaptation capacities to human pathology and falling work capacity and social integration of people is noticeable.

The work capacity of the biological and social unit of man is affected by diseases / diseases which, in disciplinary terms, even reach the medical / disciplinary process of surgery due to the harmful action of the various environmental determinants. As such, there is an excessive demand for adaptive mechanisms where post-aggressive reactions are associative stress variants.

Endogenous - exogenous associative tensions against threats to human health participate in the connection or disconnection, as appropriate, of health insurance mechanisms. From an economic, social and medical point of view, the focus is focused on maintaining the body's reactions in imposed wrinkles of efficiency. As a consequence, endogenous - exogenous associative tensions are sources of transformation of adaptive manifestations to pathological disorders.

Associative tensions should not cause disturbances, as it aggravates the body's self-maintenance capacity, and even at critical moments. As such, it is necessary to avoid the dissolution of the conventional equilibrium of the body as it can reach the appeal of the medical procedural arsenal and, as the case may be, in moments and limit situations even at the surgical disciplinary intervention.

It is concluded that by their dynamic nature, the situations, states, phenomena and medical / surgical processes are in a continuous interaction, through mutual connections, marking stochastic dependence.

The health threat by exogenous and endogenous factors is articulated with a general causal interior of the human body (in molecular biology, neuronal activity, hormone, etc.), the so-called generic recovered predisposition, as a prerequisite for non-linearity behavior of the body human.

References

Dossey L. - Space, Time and Medicine, Shambhala, Boulder, London, UK, 1982.

Gillespie M. Brigid, et al., - Factors that influence the expected length of operation: results of a prospective study, BMJ Quality & Safety, 2011; 21 1–1, Published Online First: 18 Nov 2011.

Lingard L. - Communication failures in the operating room: an observational classification of recurrent types and effects, Qual. Saf. Health Care, 2004; 13:330–334.

Marcus Solomon - Provocarea ştiinţei, Ed. Politică, Bucureşti, 1988 p. 128.

Sadideen Hazim, Kneebone Roger, - Practical skills teaching in contemporary surgical education: how can educational theory be applied to promote effective learning?, The American Journal of Surgery, Volume 204, Issue 3, September 2012, pp. 396–401.

Saragea M. - Tratat de Fiziopatologie, Ed. Academiei R.S.R., Bucureşti, 1985, p. 33–41, Subcap. D., Caracterisiticile esenţiale ale stării de boală.

Stângă L., et al., - The exogenous transmission versus endogenous selection in cardiovascular surgery, Journal of Hygiene and Public Health, vol.62, nr.3/2012.

* * * - DEX '09 2009/ MDA2, 2010.

* * * - Sentinel event statistics: 24 June 2003. Joint Commission on Accreditation of Healthcare Organizations, Available online from, //www.jcaho.org/ (accessed 25 December 2017).

Horia LĂZĂRESCU[1], *Andrei KOZMA*[2]

[1] PhD, Senior Researcher, MD, National Institute for Rehabilitation, Physical Medicine and Balneoclimatology, Bucharest, Email: dr.ka.mailbox@gmail.com

[2] PhD, Senior Researcher, MMD, MDHC, National Institute for Rehabilitation, Physical Medicine and Balneoclimatology, Bucharest; member of Academy of Medical Sciences and of Academy of Romanian Scientists

Natural Halotherapeutic Resources – Cost-Benefits in the Context of Bio-Sanogenesis

Abstract *Halotherapy is a treatment method that is based on artificially recreating the microclimate conditions of salt mines. Simulation of the natural therapeutic factors of the underground environment of salt mines and the development of halotherapheutic chambers with artificial curative environment on the surface is a problem of scientific complexity. Authors describe the use of natural resources of halotherapy by creating an artificial halotherapeutic environment for the benefit of many patients with asthma, chronic bronchitis, allergic rhinitis and chronic obstructive pulmonary disease which were evaluated clinically and have also completed a questionnaire which assessed their own perception of how their disease affects their lives. Some preliminary results indicate an increase of life quality of patients who have undergone Halotherapy. The benefits of using this type of treatment, from a bio-sanogenetic point of view, are obvious from the cost-benefit point of realizing this artificial microclimate.*

Keywords: halotherapy; halochambers; effect of halotherapy, bio-sanogenesis

Introduction

Speleotheraphy is thought to improve respiratory parameters of humans. Mentions of effects of salt mine air on the respiration capacities of miners' date back as early as the Roman times

Halotherapy is a treatment method whose development started in the early 1980s. It originates in ST. HT is based on artificially recreating the microclimate of salt mines.

For climatic imitation of the climate within a salt mine, necessary for the halotherapheutic chambers, small enough, saline aerosols that are able to reach deep within the airways must be created.

The first uses of salines were made for therapeutic purposes. Halotherapy or salinotherapy are therapies that have been practiced since ancient times, from times when man began to exploit and consume salt, he realizing and empirically sensing the effect of saline aerosols on the body. Halotherapy (HT, halos = salt) is a method of treatment whose development began in the 1980s, descending of speleotherapy in salt mines, based on artificially recreating microclimate conditions in salt mines, and has originated in the Regional Hospital of Alergology (Ukraine) of Solotvino (Slatina), where after the first scientific works that showed the therapeutic effect of the saline subterranean environment (Iu M. Simionka, 1973), in a gallery in the Subterranean Speleotherapy Section from Salt mine 8 Solotvin of the Regional Hospital of Allergology (Solotvino - Slatina, Ukraine), a salt grinder was installed that dispersed around it a mist of saline particles and where the patients with asthma used to come – patients in this hospital and in the underground speleotherapy department to inhale dispersed salt particles, in addition to speleotherapy treatment.

The problem of simulation and modeling of natural therapeutical factors of underground environment (from salt mines, caves) for the realization of models of speleotherapeutic / halotherapeutic salons (chambers) at the surface with curative properties, which can be used in hospitals, spas, etc., is of interest internationally and in the country. Ten years ago, under a project entitled "Complex medical-biological study for the innovative use of potential therapeutic environmental factors from salt mines in health and balneoclimatic tourism; solutions for their modeling" from the National R & D Plan, they foresaw the achievement, in the National Institute for Recovery, Physical Medicine and Balneoclimatology of an "experimental / functional model", and subsequently of a "final product" of halotherapy enclosure called "Speleotherapy (halotherapy) Salon with artificial mine environment."

"The Speleotherapy (Halotherapy) Salon / Room with Artificial Salt Mine Environment" was placed in a separate building within a building materials complex of rooms including the entrance hall, the proper "halotherapy salon / room", the medical cabinet, dressing room, waiting room and bathroom.

The salt walls of the "halotherapy salon / room" were built from salt lumps from the Slanic Prahova Mine, of different sizes from a few millimeters to over one cubic meter, placed and fixed to the walls of the room intended for the realization of the halotherapy area. The binding of salt lumps with each other was done by using a mixture of pasta containing 15–45 cubic millimeters crushed salt crystals. Big lumps were incorporated at the base of the walls and additionally fastened by beech spikes, through special openings to the walls of the room. This structure of the salt lump walls allowed to obtain a "mining", atraumatic safety and to achieve an environment close to the parameters of the underground salt mine environment with natural therapeutic factors used for speleotherapeutic purposes (underground treatment in the galleries of saline mines and caves possessing natural therapeutic factors and curative properties).

In the "salon", 10–12 patients can receive halotherapy procedures at the same time, being supervised by medical personnel who have the necessary knowledge, including the operation of special facilities. It should be noted that the concentration of salt (sodium chloride) in the aerosol formed by the halotherapy room comprised 0.7–1.2 mg /cubic meter air (the sodium chloride intake value by inhalation of saline aerosol for one hour being dozens of times less than the amount of salt intake through food.

In order to preserve the curative properties of the "halotherapy salon / room" environment, certain requirements are imposed on the organization of functional circuits, the number of patient series, the intervals between "salon" entrances and the observance of anti-pollution measures at the entrance to the "the haloterapeutic center" (keeping personal belongings in the closets, use of booties, gown and disposable beret).

The functional circuit is made up of several rooms including waiting - relaxation room, medical consultation cabinet and supervision of halotherapy treatment, changing rooms for keeping the personal belongings of the patients, sanitary group, technical spaces and the "proper speleotherapeutic salon". For children aged 2 to 6 years, a separate halotherapy room is recommended, for the future.

The medical circuit of the patients includes: entrance to the halotherapy center / complex, waiting in the waiting room, registration and clinical evaluation by the specialized medical staff, decision on procedures and halotherapy treatment, realization of halotherapy procedures in the halotherapy salon / room (space) in the presence of the medical staff of the halotherapy room / space / "halotherapy center". For the halotherapy procedure, 10–12 patients can enter the halotherapy salon / room at the same time.

The minimum and mandatory equipment for the medical cabinet includes: a stethoscope blood pressure meter; negatoscope, thermometer, reflex hammer, examination lamp, screen, etc.

As a result of the analysis of the literature data and of the medical-biological experimental studies on the batches of laboratory animals with induced pathology, as well as those obtained with patients with bronchial asthma and other infectious - inflammatory and allergic diseases, exposed to procedures and halotherapy treatment, "medical indications for the selection of patients with chronic respiratory pathology in view of the halotherapy treatment", the indications and contraindications for the halotherapy procedures and treatment in the Halotherapy Salon with artificial saline mine environment were analyzed and proposed.

Both women and men between the ages of 3–70 can benefit from the treatment and procedures of halotherapy with the reference that children up to 10 years must be accompanied by their parents.

Main guidelines for halotherapy procedures and treatment:

- Non-allergic / intrinsic / nonatopic asthma, allergic / extrinsic / atopic asthma, asthma bronchitis.
- Chronic bronchitis, asymptomatic or symptomatic period without negative evolution, without medication or with symptomatic medication (patient's medication).
- Chronic obstructive bronchopneumopathy (COPD), asymptomatic or symptomatic period without negative evolution (without aggravation / aggravation, without wheezing, wheez breath, persistent cough with sputum production and

short breath) without medication or with symptomatic medication (patient's medication).
- Allergic and chronic infectious-inflammatory rhinitis and sinusitis, intermittent or slightly persistent, asymptomatic or symptomatic period without negative evolution, without medication or with symptomatic medication (patient's medication).
- Pharyngitis and chronic tonsillitis.
- Atopic dermatitis.

Conditions and requirements for halotherapy procedures and treatment include: specialist physician control at the surface, the presence of the nurse in the Halotherapy Sector, the presence of emergency medication in the Halotherapy Sector or near.

Contraindications for halotherapy procedures and treatment are still quite numerous; we mention only a few of them: the complications of the asthma crisis, asthma with continuous dyspnea and the state of asthma illness with violent seizures, asthma with negative evolution, acute bronchitis, heart failure, tuberculosis, undercompensated and decompensated cardiopathy, HTA, acute renal disease, acute hyperacid gastritis, acute hepatitis or cholecystitis, diabetes, severe form and more. These also include: claustrophobia, depression, neurosis and post-operative period up to 2 months.

Social impact of halotherapy treatment

A positive social impact is created through the possibility of using the method of halotherapy, a non-medical, complementary method, for balneoclimatic medical purposes for patients with chronic inflammatory diseases, respiratory allergies (and possibly other pathologies - as a result of multidisciplinary scientific studies), thus contributing to the improvement of the health status of the population.

Chronic or allergic respiratory and cutaneous diseases or other pathologies, medical recovery (rehabilitation) and prevention of illness is done by the specialized staff of the state or private medical institutions in spaces approved for halotherapy. The selection and referral of patients for halotherapy procedures is done by the family doctor, specialist / primary pneumologist, allergologist, doctor for internal diseases or pediatrician.

Based on the experimental results obtained in the previous studies (2001–2007) and the Financing Project / Contract no. 42120/2008–2012, Contracting authority UEDISCDI, Project entitled "Complex medical-biological study for the innovative use of potential therapeutic factors of the saline and cave enviroment in health and balneoclimatic tourism; solutions for their modeling", "Medical Indications for the Selection of Patients with Certain Chronic Respiratory Pathologies for the Experimental Halotherapy Treatment in the Salon of Halotherapy with Artificial Salt Mine Environment" were elaborated.

It is important to comply with the patient's medical documentation and patient requirements: Patients will be selected for halotherapy treatment based on the referral of the family doctor / specialist doctor or the patient's wish. A medical file or a diagnosis copy of the medical record with the latest control of disease progression is required. Also, some data, such as the results of spirometry or peak expiratory flow (PEF), chest radiography, blood and sputum medical tests, atopic skin tests, allergy investigation, otolaryngology consultation, cardiology consultation, electrocardiogram and any data that helps assessing the patient's health status before applying the halotherapy treatment, are welcome.

The doctor / nurse will select the patients for halotherapy procedures based on the respective indications and contraindications, the methodology of the procedures and the halotherapy treatment, these being elaborated on the basis of the specific studies of the environment in the respective space / premises built for speleotherapeutic purposes and its therapeutical effect. In order to select patients for the halotherapy procedures and treatment, it is necessary to have a letter from the family doctor or the medical documentation of the patient (medical file or copy with the diagnosis from the medical record and the control of disease progression; some data are welcome as well, such as the results of spirometry or peak expiratory flow (PEF), thoracic radiography, blood and sputum medical tests, atopic skin tests, allergy investigation, otolaryngology consultation, cardiology consultation or electrocardiogram, and any data that helps to evaluate patient's health status before applying the halotherapy treatment), afterwards, after making the decision on halotherapy treatment.

Halotherapy procedures, regime and treatment have been established and applied on the basis of the experimental studies from previous stages of various projects during the period 2008–2012; beneficial effects were quantified by patients' answers to a complex health questionnaire (Table 1.)

A majority of the patients has reported the ability of better sleeping during the night, a decrease in the daily and nocturnally coughing episodes and also a decrease of the necessity of using their prescribed medication.

Halotherapy procedures for patients with asthma and other respiratory chronic infectious-inflammatory and allergy pathologies are based on previous studies (the first two days - up to 30 minutes, thereafter 40–50 minutes daily with interruption in the days of rest of the medical staff, the total number of days with halotherapy procedures being 15 days). The procedures are applied depending on the clinical status of the patient and on the results of preliminary clinical investigations prior to the treatment. During the adaptation of the body to the artificial saline mine at the beginning of the treatment and at the end of the tratment, 1–3 procedures of 15–30 minutes are recommended.

Clinical adaptation of patients with asthma, chronic bronchitis and chronic obstructive bronchopomeumopathy to underground conditions (i.e. 5 to 10 days of procedures), depending on the pathology and its severity. After these procedures, there is a rarity and slowing of irritable dry cough, coughing with viscous expectoration, adaptation to physical effort and normalization of sleep at night.

Table 1: Results of the questionnaires

Question	Increase	No change	Decrease
Use of medication	-	60 %	40 %
Ability to breathe through the nose	20 %	80 %	-
Ability to breathe through the mouth	60 %	40 %	-
Tiredness during the day	-	30 %	70 %
Interruption of daily work due to symptoms of the disease	-*	80 %	20 %
Interruption of night sleep due to symptoms of the disease	-*	70 %	30 %
General happiness	70 %	30 %	-
General stress caused by the symptoms of the disease	20 %	50 %	30 %
Effect on social relationships **	-	100 %	-
Effects on relations with the family**	-	100 %	-
Ability to do sports	20 %	80 %	-

Note: *an increase in the symptoms has been noticed in the first days due to accommodation to the HT chambers; **this questions were not understood by patients.

Another important aspect, in order to preserve the curative properties, is the observance of the rules of movement and behavior in the halotherapy area. Patients to whom the halotherapy procedure and treatment will be applied should be „trained" on the operation of the halotherapy room / premises, patient requirements, medical indications and contraindications, duration of procedure and halotherapy treatment and to obtain other information for the proper functioning of the „center of halotherapy". In order to preserve the curative properties of the halotherapeutic environment, it is necessary to use a special regime of entry and circulation in the halotherapy area (premises), so the entrance will be made in compliance with certain sanitary measures, being necessary to elaborate and observe the „Rules of movement and behavior in the halotherapy treatment area (premises)".

As part of these rules we mention: For the speleotherapy procedure of children up to 10 years of age the assistance of a parent or other attendant is necessary; For the entry into the space / premises for halotherapy procedures, the patient and the child attendant become aware of the „Rules of movement and behavior in the halotherapy treatment area (premises)"; Personal belongings will be left by the patient in cabinets specially arranged in the wardrobe premises - before entering the curative area; It is forbidden to enter the premises for halotherapy wearing „street" shoes and clothes, as well as with packages, purses or bags, books, magazines or other personal belongings that could negatively influence the quality of the halotherapeutic environment; The entrance to the halotherapy area (premises) will be made in shoe covers - polyethylene single use booties (or polyethylene slippers); It is forbidden to smoke, to introduce food and spirits and to use them in the halotherapy premises, as well as to use perfumes, cosmetics or other aromatics with allergic smell; It is forbidden to use mobile phones, tablets and laptops during the halotherapy procedure.

It is beneficial in order to obtain a positive response from patients that the design of the halotherapy room and the parallel use of complementary methods of treatment (e.g. „melotherapy") that do not harm the speleotherapeutic effect and fit into the recommended therapy complex for patients with the pathology mentioned in the medical indications for halotherapy, present a positive step in their relaxation.

The receiving capacity of the „halotherapy room" is optimal for 12 patients (maximum 14–15 patients) at the size and volume of the current space (see Annex 2 and 3), for each series. They enter by series (at intervals of about 120 minutes) with the duration of the treatment set by the physician, in accordance with the halotherapy methodology and pathology of each patient.

The halotherapy treatment series can be programmed daily, their number being calculated according to the capacities of the halotherapy room and the duration of the halotherapy procedures. Inside the salon for halotherapy you can enter wearing casual clothing and clean footwear using covers (booties) and single use gown.

Experience has shown that at least one day of rest between treatment belts is required to perform maintenance work on the halotherapy area.

It can be concluded, from our studies and our experience in the field, at theoretical level, that the expectations that we may have from halotherapy from a sanogenetic point of view of would be:

- Increasing the efficiency of expectoration by increasing sputum volume and secretions in the airways - which leads to improvement of the respiratory act and to the patient's feeling of release, pulmonary relief - by increasing cough productivity.
- Obtaining the bacteriostatic effect over time - which was found by reducing episodes of recurrent respiratory infections or by completely eliminating seasonal episodes. It is an invaluable benefit for COPD patients to whom an episode of acute respiratory infection may be fatal.
- Improving the quality of sleep by diminishing the edema of the superior aerodigestive duct (palatine vein, tongue base, tonsil lining pillars) often found in chronic snorting. Also, at the level of the middle and upper meatus sinus ostia, inflammatory edema decreases, leading to their reperfusion and effective drainage of the sinuses in the nasal passages.
- Increasing the quality of life by alleviating the negative effects of many forms of respiratory diseases.

Last but not least, we must mention the use of natural resources brought on site for the design of such a healing room, creating a favorable balance between the cost of installing and operating a halotherapy center with the implicit benefits obtained in the context of applied bio-sanogenesis.

References

1. Buleza, B. The effect of salt mines artificial microclimate on the individual level of humoral immunity in patients with bronchial asthma. The XIVth International Symposium of Speleotherapy. Turda. Cluj-Napoca. Casa Cărţii de Stiinţă (2012).
2. Calin M R, Calin MA, Simionca G. Indoor radon levels and natural radioactivity inTurda salt mine, Romania. Journal of Radioanalytical and Nuclear Chemistry. 2012; 1:193–201.
3. Crişan, R., Mihăescu, T. Haloterapia – o soluţie antică şi modernă în terapia afecţiunilor respiratorii. Medica Academica. (2011).
4. Enache L., Bunescu I. Microclimate and naturalionization of air insome underground enclosures (case studies: salt mines Turda, Cacica, Ocna Dej and Fundata Cave - Rasnov.Cluj-Napoca: Casa Cartii de Stiinta, 2012; 1–2: 44–46.
5. Horia Lăzărescu, Iuri Simionca, Andrei Kozma, Lucian Mirescu - Anthropological Considerations to Ensure Quality of Life of Patients Through Halotherapy Treatment; Mental Health, 2016, Ed. Universitară; ISBN: 978-606-28-0513-5; p.70–74.
6. Lazarescu H., Simionca I., Hoteteu M., et al., Surveys on therapeutic effect of "halotherapy chamber with artificial salt-mine environment" on patients with certain chronic, allergenic respiratory patologies and infectious inflammatory pathologies. Journal of Medicine and Life.2014; 7:83–87.
7. Lazarescu H., Simionca Iu. Organizational Management of the Experimental and Medical use of a "Halotherapy Chamber with Artificial Salt-mine Environment". Acta Balneologica. Journal of the Polish Balneology and Physical Medicine Association. Indexed in Emerging Sources Citation Index Thomson Reuters, Index Copernicus, MNiSW, Polskiej Bibliografii Lekarskiej, Bibliografii Geografii Polskiej, Tom LIX, 2017; Number 4 (150); p, 279–285.
8. Lazarescu H., Simionca Iu. Recommendations for use of Halotherapy Chamber with Artificial Salt-mine Environment in Medical Purposes. Acta Balneologica. Journal of the Polish Balneology and Physical Medicine Association. Indexed in Emerging Sources Citation Index Thomson Reuters, Index Copernicus, MNiSW, Polskiej Bibliografii Lekarskiej, Bibliografii Geografii Polskiej, Tom LIX, 2017; Number 4 (150); p 286–289.
9. Lazarescu H, Brailescu C, Bunescu I et al. Physical Medicine and Balneoclimatology. 2011:169.

10. Simionca Iu., Hoteteu M., Lazarescu H. Si al. Haloterapia - descendenta a speleoterapiei in minele saline; realitati si perspective de haloterapie stiintifica in Romania. Lucrare prezentata la Conferinţa Naţionala de Speleoterapie cu participare internaţionala, 06–08 Octombrie 2011, Turda, Cluj-Napoca, publicat in volum de rezumate. Editura Casa Cartii de Stiinta, 2012: 56–57.
11. Simionca Iu. The structure of the therapeutic (speleotherapeutical) factor in the salt mines – Primordial element in speleotherapy mecanism and effect. Hellenic Speleological Society. 2005; 2:426.
12. Simionca Iu, Hoteteu M, Grudnicki N et al. Environment study in order use potential therapeutic factors existing in the cavity of one salt mine for the achievement of some perspectives of speleotherapy development in Romania. Hellenic Speleological Society.2 421–425.
13. Simionca Iu., Studii de C-D în vederea elaborării unor soluţii noi de corecţie a modificărilor statusului imun la pacienţii cu astm bronşic prin utilizarea speleoterapiei în mediul subteran din unele saline cu factori curativi, Planul Național de CDI-1, Program Viasan, Proiect 441/2004. Raport Project 441/2004-2006. Rezultate stiintifice si realizari, 2006
14. Simionca Iu. Complex medical-biological study for the innovative use of potential therapeutic environmental factors from salt mines and caves in health and balneoclimatic tourism; modeling solutions theirs (Salt mines - Salina Ocna-Dej, Salina Cacica; Cave Fundata); Project 2250, Financing contract nr. 42120/2008 in National Plan of Research - Development - Innovation 2, Program 4. Partenerships in priority areas, 4. Health, Romania, (CNMP, UEFISCDI) Report, 2012 (in RO).
15. Simionca Iu. Complex study of underground environment in the Turda Salt Mine, medical-biological laboratory, in the experiment, with the purpose of evaluating the potential speleotherapeutic factors and the possibility of using the salt mine underground environment respectively in health and balneoclimatic tourism. Research Services Contract, No.310 / 2010, Beneficiary S.C. Turda Salina Durgău S.A, Performer NIRPhMB, Report, 2011 (in RO).
16. Simionca I, Grudnicki N, Buturuga A et al. Speleotherapy of patients with non-severe bronchial asthma through the therapeutic factors in Slanic Prahova Salt Mine. Correction of immune status. George Tofan Publishing House. 2009:42.
17. Stoian, Gh., Sturzoiu, Cristina, Nica, Cristina, Petrescu, Maria, Anton, M., Simionca, Iu.(Gh.), Dinischiotu, A.. Speleoterapie si Haloterapie experimentală: Evaluare biochimică în mediu salin şi artificial. Universitatea din Bucureşti, Facultatea de Biologie. National Conference of Speleotherapy Turda Salt Mine. Cluj-Napoca. Casa Cărţii de Stiinţă (2011).

Adriana GRIGORESCU[1], *Christopher DE FREITAS BRADLEY*[2]

[1] National University of Political Studies and Public Administration, Bucharest, Romania; Correspondent Member Academy of Romanian Scientists; e-mail: adriana.grigorescu@snspa.ro

[2] 'Valahia' University of Targoviste, Doctoral School, e-mail: chrisbradleymd@yahoo.com

Comparative Analysis of Health Care Systems in Romania and France

Abstract *One of the eight plus one indexes for quality of life is the health system, due to the fact that the population assistance to be in a proper physical and mental condition assure the development of the society. The health system in Romania is frequently criticized and comparative analysis with other systems from European Union or developed countries offers the opportunity to highlight the pluses and the gaps. The paper is presenting SWOT analysis of Romanian and French systems, starting from the consideration that, in nowadays a consistent number of Romanian doctors are working in French hospitals and they are highly appreciated. The conclusions are drawing few lines of concern and proposals of improving the activity in Romanian health system.*

Keywords: quality of life, health care system, analysis, quality and performance

Introduction

After World War II, Romania had a state funded Semashko health care system, its main features were: the funds needed to carry out all the activities in the system were entirely secured by the state, the state was the absolute owner of all material resources and provided health services to all the population. This system was based on the principles of centralized planning, rigid administration and state monopoly. Thus, the health care system created by the Ministry of Health was an integrated, centralized, controlled individual print axes and with limited freedom in option but accessible to all. The reform of the health system in Romania started in 1990. The problems of the health system were diagnosed in the project "A Healthy Romania" project financed and developed by the World Bank ($ 150 million) in 1992–1993 This study made a number of recommendations: (1) Creating a national public fund for independent, decentralized health insurance to manage itself; (2) Creating private alternative health insurance funds; (3) Decentralization of health services; (4) Moving focus on primary health services; (4) Hospital autonomy in the use of resources; (5) Creating and implementing an accreditation system for health service providers, both for institutions and for staff (Dragoi, 2010).

As a result of these recommendations, since 1994 the transition to a more decentralized, pluralistic health insurance system has been established, with contractual relations between the state funds and the health service providers. Currently, in Romania, the right to health is guaranteed by the Constitution. On January 1, 1999, Law 145/1997 on Social Health Insurance entered into force (Monitorul Oficial al României, 2009). The health system's considerations are: solidarity, freedom of choice by the insured of the service provider, competition between health service providers, quality assurance of medical services, patient compliance and guaranteeing the medical endurance (Gillias, 2003). The implementation of the health system reforms has seen different rhythms: advancement, stagnation, regression, return, resumption. The political changes, following the elections, have also been re-enacted in the implementation of the health system reform. Inconsistencies in health system reform have led to the current crisis of the system, with arguably the most critically acclaimed deficient health system being the Romanian healthcare system.

1. General presentation

The state of health of the population is determined by access to health on the one hand and to the access to health services on the other. Access to health depends to a large extent on external factors to the health system: genetic factors, factors environment, economic development factors and socio-cultural factors. The access to health care is almost entirely influenced by the organization of the health system. Accessibility to health care services is determined by the convergence of the offer and the demand for such services, or, in other words, the availability real-life facilities compared to demand based on real health needs (Apetrei, 2010). Disparities in access to discrimination arise for at least four reasons: ethnic or racial; Economic costs, including the costs incurred by the population (co-payments, treatment and hospitalization costs) as well as the other (transport costs, waiting times); Inadequate geographic location of facilities; The unequal quality of services of the same type.

In Romania, all four types of inequities in access to care services are evident, leading to inequities in the health status of different population groups, communities in different geographical areas and economically disadvantaged groups. These disparities are manifested by basic indicators of modest health (life expectancy, child mortality, general mortality on causes of avoidable death, mortality, years of health), but also through the low level of information on risk and health protection factors or the health care system and the basic health care package in Romania. The Romanian health system is social insurance type and aims to ensure the fair and non-discriminatory access to a package. The medical services are currently granted on the basis of the contribution to the insurance fund (6.5 % of the employee's gross salary and 7 % of the gross salary of the employee) (Dragoi, 2010). The insured benefit, on the basis of these contributions, free of charge of a package of services that are defined as legal and regulated. Primary care is currently offered by family medicine, seeking to emphasize the role of primary services as a problem-deductible filter.

Access to ambulatory and hospital care and access to free medical care or with co-payment, is done through the family doctor. Physicians no longer have the status of state employees, but become healthcare providers who conclude a contract with the Health Insurance House, the new system coordinator. Medium-sized medical staff are employed by these service providers (doctors and hospitals). The Ministry of Health maintains only the role of defining and coordinating national public health programs. A large part of Romania's population currently has a health education deficit, including a lack of awareness of the role of prevention and the habit of medical consultation. In spite of the downward trend since 1990, the mortality rate in Romania is three times higher than the average for the European Union countries and by two bigger ones than in the Eastern European countries. The maternal mortality rate, although about five times the number of deaths in 2010 compared to 2001, remains high compared to other European countries (Rotila, 2011).

At present, access to public health services in Romania is based on the principle of contributions, through the payment of a monthly fee. Children, people with disabilities and war veterans with low pay, people dependent on another insured person and without their own income have access to health services. The conditioning of access to services through the introduction of health insurance has led to the emergence of segments of the population who can not only benefit from emergency services, but also other healthcare services.

The lack information provided to the population on the need of medical insurance and on the conditions of access to medical services are usually generated by some potential applicants outside the public insurance system. In such a situations we can find groups from geographically isolated areas, with low socio-economic status, predominantly uneducated, such as Roma groups (gypsies), where the low level of education favors non-insurance behavior. According to health barometer data, more than half of the Roma people are unaware of their health insurance rights and obligations, and over 80 % of the insured people do not know at all or have only vague information about health services. The transition to the new model of healthcare provision was made without an adequate information campaign for the population (Radu, 2017).

2. SWOT analysis of the health system in Romania

It is important to understand that health services are a subsystem of the health care system and refer to the preponderant medical units and services produced by these units. Essentially, the health care system was and is a system organized and financed by the state, being made up of a network of sanitary units owned by the state, administered in a centralized structure, with the Ministry of Health at the top. Funding is made through state budget taxes and duties performed by doctors, who are also employees of the state.

Strengths:

(1) The critical examination of the financing, organization and functioning of the services, who besides its shortcomings, also highlights a number of advantages. Such a perspective is extremely important for what it is hoped to be implemented in the future. The network has recently emerged in the articles that have been developed especially in the academic field, where western experts and consultants have begun to propose various solutions on how to improve the healthcare system.
(2) The system was developed on equity principles, providing access to comprehensive services for the quasi-totally of the population. Access to services has not been influenced by the patient's ability to pay. The benefit of the absence of payment at the time of use has eroded as the medical profession's main source of income has become (in particular, perceived by the general population) totally inadequate, going as far as to conclude that the amounts claimed or received in addition from the patients by the health personnel are considered to be socially acceptable or even justified (Marinescu, 2017).
(3) Financing and organizing the system allows for effective cost control. The health expenditure outturn is relatively low. "The price" of a similar imbalance can also be attributed to the lack or limitation of access to some services, especially those requiring high expenses for equipment or materials (e.g. renal dialysis, cardiovascular surgery, transplants, articular prostheses, computed tomography, magnetic resonance imaging, etc.). In doing so, the healthcare system can be operated with reduced administrative structures and costs.
(4) The service infrastructure has been extensively developed, with an integrated network (urban and rural), clinics and hospitals. Unlike other former socialist countries, the primary care network (general medicine dispensaries) has been developed from an organizational point of view but neglected as a donation. Here are were the inequalities regarding the insurance of the medical personnel, related to the economy falls in, as well as economic disparities between counties, the urban/rural environment, etc. With the inclusion of dispensaries in the organizational structure of hospitals, competition for resources has generally caused casualties to specialized services, resulting in the detriment of general medicine. This has had a detrimental effect on the efficiency of the system, because most of the cases could have been solved at the primary level in the hospitals, rather than consuming expensive resources.
(5) There can be enough qualified medical staff with high quality medical education. In this area, given the density of doctors relative to GDP, Romania has a convenient position. However, the possibility of political interference has led to staff deficiencies, especially in the 1980s (cessation of specialist doctors training and access to cities, dismantling of post-secondary training for mid-sized staff). By the mid-1970s, there were great improvements in devastated states, illustrated by increasing the average life span, eradication or reduction of many communicable diseases, reduction of infant mortality and initiation of

national programs in the fields of cardiovascular disease, cancer, tuberculosis, mental health and dental health (Rotila, 2011). The quality of medical services also contributed greatly to these health interventions.

Weaknesses:

(1) Excessive medical care, influenced by the way in which services are organized, the vast majority of managerial positions being occupied by administrators with no managerial training has greatly reduced the chances of cross-sectoral approaches.
(2) Rigid planning, combined with the centralized system and command, has suffocated the responsibility in managing health services and in particular adapting their changing positions on healthcare. The centralized model, which imposes rigidity, often arbitrary, rules on the administration and prevented the adaptation of services to the local needs of the population, which can differ from one area to another. These norms have led to an inefficient mix of wasting in some regions and gaps in others.
(3) Regulatory planning can be considered now to be ineffective and inefficient. Although attempts have been made to reduce administrative imbalances by uniformly distributing staff and sanitary facilities, the result has been a failure. It can be observed today that the system has not managed to reduce territorial inequality, neither in the state healthcare system, nor in the provision of the population with physicians nor in the supplementing hospital beds. Funding according to historical criteria, not taking into account the different health needs of the population, has accentuated the disparities between the counties.
(4) Sub-financing of services has led to considerable delays in the introduction of new technologies needed for the diagnosis or treatment of current pathology, generating further serious deficiencies in the provision of medicinal products and sanitary materials for current use. Even after the concerns of health services in the field of quality assurance and assessment of medical care, a fundamental element of system performance.
(5) The lack of a coherent health policy after 1990 has also been favored by the inherited deficiency in the capacity to systematically analyze and develop strategies in the context of insufficient research and training in the management of public health and health services. As mentioned above, National health organizations are complex, ever-developing, organizations that produce health services. The administrative bodies within national health systems have different functions, interests, and expectations and they have a certain type of control. Health care systems are unstable because they are influenced by many factors, as well as the behavior of influencers with various interests and demands.
(6) Useful, beneficial interventions, made in the organization and structure of the national health system, may consider the following objectives: (a) Implementing new programs to improve the health status of the population and/or to adjust the volume and type of health services in line with

demographic and epidemiological developments; (b) The introduction of improved medical technologies; (c) Adapting health service production to changes in demand structure and supply of health resources; (d) Improving social justice and facilitating citizens' access to health care; (e) Eliminating the factors that influence the good functioning of the decommissioned services; (f) Transforming the health system to implement national health policy goals.

(7) Contemporary health systems are continually developing their objectives, but are not well-structured and properly managed to efficiently implement overwhelming policies. Prospective developments such as increasing health needs of the population, the advancement of medical technologies, rising health expenditures and increasing political pressure for more social security will force health care policy makers to seek maximum benefits with minimal effort and costs.

Opportunities:

(1) Health is a major social impact area that can provide arguments for policy-making.
(2) Decentralizing and giving real autonomy to health authorities and health care, as objectives in the governance program.
(3) Implementation of private health insurance, which as a consequence has the benefit of the social system from the growing burden and pressure on the insured.
(4) Effort of local authorities to implement a strategic planning project for the municipalities.
(5) Integration into the EU - increasing the competence and quality of medical attention, opportunities for the development of medical "tourism", with beneficial consequences in the field of health and economics for the inhabitants of the county/municipality.
(6) Globalization.
(7) Romania's chance to integrate into international research.
(8) Development in technology.
(9) Massive imports of cutting-edge technology.
(10) Existence of EU funds and structural funds.
(11) Existence of European and international programs.

Threats:

(1) Increasing the information level of patients, together with the progress of diversification of diagnostic and therapeutic technologies, will lead to an increase in their expectations and implicitly to an increase in the demand for complex medical services; The health system must have mechanisms to ensure the targeting of financial resources by virtue of the principle of efficiency.
(2) Decentralization and the granting of real autonomy to authorities with healthcare can also have less beneficial consequences.

(3) The emergence of private health insurance. In this regard, professional staff is a resource that must be protected, especially given the high tendencies of its migration to the private sector. The emergence of a social breakdown between individuals that can afford additional insurance and disadvantaged people who cannot.
(4) Lack of managerial capacities and abilities at the level of the insurance system. For example, hospital managers are still selected on the basis of professional medical excellence that does not always transfer to the managerial-problem area that has been insidious through inefficient management of funds, which can be difficult to quantify.
(5) The free movement of persons and the facilities created after the accession of Romania into the European Union for employment, induce the risk of migration of specialists, especially those who are highly qualified.
(6) The risk that the incidence of communicable and chronic diseases grow steadily without a coherent and concrete intervention program.
(7) EU integration - rising healthcare costs that can lead to a narrowing of the gap in access to health services between ,well-off' populations and the population just above or on the poverty line.
(8) Increased collateral costs induced either by treatment of some but very serious illnesses or due to the policies practiced by some pharmaceutical companies.
(9) Fierce international competition.
(10) The impact of globalization.
(11) Massive top technology imports without internal support.
(12) Aging of the population and migration of the young labor force.

3. Strategic recommendations for improving the healthcare system in Romania

The Romanian health system needs to be reformed from two points of view: to address the complex problems associated with the aging of the population and to focus on prevention activities that emphasize the strengthening of behavioral change among the general population. Romania lacks health programs or services tailored to the specific needs of the elderly population. The inevitable process of aging populations will lead to a great deal of health service consumption and an increase in public health spending (Enache, 2014).

In order for the health system to be able to respond to these new needs, there is a need for concrete assistance measures for the elderly: (1) Responsibility of local public authorities regarding the medical-social needs of the elderly population and the prevention of institutionalization; (2) Developing and expanding at a national level services appropriate to the specific needs of the elderly population (community health care, home care, palliative and terminally ill patients, pain therapy, daycare centers, community psychiatric centers, medical-social units); (3) Increasing the access of elderly people in rural areas to medically-diversified services (including ambulatory care and treatment for chronic diseases); (4) Developing public policies and innovative programs in geriatrics and gerontology that maintain the elderly's physical health, correct vision, hearing, and mobility issues before symptoms are aggravated; (5) Last but not least, these strictly medical services need to be doubled by the politico-social ones that provide adequate health and social services to the elderly, together with the promotion of physical activity and their involvement in social activities that increase the self-esteem, autonomy and independence of the elderly.

A country with many elderly people does not mean a country of inactive and resource consuming people. On the contrary, the pensioners' workforce needs to be reconsidered and their life experience revalued, which is an asset for the community. The second direction that the reform of the health system has to do is to focus the policies on the prevention of illness. Mortality specifies a tendency to increase the number of cardiovascular disease related deaths in the young adult as well as the elderly, as well as a significant increase in the incidence of deaths by neoplasms, especially in young women. In order to change these trends, it is necessary to promote a healthy lifestyle, a balanced nutrition, to combat inactivity and stress, as well as the consumption of tobacco and alcohol. (Legido-Quigley, et al. 2008). Also, strengthening health and social services in rural areas would improve the access of the population to such services.

4. Healthcare System in France

The model of the French health system is distinguished by its hybrid nature, resulting from a complex combination between the private sector and the public sector in terms of supply and finance. The system is based on mandatory health insurance and completed in a large volunteer private insurance. The cover is almost universal. Both the hospital and outpatient departments offer a wide range of almost unlimited health services and patients enjoy total freedom of consultation. The system seems to be performing in terms of population expectations. In terms of life expectancy and mortality, France ranks first in the EU (Johnson, et al. 2017). Public health, however, has weak points, such as the high incidence of AIDS, alcohol and tobacco use. Mortality differs a lot depending on the social class that worries more and more. Increasing health spending and deepening social security deficits, combined with slowing economic growth, persistence of high unemployment, and aging populations are a major concern. The French system is one of the most widespread in the EU.

The state plays the most important role in the French health system. It is responsible for the protection of all citizens. The central government deals with the dementia of the population as a whole and the system of social protection as a whole, controlling the relations among the various financial bodies, exercising its guardianship over the public hospital sector and organizing the professional training in the field of health. Ministry of Labor and Solidarity The State for Health, assisted by bodies such as the Medicines Agency, which forms the basis of national health policy. The High Public Health Committee chaired by the Minister of Health sets out public health objectives. The National Agency for Accreditation and Evaluation in Health (NAAEH) has the mission to assess the medical practices, quality and performance of the public and private health sector. At regional level, the 22 Regional Directorates of Health and Social Affairs (RDHSA) Implements sanitary and social equipment planning and ensures its tracking14 Through "e-health cards" that fix the number of beds on the specialty and the areas and establish rules for the installation of expensive medical equipment. The compulsory health insurance system has a comprehensive coverage (Johnson, et al. 2017).

Funding for the healthcare system is based mainly on contributions from employees and employees, representing in 1994, 12.8 % of gross income (firms) and 6.8 % of salary (employees). Retirees contribute a lower percentage. The French health insurance scheme covers 74 % of all healthcare expenditure. A share of 6.8 % of expenditure is covered by mutuality and 5 % of private insurances. Taxation contributes less than 3 %, while direct patient participation costs more than 13 % (Johnson, et al. 2017). Health insurance plays a major role in setting tariffs for private health care providers. Governance determines the level of funding Public hospitals. Public hospitals are funded by global allocations calculated on the level of expenditures in the previous year. Services are paid on a daily basis. The staff of the public hospitals is the same as the one in the private institutions and is generally reimbursed on the basis of the documents. The private hospitals are financed according to a formula combining the price per day of the hospitalization with payment based on the documents. In the outpatient sector the doctors are rewarded on the basis of the documents According to conventional rates. The reimbursable remedies are included in a list. The prices and the proportion of co-payments are set by a ministerial decree. Free OTC products that are not reimbursable are not regulated by the state.

The percentage of patients' participation in costs is on average 20 %, but ranges from zero (for strictly necessary medical treatments) to 65 % for comfort medications. In comparison to the Romanian Healthcare system, the French Healthcare System has no ceiling for the spending budget on medications (Johnson, et al. 2017).

The measures are directed towards the streamlining and reduction of the structures within the healthcare cards, so they are oriented towards the control of the diffusion of the leading medical technologies. The introduction of the principle of global development in the hospital sector seems to have helped to raise spending, but the attempts to control expenditures in the primary health care sector Welcomed a strong hostility from public opinion and practitioners One of the ongoing projects, aimed at limiting spending in the outpatient sector, is to include national targets accompanied by collective or individual sanctions when ceilings are exceeded. The National Agency for Accreditation and Evaluation in Health (NAAEH) ensures the development of quality assurance and technology assessment programs Medical records in France. The introduction of medical records is intended to avoid excessive prescriptions.

Strengths and Weaknesses of the French Healthcare system: (1) The French healthcare system offers quality service with freedom of choice and in general without waiting lists for treatments; (2) Access to medical services is equal to everyone and unlike other people, people can benefit from the treatments they need regardless of their social or work status; (3) Each has a social health insurance covering about 65–70 % of the cost of medical services and medicines. For this, a portion of the citizens monthly salary is retained (the same as in Romania); (4) Anyone can go to any specialist - even if they are a professor in a field or a private prestigious clinic. As long as you contribute to the state health insurance you will benefit without problems. If not, you pay the expenses. (5) The acute shortage of nurses, and the job is not much sought among young people; (6) There is an increasing number of AIDS patients, consumers of liquor and tobacco; (7) Mortality varies greatly depending on the social class.

Conclusions

The Constitution of Romania proclaims the principle of guaranteeing the right to health protection by establishing art. 34 (Apetrei, 2010). The State's obligation to take measures to ensure hygiene and public health. The current difficult situation of the health care system affects all its fields of activity: hospital care, ambulatory medications, preclinical investigations, prophylaxis, home care and recovery.

The Romanian legislation in the sanitary field has periodically changed, both annually with the approval of framework contracts and punctual to improve the functioning of the health care system, and the impact of these interventions has not always been beneficial to health care and drug users, among whom older people are a major category due to the present pathology At the third age. The elderly population represents a significant category of beneficiaries of the public health system targeting a wide range of services deriving from the very characteristics of the stage they are going through. That is why specialized intervention is needed both in curative and palliative care for various diseases, as well as an orientation towards geriatric programs and research to prevent the effects of an aging population.

Given that life expectancy has increased in the European Union and the proportion of the aging population - the main consumer of medical services - in the total population, modern medicines and medical techniques are becoming more and more costly, health resources are becoming an effort even for developed countries, the health system's efficiency being a topic of debate at a European level.

Against the background of economic, social and health policy issues, some mortality and morbidity indicators place Romania in last place among other EU member states. The main causes of health problems lie in the problems of the health care system, namely: limited resources invested in health care, including the pharmaceutical system; inequality in service offerings (e.g. disparities between rural and urban areas); inefficient organization and financing in the health field. The reality facing older people is in contradiction with the principles assumed in the context of accession to the European Union and promoted by the the Law on Health System Reform (Monitorul oficial al României, 2009). Medical care is also deficient for the elderly both in relation to family doctors and sanitary units (clinics, harvesting centers, hospitals, etc.).

Adherence to the European Union requires recognition of values which guides the way for those who develop public health strategies and practitioners providing direct services to the population in curative, preventive or palliative programs. These are: (1) Respect for the right to the protection of the health of the population; (2) Guaranteeing the quality and safety of the medical act; (3) Increasing the role of preventive services; (4) Ensuring accessibility to services; (5) Observance of the right to free choice and equal opportunities; (6) Assessing professional skills and encouraging their development; (7) Decisional transparency; (8) Effective achievement of equal access of citizens to basic health care; (9) Increasing the quality of life by improving the quality and safety of medical services.

Few suggestions that can improve the Romanian health care system are: (a) Rethinking the system of clearing medicines to avoid creating bottlenecks in pharmacies when free and reimbursed prescriptions are issued; (b) Implementing the patient's electronic file that will make it more effective for prescribing treatment or referrals; (c) Encouraging the development of Pharmacies' Networks or Pharmaceutical Points in rural areas, especially in isolated localities; (d) Increasing the accurate information of the elderly population on how to obtain free medication and the provision of treatments – Free (posters, pharmacy leaflets in medical cabinets and waiting rooms); (e) Leaflets and brochures sent to retired people together with the pension slip through the mail and radio and TV broadcasts on this topic at aimed at a maximum audience, etc.); (f) Developing a network of home care for the elderly;

The achievement in Romania of compatibility with health systems in the Member States of the European Union must be another challenge for the health authorities. Although there are no unified standards of health care, the European Union considers citizens' right to high quality care as a fundamental right and supports National policies for introducing product guarantee measures, services and management at the highest level within the health care system (Apetrei, 2010).

References

1. Apetrei, A. (2010). Drepturile omului în Uniunea Europeană/Human Rights in the Europen Union, Editura Lumen. Iasi, Romania.
2. Crinson, I. (2009). Health Policy: A Critical Perspective. pp. 102, SAGE Publications Ltd.
3. Dragoi, M. (2010). Sistemul de sănătate din România în context european, pp 56–72, Editura ASE, Bucharest.
4. Enache, E. (2014). Romanii, Europenii cei mai nemultumiti de sistemul de sanatate, retrieved from Ziare.com.

5. Gillias, A. (2003) What Makes a Good Healthcare System?: Comparisons, Values, Drivers. Pp 138–140, Radcliffe Medical Press Ltd, United Kingdom.
6. Johnson, A., Stoskopf, C., Shi, L., (2017) Comparative Health Systems – A Global Perspecetive, Second Edition, Chapter 11: France, pp. 200–213, Jones & Bartlett Learning, Burlington, MA.
7. Legido-Quigley, H., et al. (2008). Assuring the Quality of Health Care in the European Union: A Case for Action. pp. 112–115, World Health Organization on behalf of the European Observatory on Health Systems and Policies.
8. Marinescu, V. (2017). The Crisis of Public Health as a Media Event: Between Media Frames and Public Assesments, from Public Health and Welfare: Concepts, Methodologies, Tools and Applications. Information Resources and Management Assosciation, IGI Global.
9. Monitorul oficial al României: Legi, decrete, hotărîri şi alte acte. (2009). Volumul 21, Ediţiia 256, pp. 60, law nr. 145/1997.
10. Pahl, N., Richter, A. (2007). Swot Analysis - Idea, Methodology and a Practical Approach, GRIN Verlag, Germany.
11. Radu, D. (2017). Un uriaş sărac din Est care încearcă degeaba să imite Vestul: sistemul românesc de sănătate, retrieved from vocea.biz.
12. Rotila, V. (2011). Calitatea vieţii profesionale şi tendinţa de migraţie a personalului din sistemului sanitar: studiu cercetat si desfasurat in cadrul Cendtrului de Cercetare si Dezvoltare Sociala „Solidaritatea", Editura Sodalitas, Galati.

Ilie Ionel CIUCLEA[1]

[1] PhD in Engineering, Economist, President, General Manager, Industrial Group SC Supercom SA Bucharest, Romania, Email: secretariat@supercom.ro

Industrialization of Circular Economy in Romania

Abstract *Romania has assumed the Circular Economy. It can reinvigorate the Romanian Economy. In Romania the "Productivity of the resource" must be increased. At EU-28 level this is 2 Euro / Kg of material and in Romania it is only 0.40 Euro / Kg of material. The idea of "zero waste at the pit" is assumed, and recycling should be implemented, ie the duration of the recyclable is higher; Romania can become an example for Europe. You only need: 1) a good plan, 2) a good application, and 3) an investment. Erroneously, conceptually and traditionally outdated, the problem of waste, sanitation, collection, transportation, storage, treatment, processing and recovery of waste is considered, encompassed and cataloged among services. The Circular Economy, however, imposes a strong industrial value chain in the field, as the collection, transport, storage, technological treatment, physico-chemical, mechanical and waste processing are, in essence, pure industrial activity. In article e proposes the rapid official reconsideration of the field by moving it from the sphere of services to the industrial productive-economic system.*

Keywords: *Circular economy, sustainable development, circular industrial regime, resource productivity*

Introduction

The accelerated increase of the volume and the change of the municipal waste characteristics occur in the global tendency and correlation between 1) urbanization, 2) the generation of waste and 3) the rarity of resources in the economy, with reflection in the Gross Domestic Product in each country, including in Romania.

Circular economy is a notion currently used for a restorative industrial economy. It is estimated that global waste production by 2050 could reach 27 billion tonnes and in Romania 8–10 million tonnes. In 2016, total waste generated in the EU-28 of all economic and household activities amounted to 2.503 billion tonnes.

The total amount of waste generated is linked, to a certain extent, to the size of the population and the economic size of a country. The smallest EU Member States have generally reported the lowest levels of waste generation and the highest state, reported highet levels. However, in comparable terms, relatively large quantities of waste (approximately 6 million tonnes) were generated in Romania.

Poor management and waste elimination can have a serious impact on the environment. Landfills, for example, occupy land and can cause air, water or soil pollution, while incineration can generate emissions of environmental pollutants. Therefore, EU waste management policies aim to reduce their impact on the environment and health and improve resource efficiency in the EU. It is not the economic growth in itself that generates pollution, but the disorganized industrial way of growth determines the occurrence of pollution.

Waste generated in small and medium-sized cities is a large organic proportion, and those in large-income cities are more diversified, with a relatively higher share of plastics andpaper.

The intersectoral premises for the industrial transformation of the linear economy into the circular industrial economy are already observable. The changing composition of waste influences the choice of technologies and the waste management infrastructure highlighting the importance of their separation and the imperative need to industrialize the field for material and energy treatment and capitalization.

We appreciate that the long-term goal of policies in the field is to reduce the amount of waste generated and, when waste generation can not be avoided, to promote their industrialization and their use as resource through higher recycling and safe disposal.

1. Literature review

Industrialization / included circular economy industrialization is „the large-scale introduction of manufacturing, advanced technical enterprises, andother productive economic activity into an area, society, country, etc., or conversion to the methods, aims, and deals of industry and economic activity, particularly of an area that was previously underdeveloped economically." (Dictionary.com, Thesaurus.com, 2017)

Some analyzes (Vault.com.Inc., 2018) confirm that "The modern waste management industry can be divided several different ways. Some workers work with hazardous waste while others work with nonhazardous waste; they may be employed in the private sector or the public sector. Careers in the industry can have several focuses, from air, water, or soil concerns to waste produced by industries or government agency regulation of these industries. For industrialization, there are many types of jobs available for people interested in waste management. Some don't require a college degree and workers can spend a lot of time outside. (...). Equipment operators are needed in such waste operations as landfills, wastewater treatment plants, and some industries."

The basic idea in contemporary human society is that "The circular economy is a new way of creating value, and ultimately prosperity. It works by extending product lifespan through improved design and servicing, and relocating waste from the end of the supply chain to the beginning—in effect, using resources more efficiently by using them over and over, not only once." (UN Industrial Development Organization, 2017)

Kobza Natalia and Schuster Anna (2016), consider that "global development will be steered by the 4th Industrial Revolution that has come to a new dimension.

Its side effects can fundamentally alter the way we live, work and function. Most undoubtedly its complexity and transformation will be something that the humankind has never experienced before. It can unfold in many ways, but the reaction to that should be firm, integrated and comprehensive. Especially, the global economy should adapt to those changes and stream development into the right direction."

Yvetot Christophe, (2017), emphasizes that "Developing Recycling Industries requires the establishment of sustainable business models centered on e-waste dismantling facilities. Also, policy / law development, awareness raising, capacity building and design of collection / processing schemes, financing arrangements are required. (...) On this basis, it is necessary to seek the strengthening of regional e-waste management capacities and infrastructure."

2. Research Method. Data Collection and Preparation

2.1. European legislative package "Circular Economy"

The European Commission has come to formulate and endorse some concrete measures in the "Circular Economy" legislative package where waste industry / industrialization is central. These mainly consist of:

- Introduce mandatory recycling rates for different categories of waste, based on EPR (Extended Producer Responsibility) obligations, to companies that place later on waste in the market.
- Introducing the obligation to redesign the products with two objectives: a) to increase the proportion of raw materials from recycling, and b) to increase the recyclability of the products at the end of the life cycle, together with the rewriting of the European Waste Code for the reconsideration in industry of certain waste secondary raw materials.
- Adoption of economic instruments to promote re-use and stimulation of industrial symbiosis and greener products.
- Increase the municipal waste recycling rate to at least 65 % by 2030 and to waste packaging by at least 75 % by 2030.
- Capping the final disposal rate for all categories of waste to a maximum of 10 % by 2030, including through fiscal and coercive instruments, such as the ban on the storage of separately collected waste and the surplus disposal of waste.
- Reducing food waste by 50 % by 2030.
- Introduction of minimum standards and obligations to water users on mandatory recycling rates, by sector.

2.2. Legal obligations resulting from the Circular Economy Package

The legal obligations resulting from the "Circular Economy" package relate to municipal waste and sanitation services, as well as to the industrial sectors that place on the market goods and packaging which, after use, have to be recovered for their economic value or to minimize the impact on environment. In the context of the rising volatility of basic commodity prices in recent years, the European economy / industry has experienced one of the most protracted periods of economic downturn, which is dependent on primary resources imported from other continents.

In the Romanian economy, some firms have made progress in implementing circular economy models and have already reached maturity under conditions of industrial symbiosis with the promotion of sustainability over the overall value chain. However, Romania does not consistently apply the circular economy. If we look at some basic macroeconomic indicators on resource efficiency, we can conclude that the situation is inadequate. Prospects are worrying if we fail to focus the employers' and government attention on rethinking the industrial trajectory of the waste economy to move quickly to the effective circular economy. (Ciuclea I. I., 2017)

Romania has the lowest performing economy in the EU, because every kg of primary resource extracted from the natural environment and used in production generates an economic value of € 0.34, 1.5–4 times lower compared to the countries in the central block and East European, more than 6 times lower than the EU average, more than 10 times lower than in the Luxembourg, Netherlands, and UK economies.

In terms of domestic consumption of resources, Romania recorded an increase of more than 3 times this over the period 2000–2017, while the average for the EU decreased from 16.8 to 13.3 tons / capita. At the same time, it can be noticed that in the last years we are dealing with economic growth located far from the principles of the circular economy (Romania uses more and more natural resources but produces low economic value). No other EU country recycles less than 10 %, but in Romania the recycling rate of municipal waste is 3 %. So, in Romania, decoupling economic growth from pressure on the environment and natural resources has not been achieved, and as far as waste is concerned, the country goes in a whole different direction than the overwhelming majority of EU economies.

3. Transition to the Circular Economy Based on the Industrialization of Waste in Romania

3.1. Economic growth and competitiveness through the industrialization of waste

On January 18, 2016 in Bucharest, the minister in office and the former ministers of the environment in Romania in the last quarter of a century signed a "Declaration on environmental protection in Romania" in which point 6 states: "We agree that the implementation of the new Package of the European Commission's Circular Economy will strengthen economic growth, boost global competitiveness and create new jobs, while helping to close the circuit in the life cycle of products, bringing both environmental and economic benefits."

Waste as defined in Article 3 (1) of Directive 2008/98 / EC as "any substance or object which the holder discards or intends or is required to discard" if not collected and processed industrially can constitute an enormous waste of resources, both in terms of materials and energy.

Almost two-thirds (64 % or 3.2 tonnes per capita) of the total waste generated in the EU-28 were major mineral waste. Generally, those EU Member States with larger shares of major mining waste were those that were characterized by relatively important activities in the extractive industry, such as Romania, and / or construction and demolition activities. From the waste generated in the EU-28 in 2016, approx. 95 million tonnes (3.8 % of the total) were classified as hazardous waste.

3.2. Industrial waste treatment

Approximately 2.3–2.5 billion tonnes of waste (including waste treated in the EU) are treated annually in the EU-28. Nearly half (47 %) of treated waste is subject to disposal operations than incineration. Another 36.2 % of the treated waste is subject to recovery operations, other than energy recovery and backfill operations. Some Member States have had very high recycling rates (Italy and Belgium), while others have promoted the use of landfills (Romania, Bulgaria).

The long-term goal is to turn Europe into a recycling society, avoiding waste and using inevitable resources as much as possible. Appropriate waste management is a key element in ensuring resource efficiency and sustainable growth of Europe's economies (in line with the Europe 2020 Strategy). Accordingly, the revised Waste Framework Directive introduces a five-level waste hierarchy where prevention is the best option, followed by re-use, recycling and other forms of exploitation through industrialization, the disposal of, for example, waste, being considered as the last solution. (Ciuclea I.I., 2017)

Various companies with an industrial profile join their activity in integrated waste recycling parks in Romania. This is why it is useful to have an integrated approach to everything that means collecting and treating waste categories by reconsidering the collection service as an implicit phase of the industrial technological chain in the field. In this way, the recycling circle must be closed by industrialized systems of collection, treatment, recycling, which in fact means industrialization to save natural resources of raw materials and energy. For example, the treatment of waste electrical and electronic equipment, treatment and recycling of portable batteries and accumulators, alkaline and carbon-zinc batteries, distillation equipment for the recovery of mercury from the fluorescent powder collected from fluorescent lamps and vapor lamps mercury and high intensity discharge lamps, etc., are pure industrial alignments in the Romanian waste economy.

4. Transfer of Responsibility and Circular Economy in Romania

Responsibility Transfer Organizations (OTRs) are those who are (or should actually) deal with recycling. The Ministry of the Environment currently has 9 authorized OTRs. Yearly, OTRs are audited by the AFM, and official reports show that all these bodies have complied with their obligations. According to the legislation, OTRs are required to send monthly reports to each customer announcing the quantities of recycled packaging from the producer, which shows the effectiveness of industrialization in the field. However, there are situations in which manufacturers have been informed by an Amending Statement that the waste taken up has been recycled at a rate of0 %.

The Circular Economy in Romania implies the need to develop an updated strategy with an Action Plan based on a Roadmap to achieve environmental targets with the waste industry. It is right that formalising the industrialization of the waste economy is contributing to: the pragmatic, realistic completion of Romania's National Strategy for Sustainable Development (SNDD) - the 2020–2030 horizons; conclusion for Romania of the European Commission's package on the circular economy; industrialization of the waste domain is a step of Romania towards the circular economy; by moving to a circular economy based on the industrialization of waste, cost reduction and job creation will be achieved; in order to increase the implementation of circular economy measures in Romania through the measures adopted by the Parliament and the Government, the industrialization process can turn waste into a resource, thus turning into the economic circuit; the recycling market is of great value and, on this basis, the green industry is encouraged; through the industrialization of waste, Romanian localities adapt to the European and world environmental requirements; industrial companies are involved in environmental protection, they can promote the transformation of waste into resources (secondary raw materials) for industry in Romania.

On this motivational alignment, with legitimacy and realism, we launch the major initiative "Industry in Romania based on the industrialization of waste economy." Industrial waste recycling is a major business proposition. It is noticed that the recycling plants in Romania import waste because of the dumps that absorb almost all the waste by depositing them. Most waste, especially municipal waste, is collected in bulk. The mixture of recyclable with biodegradable and even hazardous ones makes recycling impossible or very difficult due to the high degree of contamination of the materials.

Almost 98 % of the waste generated in Romania is deposited at the landfills, more recently called "ecological deposits", which can not be "ecological", as long as there is only a garbage collection, ie pollution. Current legislation on waste management obliges Romania to recycle or reuse 50 % of household waste and 70 % of construction and demolition by 2020. Collection should be done on different fractions: plastic, metal, paper, glass, electronics, biodegradable, construction waste. They should be grouped according to the quality of the waste so that it can be later delivered to industrial recyclers or energy recovery industries (incinerators, cement factories, biogas plants). The speculative and tax evasion is in the area of independent collectors, other than sanitation firms, caused by the inertia of local authorities (mayoralties, county councils) that still do not pay enough attention to the way waste management is done. (Ciuclea I.I., 2017)

The concept of circular economy says, very concisely, that in order to harmonize the sustainable development needs of humankind in the long run, it is necessary to optimize the consumption of resources, so as to scatter as little as possible and reuse as much as possible. Improving the use of resources in industry must reach such a threshold that the amount of net natural resources consumed (ie those extracted for the first time from the natural environment) will not jeopardize their natural recovery rate in sufficient quantities for future generations.

5. Risks and opportunities for waste. The need for circularity and industrialization of waste

In the first place, for the waste industrialization issue, synthetic Risks from Conventional Waste Management and Opportunities from Integrated Solid Waste Management are emerging.

We appreciate that for the risk assessment in the Romanian economy / circular industry, at least 5 metric operators (measuring operators) are required to know the feasibility of advancing industrial production systems, so in relation to identifying and counteracting risks. These metric operators may be: 1) country risk, 2) financial risk; 3) economic risk; 4) Composite Risk Index and 5) Rating (using Institutional Investor's Country Credit Ratings).

In the case of the Romanian waste sector, the risk of industrialization shows that the variation of the economic results from the treatment - recovery can be assigned a convenient probability. Risk analyzes are already in place that can be used to assess investment alternatives and to define preventive measures to reduce the likelihood of negative factors occurring in the waste industry.

Risks due Conventional waste management	**Opportunities from Integrated Solid Waste Management**
• Low efficiency, undesirable effects on health (diseases caused by environmental vectors), environmental problems (deterioration of underground water quality due to contamination) and social problems (informal / unmanufactured garbage groups working in unsafe conditions). • Development activities and consumption-based lifestyles lead to an increase in the amount of waste. Valuable resources remain unused. • There are no extensions in terms of innovation and job creation.	• Combining centralized and decentralized decision-making options with efficient pollution control systems (in leachate and gas capture systems), resulting in economic gains due to increased efficiency, reduced global costs, minimal environmental impact and social acceptance. • Strategic waste minimization planning and green procurement programs leading to more sustainable consumption patterns, along with economic development

Risks due Conventional waste management	**Opportunities from Integrated Solid Waste Management**
• Not all stakeholders are involved, neglecting the community's contribution to inadequate environmental conditions and poor private sector involvement. • Dangers to workers' health and the prevalence of negative social situations. • Not paying attention to other new waste streams for special handling as well as recovering resources from their contents.	• Facilitate the recycling of valuable resources (plastic, glass, paper and metals), recovery of alternative energy sources (waste fuels), the recovery of biogas or compost from biodegradable waste • Encourages innovative technological development in newer areas, such as energy waste and recycling, and promotes green jobs that ensure safe working conditions • Ensures multi-stakeholder involvement in decision-making by involving non-governmental organizations (NGOs), the private sector, residential and commercial communities, and the government. It increases the formal economy and provides safer working conditions

Source: Orig. Author, 2018

However, in an adaptive market, ministerial collective decision-makers and managers are operationalizing their organizational and leadership intentions, respectively seeking to achieve the conventional expected results of the industrialization of waste.

6. Recognition of waste as an industrial sector in Romania's New Economy

Since 1972, several Western European countries (West Germany, France, Austria, Belgium, the Netherlands, Italy, Marie-Brittany and the Scandinavian countries) have resorted to the trade, exchange and industrialization of waste. The use of chemical waste recycling processes has proved to be a success story of the stage. On this occasion, new technologies of industrialization and valorization were developed.

The concept of waste industrialization has two meanings: in a broad sense 1) it is a cumulative process that structures the local social, regional and national county social system, through the intensive use of machine systems; it allows for the increase of the goods, with decreasing costs, including the idea of increased material productivity, environmentally friendly environment and the drive effect

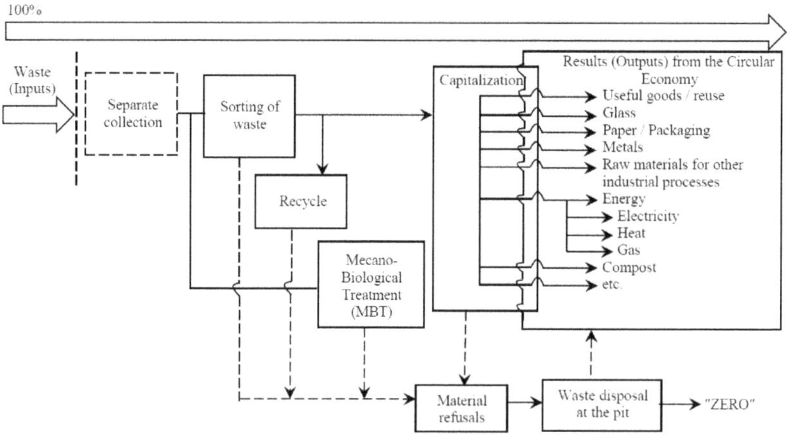

Figure 1: Proposal for a stream of industrialization of waste in Romania in the Circular Economy

Source: Orig. Author, 2018

generated by the sorting, treatment and waste processing systems. In a narrow sense, 2) the industrialization of waste contributes to substitution of imports and, progressively, to the use of raw materials on the spot.

Future industrial production will develop in symbiosis with modern information and communication technology. These systems make possible a self-organized production in which operators, machines, installations, logistics and products communicate and cooperate with each other directly. (Figure 1)

The network includes all phases of a product: from idea, through design and production processes, including logistics and calculation, tracking product and service usage to recycling.

For the industrialization of waste in Romania, an organizational concept consisting of principles that support companies in the identification and implementation of industrialization scenarios is needed, such as: a) interconnection of the waste domain with the other industrial sectors at the national level; b) transparency of waste information; c) technical assistance for the elaboration of projects technological lines for the collection, transport, sorting and industrial processing of waste; d) decentralized decisions.

A Working Group on Waste Industrialization is set up within the Ministry of Economy, which includes education and research experts, production, developers of industrial strategies, programs and tactics at national level. The Working Group on Waste Industrialization also aims to boost the merger of technology information technologies with classical production technologies and thus pave the way for new products from waste.

The process of waste industrialization is complex and involves greater specialization in production and an increase in the capacity of waste material processing. If general industrialization has negative effects on the environment, increasing pollution, we find that the industrialization of waste, on the contrary, helps to ensure industrial sustainability in terms of protecting the environment.

From the recent economic history (1990–2018) it is noted that in Romania deindustrialisation was used as a way of recovering the past. The concept of "eco-business" occasionally introduces the notion of "environmental industry". Emphasis is placed on the "clean up of pollution", environmental protection (waste management, elimination of atmospheric pollution, sewerage, wastewater treatment, etc.). They form the historical essence of the environmental services sector. As environmental issues have become stronger, the need for new technologies and new waste markets has emerged.

Conclusions

It is proposed to resort to the formation of industrial clusters in the waste sphere and the transition to projected industrial energy clusters. Complementarily, the idea of formalizing an "economics of industrial resource efficiency" is advanced, measuring the values of the interrelationships in the block-schemes for Economics-Energy-Materials-Technologies and the environment for eco-energetic industrial applications.

We appreciate that it is useful to transfer ecotechnology in all economic productive spheres, nationally and globally. There is a need for "fluctuating energy", which can be obtained industrially from diversified non-renewable and / or renewable resources. Wastes, after industrial processing, are assimilated as "fuels" in urban ecotechnological plants and can be considered as "energy storage" (thermal energy).

There are already schemes for the industrial recovery of energy from Integrated Waste Treatment Plants in "urban mines", as well as process schemes of industrial industrial systems.

It is noted that the prices on the market of industrial enterprises' achievements can be distorted by environmentally harmful subsidies, promoted and granted by public authorities, avoiding good industrial environmental practices. The thesis is about transferring taxes on activities and actions affecting the environment, which helps to strengthen the economic industrial framework. It is proposed to systematise the most relevant environmentally damaging subsidies and to draw up phases and procedures for their gradual phasing out, transferring taxation to work on taxing the environmental impact.

We are proposing that the incineration of waste that can be recycled in a technically and economically feasible and environmentally safe manner is not supported in Romania. Instead, there should be support for the industrial use of waste materials in accordance with the waste hierarchy in order to ensure the supply of raw materials to industry and to bring Romania closer to a "recycling society".

In the new circular economy industry, it is proposed to introduce a waste trace information system to identify their route points. On this basis, we are advancing the following proposals:

- Including the phrase "circular economy" in the name of the Ministry of Economy.
- Allocating to the current ministerial sub-structures the tasks related to the "circular economy of Romania".
- The inclusion in the theory, practice and normalization of costs and elements of influence in the circular economy, with the development and approval of appropriate methodologies in the field.
- The inclusion in the Public Budget of the Public Investment Chapter, together with the private ones, in the circular economy.
- Providing facilities to investors in infrastructures and eco-technologies related to the circular economy.

References

Ciuclea Ilie Ionel, et al., Incipienţa Economiei Circulare şi instaurarea dominaţiei eco-tehnologiilor, Conferinţa Internaţională, Dezvoltare durabilă în condiţii de instabilitate economică, Universitatea Academia Comercială Satu Mare, Ediţia a V-a, Satu Mare, 24–25 iunie 2016;

Ciuclea Ilie Ionel, Bazele Economiei Circulare. Ecotehnologii circulare pentru materii prime în infrastructuri energetice urbane, Editura monitorul Oficial, Bucureşti, 2017;

Ciuclea Ilie Ionel, et al., Expression of circular economy and waste abolition in smart cities,/Draft, Conferinţa Zilele Academiei de Ştiinţe Tehnice din România, Ediţia a 11-a, "Oraşul inteligent", Academia de Ştiinţe Tehnice din România, Universitatea "Petru Maior" din Tîrgu-Mureş 6–7 Octombrie 2016.

Kobza Natalia, Schuster Anna, Building a responsible Europe - the value of circular economy, IFAC-PapersOnLine 49–29 (2016) 111–116.

Yvetot Christophe, UNIDO: Circular Economy and Sustainable Industrialization Pathways in the Developing World, Institute for European Environmental Policy (IEEP), www.slideshare.net/IEEP_eu, Published on Nov 23, 2017.

* * *, - Circular Economy, All 'round the world: Embracing the circular economy, UN Industrial Development Organization, 2017.

* * *, - Industrialization/ included circular economy industrialization, Dictionary.com, Thesaurus.com, 2017.

* * *, - Waste Management, Vault.com.Inc., http://www.vault.com/industries, New York, 2018.

Vlatko CINGOSKI[1], *Biljana PETREVSKA*[2]

[1]Faculty of Electrical Engineering, University "Goce Delcev" Stip, Macedonia, Email: vlatko.cingoski@ugd.edu.mk

[2]Faculty of Tourism and Business Logistics, University "Goce Delcev" Stip, Macedonia, Email: biljana.petrevska@ugd.edu.mk

Preserving Environment by Clean Energy Public Transport: The Case of Skopje, Macedonia

Abstract *Being consecutively ranked as one of the most polluted cities in the world, Skopje, the capital of Macedonia, serves as a suitable ground for introducing new, environmentally friendly public transport. The paper argues the justification of utilization of a monorail as technologically and operationally sound long-term sustainable transportation system. Replacing the current city transport based on diesel buses, with new electric driven monorails, enables sustainability, emissions reduction, and clean energy utilization. The research findings indicate that with only two suitably designed monorail lines, almost 70 % of all city public transportation needs may be covered. Such fast, reliable and modern concept will contribute to air pollution reduction in a large manner. Despite the common claim that monorail costs are unpredictable and extremely high, the study evidence some stylized facts to be reasonably consistent, yet, with a necessity for more in-depth feasibility analysis. The practical significance of the paper is that suggests valuable recommendations for projecting a monorail, as probably the only permanent solution to the slow and inefficient public transport of Skopje, and improving environmental footprint in the same time.*

Keywords: *Clean energy; Monorail transportation system; Environment impacts; Skopje*

Introduction

Constant increase in urban air pollution particularly from road transport and traffic congestion is becoming a growing concern and a very delicate issue for large cities. Skopje, the capital of Macedonia, is facing with rapid use of motorized transport, which is expected to continue to increase in the coming years, potentially diminishing air quality. With more than 650,000 inhabitants and a daily inflow of almost 20,000 people, Skopje is very busy economic and administrative centre in the region, which is rapidly facing a poor air quality. In the winter of 2018, Skopje was ranked for several times at the unfavourable first place on the list of the most polluted cities in the World. It was noted over 374 µg/m^3 of PM_{10} and PM_2 particles, being almost ten times more than the critical values, and toping other largely populated and polluted cities like Kolkata (India) 361 µg/m^3, Dhaka (Bangladesh) 329 µg/m^3, or Lahore (Pakistan) 232 µg/m^3.

This results in life quality reduction, along with aggravated potentials for public transportation and commuting within the city. The thorny problem that Skopje encounters is the traffic organization including reduction of traffic congestions, air pollution, and parking issue. With the gradual increase of its population, it becomes very difficult to commute from one to another part of the city in easy, fast and convenient manner. The streets became too narrow to accommodate the increased number of vehicles and the duration of rush-hours sharply increased spreading almost over the whole working day. Although not being the major, traffic is definitely one of the largest air pollution factors along with industrial plants and household heating facilities.

Many countries that face similar environmental problems along with traffic jams, over-crowded traffic and poor public transportation system, firmly determined to construct type of public transportation system that completely differs than Skopje's. China, Malaysia, Korea, Russia and many more introduced the monorail (MR) technology. By following many positive world-wide examples, Skopje may have modern, ecologically friendly and long-term sustainable city transportation system. The main benefits that MR transportation structure provides are:

- It occupies less space since it is elevated above the ground, provides better traffic safety, and it is faster and more secure.
- The construction of the driving system is easy operational and straightforward for maintenance, and provides fairly cheap and simple driving.
- It is almost noiseless, environmentally highly acceptable and recommended for very densely populated central city cores, thus avoiding collisions or traffic accidents.
- It may be easily accommodated within the current transport system enabling transportation of people and goods directly in the city centre by using the so-called hide-in stations, which may be embedded in or side by the existing buildings, shopping malls or any other facilities. All new stopping stations may get added-value by gaining inter-disciplinarily purposes like shopping, meeting and/or marketing places, etc., allowing passengers to get on/off the MR above the main street and
- Keep green areas under the tracks and among pillars enables environmentally friendly footprint of the facility, so cars, people and any other traffic under the tracks may be unobstructed, leading to increase of the space usage.

This paper elaborates a project idea of introducing a new sustainable city transportation model based on light and electricity driven monorail system (Kato et al., 2004; Kuwabara et al., 2001; Nehashi, 2001). In order to meet the aim, the paper is structured in several sections. After the introductory part, the following section presents a brief overview of the literature that explores the issues of clean energy and public transport. This is followed by a section that gives a snapshot on the current city transport system, and a section that presents some stylized facts on MR transportation system applicable to the case of Skopje. The article's final section offers main conclusion and posts some recommendations.

1. Literature review

There is a large body of literature that elaborates the necessity of developing intelligent energy systems for efficient energy processes and mitigation technologies for the reduction of environmental pollutants. In this manner, Yann (2015) explores many areas of clean energy systems, along with the environmental, social and economic impacts. Norman et al., (2006) assess the energy use and greenhouse gas (GHG) emissions by considering public transport as a major element of urban development. They conclude that the most targeted measures to reduce pollution should be aimed at transportation emissions. Barrero et al., (2008) argue introduction of different types of mass transit electric vehicles (battery electric buses, trolley buses, trams, metro, light rail) which enable large reductions in terms of emissions. Ozzie (2012) even discusses the issue that many environmental groups steer their platforms away from energy reduction strategies, driving instead toward the glowing symbolism of green energy production.

On the other side, many academicians argue the role of public transport within the scope of preserving the environment. Namely, Shapiro et al., (2002) emphasize the vital role of public transport in improving energy efficiency and the environment, noting that it is often under-appreciated transportation. Banister et al., (1997) try to understand the links between transport, energy and urban form as part to create sustainable cities. Thackeray et al., (2012) argue the major advances made in lithium-battery technology by the discovery of new materials and designs which enable sufficient energy for use in vehicles, thus making incentive to harness alternative sources and means of vehicle propulsion. Næss et al., (1996) detect that urban form variables have a significant influence on the inhabitants' average energy use for transportation. In their multivariate study they found that a high population density seems to be beneficial if the aim is to reduce energy use.

Furthermore, in the line of building a system of energy conservation strategies, Tzeng and Shiau (1987) suggest an application of a multiple criteria decision-making method to evaluate the possible alternatives. On the other hand, Azar et al., (2003) discuss several energy scenarios that may meet cost-effective fuel choices in the transportation system. For that purpose, they used a global energy system model and found that the oil-based fuels remain dominant in the transportation sector over the next 50 year, thus yielding in environmental pollution. Schipper et al., (1992) investigate the structure of energy use for public transport, and even back in the 90-ties concluded that more energy-intensive modes of transport provoke increase of energy use, thus leading to pessimistic outlook for future energy use.

Table 1: Operational data for Skopje Public Transportation Company (JSP) for 2016

Number of bus lines (Urban/Suburban)	82 (38/44)
Transportation length [km] (Urban/Suburban)	1,252 (428/824)
Yearly distance travelled [km] - Urban area - Suburban area	18,935,970 11,379,926 7,556,044
Total number of passengers/year - Average number of passenger/month - Average passengers/hour	45,925,737 3,827,144 7,070
Total number of busses	428
Average age of the busses [years]	10.09
Average consumption of diesel fuel/year [l] - Monthly - Daily	7,764,418 647,035 21,214
Average achieved commercial speed [km/h]	19.47
Average price per ticket (EUR)	0.55

Source: JSP (2017)

2. Public transportation system in Skopje

The Public Transportation Company (JSP – Javno Soobrakajno Pretprijatie) runs the public transportation system for the city of Skopje as of 1947, and until 1989, was the only enterprise for the city public transport. Today, JSP has over 80 bus lines and carries over 50 million passengers (Table 1).

Yet, the average age of buses (over 10 years) the diesel fuel spent daily (over 20 thousands litres), monthly (over 640 thousands litres), and yearly (over 7.7 million litres) points to extremely serious indication for substantial negative environmental implications. Adding the extremely low average achieved transportation speed (< 20 km/h) due to narrow streets and congested traffic, provokes unfavourable interest for the current transportation system. Despite the low ticket price, the average number of passengers is over 7 thousand/hour being insufficient to fully cover the operating costs.

Such public transport strongly initiates necessity to make severe changes, being focused on sustainability and clean energy.

3. MR public transportation system

MR is a modern, economical and environmentally friendly, fast and widely-used way for urban transport, particularly applicable for large city environments, thus many countries apply it due to many advantages. Today, such systems are widely used in almost all major world cities in the United States, Japan, Germany, Australia, France, Sweden, South Korea, Taiwan, Canada, China, etc.

From a technological point of view, the MR may be considered as long electricity driven bus that moves along a single rail above the ground. Due to its narrow rails, it provokes less negative economic and environmental impacts compared to light or heavy rail systems. Commercially, there are three major MR types:

1. Monorails that envelope/straddle a track (Figure 1a). It envelopes and straddles a narrow deep track being supported by two bogies and guided by rows of stabilizing rubber wheel along each side of the track;
2. Monorails that run on top of a track or a slab at the surface (Figure 1b). It has a unique central guide rail on top of the track that prevents uplift and derailment of the vehicle; and
3. Suspended monorails under a track which is above the vehicle and the propulsion motors and bogies are on the top of the vehicles (Figure 1c).

Based on desk research and taking into consideration the location of Skopje, the average number of potential passengers, as well as the location of various strategic urban units, the research revealed possibility of proposing construction of two perpendicularly positioned MR lines. Figure 2 presents two MR lines, whereas: Line 1 would start from the municipality of Gjorce Petrov to Novo Lisice, with future potential line extensions to the municipality of Saraj and the recreation center Matka on one side, and the Skopje International Airport on the other side; and Line 2 would start from the suburbs of October 11, through Kisela Voda and the Koco Racin Boulevard towards the municipality of Chair and Butel, ending in the vicinity of the Skopje central Cemetery.

The benefit of such MR system in Skopje will be three folded: (i) It will cover almost 70 % of all city public transportation needs; (ii) New electric driven monorails will enable long-term sustainability; and (iii) Air pollution will be substantially reduced due to clean energy utilization by replacing the diesel-fuelled busses as one of the largest sources of air pollution in the city.

Yet, constructing the proposed MR lines in Skopje is ultimately related to financing, which is generally the biggest challenge for a large-scale project, like this is. Despite the common claim that MR costs are unpredictable and extremely high, there is an evidence that they may be reasonably consistent. The practice shows that almost 85 % of the investment costs stand just for three items: civil works, monorails and/or special vehicles, and monitoring and control system. Table 2 presents some insights for construction costs of the Urbanaut® type monorail.

Based on findings in Table 2, some initial projection of financing is made. Accordingly, construction of two MR lines, as proposed for the city of Skopje, with a total length of approximately 16 km might cost between 120 (single line) and 220 (dual line) million euro. These lines will be the backbone of the whole future MR public transportation system. The suggestion is to be constructed as dual lines allowing passengers' commuting in both directions, as well as enabling further

a) Straddle type b) Urbanaut® type c) Suspended type

Figure 1: Most common types of MR structures today worldwide

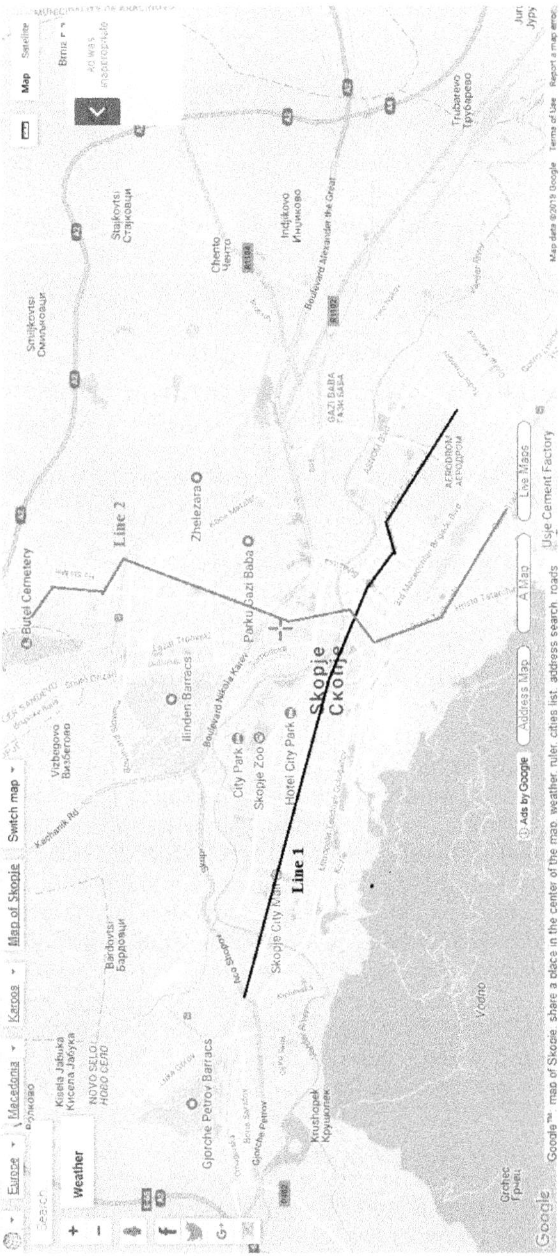

Figure 2: Proposed MR lines for Skopje

Legend: Line 1 (Gjorce Petrov to Novo Lisice); Line 2 (11 October to central Cemetery).

Table 2: Typical cost for construction of Urbanaut® type monorail [million EUR/km]

Type of activity	Type I (single line)	Type II (dual line)
A. Elevated Guideways, Including Foundations	3.20 (42 %)	5.85 (41.8 %)
B. Passenger Loading / Unloading Facilities (2 Stations)	0.75 (10 %)	1.20 (8.5 %)
C. Maintenance Yards & Operational Control Facility	0.50 (7 %)	1.00 (7.2 %)
D. Electrical Power, Signals, and Moving Block Control	0.45 (6 %)	1.00 (7.2 %)
E. Rolling Stock (3 Single Vehicles or 3 Car Train)	1.80 (25 %)	3.25 (26.8 %)
F. Fees & Contingencies of A, B, C, & D	0.75 (10 %)	1.20 (8.5 %)
Total cost (Intermediate Size) [million EUR/km]	7.45 (100 %)	13.5 (100 %)

Source: http://www.urbanaut.com/

extension of the system with other single MR lines to other areas. In the first phase, all stations of the MR system may be well connected with other city's suburb areas that already have active bus lines. This will support utility and increase number of passengers for the MR system at least for additional 50 %, thus achieving usage rate of more than 10,000 passengers/hour. This undoubtedly will improve the feasibility of the whole project.

Therefore, the expected number of passengers may expand at approximately 65 million/year, allowing the average price of at least 1EUR per single use. However, more detailed feasibility analysis is required, leading to financial justification, whereas, everything that may result in investments return rate under 12 years, is strongly acceptable. Due to fact that construction costs for MR is heavily depended on many issues (like: total length of the system, terrain topography, location and current utilities, passengers' requirements, speed, number of stopping stations, etc.), it is necessary for the case of Skopje to make more in-depth feasibility analysis.

Furthermore, a kind of economic evaluation is the cost-effectiveness analysis, which can give strong guidance to decision-makers on what are preferable instruments or packages of instruments to use. Even more, establishing a predictable and consistent policy and regulatory framework may be very important in assisting to attract the private sector financing (Gwilliam et al., 2004: 77).

Conclusion and recommendations

The research does not attempt to provide a detailed map applicable to solve pollution problems of Skopje, but rather to suggest framework for serious consideration for answering profound issues, like the nature of urban air pollution, pollution sources, and available resources. Moreover, the study intends to propose some scheme in which local and central policy makers may approach to selection and implementation may occur from internationally based experiences. It places a special emphasis on how to coordinate policies across many sectors that are closely linked to the mitigation of air pollution from city urban transport, in the first line environment, transport, and energy. Greater use of public transportation offers the single most effective strategy currently available for achieving significant energy savings and environmental gains, without creating new government programs or imposing new rules on the private sector.

In this line, the study posts some valuable recommendations for developing MR as probably the only permanent solution that would improve environmental footprint of Skopje. So,

- Skopje is a "flat" city being longitudinally aligned along the river Vardar. Seven municipalities within the city (Gazi Baba, Aerodrom, Cair, Kisela Voda, Karpos, Centar and Gjorce Petrov) are located opposite to the city centre giving the opportunity for easy coverage with MR.
- Skopje has very unfavourable environment history, so investing in environmentally acceptable long-term public transport would be very useful. This might be promoted and supported by the Government, city authorities and various European environmental funds and
- Macedonia is heavily dependent on import of petroleum and natural gas, which instead of being used for transportation, may be used for electricity generation, thus enabling electrically driven MR transportation systems.

By proposing a monorail and electric powered vehicles as efficient public transportation system, Skopje may significantly reduce emissions and achieve pollution reduction. Although being defined as an expensive alternative, MR massively declines the lifecycle GHG emissions. Only with two suitably designed MR lines of about 16 km, almost 70 % of all city public transportation needs might be accommodated. Since it will be positioned above the ground level, the city will gain more green areas, parks, bicycle tracks and parking spots thus enabling environmental improvement. Yet, the proposed project requires considerable economic policy dimension that is heavily dependent on cost-benefit analysis. Hence, Skopje must design and adopt air pollution strategy appropriate to its own circumstances. Namely, environmental and ecological impacts are important, but are only one aspect of urban transport policy, vis-à-vis economic, financial, social and distributional concerns which also come into play. The various dimensions of policy impact have to be balanced in local and national political process.

References

Azar, Christian/Lindgren, Kristian/Andersson, Björn A.: Global energy scenarios meeting stringent CO_2 constraints-cost-effective fuel choices in the transportation sector. Energy Policy, 31(10), 2003, pp. 961–976.

Banister, David/Watson, S/Wood, C: Sustainable cities: transport, energy, and urban form. Environment and Planning B: Planning and Design, 24, 1997, pp. 125–143.

Barrero, Ricardo/Van Mierlo, Joeri/Tackoen, Xavier: Energy savings in public transport. IEEE Vehicular Technology Magazine, 3(3), 2008, pp. 26–36.

Gwilliam, Ken/Kojima, Masami/Johnson, Todd: Reducing air pollution from urban transport. World Bank, Washington DC, 2004.

JSP – Javno Soobrakajno pretprijatie: Yearly work report for JSP - Skopje for 2016, (in Macedonian), Skopje, April 2017.

Kato, Masamichi/Yamazaki, Kenichi/Amazawa, Toshiharu/Tamotsu, Takayuki: Straddle-type Monorail Systems with Driverless Train Operation System. Hitachi Review 53(1), 2004, pp. 25–29.

Kuwabara, Takeo/Hiraishi, Motomi/Goda, Kenjiro/Okamoto, Seiichi/Ito, Akira/Sugita, Yoichi: New Solution for Urban Traffic: Small-type Monorail System. Hitachi Review 50(4), 2001, pp. 139–143.

Nehashi, Akira: New Types of Guided Transport. Japan Railway & Transport Review 26, 2001, pp. 58–67.

Næss, Petter/Sandberg, Synnøve/Røe, Per Gunnar: Energy use for transportation in 22 Nordic towns. Scandinavian Housing and Planning Research, 13(2), 1996, pp. 79–97.

Norman, Jonatan/MacLean, Heather/Kennedy, Christopher: Comparing High and Low Residential Density: Life-Cycle Analysis of Energy Use and Greenhouse Gas Emissions. Journal of Urban Planning and Development, 132, 2006, pp. 10–21.

Ozzie, Zehner: Green illusions: the dirty secrets of clean energy and the future of environmentalism, University of Nebraska Press, Lincoln and London, 2012.

Schipper, Lee/Steiner, Ruth/Duerr, Peter/An, Feng/Strøm, Steinar: Energy use in passenger transport in OECD countries: Changes since 1970. Transportation, 19(1), 1992, pp. 25–42.

Shapiro, Robert/Hassett, Kevin/Arnold, Frank: Conserving energy and preserving the environment: the role of public transport, Report for the American Public Transport Association, 2002.

Thackeray, Michael/Wolvertonb, Christopher/Isaacs, Eric: Electrical energy storage for transportation-approaching the limits of, and going beyond, lithium-ion batteries. Energy & Environmental Science 5(7), 2012, pp. 7854–7863.

Tzeng, Gwo-Hshiung/Shiau, Tzay-An: Energy conservation strategies in urban transportation. Energy Systems and Policy, 11, 1987, pp. 1–19.

Urbanaut® homepages, http://www.urbanaut.com/, Accessed March 2018.

Yan, Jinyie: Handbook on clean energy systems. John Willey & Sons, 2015.

Ilie Ionel CIUCLEA[1]

[1]Economist, PhD in Engineering, President, General Manager, Industrial Group SC Supercom SA Bucharest, Romania, Email: secretariat@supercom.ro

Life-Cycle Curve of Waste-Type Products

Abstract *The paper presents the procedure for analyzing the evolution of the environmental enterprise from the composition of the entity's scheduled development curve to the residual product life cycle. There are presented elements that are part of a general strategic and tactical model of Romania's alignment with the trends and trends in the field of waste and waste utilization in the circular economy. The new concept of inter-economy and bio-etalon is first introduced in literature. It is argued, as an original contribution, that raw material for goods and goods goes through compromises, and waste reuse policies record difficult decisions / choices about production, distribution and consumption. The idea of introducing into Romania the circularity of the economy, consisting of ecological business conditions, is realized by the exploitation of the waste for the production of new goods, given the product life cycle that undergoes radical transformations in the modern economy.*

Keywords: *waste, raw material management, circular economy, bioethalon, product life cycle*

Introduction

Biological processes are manifested in nature as far as the biosphere is the area of exploration and exploitation of the materials involved in products with clearly defined life cycles. Any imbalance in the normal environmental cycle or disturbance to the environmental balance has the significance of pollution, as the process quality or the quality of the modified ecosystem shows that quantitative exchanges produce qualitative changes. The introduction by man into the environment of a certain amount of "some material" as a result of his productive-reproductive activities can cause proportions of accumulations that exceed the "reception" tolerances, reaching the perceived disruptions and deteriorations / classified as harmful. The residues material from productive and non-productive consumption contribute to these disturbances, thus generating what conventionally means pollution.

On this basis, investigating the waste problem in Romania (2018), we can see the market position of the environmental enterprise given by the following aspects: if the company is active on the waste market, from collection to total embedding in production-reproduction through specific, specific economic circularity; whether the environmental undertaking has a "strong" position on the specific waste market and how it benefits from the positioning in question; if the firm occupies a market segment or the quasi-totality, or the whole of the specific market, through the conceptual and operational dominance of production-reproduction designed for waste products and goods; whether the environmental undertaking is responsible for the conditions of the waste market (expansion or restriction); whether the entity proves relevant to the level of competence with regard to the organization of local, national or international waste marketing; how the environmental undertaking's mission is highlighted by the efficiency of collection channels - processing (treatment) - total raw material incorporation (up to zero waste).

Examining the environmental enterprise's production cycle means the intention to look for shortening formulas - making the "collection" – "zero" waste route more efficient 'in close connection with product life cycles. Of course, the quasi-continuous examination of marginal cost / price developments (amelioration or erosion) in the field is envisaged. On this basis, there is a distinct setting on which work segment investments are made: on collection, transport, storage, treatment, finality of total waste incineration (thermal power plants, electric, etc.).

The above elements help to determine the influence of product lifecycle on defining the profile of the environmental enterprise (feasibility, reliability, quality, etc.).

1. Literature review

In the literature in Romania and in the world, there are quite in-depth narratives related to the life cycle of the product. The concept / phrase "Product Life Cycle" refers to the average life of a product. It is customary to use the analogy with the condition of man in time (products, in analogous context, are born, develop, mature and aging, fall into decline).

Disposal / sales are influenced by the life of the product. Exiting the product will change its status, becoming waste. From now on, the waste is covered by specific industrial processes. The societal interest is that the lifecycle of the product is as long as possible, even by resorting to its re-insertion into new products from waste.

It is noted that "Life Cycle Assessment is a tool for assessing the environmental impacts and resources used throughout the product life cycle, ie from raw material acquisition, through production and use to waste management." (Göran Finnvedena, et al., 2009) At the same time, we find that Life Cycle Thinking and Assessment can help policy makers choose the best environmental options. In fact, "Life-cycle thinking and analysis can help reduce negative environmental impacts of waste generation and management. This includes looking at ways to reduce waste production, increase recycling, and dispose of waste in a more environmentally friendly way." (Balkau Fritz, et al., 2004)

Nelen D. (Nelen D., et al., 2013) show that "The European Waste Framework Directive (2008/98/EC) explicitly specifies the hierarchy for waste management: prevention, preparation for re-use, recycling, other recovery actions, disposal. When selecting waste management options, this waste hierarchy should be followed. A deviation can only be justified by Life Cycle Thinking (LCT) on the overall impacts." So, the life cycle concept of products is related to an analogy with biology. At the same time, Romania meets benchmarks in the field.

The analysis of the life cycle cost of a product is a technique for highlighting the comparative values of the costs to be incurred over a certain period of time. In essence, "Life Cycle Assessment" is an environmental management technique. Durand Pascal, (2017) in his report to the European Parliament he states that it is necessary to take the following suggestion: "Stresses that a balance must be struck between the extension of product lifetimes, the conversion of waste into resources (secondary raw materials), industrial symbiosis, innovation, consumer demand, environmental protection and growth policy in all the phases of the product cycle, and considers that the development of increasingly resource-efficient products must not encourage short lifetimes or the premature disposal of products".

For the study area we think it is true thesis of Căpăţână Veronica, (2016), that "Studying life cycle factors is important for estimating the life expectancy of some products. The marketing strategies used are not the same throughout the life cycle, they can be informative in the launch phase or persuasive in the phase of increasing or maturing."

It is important, however, to identify new links between Life Cycle Assessment and municipal waste management. The Ministry of Environment of Romania, (January 2018), officially states that "The latest statistics on the management of solid municipal waste in the EU show that there are large differences between Member States. The most striking difference is when comparing the ratio between storage and recycling. Storage that is the worst management option in the waste hierarchy is unfortunately still the main means of waste disposal in some EU Member States." In fact, it is noticed that, in essence, there is still a real waste management gap at the global level. Also, the Romanian Ministry of Environment shows that the "loop closure" of the product life cycle through recycling and reuse has benefits for both the environment and the economy. (Ministry of Environment, 2018)

2. Research Method. Data Collection and Preparation

The basic issue agreed in product life cycle research has been associated with the requirement of fully capitalizing on products that have become or will become waste in the Circular Economy.

By adding new elements to characterize the competitive advantage for environmental enterprises, innovation / innovation is being invoked in Romania to win the competitive advantage for the production of new products from waste.

A number of 16 small and medium-sized enterprises in the environmental field (sanitation, waste collection and processing) in the Development Region no. 8 Bucharest-Ilfov (2016–2018) and it is found that, generic and representative, the environmental firm to be competitive concerns: knowledge (awareness) of the innovation promoted by competitors; valuation of costs from idea to product /

new final service from market waste; elaboration of a program / program outline a) research, respectively b) development of the waste recovery technologies in the company, in harmony with the strategic directions of advancement of the entity in the Circular Economy; orientation towards internationalization in the field; defining weaknesses and strengths in research and development work in the field.

In the context of complementarity and joint articulation to gain competitive advantage, productivity, material and financial resources, profitability, managerial performance, attitudes of managers and employees, social responsibility (public) of the company, etc. were examined / assessed. for the use of waste to make new products and goods.

As demonstrated by the discussion, analysis and debating sessions of the Industrial Group S.C. Supercom S.A. Bucharest, (2018) the size and intensity of the competition on the environmental waste market determines the organizational entities in the field to assess their own competition potential. The costs are those that induce differences / differences between competitors. We see that the cost advantage is more sustainable than the price advantage.

The competitive advantage of costs can give the environmental firm the opportunity to cover (accept) the market in the field, and the competitive price advantage, most often / often, provides coverage / occupation of only segments or niches of markets. (Figure 1)

On this line of analysis, we find that if an environmental undertaking in Romania does not master the full competitive advantage for its forwarding direction, the chances of successful success are affected.

As a rule, combinations of competitive advantage sub-sequences for “waste” products can not be achieved radically as the “waste” product is generic “univalent”, lacking its “functionality” parameter with respect to “functions / functionalities” other (manufactured) products on the market (on the same market). Instead, if an environmental firm formulates a clear and consolidated “strategy for multi-competitive advantages,” the philosophy of action is changing. “Pluri-Competitiveness” becomes “unit”, a programmatic standard for the organizational behavior of the respective environmental firm. In the end, focusing on the integrated competitive advantage means the strategic direction of the organizational entity in question.

In this context, the original proposal of competitive parameterization of the activities of environmental enterprises in Romania can be introduced with the help of bioethalon. Typically, in any enterprise (including environmental organizations), it is frequently used to analyze resources for their quantitative, qualitative, value, structural knowledge to be used in relation to efficiency and return criteria. In this way, the control and identification of critical situations is carried out, or the potential (reserve) for the use of resources in order to obtain the competitive advantage is emphasized.

However, in our opinion, the significant requirement in this field is to proceed to the audit of resources, which is assimilated in the value analysis formula, quasi-permanently cross-linked to cost-benefit requirements.

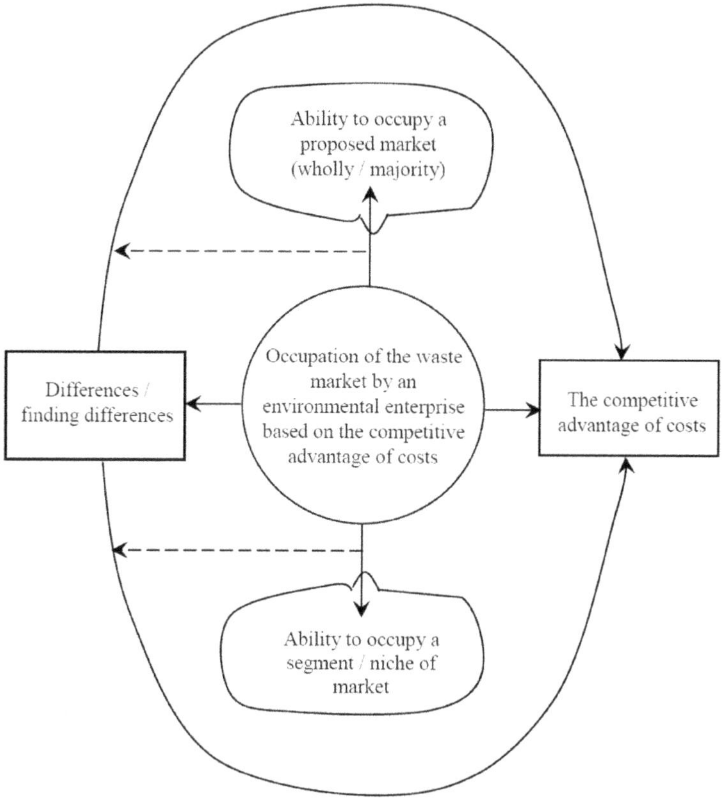

Figure 1: Relational foundation of the occupation of the waste market by an environmental organizational entity by assuming the competitive advantage of costs in the Romanian economy

Source: Author, 2017/ 2018

The structural segment of value-added, returned to the enterprise, is the key in assessments (audit). As a result, environmental enterprises can proceed with the operationalization of at least three auditory methods: 1) analysis of value added (value added); 2) comparative analysis and 3) redundancy analysis.

The dynamics of waste business, however, fall into a product-life cycle of products ("waste") technologically, commercially and financially driven. (Figure 2)

The product (the material, the "waste" of interest), the market, eco-technologies, competition, prices, gambling limits for income, etc. are the elements that by the importance coefficients (appraisal scores), then the significant increase (which is the most prolific phase / stage), maturity and cyclic closure by decline.

(Elements)	Launch	The onset of growth	Significant growth	Maturity
Market				
Product / Material / Interest for waste	(- , +)	(+ , -)	(+)	(±)
Eco-technologies	(+)	(+)	(+ , -)	(-)
Competition	(-)	(-)	(- , +)	(±)
Prices	(+)	(+)	(+ , -)	(-)
Intervall of marginal interest	(-)	(-)	(+)	(±)

Figure 2: The life cycle of "waste" products and their contribution to economic / social development

Source: Author, 2017/2018.

In fact, the "decline" is quasi-continuously postponed, because the "zero" waste society is still not implemented and the predictions in the field refer to the "ideal", not to a predictable future of this state (with "zero").

At the same time, it is useful to seek out the environmental enterprise's effectiveness in a waste business portfolio. For the first time, we advance the procedure of analyzing the evolution of the environmental enterprise from the composition of a) the planned development curve of the entity with b) the life cycle of "waste" products. (Figure 3)

In principle, any environmental organizational entity proposes the advance at least linearly, thus marking the quasi-continuous development. In the initial phase, the start-up decision with eco-tech investment infrastructure shows an effort with relatively stagnant results in terms of benefits. It is the reflection of investment spending in the enterprise's operational future.

The composition relied on by the new conceptual process in the present paper leads to the delimitation of three areas of existence / existence of enterprises with the object of exploitation and recovery of waste:

Z_1 = Stable area for business with waste.
Z_2 = Scheduled area for waste business (where phases and stages are under way for eco-technology, waste disposal, market, and efficacy).
Z_3 = Forecast area (covered by the life cycle of waste products); the life cycle curve decline is below the level of the areas Z_1 and Z_2.

In our appreciation, the operational, strategic and tactical goal of the environmental enterprise must be found in the area Z_2 (Scheduled area).

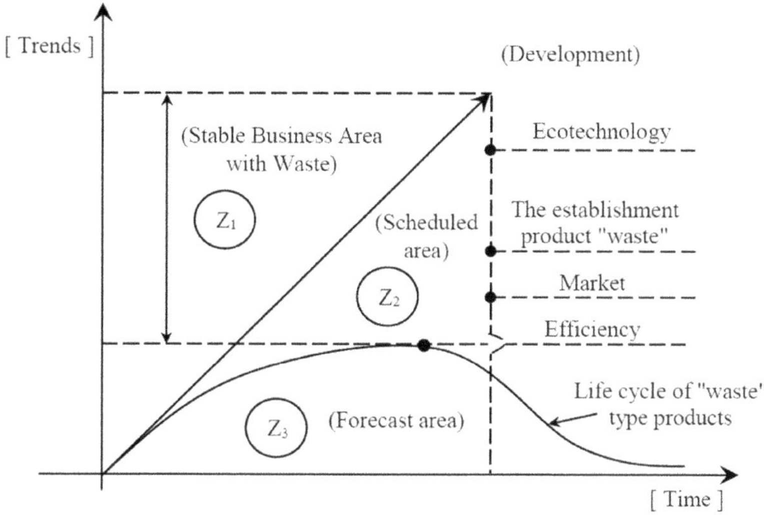

Figure 3: Intervals identified for the constitution of the stable business area with waste

Source: Author, 2017/ 2018

Assigning coefficients of zonal importance, we can see:

$$Z_2 > Z_1 > Z_3$$

$$[\{Z_1\} \ast \{Z_2\} \ast \{Z_3\}] \xrightarrow[(Z_3 \to 0)]{} MAX\{Z_2\}$$

(1)

Elaborators of environmental business operation / operation programs should be aware of the decline of the life cycle of the “waste” product, tend to lead the entity to the stability zone, but more than anything else to maximize operational, strategic, tactical and as efficient site on the programmed area (on the programmed area Z_2). In fact, the recyclable products / goods have to cope, in a multiple competition regime, with products / goods of the same category / family as well as with the absolutely new ones on the market, with an up-to-date life cycle.

The concluding remark in this field is that in Romania the companies in the field of waste and waste recycling activities have their own opportunities, strongly consolidated on segments, niches, areas, etc. when they adhere to eco-technology and are essentially engaged in Circular Economy.

3. Conclusions

Life cycle cost analysis of a product is a technique for highlighting the comparative values of the costs to be incurred within a certain timeframe.

Storage is the worst management option in the waste hierarchy. Essentially, there is still a real waste management gap at the global level.

The size and intensity of competition on the environmental waste market determines the organizational entities in the field to assess their own competition potential. The cost advantage is more sustainable than the price advantage. The competitive advantage of costs can give the environmental firm the opportunity to cover (accept) the market in the field, and the competitive price advantage, most often / often, provides coverage / occupation of only segments or niches of markets.

If an environmental firm formulates a clear and consolidated "strategy for multi-competitive advantages", the active philosophy is changing. "Pluri-Competitiveness" becomes "unit", a programmatic standard for the organizational behavior of the respective environmental firm. The significant requirement in the field is to pass on the resource audit, which is assimilated to the value analysis formula, quasi-permanently cross-linked to cost-benefit requirements.

Elaborators of environmental business operation / operation schedules must be aware of the decline of the life cycle of the "waste" product, tend to lead the entity to the stability zone, but, more than anything else, maximize operational, strategic, tactical, and as efficient site layout.

References

Balkau Fritz, et al., Why Take A Life Cycle Approach? United Nations Environment Programme, Division of Technology, Industry and Economics, First 2004.

Căpăţână Veronica, Ciclul de viaţă al produsului, /prezi.com/, 17 February 2016.

Durand Pascal, - Report on a longer lifetime for products: benefits for consumers and companies, Committee on the Internal Market and Consumer Protection, motion for a European Parliament resolution, The European Parliament, 9 June 2017.

Göran Finnvedena, et al., Recent developments in Life Cycle Assessment, Journal of Environmental Management, Volume 91, Issue 1, October 2009, Pages 1–21.

Nelen D., et al., Life cycle thinking as a decision tool for waste management policy, Metallurgical Research & Technology, Volume 110, Issue 1 (Social Value of Materials), 2013, pp. 17–28.

ISO 14040: 2006. Management de mediu. Evaluarea ciclului de viaţă. Principii şi cadru de lucru.

ISO 14044:2006. Management de mediu. Evaluarea ciclului de viaţă al produsului.

"Închiderea buclei" ciclului de viaţă al produsului prin reciclare şi reutilizare, cu beneficii atât pentru mediu, cât şi pentru economie, Ministerul Mediului din România, /www.mmediu.ro, 17 January 2018.

Daniel CIUIU[1], *Marina BĂDILEANU*[2], *Izabell Luminița GEORGESCU*[3], *Svetlana CIUMAC*[4]

[1]Technical University of Civil Engineering; Institute for Economic Forecasting, Bucharest Romania, Email: dciuiu@yahoo.com

[21]Centre for Industrial and Services Economics, Romanian Academy, Email: badmarina@yahoo.com

[1]Centre for Industrial and Services Economics, Romanian Academy, Email: georgescu_izabell@yahoo.com

[4]Center of Political Research and International Relations of the Institute of Legal and Political Research of the Academy of Sciences of Moldova, Email: svetlanaciumac@gmail.com

Homogeneity Of The Granger Causality And Applications For Generated/Recycled Waste Dependence On Welfare

Abstract *The main objectives of this paper include extending the classical homogeneity tests for panel data (data series, for the 2002–2016 period, on generated / recycled waste, GDP_{PPS} per capita and HDI, for 15 EU countries), testing Granger causality homogeneity and, if the homogeneity hypothesis of the Granger causality proves true, identifying the source of this homogeneity. The two sources considered are: (i) the lack of Granger causality for all countries and (ii) the existence of a common Granger causality for all countries considered. Among our findings we mention that in all four cases we have homogeneity of the Granger causality. In the case of the dependence among the amount of recycled waste on GDP_{PPS} per capita, this homogeneity comes from the effective Granger causality, whatever the considered country. In the other cases, this homogeneity is due, obviously, to the lack of Granger causality.*

Keywords: *Granger causality, panel data homogeneity, generated/recycled waste, Gross Domestic Product at Purchasing Power Standard (GDP_{PPS}), Human Development Index (HDI)*

Introduction

The general perspective of this paper is given by the precarious situation of waste selective collection and recycling activities in our country. The European Environment Agency (EEA, 2016) draws attention to the low waste recycling rate in Romania (13 %), and emphasizes the need to develop the infrastructure required for separate collection and recycling of municipal waste and the long distance yet to go through to reach the 50 % objective recycling rate established by the adoption of the Framework Directive 2008/98/EC on waste. Romania's Development Strategy over the next 20 years, elaborated within the Romanian Academy, states that in order to increase the recycling rate to 50 % by 2020, the authorities should commit to an exceptional effort, even if a derogation period is granted until 2025 (Platon and Constantinescu, 2016). European Union statistics provide the ranking of countries according to the share of municipal waste treated by recycling or composting in total generated municipal waste in 2015. On the top five places we find Germany, Austria, Slovenia, Belgium and the Netherlands with weights between 67.7 % and 51.7 %, while on the last five places - Croatia, Slovakia, Greece, Romania and Malta with weights ranging between 18.4 % and 6.9 %. Thus, in 2015, Romania ranked 27 of the 28 EU countries (Eurostat, 2017).

Given this situation, the present paper aims to identify a possible causality relationship between the quantities of waste generated / recycled and the population's living standard. To express the standard of living, we have selected two indicators, ie the Gross Domestic Product per capita at Purchasing Power Standard (GDP_{PPS}) and the Human Development Index (HDI) respectively. If this relationship of causality exists, we will estimate its homogeneity in the 15 EU considered countries. The best and worst situated European countries were selected from the above mentioned ranking (according to the success of waste recycling activities).

The four considered time series (for the 2002–2016 period) refer to the generated and recycled waste quantities and the GDP_{PPS} per capita (extracted from the Eurostat website) and the HDI (extracted from the United Nations' Development Reports), for 15 EU countries. The objectives taken into account by the authors include: extending classical homogeneity tests for the panel data, testing the Granger causality homogeneity, and, if the Granger causality homogeneity hypothesis is verified, identifying the source of this homogeneity.

1. Literature review

The literature offers a multitude of models used to predict the generated quantities of municipal waste. The most commonly used independent variables include population, income or GDP per capita, education, age etc. These variables have been grouped on criteria such as: production, consumption and waste treatment operations. Other independent variables take into account seasonal variations of generated waste, consumption, environmental taxes, household income, employment, urbanization, gas, water and electricity consumption. Indicators such as the number of household members, the level of education by age group, household consumption habits etc. are also taken into account. It has been shown that the amount of waste generated depends on the size of households, their level of income and education (Kolekara, Hazra and Chakrabarty, 2016).

The Granger causality tests' popularity is incontestable, taking into account the thousands of articles published in indexed journals. However, there are authors considering that causality tests can sometimes lead to erroneous conclusions. It is obvious that we must take into account the limitations of the Granger's proposed method, such as the lack of theoretical knowledge regarding the mechanisms underlying the studied phenomenon, the divergent results of applying different causality tests on the same data series (tests confirming the null hypothesis and others infirming it) that contradict the third proposed by Granger axiom (causality is constant over time), the aggregation of data series that also can affect the final results (Maziarz, 2015). Because the series are not stationary, we use the Toda-Yamamoto version of the Granger test (Jula and Jula, 2010), where the number of lags is the sum between the value of p from the VAR model and the maximum integration order.

When performing the Granger causality test and the classical homogeneity tests for panel data, two models are compared. This comparison is following defined steps: determining the coefficients, the sum of the error squares for each of the two models and the corresponding number of degrees of freedom; calculating the Snedecor-Fisher statistics; comparing the Snedecor-Fisher's statistics to the Snedecor-Fisher quantile distribution, with 10 %, 5 %, 1 % thresholds. The null hypothesis is accepted or rejected based on the outcome of this comparison. In the above mentioned tests, we have a basic model with the fewest restrictions and a restricted model (Jula, 2003). The basic model is the most heterogeneous for panel data (N regression models, when testingthe total homogeneity or the model with specific fixed individual effects; the model with specific fixed individual effects when testing the total conditional homogeneity). In the case of the Granger causality test, the basic model is the one with 2 * d + 1 coefficients (with a possible Granger cause). The restricted model adds restrictions to the basic model: related to the cross-sectional independence of some coefficients (these coefficients are equal for all cross sections), while for the Granger causality test, the restrictions are related to the absence of a Granger cause (the corresponding coefficients are restricted to zero).

An extension of the Granger causality in the case of the existence of a cyclic component is presented in Ciuiu, Bădileanu and Georgescu (2015). A test to integrate a cross-section in a panel is presented in Ciuiu and Simionescu (2016). Simionescu, Ciuiu, Bilan and Strielkowski (2016) provide tests for homoscedasticity and self-correction of errors.

In Baltagi (2005) and Jula (2003), the coefficients of the model with specific fixed individual effects are determined by regression without free term for all sections, after all the variables have decreased with the average per section. In our C++ pangr.cpp program, we have solved the problem using the least squares method by replacing the free terms in the first equation corresponding to each cross section. It follows that we should calculate for each cross-section (in our case, each of the 15 EU countries) the variance-covariance matrix of all variables, and the average of these matrices. Analogical to classical solution, a linear system results with unknown coefficients of the explanatory variables. The matrix of the system is given by the mean of the variance - covariance matrix of these variables, and the right member - by the average covariants between the explanatory variables and the resultant variable. The free terms result, in both cases, from the first equation of the regression for each country. In Păltineanu, Matei and Mateescu (2010) there are presented numerical methods to compute an integral and to solve a Cauchy problem, among which we mention the Simpson method for the integral and the Runge-Kutta method for the Cauchy problem. In Văduva (2004) there are presented methods to simulate a normal random variable and consequently for random variables connected to the normal distribution (Student, χ^2, Snedecor-Fisher).

2. Methodology

The methodology includes, among others, a series of tests added to the three classic homogeneity tests for panel data (Jula, 2003; Baltagi, 2005) applied to both the extended model (including Granger causality coefficients) and the reduced model (only the coefficients related to the preceding values of the resultant variable), as follows: three tests on the homogeneity of Granger causality, as well as total homogeneity / fixed effects conditioned by this homogeneity; three Granger causality tests, ie: the extended model in which the Granger causality coefficients (for the GDP_{PPS} and HDI time series) are identical and the other coefficients depend on the country is compared to the totally heterogeneous reduced model; the fully homogeneous extended model is compared to the totally homogeneous reduced model; extended model with specific fixed individual effects is compared to the reduced model with fixed individual effects. For the Granger homogeneity test, we denote with N the number of cross sections (in our case countries), with T the number of time moments, and with K the maximum sum between the integration order and the order of the VAR model for the N cross sections and the two time series. The extended model is:

$$Y_{i,t} = \alpha_i + \sum_{j=1}^{K} \beta_j \cdot Y_{i,t-j} + \sum_{k=1}^{K} \gamma_k \cdot X_{i,t-k}.$$

In the reduced model, the last sum in the previous equation is null as the coefficients of the possible Granger cause become zero. Below (Table 1), we show the numbers of freedom degrees needed in computing the Snedecor-Fisher statistics that are used in our tests.

We mention that for the reduced and extended models with no Granger causality, the sum of error squares is the same; only the number of freedom degrees is varying.

For the estimation of the model coefficients, of the errors' dispersion of these models and the Snedecor-Fisher statistics used in the tests performed, the pangr.cpp program developed by the correspondent author is used. For the calculation of 10 %, 5 % and 1 % quantiles by both Runge-Kutta and Monte Carlo methods, as well as for the determination of the errors using the Simpson and Monte Carlo methods, the cuantcls.cpp program was developed by the same author. The above

Table 1: The numbers of freedom degrees for extended and reduced models, with or without Granger causality

Panel\Granger	Extended model	Reduced model	Extended model with out Granger causality
Totally heterogeneous	N(T-3K-1)	N(T-2K-1)	N(T-4K-1)
Totally homogeneous	N(T-5K-2)+2K+1	N(T-3K-2)+K+1	N(T-5K-2)+K+1
With specific fixed individual effects	N(T-5K-1)+2K	N(T-3K-1)+K	N(T-5K-1)+K
With the same Granger causality	N(T-4K-1)+K	It is not calculated	It is not calculated

Sources: For the numbers of freedom degrees in columns 2 and 3 and lines 2, 3 and 4 of the table (Jula and Jula, 2015) (in our case, the value T of the number of time moments becomes T-k to access the previous values of the explanatory variables); for the rest of the freedom degrees - own determinations.

mentioned numerical methods, respectively the Monte Carlo one are applied because in the Snedecor-Fisher distribution statistical tables not all of the degrees of freedom pairs are presented.

3. Applications

For Granger causality, we determine the maximum integration order for each of the four variables. For all of these, the computed integration order is 2. As we have to add the order p of the VAR model we obtain, usually, p=1. For some countries and one of the four models, p=2. Hence, the maximum $K=p+d_{max}$ is 4. According to the number of freedom degrees formula for total homogeneity (Table 1), for K=3 and K=4 this number becomes negative.

If we solve the equation equalizing with zero the above number of degrees of freedom, K is linear increasing on T for N=15 (our case), N=28 (EU), N=33 (EU+candidate countries), N=49 (Europe) and N=193 (whole world). The slope is decreasing on N. In the extended linear regression model, the waste generated in the current year depends on the quantities generated in the previous two years, as well as on the GDP_{PPS} per capita of these years (thus, the linear regression starts with the 2004 year). Next, we present the results of the regression models for the generated / recycled waste according to the GDP_{PPS} per capita. As for the recycled waste, we have found that this is the only case where we have Granger causality (GDP_{PPS} per capita is Granger cause for the amount of recycled waste). For the generated waste by GDP_{PPS} per capita, Table 2 depicts the results:

For the recycled waste by GDP_{PPS} per capita, we have the following table of results (Table 3).

Table 2: Regression equations for the 15 countries' panel, for generated waste by GDP_{PPS} per capita

Model	Regression equation	Romania's case (i=13)	Errors' variance	Freedom degrees
Extended totally heterogeneous	$Y_t = A_{0,i} + A_{1,i} \cdot X_{1,it} + A_{2,i} \cdot X_{2,it} + A_{3,i} \cdot X_{3,it} + A_{4,i} \cdot X_{4,it}$	A_0= 205.71, A_1=1.017, A_2=-0.439, A_3=0.016, A_4=-0.024	360.384	120
Extended totally homogeneous	$Y_t = 5.789 + 1.203 \cdot X_{1,it} - 0.239 \cdot X_{2,it} + 0.00425 \cdot X_{3,it} - 0.0039 \cdot X_{4,it}$		1604.043	50
Extended fixed effects	$Y_t = A_{0,i} + 1.069 \cdot X_{1,it} - 0.282 \cdot X_{2,it} + 0.00347 \cdot X_{3,it} - 0.00485 \cdot X_{4,it}$	A_0=78.368	1055.144	64
Extended Homogeneous Granger causality	$Y_t = A_{0,i} + A_{1,i} \cdot X_{1,it} + A_{2,i} \cdot X_{2,it} + 0.00381 \cdot X_{3,it} - 0.00565 \cdot X_{4,it}$	A_0=87.01, A_1=1.339, A_2=-0.555	606.274	92
Reduced totally heterogeneous	$Y_t = A_{0,i} + A_{1,i} \cdot X_{1,it} + A_{2,i} \cdot X_{2,it}$	A_0=47.683, A_1=1.442, A_2=-0.59	501.672	150
Reduced total homogeneous	$Y_t = 11.578 + 1.249 \cdot X_{1,it} - 0.275 \cdot X_{2,it}$		1669.527	108
Reduced fixed effects	$Y_t = A_{0,i} + 1.124 \cdot X_{1,it} - 0.321 \cdot X_{2,it}$	A_0=60.46	588.894	122

Source: own determinations.

Table 3: Regression equations for the 15 countries' panel, for recycled waste by GDP_{PPS} per capita

Model	Regression equation	Romania's case (i=13)	Errors' variance	Freedom degrees
Extended totally heterogeneous	$Y_t = A_{0,i} + A_{1,i} \cdot X_{1,it} + A_{2,i} \cdot X_{2,it} + A_{3,i} \cdot X_{3,it} + A_{4,i} \cdot X_{4,it}$	A_0=-0.65, A_1=0.623, A_2=0.17, A_3=-0.00035, A_4=0.00052	9.289	105
Extended totally homogeneous	$Y_t = 1.368 + 0.946 \cdot X_{1,it} + 0.026 \cdot X_{2,it} + 0.00009 \cdot X_{3,it} - 0.00009 \cdot X_{4,it}$		45.407	35
Extended fixed effects	$Y_t = A_{0,i} + 0.781 \cdot X_{1,it} - 0.012 \cdot X_{2,it} + 0.00023 \cdot X_{3,it} + 0.00001 \cdot X_{4,it}$	A_0=-1.798	28.116	49
Extended Homogeneous Granger causality	$Y_t = A_{0,i} + A_{1,i} \cdot X_{1,it} + A_{2,i} \cdot X_{2,it} + 0.00031 \cdot X_{3,it} - 0.00001 \cdot X_{4,it}$	A_0=-2.395, A_1=0.466, A_2=0.254	14.418	77
Reduced totally heterogeneous	$Y_t = A_{0,i} + A_{1,i} \cdot X_{1,it} + A_{2,i} \cdot X_{2,it}$	A_0=0.342, A_1=0.916, A_2=0.155	10.935	135
Reduced total homogeneous	$Y_t = 1.439 + 0.949 \cdot X_{1,it} + 0.024 \cdot X_{2,it}$		45.439	93
Reduced fixed effects	$Y_t = A_{0,i} + 0.821 \cdot X_{1,it} + 0.029 \cdot X_{2,it}$	A_0=0.77	13.199	107

Source: own determinations.

Table 4: Generated waste by GDP_{PPS} per capita

Degree1	Degree2	F	quant1	quant2	quant3	quant4	quant5	quant6	err1	err2
70	120	1.4649	1.31	1.40	1.62	1.31	1.41	1.62	0.0333	0.0322
56	120	1.2032	1.32	1.44	1.67	1.31	1.42	1.69	0.1998	0.1986
14	64	0.8579	1.61	1.85	2.36	1.62	1.85	2.33	0.6059	0.6120
42	150	4.9860	1.35	1.47	1.72	1.36	1.50	1.64	0.0001	0.0009
28	150	0.2424	1.41	1.54	1.85	1.41	1.56	1.79	0.9999	0.9956
14	122	13.1558	1.55	1.77	2.23	1.55	1.83	2.14	0.0001	0.0000
28	120	0.8278	1.42	1.57	1.89	1.43	1.54	1.90	0.7121	0.7059
42	92	0.9592	1.39	1.52	1.81	1.40	1.46	1.79	0.5494	0.5503
28	92	0.4615	1.45	1.60	1.93	1.45	1.57	1.95	0.9909	0.9862
2	92	16.060	2.41	3.22	4.71	2.24	3.34	4.65	0.0198	0.0012
2	50	31.2045	2.44	3.29	5.26	2.37	3.41	4.89	0.0231	0.0000
2	64	2.0451	2.46	3.27	4.83	2.56	3.11	4.95	0.1409	0.1376

Source: own determinations.

The tests are presented in the following order: three classic tests for the extended model, three classic tests for the reduced model, Granger causality homogeneity test, and three Granger causality tests. We are comparing the Granger homogeneity model with N = 15 regressions in the reduced model, then the two models of total homogeneity / fixed individual effects extended - reduced. The tests results are summarized in the following tables (Tables 4–7). Each test is associated with a line in the table; the order of the columns refers to degrees of freedom, followed by the F statistics, the 10 %, 5 % and 1 % quantiles (calculated by solving the Cauchy problem using the Runge-Kutta method), the same quantiles calculated using the Monte Carlo method, the last two columns being allocated for the estimated errors (calculated using the Simpson and Monte Carlo methods).

In the case of Granger causality tests (the last three tests), in all four cases, we found a Granger cause only for the first two tests: (i) when comparing the model with the same Granger influence to the totally heterogeneous reduced model, and (ii) when comparing the totally homogeneous models. So, when Granger's causality coefficients are country independent, the other three are all either country dependent or independent.

Conclusions

As to the extended model, from the data presented in Tables 4–7, it is noted that only in the case of the amount of recycled waste depending on GDP_{PPS} per capita,

Table 7: Recycled waste by HDI

Degree1	Degree2	F	quant1	quant2	quant3	quant4	quant5	quant6	err1	err2
70	105	1.4417	1.32	1.43	1.65	1.31	1.41	1.61	0.0443	0.0466
56	105	1.3111	1.34	1.45	1.70	1.32	1.43	1.66	0.1166	0.1181
14	49	0.5394	1.64	1.91	2.46	1.66	1.92	2.61	0.8968	0.8852
42	135	5.9872	1.35	1.48	1.74	1.32	1.48	1.73	0.00001	0.0017
28	135	0.2087	1.42	1.57	1.86	1.42	1.58	1.86	0.9999	0.997
14	107	15.2263	1.58	1.78	2.25	1.54	1.78	2.08	0.00001	0.0001
28	105	0.9254	1.43	1.59	1.91	1.41	1.56	1.82	0.5777	0.5808
42	77	0.7907	1.40	1.54	1.84	1.41	1.53	1.91	0.7951	0.7901
28	77	0.4403	1.46	1.62	1.98	1.46	1.61	1.97	0.9915	0.989
2	77	13.3605	2.44	3.22	5.19	2.37	3.20	5.20	0.0165	0.0001
2	35	29.6472	2.52	3.36	5.79	2.60	3.21	5.80	0.0184	0.0000
2	49	0.96	2.45	3.28	5.13	2.40	3.28	5.13	0.3919	0.3805

Source: own determinations.

Table 5: Recycled waste by GDP_{PPS} per capita

Degree1	Degree2	F	quant1	quant2	quant3	quant4	quant5	quant6	err1	err2
70	105	0.9441	1.32	1.43	1.65	1.31	1.41	1.61	0.5978	0.5999
56	105	0.7734	1.34	1.45	1.70	1.32	1.43	1.66	0.8543	0.8545
14	49	0.5374	1.64	1.91	2.46	1.66	1.92	2.61	0.8981	0.8872
42	135	5.9872	1.35	1.48	1.74	1.32	1.48	1.73	0.0001	0.0017
28	135	0.2087	1.42	1.57	1.86	1.42	1.58	1.86	0.9999	0.9970
14	107	15.2263	1.58	1.78	2.25	1.54	1.78	2.08	0.0001	0.0001
28	105	0.3455	1.43	1.59	1.91	1.41	1.56	1.82	0.9909	0.9954
42	77	0.7911	1.40	1.54	1.84	1.41	1.53	1.91	0.7946	0.7897
28	77	0.4417	1.46	1.62	1.98	1.46	1.61	1.97	0.9913	0.989
2	77	12.6917	2.44	3.22	5.19	2.37	3.20	5.20	0.0159	0.0001
2	35	29.0324	2.52	3.36	5.79	2.60	3.21	5.80	0.0182	0.0001
2	49	0.6148	2.45	3.28	5.13	2.40	3.28	5.13	0.5458	0.5412

Source: own determinations.

Table 6: Generated waste by HDI

Degree1	Degree2	F	quant1	quant2	quant3	quant4	quant5	quant6	err1	err2
70	105	1.4393	1.32	1.43	1.65	1.31	1.41	1.61	0.0451	0.0475
56	105	1.0921	1.34	1.45	1.70	1.32	1.43	1.66	0.3443	0.3474
14	49	0.8340	1.64	1.91	2.46	1.66	1.92	2.61	0.6302	0.622
42	135	6.0393	1.35	1.48	1.74	1.32	1.48	1.73	0.0001	0.0017
28	135	0.3479	1.42	1.57	1.86	1.42	1.58	1.86	0.9990	0.9961
14	107	16.0718	1.58	1.78	2.25	1.54	1.78	2.08	0.0001	0.0001
28	105	0.7571	1.43	1.59	1.91	1.41	1.56	1.82	0.8009	0.8051
42	77	0.3934	1.40	1.54	1.84	1.41	1.53	1.91	0.9993	0.9974
28	77	0.3645	1.46	1.62	1.98	1.46	1.61	1.97	0.9964	0.9933
2	77	15.8179	2.44	3.22	5.19	2.37	3.20	5.20	0.0086	0.0001
2	35	29.8179	2.52	3.36	5.79	2.60	3.21	5.80	0.0183	0.0000
2	49	1.9371	2.45	3.28	5.13	2.40	3.28	5.13	0.1579	0.1536

Source: own determinations.

the total homogeneity of the model appears. In other cases, we found only the model with specific fixed individual effects (ie the free term in the linear regression model depends on the country, the value of the other coefficients being independent of the country considered) and total conditional homogeneity. Regarding the reduced model, we noticed the identity of the conclusions for all four analyzed cases and the three classical tests. More precisely, we do not have total homogeneity, we have the model with specific fixed individual effects. From the model with specific fixed individual effects does not result total homogeneity. In other words, the significance of Snedecor-Fisher statistics is 1 % for the total homogeneity test and for the conditional total homogeneity test. In contrast, for the specific fixed individual effects test, the Snedecor-Fisher statistic is insignificant with an error of more than 10 %.

In case of Granger causality homogeneity analysis for the GDP_{PPS} per capitaand the quantities of waste generateddata series, it was found that neither of the two models (the first one refering to the waste generated according to the previous values of this waste and the GDP_{PPS} per capita - the previous year and two years ago - and the second one taking into account only previous values of generated waste) is totally homogeneous; theseare models with specific fixed individual effects. Also, for these models, the conditional total homogeneity test is valid only for the first model. When comparing totally homogeneous models, it would result that GDP_{PPS} per capita would be Granger cause for the amount of generated waste, but it is not the case. In contrast, when comparing models with specific individual fixed effects, it results that GDP_{PPS} per capita is not Granger cause for waste generated.

As to the homogeneity of Granger causality for the GDP_{PPS} per capita and the quantities of recycled waste data series, we found total homogeneity for the first model (where recycled waste according to the previous values of these wastes and GDP – one year before and two years ago) because the Snedecor-Fisher statistics becomes insignificant in relation to the quantiles determined using the program cuantcls.cpp. For the first model, the existence of specific fixed individual effects was also found. In this case, all Snedecor-Fisher statistics are insignificant (including the one for the total homogeneity test, which in the case of generated waste was significant). For the second model (which only takes into account previous values of recycled waste), the results are similar to the generated waste, namely: we have no total homogeneity, but we have specific individual fixed effects, and for the third test we have found no conditional total homogeneity.

References

Baltagi, Badi H.: Econometric Analysis of Panel Data. John Wiley & Sons Ltd 2005, Third edition.

Brockwell, Peter J./Davis, Richard A.: Introduction to Time Series and Forecasting. Springer-Verlag 2002, Second Edition.

Ciuiu, Daniel/Bădileanu, Marina/Georgescu, Luminiţa Izabell: Granger Causality Test and Chow Breakpoint Test on the Romanian Day Ahead Electricity Market. Procedia Economics and Finance 22, 2015, pp. 601–609.

Ciuiu, Daniel / Simionescu, Mihaela: Phillips Curve in Some European Union Countries: A Panel Data Approach. In: Dobrescu Emilian / Păuna Bianca / Saman Corina (eds.): Selected Issues in Macroeconomic and Regional Modeling. Nova Publishers: New York 2016, pp. 49–63.

Jula, Dorin: Introducere în econometrie. Ed. Professional Consulting: Bucureşti 2003, pp.194–197; 203–213.

Jula, Dorin/Jula, Nicoleta: Introducere în econometrie. Ed. Mustang: Bucureşti 2010.

Jula, Dorin/Jula, Nicolae-Marius: Prognoza economică. Ed. Mustang: Bucureşti 2015.

Kolekar, K.A./Hazra, T./Chakrabarty, S.N: A Review on Prediction of Municipal Solid Waste Generation Models. Procedia Environmental Sciences 35, 2016, pp. 238–244.

Maziarz, Mariusz: A review of the Granger-causality fallacy. The Journal of Philosophical Economics: Reflections on Economic and Social Issues VIII (2), Diu Libertas International University, Rosetti International, 2015, pp. 86–105.

Păltineanu, Gavriil/Matei, Pavel Mateescu, George Daniel: Analiză numerică. Conspress, Bucharest, 2010.

Platon, Victor/Constantinescu, Andreea: Deşeurile. Materiale reciclabile. In: Bogdan, Simionescu: Resursele naturale. Rezerve strategice, ce folosim şi ce lăsăm generaţiilor viitoare (Vlad Ionel-Valentin (eds.). Strategia de dezvoltare a României în următorii 20 de ani, vol. III, partea 1). Ed. Academiei Române: Bucharest 2016, pp. 113–122.

Popescu, Theodor: Serii de timp: Aplicaţii în analiza sistemelor. Ed. Tehnică: Bucureşti 2000.

Simionescu, Mihaela/Ciuiu, Daniel/Bilan, Yuriy/Strielkowski, Wadim: GDP and Net Migration in Some Eastern and South-Eastern Countries of Europe: A Panel Data and Bayesian Approach. Montenegrin Journal of Economics 12(2), 2016, pp. 161–175.

Văduva, Ion: Modele de simulare. Ed. Universităţii Bucureşti, 2004.

Eurostat factsheets: Energy, transport and environment indicators, 2017 Edition, Statistical Books, Eurostat, doi:10 2785/964100 KS-DK-17-001-EN-N.

European Environment Agency (EEA), 2016, Municipal waste management, Country fact sheet: Romania (http://wmge.eionet.europa.eu/sites/etc-wmge.vito.be/files/Romania_MSW_2016.pdf), accessed 22 March 2018.

Eurostat, 2018, Municipal waste by waste operations, Waste generated, http://ec.europa.eu/eurostat/data/database, extracted on 23.02.2018.

Eurostat, 2018, Municipal waste by waste operations, Material recycling, http://ec.europa.eu/eurostat/data/database, extracted on 23.02.2018.

Eurostat, 2018, Main GDP aggregates per capita, http://ec.europa.eu/eurostat/data/database, extracted on 23.02.2018.

United Nations Development Programme, Human Development Reports, Human Development Data (1990–2015), Human Development Index (HDI), http://hdr.undp.org/en/data, extracted on 23.02.2018.

www.ingramcontent.com/pod-product-compliance
Ingram Content Group UK Ltd.
Pitfield, Milton Keynes, MK11 3LW, UK
UKHW020833290926
15470UKWH00004B/1318

9 783631 792049